THE CONVOLUTED UNIVERSE

Book Two

By
Dolores Cannon

PO Box 754
Huntsville, AR 72740

WWW.OZARKMT.COM

Printings 2005, revised 2007,2009(2),2010(2),2011(2),2012,2013, 2014,2015,2016,2017,2018,2019(2),2020(2),2021(2),2022(2), 2023(2)

For permission, serialization, condensation, adaptations, or for our catalog of other publications, write to Ozark Mountain Publishing, Inc., P.O. box 754, Huntsville, AR 72740, ATTN: Permissions Department.

Library of Congress Cataloging-in-Publication Data
Cannon, Dolores, 1931-2014
    The Convoluted Universe - Book Two, by Dolores Cannon
    The sequel to *The Convoluted Universe - Book One* provides metaphysical information obtained through numerous subjects by hypnotic past-life regression.

1. Hypnosis   2. Reincarnation   3. Past-life therapy
4. Metaphysics   5. Lost Civilizations   6. New Earth
I.   Cannon, Dolores, 1931-2014 II. Reincarnation III. Metaphysics
IV.   Title

Library of Congress Catalog Card Number: 2005925749

ISBN: 1-886940-90-8/978-1-886940-98-7

Cover Design: Victoria Cooper Art
Book set in: Algerian, Umbra BT, Bell MT
Book Design: Julia Degan

Published by:

PO Box 754
Huntsville, AR 72740

WWW.OZARKMT.COM
Printed in the United States of America

The most beautiful thing we can experience is the mysterious. It is the source of all true art and science.

Albert Einstein

A human being is a part of a whole, called by us "universe", a part limited in time and space. He experiences himself, his thoughts and feelings as something separated from the rest ... a kind of optical delusion of his consciousness. This delusion is a kind of prison for us, restricting us to our personal desires and to affection for a few persons nearest to us. Our task must be to free ourselves from this prison by widening our circle of compassion to embrace all living creatures and the whole of nature in its beauty.

Albert Einstein

The author of this book does not dispense medical advice or prescribe the use of any technique as a form of treatment for physical or medical problems. The medical information included in this book was taken from Dolores Cannon's individual consultations and sessions with her clients. It is not intended for medical diagnosis of any kind, or to replace medical advice or treatment by your physician. Therefore the author and the publisher assume no responsibility for any individual's interpretation or use of the information.

Every effort has been made to protect the identity and privacy of the clients involved in these sessions. The location where the sessions were held is accurate, but only first names have been used, and these have been changed.

TABLE OF CONTENTS

Section 6: Time Portals

Section 7: Energy Beings and Creator Beings

Section 8: Stepping Off the Deep End

Author's Page

SECTION ONE

BENEFITS OF

PAST LIFE THERAPY

CHAPTER ONE

MY BEGINNING IN HYPNOSIS

My adventures in the field of hypnosis have resulted in twelve other books besides this one. I often feel like the characters on "Star Trek" who go where no man has gone before. I have traveled through time and space to explore the history of the past, and the possibilities of the future. I have journeyed to unknown planets and dimensions and conversed with many so-called "alien" species. I have seen the wonders of lost civilizations and received information about their demise. All of this has been done without the use of time machines so common in Science Fiction. The only thing required for this adventurous work is the use of the human mind. Everything known and unknown is hidden in the recesses of the subconscious where it awaits discovery. This is my work and my passion. I consider myself the reporter, the investigator, the researcher of "lost knowledge", even though most of my work is hypnotherapy through past-life regression. I consider my work as dealing with the unknown, because I have discovered a method or technique of hypnosis whereby the realms of the mysterious and unexplored can be probed and examined.

Soon after I began working in this field I found that my work was veering away from the mundane into "lost knowledge"; so-called because I found I was discovering information that had been forgotten, buried or never known in the first place. We are moving into a new world, a new dimension where this information will be appreciated and applied. It was buried and lost, or held back for definite reasons. Many lost civilizations misused their powers and did not appreciate what they had accomplished, so the knowledge was taken away. Maybe it is time for these talents, powers and knowledge to come forth again and be appreciated and applied in our time period.

Of course, the main object of my work is therapy and helping people recover from or resolve their problems. But the most exciting and fulfilling part of my work, the gravy, the icing on the cake, is to discover history. And to bring information and new theories back to our time. It is truly like discovering buried treasure. They say, nothing is really new. We are only recovering knowledge we all once had in other lives, but have forgotten over the eons of time. Yet in my work I have discovered it has never truly been forgotten, because it has been stored in the computer banks of the subconscious mind. It has only been waiting for the proper time to be brought forth once again. This is what I have attempted to do through my work with hypnosis.

I lecture all over the world constantly on the subject matter of my books. I always start my lecture with a short personal background so the audience will understand how my information is obtained. I have been accused of making up the cases in my books, of being a wonderful fiction writer. To me that would be an even greater feat, to invent the material I write about, instead of just reporting the facts that come forth in deep trance. I have truly discovered a way to open the proverbial Pandora's box. The material continues to pour forth from my subjects' subconscious minds. All I have to do is organize it and put it into books. And that is no small task.

My roots in hypnosis go back to the 1960s, so I have been involved in this field for approximately forty years. In those early days of my work the induction process was time-consuming and tedious. It involved what I call "watch the shiny object" where something is dangled or swung in front of the subject while the hypnotist proceeds with the induction. And the long, drawn-out process involving the relaxation of all the parts of the body. Then there were various tests preformed to judge the depth of trance before the hypnotist could proceed. Some of these procedures are still used today and are still being taught, although mostly they will be seen in movies or on TV for dramatic affect. Most hypnotists have progressed to much faster methods. This was how I developed my own technique, by the process of elimination of those parts of the induction that were time-consuming and unnecessary. Modern techniques involve the use of the voice and imagery and visualization.

I first became involved with reincarnation and past-life regression in 1968. My husband, Johnny, was career U.S. Navy for over twenty years, and had just returned from duty in Viet Nam. We were stationed in Texas and trying to return our lives to normal after a four year separation caused by the war. My husband (who was the main hypnotist) and I were working with a young woman who was having problems with nervous eating. She was overweight and having kidney problems, so her doctor suggested that maybe hypnosis could help her. Up until this time we had only done conventional hypnosis focusing on habits; mostly working with people who wanted to stop smoking, lose weight, etc. We never in our wildest dreams thought anything beyond that could be accomplished. While working with the woman, we regressed her backward through her life looking for significant events when she suddenly jumped into another lifetime as a flapper in the roaring twenties in Chicago. To say we were surprised is putting it mildly. We watched as she transformed into a different personality with different vocal patterns and body mannerisms. She literally became another person before our eyes. This was our first exposure to reincarnation. The entire story of this event is told in my book *Five Lives Remembered.* This was the first book I ever wrote and it has never been published. I don't know if it ever will be because it seems too mundane now in the light of the events that have occurred in my career. But some people think there might be an interest in the story of my beginnings in hypnotism.

As we worked with the woman, our curiosity made us want to know more about this reincarnation phenomenon. We wanted to find where the hypnosis would take us. We regressed her through five different and distinct lifetimes to when she was created by God.

5

All the sessions were recorded on the portable reel to reel tape recorder of those times. It was called "portable" although it was extremely heavy and used large eight inch reels of tape. In those days there were no instruction books to guide a hypnotist should this sort of thing occur. The only book of this type that was in print was *Search For Bridey Murphy*, by Morey Bernstein. That book was then considered a classic, but now it is so mundane it would not even be published. It came at the right time. So we had nothing to guide us as we traveled back in time with the woman, and literally watched her become the other personalities as we went through each time period. We invented our own rules as we went along, and the results were remarkable. Also during the experimentation, because no one had told us it couldn't be done, we progressed her into the future to see what we would all be doing. She saw us living in a country setting and we had grandchildren. We did not tell anyone the identity of the woman we were working with. Yet several Navy friends heard about it and came to the house to hear the latest installment, the latest chapter. The experience changed our lives and belief system forever.

1968 was a very significant year in my life because *everything* changed forever. My life would never return to normal. My husband, Johnny, was almost killed in a horrendous automobile accident on his way to the Naval Base one night. He was hit head-on by a drunken driver, and mangled into the wreckage of our Volkswagen bus. The doctors said it was a miracle he lived, because his injuries were so extensive that he should have died that night. One reason his life was spared was because a corpsman who had just returned from Viet Nam was traveling in the car behind Johnny's. He was accustomed to treating emergency injuries on the battlefield, and so he was able to treat Johnny before he bled to death on the highway. By the time the emergency crew arrived from the base the corpsman had controlled the bleeding, but Johnny was still mangled into the wreckage of the car. It required extensive work by the fire department to free him. He was then transported by helicopter to the Naval hospital in Corpus Christi

When I arrived at the Intensive Care Unit five different doctors came in one by one and gave me several reasons why he could not possibly survive the night. They were perplexed that I was not upset. I told them they were wrong. He would not die. But of course, I could not tell them how I knew this. How could he die if he had been seen in the future with grandchildren? I knew it was true. I believed in what we had done and what we had discovered. If I was going to believe it, I had to believe it *all*. This belief helped to preserve my sanity during a horrible time.

I did not realize it at the time, but the belief system of many people on the base was also being tested. Some said that the accident was a punishment from God, because we were delving into something that was considered working with the Devil; exploring reincarnation. We were peering around corners into the darkness, opening doors that were better left closed. I could not believe that, because during our work with the woman we had been shown a God that was loving and kind, not vengeful. I could not fathom the reasoning behind what had happened when my world had been turned upside down, but I definitely knew that our curiosity and quest for knowledge into the unknown was not a punishment.

How ironic for Johnny to survive the war only to die from the negligence of a drunken driver. But this was not to be. The doctors called him the "miracle man", because against all odds and defying all logic, he survived. This was the beginning of the nightmare that was to last for many years.

After months in Intensive Care and spending a year in the hospital (eight months of which was in a body cast) he was discharged from the Navy as a disabled veteran. This was when we decided to move to the hills of Arkansas where we thought we could live on a pension and support our four children. At that time it was a necessity, but later I was glad to have this sanctuary in the hills as my retreat. Johnny spent twenty-five years confined to a wheelchair. As a partial amputee he could walk outside with crutches, and drove a hand-controlled car. During that time I was completely focused on my husband and the children.

My adventure into reincarnation with hypnosis had to be put on the back burner as I adjusted to my new life. My interest in hypnosis was not to be rekindled until the children began to leave home: getting married or going off to college. Then the "empty nest syndrome" hit, and I was faced with the question of what I was going to do with the rest of my life. I decided to do something very unusual, not what the "normal" woman would do in this circumstance. I decided to return to hypnosis, even though I had no idea where I would find clients in the hills of Arkansas. I just knew that this was something I wanted to do. But I did not like the old fashioned long-drawn out induction methods that had been popular in the 1960s. I knew there must be easier and more rapid techniques. So I studied the newer methods, and found that the trance state could be induced through imagery and visualization. I no longer wanted to focus on regular hypnosis to help the person break habits: stop smoking, lose weight, etc. My interest had been kindled in reincarnation, and that was what I wanted to focus on. In the late 1970s and early 1980s there still were few books in print to help the hypnotist in the field of past-life regression therapy.

So I had to invent my own technique. I soon found that most of what is taught in traditional hypnosis is unnecessary. So I began to remove some of these steps, and substitute quicker methods. As long as the person is not being harmed I believe the hypnotist can experiment to find out what works and what does not. After all, in the beginning someone somewhere had to discover how to create the most effective trance state. I knew I was blazing new ground, entering new territory. Now, after almost thirty years of honing and perfecting my technique, I developed my own method. I like to work in the somnambulist trance state (which is the deepest possible trance state), because I believe that is where all the answers are. Many hypnotists will not work there, because they say "strange things happen there". Anyone who has read my books knows that strange things do indeed happen there. Most hypnotists are trained to keep the client at the lighter state of trance. At that level the conscious

8

mind is very active and often interferes and interjects. Some information can be obtained at that level, but not the complete cooperation of the subconscious mind that occurs at the somnambulist level where conscious mind interference is removed. The person normally does not remember anything and thinks they merely fell asleep. The normal odds are that one out of twenty or thirty people will automatically and spontaneously go into the somnambulistic state of trance. But in the technique I developed the opposite is true: one out of twenty or thirty *will not* go. So it is a very effective method of removing the conscious mind and allowing the subconscious to find the answers. This is the method I teach now in my hypnotherapy classes, and my students are reporting the same amazing results.

When I began my therapy in earnest in the late 1970s, I soon discovered a pattern. This was before I discovered my method to contact the subconscious mind. After that the pattern became even clearer. I found that most problems that people have: physical, mental, allergies, phobias, or relationships, etc. could be traced back to events that originated, not in the present lifetime, but in other lives. Many of my clients had spent years going from doctor to doctor in the medical and psychiatric field, and they had little success in finding the answers to their persistent problems. This was because the doctors were only focusing on the obvious physical symptoms and events that had occurred in the present lifetime. Sometimes the problem can be traced to events that occurred in childhood, but in the majority of the cases I have worked on, the answer lies buried further in the past.

I believe past lives exist on another vibration or frequency. When we regress to those lives we change frequencies to see and experience them, just like changing the channels on a radio or TV set. Sometimes these other frequencies are too close or overlap and cause static or disease.

In my technique I have the best results by contacting (what I call) the subconscious mind. At a crucial point in the session after the subject has located the past life that holds the answers to the problems in the present life, I then ask to speak to the

9

person's subconscious. It always answers and gives the desired information.

In traditional hypnosis the practitioner is taught how to receive answers from the subconscious by the use of hand signals. This is where they ask the person to raise one finger for "yes" and another for "no". To me this is extremely slow and very limited. Why use this method when you can speak directly to the subconscious and it will answer you verbally? With my method you can converse and have a two-way conversation with it, and you can find the answer to absolutely anything you want to ask.

My definition of the subconscious is: the part of the mind that takes care of the body. It regulates all the systems of the body. You don't have to tell your heart to beat or yourself to breathe. I identify this as being the job of the subconscious, because it is constantly monitoring, and it knows everything that is going on in the person's body. That is why we can obtain answers to health questions using this method. I have found that *every* physical symptom, disease or malady is a message from the subconscious. It is trying desperately to get our attention in one way or another. It is trying to tell us something, and will persist until we finally understand. If we don't pay attention the disease or problem will continue to worsen until we have no alternative, or until it is too late to reverse the situation. I know this is true because the same symptoms have related to the same problems in many people's present lives. I only wish the subconscious could find a less painful way to deliver the message. I often say, "Wouldn't it be easier to just hand them a note?" The subconscious thinks it is relaying the message in a direct, forward way that the person should understand, but this is often not the case. We are too focused on our everyday lives to wonder why we have persistent backaches or headaches, etc.

When we have the session and discover the reason for the discomfort (and often the reasons can be so extraordinary that I do not think anyone could make the connection consciously), then the message has been delivered, and the discomfort ceases.

10

There is no longer any reason for it to remain since the message has been delivered and understood. The person can then return to health, *if* they make the required changes in their life. It always goes back to the responsibility of the person. The subconscious can only do so much, and the free will of the person is always respected.

I know these statements sound radical and do not fit with traditional methods of treatments, but I can only report what I have discovered and observed from helping thousands of people.

I also believe that the subconscious is the record keeper, the equivalent to a gigantic computer. It records everything that has ever happened in the person's life. This is why this information can be made accessible through hypnosis. If the person were asked to return to their twelfth birthday party they would be able to remember every event of that day, including the cake, those who attended, the presents, etc. The subconscious records every tiny detail. Much of it I think would be superfluous, and I wonder what the subconscious does with all the minute details. For instance, at any given moment you are being bombarded by thousands of bits of information: sight, sound, smells, sensory and much more. If you were to be consciously aware of all of this, you would be overwhelmed and unable to function. You must focus on only that information that is necessary for you to live your life. Yet the subconscious is always aware and constantly recording and storing this information. For what? We will explore that further in this book. This could also explain where sudden psychic revelations and intuitions come from. It is part of that information that we are receiving on another level that we don't necessarily need. But since it is there it occasionally leaks through into our conscious world. When this occurs it is considered a miraculous phenomenon, although this vast store of information is always there, and ready to be tapped into with the proper training.

The subconscious not only records everything that has ever happened to the person in *this* lifetime, but everything that has ever happened to them in all their past-lives, and existences in the spirit state. Much of this has no application to the present

11

life. It can be tapped into for curiosity's sake, and it would be interesting to the person. But what purpose would it serve in answering the problems of the present lifetime?

This is one of the mistakes that many hypnotists make. They see no value in taking the person to a past life, unless it is just for curiosity, fantasy or enjoyment. (Although many of these past lives are far from joyful.) This is the reason I developed my technique. I take the person to the lifetime that is most relevant or appropriate to the problems in their present lifetime. I never lead. I allow the subconscious to take the person to the life it considers to be the most important to view at the time of the session. I am always surprised, whether the lifetime is boring or mundane (which 90% of them are), living in ancient or modern civilizations, or dealing with aliens and life on other planets or dimensions. The subconscious makes the connection and it is always one that I or the subject would never have consciously made. Yet it makes perfect sense when viewed from this perspective.

When I contact the subconscious, it always amazes me because it becomes obvious that I am not speaking to the client's personality, but a separate entity or portion of themselves. I can always tell when the subconscious is reached and answering the questions. It always speaks of the person in the third person (he, she). It is unemotional and seems to be removed or detached from the problems, almost as an objective observer. It will chastise the person because they haven't been listening. Sometimes the subconscious' first remark will be, "Well, finally I am going to have a chance to speak. I've tried to talk to (Jane or Bob) for years, but they won't listen." The subconscious can be so objective that it sometimes sounds cruel. It pulls no punches, but tells the truth about the situation, as it sees it. When it has finished brow-beating the person in order to get the point across, it always tells them how much they are loved, and how proud they are of them for any advances they have made. This part also recognizes me, and often thanks me for putting the person into this trance state and allowing this process to occur. It often speaks of itself in the plural (we) as though it is

12

not a single entity, but several. This is explored further in this book.

Skeptics won't understand or believe this, and they would have good reason not to, *if* this contact was happening through only one person. But how can people argue that this is fantasy, fraud, hoax, deliberate manipulation, whatever, if it is happening through *everyone* I work with, no matter where in the world they are located? I have approximately 90% success rate with the hypnotic technique of taking the person to the appropriate past life, and of these about 90% success in contacting their subconscious. The subconscious always speaks the same way, and answers the questions in the same manner. This would not happen if it were a random circumstance

The people I have had the most difficulty putting into trance are usually high-powered businessmen, those who are judgmental and analytical. Instead of relaxing and going with the suggestions, they want to try to maintain control over the session. There are others who say they are ready to find the answers, but secretly they are afraid of what will come out, so their conscious mind sabotages the session. But as I said, these are only about 10% or less of the clients that I see. The rest (90%) always find a past life. So I believe this is very persuasive evidence in favor of reincarnation.

This has made me wonder. If this portion of the person's mind seems to be the same in every instance, what am I contacting? If it only belonged to the individual person I am working with, and only has access to their information (which is the logical way to look at it), then why and how can it tap into information on a grander scale? The subconscious itself supplies the answer to that question in this book, because as my work expands I am aware that more is going on, and I am ready (or I think I am) for more complicated explanations.

I now know I have been limiting it, and simplifying it. It is actually like communicating with a computer terminal connected to a giant database. The database transcends time, space, and all limitations of individual consciousness. This is the amazing part of my work. I seem to always be speaking to the

13

same part (or entity or whatever it is), a part that I have now discovered appears to be all-knowing. It not only has the answers the client is seeking, it has answers about anything that I wish to ask. An all-knowing part of something that has access to all information. Some people may choose to call this part the "Total Self","Higher Self", the "Oversoul", Jung's "Collective Unconscious", or "God". These could all be relating to the same thing under different names. I just know that I have found in my work that it responds to the name of "subconscious".

There are many other terms in science and religion that could attempt to explain this portion I have succeeded in tapping into. Whatever it is, it is a joy to work with, mostly because of my curiosity and desire for information. I love doing research in libraries, and this is like having access to the grandest library of them all. So journey with me as I explore more of the complicated metaphysical concepts. I know I don't have all the answers, but I have succeeded in scratching the surface a little deeper. Maybe your minds will be stimulated by what I have found. Keep searching and asking questions. That is the only way the answers will be found. Remember the saying, "A parachute is like the mind. It only works if it is open."

CHAPTER 2

NORMAL PAST LIFE THERAPY

People don't realize the power their own mind has to cure themselves. My technique allows access to that part of their mind that can find the cause of their problems. The subconscious can be very literal in the physical symptoms it uses to deliver its messages. If more people became aware of this they would listen more closely to what their body is trying to tell them.

From the thousands of sessions I have performed I can usually identify a pattern or sequence of symptoms that indicate the possibility that the person's physical problems may be coming from current events in the present lifetime. For instance, if someone tells me they have persistent back pains or shoulder pains, I will ask if they are carrying a heavy load in their life. Invariably, they reply that they do indeed feel that way because of their home life, work environment, etc. and feel they are under a lot of pressure. These types of conditions manifest as discomfort in the back or shoulder area. Pains in the wrists and hands can mean they are holding onto something in their life they need to let go of. I have found that pains in the hips legs or feet mean they are in a situation where they can go in a different direction in their life. It usually involves some important decision that would radically change their life. It manifests as discomfort in that part of the body because the subconscious is telling them they are afraid to step out, to take the next step, so the pain is physically holding them back. Stomach problems are sometimes caused by the person not being able to "stomach" something going on in their life. Cancer, especially in the intestines, is holding things inside until it causes stress and begins to eat away at the organs because it cannot be released. Epilepsy can be the inability to process or

15

deal with a high level of energy present in the body.

I have had subjects who choked when they ate certain foods, or when they took certain medication. In those cases the subconscious said they did not need to take the pills, because they were causing more trouble for the body. The reflex caused choking and discomfort as a form of rejection, in order to keep the person from ingesting the offensive food or medicine. The subconscious can be very dramatic and controlling sometimes.

While some of the answers can be found in the present life circumstances, the majority of my work focuses on other lifetimes. I will present a few of the "normal" past-life regressions to show their use in working out problems that the subject is experiencing in the present life. The rest of the book will focus on the abnormal or different type of regression, and how the subject was also helped by exploring these.

It must be remembered that these explanations can not apply to *all* cases verbatim, as the only cause for the malady or discomfort. There can be no blanket statement that: overweight is always caused by this, or migraines are always caused by that. The explanations are as varied as the person, and the subconscious can be very clever. The hypnotist must be flexible and use their own instincts to ask the proper questions. The answer and solution that applies to one person may not be the answer for the next.

An example of past lives influencing the present by creating physical problems: many cases of arthritis stem from being tortured on the rack or by similar contraptions in dungeons in medieval times. Mankind has a history of doing terrible things to each other, and this is sometimes carried in the body memory.

I had an interesting explanation for fibroid tumors in the uterus. The woman had had several abortions. She had good reasons for them because at the time she already had several children, and was having a very difficult time trying to work and support them. She felt under the circumstances she could not add to the burden by having more children. She said the abortions did not bother her and that she had come to terms with it, but her subconscious and her body knew otherwise. She began having problems with fibroid tumors. During the session her subconscious said she was feeling more guilt than she realized, and the fibroid tumors represented unborn babies. Once she came to terms with this the tumors began to shrink, and disappeared without the need of surgery.

Sexual diseases: herpes/hysterectomy/cysts on ovaries/prostate problems, etc. have been traced to sexual misbehavior or mistreatment of the opposite sex in other lives. These can also be a method of keeping the opposite sex away in this life, or be self-prescribed as punishment. A woman had endometriosis, problems with her female organs that affected her back. She never had any children although she had been married for 19 years. Her doctor wanted to operate and remove her ovaries and tubes to clear up the sexual problem. Her past lives revealed: female organ problems sometimes stem from a pattern of living several lives as priests and nuns who had to be celibate. This caused the suppression (repression) of sexual feelings and activities.

Vows in other lives are very powerful. Especially vows of poverty often carry over and cause money problems in the present life. These must be recognized as necessary in the former life, but now they can be renounced as inappropriate.

Sometimes the person has been one sex throughout many lives and suddenly find themselves in the body of the opposite sex. They develop diseases and problems as a way of rejecting the body, especially the parts of the body that have to do with the hormones. I have found this is also one explanation for homosexuality. The person has had many lives as one sex, and have difficulty adjusting to life as the opposite sex.

I have had many subjects who suffer from migraine headaches, and these can often be traced back to past lives that deal with trauma to the head. Blows to the head from either humans, weapons or animals are usually carryovers to remind the person not to repeat a mistake in this life that may have caused their death in the other lifetime. One case was a woman reliving the lifetime of a young man shot in the head during the American Civil War. There was a case in England where the woman had terrible headaches all her life that originated on the bridge of her nose and extended upward across her forehead and over the top of her head. No medication could give her relief. We found the cause came from being struck by a sword in that exact place on her head during one of the numerous wars that have been fought in Europe down through history. The understanding of the cause is enough to take away the physical problem.

One migraine case went in a different direction. The woman client was a travel agent, and as such she could travel all over the world. Her headaches developed after she left Indonesia and was returning home. It was a very beautiful and relaxing vacation, and she had felt very much at home there, so she could not associate the onset of the headaches with the vacation, since nothing traumatic or unpleasant occurred there. During the regression, she went to a very idyllic lifetime in that part of the world with a wonderful family and a man who loved her very much. Her subconscious explained that when she returned to that part of the world it triggered the memories of the wonderful life, and she was upset at having to leave it again. This created the headaches. She longed to return to the place where she had been so happy. My job was to convince the other personality that even if she were to return and live there it would not be the same, because the people she loved were no longer there and the circumstances were different. She would be unable to recapture that lifetime, so she would have to find happiness in the present one, perhaps with the same people since we tend to reincarnate with our loved ones. Once this was understood the headaches disappeared immediately and have not returned.

There are also many explanations for being overweight. Some are easy to predict: the person died of starvation in another life, or caused others to starve. Sometimes the weight is protection. The person puts on the padding to protect themselves from something (either real or perceived) in the present life, or as an effort to make themselves unattractive in order to keep from being hurt. My job is to try to find what they are protecting themselves from, etc. Often the person is the last one to realize this is the cause, yet when it is explained under hypnosis it makes perfect sense. Then the client can make a recovery.

I have also had unexpected explanations for being overweight. One woman went back to a lifetime where she was the leader of a clan in Scotland. The job was very demanding and she greatly felt the responsibility of it. When the man died he still felt this, and dropped a very important clue when she said (after the death), "I will never be rid of the *weight* of this responsibility." Very important words that the subconscious had taken seriously and carried forth to the present life.

An unusual case was described in *Legacy From the Stars* where a woman saw herself as an alien who crashed on Earth through an accident, and was taken care of by natives. He had many abnormal abilities that attracted attention. One was that the different gravity on Earth caused him to float unexpectedly. This triggered the desire to keep herself from floating and attracting attention in the present lifetime by adding extra weight, even though it logically did not make sense.

Another unusual explanation for overweight came forth when a client, Rick, wanted help with his weight problem. Nothing seemed to work, especially diets that had him eating

19

only select things in exclusion to others. During regression he went immediately to a life in some type of ancient culture. The buildings and structures did not sound like anything I have encountered or read about in history. Some of the description reminded me of the Aztecs, especially what the archaeologists have discovered. There was a rectangle courtyard surrounded by strange structures that were used as viewing stands similar to bleachers. An athlete from each of the communities competed in a game. Rick was an athlete who had been trained to do this. This game was very important because it decided the ruler of the combined communities for a season. The ruler would be rotated each season, and this was decided by which athlete won the game. Rick wore a strange uniform and his face was painted with streaks of paint. The idea of the game sounded like basketball. They ran around the court with a ball and had to throw it through a stone hoop that was mounted on the side of the courtyard. This is why I thought of the Aztecs, because the archaeologists say they uncovered a ball court in Mexico where the Aztecs played a similar game, but they claim it was played with a human head that was thrown through the stone hoop. If this is the same location, did the game deteriorate into using human heads, or are the archaeologists incorrect?

Rick was a very good athlete and won consistently. This meant that his side chose the leader for many, many seasons. He did not like working so hard, and often wished that the leaders would play instead. He was not allowed to marry, and was restricted to a strict diet that was designed to keep him lean and in wonderful physical shape. He often envied the other people because they were allowed to socialize and eat anything they wanted. His diet consisted of turtle meat, some type of white root, plenty of water, and a bitter tasting white liquid that was extracted from some fleshy plant. He had to drink the liquid every morning and evening. It often made him a little sleepy, but was essential because it was supposed to keep his muscles fit. He hated the taste and never got used to it.

Eventually he became tired of playing the game, and tried to find a way to get out of it. The people loved him, but after a while they were becoming bored because of his consistent winning. The other communities did not like it, because they did not get a chance to rule. He decided he would lose, but it could not be too obvious. When he began losing it was decided to replace him. Then he was allowed to live a normal life, including eating anything he wanted. He decided to go and live with the opposing community, because they were so happy to finally get a chance to rule. There he found that their athletes were not on restrictive diets, but normal food. He was happy there, but he did not live much longer. When he was dying he felt as though his insides were on fire. The medicine man said it was a result of the white liquid he had been forced to drink all those years. It had damaged his body.

When we spoke to the subconscious the connection was obvious between that life and his weight problem. The subconscious said the drink was a drug, a narcotic that caused his heart to beat faster and the digestion or metabolism of the body to be speeded up to produce good muscles and faster speed. It eventually ate holes or ulcers in his intestines, and this was what killed him. When I asked about helping him with his weight problem, the subconscious said it was not that simple. There were many factors involved that were all intermingled. Because of the authority figure (the ruler) forcing him to do something that was not in his best interest, he had learned to be suspicious and not trust those in authority (government, church, doctors, etc.). Also eating became associated with pleasure and social activity. It would be difficult to separate all these components, and he was in good enough health that the subconscious did not think it was worth it anyway. It was obvious why Rick did not do well on diets that were restrictive, where he could only eat certain foods. This brought back the memory of the other life. He now loved to cook and to eat a large variety of food. This was an unusual reason for being overweight, and one that would be difficult to help.

When Rick awakened he did not remember anything, but he wanted a drink of water because of a very unpleasant bitter taste in his mouth. He said it reminded him of a time when he was a

21

child and exploring the woods with his friend. They found some fleshy plants and chewed on them. (It was a wonder he didn't hurt himself, because many plants in the woods are poison.) It had a bitter taste. I told him about the white liquid that he had drank for many years in that other life. He had brought this taste forward. He was fine after drinking some bottled water.

I have traced many cases of asthma back to past lives where the person usually died from smothering, or something to do with the lungs or the breathing, such as their environment (dust, sand, etc.). One significant case occurred early in my work. A doctor came to see me who had had bouts of asthma for many years. He was using an inhaler, but knew this was habit-forming so he wanted to get off it. He knew enough about the paranormal and metaphysics to think the answer might lie in past lives. He went back to a lifetime as a native living in the jungle in Africa. This was during the time when the French were mining asbestos underground. They would capture natives and take them into the mines to work as slaves. He was one of those captured and taken underground. The constant exposure to the asbestos fibers during the mining procedure created physical symptoms in the natives, such as bleeding through the mouth from the lungs. This would create breathing problems and eventually kill them. When this happened the French miners would just take the body into the jungle and capture another native to take their place. The man began to have the familiar symptoms and knew he would die from the irritation to his lungs. In his culture it was not wrong to commit suicide if you were in an unbearable situation, so he plunged a stake into his right shoulder area and died.

When I communicated with the subconscious it was explained that the memory of that life had been carried forward, and under times of stress the breathing problem would return in the form of asthma attacks. Now that the doctor understood where the problem originated, it could be taken away. When he awakened he said, "I always wondered why I sometimes have pains in that area of my chest." He was rubbing the exact location where he had driven in the stake. This doctor subsequently became a good friend, and about four or five years after the session I asked him about his asthma. He smiled and said, "Oh, that's right! I *used* to have asthma, didn't I?"

Many fears and phobias can be easily traced back to the way a person died in a past life. Fear of heights, fear of the dark, claustrophobia, agoraphobia are easy to understand when viewed from this perspective. One such case (out of hundreds I have worked with) was a woman who was claustrophobic, had a terror of having her hands or feet bound, and who couldn't sleep all night without waking up every hour. She had an incident of deja vu when she visited the National Historic Site at Fort Smith, Arkansas, where there is an old museum and courthouse. This was where Judge Parker, the infamous "hanging judge" held his court trials from 1875 to 1897. They have also preserved the jail and reconstructed the gallows. She knew she had been there, and that it had been a horrible experience. The trip was an eerie experience for her.

During the session she went back to a lifetime when she was a Confederate soldier who had been captured with several others. They were crammed into a room that was a dark space with very small windows. The fear of having her hands or feet tied came from being shackled to the wall with chains. The inability to sleep through the night was caused by not getting much sleep in such a situation, and also the fear of what was going to happen. During the next few days they were all hung.

This case is only one example of how deja vu experiences can be an unconscious reminder of a past life. As well as the fascination with certain time periods and cultures (countries). These attractions are not always negative, but they carry a strong emotion that indelibly carries over through various lifetimes.

Another client was a professional nurse, who has a masters degree in psychology. She had been going to a therapist for quite a while, trying to find the answers to her problem, but wasn't having much success with it. The only conclusions they could come up with was that something happened in her childhood that she did not remember. It still didn't answer her questions. She was having problems with her oldest son. When she became pregnant with him she was not married, and wanted to have an abortion. The father of the child eventually wanted to marry her, and talked her into having the baby. But ever since the baby was born there was the feeling of being threatened by him, intimidated by him. She thought maybe he might have almost realized that she tried to abort him. Even though he was now an adult there were still problems.

During the session she went immediately to a scene where she was a man and was *extremely* angry. She had her hands around someone's throat and was choking him. As we were able to see who the man was, she said it was her son in this life. He had found him with his wife, and was going to kill him. The wife, she suddenly flashed on, was her mother in this present life with whom she has a very bad relationship. She killed the man who was now her son. The authorities came and took her (him) away and put him into a horrible prison cell that was full of rats and roaches with no windows to the outside. Very dirty, very dismal. Eventually he died in that place. The son came back in this lifetime so they could work out the negative karma, but he came back with a great deal of resentment toward her. It was no wonder she felt threatened and intimidated by this boy.

In her present life she could never understand her absolute disgust for alcoholics. The smell of alcohol, the way they talked and the way they acted, really repulsed her. When we asked about that, she definitely associated alcohol with that scene

24

where she was choking the other person. Maybe both of them had been drinking, and this added to the extreme anger. Whatever it was, it resulted in terrible consequences. So she had to come back in this life with all the people involved to try to work out the negative karma. By realizing this and seeing it really belonged to this other lifetime, she could forgive herself and all the participants. We could leave it in the past, and this would solve the entire problem.

In my work I have found there are as many ways to repay karma as there are stars in the sky. But the *least* desirable way to repay a murder is come back and be killed by your victim. There does not solve anything. It just keeps the wheel of karma turning, and only breeds more karma. I was told the best way for a murderer to repay for his crime is the "soft way", through love. For instance, the person who was the murderer would be put in a position where they would have to take care of their victim. They might have to devote their entire life to taking care of that person: a dependent parent, a handicapped child, etc. They would not be allowed to have a life of their own. This is a much wiser way to repay than "an eye for an eye".

Her psychologist had told her he didn't object to her having past-life therapy, but he didn't believe in it. Yet she would never in a million years have been able to find the cause of these problems through traditional orthodox therapy. I would have liked to have been a fly on the wall to see what he said when she told him she no longer needed further treatment. She has found the answers in this form of therapy.

Another case in New Orleans, was a very overweight young woman who desperately wanted to have a baby. She had been on fertility drugs, and nothing worked. She had a terrible time with her periods and was bleeding for months at a time. The only solution was to put her on birth control pills to try to regulate her periods, which defeated the purpose of trying to conceive. She was also trying to lose weight. During the regression I asked about the inability to have a baby. The subconscious said in her last lifetime, she was a foster parent and had as many as eleven foster children. As soon as one would leave the home, another would come in. She was very good with this succession of children, and very much enjoyed them, but in this lifetime they were giving her a rest. They said not to worry, she would have a child. Her body was being regulated now, and was beginning to return to normal. The overweight was a trial she had to go through, especially as a young person and on into adulthood, to see if she could take the teasing and the vicious remarks even adults made. She had now passed the test, and was being allowed to lose the weight. By the time she gets to the point where she can have a child, the body will be in good condition. And, of course, the child will be coming at the time it is supposed to come.

She had also been overly sensitive all her life, with periods of depression, feeling all alone and deserted. She finally had a breakdown where she couldn't stop crying. From her notes, she said, "I feel very empty inside. I often feel like the life I lead is uneventful and bland. Sometimes I feel like I am resting. Other times I fear I am waiting for disaster to strike. Always the sadness is there. How do I identify it, and what do I do to change it? The sadness has been a part of me since I was a small child, eight or nine years old." The subconscious made a very interesting comment. It said she was supposed to have been a twin. The other entity made an agreement to come into this life with her, but at the last minute changed its mind and decided it did not want to come at this time. So the other "body" did not develop, and she was the only one born. All her life she unconsciously felt that the other part, the twin that was not there, had left her alone and abandoned. There was the feeling of sadness, that something was missing, along with the depression. That was the reason: she was missing this other entity that was supposed to accompany her in this life. I never said it, but I kept wondering if it could be possible that the baby she will have in the future may be this other entity finally

26

deciding to incarnate.

When we told her mother about this, she said that was a real shocker, because she had never had any indication. The doctors never told her there was a possible twin. My client was born in 1972. I don't know if they were looking for what is called the "phantom twin" or the "disappearing twin", which is a phenomenon now. Later when we all ate supper together, her mother said that when she was born there was an unfamiliar substitute doctor. Maybe her regular doctor would have told her if there was any indication of an extra baby. I suppose we will never know.

I have found other cases of infertility caused by dying in childbirth in another life. An attempt by the subconscious to keep it from happening again. Sometimes the subconscious uses strange logic.

This regression took place in San Jose, California, in May 2000. A woman had extreme sadness all her life, depression, etc. She had a repeatable pattern in her life of abandonment, rejection, the feeling of being unworthy, the throw-away child, and fear of "what"? She had been abandoned as a little child and raised in an orphanage. There were troubles with men, marriage, jobs, always the feeling of not being worth anything and not able to accomplish anything. She also suffered from migraines, which I began to think were her way of punishing herself. A very dismal, pitiful person.

We went through an important lifetime that explained her situation. She saw herself running through the streets of a city carrying a year old baby. All the people were running frantically, screaming, because they were being chased by many soldiers on horseback. Obviously some type of invasion was going on. In fear for her life, she was trying to find someplace to hide. Her baby was crying, and she was afraid that would cause attention and they would find her. So she put the baby down next to a wall and ran to hide inside a building. She thought, surely no one would harm a baby. But as she watched, the soldiers rode down the street and killed the baby. She was so overcome with grief that she didn't even care when they found her and raped her, before killing her. She blamed herself for the death of the child, thinking she should have kept it with her. Either way they both would have died, but she was not thinking of that. She only blamed herself for abandoning the child. She was distraught even on the spirit side.

She brought the grief and torment forward into this lifetime and repeated the punishment pattern. I asked her if she could forgive the soldiers for killing her baby? She said, yes, she could, because they were just doing their "man" thing. But she could never forgive herself for deserting the baby. After much negotiation with the subconscious, I finally got her to forgive herself. It was very difficult, but was a relief when she was able to do it. When she awakened and we discussed it, I told her she had been beating herself up for too many lifetimes, and it was time to let it go. Besides, if we had taken her back further into prior lifetimes I would be willing to bet we would find that she was repaying karma for doing the same thing as a soldier. What goes around comes around. She felt a tremendous relief after the session. The feeling of unworthiness disappeared and was replaced by one of hope and expectation. I felt she had made a turning point in her life. It was time to stop punishing herself, and start living.

This next regression involved a very pretty young woman from Czechoslovakia who is living in London. She had been studying metaphysics for several years at the College of Psychic Studies, but did not have any degrees yet. She knew the information, but always stopped short of taking the final exams or writing the final essays, etc. Her main concern was eczema all over her entire body. She had this since she was three months old. Nothing the doctors tried had much effect. As a child she was hospitalized for several months trying to find something that would work. She had been on steroids, but they had side effects. She tried Chinese herbal medicine and got some relief, but it also caused stomach infections. She was currently using a cream that kept it from appearing so bad on her face. In the worst stages her whole body itched and burned. She wanted help relieving this, although she had had this for most of her life and it was definitely a part of her. She felt if it were removed, then a part of her would be taken away. It would have to be replaced with something.

As soon as she entered the deep trance she saw a bright light, and realized she was looking into a fire. The fire was at her feet and was spreading up her body. She was becoming upset so I moved her to where she could observe it objectively. She saw that she (as a man) and others were tied to stakes in a field near some woods, and were being burned at the stake. As we went back to the beginning of the story she saw that she and several other men lived in a large manor house or estate and were gnostics. They lived quietly studying and writing in large books, not bothering anyone. However the local officials thought they were dangerous and working with the Devil. The officials were spurred on by the religious community, who also saw them as a danger. One night they were awakened by dogs and men bursting into the house. He and some of the others ran through the woods chased by men and dogs, and were captured. They were taken to a place in town where they were horribly tortured, trying to make them reveal where they had hidden the books. During the torture there was a lot of damage done to his face, especially the jaw and eye (which have given the woman trouble in this life). Finally, when they couldn't get any more information the gnostics were taken to a large room for a mock trial. By that time he was in much pain and was completely disoriented so that he could not participate in the trial, or answer any of the accusations. He just sat there in a stupor and heard everything going on around him as though in a dream. It wouldn't have mattered anyway, because the trial was just a sham, a formality. They were then taken out to the field near the woods and burned at the stake. He and the others had done nothing wrong. They only possessed secret knowledge that they were attempting to preserve. She said some of the books had been hidden where the people in that day would never find them.

This has happened countless times down through history. There have always been groups of gnostics trying to preserve knowledge, and there have always been other groups trying to gain that knowledge to use for their own purposes. This was the real reason for the so-called "witch trials" during the Inquisition. The Church was trying to get rid of those who possessed secret knowledge that they had been unsuccessful in trying to obtain. Now we know that nothing is ever lost. The knowledge was hidden in the safest place of all: the human subconscious.

The subconscious acknowledged that watching the fire move up the body was the cause of the eczema. The burning and itching was symbolic of that death. It was easy to see why she was unable to finish her metaphysical courses in her present life. She was unconsciously afraid that the same thing would happen again if she obtained knowledge, although this had not kept her from seeking and studying it. I had to convince the subconscious that being burned at the stake would be very unlikely to happen again, because she was living in a totally different time period. The eczema could also be taken away because the cause was recognized, and the need for it was gone.

I remembered her statement that if it was taken away it would have to be replaced with something else. She was shown another life in Holland so she could see that at one time she possessed a strong healthy body. She really liked that body, so the subconscious said she could replace the eczema with the healthy body vision of the Dutch girl. This made her very happy and she agreed to allow it to happen.

A woman client had lower back pain stemming from a disk problem, and her doctors wanted to operate. She relived a past life as a black soldier in Korea. There were bombs exploding all around. He was hit in the back, and it threw him into a ditch full of water. Paralyzed, he couldn't get out, and drowned. He came back too soon and carried the memory in his back. This also explained her fear of enclosed spaces and not getting air. (Also occasional bronchitis.)

I have found in my work that there are more souls waiting in line for handicapped bodies than normal ones. This is easy to understand from the spirit viewpoint. The plan for reincarnating on Earth is to repay as much karma in one lifetime as possible, to avoid having to return again and again. More karma can be repaid through a handicapped body. The soul is learning great lessons, and also the caretakers (parents, etc.). And these people have agreed before coming into this lifetime that they will take care of the individual and help them as much as possible. Everything in life is about lessons, although some are more difficult than others. Also, what lessons are being learned by everyone who *sees* the handicapped person? How does the observer react? The handicapped are teaching everyone they come in contact with. Thus they are not to be pitied or shunned. They are to be accepted and admired for choosing a difficult path in this lifetime.

People who are adopted know this is going to happen. It is all planned, and from the other side the arrangements are made between the biological parents as well as the adopting ones. The biological parents have agreed to give the genes that design the physical body, and they learn a lesson by giving the baby away. The adopting parents have agreed to raise the baby in the environment it decided it wanted, in order to learn the lessons it desires in this life. Yet plans are not set in stone. There is always free will (not only the person's, but everyone that they come in contact with). All those involved can change the outcome.

The following case goes back to my first love: the discovery of lost or unknown knowledge. It is an interesting bit of *possible* history.

A man in England was the director of a printing company, especially good with people skills and negotiation. Yet he felt trapped by his job and responsibilities, especially marriage. He had developed a disturbing habit of squinting and blinking his eyes. It was annoying to him, and he thought it made him appear strange when talking to people in his work. He tried to pretend that it was merely an eye irritation. He was also sensitive to light.

He mostly wanted to know if he should change his direction in life, get a different job and perhaps leave his wife and four children to pursue a life with his girlfriend. Some of this could be the result of his age (in his 40s), when some people begin to question their path, and think they have "missed the boat". He had many dangerous hobbies: hang-gliding, scuba-diving, mountain climbing. He loved the excitement and danger of many pastimes that were the opposite of his job (which he was now finding boring.)

His regression was very strange, and I am wondering if we tapped into an unknown piece of history from World War II. At

32

first he went into a mundane life as a blacksmith with a family living happily in a small town somewhere in the American West. There was nothing unusual about the life, and I asked him to move forward to an important day. When he did, he suddenly gasped in horror and said he was seeing the mushroom cloud of an atomic explosion rising high in the sky. Then an extremely bright light that overwhelmed him. Naturally, I thought it had to be the atomic explosion at Hiroshima or Nagasaki, because those are the only ones I was familiar with. But it wasn't.

He exclaimed, "It was too much power! They must have made a mistake! It was far more powerful than they intended!" He was totally in shock, and then began to convulse and tremble and shake. He could not talk to me because he was so caught up in the physical reactions. I put my hand on him to calm him, and asked him to remove himself from the scene and view it from an objective position, so he could explain what was going on. It took a few minutes before he was able to do this. He was so caught up in the vibrations and convulsing that he couldn't speak. Almost as though he had been caught up in a violent shockwave. When he was finally able to talk, he said he was a member of a scientific team that was experimenting with this type of power. This was happening in Germany, which totally surprised me. They were in a mountainous area and had a laboratory in a canyon between two mountains. He thought he was Russian instead of German. Each of the scientists had a piece of the formula or equation. They had to put it all together to make it work. Nothing could be done separately because each one did not know the other parts. He had been chosen to participate because of his excellent knowledge of physics and mathematics. The scientists understood the concepts on paper, and the way it was supposed to work, but had not actually tried it. They were involved in a war and were trying to find a new weapon. It didn't matter if people were killed, because they were trying to save their own people. Apparently they were experimenting when the explosion occurred, intentionally or by mistake. But he was in awe of the power of the explosion. He did not think it was supposed to be so big. He thought they

33

were working on something that could annihilate a large area, but he gasped that this would destroy an entire city or more. It was far more powerful than he (and he presumed the others) had possibly imagined. As he looked down on the scene from above there was nothing left. The laboratory and everything was totally destroyed. As long as he viewed it from this position he was able to talk coherently and objectively. If he talked about the explosion and drifted back into the scene, he would start the shaking and convulsions again. So I had to calm him each time and remove him back to his safe vantage point.

His subconscious said he was allowed to relive this life so he could see that if he had survived something of this magnitude, then nothing could bother him. He would be able to survive any situation in life. (Although literally he did not survive, but his soul came out of it unscathed.) This explained the squinting, blinking and aversion to bright light in his present life when he was in a stressful situation. It was trying to remind him that he could handle anything.

Was Germany experimenting with atomic power before or at the same time the United States was? People have told me that the Germans were involved in experimentation with "heavy water". Maybe this was the reason they did not succeed. Maybe their top scientists, who possessed all the separate parts of the knowledge, were all killed at once in this fatal experiment, and there was no way they could quickly get back to that level in the experiment. People I have told about this said that someone would have noticed the cloud and repercussions. Maybe not. We were experimenting in White Sands, New Mexico, for years before the actual A-Bomb was dropped on Japan. They were conducting experimental explosions out in the desert. If someone saw it from a distance they probably would not have known what they were seeing. Remember, this was the most carefully kept secret of the war: the development of the atomic bomb. Only those in a position to know knew anything about it until the final dropping of the bombs on Japan. Maybe the same thing was happening in Germany. He indicated that the laboratory was located in an isolated spot in the mountains.

Maybe (like White Sands), they were located miles from civilization, so who could have known about it? If someone saw the explosion they would not have known what it was, because nothing like this existed in mankind's point of reference. Even normal bombing was horrible enough. This was probably Germany's best kept secret also. After the war, top German scientists came to the U.S. to work on our rocket program. We do know they were experimenting and successfully launching rockets (V-2s) during WW II. I think it is entirely possible that they were also experimenting with atomic power. We just beat them to it. Our atomic bomb was originally intended to be dropped on Germany, but the war ended before it was ready, so it had to be dropped on Japan to see if it would work. This is a fact of history. (See my book *A Soul Remembers Hiroshima*.) I think it is entirely possible that both countries were working on secret projects, and may have been aware of each other's progress.

All of these cases found answers that would never be accepted or even looked for by the logical medical community. Yet they make prefect sense through the logic of the subconscious mind. They also show how the therapist must try to convince that part of the client that the problem is no longer necessary. That the problem belongs to another body that ceased to exist many years ago. There are no books to teach the hypnotherapist what to do or say. Much happens on the spur of the moment, and it just goes back to "common sense" when trying to handle an unexpected situation. The main thing is that the client must be protected at all times. We must practice by the same oath as members of the medical profession: "First do no harm!"

These samples are only very few examples of the thousands of cases I have performed for therapy. I tried to choose some that would show the variety of explanations for physical and other problems that a client might have, and how it can be

35

traced to another lifetime. Also, this demonstrates the ease that the problem can be handled with the invaluable help of the person's subconscious. The skeptics will say that the person was fantasizing a story that would explain the physical problem. If that were so, why did they choose something so bizarre (and often gruesome) to offer an explanation? There are much simpler ways of doing it if they wanted to create a fantasy existence. If these cases are looked at objectively, it will be seen that they definitely do not exhibit the characteristics of fantasies. Even if it were their imagination, the main thing is that they found the answer to their problem. And with the answer came freedom. That is my greatest compensation for the years of work: being able to help others.

Of course, the questions are an essential part of the whole process. I have been told many times by "them" that the way the question is asked is of extreme importance. Questioning becomes an art. If the question is not asked correctly I will only receive partial information or none of any importance. The question must be phrased precisely, and this is what I have learned while developing my technique for almost thirty years. Practice is very important to the development of any technique of therapy.

Once a person has accepted the reality of the concept of reincarnation the next step is to understand that Earth is not the only school a person can choose to attend. We all have had lives on other planets and even other dimensions where it is possible to not have a physical body. It is possible to be an energy being. We are not limited by the physical world we know as Earth. Anything is possible. This is what I explore in the following chapters. Other worlds, other realities, other possibilities.

This chapter has focused on "normal" past-life therapy cases. The next chapters will focus on the "abnormal" or unusual cases where the client still obtained valuable information dealing with their problems, even though the subconscious took them down unusual and unfamiliar routes to get there. Along the way it also supplied invaluable information for my curious mind as the reporter and researcher of "lost" or unknown knowledge.

SECTION TWO

ANCIENT KNOWLEDGE AND

LOST CIVILIZATIONS

CHAPTER 3

THE CAT PEOPLE

(A DIFFERENT SPHINX)

This was a private session I conducted in June, 2001, while in Kansas City, Missouri at the Unity Church Convention.

In my hypnosis technique I regress the subject to a past life by having them descend from a white cloud. It can have very predictable results in normal past-life therapy, but often the results are unpredictable and anything can happen. That is the excitement of my work, because I never know where the person will go. In this case, when Jane came off the cloud she was surprised and confused to find herself in Egypt. She could see the pyramids, but her attention was more focused on a beautiful temple that stood on a rise nearby.

"The pyramids today are ruined. They look older. I'm seeing them as they look now, but I knew them then, before they were ruined. I remember when they were new and shiny and beautiful. The paintings were so gorgeous. I can see the paintings in the ruins before they had been beaten away. It's like *home*. I knew these places. This is my comfortable area. That's why I came there. Isn't that funny? I'm going back into the *then* instead of the now. Back when they were, oh, oh, so gorgeous. I can see the gold statues in the temple. I put my face against the gold figure, the gold cat. And it's funny how gold has such a warmth to it. There's an energy in that gold. I work with the Pharaohs, and I'm one of the few allowed in the temples. I've gone to a temple where I feel such great love. I see it all. Oh, my goodness! All those people."

39

D: *Are people there?*

J: Not in this spot. They're not allowed in here. It's one of the few places that truly only the chosen are allowed to sit. I'm trying to get more comfortable in here, because the cognitive part of me keeps coming up saying, "This is ridiculous!" And I'm telling it, "Shut up!"

This often occurs when the person first enters a past life scene. The conscious mind tries to distract and confuse. Anyone who attempts meditation the first time knows exactly how the mind can jabber and try to stop the process. The best thing to do is ignore it. As the person goes deeper into the description of the scenes the conscious mind shuts up, because no one is paying attention to it. The hypnosis technique that I have developed is designed to push the conscious mind to the side so that it cannot interfere. You close it off and allow the subconscious to supply the information freely. Without the conscious mind's questioning and interference the information is more pure and accurate.

D: *Don't worry about that part. Just tell me what you're seeing.*

J: I feel others wouldn't dare come in here, because it's not safe for them, because of the energy. This is the temple of the white light. This is where it exists here on this plane. And I need to walk into that light. (All of this, since she entered the scene, was said with a sense of awe and disbelief.) And there's such a presence in that light.

There was so much awe and reverence I knew I had to draw her attention back to describing her surroundings so we could find her location.

D: *Is the temple a separate place from the pyramid?*

J: When I floated down from the cloud I came to this temple. I don't even think they've discovered this yet. They're getting closer. You go through the tombs and that's where the dead go. But this is a temple where the living come.

40

And this is where I live. This is where I work. This is what I was born for.

D: *But you said there were other people?*

J: There are helpers in there. They bring the others to us that work here, that work in the light. They come to us for advice. And it's so funny, because they think we're the ones that know, but it just comes through the light. And they wouldn't dare walk in the light.

D: *You said there is a lot of energy in that place. The average person can't be in that energy?*

J: Not in that spot. Not in the white light.

I asked her to describe herself and she was confused again, because she wasn't sure if she was male or female.

J: (Confused) I keep going back and forth. One minute I feel like I'm female, but then I feel like I'm a male.

She was wearing a long flowing white robe, but she did not have any hair. Her head had been shaved.

J: We don't want it to interfere. I feel almost like I'm female, but I'm not, because we stay away from being female and male. (Chuckle) But I think this body would have been ordinarily categorized as female, because I think I can feel my breasts. I'm really, really skinny, so there's not much to my body.

She was wearing elaborate jewelry described as something made of gold and stones that clasped onto her lower arm and twisted around her wrist, extending out onto the fingers.

J: They deck us out great. (Laugh) It's more for them than it is for me. The people that come to be healed, they like that kind of fancy stuff. It makes them feel like they're getting ... let's see? What would we call that now? "More bang for the buck." (Laugh) That's why there is a statue of a gold cat, and they make our jewelry out of gold, because those that make the jewelry feel something in the gold. It's like a love in that gold alchemy. That's it! It's in the alchemy. They make us these jewels. (Surprised) By golly, the gold helps. That's *it!* The way it lights. That's the pure energy coming through. And it goes through the gold, so that when I touch the others for the healing, it keeps them from being hurt.

D: *Would they be hurt if you didn't have the gold?*

J: Yes, it's like a synthesizer from the etheric into the physical. When I go into the light, I take off my jewelry. And I think sometimes I even take off the robe, because I don't want anything between me and that incredibleness. And then I put on the robe, so that shields them from the body energy that I get.

D: *So you produce more energy when you're in that energy field?*

J: Oh, no. I just carry it. It's such a wonderful feeling. It gets into your ... into the atoms. It's so wonderful.

D: *It doesn't hurt you, but you have to shield it.*

J: From the others. It is too powerful for them. It's like, you touch them and they go "Poof!" (Laugh) It's nothing personal. That's why I have to watch for them.

D: *Is this energy in one part of this temple?*

J: Yes. We have our own stone in there. And those that carry that energy, when we get close to that stone, it just comes alive.

D: *Where is this stone?*

J: The people come in the front, and there's the hall where the regulars can be, and the people gather. And then there's the area where the energy starts to change a bit. Then they go into the other part, where they've put more artwork, and put jewels in the walls. And then there's the area where we keep the stone that's far and away from the others, so it's safe. And there are curtains to help shield them.

When I did my research I found that the old temples in Egypt were designed the way she said they were. The temple was considered the House of the god, not the house of the priesthood. The highest priest was the Pharaoh, who appointed high priests and others to perform his duties to the gods. There were two parts of the typical temple: the outer temple where the beginning initiates were allowed to come, and the inner temple where one could enter only after proven worthy and ready to acquire the higher knowledge and insights. The worshipers were never allowed further than the outer court, where they could leave their offerings. The statue of the god to whom the temple was dedicated was located in the inner temple. But in the case of the temple in this regression there was something more powerful located there.

In *Jesus and the Essenes*, there was also a giant crystal in the library at Qumran that the Essene students channeled their energy into, and it was directed by the Master of the Mysteries. Jesus learned to use this energy while he was a student there. This crystal was also in a protected area so the students wouldn't be hurt by getting too close. This is also similar to the Ark of the Covenant, which was kept in the Holy of Holies behind the veil in the Temple at Jerusalem. Only qualified priests could come in contact with it. In *Keepers of the Garden* Phil discussed a past life on another planet where his job was as an energy director, where he directed energy that was directed to him. So it appears that many in olden days had access to similar powerful stones, and also the knowledge of how to use and direct the energy that they contained. This is part of the ancient knowledge that we have lost. It seems to be time now to bring this information back to use in our time period.

D: *The average person doesn't go into the room where the stone is.*

J: Not past those areas. It's not safe.

D: *They don't have the training to be able to take that energy.*

J: It's the letting go-ness. That's what I've worked so hard in this life for, is just to let go. (A revelation.) Oh, isn't that amazing! Those of us who can work with the sacred stone, we put a little piece of it in the pyramids for those Pharaohs. And that's why people can die if they go into those parts of the pyramids. Actually that stone is so powerful there can only be one little piece in there. And those that went into the pyramids afterwards – into the *now* time – the tomb raiders, they talk about the curses. There's not a curse. It's the stone.

D: *It is just energy, and it's probably not compatible with everyone.*

J: NO! NO!

D: *And they perceive it as something negative.*

J: But see, the stone manifests anything. That's the secret of the stone. And if their heart isn't pure, that's why they can be destroyed, because they come near that pure energy.

D: *They manifest what they're afraid of, whatever it is.* (Yes) *That makes sense. But what kind of stone is that main one?*

J: That's funny, because you would think it would have to be a special stone. But it's the dual thing. Crystals work good, and it's hard to find a good pure crystal. And then you have the pure crystal, and you take it into the sacred energy. And that's what makes the crystal special. It's not that the crystal itself was special. (Chuckle) Isn't that funny? People are buying all these crystals now, and they think it's the crystals that are helping them. (Chuckle) It's the energy. It's not the crystal itself. It is that divine energy.

D: *But it is like a crystal stone?*

J: Well, no, that's the only thing that can, on the physical, hold it, besides these bodies that have agreed to it. We use the large crystals though, because when we go into our common place, and we open up to that energy, that pure crystal can hold that for us. It's kind of like those energizer batteries. We can store it in there, and then we go out and we work with the people.

D: *You're able to take the energy with you and use it.*

J: Yes, and give it. And then try to help them see. We can give them a real good blast of it, because the alchemy of the gold on the bracelets helps so they don't get hurt. And then that energy stays with them a little longer. I can just touch them and they get it pretty good, but that jewelry amplifies it. It also shields them from themselves, because that

44

bright pure energy is too strong.

D: *Where is this energy coming from?*

J: That comes from other light sources. From the very ends of it. (Softly) The God source.

D: *How can it be directed into that one chamber? It would be everywhere, wouldn't it? It would be dissipated.*

J: When we reincarnate onto this physical realm, those of us that can carry the energy, make an agreement. And we actually have that energy inside. There's an alchemy in that body. And that gives that body some pretty hard times when they incarnate. That's why Jane's kidneys kept shutting down in her present life, because it was the filtering of the karma of that soul, that spirit. Because no matter what, we have to have those bad experiences, because we want to be all knowing. But those energies exist. So when they come into this body in a very powerful state, there is so much cleansing. *So* very much cleansing, that those kidneys couldn't handle it.

Jane had several bouts of illness as a child and almost died. She spent months in the hospital as the doctors fought unusual and unfamiliar symptoms.

J: That's why she got so sick and why she had to be in the hospital. It was that energy that she brought with her.

D: *But wouldn't that energy have been left with the body in Egypt?*

J: Well, technically no. That white energy in the temple of healing – that's what it is, a temple of healing – we could put the energy into the crystal so it would be faster for us to come in and re-energize ourselves. And that gave it a focus.

D: *But I would think when the soul left that body, that the energy would have been left with that body. And not brought forward. Because the body in Egypt is the one that was directing it, working with that energy.*

45

My first concern is to help heal the body in the present incarnation. So I was trying to separate the two personalities so the carryover would cease to harm Jane's body.

J: Yes, but we're here to bring that energy in. It's actually spirit that carries that energy. And that spirit goes with that body. So it's the spirit that *owns* that. And so it's the degree that the spirit is going to be in that body on the physical. I didn't think it was that technical, but it really is. In Egypt, in that time in that body, the alchemy of the physical was one thing. But the sugars, the *contaminants* of the body in this physical time, the environment, the air. Even the sun is different. In Egypt you could almost go out and be healed by the sun. And now in this life there's so much garbage in that air, that the present body, when it went out to play, and would try to heal itself, couldn't. When this body had surgery it was difficult to handle the pain. She could have said, "No, I'm leaving this body. I'm out of here." And *this* body was really fortunate, because of the incarnation team, the parents, the love. The love, especially of that mother to this body. (Chuckle) I could hear her calling for me to incarnate from the other side. And I waited a while, because I knew this life wasn't going to be a lot of fun.

D: (Trying to get her back to the original story.) *But it's interesting to me that the spirit could bring that energy forth.*

J: But see, that's what spirit is, it's an energy. We are all a spark of God.

D: *Yes. But the physical body in Egypt was exposed to that energy and knew how to work with it. That's why I was surprised that that energy would still remain with the spirit.*

J: It really wasn't that they were separate. In the ocean of love and mercy, it's all that bright white light. And then we break off in that little spark. And then we incarnate. And when she came into that incarnation in Egypt, a lot of that white light came with her. And then we wanted to bring that white light into *now*. And when we did that, because of the environment ... I mean, it wasn't *that* energy then and this energy now. Because it's *all* now. It's just a whim, and this part of the whim, because of the environment, that's the problem.

D: *But the energy, you said, comes from the all-powerful, the Source. And it entered into and directed this crystal. Were you trained to know how to create this energy and direct it?*

J: No. You're born with it. You learned it. But it can't be taught on this plane. You carry it with you from your other schools on your other planes.

D: *I was wondering if you were taught with others how to create this energy with the crystal in that place.*

J: No, back then it was tougher on the parents, because the kids just did this stuff. How do we say this? We just did it. The child just did it. And that's why this child had to be away from the parents and from physical things, because the body did things. If those parents would have seen that, they would have freaked out. They would have been too shocked. Because as a child, when you incarnate, you just do it. And at the time of the pyramids when that child was born, things happened when that child was tiny. So the parents knew this infant was to be taken to this school. Taken to the temple, where those who also did these things were able to raise that child, because those parents knew they couldn't.

This was similar to the case of Molly, told in another chapter, who had amazing abilities in this life as a baby and very young child, which totally frightened her parents.

D: *It has to be in a different environment.* (Yes.) *But there were others there also with you.*

J: And they were born just like that too.

D: *And they were brought there. But you said this temple is near the pyramids? You can see them.*

J: Yes. The pyramids are off. They had the temple at a height, a higher place. And then you can look out, and you

47

can see where the pyramids are.

D: *But you don't think that temple has ever been discovered?*

J: No. The temple was left to dust, because it was its time. It wasn't its time to be known, like it was for the pyramids. And there's something about the Sphinx. The cat part and then the face part. That's funny. It's almost like somebody knew. It's like my attachment with the cat statue. The temple had to be dissolved. That's why they built the Sphinx.

D: *The temple was there before the Sphinx?*

J: Yes. And the only thing that was allowed to be a reminder of that temple that was destroyed, was this Sphinx. It represented the cat people. They called us the cat people, because we had our golden cats and we had our temple cats. It was for those people who needed our help. The life they were in, they wouldn't come to the temple. So we'd go to them in cats.

D: *How do you do that?*

J: You see, cats are very special. That's why they have that attitude. (Chuckle) We could pick them up and we could communicate with them mentally. If you ever try to talk to a cat on the physical, they'll look at you like you're crazy. Unless you're one of us, and then they understand. But we would hold the cat and we would talk to it. And then we'd send it off to help someone. After they were done, they would come back, and tell us what had happened. But that's why they built that Sphinx with a cat body, or the lion. Of course, that's the greatest cat of all. We had lions in the temple. They were our best cats. But, you know, if you sent a lion out amongst the crowds of the people they'd .... (Loud laugh)

D: *They wouldn't like it.* (She was still laughing at the mental picture.) *And then when they came back, you were able to understand what the cat ....*

J: Yes. Because we visualized, and the cat would show us that they had gone, and had rubbed that person. And maybe that person opened up to the cat, and they were able to hold

48

them and hold them. And they got the energy that we sent them.

From encyclopedia:

"In Egypt, cats were kept as pets not only on account of their helpfulness, but because of their beauty, intelligence and grace, and were associated with the gods. In Egypt they were sacred to the chief god, Ra, who sometimes took the form of a cat, and Isis, the chief goddess, was portrayed with a cat's ears. Moreover, the Egyptians revered a cat-headed goddess, Pasht, who was closely related to Isis and from whose name it is believed the word 'puss' has been derived. Cat temples, and also cat cemeteries containing thousands of bodies of embalmed cats, have been excavated in different parts of Egypt. Many other animals were sacred to the Egyptians, but none except the bull was worshiped over the entire country like the cat, which they immortalized also in pyramid texts and in their jewelry, pottery and furniture."

Maybe the archeologists didn't fully understand the role that cats played in that culture.

D: *Were you there when the temple dissolved?*

J: No, I was there early on when the temple was new. When it was functioning with energy. When I was helping them. If I were to go back there in the now, I could only find it by that pile of dust that it is. In configuration to the view.

D: *Was the destruction done on purpose?*

J: Yes. The people needed to go into that time of darkness.

D: *Was the dissolving done by the people like yourself that were living there at that time?*

J: No. Oh, I think they thought they were responsible for it. That the energy itself, the divine source, was angry. And said, "Fine, if you don't want my help, then I shall cease to exist there for you." And it was just ... *gone*. There was no need for it to be on the Earth plane. It just "swoosh".

D: *What did it mean by "if you don't want my help"? Did the times change after you were there?*

J: Yes. People believed more in the gold that we wore, than in the energy we put into it. So they started making those statues, those damn statues. And they prayed to those stupid statues. And they prayed to that gold. And they said, "Now I'm healed because of the gold." We tried to teach them that it wasn't the gold. That it was the energy, but they couldn't understand that. In that life I decided to take off the gold once and heal somebody, because I could see where they were going. And I touched them, and they died. It was too much energy. They even cursed me then. They thought I killed them. And they dragged me out, and then they stoned me to death. After I didn't wear the gold, that's when those crazy fools got the idea that it was the gold that was healing. They didn't know, of course. They couldn't understand unless they had a child come into their life like we were. And even though the parents tried to explain, it was too late.

This part about the temple dissolving sounded very much like what happened to the temples of the Sun and the Moon in the Bartholomew story in *Book One*.

D: *I would have thought that the energy could just leave, but the building would remain.*

J: Because of what we had been able to do, it was like molecularizing God, in a sense. And every little piece of that temple had that energy in it, especially in that one area. And that's why it had to be dissolved, because if the people had walked in there later, they would have been killed. And so, they took out all the gold, because of the energy that the gold had. The gold still healed people.

D: *So it did some good.*

J: Oh, yes. But the temple itself, and the piece of quartz, the sacred stone, turned into dust when it was dissolved. (A revelation.) Oh, for heaven's sakes! When you look at the grains of sand now in that area, you'll see little crystalline pieces. And that's the little pieces of the sacred stone. But the stone had to be broken down into those tiny fragments in order for it to not kill any more.

D: *But there is still a lot of energy in that area, isn't there?*

J: *Oh, yes!* And we call it, a rose is a rose is a rose. And when the divine agrees to something, it doesn't just change its mind like a human does. (Laugh) Yes, what it does it does.

D: *So the temple was there at the same time as the pyramids.*

J: Yes, the pyramids were the oldest.

D: *The Sphinx came later?*

J: Yes, because after the temple was gone, even though the people didn't understand what we did, they were grateful for the gold. And the mystery of the cat people became like a legend. The priests weren't able to continue what we did because they didn't know our secrets. Creating a legend was the best they could do.

D: *What were they using the pyramids for at that time?*

J: They were like the satellites from that temple. As I said, we took a little piece of the sacred stone from our temple and put it in the pyramid, because it was to honor the great ones. The great Pharaohs. And they were great. They were the ones chosen to work with the people. The Pharaohs were born with their secrets, just as we were born with our secrets to heal and help people. And we of the temple were of foreign energy, and those of the pyramids were of another energy. And the pyramid energy had more of the negative. That's why it still exists, because it was able to assimilate into this environment so much easier. And it was a way of trying to carry and explain some of the great temple. (Pause) We were the ones that survived Atlantis and its destruction. That was the first place where that energy was brought in. And that's where we learned first that the energy had to be shielded. It had to be in that special temple, because that was the first place that the divine energy was used. And as soon as those crazy people started getting their crazy ideas ... you can't have any negativeness around that divine. It's not that the divine is going to point at it, and say, "Oooh, that's bad!" That's not it. The divine doesn't do that. The divine is beyond the good *and* the bad. But what happens is, if you have that negative and you bring that into the divine again, it exponentiates. That was the amazing part. It wasn't even that at the Atlantean times. It wasn't that they were evil. It wasn't that they were vicious, but it was the beginning of the negative. I guess the Great One realized that we weren't learning enough being positive. It is that spirit *is*. Spirit never stops. And we cannot walk away from one body into the next.

D: *You just carried the information from one life to the other.*

J: Yes. There were actual ones that were told about Atlantis coming to its end. That was so hard for us to face, because we believed that we could teach. And it wasn't that we couldn't teach. The alchemy of the bodies was changing. And that was part of what was leading to the destruction of Atlantis. That's why it had to be destroyed in total again in Egypt, because that energy couldn't be let loose.

D: *The energy had become too powerful?*

J: Yes. I've left that temple and I've gone to old Atlantis now. I can understand it better if I have my feet in Atlantis, because, oh, that was so beautiful. And I was so upset when they said it had to come to an end.

D: *But the energy was being misused in Atlantis, wasn't it?*

J: Oh, yes. They called it the next step. Can you imagine that? They called that the next step. I called it cliff jumping. Because what if I could jump off of a cliff and go "splatt"! What have I learned? I learned that I can "splatt". What's your point? But they said that it wasn't the splatt, it was the fall. Learning from the fall. Again, we're trying to see a direction, and we're talking of evolution. It was what we were trying to evolve into. The alchemy of the body started to change. The alchemy of our bodies then ... oh, my, what our bodies could *do!* These bodies can *still* do it. But the alchemy started to change, and so the energy started to change. Then we couldn't get near the pure. We had to get further and further and further away from it. And that's why now we can go back to that body. That's still hiding in there under all those layers.

D: *It still has the knowledge?*

J: Yes. And that's why we can look at it and say, "Okay, I'm going to heal this." (Chuckle) And that's why this body has a real hard thing to cure here with this part, (She pointed to the center of her forehead) because it couldn't accept that divine part.

D: *The third eye part?* (Yes)

I wanted to return to information about the Sphinx.

D: *You were talking about the Sphinx. You said that was created later in memory of the Cat People. Did it have a face like it has now?*

J: No, it was more a womanly face. They redid it later.

D: *That's what I've heard. People have said that the original face was different.*

J: The original face was beautiful. It was a woman. It was a beautiful, beautiful woman. Oh, I just saw something! The one that they stoned? That was her face they put on there.

D: *The one you were in that lifetime?*

J: Yes. I didn't realize they thought I was that beautiful. (Chuckle) I wasn't. It was their guilt for stoning me. But they stoned me because they feared me, because I killed somebody. Never before had I killed somebody. All I wanted to do was show them that their damn gold wasn't what was curing people. – There was also the headdress. I wore a headdress too when I did that healing. It came down onto the shoulders. Oh, that's why my shoulders bother me! From that damn headdress. It was so heavy.

53

Oh, and that's my guilt. That's it! That's why the shoulders bother this body, because I thought I caused the destruction of the temple.

D: *You didn't though.*

J: Oh, no. I know that now.

D: *What does the headdress look like? I'm trying to get a mental image of what the original face looked like on the Sphinx.*

J: The headdress had like a shoulder arch, and then it came up, and then it went across. And it had a rise to it. They tried to make it kind of like a sun around the head. They were trying to represent that glow of energy that we were trying to radiate out. It fit over the head. And out to the shoulders, and down this way, out to the paws. And so they put that part onto the cat body. *Originally,* it was our shoulder piece to that headdress, because it was like a mantle that we put on. (Apparently here she switched and began describing her own headdress again.) And there were jewels across the top. Maybe it was like diamonds, maybe it was like crystals, but that part was clear, and it was set into the gold. And it was *horribly* heavy, is what the damn thing was. And the memory of it caused shoulder pain in this present lifetime. The pain was also caused because I thought all this time that I caused the destruction of the temple. The paws came out from the shoulder part of the headdress. It was like, if you laid the cat down, and then you set the mantle on top of it so that the paws came out at the end. But this was part of the mantle of that headdress.

She made hand motions showing the shoulder piece coming down as far as her wrists, with only the hands sticking out.

J: And that's why the head of the Sphinx would have been so much bigger, because of the headdress. And that's why it fell apart, because that mantle piece couldn't take the weathering.

D: *Did they change the head on purpose, or did it just come apart?*

54

J: Well, it was the female thing. The Pharaohs, the guys with the pyramids that are still there. They weren't too keen on having this big woman thing there. (Chuckle) So they made it more generic, because it doesn't exactly now look like a man or a woman.

D: *Right. The head's too small for the body.*

J: Yes, *way* too small for the body. The Pharaohs made that smaller, because they wanted to put us in our place as the time went on. The body was that of a cat. And so proportionally they tried to put the head of a human onto a cat. And then they did the calculations. What's sixty-two times? Sixty-two times the size of the body of the cat, would have been the ratio. Sixty-two, something like that. Maybe that was it. You've seen the things the Pharaohs wore over their heads. They took that from us with our mantle.

D: *There is talk of something underneath the Sphinx. Do you know anything about that?*

J: Maybe that's some of our old temple. Maybe he built the Sphinx on top of where our temple was? Is that it? Secrets?

All during this session Jane seemed to be receiving information that surprised her, that she was not logically expecting. Also, many of her answers were almost whispered. Very soft, but the tape recorder was able to pick it up.

D: *People have said maybe there is something underneath the paws of the Sphinx.*

J: Under the *body* part. They did keep some of our secrets in that body part, before the temple was destroyed. Because we did record some of our learning. The learnings were kept.

D: *Can you see where this would be located?*

J: Yes, the kitty sits on it. (Chuckle) Have you ever seen a cat when it's caught a mouse, and it's proud of itself? He'll lay on it. That's what this Sphinx's been doing. (Laugh) He's laying on his great catch, on his great prize. The paws, maybe that could be the way they enter into it. Sure, sure, that's it. That's where you go in. I can almost see it. Under the paws there's an entrance. And they did it like that on purpose, because in our original temple ... remember I told you how we put the most energized part in the back? I think maybe they might have kept some of that sand from the temple that was destroyed. (Laugh) And no one ... (She found this amusing) this is cute. They are going to go under those paws, they're going to find the entrance, they're going to be all excited. They're going to go back in there, and they're going to find (Laugh) ... dust and sand. And they're going to say, "For this?" (Laugh) They'll say, "Oh, well, this was already raided."

That would certainly be a shock to the discoverers, because they would not realize the importance and symbolism of the sand attached to the original energy of the healing temple.

D: *They're hoping to find records and things like that.*
J: There are the records. But it will take them a while to try to decipher those, because it was *our* secret language.
D: *Is there a way to get back into that part if they find the entrance?*
J: Labyrinths? I think they made it a labyrinth. (Pause) I'm not supposed to say.
D: *You're not supposed to say what?*
J: Well, those who weren't destroyed in the temple were angry. So they made this very, very difficult. And they're not going to make it any easier for anybody. Those things were buried. But when people get in there, they're going to find a whole different language that they haven't found before. Different from what they typically think was spoken then, because we had our own ways. And it wasn't that we had our *own* ways. It's what we were told. It was so nice to be able to be in the temple, because it was such a different way of being than it was outside of the temple. We had our own languages. We had our own skills. We

had our own ways of doing everything. But it *had* to be different, because our energy was so different. And it was the same thing in Atlantis, in order for us to learn more. We had to set up the temple, because with our discussions with the divine and what we were trying to learn here, we begged to still be able to teach. But the divine said, "They won't learn." And we said, "You have to give us a chance." And the divine said, "All right, here." That's what it did. And he said, "But you have to be *totally* separate, totally different, totally ...." So when they get in there, they're not going to understand what they find. I don't even know if the hieroglyphs ....

D: *The carvings?*

J: Yes, yes. I don't even know if they'll understand those. They're going to be so amazed. I just wonder if they're going to be allowed to finally get in there. But I suppose, with the things that are coming, the things that are coming ... (Softly) maybe. They'll be so confused. (Laugh)

D: *Can you see, will the entrance under the paws be hard to find?*

The reason I was trying to pursue this and get more detail was because I had a session with a friend about the same thing only a week or so before. She is working with investigators in Egypt, as a psychic, to try to discover the hidden tunnels. She had already been down into a part under the paws, between the Sphinx and the pyramid. She was planning on returning to do more investigation.

J: It's hidden in plain sight. It's so obvious. Energetic-wise, I think if I went there I could just say, "Start diggin' here, boys." It's very deep. They went out of their way to make it complicated, but not impossible. The ones who did this understood what the logic would be *now*, and so they used that against them. (Chuckle) So if they try to do a logical progression on it, they're just going to get further away. (She found this amusing.)

D: *But when they do get under there, they're going to find a labyrinth.*

57

J: That's what's going to slow them down, because there are so many different dead-ends. And there's a lot of area between where the paws are, and the back.

D: *But only the right people are going to be able to find it, aren't they?*

J: Well, they're the ones who have asked. They've asked to be able to bring that into the now, because it's going to take them so long to understand it. It may not be so shocking for them, because the pictures are going to show that the body can heal itself. But they're not going to understand.

I then asked questions that Jane wanted to find out about. This was the real purpose for the session. I will only include remarks that relate to the story. The rest may not be pertinent.

I asked the subconscious how that life in Egypt related to the events in her present lifetime.

J: The big experience was realizing that she didn't destroy the temple. Also the shoulder thing. She carried a lot of that in this lifetime.

We now knew that the discomfort could be taken away, because we had found the source of the problem.

J: What she needs to understand is that the divine, yes, can control. And sometimes when we come into the physical, we think we're just trying things, but that's not it. She thought she was the cause of the destruction of that temple.

D: *She didn't have anything to do with it, but she was stoned.*

J: It was time for the people to be shown that it wasn't the gold that did the healing. But the divine knew, and she was shown she would be stoned for that. Now why would she forget that? Oh! She forgot because it was so terrible. That makes sense. But it was time for the consciousness to make that change. The people needed to make that change. Except that was a great step *down.* There were thousands involved when she was stoned, and it was a great tragedy.

58

D: *Yes, it was, because many of the abilities and the use of energies were lost at that time.*

J: And that's why she's earned the privilege to bring that back in this life.

D: *This is why she came into this life with so much energy, that she had to be in the hospital as a baby. To learn to assimilate the energies, so the body could handle it?*

Jane had to stay in the hospital for months as a baby because of unusual symptoms that the doctors never could understand. Apparently it was an assimilating time so the body could adjust to the high energy she was carrying into this lifetime from the lifetime in Egypt. But this has also now been traced back before that to the lifetime in Atlantis when the use of these energies was commonplace.

J: The divine has been working with people so that they have those out-of-the-ordinary experiences. That's natural. Back in Atlantean times if you didn't, there was something wrong with you. It was a natural thing to do. And what we did with it then in Atlantis ... we walked into the negative. And after walking so many years deeper, deeper, deeper, deeper, into the negative, now we've learned where our negative takes us.

Jane was allowed to remember this knowledge so she could use it for healing in her present lifetime. The energies were available, they had never really gone away. They had been waiting in a dormant state until she would reincarnate into a lifetime where she could make use of them. The knowledge of how to use these abilities would come to the surface of her conscious mind, and it would become very easy and natural to use these energies for her healing work. I am finding many, many of the people alive now are tapping into these dormant energies, because now is the time to revive them and put them to positive use.

J: They built the Sphinx for her, because they loved what she did. But they also feared it, and that's why they buried the secrets deep underneath it, because they felt she was the only one that knew that. And so when she died, that temple was destroyed. There was such great fear, and they buried those things deep. And they built the Sphinx to honor her, and hopefully to appease her so she wouldn't harm the people any more.

It must have also been very frightening to the people when the temple was totally destroyed and dissolved to a pile of dust and particles. It is easy to see how unnatural events can create legends, monuments and idols to symbolize what occurred. In later years people would not have the full story about the events (because of their unnatural components), and other explanations could be brought forth by those in power. Especially if they want to discredit the original events. This has been the role of many rulers and priests throughout history, and the reason why much of our history of the Earth (especially the ancient times) has been lost. Part of my work has been to bring this history back to our time.

There was a strange and rather unusual aftermath to this session. We were in Kansas City, Missouri, attending the Unity Church Conference. My daughter, Nancy and her children were at the hotel where the conference was being held, selling my books at a booth. When the conference was over, we were going to head back home to Huntsville, with a stopover at my daughter Julia's home in Lamar. As we were trying to find the correct street to lead us to the highway out of the city, we became lost and went down an unfamiliar street. We passed a huge Masonic temple. I was completely astounded as I saw two very large statues, one on either side of the steps leading into the building. They were statues of lying sphinxes. And they had the face of a woman and an unusual headdress that came over her head and down the back halfway, over her shoulders and down to the wrist of the paws. Both statues appeared to be identical. I was flabbergasted and began telling Nancy about the coincidence with the regression I had just finished. We drove on for several blocks before I asked Nancy to turn around and go back. I wanted to get out and look at the statues more closely. I also wanted to take some pictures. We drove back and parked. I got out and walked all around the front of the temple, taking pictures of the statues from all angles. I wanted visual proof and something substantial that I could refer to in a book, and also to help in my research. I kept wondering why the Kansas City Masons had this symbol of the sphinx. It was definitely a departure from the traditional version of the one in Egypt. I knew I would have to research the background of this symbol. I also now knew that the regression had some basis in fact, and that I should write about it. Who knows what I might uncover? I also know it was no mistake that we went down the "wrong" street.

Ever since I had this regression I have attempted to find through research some evidence that a woman-headed sphinx really did exist, but to no avail. I have found mention that a second giant sphinx was thought to have existed on the opposite side of the Nile, but I have not been able to find anything else about that. I have been told that there are many, many sphinxes in Egypt, and some of them have a woman's face, but usually are depicted with wings. An Internet site said, "Rarely was the Egyptian sphinx portrayed as a female. When it was, it symbolized the goddess Isis and/or the reigning queen." This same website said that in ancient times a Sun temple once stood in front of the Great Sphinx to receive offerings to the rising Sun. (Again the reference to gold represented by the Sun.)

There are also many, many pyramids of varying sizes in Egypt. The main Sphinx and pyramid near Cairo are the ones we are most familiar with.

If I could find out nothing more about the ancient sphinx, I decided to find out why the Masons in Kansas City put the statues of woman-headed sphinxes at the entrance to their Temple. I met with surprising results. The magnificent structure is the Scottish Rite Temple located at 1330 Linwood Blvd. in Kansas City, Missouri. It was built in 1928, and Jorgen C. Dreyer was the architect and sculptor of the sphinx statues. I was finally able to contact someone in authority at the Temple and he was confused by my question, "Why do the sphinxes at the entrance of the building have the face of a woman?" He said no one had ever asked that question before. He said they go past those statues every morning coming to work, and had never questioned it. But, yes, why would a Masonic Lodge, a male-oriented organization, have statues of a woman at their entrance? He said that the building and statues were supposed to be an exact copy of the Scottish Rite headquarters in Washington, DC. This was built in the late 1800s during the Napoleonic Era, when Egyptian architecture was strongly influencing buildings in America.

I went on the Internet to find more information about this building in Washington that preceded the one in Kansas City, but the mystery deepened. They were supposed to be exact copies of each other. The architecture of the building was, but not the statues. The sphinxes in Washington that flank the steps are male. They are not identical, one having its eyes open and the other with the eyes shut. They are said to represent Wisdom and Power.

I tried to find more information about the sculptor, Jorgen C. Dreyer, to discover why he carved the statues as female. There was information about the man and the building, but not his motives. From the Kansas City Library website: "The Scottish Rite Temple sphinxes were completed in 1928 and weigh 20,000 pounds apiece. Each of the two female heads atop lion bodies with griffin details wears a medallion that represents the Masonic order." I attempted to find out more by researching the newspaper files about the date of dedication of the building in 1928. I thought there might be a mention of why

62

the statues were designed the way they were. But again no luck. The Kansas City Star no longer allows anyone to see their archives. How do they expect people to do research if we cannot have access to old newspaper files?

I also had no luck in finding any mention of "The Cat People", except that it was known that cats were highly respected and worshiped in Egypt.

So I decided to go ahead with this book even though I do not like to leave loose ends. Maybe someone out there has the answers and can share them with me.

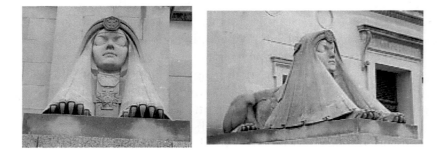

Woman headed sphinxes at the entrance to the Scottish Rite Temple, Kansas City, Missouri.

Power   Wisdom

Male headed sphinxes at the Scottish Rite Temple Headquarters in Washington, D.C.

CHAPTER 4

THE GODDESS ISIS

This session was done while I was in Las Vegas, Nevada, speaking at a conference in April, 2002. Ingrid was a small woman in her fifties who had been raised in South Africa. She had an accent, but I became used to it during the session. Accents always give me problems. I have to listen very closely. Sometimes the subject will not go as deeply if English is their second language, but in Ingrid's case it didn't seem to make any difference. She went deep quickly. I did not even have a chance to ask where she was when she descended from the cloud. She began with an emotional outburst. I had to turn on the microphone quickly.

I: I came here to make peace! Others do not understand our ways. They fight so much. They destroy so much. We have been trying to bring some balance, but they do not understand.

She was so emotional she was on the verge of tears. I wondered what caused this outburst. Was it related to a past life, or was it something Ingrid had been holding inside for a long time?

I: I didn't want to come here, and my elders *forced* me to come here, because the planet *needed* a change. And I came. (Crying)
D: *Have you been on Earth for a long time?*
I: I was here thirty-six thousand (36,000) years ago, in the time of Memphis. (Her words were difficult to understand because she was sobbing in between.) I then came from

Sirius to make good the destruction on this planet.

I cannot lead, but must allow the subject to tell their own story. Was she referring to the destruction of Atlantis?

D: *Were you living at the time of the destruction?*
I: I came *after* the destruction. To help the people. The race that was on Earth.

The emotion subsided. She was easier to understand.

I: The survivors. To teach them the new ways. To teach them love. To teach them harmony. To teach them oneness.
D: *Did others come with you?*
I: There were a few of us that came in the ship. We landed in the place that you know as Egypt. Some of the survivors were there, because that was part of Atlantis. A major portion of Atlantis is under the ocean. And much new land emerged. Egypt was part of Atlantis.

Her pronunciation was very deliberate, as though the names of these countries were strange and difficult to pronounce.

I: Some of the survivors were in Egypt. And there were others on little islands, who moved after a while to other high land.
D: *But you had been living on what you call "Sirius"?*
I: Yes. We are a very highly evolved race or frequency or energy level. We eat of the light. We do not eat physical things, as you do on this planet.
D: *But you said the others made you come?*
I: There is a council of elders on our planet that oversees much of the cosmos. They are responsible for life and for creation. They create many of the species, and many of the planets. This is their job.

This statement about the creation of our species did not surprise me, because I have received the same information through many of my subjects. It resulted in my books, *Keepers of the Garden* and *The Custodians,* which cover the material in detail.

D: *Do they have to physically go to those planets to do this?*
I: They don't necessarily have to go physically, but sometimes they do. When they *re*program things. When they *re*structure things. When they *remake* species that are *totally* – what can we say? – have gone astray. When the frequency and energy levels are not useful to peace and harmony.
D: *Originally did you create the animals there and physically take them to the planet?*
I: They were not *physically* taken to the planet. We *designed* them where we were, and then physically came here to energize them. With the substance of whatever frequencies the planet Earth has; the energies and the frequencies of this planet.
D: *So you also went to many other planets?*
I: (Interrupted) Oh, yes! We have inhabited, not only this planet, but many, many more. Because we are the *gatekeepers* of this planet, and many, many more. We are concerned about what is going on here. Don't you see? (She became emotional again.) With the destruction that is going on. (Sobbing) We gave them free will, but to experience *love,* not disharmony and *destruction.* They have gone astray.
D: *But you said you didn't want to come. Why did they send you?*
I: (She calmed down.) They sent me the first time after the deluge of Atlantis to help the species. There were others that came with me. There were many of us. And then when the species was ready to be self-sufficient, we left.
D: *Did you have physical bodies at that time?*
I: We had to change our structure to align with the more base level of the Earth species. So we took on physical bodies to

67

be – what can I say? – to be more aligned with the structure and the energies and the frequency levels of this planet. Which is very low, and we would call it "very base". The star system you call "Sirius", the brightest star that you see in the heavens, that is where we come from.

D: *What did you look like in your original form at that time?*

I: We are now light bodies. Just energy frequencies. You see us as light. You don't see us truly as a physical form, just beings of light.

D: *Then you were living on one of the bodies that orbit Sirius? Is that what you mean?*

I: We live *in* Sirius.

D: *But I think of a star as being like our Sun. It would be very hot and very bright.*

I: It is not just bright. It is *brilliantly* bright. But our frequencies and our energies are in alignment with that system. Like your bodies are in alignment with the Earth system, ours are too with *our* system. Our frequencies resonate with the star you call "Sirius".

D: *You would be an energy that was part of that sun, as we call it?* (Yes) *That was what I was trying to clarify. You said there is a council there. Are they located also on the star?*

I: They are located there, and they are also located in what you call "the central sun". We are continually in contact with what you would call "the Lords of the Word".

I couldn't understand this. I thought she was saying Laws, but she corrected me and said it was "Lords of the Word."

I: The Lords of the Word of the Cosmos, or as you would call it "the Word". And as *we* would call it, "the Cosmos", or "the Lords of the central sun", or the higher beings, or the light beings of the central sun. That are part of what you would call "God" or God*dess*, or where our light begins from.

D: *I have heard of the council, but I was never sure where they were located. But these are the ones that take care of all of the planets?*

68

I: Of the whole Cosmos.

D: *They make all the rules and regulations.*

I: Yes. There are many laws, but they are not controlling laws. They are laws made from love. They are laws that work with *freedom*, and with love.

D: *Were you always an energy being, or did you have other lives?*

I: I had the ability to mold to the energy frequency. I sometimes had to take a physical form to raise vibrational frequency of energy levels. Not only on your planet, but sometimes on other planets, too.

D: *But at that time when you were first told to come, the council knew something was going to happen to Atlantis?*

I: The council waited for the deluge to happen in Atlantis. It was time. It was too late to save Atlantis. But they needed to assist the planet, and the survivors, and the ecology system, and other life forms. Assist them and help them in their survival.

D: *Because there was much turmoil at that time.*

I: Oh, there was. Too much. Much too much. It was the turning of the axis as well, so you can imagine the problems and the destruction with something totally lop-sided.

D: *So your job was to land in Egypt and help the survivors there.*

I: Yes, and I lived there a long, long time. I lived from my time of arrival, and from my time of taking an Earth body, to be able to be part of this frequency. And to be able to resonate with this frequency, I had to take on an Earth body. And that Earth body was in a physical form for at least six hundred years. Most of us lived for about that time, until the people became more self-sufficient. Then we left.

D: *So you were living with them that entire time, with this physical body you had fashioned.*

I: Yes, we did. And some of us intermarried with the Earth species to give it a *higher* being to assist when we left.

D: *Did the people know you were different?*

I: Oh, they did. They called us "gods", because they *knew* us. This is why I was known as Isis, the goddess. I was the woman, Isis, the goddess. I took the body of the female. And my name then was not as you know it as Isis. They have changed it somewhat. I was Ezi (phonetic). That was the original name. Ezi, which you now call Isis. We were helping the people. We made them understand all about ecology. We taught them about the different herbs. We taught them about the different healing methods. We taught them how to raise the frequencies. We taught them about oneness. We taught them about what you call "God". What we know of the kind creator. We taught them about Him. We taught them about how to love one another, to respect one another, to respect one another's space. And respect all life. That *everything* was part of the one. That there was no separation.

D: *I suppose they were ready to hear this after the destruction.*

I: Oh, they were very, very ready. They were ready to turn around. They were really ready to change.

D: *Did you also teach them how to build the buildings?*

I: Oh, yes. The pyramids are ancient, my dear one. More than twelve thousand years old (12,000). They are ancient, ancient, ancient. More than you can think about. It was done with a form of light energy. Those big stones that you see were done with light energy.

D: *Did your people from Sirius do it, or did you teach the others how to do it?*

I: We were partly responsible. But some of the species that we created by intermarriage also resonated with some of our frequencies. And they too could work with the light energy, and teleport most of those massive stones and structures. And design things exactly and in accordance with what we had planned, so that they were in alignment with the planet, and in alignment with Sirius. And in alignment with receiving the frequencies and energies with whoever went into these huge temples. They were really temples of healing. They are not, like people think, temples of burials. They are not.

Jane said the same thing in Chapter Three, "The Cat People."

D: *I've never thought they were tombs.*

I: They are not where people go after they die. They are temples to raise frequencies. To raise energy. That's what they're for. Much of the energies are not as powerful as they were, but there is some frequency left. What has happened over time is that people have come in with changes in energies and vibrations. And they have spoiled much of the original essence of those temples. They have debased it.

D: *Many years have gone by too. That would make a difference, wouldn't it?*

I: It does to a certain extent. But if the people had gone there with pure intention, then their vibration would have been much, much higher. And it would have remained as it was done, and would have assisted many, many, *many* people.

D: *But the world didn't stay that way.*

I: It didn't. They have made the energies and the vibrations so tainted, all life forms. And they have polluted the ocean. They have polluted the land, the rivers, everything. *Everything.* The oceans, the forests, the mountains, their energy is everywhere. We breathe in those things too. It's everywhere. It's everywhere. Everything alive is affected.

D: *You can't get away from it now.*

I: No, it's everywhere, everywhere.

This was making her upset again. I had to change the subject.

D: *I have been told that in Atlantis they had the abilities to do things with their minds.*

I: They misused their minds. They worked a lot with crystals. They used the light of crystal energy to do much of their work. They were open to this, but they didn't know as much as *we* did. They didn't know as much of the light

71

therapy, as they knew of the crystal energy that they worked with. They misused the crystal energy. After the destruction, we showed them how to do things the right way, and to clear their minds.

D: *What about the Sphinx? Was that built about the same time as the pyramids?*

I: The Sphinx was built about the same time, within maybe a thousand years. The Sphinx was built more by the Atlanteans, because they used the Sphinx for some of the burial sites. You will notice there are chambers under the Sphinx that were used for burial sites, or what you would also call "tombs". That was the purpose of the Sphinx. And the lion was the protector of those tombs. That was the Atlantean belief system. It depicts the lion energy. The lion is the king of the beasts. And it is supposed to be protecting and roaring at any would-be grave or tomb robbers.

D: *They have found some hidden chambers underneath the Sphinx.*

I: There are many, many more that they still need to find. And as far as the Hall of Records, it is not under the Sphinx. It is under the main pyramid. There are also tunnels under there. Many, many tunnels that lead to far off places in the middle of this planet. To races that you don't know about. You can be led from those tunnels to other races that inhabit this planet, that live below the surface.

The underground cities will be expanded upon in the next chapter.

D: *But the people now that are in charge of the pyramid don't know these things exist?*

I: They are aware of certain things, but because of the belief system, because of the religious doctrine that they have, they don't want people to know they've had past lives. That they've been other life-forms. That it is not their religion that reigns supreme. That there are other forms of worship other than their form of worship. That there are other means of going to Source than only *their* means of going to Source.

D: *Are they aware of the openings to go beneath the surface?*

I: Oh, they are aware of the tunnels. Some they have closed. There are some that are open. But they are afraid of bringing that into the public. As well as being afraid of the unknown themselves.

D: *So they don't let people know the tunnels are there.* (Yes) *But they can be accessed from within the pyramid?*

I: They can be accessed *only* from the great pyramid.

D: *But they have never explored them themselves, because they are afraid?*

I: They are very, very afraid of the unknown. If they bring this to the Westerners, then the Westerners are not as – what you would call – "chicken". They are not afraid to explore. They may have ways and means of going through this tunnel without suffocating, or being asphyxiated. They would be able to go through these tunnels, but they would be wiser not to. Because these tunnels are very, very long. Miles and miles long. They don't want anyone to know about them. Number one would be the risk. And number two would be because of the belief system.

D: *Were your people responsible for building these tunnels?*

I: Yes, we were. It was very simple for us. We just used light energy. And our form of transportation too was very, very simple. We travel through light.

D: *When you made the tunnels did you use your craft?*

I: We didn't necessarily have to use the craft. We could just mentally envision what we wanted to do. And then create it with our minds.

D: *Why did you make them go under the Earth?*

I: There was a surface species that wanted to experience that. They were a very evolved species. They wanted to be away from the madness on the surface. So they decided to help Mother Earth and go to the middle to assist her. Because, as you know, she is a living being. So they are part of her helpers, and part of her assistants. And they work very closely with her. They are very, very evolved.

D: *Were there any people living under the Earth before that?*

I: Not to my knowledge. But this came about after we came here.

D: *And they made the tunnels and then some people wanted to live there?*

I: Yes. They have a frequency level and vibrational level where they don't need a physical sun, as you do. But they have means of obtaining light from the physical sense.

See Chapter Five, "The Hidden City". Also mentioned in *Keepers of the Garden.*

D: *Were the tunnels built before the pyramid?*

I: The tunnels were built after the pyramids were made, because these were not to be known to everyone. Only just for the chosen few.

D: *Are there still remnants of these people living beneath the surface?*

I: There are many of them still alive, very much alive as you and I.

D: *Have they ever tried to come up the tunnels onto the surface?*

I: Oh, they have. They are very, very evolved. They have ways and means where they sometimes surface. And they have ways and means where they go back. It is very simplistic for them. They use different frequencies and different light therapies to do that, because they know light therapy.

D: *It sounds as though they took what you were trying to teach and kept it pure. While the others on the surface contaminated it.*

I: They did. They decided to keep the purity, and to help evolve the planet when she was ready to move and to shift to a higher vibration, and to a higher frequency. Which she is presently in the process of doing.

D: *Are there other openings in other parts of the world that could access these people living under the ground?*

I: To my knowledge, in some of the other pyramids. I see the Yucatan, the pyramids there. And there is one more, I think, in Bolivia. We didn't know it as Bolivia, as you know it now. It was a different name.

D: *But other people made these openings so they could access the same place.*

I: It was the same race that we created that went there, because transportation was very easy. We transported through light energy and through light frequencies. And wherever there were people that needed help, we went there. And pyramids were built there to teach them the higher ways. And then at the same time we created these tunnels too, as some of us needed to go with them. To work closely with the Divine Mother. To help her in her process of evolution.

D: *You said you lived in Egypt for six hundred years. Were you known then as the priestess Isis – and you said you pronounced it differently – for the whole time?*

I: Yes, I was. I was known world and wide. I was known on this whole planet. And so was I known in many other spheres as well.

D: *But you didn't intend to be worshiped, did you?*

I: It was utter nonsense that they worshiped me, because of who I was, because of the power I had, because of the frequencies and the energies that I carried. They looked upon me as someone who could help them and assist them. It was not mostly a form of worship, but more a sign of respect.

D: *Then after six hundred years, had they evolved to the point that you thought you could leave?*

I: We had by then created enough species by intermarrying to have that frequency and that energy level to assist the race at that time. And even the ecology at that time. To bring a balance on this planet. So after six hundred years many of us that came in original form left. We left the hybrids, and those that were created from us, behind to carry on the work.

D: *At that time did you go back to Sirius?*

I: Yes, we left our physical bodies and went back to Sirius.

And took back our old form.

D: *If you were back home again, why did you decide to return to the planet Earth now?*

I: This time we have decided that there should be *many* of us. And there *are* many of us that are here to make good what was done in the Atlantean times. And this time to avoid that kind of deluge. Because we see that this time with more and more people awakened, there may be things that will happen, because, as you say, that debt has to be thrown away into your garbage can. So this is what we're doing. We're clearing the debt. Resurfacing all the negativity to clear the air. So that things can become more balanced, more harmonious, and more peaceful. There will be problems. Geophysically, geologically, there will be problems with the human races who are fighting one another. But do not be stressed out or angered by it. Stay in your place of love. And believe that all is in divine order. And believe too, that all will be well. And all *shall* be well. It won't be as bad as it was during Atlantis. This is why many of those that were in Atlantis have come back at this time, to make good the wrongs that they did then.

D: *When you went back to Sirius after the time in Egypt, did you stay there until the present incarnation?*

I: Yes, I did. This is my first incarnation since then.

D: *But you came back this time with a physical birth. Isn't that true?*

I: Yes, I did. But it was enough for the frequency and energy that was in that physical form. It was a very small fraction of myself. And then after Ingrid got ready to take on my essence, I've been coming more and more into this physical body, to integrate with this body.

D: *Why did you decide to do it in that way, rather than create a body again?*

I: It was better to do it this way, because your planet has a different frequency level and a different vibrational level. After the deluge it was much easier to do that, because they were looking for answers. They were looking for gods. And we came as gods.

D: *So now it's easier to come into the body of a baby.*

I: It was easier to come in this time of frequency, because the deluge hasn't happened. It is a different form, and a different form of events that are taking place. This is not *after* a deluge, but trying to *prevent* a deluge.

D: *I see. I was thinking it would be harder on you, more limiting in this way.*

I: This is why a very small aspect of myself came in then at birth. Many times as a child I looked at the stars and I asked them to take me home. I couldn't understand the people. I couldn't understand people suffering. When I saw beggars as a child in Africa, I cried.

D: *But the other way you had so much more power and abilities. It must feel very frustrating to be limited in this way.*

I: It is limiting in many ways.

D: *And you had to live a life that is frustrating as a human too.*

I: It was very, very, but I had to learn the ways of the human. I had to learn the ways of sorrow. I had to learn the ways of different religions. I had to learn the ways people conduct themselves. Of all kinds of human feelings and emotions and experiences that the human goes through, for me to truly understand. So it had to be done in a different way, because there is much more of your race now than during and after the deluge of Atlantis.

D: *But you said a part of you, your essence, came in as a baby. And that more of it is incorporating now?*

I: Yes, more and more of it is being incorporated into this physical body. This physical body's frequency and vibration is being raised by the day. She's been doing a lot of night work. We are working with her DNA. We are working with other aspects of her physical body as well. She doesn't know it, but we take her away many times in her sleep state, and work on her. The conduit told you earlier that her chakras spin all the time. And this is what happens to her all the time. When she's lying down or in a quiet state, or talking to someone, her vibration is continually spinning and being reintegrated all the time. Now she understands

77

what is going on with her. She didn't understand.

D: *That's one of the questions she wanted to ask: Why she was feeling the vibration and the ringing in her head?*

I: Now she understands, so she won't be questioning any more. But will be more accepting of what is going on.

D: *That the energy is just incorporating more and more, and changing.* (Yes, yes.) *Is this one of the reasons why when she went to Egypt for the first time she had those experiences?*

When Ingrid went to Egypt with a tour group a few years ago, she had very emotional reactions when she visited the ruins of the Temple of Isis. It affected her so strongly physically that she had to cut the trip short and return to the States. It took several weeks to return to normal mentally and physically, but she could never understand the extreme reaction. This was one of the questions she wanted an answer to.

I: She was told to reclaim her path, but she hasn't been doing so. She has been, as you say, (slowly and deliberately) procrastinating. It is a difficult word for me to say. She must know what she has to do, and get cracking, as you would say. And start doing what she's supposed to do.

D: *But that's human to hesitate.*

I: I know. She gets all these human feelings and emotions that she was so integrated with, trying to learn the human experience. It has, to a certain extent, burdened her down. I think it is now time for her to move forward. She must move forward. It is good for her to keep her Isis connection quiet, because people would not understand. People would have the wrong impression. They get into the egotistical mode. And this is why she shouldn't mention this to anyone.

D: *She can only share it with those she thinks will understand.* (Yes) *But that's why when she went to the Temple of Isis, she had those reactions.*

I: Yes, much of her energy was activated then. Much of herself was activated then. Because she had parts of herself

78

when she was in physical form in that area. She lived for a long, long, long time in that place. So when she went there she picked up her energy from the frequency levels there, and integrated that. And that was her purpose for going there really, because that was part of her integration. She integrated with all those energies there. With the ground, with the river, with the trees. All life forms she integrated with when she was there.

D:	*It was more or less to trigger and activate it.*

I:	She will not go back to Egypt again, because it's not really necessary for her to go back. It depends on world events. There are many things going on in the Middle East. And there are more things to come.

D:	*They were worried about her at that time, and they took her to the hospital.*

I:	That one time she almost died. And we kept her alive.

D:	*She was carrying too much energy back with her.* (Yes) *Can you help her to know that it won't happen again?*

I:	We will help her in every way possible. We will ensure that it doesn't happen.

D:	*She was raised in South Africa. Why did she have to leave there? It was a very traumatic and drastic decision to move from there.*

I:	It was part of divine order. It was the will of spirit that she comes to the center. It was the will of the council that she comes here, because this was the country that needs the love vibration. It is this country that needs to understand oneness. That needs to understand love. That needs to understand respect for all life, because it is the greatest power on this planet.

D:	*So it was part of her destiny to move her energy to this country.*

I:	The world really needs to awaken to love. It really needs to respect people's place. It really needs to make peace. It really needs to create a balance. These level of frequencies. You don't need to go and kill because you need oil. You don't have to create circumstances because of power and greed. You don't create those things at the expense of lives. You don't create those things just to have more financial

79

power. More greed and more control. It's a state now of sharing. You should share your global resources. You should feed the hungry. You should love one another. Respect and love.

D: *This is very difficult, because those in power are the ones that control all these things.*

I: We are coming to a stage where now there's so much of life's energies coming through. There's so much of higher frequencies that are being beamed onto this planet. The people will have no alternative but to change. All the rigid structures that are made up to now will all fall out. They have no alternative, but to break and to collapse. They will all collapse with the power of the light, or with the power of love. It is too powerful. There's nothing that supersedes the power of love. Love is all there is. Love is what you breathe. It permeates the universes, the cosmos. And love is what everything is created from.

D: *That's true. It's going to be interesting to see how it can overpower the power structures, because they control everything.*

I: They will be the masters of their own fall. They will create their own destruction. They will create their own fall. They will be truly responsible for whatever happens to them.

We were told that Ingrid's health problems were being caused by the pressures of a bad marriage to a dominating man. It didn't happen because of karma, because she had never lived on Earth since the lifetime in Egypt. There can be many reasons to experience a negative lifetime with another individual besides working out karma from other lifetimes. In this case it was to learn to deal with human energies. And as we know, some of these can be negative. Of course, this is difficult for the human because they have no conscious memory or knowledge of what is involved.

I: She had to understand the human psyche, human behavioral patterns, humans' lies and deceits. And the way they conduct themselves. The only way she was to learn it, was to experience it.

Ingrid's speech pattern had changed to a clipping, shortening of the words. This had occurred in the beginning, but then straightened out. It sounded like someone having difficulty with words, as though this method of communicating was awkward. She was sometimes separating the longer words into syllables. It sounded awkward and unnatural. Toward the end of the session, her voice once again returned to normal.

I: Ingrid works more with the whole energy and frequency system. And brings the vibration of the divine love energy into their frequency system. By just bringing in this divine love, love permeates and supersedes everything else. It transforms and transpirits everything. Love is the most powerful force in the world. If people tell you that the opposite of love is fear, it is not so. Love just is. Love has no opposite. Remember that, dear one. Love has no opposite. Love just is. It is the answer to *everything.* Everything. Wherever there's disharmony. Wherever there's pain. Wherever there's hunger. Wherever there's sorrow. Just send love. Not only to humanity, but to all life. To the rivers, the oceans, forests. To the animals, the birds, the bees, the air that you breathe. To the whole cosmos, because you are part of the one. We are all part of the one. There is no separation.

When I did research about the Goddess Isis it became obvious that she was associated with the things that Ingrid said she came to Earth to do. She instituted marriage, and taught women the domestic arts of corn-grinding, flax-spinning and weaving. She introduced the practice of agriculture, and the arts of medicine. How fitting for her to be remembered that way, because she said she came after the destruction of Atlantis to help people rebuild the Earth. She is considered the primary feminine archetype, or energy representative of nature's divine fertility. She is the focus of divine motherhood, and the queen of all regeneration. She is tied to monthly lunar cycles and the yearly growing seasons. She wanted people to learn how to take care of the Earth. Isis embodies the strengths of the feminine, the capacity to feel deeply about relationships, the act of creation, and the source of sustenance and protection.

Another thing I found that goes along with this session was that Isis was also called Eset. This is similar to the phonetic name Ingrid gave of Ezi, and could be the same when you take into consideration Ingrid's accent.

Isis played an important role in the development of modern religions, although her influence has been largely forgotten. She was worshiped throughout the Greco-Roman world, mostly as the personification of the feminine qualities. With the advent of Christianity, many of the chapels of Isis were converted to churches. During the fourth century when Christianity was making its foothold in the Roman Empire, her worshipers founded the first Madonna cults in order to keep her influence alive. Some early Christians even called themselves Pastophori, meaning the "shepherds or servants of Isis", which may be where the word "pastors" originated. The ancient images of Isis nursing her infant son Horus inspired the style of portraits of mother and child for centuries, including those of the "Madonna and Child" found in religious art. Thus the images of Isis with the infant Horus became the Virgin Mary holding Jesus.

CHAPTER 5

THE HIDDEN CITY

I went to Memphis, TN, to speak at the Unity Church in the summer of 2001, and stayed for a week to do private sessions at a motel with a kitchenette.

When doing this type of work you have to be prepared for the unexpected. It was happening more often now that when I had a session with someone, they would not go into what would be considered a "normal" past life. Almost as though we are being told that the person must become aware that they are more than they imagine. They have a much more colorful soul life than they could possibly be aware of. Maybe this is the time in our history when we must become aware of these other parts of ourselves. It was not unusual for my subjects to go to other planets, to other dimensions, to lives in long lost civilizations. Wherever they went, I had to ask questions pertaining to what they were describing. Because they were definitely seeing it for some reason that was important to their current life and their current rate of growth and understanding.

Thus it was with Mary. When I had her descend from the cloud, she began to describe her surroundings at once without any encouragement. They did not sound like anything I was familiar with in history. She found herself inside a huge incredible building. There were many large rooms with tall ceilings, and the architecture was like nothing she was familiar with. It was very unique. There were huge wooden doors covered with incredible ornate carvings. As she looked out of a large window onto a courtyard, she saw a lake with a little bridge that seemed rather oriental. The size of the building was immense, and indescribably beautiful. Everything about it was elaborate and the colors were royal and rich.

I asked her to describe herself and she was a male dressed in a very beautiful elaborate robe made of red and gold velvet-appearing material. She was also wearing a headdress that she couldn't see, and her shoes were of some type of wood.

When I asked her to see what type of work she did, she found herself in one of the many rooms in this huge place.

M: I believe I'm a monk or some sort of spiritual person. There are other people here now. They're dressed more plainly than I am. Not all alike, but just simple. There are books everywhere in this one room that I've gone into. They're all sizes and shapes, and they fill the room, floor to ceiling. There are books everywhere. Books. Records.
D: *The kind of books that you open up?*

I wanted to distinguish between books and scrolls. This would help me to find the time period.

M: Yes, you can. I'm on a higher level looking down into the room. And there are people on the lower floor bustling around doing things.
D: *This room sounds like some kind of library. Is that right?*
M: It does seem to be. I think some of the people are caretakers of the books. They seem to be researching, or recording. It feels like an ancient hall of knowledge. I think this is some vast collection. This is so *vast.*
D: *What is your responsibility if they're doing the care-taking?*
M: I'm not quite sure. I see also, some walls of rock now. (A sudden revelation.) It seems as if I am underground. This seems to be another part of this vast complex. It almost makes me wonder if it's all underground.
D: *Well, earlier you saw a lake and a bridge.*
M: I wonder if it's a large underground city. It seems to be. One of my first impressions was what we would think of as Shambala (had difficulty with the word) or a Shangri-La, or something like that. It was because it was so vast. But the rock and the tunnels and the steps make me think that it's hidden. The whole place is a hidden place, even though it

has light and water. And I see tunnels. It's like a place that's closed away. Hidden. It is for protection. To preserve the records.

One of the main themes that keeps running through the regressions I have been doing in the past few years seems to be that we are recorders or accumulators of information and knowledge, and the main job is to preserve this in various forms, even by encoding it into our DNA or subconscious, so it will not be forgotten. Knowledge seems to be very important in the scheme of things. Maybe because the Source or God needs us to accumulate all the information we can. The ETs also are accumulators of knowledge and information. This is one of the main purposes for the implants (especially those in the nasal cavity), to transmit and record information. The more I explore this I keep finding that *everything* is recording. There will be more on this in the other chapters.

D: *You mean by putting the records underground, it's a safe place?*
M: Yes, it's a safe place. There are pyramids above ground, but this is very deep underground. I got a picture of a pyramid. But now I'm getting a picture of a high mountain range also, so it can't be the pyramids we are familiar with. There are steps that go up to this place that are honed into the mountains. Things that are not known. Things that are hidden in the mountains. The pyramid is in the mountains. (Surprised) This is a space-port. And there is a world on the outside and a world on the inside.
D: *These steps that you said were honed into the mountain. Where do they go?*
M: They go into the entrance to this hidden city.
D: *So the pyramid is outside, but the entrance goes inside the mountain range?*
M: Yes. The pyramid is not what was important. It was thought that was what was important, but it is not. What is important is what is in the mountains around it, behind it, beneath it. There is the hidden.

85

D: *Is the pyramid used for anything?*
M: No. It is just a marker.

In the "Isis" chapter she said the entrances to tunnels leading to the underground cities were located near pyramids.

D: *But you said it is a space-port.*
M: It *was* a space-port, yes, when this was originally built, a long time ago. I see this huge, huge, deep, deep, deep opening into the earth. This place is being built. (Long pause)
D: *What are you seeing?*
M: I just see this incredibly huge, very deep crevice opening into the earth. And I know there are ships that are going down into this. And they're taking supplies. They're taking people. And they're taking materials. They are building underground. It's almost as if it was an opening of what I would call a volcano, only I don't know how big they are. But it's going down, and I get to a point where I can't see. It's so dark into that. That was the way they went into the entrance, to take the supplies to build this underground place. By just zooming down through an incredible crevice, like a volcano. And going through *huge* openings.
D: *This was done so people couldn't find it?*
M: Yes, it was a long time ago. There are primitive people that live over the other way, down the mountain in the valley. They live in something like a hut-type thing. They are the native people. They are frightened. And there are many things in the sky overhead.
D: *That's why they're frightened?* (Yes) *You said they are bringing people and supplies.*
M: Yes, we have to go inside. I was just seeing the cavern. As you go down deeper, you can see light at the bottom.
D: *They found a way to create light down there?*
M This is technology that has come from other places. This is not of Earth.
D: *Why would they choose to come there, and build this city inside*

that mountain?

M: There is a war destroying the planet.

D: *Is this taking place on the planet Earth?*

M: Yes, I believe it is. It was a war that destroyed a great deal of the surface. Much, much destruction.

D: *Are these people fighting the natives?*

M: No, they were all other people from outside. They were evil ... they were bad. They were *mean*. They came to this planet. They were very fierce. Very powerful.

D: *Was the other group here in the beginning?*

M: There are more than one. There are many, many groups. One group .... (Long pause)

D: *What are you seeing?*

M: An image of something that looked like a glacier up by a lake. And there was ... what I would call a ship, that is very odd-looking. Nothing I would ever even see in Star Trek. Long and sleek, but with different appendages.

There was a long pause as she observed. This is when it becomes frustrating, when I can't see what she is seeing. She attempted to describe.

M: They were doing something nearby. There's some sort of ... I don't know what this is that I see. It's like a plant, some sort of a factory. And I feel that they're taking resources. They're mining. There is a large, large apparatus that .... I just see things that I don't know what they are.

D: *You said they're around this glacier?*

M: The glacier is up high. But some of this begins to come down into the lower part of the mountain and the valley.

D: *That's where they're doing the mining?* (Yes) *What connection does that have with the war you were talking about?* (Pause) *You said there were several groups.*

M: I see that there are missile type things being fired, and launched. I see that the glacier came about because of these wars. I see this incredible *light*. Much of the outer surface of this planet was devastated by this light. Incredible

87

explosions. Many people left on spaceships and went away. Some are living underground. Many were destroyed.

D: *You said the glacier came about because of this?*

M: Yes. What they were doing caused sinking of lands, rising of lands. It caused days of darkness. Cold. Destroyed, destruction. Massive destruction. I know I'm here to help. I'm here to watch over the records.

D: *So that's why they have transported these records.*

M: Yes. The knowledge.

D: *Where did they get these records that they're trying to save in this vast library?*

M: It's the knowledge that we didn't ever know we had. There were flourishing civilizations. Atlantis. Lemuria. Technology we had received from others. How the DNA had been mixed with the humans.

D: *This is all part of the records?*

M: Yes. This incredible, incredible place.

D: *And your job is to protect this knowledge and watch over it?*

M: I'm not quite sure. I don't record it. I don't care-take. I think I'm an advisor or .... (Long pause) I see myself going along a lighted stairway. It's not tall, it's small and it just goes into this space. It's very well lit. It has crystals. (Pause) Other beings meet me in this room. They come in their light. They are not a real body. They affect a form of a body, but they are very, very beautiful. (Long pause) And there is this ball .... And it has all this pretty color and it radiates and emerges. And I feel like they communicate with me. (Long pause) Like I'm the one they talk to, and then I go and I tell the others.

D: *But you have a physical body, where they don't.*

M: I do have a physical body. And I live underground there.

D: *You saw them bringing the things earlier when they were building it. Apparently it's already finished now. Is that what you said?* (Yes) *Can you go to the surface again and live there, or do you have to remain underground?*

M: Some will return to the surface. Others will not choose to. But the surface will become habitable again in time.

88

D: *Are these records of Earth, or did they come from somewhere else?*

M: Earth and others. It's like *all* knowledge.

D: *And these beings brought it down there so it wouldn't be destroyed?*

M: They're very, very loving. They are there to help us and teach us. I'm their voice, I think.

D: *Were they afraid all of this would be destroyed when the war occurred on the surface?*

M: Yes, it was to protect us. It was to protect and to save, and to help us down the road.

D: *Did they bring humans underground?*

M: Yes, there are many different beings underground.

D: *When they built this beautiful city, was this after the destruction of Atlantis?*

M: The building of the city began before the destruction. It was known that this was pending. That this was at hand. It was known. The violence had shifted. The building of the city, and the accumulation of records began long ago, even before Atlantis. Long before Atlantis.

D: *I have heard there were many civilizations before and after Atlantis.*

M: There were very highly advanced cities. And also very primitive places during the time of Atlantis. I'm seeing the outside world now. And I see gates into a city that is surrounded by mountains, but it's sitting on the water. This is above the ground. The other one was already there under the ground.

D: *Was the one above ground built by humans?*

M: Humans who were more evolved than humans that we know of now. That city was more populated. The underground city was in a sparsely populated area. Human and extraterrestrials did live and co-exist here. There were those who were here to help, and there were those who came to conquer. Part of the humans had become much more evolved. Other humans were very, very primitive. More animal-like. And there is a place where humans were treated very, very badly. Very poorly. Mutations.

89

D: *Was this at the time of Atlantis? If we can get a time sequence.*

Of course, I was thinking of the mutations of half-human/half-animal that occurred during the time of Atlantis. I didn't know if this was the time period she was speaking of.

M: One is a little before the other, but close. (Long pause) Council! There's a council. There is a meeting to decide to stop the evil ones. A large meeting. Galaxies. More galaxies. More peoples.

D: *They want to stop some of the ones who were doing mutations?*

M: Yes, they were being destructive. They were controlling. Cruel deeds. The time between these two is so close, it is hard to give specific — ten years maybe. One area of the world was largely evolved and thriving. Another area very primitive, being plundered, being mined. Mined for gold. They were warrior-like. They were trying to keep their deeds hidden. They were close, but not in the same area. They were discovered. And there is a council in a high place discussing this. They don't like what this group is doing. A large table. A lot of discussion.

D: *Do they make a decision?*

M: Yes. They decide they *must* protect, must stop. (Long pause) They ask them to leave. To cease, to leave. This leader, this spokesperson, dressed in a lot of metal. Almost seems as though he has a bird-like headdress. They don't think this council is a true threat. And they say they have every right to this planet also, and refuse to leave. They have been bringing weapons. There is the space-port. There are weapons on the ground. They want this space. They had been preparing for any attack. Their consciousness is warlike, therefore they keep many defenses.

D: *So they don't think they have to obey the council.* (No) (Pause) *You can condense time and tell me what happens as a result of their actions. What did the council decide to do?*

M: That's when they decide to move the people to a safe place, and to relocate. The threats are known. This could be very costly, very devastating. There is much movement to relocate the people, but everything happens too quickly.

D: *But don't the negative ones know if they go to war they will also destroy what they came for?*

M: They really, really did not think. There has been mass destruction. There have been many galactic wars.

D: *So they're not thinking that it will also defeat their purposes?*

M: No, no. The Creator has given free will. They have been allowed to let the dark side flow. It has been allowed to be. So when the stand is taken from those who are of the light, the earth falls into a period of great darkness. There is very little that survives on the surface. Very little. There are some places that were shielded, but much, much is destroyed. There are great changes. There are other planets around that are affected also by this, that are actually totally annihilated. This is not just of the Earth. It was a galactic war in this system.

D: *Which other planets were affected?*

M: In this galaxy, in this solar system, Mars was greatly affected. It was not always the barren planet that it is now.

D: *We were told that it happened because of a war on Mars.*

M: These wars were related. Some of the damages were part of a galactic war.

D: *So it wasn't the repercussions of what happened on Earth. You mean it was going on at the same time?*

M: Seems to be what I understand. It was many groups. I seem to feel that I was amongst that council of twelve. I don't know why I said council of *twelve*, because there are more there at the table.

D: *Maybe they were the most important ones.*

Note that the group that first gave us information through Phil in *Keepers of the Garden* identified themselves as the Council of Twelve.

M: And I was a liaison between, assigned to watch over that underground city for a very, very long time.

D: *Then the destruction on the surface did not affect the underground cities.*

M: No, it was safe. It still exists.

D: *Let me tell you something that I'd heard in my work; that Atlantis went down because their own scientists were doing things they shouldn't have.*

M: Many in Atlantis had become of the dark side. They were not always that way. The misuse brought about the galactic war. It was all interconnected.

D: *So the negative beings became aligned with the people of Atlantis?*

M: Yes, many fell into the dark side. It was all happening at the same time, and perhaps earlier. There were many in the light that had great foresight. Who had great powers that we don't know of today. (Long pause) All of this could have been stopped, but it would have gone against free will. It was necessary to allow all that was and has been, to be. It has gone and come full circle of Earth's millions and billions of years. And there is much, much knowledge. Much, much change that is to come. Much is to be known.

D: *I've always thought the Atlanteans did it to themselves.*

M: There was more going on. They did not begin the experiments without the interference of the negative dark ones. It is like they forgot who they were. They forgot their enlightenment. They became caught up into the material world, and this began the imbalance that brought all of the destruction.

D: *You mean they were working with the negative ones?*

M: Yes. They were lured by the dark side.

D: *So the negative ones were helping them, giving them the knowledge?*

M: Yes, they were tempted.

D: *The council allowed this war to take place even though they knew the circumstances; the results.*

M: It had to do with free will. And to learn. Consciousness went very far into the realms of darkness to learn, to explore. I keep seeing a huge turning, like a wheel, but it's not a wheel. It's like seeing a solar system turn full circle.

D: *Like cycles?* (Yes) *So after the destruction, did it take a long time before life and civilization came back to the surface?*

M: Yes. Some of the indigenous ones were transported back to the Earth. And they began new civilizations. Like starting all over again.

This will be referred to later in this section. One of my clients reported a past life when he and many others were taken off the planet just before a catastrophe, and returned afterwards to start their lives anew.

D: *And you said this also caused some of the glaciers to form?*

M: Yes. It changed the Earth.

D: *But weren't there some that carried the knowledge, who lived on the surface?*

M: Yes, there were. But it has been passed down and hidden for fear of the ... those that wanted power and control have always ... the dark forces have come back. After the earth began to heal, they did come back in smaller numbers, and they have worked with governments. They are not human of appearance necessarily. Some are humanoid type. Some are reptilian-looking. Some are hybrids, who are human and alien. They have come back. Many though of the dark side have turned to the light. But there are those who still try to hold on to control and to power. There seems to be things that I'm not allowed to see. I can only go so far with it. I don't understand why I can't know exactly time, and I just see images. And I keep feeling that I was like a liaison person.

D: *Yes, I've been told before that there are some things we are not ready to see yet. We are not allowed. It has to go in a time sequence. But do you feel as though you're being shown this now, because it's coming full circle?*

M: Yes. There is really a lot of beauty to come. There are changes that are coming. There is light where there was

93

darkness. Like a matrix of ... we cannot see what is right in front of us. It's like looking through a veil. It's there in front of us. Distorted images. Distorted information. It will change.

I then asked to speak to Mary's subconscious to try to find more information that she was not allowed to see.

D: *Why was Mary shown this? We were looking for something of significance, and this is of great significance. But why did the subconscious choose to bring this forward for her to see at this time?*

M: She has always felt that link with Atlantis. That she was there. That it was so. That it truly did exist.

D: *But this showed that she was connected more with the underground city.*

M: Only for a time. She went there to oversee. To be a liaison. She was always there. She was chosen for the mission.

D: *Her job was to oversee the knowledge and the hidden records.* (Yes) *But why was she shown this at this time? What does this have to do with her present lifetime?*

M: (Big sigh) She senses many things, and yet she has been afraid to know some things. Some things she was not ready for. And some things were not, even yet, time to know.

D: *The subconscious is very wise when it allows those things to come forward in their time. Does this mean she is going to have something to do with this in her present lifetime?*

M: There's a communication. There's a door, a portal, an opening, that she has her hand partly through. But she has not yet stepped through. She puts her hand in, and then she pulls it back. It is a connection between herself and her guide, angels, through the portal. The communication of connecting consciousness. Becoming one and moving in and out of each other. The door, the portal will open where she may see that which she has longed to see. The spirit world as she recalls it. Other dimensions. She chose to come to the Earth life after she left the place of the liaison.

94

There were many that came to Earth, that chose a physical body.

D: *They decided to come and help?*

M: Yes, they had a choice. They didn't have to.

D: *But she still has this memory that there was more beyond this physical. Is that what you mean?*

M: We are all timeless. There were other lifetimes. Other dimensions. Other realities.

D: *The information that she was giving about the wars and the underground city, would I have permission to use that information in my work?*

M: Yes, you have permission. More knowledge will come to you that will make this more complete than it is today. There are some gaps that could not be filled for you today, that will be filled at a later point. You will understand more clearly. You are already writing this, have written this, this is in process. There is more knowledge that you will have. It is not clear at this point where it will come from. There is a door opening for you to this well of knowledge. It is closed at this moment for you. It is this same door that you will be allowed to go in and review the knowledge. You may be taken there through another entity, or you may be taken there on a spiritual journey with your own guide. This is a real and marvelous place. The door is closed at this moment. The door will open for you and you will have a warm welcome.

D: *This city that was underneath the ground, is that city still there?*

M: Yes, it is still there.

D: *Is the information, the library, still there?*

M: Yes, it is still there. There are many, many complete underground cities.

D: *I'm glad to hear that, because to me the destruction of knowledge is a very terrible thing.* (Yes) *That's my job, to try to get it back.*

M: Yes, it is. It is your mission. And it is your mission to help others remember.

D: *That's what they've told me. It's not to find out more, it's to remember more.*

It took three years, but they were correct. More information did come through in 2004 after I opened an office in Huntsville, Arkansas, and began seeing clients on a regular basis. Bob was a man who had moved from the north after his wife died. He came to our area sight unseen, bringing just his books and his dog. He had left everything behind. When he bought his house by the lake the former owner left all her furniture, so everything worked out fine. A new life in a new area, even though he knew no one.

He was a voracious reader, especially consuming everything he could find about metaphysics. He owned some rare, one-of-a-kind books. This was his passion. Yet I believe the information that came through during his session would be difficult to find anywhere. I do not believe he was being unconsciously influenced by his reading.

He had difficulty seeing anything at the beginning of the session. Although he felt he was standing on something rock solid he could not see anything but gray all around him. After several attempts to trigger visualization I asked him to imagine what his guide or guardian angel would look like. He saw a beautiful blond haired woman in flowing, shimmering blue robes. He felt comfortable with her and agreed to allow her to lead him somewhere that would be appropriate. He took her hand and she led him downward through an opening into an underground tunnel. The tunnel unexpectedly came out into an unusual place.

B: We're in this large open air space. But I can sense that there is a roof above our heads. A much different distance above. It is like being inside a cavern. A very, very large one. It is very nicely lighted. There are trees everywhere. I sense that it is a very gentle place to be. Many very beautiful buildings in all pastel shades. There are trees and lawns and gardens, and beautiful flowers, and animals running every which way.

D: *This is all underground?*

B: (Excited) Yes! Yes! Yes! It is very well lighted. It seems to radiate from a central sun that can be seen quite easily. It's not the same brightness as our Sun on the surface. Grayish in shade, but it puts out a beautiful light. The buildings here and everything else looks just like it would if you were looking outside in our sunlight. And it maintains a temperature of approximately 72 to 75 degrees, and it never gets hot. It does rain, but that's of course programmed into it.

D: *Hmmm, this sounds unusual to have all of this underground, doesn't it?*

B: Well, it's been there for many, many millions of years. And of course their technology now is far surpassing ours to the point where some of us come and go from here quite often. But we never realize we do. And I have been one of those people that have been there many times in the past.

D: *You said there are also animals down there?*

B: Oh, yes! Yes, yes. Many animals that we see on this planet all the time. But there are many other types there that people wonder about. That you never see that often. For instance, there is one that is a big swimming animal that they only get glimpses of. A Loch Ness monster type of thing. They come up from underground channels through the earth. And occasionally they swim into them and pop up in above ground places, because they can go either way.

D: *So there's water down there too.*

B: Oh, yes! Actually there's almost as much water down inside the planet as there is on top. It gets there by flowing through the various fissures through the actual crust of this planet. And some, of course, comes in from the polar openings on both ends of the planet.

D: *You said there are cities under there?*

B: Yes, everything that you could ever hope to imagine, including one of the greatest computers in the entire

97

universe. Far, far in excess of anything on the surface.

D: *What does* that *look like?*

B: Actually it isn't just a little piece of something, like we see here. But it's literally acres and acres and miles and miles, all self contained. It stores all the main universal knowledge. You can walk along these nice beautiful garden paths, like it you were on a twenty acre farm, for instance. There are flower beds, little patches of roses and all sorts of other really exotic plants. You could walk down these little pathways, and go into various garden plots or flower plots. And you could find yourself in a raised chair, or it's more like a lounge bed. And you get on it like you would try to get on a hammock. And it doesn't swing, it sort of stabilizes. But as you sit down into it, and then pull your legs over onto it and lean backward, it encases you like a banana peel. It's a machine which you can then ask a question, and automatically you can travel anywhere in the universe that you want. You can do it that way. It's also a learning machine. It will teach you anything that you need to know, or want to know. Or it's also a virtual reality machine which will allow you to travel. You can use that type of conveyance. Or if you don't want to use that, we do a more physical body transport. You can go up the little steps into what they call "portals", but basically what surface people call "stargates". You walk in there, and you can literally transport yourself *anywhere* in the known universes that you want to go. You take your body with you, and you can also come back. There are also high speed tunnels interwoven like a spider web, where trains will pass through the interior of the Earth at more than 3000 miles an hour. That's very commonplace. It takes a mere matter of an hour to go someplace. This is only one of the planets in the entire known universes. But it's pretty much generally the case, because they're all hollow. Most have civilizations living inside. And we have a continual fleet of interstellar ships that travel between all of these worlds on quite a regular basis. You sometimes see them here, but generally, we have these so-called "cloaking" devices that sort of crop out of these Science Fiction movies you people show on the surface television systems. Called "Klingon cloaking device"? All of the ships have them. It is just standard procedure.

D: *Why would people want to live underground rather than on the surface?*

B: It's safer. There are secondary reasons. You have on planet Earth something that is called the "frequency" barrier. The frequency barrier is lessening now, because you're traveling close to the new frequency change on planet Earth. That's basically what everybody is waiting for. That's why there's so much interest from intergalactic races. We can come here and watch all this happen. Because while you can't necessarily see it on your Earth instruments, we're aware of it. And now we can gauge this on our instruments that are much more refined that yours. So we're all waiting, because it's upcoming very shortly.

He was speaking of the frequency changes leading up to the creation of the New Earth. See Chapter 30.

D: *But we don't think of the Earth as being hollow, because we think there is magma at the center of the Earth.*

B: But that's one of those cute little stories they get you to believe on the surface. They tell you all sorts of untruths. Actually your surface of this planet is 800 miles thick. Underneath *that* it's entirely hollow. The sun that we have inside is 600 miles in diameter. It was *brought* in millions of years back, and installed there. – But the people who remain here are going to be inside the planet. It's not affected inside. It's only affected on the outside. The eight hundred miles within that crust is where your planetary magnetism actually comes from. It's not the center. Your volcanoes all come from the friction of rocks sliding back and forth within the frame. The center is very hollow, and of course, has the sun as I've indicated. All other planets are very

99

similar to this same construction. So with the friction of the rocks sliding upon each other, that builds your volcanoes. All your volcanoes are subsurface. Maybe a couple of them go down two or three hundred miles, but they don't go all the way to the center of the planet. The center of the planet is not magnetic. Because if that were to happen I would suspect – and I am not one who can really speak upon that kind of thing – but if a major other planetary body coming into the solar system brushes by Earth. This is what you would have happen. (Slapped his hands together.)

D: *It implodes.*

B: No, no. You would have a draw like a magnet. A magnet would literally suck a planet with a solid molten core right into it. And wouldn't let it necessarily release. The other planetary body is designed so that when it flows by Earth it will be magnetically drawn to one end or the other. Whatever end is like a magnet. North attracts south, as it would. If the planet Earth were a solid body, it would literally connect. And it would not release. But in reality, it is not that strong, but the pull could cause the planet to *tip over.* Whatever strongest pull comes in. Whatever strongest side.

D: *Have you had many lives under the planet?*

B: I've been inside several times in the course of my lifetimes on this planet. You see, it's different there. Because outside you have lives, or other places you have lives. And inside planets you literally can live forever if you want to. Actually most of my lives were out and about some place or another.

D: *Other planets?*

B: Yes, you move around from one lifetime to another. It's whatever you need to accomplish. The whole universe is just like a super big school. You go from one place to another, depending on what you need to learn.

D: *Do you stay very long at each place?*

B: Whatever length of time you need in order to complete your lesson or whatever you're working on. Your project.

100

And don't forget, some of us are millions of years old. We live forever, technically.

D: *So coming to Earth is rather like going back to kindergarten, isn't it?*

B: Oh, yeah, it's a bit of a trade off. But sometimes you do it for a refresher course. (Laugh) A hell of a way to do it, when there are so many billions of things you can do in the universe. Planets you can visit. Lifestyles. All sorts of things. It's unlimited. But in my life as Bob it's very low key. It gives me a chance to clear out my mind, and lie back and let the whole thing go. Just sort of sit there and observe, and watch people. It's a vacation. What other people do on a vacation, I'm doing here now. I am an observer.

CHAPTER 6

ESCAPE FROM ATLANTIS

I have found several examples of people escaping from the cataclysm that caused the destruction of Atlantis. Everyone did not perish even though the upheavals reached around the world. Many were able to find their way across the seas to other countries, and tried to preserve their way of life in a totally different environment. The following is one example:

Marie was a nurse working in an obstetrical unit in a hospital. She came to my office in Huntsville in 2004 seeking the answers to problems, just like everyone who comes. The session, however, was not the usual past life, and at first did not seem to have any relation to her present life. When she came off the cloud she said she was floating out in the middle of the ocean.

This can mean several different possibilities. A sea creature, someone swimming, or someone coming in on the day of their death and they are drowning. However, her voice did not display any fear as would occur if she went in on the day of her death.

As she looked around she saw she was in a little boat. "The sea is calm right now. And I feel like it's going to get worse before it calms again. Everywhere I look there's water all around. There's nothing else but water. It's a wooden boat. It's not very large. Could hold three or four people. I feel we're out in the ocean. And we don't have much control over where we're going. We're just more or less drifting. I think we have some oars, but they don't make much difference, with the size of the boat and the size of the water. We're in the current, and it just more or less takes you where it wants you to go."

D: *Then you're not trying to go any certain place?*
M: I feel like we're leaving some place, and we're trying to find a place of safety.
D: *Do you know where you're going?*
M: No. Wherever the boat takes us. We have no choice.

102

There was one other person in the boat. "I feel it's a very close friend. A close companion. I'm not sure if it's male or female. It's someone that I have a very close relationship with." She saw that she was a middle-aged man dressed in a rough cloth robe tied with a rope belt.

D: *What are you doing in the boat?*
M: I feel like we had to leave. And ... I feel like I'm from Atlantis or Lemuria. And that our island was no longer going to be, and we had to leave while there was still time.
D: *Did you think a small boat would be safe?*
M: I don't think there was much choice. Many others had left. And we volunteered to go in the smaller boat, because the others took the bigger boats. They would have definitely been safer. It was something that we knew was going to happen, that we had to leave. And we allowed the others to leave first.
D: *Was something happening when you left?*
M: It had been going on for a while. And we knew that our world would be no more. And then we tried to make preparations for it. And take the things that we needed. We didn't want the whole civilization to end, so we took remembrance of it. Some information, some crystal things that would help us in the new world.
D: *Are these some things you used?*
M: Yes, they are part of our civilization. And they were things that we could carry with us that would be helpful, if we needed them in establishing a new life.
D: *What was your job, your occupation?*
M: I was in the temple. (Long pause) I spent my time learning about the use of energy. And making our world a better place for different forms. I worked with healing and helping others. I was not one of the exalted ones. I was still a student, but I was making progress. I was learning, but I was also teaching. I would help others.
D: *This other person that is in the boat with you, were they one of the students?*

M: They were also in the temple with me, and they would work along side. It was like an assistant.

D: *You were being taught, and you were using the energy?*

M: Yes. Crystals, and the use of energy. And how to create things. How to change situations. How to heal. How to help people who had fallen out of balance. I could do these things, but I had not perfected it. I was still learning the combination of one's mind and the presence of energy. That you could alter it, and help bring it into a physical form. And then it might be used for the good of all. The manifestation to be used in the community, or even for individual use, or that the followers of this way could use.

D: *That's good that you were working with the positive.*

M: Yes. I was becoming better at it. I was able to influence weather patterns if it was so needed. Then again, my interest centered more on the helping of others. Their physical and mental ailments.

D: *They would come to you at the temple?* (Yes) *And how did you heal them?*

M: We would use crystals sometimes. Sometimes we just used the manipulation of energy through touch. Sometimes we wouldn't even need to necessarily touch them, but just bring them the energy with the hands.

D: *So these crystals were very powerful.*

M: Yes. They would amplify the energies that you would send out. And they would make them even stronger. Sometimes they would help to change the energies into positive.

D: *You said you were controlling the weather patterns. Why would you want to do that?*

M: If we had a period of time when there was too much drought, and went without water. Or if there were storms that threatened to destroy where we were. We could try to alter the energies so it would not be so devastating. There was much unrest in the area. There were many people with negative energies. And so you would try to counterbalance that.

D: *In the same land that you lived in?*

104

M: Yes. There were those who were experimenting with the dark side of the energies and the powers. And they were creating chaos. They were creating unrest among many of the people there.

D: *So it is possible to use the energies in the negative way also.*

M: Yes, it is. That's not the way the energies were ever meant to be. But because of so many entities or energies, the entities' thought patterns had altered it. They learned how to do it. There were negative forces creating all sorts of problems.

D: *You would think they would know that wasn't the way to use it.*

M: There are many that are not that far advanced. That have not understood the way things should be.

D: *Because everything you send out comes back, doesn't it?*

M: That's correct.

D: *There was nothing you could do to help combat the negative?*

M: There were many things that we did to combat it, but it finally became too overwhelming. And there were more negative vibrations and energies that were sent out, and more people being drawn into it. We became afraid. And finally there was no more that we could do at that point in time, at that place. So we had to do what we felt would be the best way to save our knowledge and our ways. And that is why many people decided to leave. To go out into the boats and take with them the things that they could.

D: *What did you see that was going to happen, that would make you do something so drastic?*

M: The land that we lived on was breaking up. There were many earthquakes. And it was going to be pulled underneath the ocean. And we knew we couldn't stop it.

D: *So there were already earthquakes occurring?*

M: There had been, yes. We knew that it was just a matter of time before we would have a totally new realm of existence. That some of us would be leaving their physical bodies. And that others of us would try to save some of the remnants of the old world, and take it into the new.

D: *You would think that the people that were using the negativity would have stopped it when they saw what was happening.*

M: They were drunk with the ability to alter things, to change it with the power. They didn't care. There were some who planned to leave also by boats.

D: *Do you know what specifically they were doing with the negative energy? What they were using it for?*

M: They were trying to turn people away from the light. Trying to turn them away from the positive. And to only be afraid and see the negative things. They wanted to have them under their control. So they would be their leader, and they would have many people that were afraid and would only listen to them.

D: *By using fear.* (Yes) *But some of them also tried to get away when they saw what was happening.*

M: Yes. It had gone too far. And the land and the area could no longer take any more of the disruptions. It would not be able to exist much longer. That it would be going underneath the waters.

D: *You said the bigger boats were already taken.* (Yes) *So many people knew what was going to happen. Then you and your assistant took the smaller boat. And you have some of the crystals with you?*

M: We have crystals and we have some scrolls. Some teachings or information that we want to preserve. Many people have copies. Many have more items with them in the hopes that some of us will make it. Not everyone set out in the same direction. We all tried to go in different directions. Again, in hopes that we would be able to continue with some of the learnings, the teachings, the information that we have.

D: *So none of you really know where you're going.* (Pause) *You've not been to these places before?*

M: Some have traveled. Mostly by boat, but they were also able to visit in their sleep. They were able to go in levitation. (Meditation? It sounded like: levitation.) They were able to move about in that way. They didn't necessarily need the physical with the boat. But at this time

106

with so much energy disruptions and the powers — it was almost like a horrible vicious storm — that we were not able to use some of those methods of travel. We had to go by boat.

D: *But also you couldn't have carried these things with you if you went in the spirit form.*

M: That's true.

D: *You had to take physical objects with you.*

M: The information would be preserved forever in the etheric realm, and in the higher realms up above, but it would not be as easily accessed in a physical form if we did not take those things with us.

They had not seen what happened to the land because they were already out at sea. They just wanted to get away, and were going wherever the current was taking them.

D: *Do you have any food with you?*

M: Yes, we have some. We ration it out. And we've learned to exist on a very small amount, because we want it to last as long as it can. Because we have no way of knowing how long it will take to reach land.

D: *What kind of food do you have with you?*

M: It is like a highly concentrated form of energy. It's some sort of a grain. And little cakes that we can eat. Our water, of course, is very valuable, and we only take sips of that. Because you're only able to carry so much. And so we try not to use the paddles much. We try to conserve our energy. And we sleep as much as we can. We eat as little as we can.

D: *That's make sense. Because when you're sleeping you're not using as much energy.*

M: That's right.

D: *It doesn't sound like the kind of food that would spoil.*

M: No, it will keep for long periods.

D: *Have you already been out to sea for a while?*

M: (Pause) I'm not sure if it's days or weeks. But it seems like a while. We can mark on the boat the passing of each day.

D: *But it still is just like one day after the other.*

M: That's right. Especially when you sleep a lot. And you wake and you go back to sleep.

I moved him ahead in time to see what happened, because he could have been floating on the ocean for quite some time.

D: *Do you find a place to stop?*

M: Yes, we do. There are many people standing and watching us as we come ashore. Wondering where we have come from, and in such a small boat. And we think it's in ... it looks like it's in Egypt where we've come ashore. The people standing around, they have darker skin.

D: *Can you understand each other?*

M: We're able to communicate telepathically, but language, there's a barrier.

D: *Can they understand you telepathically?*

M: Some are able, but we are able to understand them more than they can understand us.

D: *Has anything happened on the land where they live?*

M: There has been many storms, and changes of the seasons. They know something unusual is occurring. And they're frightened with it. The seas have been unsettled, and the weather has been unusual for them. And then with people arriving in a small boat, and looking obviously different, that makes them even more suspicious.

D: *Are you able to tell them what's happening?*

M: We do not share with just everyone general knowledge of what has happened. We just said that we've lost our home, and that we sailed for much time in a boat to get here. And it seems like there's someone there who can translate. But we do not tell everyone we come in contact with the general story of the whole ordeal. And they don't have a good understanding of the whole civilization from which we came.

D: *Their civilization is not so advanced?*

M: No. It's not like ours was.

D: *Will they allow you to stay?*

M: Yes. We're kind of an oddity for their curiosity. They allow us to come.

D: *What are your plans now?*

M: The immediate plans were to recover, and to just get some food and water and shelter for a while. And there's a man who takes us in and allows us to stay with him.

D: *But the things that you brought with you survived? The crystals, and the scrolls and the information.*

M: Yes, they did. We keep them wrapped up in our ... it's like a cloth. It may be even like a bolt of material that we have those things wrapped up in. We are afraid that they could be destroyed, or someone would steal them if they saw them.

D: *If they knew what they were.*

M: Yes. We hide them in a cave.

D: *Do you think you will be able to teach anyone about the knowledge?*

M: We are fairly certain that there are people here. There are teachers, or there are fagists (phonetic) (?) that we could share these things with. And once we realized if they were to be trusted, then we could gradually begin to share these things with them.

D: *That will take time. And you have time now, don't you?*

M: Yes, we do.

D: *At least you've found a place to stay. You don't know if the others made it or not.*

M: There have been reports of some others that have come ashore at different places. And so we know that some people in different areas have made it. Some we have not heard of. But we know that there have been some others that have survived.

D: *It shows that the knowledge will not disappear then.*

M: It's a very joyful news to hear that there are others. That we are not the sole survivors. The responsibility was to continue carrying this information and these gifts.

I took him ahead to an important day in that lifetime in order to progress the story.

M: We have found a place to store the crystals, and the scrolls. We feel that we can rest now that we don't have to worry about their well-being at all times. We have shared some of the information, but these people are not ready for all of it. So we must take these things and put them away for now.

When I asked where they had hidden them, he became apprehensive. I had to convince him that I was no threat, that it was safe to tell me.

M: It's stored away ... it's within a pyramid. But it's almost an inter-dimensional type of storage area. It's not one that could be found unless you know how to access it. You would not easily see it, or know that it was there. It will take certain energies for the items to become noticeable. For them to appear. The items are physical, but they are stored in like ... an area with ... it's like they're there, but you can't see them. It's like an inter-dimensional space. A box that we have put them into and then closed. And only certain energies can open the door to this, and then they would be visible.

D: *Is this inter-dimensional space something you knew how to create?*

M: I had help from some of the others that survived, and we met up eventually. By working together we were able to create this space.

D: *So it's not a* physical *place within the pyramid.*

M: It is a physical place, but it's like it's invisible. It's there. And as long as it's sealed ... a person cannot just walk by and see it. It has to be a certain mental energy, knowledge, and even some symbology, some symbols are needed in order to open this.

D: *But is it like you put it in a wall?*

M: Yes, it's similar to that. It's like on the inside of one of the large stones. It's there, but you can see no way to get inside of it. There's no indication that it's there.

D: *There's no way to physically open it.*

M: That is correct. You couldn't physically open it. It has to be done with energy. It has to be a certain thought pattern. And it has to be the right person with the symbols. They have to carry in their energy field these symbols that are needed to unlock the stone.

D: *It's not physical symbols that they know about?*

M: Before coming into carnation. Before being carnated here, they were aware of that, and the symbols were in their energy field.

D: *So they were put there before the person was incarnated?*

M: Yes. And sometimes they had to earn them. They had to learn certain things or go through certain tests for those symbols to become functioning. To be activated. In order for them to work. So maybe if the same person was at the right spot at the certain time, nothing may have happened. They needed learning. But now if they had achieved certain things in this lifetime. If they had passed certain tests showing their true intentions, their good intentions, then that would activate these symbols in their energy field. And if they were to go there, then they would be allowed to open this. To know where to go. And with their mental thoughts it would open like a key. And there's more than *one* person with these. There has to be many, in case one fails.

D: *That would make sense. When people incarnate, do they have certain symbols that are put into their ... spirit, aura or whatever?*

M: Yes, we all carry those. And that's how sometimes we compliment each other, or we recognize each other. We don't see them with our physical eyes, but our body knows it, or our energy field knows it. And we may experience certain sensations. There's either revulsion or attraction, or feeling of well-being.

D: *So these symbols are important.* (Yes) *Are these symbols created on the spirit side?* (Pause) *I wondered where they come from.*

Who decides to put them into the ... I guess aura field, for lack of a better word?

M: They are part of the universal mind. The universal intelligence. And they coincide with what our life plan is before we are incarnated. They are like keys throughout our life. If we go to a certain spot or a certain place, if we meet a certain individual, and the key fits in the lock. Or the two symbols merge. Or opposing symbols. They'll help us to know what we should do. Sometimes it can unlock memories. Sometimes it can trigger a response within us that helps us to make decisions, and change our life. Our life styles, our life decisions. So they're almost like a little guidance system. That at a certain time it can be activated and help us know what to do, when to do.

D: *But these are things that the average person doesn't know about, and we're not aware of.*

M: No, but we all have them.

D: *And usually you can't see them or know they're there.*

M: Some people are able to, but most of us cannot see with our eyes.

D: *You just get feelings, instincts.*

M: Yes, yes. That's it.

D: *That's important. And that means that symbols are very important to the universal mind.*

M: That is correct. It's a universal language.

This goes along with the information I have received and reported in my other books. That the ETs communicate in symbols, and these contain blocks of information and concepts that can be transferred mentally. Also it partially explains the numerous reports I have received of people receiving a flood of symbols entering their mind. Some have reported lying on the couch in their living room, and seeing a beam of light come through the window containing numerous geometric and other symbols. This beam of light concentrates on their forehead area. Others have reported a compulsion to sit for hours drawing symbols or unusual designs. (Many people have sent me copies of their drawings, and it is amazing that they seem to be similar.) The ETs have told me that the Crop Circle symbols contain blocks of information also. The observer doesn't have to be inside the circles to receive this. Just seeing the symbol in a magazine, newspaper, etc. is enough to download the information. They have reported various other ways that the download occurs. They said it is their language. The person receiving it doesn't necessarily have to understand it. It is implanted into the person's subconscious on a cellular level. The purpose is that eventually they will need the information, and they will have it and not even know where it came from. Which brings up the question: if we incarnate with a symbolic pattern imprinted upon our soul, aura, however it is done, does the download from the ETs add to this pattern, or activate it? He did say that this pattern changes as the person goes through life experiences.

D: *I know there are many, many pyramids in Egypt. Did you put them in a large one?*

M: (Pause) I'm thinking it's in the paw of the Sphinx, instead of the pyramid itself. I believe so. There are many underground tunnels and chambers in there. I think it was placed – if I am looking at the Sphinx – it would probably, I believe, be the left paw.

D: *Do these tunnels go underneath the pyramid also?*

M: Yes. There are many of them underneath the pyramids.

D: *But most people don't know how to access these, do they?*

M: No, only certain initiates, the priests, certain royalty. The average common person does not know. There's rumors that they exist, because they had to be built. And there's always leakage of information that comes out. But the

113

average person does not know the particulars. They've only heard rumors that they exist.

D: *But if the Sphinx and pyramids were already there when you came there, have you ever heard any stories about who built them?*

M: (Pause) Yes. I believe that the civilization – even though it was not as far advanced as our own – had been given some help from the extraterrestrials. Because the general intelligence level of that particular society was not that highly developed. They gave them information. But, again, to a small portion of the people. It wasn't all of them. And many of them were more followers than independent thinkers.

D: *Did you ever hear how they were able to build with such large stones?*

M: It was done with energy manipulation. It was done with a type of gravitational device. Levitation. It would have been almost impossible physically to build those.

D: *Where you came from, would you have been able to do something like that?*

M: Yes. Although my expertise was not in architecture or the building of things, I did know the basics of manipulation of energy. And levitation. Most of the students, the initiates, those that worked in the temples, they all knew these. That was part of the learning. Of levitation and the use of energy.

D: *So this was something everyone was taught.*

M: Yes. And there were those that were very far advanced in those things. In architecture and creating material things. It wasn't just material. It wasn't just third-dimensional. It was an interweaving of the material and the higher vibrations, which would be closer to spirit manifestations. They weren't just physical.

D: *But you said these people that lived in Egypt weren't advanced enough to have done this by themselves.*

M: No. There were some who were more advanced, and more willing to listen. And were more open ... usually those more educated than the common person who lived there.

And they were given this information in hopes that it would help the civilization advance. And so they were contacted by the extraterrestrials, those that watch over. And they came and they helped them with these things. And because of our knowledge and where we came from, we were able also to help in their learning and progression.

D: *Why were the pyramids built? Did they have a purpose?*

M: (Long pause) They were very compact sources of energy. They weren't like a crystal, but they almost were able to amplify and help in the creation of many things within the pyramid. And within the vibration of the pyramids. They were centers of learning, but also it was like entering another dimension, because of the energy that they held. And they were able to amplify and actually also to transmit vibrations and energies to other areas. It was like a giant energy field or force – maybe not necessarily a force. It was a center of much power and energy.

D: *So that was why the extraterrestrials wanted these to be built?*

M: That was part of the reason they were built, or the function of them. The extraterrestrials just want mankind to create a world of more harmony, and more peace. And a happier place to live in, rather than one of poverty and pain and despair. They were hoping that we would be able to use this information and these gifts to expand that possibility.

D: *It has to be people who have the knowledge of how to use it.*

M: That's right. And that is why there were only certain individuals that were given this knowledge of the powers of the pyramids, and the possibilities that they could help to develop in that area. But also with that power comes the possibility – just like Atlantis – of the negative.

D: *Of the misuse.*

M: That is correct. (Big sigh) The free will, it can be turned either way.

D: *That's why it could go either direction. But rather than using your scrolls and your crystals, you decided to hide them there where they would be safe.*

M: Yes, the people were not ready for all of the information.

115

And they were not using it as it should be used. There was already abuse of the powers in some of the areas, where it could turn into another Atlantis very easily. If they would have the knowledge and the use of the absolute power.

I then decided to move Marie ahead to the last day of the man's life, because I didn't think there would be anything else to learn after he had hidden the secrets away.

M: I am very old. And my body's remained in fairly good condition, because of my knowledge of healing and the use of energy, and the thoughts that our teacher told us form the physical. But my body has aged. And is very tired. And I'm ready to leave.

D: *So there's nothing wrong with the body.*

M: It is aging. It has changed from the effects of this Earth life. There is nothing horribly wrong.

D: *Did you live there in Egypt for a long time?*

M: Yes. I want to say maybe forty more years.

D: *And so you were able to pass along some of your knowledge.*

M: Yes, I was. I shared what I thought was appropriate with the learned. Those that had been trained in the ways. But again, I was not able to share all of it because it wouldn't have been appropriate at that time.

D: *Yes, but you did much with your life.*

M: I tried. There was always some wrong decisions. Sometimes you would tell people things or teach them, and they would not ... just like any time in their life, people will take it and some use it, and some do not. And some misuse it.

D: *That's the same way it is everywhere.* (Yes) *Is there anyone with you on the last day of your life?*

M: No, I'm alone. I'm not afraid, but I know I'm ready to leave.

After he had moved out of the body to the spirit side, I asked him to review the life he had just left and see if there was a lesson that he learned.

116

M: I think I needed to learn patience, because I was always eager to learn, but I wanted to learn more. And I never felt like I was where I could be. I would reach one milestone, and it was never enough. I thought that I should know more, and know more faster. And that was a very hard lesson.

D: *Do you think you learned it?*

M: Can anyone ever learn it? That is a tough one. Yes, I learned to be more patient.

D: *You also had a great deal of knowledge.*

M: Yes, and that was another part of the lesson. (Big deep sigh) To learn the use and the giving out of the knowledge. The responsibility that goes with it. That if you were given that knowledge, you must learn to use it wisely. That sometimes it is meant for others, and sometimes it is not. And if you give it to the wrong person at the wrong time, it can be disastrous. And if you give it to them at the right time it can cause wonderful, wonderful results.

D: *So you have to be discriminating.*

M: That is correct. And it is a very great responsibility.

I then had the entity recede and integrated Marie's personality back into the body so I could speak to her subconscious.

D: *Why did you pick that lifetime for Marie to see today?*

M: Because it very much parallels what she is going through today. She is on a path of learning. And she has great opportunities to do much to change this world. To help bring the new world in. It is a very great responsibility.

D: *But on the surface it doesn't appear similar really.*

M: She has the ability to do much good in this world in relation to the use of her energies, her knowledge from all her past lives. She is able to communicate with many. Or she will be when she is able and when she is ready. And if she does not do this at the proper time, in the proper sequence, then there will be many valuable things lost. And it is very important that she understands that: number one, patience is very important. That all things will come when it is time. And secondly: as she obtains these powers and these abilities, to use them very discriminately. And although the desire is correct, to help others, you do not always help them by the easiest path. And sometimes they must learn for themselves. And so to give to them everything, that on the *outside* looks like they could use or they need, it is not always the right decision. She must give to them, when the time is right, possibly a little less than what they could actually use.

D: *Where will this knowledge come from?*

M: This knowledge that she has had, that she has learned from all the past lifetimes. And when the right time appears, it will be given to her.

D: *It will all come back, you mean?*

M: Yes. And it has been arranged that parts of her ... of *me*, of the oversoul, at the right time will enter in, and bring with it these gifts. These energies and this knowledge that she needs in order to move to the next step, to the next level.

D: *But her present personality will still remain, won't it?*

M: Yes, very much so.

D: *It's just like an overlay, or a merging? Of the one that has the information.*

M: That is correct. It will just be merged with her present being.

D: *Then she doesn't have to study, or take any classes?*

M: Yes, she still needs to do these things. It will help to trigger memories. And it will help her in the relearning. It is very hard sometimes to just bring in these certain thought patterns. And by relearning them with the different circuitry of her mind, it will help her in this present lifetime. She's being trained from this side.

D: *She has another question. Why does she get so seasick? She loves the water, and the dolphins, but she gets so seasick.*

M: The energy level of the ocean is very high. It creates very forceful energies. And because her body, her essence, is a

118

transmuter of energies, she can only absorb so much before she physically begins to feel it. It also has to do with her extended period of time on the ocean when she first left Atlantis. It was very stressful being on the ocean. And again, the energy levels were very high. Although she had some power and ability over the elements, and the ability to alter energy to keep the oceans from being too violent, she was in a weakened state from lack of food and water.

D: *The trauma of the situation.*

CHAPTER 7

ANCIENT KNOWLEDGE

This session was held in May 2002 at a ranch outside of Bozeman, Montana, where I was staying in a guest house. I went to Bozeman to do some talks, but the main reason I went there was to finally meet Leila Sherman, the 100 year old woman who photographed the picture of Jesus that I used for the cover of *Jesus and the Essenes.* I knew this might be the one and only chance to see her. A woman was working with Leila on producing and marketing the picture. Leila told me she thought she was ready to die, but when they put together the website www.christpicture.com and the marketing plan, it was so much fun that she said she thought she would stay around another 100 years. Leila lives in a retirement home, but is still very active and able to take care of herself. She said she is the oldest in the home, and the only one that doesn't require assistance.

Lorraine flew from another state to be in Bozeman at the same time. She was a healer and was working with doctors and hospitals to introduce and combine natural healing with traditional methods. In the large city in which she lives, she is working with five hospitals and beginning by teaching the nurses. She is very intelligent and thinks this will grow into something very important.

In the session, when she came off the cloud, she found herself as a 14 or 15 year old girl with long, reddish-brown hair, in a peaceful setting that I thought was probably a coastal sea town. That's what it sounded like, but I was to find out differently as we progressed. She described her house as sitting on the cove, and very large with archways that looked out on both sides at the water. She wanted to live a normal life there with her parents and brothers, but a powerful group on the island had other plans for her. They had discovered she was different from the other people, and wanted to use her abilities. She was to go to live in a large temple on the hill above the town.

L: I have the gift. I can see.
D: *You can see what?*
L: (Whispered.) The future. (Long pause) I can see the future. They want to teach me how to direct it.
D: *Even though you have the gift, you don't know how to control it. Is that what you mean?*
L: No! They want to control it – through me. (A whisper) The order. The men who run everything. The sea. The people. I am to go live in the big temple on the hill and do as they tell me to do.
D: *The men in the temple are controlling things?*
L: (Curiously). Yes. They will control me. I want to stay with my family. I want to sail away on the ocean. My brothers can do what they want. I want to sing. I'm not allowed to sing. Things happen when I make those sounds.
D: *I don't see anything wrong with singing. What happens when you make sounds?*
L: Whatever I want! – The men on the hill are afraid of me.

I assured her that she could talk to me about it, because I was not a threat to her. "What kind of sounds do you make?" Lorraine had her mouth puckered as though she was making an oooh sound. "You're moving your mouth, but I can't hear anything."

L: You don't hear the sound? It's like the wind. It's sounds of the wind.

She then began to make an eerie, shrill, elongated tone. It was gradual, but constant, from Oooooooooooooooooooh (middle tone) Oooooooooooooooooh (high tone) Oooooooooooooh (higher tone, then too high to hear) and then down again Oooooooooooooooooooooh (middle tone). Later when Lorraine listened to the tape, she said that was a sound that would be impossible for her to make. Especially the part that gradually grew higher in pitch until it was too high to hear.

She explained what the sound did, "That opens doors." I didn't understand what she meant. Physical doors? "You can walk through those doors. They can't see them." So it obviously wasn't physical. She was referring to something apparently in the unseen world.

L: They are gilded doors with jewel encrusted edges and white and colored light in the center. They are not – really – physical doors. They are openings, portals.

D: *Where do you see them?*

L: In front of me. There in the space.

D: *When you're outside?*

L: No, wherever I am, they are with me. They're in space. The sound creates the doors and opens the doors. When they open up, I can go through into the doors.

D: *And nobody else can see these doors. When did you first find out you could do that?*

L: I was five. My family, my uncle. I told them things that I could see through the doors. They thought I was making stories – and that I was funny.

D: *What did you see through the doors?*

L: (Whisper) I see the future.

D: *How did you know it was the future?*

L: Because I would tell them the stories and then they would happen. They started to believe when I was eight. Then the men on the hill took me away. They started testing me. I was put into the room where I was made to perform. And they would write what I would tell them. And then they started training me to change what I saw. They wanted me to change it to help them. To redirect it. Make good things happen for them, and the tragedy to go to someone

122

else.

D: *So you saw negative things?*

L: I could see everything. I knew what was coming. There were three windows inside the doors. I can see how it can be. Three different ways it could happen.

D: *So the future is not just one way.*

L: (Whisper: No.) I could change it. Send it elsewhere. Move it. Make it different.

D: *Is that allowed to be done?*

L: It's like luck. The good luck comes, the bad luck has to go somewhere else. They didn't see that. They thought they could take all the luck and keep it. They took it for themselves and controlled everyone. We live on a large island, lots of coves. I saw it from the cloud as I was coming down. It's beautiful. And they have tall structures on the top of the hill and they rule all of the people below.

I thought it sounded like some type of organized religion.

L: No church yet. It's not yet religion. It's power. It's the temple. It's the place of all being.

Apparently we were further back in time, before the beginning of organized religion. But it doesn't matter, power and greed have been present since the beginning of man living on Earth. There seems to have been a constant battle between the forces of good and evil.

D: *And they wanted to control everyone that lived on that island by changing what you saw?*

L: They do. All the minds with the power live in the temple. I have to go live in the temple. I have to leave my family.

D: *How does your family feel about it?*

L: They've become very prosperous because of what I have done. I gave them the luck. You think it and it happens. And you take it in and give it that direction and send the other to someplace else. It's just a direction. They would

123

have total control of all of the power if I go live there. I am to show them how.

D: *Do you think you can show them how to do it?*

L: No. (She began making the ooooh sounds again.) All I'm doing is opening the window. The portal opens with a sound. And then I can see more through the door if I look. The sound carries waves. And the waves push open the window. And I can look at what is to come.

D: *But you said you're supposed to teach them how to do it?*

L: Yes, they think they can learn it. (Chuckle) I don't know where it comes from.

D: *How can you show them how to do something if you're not sure how you do it?*

L: I don't know how to *not* give them the information. They make me do it or my family will suffer.

D: *I see. But they are men, they probably couldn't make the sounds in the same way.*

L: (Whisper) No, it's not possible. I learned this year how not to tell them the truth. I'm going to make them do things the right way. I'm learning from my uncle how to control their power. But I have to pretend I don't want to know. And then they teach me more and more. Soon I'll have all their knowledge. Each of the group have different gifts in different areas. And they know different things of how to control the minds of the people. And they are teaching me each gift. – I have to do something. They're doing it for the wrong reason. They're going to destroy us. They take all of the positive energy and they're dumping all of the negative energy into a hole. And it would soon be very large ... and it will erupt.

D: *It has to go somewhere, is that what you mean?*

L: Yes, they don't see that! Everyone thinks you can have only good. I don't know if I will be able to have all of their knowledge in time.

D: *What do you see that's going to happen?*

She hesitated, then started crying.

L: Everything comes apart and falls into the ocean.

D: *Do you try to tell them?*

L: Yes. They say it's up to me. To send it and change it. I could do it, if they used their power in the right way. But they don't and they keep giving more of the bad side into the hole. And it's growing, and they become more and more thoughtless and careless. I'm afraid I have to control them. As soon as I know all of their gifts, I can take their power from them, and redirect it back to the people.

D: *That's your plan?* (Yes.) *Did you go to live with them in the big temple?*

L: Yes. It's beautiful. It has many stairways and columns. And archways that look down to the water. And there are large colorful birds. And beautiful music. It's very beautiful. I have a black leopard. (I was surprised.) Her name is Sasha. She's my pet. She hears my thoughts. She is with me all the time.

D: *I would think that a leopard would be dangerous.*

L: (Chuckle) She can be. But she chooses not to be.

D: *Do the other people also have animals for pets?*

L: Yes, many of them do. The animals are everywhere. They live in harmony in this large place. There are large corridors and many beautiful rooms here. I speak to the people daily. I lie to these people. I tell them what the men want me to.

D: *What do you lie about?*

L: The danger of living with so much, with so many gifts. No one is ever sick any longer. We've learned to heal. I must be about 25 now.

D: *How do you do the healing?*

L: We no longer do healing.

D: *When you did it, how did you do it?*

She made the shrill Ooooh sound again.

D: *Tell me what you're doing.*

L: I was rotating the ceiling to line up the light.

D: *(I didn't understand.) What light?*

L: We are light inside. It gets fractured, and must be realigned to flow. And everyone is taught the tones to realign their light.

D: *You said you were rotating the ceiling. What did you mean?*

L: I use the colors and the tones through the light to realign them. There's a pattern on the ceiling of the solar system. And the colors and the tones have to match. The colors are in the light panels on the ceiling. They look like short bursts of light in different colors. It appears to be a solid piece of glass, but it's tiny lights of color. Some kind of tubing connecting them. And the lights look solid, but they're little flashes of light inside the different panels. Creating the panel. The solar system pattern changes for each person who comes under the light. It's read by a light in your wrist, and it is displayed on a pattern on the ceiling. Then the lights align and they come down through the base of your skull. And into the body and it realigns your light.

D: *Then it's a machine of some kind?* (Yes.) *So the pattern of the zodiac changes for each individual person.*

L: It's their chart. I used to do it myself individually for these people. And eventually I taught them to use the tones themselves. We have no more disease.

D: *Is there anything else on the ceiling, or just those patterns, and slabs and the light?*

L: There's a large object in the center that directs the beams. It's a series of crystal looking objects placed at certain segments of space. And the light fractures through it as it rotates very quickly. Very, very quickly. You don't see it moving. You just have to know it moves. It shoots shards of light through the glass, and numbers are clicking and it pulls the lights from the colored panels (Said with a tone of discovery). It bounces it through all the little layers of crystals till it reaches the numbers that make the individual's personal pattern. And then it shoots it at the base of the skull down through the body's points. Little points in the body that correspond with each of the lights.

And back up through the root chakra and out through the crown chakra.

D: *And this heals the person?*

L: It aligns their individual light!

D: *And everyone has their own pattern?* (Yes!) *And this finds the pattern so the light can activate it and heal the person?*

L: Yes, we know how to align the light. When the light is fractured, the information of disease in these bodies goes away. As long as their light is aligned, the bodies do not age.

D: *And there have to be certain tones that will activate this.* (Yes.) *Do the men know how to do this?*

L: No. Just me. I'm in trouble for doing that. The people were charged much of what they had to be healed. Only the wealthy could be healed. They're very angry with me for teaching the others how to heal themselves. But it doesn't matter. Our way of life is coming to an end.

D: *Is that what you see?*

L: Yes. All of the bad luck is growing to a size and proportion that will erupt. And they don't care; they don't believe me. It's up to me to change it. To send the bad luck someplace else. They have chosen a spot. It's a land where many people live. They're not rich people. They're the support of our system though. And they don't think they need them any longer. The fishermen, the farmers. They used to support the land. They don't need them as long as they have me to direct the luck!

D: *What are they going to use for food?*

L: They don't need it any longer.

D: *They don't have to eat?*

L: Not like we did.

D: *So these people are dispensable?*

L: They think so. That's incorrect, because people are the only thing that is important. What they don't know is that it will take everything with it. Not just those people, all of us, because it's so large, so powerful.

D: *Did you learn all of their knowledge?*

127

L: Yes, but I don't have enough yet. I don't believe there'll be enough time. I need to come full circle in all the knowledge to control them. To be able to change what we're doing and accept the bad luck. And let it out a little at a time to relieve the pressure it is sitting on, so it doesn't erupt. They think I can send it out and destroy others far away. And that it will go away. But what they don't realize is, it's so large it takes all of us with it.

D: *So, what happens?*

L: (Long pause) I let it destroy us.

D: *Did you direct it a little at a time?*

L: No. That was what I wanted to do, but I was not allowed to. No one was willing to live with the bad luck. To let it out a little at a time would mean people would live with failure and famine and disease and disharmony. I didn't tell them it was coming. I let it erupt. (Woeful) And it took everything. It all came apart. There was a very long, low rumble under the earth. Everything started falling around us. We rolled into the sea.

D: *The whole island?*

L: (Whisper) Everything.

D: *What do you see when this happens?*

L: (Faint whisper.) Horror ... horror! Everything was destroyed. Nothing survived. It was like earthquakes and atomic bombs all at the same time. Just tremendous power. Red and black and dark from the bowels of the earth. Erupting and taking all with it, so that everything was even again.

D: *It all balanced out again?* (Yes.) *Where are you as you watch this?*

L: I'm standing between a column under one of the arches looking out at it happening. It looked like the earth opened up to swallow everything, and belched it back up. There are black clouds in the sky and fire. And all of the art and beauty is gone. I'm gone too.

She began making gasping sounds. I gave suggestions that she could watch the scene as an observer if she wanted to, so she would not experience physical sensations.

L: (Whisper) Water. I drowned. From our high vantage point we were the last to go. (Whisper) We watched them all die.

D: *So are you watching it from above now after you're out of the body?*

L: (Strong and clear) Yes!

D: *What do you see from that perspective?*

L: Things falling into the sea. Dead bodies and animals floating in the water. My family's with me. They're all with me!

D: *How do you feel about what happened as you look at it from that side?*

L: It's a grave mistake to allow the greed to control the power. It was terrible greed. There's a scale of things: animals, trees, plants, humans. And somehow the negative side of the forces dominated the positive side.

D: *But it really wasn't your fault. You don't have to feel responsible for anything.*

L: I feel sad that I failed.

D: *You were trying to do the right thing.*

L: Yes. The sea has settled down. It's calm now. Pink sky is back. There's nothing forever; just water.

D: *What eventually happened?*

L: We came back to a land that was desert.

D: *Did the land eventually reappear?*

L: (Curiously) Yes. The waters receded. It's very pretty here.

D: *Why did you decide to come back to a place that is desert?*

L: To begin again. We must do it right!

D: *Do you still have the same powers?*

L: No! We're simple people. It's safer. It takes time ... many, many generations. And in time comes understanding. We will build again to that level, but this time we will take it the right way. And the men will not rule! No greed.

D: *Do you think you'll be able to bring back the knowledge and power you had at that time?*

L: It's coming. We'll have it.

D: *But, people being people, do you think they will be able to control or direct it this time in the right way?* (Yes.) *Do you think they're ready for it?* (Yes.) *Because you know there's always those greedy people in the world that want to control everything.*

L: They are exposed. They're not in contact with the power. They will be out of habit. The keepers of the power won't let them control them any longer.

D: *Who are the keepers of the power?*

L: The women. They are leading the world with love.

D: *You mean this time the men won't be involved?*

L: No, they're involved. They take much longer to come to the power.

D: *The women will be the ones deciding how to use the power. Do you think this time it will be used in the right way?*

L: For many, many years. Hundreds and hundreds of years.

D: *Will this be the entire world or just a certain part?*

L: The entire world.

D: *Will it happen quickly or will it take time to change the world?*

L: It takes time.

D: *You have to start somewhere, don't you?*

L: Yes. For that knowledge that has been misused.

I then asked for permission to speak to the subconscious so we could find out why this lifetime was chosen for Lorraine to see.

D: *Why did you choose that lifetime for her to see at this time? What were you trying to tell her?*

L: That her thoughts are okay. The old way is going away and the new way is coming. It will never be the same. She must prepare herself to be alone.

D: *What do you mean?*

L: It is in the female energy that her role is played.

D: *But she's married.*

L: (Pause) Life has a different path for her. We cannot tell her any more about that at this time.

This is one way I know when I am communicating with the subconscious. It can be very objective with no emotion, and it can be very blunt. Sometimes even cruel.

Many times when Lorraine was relaxing or meditating she had seen the room where she did the healing, with the crystal and zodiac signs on the ceiling. The subconscious agreed, it was the same room.

D: *She feels she has this healing power, but she can't quite reach it.*

L: She is to bring that back. It is always the same. From what starts in the beginning will be finished.

D: *She was trying to use it in the right way. What happened wasn't her fault, was it?*

L: There is no fault. There's nothing to regret. The power was closed off for awhile, until everyone understands the balance of power.

D: *It sounds like she's mostly supposed to teach women, yet most doctors are men.*

L: Many more women are becoming physicians. You will see in the future, very few men will be physicians. The healing comes through the female. Positive energy. That is where healing begins; it is where life begins.

D: *They underestimate the power of the female energy, don't they?*

L: They have controlled it forever.

D: *Mostly I think because they're afraid of it.*

L: Umm, they should be. We brought her to you so she could find some answers. We hope that she will take what she saw today and be able to use it.

This session contained information about the destruction of Earth in the far distant past. I have been told that the civilizations of Earth have risen to remarkable development only to completely disappear many, many times. This has occurred long before "modern" man appeared on the scene. There is a huge chunk of history that we know nothing about. That is part of my job: to regain this lost knowledge.

In another of my sessions the subject described a similar group of highly developed people living in a civilization far in the past. Rita, a television producer, found herself in a very large hall with columns. The ceiling was a dome 60 feet high. The walls were made of beautiful golden alabaster or agate. The floors also seemed to be made of alabaster set in geometric designs with a thin layer of silver separating them. There was a very wide staircase of three or four large slab steps leading up to an elevated, central area underneath the dome. This was where she and eleven other women worked.

"This round chamber is a very special place that we gather to do certain kinds of work. The domed structure is at the center of this building for an energetic purpose. It is here that we invoke energy with intention for the purpose of adjusting the energy fields."

They were dressed in loose fitting lightweight garments tied with a loose cord around the waist. It reminded her of the drawings of classical goddess-type beings. The clothes were light pastel shades. She was in her early 30s with dark red hair and pale skin.

"There are no males allowed in this building. Only the females do this work. We're not the only group of females that do this. There's a group of old women that work with a different kind of energy. All I know is that there are elder women that do this, and we're the younger women. There is one elder woman in our group. We have to take over the work because its their turn to not have to work so hard. When different types of energies are needed with their old ways of knowing, then they come in for that. That's very specific to their lineages and their ways of knowing. We're the younger or

132

the next generation. So they train us, and now we're old enough and experienced enough that we still have one wise one with white hair that works with us. And we can teach the younger ones. The knowledge must not be lost."

When they had all assembled she described the ceremony or ritual that they used to begin the energy work. "It is very quiet. The elder one sets the tone, literally. It's a tone. I don't know where its source is coming from, but she's calling for it or creating a tone in the room. And the tone is operating in a circular, clockwise fashion. She calls for the tone and it sets the vibratory frequency in the room for the work we'll be doing. Then we must prepare our own auric fields. We go inside our auric fields and create a blue egg around each of us for our protection. But it's for more than protection. The blue egg takes us into a place where we can hear and see more clearly. It's almost like a place of both transmission and receiving. So there's a blue egg, and we receive and transmit both from this special energy field surrounding each one of us."

They had met to work on a particular problem of great importance. "Something's having an effect on the vegetation outside in the region, and there seems to be an issue with the Sun. What I'm getting is something to do with Sun spots, solar flares, something of this nature. We're having issues at this time on the Earth of some interference, some radiation level from the Sun that's affecting the vegetation and the beings here. It's disturbing the energy fields of some individuals and some plants, and they're not responding well to it. It's very intense, and we're trying to make corrections in the output. We can feel it in the vibratory patterns around us."

I thought the Sun would be a big object to work on because it has so much power. "Not for us. We can't alter the Sun itself, but we can ameliorate the intensity of the effects that the Sun's anomalies are having on some of the people. Because it's frying and hurting and damaging some of the people's emotional fields. The atmosphere seems to be thinning, because every time there are extraordinary events of the Sun we're very subject to the influences of it. It's very noticeable and uncomfortable to all

133

living things here. Fish too. The water too. The water's hot."

She then continued with their ritual process. "We all do our massive prayer together and speak with the beings that intercede and work between ourselves and the Sun, asking for the effects to be ameliorated. Asking and invoking a protective layer that in essence is like a protective bubble to shield us from some of the effects here that we have created."

Of course, I wanted to know more about the beings they were in touch with. "They're great beings like the devas of nature and the spirit of the Sun, and everything that operates in between. There's a hierarchy of angelic and devic beings that operate between the Sun and ourselves as agents in a cooperative fashion. This allows the assimilation of the energies of the Sun to be utilized and absorbed and taken up in a proper manner on the planet. Something's changed. This is very major. I don't know that we can continue to have their support in this way. We're at a turning point. I'm feeling much sadness, and my whole body is shaking. We've always been able to call on the beings to help us, and they would if they could. But they can't do it now. This is a very intense period of time."

All twelve of the women stood in a circle to invoke the protection. "We go into the blue eggs or we can't function. It's a protective barrier between the elements happening on a vibratory level here so the twelve of us can function. This will go on for a long time. We can stand for a long time. We don't feel our bodies. We're not aware of our bodies. We're asking permission of the devic beings for help, and permission both to project our energies out into what would become a protective bubble of sorts to give us insulation one more time. We're running out of time. We've had this granted to us many times to avert a certain fate, an ecliptical type of event. Eclipse is a word that is prominent here. This is the eclipse of an event and I don't know what that means. An ecliptical time, whatever that means. Now we're facing a time when we don't know that they're going to let us keep evoking the protection of the beings, because of the fear of the people that are on the planet now. Because things are changing dramatically and rapidly now.

Everything is being affected here and we know that we can only stand here and ask, and we accept whatever is going to be. That's all we can do. We've been very affective in holding this off in times past. We've worked with these energies before, this is not the first time. They've been working with us for generations and generations. We're on a very different length of time here as generations are very long periods of time. And over the course of the last several generations we've been invoking this same protection. It worked in the past, but we are at an understanding that this is coming to the end. We have to do what we can."

In spite of their best efforts they failed. She made a strange statement that I did not understand. She said, "We can't continue this way any longer. We go to sleep now. There's no other procedure after this. We all have to go to sleep for a long time." I asked for more explanation. Did she mean they died and would be leaving their physical body?

It was partly that, but more. "It means that after our bodies can't withstand the impacts of this radiation any longer, our bodies are going to die away, and then we'll have to leave the bodies. I'm like everybody else. I'm afraid too. The ways as we've know it are going to be consumed by some force that appears to be portions of the Sun. That's going to be consumed and we won't exist anymore, as we've known at this point in time. This will be the end of an epoch. But it's going to be a long time before we can come back and resume operations We have to go through a sleeping period where we have to let other things happen, apparently to get back to a point to start back where we were and to rebuild this golden time. We're going to be asleep for a while. It means that our conscious knowledge is not going to be what it is this day. It's not going to be what it was before us and previous generations. It's going to go to sleep and close down, while we go through this darker cycle. It can come back awake again when the time is right, and there will be times and places like this again in a new way. With these feminine beings once again coming to invoke all the forces, and all the devic beings of the Sun and the atmosphere and the Earth spheres and the cosmos, all coming together to work again. To go back into a golden time like this alabaster with which we were surrounded. We're going to be joining together again one day in a new way. Signaling the waking up again. We're very sad. The knowledge will go to sleep until... it's almost like it was preprogrammed in us that there would be a time when, just like Sleeping Beauty, we would wake back up, and it would be very beautiful once again."

Apparently she meant that the knowledge and their human ability to use it would be shut down for a long time, until the time was right for these abilities and talents to be brought forth to Earth again. I was told this was what happened after the abuse of the abilities in Atlantis. It was like blowing a fuse, and the human mind would be unable to revive it until the time was right. It had to be closed off to mankind. I have also been told that they think we have reached the time of awakening now, and these abilities are beginning to resurface in many humans. I know it is happening with the people that come to me for sessions. One purpose of the session seems to be to let them know that they had these abilities, and that they can have them back now.

From her out-of-the-body perspective I knew she could see everything that happened, so I asked her to tell me what she could see. "It fries everything! Everything! The life forms can't survive the radiation. We are fried by radiation, but it's permeated with this golden energy and light. I don't understand any of this. It's all gone." I asked about the buildings. "I don't think it's even relevant anymore. Everything that had to live within that frequency, within that dimension, all things that are delicate that are sustained on the proper electro-magnetic balance, the proper levels of radiation, proper temperature and humidity levels. As all of life is sensitive to everything within that range of life as we know it, which includes the plants and the animals, is not there now. It's ending."

Then she described what it looked like after things had quieted down. Apparently it was not the end of mankind, because she did see some humans surviving. "It's very dark.

People are back. It's just a different place. It's a different geographic location. It's much darker. The land mass would appear to be what would be called the Middle East, maybe in Africa. It looks similar except there's more land mass between the Middle East and Africa."

I wanted more information about the cause of the catastrophe. "They were experimenting and playing. They were utilizing energy, because we had gotten far away along in our knowledge of energy and light and crystal/silicone powers. And we harnessed much of it, except that apparently this was pushing it to the limits. I didn't work in that area. That was not my job. I was here in the domed area, because I was female and that was what I did. But there were others, the males, on the outside and they were allowed to work with the energies. There were also some females that were allowed to work with it too. And they worked together with these generators and crystals and things like that. I can see them now. They're really amping it up, but they're creating some real problems that we can't reverse. And it's not working well with the effects of the radiation from the Sun interacting with what they've created. It had a very devastating effect. There was no way to stop it. They created it. They overdid it. Because they disturbed the radiation balance here greatly. They made it so that we were totally vulnerable and had absolutely no atmospheric barriers to protect us from the Sun and its radiation. And that somehow interfaced with what they were doing. They destroyed, they evaporated our protective barriers, because we're not supposed to be totally subject to the effects of the Sun. We're too close to it. All sorts of extraordinary sophisticated elements were already in place for our protection, and they were destroyed. They were playing with power sources. Now we get to go back into dark. We now have to figure things out all over again."

I asked, "Was your area the only area of the Earth that this happened to, or were there other places in the world?"

"That's the land mass and area that was fried. However, there were major problems elsewhere. I don't even know how much time has elapsed. There's life. It's bleak. It's tenuous, but it's there in this Middle Eastern area, and extends into Africa. There's some vegetation, but not much. There's not much sophisticated anything. It used to be very verdant. I'm only seeing where I was before. It's not there. That's finished. But there were environmental effects that did affect other areas too. It wasn't just localized, and it took a long time for life in a certain sense to really re-establish itself, because other areas seemed to be affected. And what was left just wasn't that pretty and pleasant. They weren't the most desirable places to go, but we had to go there. And there was not much foliage and it's not attractive. It's dry."

I wondered if this was what caused the deserts, which are the largest in the world, to form in that area. "It very well may have, because there's not much vegetation that has reformed. As I look at it into the future, there's a lot of black dark energies. There's a lot of parched, dry, what we know as desert looking regions. Craggy, deserty brown. Not a lot of foliage at all, but little tiny bits of scruffy bits here and there. Nothing like what we knew. We had beautiful crops and beautiful plants, and such a beautiful way to raise the plants. And had the energy to raise them in totally beautiful and unique and clean ways. Everything flourished tenfold compared to modern times with no chemicals at all. Just because we knew how to use energy well to grow our crops and for an abundant yield without ever depleting or debilitating anything. And now I don't even see how we're going to live on this crappy looking land."

"You said you had to go to sleep for a while."

"Yes, and that power didn't wake up. That knowledge didn't wake up. All that woke up was our primitive minds and bodies; survivalist. The soul is shielded from ourselves. We didn't really even know what the soul was anymore."

"So you started over again in a more primitive lifetime?"

"Not primitive as in cave people. We are people, humans that we know now. But primitive as in it is just a desperate, hungry kind of existence. No bounty. No plentifulness anymore. The knowledge was gone. And the food and plants. You don't even see any animals around here. A few little things

138

that crawl. Only those that can survive really harsh environments are here. That's all. We even eat some of those things. – One of my last understandings was we had so much beauty here, and so much help was given. And so much interface from so many dimensions and realms, that made this such a beautiful and liveable and abundant, verdant life experience for us. And we did not respect that. We didn't respect all the intricate levels of intelligence it took to make this place function as a holistic entity. There were many among us who didn't respect that, because they were so obsessed with just amping up. More power is better power, and they took the actual sources of crystalline and silicone and everything and these elemental forces. And they amped it up so much thinking more would be better. I'm not clear on why they thought this because I wasn't involved in the energy field, in energy production as they were. I'm still not quite clear even from my perspective exactly what they thought they were doing. We already had everything. We didn't need anything more. I don't even understand why they thought we needed more power. There must have been something they were trying to accomplish or achieve or remember. I don't know."

"Do you think there was a lesson there?"

"More is not better. Abuse of energy, abuse of power, going against the entire devic, angelic, natural order that was beautifully created for us. Going against all of that by dismissing it as though it had no meaning, because power is power. Raw power and their experiments, to a few, seemed to be more important than honoring what was already existing here that was protecting us. Because they didn't understand there's a greater power than anything they could have conceived that could fry us. It appears that we are doing some similar things now. History is repeating itself. But there was much damage to all of the souls and beings that lived there. Much damage, great sadness. Great shock, sadness and just darkness and damage descended upon those souls. We were all there at that time and we agreed to be there at that time. Some were record keepers. Some were there simply to keep the record for when we woke up. Others were there to actively precipitate the event, and granted, it wasn't the smartest, wisest thing to do. But it was done and everybody played their role exactly as they had agreed to do coming in. I don't understand why it had to be this way. There must have been some kind of process that we needed to go through. I don't understand why it ever had to go that way, but it did. So now that necessitated the process that followed."

I then called forth the subconscious to ask why this lifetime had been chosen for Rita to see. What could this possibly have to do with her present life?

It said, "This is where the heart was hurt. This is where the entire soul was hurt. Everything was hurt for many. This is where we fell. It was very shocking to all levels. Every level. An assault to the soul. At the astral levels, every level of the being was so shocked. It couldn't be allowed to remember, because the anguish of knowing what had been would allow such deep depression in the days of 'not so much' that were ahead. The darker days ahead. There was just no point in remembering that because it would be a long time coming back. Rita's heart center has been protected for too long, and the same protection is now no longer appropriate. She can bring the memories back. This is a very important period of time for all. It's interesting to see that we've once again learned how to grow things, and make things abundant. And we have a proliferation of animals and plants and everything. And we're destroying it again. This cannot be tolerated."

Science had gotten out of hand during that time, and scientists were playing at controlling the weather and the atmosphere. "Apparently they did something that allowed us to become extraordinarily vulnerable on an electro-magnetic level. We became very vulnerable to the influences of the Sun and its anomalies. They were responsible for this thing. Somehow there was a thinning of a protective barrier from the Sun. And the Sun is doing what it can do if the Earth is not properly insulated."

This group that she was part of knew that this negative use

of nature could only spell disaster. They tried to use their positive energy to counteract it, but were unsuccessful. The misuse of the energy succeeded in tearing a huge hole in the ozone layer. The direct power of the Sun came through and burnt the Earth in certain spots. Many millions lost their lives and the climate was changed. Huge deserts formed where the direct power came down and life and fertility never returned to those areas. This sounds frighteningly familiar to our own time period. How many times does history have to repeat itself before mankind finally gets the message? The Earth is a living being, and will rebel if too much damage is done. And it has the power to counteract if mere mortals think they have the power to try to rule it.

Another example of a civilization that was destroyed in ancient times:

Carol is a highly gifted psychic who works with the police, and also with people all over the world who are trying to uncover lost information from historical sites. We have been friends for many years, and this session occurred when I visited her at her home in Little Rock, Arkansas. We were looking for information that would help in her investigations in Egypt. As usual, I began by having the subconscious take the person back to the most appropriate past lifetime that can explain what is going on in their life now. Carol went under very quickly, but as a psychic she was used to the trance state; plus she knew and trusted me.

She came off the cloud in an unfamiliar environment and had difficulty describing what she was seeing. "They're dwellings, but they're stacked on top of each other." They were constructed out of clay of different pastel colors. "I have nothing to compare it to. They are staggered. Many, many individual dwellings with openings, staggered one on top of the other. Like a mountain or a hill of dwellings." They were not built into a mountain, but were erected like a mountain or cliff.

141

"Some jut out more than others. Some are recessed, and some are not. And some of the ones that are recessed are for walkways. They're very strange. There are buildings on my left that are not in this mountainous stock. They are also very strange. Roofs slanted oddly. Flat, odd angles. There is not much vegetation. Only this large city of strange buildings."

I asked for a description of herself, and she saw that she was a young girl about fourteen with red hair and very light skin. She was dressed in a loose layered tunic type garment tied with a cord at the waist. The most notable thing was that she had a large red stone on a chain around her neck. Her voice became childish as she identified more closely with the personality.

C: A necklace. (She grabbed this word as though it was not one she would have thought of.) With a red stone.
D: *It sounds beautiful.*
C: Pretty, no. A tool. It's natural. It's very long. It's not perfect. It's a tool to use ... (She was having difficulty with the language, and finding the proper words. She was speaking primitively, often using one word instead of a sentence.) Heart. Used for heart. Open. Keep heart open.
D: *Do you know how to use it that way?*
C: I've always known. Each one of us knows which way we're supposed to use these stones. Each one of us does.
D: *Are there different stones for different things?* (Yes) *Do each of you have a different stone?*
C: Each one of us, yes. Mine is the red one. To keep the heart open and flowing with oneness.
D: *You said there are others. Are there a group of you?*
C: Yes. And we have always done this.
D: *Even as a child?*
C: Always.
D: *Did anyone teach you how to use it?*
C: (Confused.) Teach?
D: *Show you how?*
C: Umm. Many.
D: *Many people showed you ....*

C: (Interrupted) People, no. Not people. People don't know. People don't understand.

D: *You mean the average person doesn't understand how to do this?*

C: No, we help them.

There were twelve boys and girls in her group, and they were all about the same age. Her answers were given in the simplest way. Almost childlike.

D: *But you said you've always known how to do this. And someone else showed you how?*

C: (Confused.) Ummm. I need name for this.

D: *Well, maybe not a name, but just a description. You said they're not the ordinary people?*

C: They're not human. (She had difficulty finding the words to describe them.) They're the beautiful ones.

D: *What do they look like?*

C: Shimmery, beautiful. They are of the Source. The oneness. They make me remember who I am. But not always.

D: *Why not always?*

C: Not safe.

D: *Why wouldn't it be safe?*

C: Trial. Too much attention.

D: *From the people in the city?*

C: No. Dark forces. We're safe. We are protected. (That word was said as though it was a strange word.) But if we bring too much attention – for we are still young – it could be dangerous to our physicality.

D: *So it's not the people in the city you have to worry about?*

C: Ummm, no. They're at an age of understanding and openness. Not all. But on the most part. They're young in their wisdom.

D: *Do you have a family there?*

C: Family. Yes.

D: *Does your family know what you were taught?*

C: They had no choice. They are our family. They're physical, and we love them. But they don't fully understand.

D: *You said they had no choice. What do you mean?*

C: (She had difficulty finding the words.) Compelled? (Confused) I don't have full knowledge yet. They must allow us to do what we need to do. They cannot stop us, nor would they really want to. But they understand that we are different. And so, because of that, they do not try to get in the way of what we do. But they don't understand why they are compelled to allow us to do what we need to do. They don't know why. They are compelled.

This was similar to those in the earlier chapters who were born into normal families that couldn't understand their special abilities. In the other cases the children were given to the temple to raise, because their parents didn't understand them. In this case they were allowed to develop and practice their abilities without the interference of the parents.

I wanted to know more about the special stone that she wore around her neck. "You said the others in the group have different stones. Are they for other parts of the body? Like yours is for the heart?"

C: Yes, yes. Energy. Energy centers.

D: *What are some of the colors that they have?*

C: Blue. That is to help with communication. With speaking the word, with channeling, with bringing forth information. (This was said very deliberately, almost as though the words were unfamiliar and difficult to pronounce.) Yellow. For health. Sacred balance.

D: *You mean balancing between the spiritual and the physical?* (Yes) *Are there other stones?*

C: Other stones, yes. Green. Green is for the healing. Green is also for maintaining balance with earth energies. And plants. It helps with communication with plants.

D: *Oh, you can communicate with the plants?*

C: (Emphatic) Yes! So they teach us.

D: *I've never thought of that. What can a plant teach you?*

144

C: How to use them.

D: *Oh? How can you use the plants?*

C: In whatever way that they were created for. (As though anyone should know this.) To help people. To help other plants. To help environments. To help animals. To help with creating oneness. They can do *anything!*

Her tone of voice was one of disbelief that I didn't know these things. It was so obvious and fundamental to her, it should have been the same to me.

D: *I guess I've never thought of it that way. Do you use the plants to help people?*

C: Yes. We are told what to do. They know how they need to be used.

D: *I guess I was thinking of picking leaves or whatever.*

C: We don't have to destroy the plant to use the plant.

D: *I thought of using the plants, or the leaves, berries or flowers. You don't have to do that?*

C: One can.

D: *How would you use it if you didn't destroy the plant?*

C: (Simply, as though speaking to a child.) You use the *consciousness.* The vibration and the essence. And ask them to do what they do.

D: *Ah, I never thought about them having a consciousness.*

C: Everything has consciousness. But we have to be very careful in how we use it, because it would bring attention.

D: *The other people just don't understand, do they?*

C: It doesn't matter. Some do.

D: *This city you live in, do you have transportation in the city?*

C: (Confused) Transportation?

D: *How do you get from one place to the other?*

C: (Pause, still confused.) For who?

D: *Well, if you were to go from one part of the city to the other. How would you do that? Or even outside the city? (Still confused.) I guess I'm just curious about the city.*

C: The city? Movement? *(Yes)* Vehicles? (An unknown

word.)
D: *Yes. Do you know that word?*
C: Through mind of now.
D: *Mind of now. What does that mean?*
C: (Confused and frustrated pause.) Translating. Translating through word mind of now. (Deliberately) Translating this time through mind of now.
D: *Translating this time through mind of now. (I didn't understand, but I went along with her terminology.) Are there vehicles? You used that word.*
C: Vehicles. (Had difficulty explaining.) Singular vehicles. Some double vehicles with movement. And normal movement. And like ... magnetic?
D: *Can you sit in these vehicles and go places?*
C: Sit in, yes.
D: *Do they go over the ground?* (Hesitation) *Over the surface?*
C: Sort of, yes.

This was becoming more difficult the deeper she went. I knew she was identifying more and more with the other personality, and was having more difficulty describing things in terms we could understand. She was completely disassociated from the mind of Carol, but was attempting to use her vocabulary.

C: I can't....Try and translate through mind of now. Electro-magnetic.
D: *You just get into the vehicle, and then what do you do?*
C: Go!
D: *You are just able to do it?* (Uh-huh) *By using the mind of now.*

I didn't understand that she was referring to the mind of Carol. She meant she was translating through Carol's mind using her vocabulary.

C: No. Translating through mind of now.
D: *(I still didn't understand.) Translating through the mind of now*

you are able to make the vehicles move. Is that right? (She was frustrated: No.) *I'm sorry I'm having such a problem, because I do want to understand.*

C: I am translating to you what is here through the mind that is .... (Confused)

D: *Now I think I understand what you mean. You're trying to find the words. Is that right?* (Yes) *And the other mind, your mind, does not have the same words.*

She was relieved that I finally understood. She was finally able to get it across to me.

D: *Do the best you can. That's all I expect. Do the very best you can with the words that you can find. How are these vehicles powered?*

C: (Slowly) Electro-magnetic ... pulse.

D: *Do you have to steer it some way, or how do you make it go?*

C: Thought.

D: *Your mind must be very powerful, if you can do this. Just think where you want it to go?*

C: The vehicle is compliant.

D: *It complies with your thoughts.* (Yes) *Does everyone in the city have the same ability?*

C: (Hesitant again.) Some. Some cannot. Then they can be taken by those that can.

D: *I see. The ones that don't know how to do it have to be taken by someone else. So the city is a good place to be.*

C: Yes, for now. Dark times are coming.

D: *How do you know dark times are coming?*

C: (Sadly) We know. (Almost crying) We know.

D: *What is it that you see? (She was crying.)*

C: All's going to be lost! Gone!

D: *What do you see happening?*

She was openly crying, and it was difficult to talk.

C: (Between sobs) There's going to be a darkness ... and a

shift. And there's *nothing* we can do.

D: *Who's going to cause the darkness? Can you see that?*

C: (Sobbing) I don't know all of it. They won't wake up. They won't enlist ... into the awakening process. The process of the oneness.

D: *You don't know what causes the darkness?*

C: It's coming. (Hesitation and confusion.) The dark forces? Not from here.

D: *They're coming from somewhere else?*

C: Part of it. It's terrible. We can't dwell on that. We know it will come. But we will do what we can *while* we can.

I decided to move her away from that scene to find out what was going to happen. I instructed her to move forward to an important day, and asked her what she was seeing. She was there instantly, and seemed upset. She was just groaning.

D: *What's happening?*

C: (She didn't answer for a few seconds, but I could tell from her facial expressions that something was happening.) I'm gone. (Simple and direct, no emotion.)

I knew I would have to move her backwards to before the event if I was to find out what happened. I instructed her that she could watch it as an observer if she wanted to. It seemed to be something traumatic, and it would be easier if she was viewing it from an objective viewpoint. Her facial expressions indicated emotion. She then took a deep breath, and began telling me what she was seeing.

C: Circle. We're all in circle. And we're moving in circle, and there's something in the center. (Confusion as she tried to explain what was happening.) It's an obelisk that has a stone on top of it. And we're going around it. Counter ... counter-clockwise.

D: *Why are you doing the ceremony?*

C: To bring light. The darkness is coming. We *must* do it as

148

long as we can.
D: *Then what happens?*
C: There are explosions. There are ... explosions of darkness, rumbling, rolling. Screams! We must continue.
D: *Where are the explosions coming from?*
C: They're coming from the west.
D: *Do you know what's causing the explosions?*
C: I don't know. There's ... (Total confusion, she was unable to form words for what was occurring.) Earth ... shifts. Something exploding, which makes many explosions. Don't know. Darkness. A darkness that's ... you can *see* it coming. We must keep the light. For the connection, and hope.
D: *Then what happens?*
C: (Big sigh) It's over!
D: *What caused it?*
C: Everything. It's like ... (confusion) explosions? It's like a huge wave. Of water. (Confused.) Energy. Water. Explosion. Heat. Everything that was ... (frustrated) there is a word. Debris? Mountains of debris.
D: *Oh, that kind of a wave, of debris. Then you wouldn't be able to run away from something like that, would you?*
C: No. We had to continue.
D: *As long as you could? (Yes) And then you were hit by all of this darkness and explosions. (Yes) Is that when you left your body? (Yes) Did you all leave the body at the same time? (Yes) That was good. At least you weren't alone, were you?*
C: No, we weren't.
D: *As you look down on it from that perspective, can you see what happened?*
C: Earth ... change. *Huge* earth change. The shift!
D: *Did it happen everywhere?*
C: (Confused, then:) Yes. Massive.
D: *If this happened every place at once there must have been many people that lost their lives.*
C: Millions.
D: *As you look at it from that perspective, you can see more now,*

because you're removed from the body. Do you have any idea where this place was? Did it have a name or anything that people called it?

C: (Big sigh.) Not that you would know now.

D: *But it sounds like it was a civilization.*

C: It was. It was.

D: *Very advanced. Except your group was more advanced than the others, weren't you?*

C: We had to be.

Many experts and archaeologists deny that these ancient civilizations could have existed. They argue that if it were true they would have found some evidence of them. This session explains why that might not be possible. Not only are some buried beneath the waters of the ocean, they are also buried beneath mountains of mud and debris, and under the relentless shifting sands of deserts. As such it would be very unlikely that any artifacts will ever be found. The same thing would happen if our current civilization were suddenly buried in a monumental disaster. All of our wonderful structures and technology would suddenly disappear. And people of the future would never know we existed in such an advanced state, except through legends that might be passed down. So I tell the skeptics not to be so certain that these wonders weren't there in the past. We may be speaking of our own future.

D: *When you were in that life, you spoke of other beings that taught you things. (Yes) On this side as you look at it, do you know any more about who those beings were?*

C: Our guides. There were also many, many others, that helped and assisted. That were spiritual beings from other ... space? Dimensions?

D: *Why were they helping your group?*

C: Ours was not the only one. There were other groups as well.

D: *But they were not giving this information to the average person.*

C: Could. The people didn't *want* it. Only *some* wanted it. But then those that *did* want it, wanted it for personal ego. That would have been wrong.

D: *But it's okay now, because you survived it, didn't you?*
C: Always survive. Cannot *not* survive.
D: *That's true, because no one can really kill you. You never die.*
C: That is correct. But we have limited spaces to accomplish while in the physical. And there's never enough time.

I then moved her away from the distressing scene and brought Carol's personality back into the body, so I could ask the subconscious questions.

D: *Why did you choose that lifetime to show to Carol?*
C: It has always been the same. We always come back together. We always do this in the same time frames when we come back together.
D: *You mean the group?*
C: Yes. We come back separately, but not at the same time frame.
D: *In the past, you mean?* (Yes) *But now you're all back together again?*
C: Many of these were lost. In that lifetime. In between. And in this lifetime.
D: *You mean they aren't all back together again?*
C: Many were taken from other groups that were doing similar work, in order to bring a balance, so that work could be done.
D: *What connection does that lifetime have with her present lifetime?*
C: The knowledge. The oneness. The knowledge of the consciousness. All things that are one can connect, and all knowledge can be used and brought forth for change.
D: *Do you mean we're going through the same thing all over again?* (Yes) *It does sound similar in some ways, doesn't it? Is she supposed to bring this knowledge forward to our present lifetime?* (Yes) *In that lifetime she had much knowledge dealing with stones and plants, didn't she?*
C: More. Knowledge of harmonics. Knowledge of frequencies.

151

Knowledge of getting information through frequencies from anyone or any*thing.* Time travel.

D: *This group was able to do that by the knowledge of harmonics and frequencies?*

C: Yes. The brain is ... (looking for the word) holograph.

D: *Holographic. How were they able to do the time travels?*

C: Portals.

D: *And she knows how to find these portals?* (Yes) *So she has that knowledge from that lifetime?*

C: Yes. And from others that key into this one.

I wanted to know if Carol would be allowed to bring the knowledge back to her present lifetime, because nothing is ever lost. It's always there waiting in the subconscious if it's advisable to use again. The subconscious said there was a problem because she had a deep-seated fear, because she had used this knowledge in many other lifetimes and there had been extreme danger in some of them. This fear had been implanted for her protection, so she wouldn't be exposed and have the possibility of danger to her physical body. The subconscious agreed that it was now time to release the fear so she could bring the knowledge to our present time. It instructed me that it had the key, but I was the one who had to activate the procedure to unlock it. I was told I had to call forth the sentinel. This was new to me. I asked what it meant.

C: The sentinel of internal/external knowledge.

D: *And this sentinel can allow it to be released slowly in a safe manner?*

C: Slowly is not required.

D: *But safely.*

C: Safely.

D: *We don't want to over-flood her mind. It has to be released in a way that she can handle it.*

C: Yes, but protection ... fear ... implant must be removed.

D: *The sentinel sounds like a very important person. Does he have the power to do this, and allow the information to be released in measured doses that way?*

C: I give you permission to unlock the fear protection implant. All else will fall into place. I now unlock the fear protection implant. Permanently.

D: *And the knowledge will only be used for good. For positive. Isn't that correct?*

C: Only for good.

D: *And so the information will begin to come back, that's been hidden for a long time.* (Big sigh) *And she will be able to use it. That's very wonderful. I thank you for allowing it to happen. Without you, it couldn't have happened.*

C: Without *you* it couldn't have happened.

D: *But I'm just the tool to help get to the information that Carol wants to use. I thank you for allowing it to happen. How are you going to release the information? Will it be done in dreams, or intuition?*

C: Knowledge. She will *know* it. She will remember.

These examples show that in the past many of us have gained great knowledge of how to use the powers of the mind. Even though we have forgotten these abilities, they are still there awaiting the time of their revival. Many of the people alive today are carrying these memories of how to use the mind, and this appears to be the time for this to be reactivated and used for the good of our planet. These are indeed the special people. And my work shows they are much more plentiful that anyone suspects. The time of reawakening is now!

CHAPTER 8

TAKEN TO SAFETY

Through my work with the ETs and my regression work I have been told many times that if the Earth faced destruction, or if another mass catastrophe were to occur that would threaten the human race, that the ETs would take us off the planet. There have been several versions of this in my work. In one of them they said another planet was being prepared that would be almost identical to Earth. It would be topographically different, but humans would be able to survive there. It was called the "New Eden", and animals and plants were already being prepared there so the humans would feel comfortable. Another scenario would be that people would be taken onboard spacecrafts to await the calming down of the Earth after the cataclysm. In either case I assumed it would take thousands of years for the Earth to calm down and become inhabitable again, because everything would have to start over, depending upon the severity of the catastrophe. If the survivors were taken off Earth to await this, I assumed it would have to be their descendants who would be brought back to reestablish civilization again (even if in primitive stages). I have been told this has happened many times down through Earth's turbulent history, that civilizations have been destroyed and life must begin anew. The most important message from the ETs is that the human race must not perish! They have invested too much time and energy into our development to allow us to destroy ourselves completely through our own stupidity.

These were my assumptions in our logical way of thinking. That it would have to be the descendants of the original survivors who would return to repopulate the Earth, because of the incredible length of time that would be involved. During the following regression I found that my assumptions were wrong.

154

When Marian came off the cloud she found herself as a male in his thirties with long black hair, dressed simply in a short robe tied with a cord. He was standing on the edge of a forest looking out across a grassy plain at a small town. This was his destination, and he had left his own village two or three days earlier. When he entered the village there was a lot of confusion among the inhabitants. "Something's going on, and the people don't understand. They are very disorganized. They are walking around, running around, trying to find out what's happening." It seemed as though no one knew exactly what was wrong, but they were reacting in the same way that animals can sense danger. He also felt apprehensive.

"I'm supposed to get this group in this village to join with my group or village. I'm sort of like an emissary, but it's like, okay, where do I start with this mess. There's a natural leader that will be the person that really pulls it together. I have to seek out the person that can help me accomplish what I need to accomplish. It may not be the official ruler. Something is happening. This is not the only place. Something's going on to disrupt things. It's affecting everybody. This is why we must band together."

When he found the person he was seeking, it was a woman. "She's in one of the houses. She's of like mind. She knows that things need to be gotten control of. That organization needs to come to the people, to the group. And she's willing to work with me. She's calm. She's respected."

He knew the people would listen to her, and he stood in the background as she talked to the people. "I'm confirming what she needed to know and do. So she goes out and does it. She starts talking to them, so they begin to listen. Because they need it. They want it, because they're scared. They need some kind of guidance and apparently the leader isn't providing it."

I had no idea where this was all going, because it was vague as to the cause of the confusion, and Marian's role in all this.

But I could not lead. I had to let the story unfold by only asking questions. I asked, "What are you deciding to do?"

"Let her work with them for a while before she presents the idea of an alliance. Of getting together with other villages, so we can discuss strategy. There are other people that went out to other villages. It's going to be kind of like a council. There's a threat that's common to all of us. It's not other people threatening."

I thought maybe it could be an invading army, because that happened countless times down through history. "It's hard to define, because I don't understand it either. I can't say if it's Earth changes, or if it's coming from outside. Nobody's quite sure what it is. If we can organize, we can get through this."

I decided to take him forward to see what was happening, in the hope that it might become clearer. All the people were gathered in a large clearing. She led out a big sigh, and said, "It's crazy." After a pause, she reluctantly told me what she was seeing. "I see ships. Alien ships. They're coming down. It creates fear, but they're not hostile."

He described the ships as "Sort of round, but not ball shaped. More oval. They're not little two or three man things. They are bigger. They can hold many people." The ships were not landing, but hovering over the ground.

D: *What do you do?*
M: (Hysterical laugh) Try and pretend I'm not afraid.
D: *Did the people know something like this was going to happen?*
M: We have never seen anything like this in our life. Maybe on a psychic level we knew. On an animalistic level we knew something was coming, but we didn't know what it was. That's why we were organizing. There was a threat. But nobody understood the threat.
D: *So it was something you couldn't have really prepared for.*
M: No, but we had to. Because otherwise people would just be running around crazy. And so you have to be organized. And all the people from many villages are here.
D: *What happens?*

156

M: We have to leave. Everybody has to go in the ship.

D: *Is somebody telling you that?*

M: No, I know it. I just know it.

D: *Why would you have to leave? This is your home.*

M: Because something's going to happen. And if we don't leave we'll be killed. So this lady from that village, and me from my village are here with the people that went to different villages. We know we have to get the people to go.

D: *Do you have any idea what would kill you? What would happen if you don't go?*

M: Something that's going to happen to the Earth.

D: *Are the people willing to go?*

M: They're all scared. It's hard. I can't let them know I'm scared. Me and this woman, and other people from other villages are going to help lead them on these ships. We're trying to round them up. Some go willingly. They're willing to follow. And others, you have to encourage them. They think it's crazy.

I asked for a description of the inside of the ship after everyone was onboard.

M: It is good sized. There's room for everybody. And it's not crowded.

D: *You said there are several ships?*

M: Yes. In different places. You can look in the distance and see them. You can take stuff with you if you want. Or animals and whatever you think.

D: *Can you see the people that have come with the ship? What do they look like?*

M: (Chuckle) They're trying to look non-threatening. They're trying to smile, and hold out their hand, and be friendly. Be careful of who they approach.

D: *Do they look human?* (Yes) *It's not as frightening that way. Well, if the ones that will come get on with their animals and whatever, what happens then?*

M: (Long pause) The ships go out into space and heaven.

157

D: *How do you feel about that?*

M: There's a lot of work to do. In terms of talking to the people, and telling them it's okay. It's the right thing to do. And it'll be all right. I'm starting to relax. I'm so busy.

He was able to see outside the ship, and the Earth below. I wanted to know what it looked like. He sighed deeply as he tried to describe what he was seeing. "The Earth looks like what I would imagine solar flares look like. Things flaring up from the Earth. I can't say they're volcanoes. I don't know what it is."

D: *Can you ask one of the people on the ship what is happening?*

M: I could. They're busy, but I could though.

D: *Just ask them what's going on down there?*

M: Just planetary changes that you wouldn't understand. (Chuckle) You could try. (Laugh)

D: *Yes, let him try.*

M: It's kind of a cross between a volcano and a comet and a nuclear explosion. That's the closest he can describe that I can understand. They knew it was coming, and that's why they wanted to take as many people off as they could. And we'll go back.

D: *Will you go back right away?*

M: He starts to explain that we can be held in a situation where time goes by, but *we* don't change. And then we'll just go back.

D: *That's an interesting way to put it. Time will go by but you won't change. Can he explain it any better?*

M: It's not suspended animation. Time will go by, but you won't .... (Very softly:) How do I explain it? Time goes by on Earth, time does not go by on the ship. The Earth will go through stuff, and the ship won't.

D: *It's kind of like two different — I don't think "time periods" is the right wording.*

M: Time goes by there, time does *not* go by here.

This is very similar to the concept they have told me, that time is an illusion. Time passes from the human perspective: hours, days, weeks, months, because we are trapped in that concept. They have no concept of time and thus it does not exist for them. This is one of the reasons they can travel so easily through time and space without restrictions. They said that mankind is probably the only species in the universe that has found a way to measure something that does not exist.

D: *Are they going to keep you on the ship until it's time to go back?*
M: Right. It's not going to be very long.
D: *But on Earth it would be much longer.* (Yes) *So you won't go anywhere else. You'll just stay on the ship.*
M: Just hover.

That answered the question I had earlier. I thought they would have to be taken somewhere where they could wait out a catastrophe, and not be able to return until the Earth was capable of supporting life again, which could be thousands of years. If they were not trapped by the concept of time, it would be rather like watching the events like a fast forward on a video tape.

M: That is good that it will not take long, because the people won't get that upset. There is plenty of room, so some of them brought their animals with them. (Laugh) It's like a Noah's ark!
D: *(Laugh) That's what I was thinking. It sounded like it.*
M: We won't feel like it's a long time on the ship.

I moved him ahead so he could see what was happening on the Earth below.

M: It's almost like the fourth of July. You know, one of those cones that go off. That's what it looks like is going off in different parts of the Earth. There were fires, and clouds of ash. You can see the colors changing.

159

D: *What do you mean by the colors?*

M: When it first went off, there were the greens and the blues and the white cloud things. And then these flares. And sometimes there were gray clouds. Then the gray, and the ugly brown and gray yucky clouds slowly clear up. And then things came back to the blues and the greens and the whites.

In a short period of time, he watched what would have taken thousands of years to happen. He then moved ahead to when they were all returned to the Earth.

D: *Do they take you back to the same place?*

M: It's hard to say. There are trees and stuff again. They came back. But there are no villages and no manmade stuff around. There are no animals except the animals we took with us.

D: *When they let you off, did they stay with you?*

M: They told us that we were going to just have to start over.

D: *So it's not their responsibility to help you?*

M: They just tried to help people see that they will have to use their skills, whatever they know.

D: *It's hard to begin all over again.* (Yes) *At least they saved everybody.*

M: Right. And they work with the people to boost their morale and give them confidence. Tell them why it can be done.

D: *Do you know if everything was destroyed?* (Yes) *The whole world?* (Yes) *Then do they leave?*

M: Yes. They're going to continue their functions.

D: *You're going to have to begin again. That showed a lot of perseverance to do all of that.*

I then moved her forward trying to find another important day, although I didn't think anything could be more important than what he had just been through. He announced, "I don't live much longer. Something happens to me. There's an accident. A tree falls during the rebuilding process. It crushed me." I then had him move to the spirit side and look at the life from that perspective. I asked what he had learned from the life. "Sometimes you have to go with the unknown."

I then integrated Marian's personality back into the body, replacing the other entity, and brought forth the subconscious.

D: *Why did you pick this strange lifetime for Marian to see?*
M: It's going to happen again.
D: *(This was a surprise.) You think so?*
M: It's going to happen again. There's going to be Earth changes. And the ships are going to come again.
D: *What's the connection with Marian's life now?*
M: Because she knows it's going to happen again. She went through it once already, and she's going to be living when the Earth goes through it again.
D: *The man could see something happening from the ship. What happened to Earth?*
M: There were lots of changes. Lots of disruptions. It's a cycle.
D: *Was it caused by man the last time?*
M: No, it's a cycle. A natural cycle.
D: *That the Earth goes through?* (Yes) *But it was not meant for all life to perish, was it?*
M: No, they don't want everything to be wiped out.
D: *That's important, because it's a lot of work to start all over again. What did they mean when they said, "Time would go by on Earth, but not on the ship"?*
M: Because that's the way time is.
D: *It must have taken a long time for the Earth to come back to where it was habitable again. Yet the people on the ship didn't change.*
M: Time is where you focus. On Earth you go step by step by step by step. You don't have to when you're not on Earth. You just focus and you're there. If you focus over there, you're there. There's no time scale. You are *out* of scale, because they don't need a scale.
D: *It's always hard for our minds to understand.*

161

M: It's going to happen again. I'm not even sure if it's going to happen in this lifetime or not. I mean *Marian's* lifetime. But the job is to make people aware. The *plan* is for her to slowly uncover information, so it won't overwhelm her. But the information's there, and she has to uncover it. And it has to do with this ... off-world stuff. This Earth project stuff. She has to get people to see what's out there. Get people prepared. *More* people aware. That there are more things than rush and hurry in this world. There are more things than just going to the grocery store. She needs to open their minds. They have to wake up. They aren't stupid.

D: *I've been told many times that people are really hurting the Earth. Is that what you mean?*

M: (Big sigh) It's beyond that. Stopping hurting the Earth would have slowed things down. It's going to happen. Period!

D: *There's no way to stop it now?*

M: No. It's on the way.

D: *What is it she's supposed to do?*

M: Just keep waking people up. It may not happen in this generation. But the more people that are aware that things can happen to the Earth itself, the more people will be ready and willing to go on the ships.

D: *It will be the same thing again?* (Yes) *They will come to take some?* (Yes) *But there will be some that won't want to go?*

M: The meek can have the Earth.

D: *I guess the meek would be those who are afraid to go.*

M: She must tell people of things they have never thought of. Things that they've never looked at. Things they've always thought were weird and laughable.

D: *You mean metaphysical ideas?*

M: Right. It doesn't have to be UFOs.

D: *This would be a way of advancing?*

M: It would be a way to save your butt.

It is amazing that I keep getting these pieces of the puzzle

162

from so many people all over the world. It is my job to put the puzzle together, and as I do that it begins to make some sort of sense, even if our conscious reasoning can't quite grasp the enormity of it all. There seems to be much more that is just out of reach.

SECTION 3

ADVANCED BEINGS AND KARMA

CHAPTER 9

CHILDREN CREATE KARMA

A case I did in California in 2001, showed the difficulty souls, who have not known Earth life, have adjusting to this hectic planet. A young woman came to see me while I was in San Jose for an all-day lecture for the A.R.E. group (Edgar Cayce Foundation). I usually try to see people who are on my waiting list for private sessions and I schedule them around my talks. Susan was overweight, and I immediately thought this would be one of the problems she would want to investigate. But her main issue was that she and her husband wanted to have children, and she had not been able to conceive. I always direct the subconscious to take the person to the most appropriate lifetime to explain the problems they are having in this present lifetime. This was the procedure I followed with Susan.

When Susan entered the deep hypnotic state, instead of finding herself in a past life on Earth, she floated through space and found herself standing in front of a big metal door with a large X on it. The X was composed of four triangles, and as we talked, the triangles all opened outward so she could enter. Through the doorway she could see she definitely was not on Earth. She was on a cliff overlooking a valley, and everything: rocks, dirt and sky, had a reddish color. She saw a large dome in the valley, but there were no trees or vegetation. She immediately knew that you couldn't breathe the air. No one was safe outside. She knew there were people in shelters down below the surface, and that was where she had to go. She found the entrance in the side of the cliff and went down into a very dark area beneath the surface where the people were hiding. Susan appeared to be a tall, thin, blond male. "No fat!" she chuckled.

Her job was to deliver supplies to various outposts on planets in their two sun system. This was one of the stops enroute and her job was to check on the people, and see what they needed. The people had food, but water was in short supply. They could not go to the surface, but had to live crowded together underground. The people appeared human, but were dressed in rags. The dome contained engines and had something to do with generating power. Apparently it also filtered the air that reached the underground shelter. She explained that there had been a war many, many years before that had destroyed the atmosphere and made it hazardous to the surviving population. It had been caused by something like a nuclear bomb, and life had not returned to the surface because the air was contaminated. They had adjusted to this type of life, and built the underground shelter, but now a new danger loomed. Another group had discovered the planet and was trying to take it over for the minerals it contained. So more fighting was occurring, making it doubly dangerous to be on the surface.

When the fighting slowed for a while, she went back to the surface and returned to her small scout ship and left the planet. I then asked her to go to an important day in that life. I always choose an important day, because in most lives (even in our present ones) the days are very much alike. What one person considers an important day, another does not. Many times these are mundane, but that is because the life is mundane and there is not much to alter it. Susan's life was no exception. Even though it appeared to be taking place on another planet, it seemed to be very ordinary. Just a man delivering supplies to one outpost after another. Even the place where he obtained the supplies (a barren planet) seemed nondescript. This time when I asked her to move ahead to an important day, she suddenly announced, "I'm crashing!" It didn't seem to bother her to say this. She was unemotional and detached as she described the feeling of falling. "We hit something, or something hit us. The front of the craft is half gone. I don't know what happened." She had already exited the body before the ship crashed back into the planet.

I could not understand how this strange otherworldly life could explain Susan's inability to conceive. The subconscious' logic always surpasses mine, and the answer it supplied was not one that I expected.

The subconscious had shown her that lifetime so she would remember where she came from: the planet with two suns. Susan had dreams since childhood about a place that was not Earth that had two suns in the sky. She even drew pictures of this strange place, but she could not understand where these memories came from. The subconscious said the reason she was not having children was because she was still identifying with the other personality who crashed.

Her other lives had mostly been on other planets, and when she decided to experiment and try living on Earth she had difficulty adjusting. She did not like it here, and wanted to leave and go home. She said, "There is too much responsibility. Too much everything. Too hard. More challenging."

Her other personalities had mostly been in a body that had no sex organs and could not be defined as either male or female. This is called "androgynous", and many ETs that I have investigated are living this way today on their worlds. She did not like being female or having sex parts. She said, "There's no sex when there's no sex." These other beings did not reproduce, but were "made". This usually occurs by a cloning process and thus does not need sex to reproduce.

I tried to explain that I understood her identification with the other personalities, but in order to have a child in this life, sex was the only way humans know how to get children here. She replied that she didn't want to be human. She didn't like this world at all. She felt she had learned enough and wanted to go. This is always a warning sign, and I knew I had to proceed with caution. Even though the conscious personality of Susan seemed to be well-adjusted and wanted to have children, this other part of her was a total opposite. It did not like it here and wanted to leave. My job is always to protect the person I am working with, and not allow any danger to befall them, even if it is from another part of themselves. She kept insisting, "I'm done now. I'm done. I'm done. I want to go."

She also insisted that she did not need to have a child. A child would cause connections to the Earth. She wanted to sever all connections. She did not want to create karma with a child that would cause her to come back here. If she had no ties to Earth then it would be easier to return to her home planet. This experiment had not turned out like she thought it would. The cause of her being overweight was to protect her against sex so she wouldn't have children. I have heard this before when people subconsciously cause themselves to be overweight to make themselves unattractive to the opposite sex, and the padding of the extra weight acts as protection and puts up a barrier. So even though the conscious mind of Susan was saying she wanted children, the subconscious part had another scenario.

I attempted to argue with her. She said she liked children and liked to work with them. So I suggested that since she had loving tendencies she would be a good mother. If she had one of her own, she could teach it all kinds of wonderful things, and that would be a new experience. It would be a challenge to teach a child how to live in this world. It would be a gift that she could give to this planet. She was still afraid of creating connections that would tie her to this world. "It would make me come back here again and again. I don't like it here. I don't like connections."

She was very insistent that her life would be short. That is was almost time to leave because she wanted to go home. I argued that if she cut it short she would only have to come back and do it again until she completed her obligations. She definitely did not want that to happen, because she wanted out. So I thought I was making some headway by my persuasions. She had been having dreams of her home planet most of her life, so she would not forget where she came from and get stuck here. It is too easy to forget once the soul enters the body. The person gets caught up in this world and its unique problems. When I talked about her losing weight, she said this world was too heavy. One way to get rid of the weight was to just leave her body. She was certainly determined. I can only hope that my positive affirmations were getting through her stubbornness. I kept insisting that she couldn't leave until she had completed her responsibilities. She didn't need to get caught in the cycle of coming back to Earth. That is a harder cycle to break.

This was a difficult case because I didn't know I was going to encounter such resistance from Susan's subconscious. I was to later discover other souls who volunteered to come into this world at this time to help. They also did not want to have children because it might tie them to our world. They had to remain free of karma so they could leave when they finished.

It is interesting that many of the people I have worked with in the last few years regress to lifetimes where they were light beings living in a state of bliss. They had no reason to come into the Earth's density and negativity. They all volunteered to come to help the Earth at this time, but had no idea how difficult it would be once they were in the body.

I have encountered what I consider to be several different waves of souls that have come in at various times. The first wave were souls like Phil in my book *Keepers of the Garden*. These are now in their forties. They had a difficult adjustment and many wanted to commit suicide in order to return "home". They normally have a good home life, excellent occupation and everything that we would consider to make up a good life. But something was missing because they never felt they belonged here. They didn't like the violence and ugliness they found in this world. They wanted to return home even though they had no idea, consciously, where that home might be. I have heard from many people all over the world who think they are of this group. They thought they were the only ones in the world that felt this way, and were very relieved, upon reading my book, to find they truly were not alone.

A second wave that I discovered, came about ten or more

171

years later. These are now in their twenties and thirties. Some of these have adjusted very well. Under hypnosis, they say they are simply here to act as a conduit or channel to conduct the type of energy to the Earth that is needed at this time. These people lead very nondescript lives, often unmarried with no responsibilities (especially no children). They have jobs that allow them plenty of free time to explore their true interests, which seem to center around helping people. They appear to have no problems and have adjusted to this world much easier than the first wave.

The third wave is definitely the special children (so-called the Indigo Children) who have come and are still coming in. Some of these are now in early puberty. These are indeed the special ones, and have been called the hope of mankind. They need to be understood because they function at a different level and frequency than other children their age. There have been many books written about these children, and I have spoken at conferences focusing on them. They are indeed different. Even their DNA has been proven to be different. In my work, I have been told to emphasize that they not be put on drugs, especially Ritalin, which is a mind altering substance. They are bored at school and are sometimes disruptive because they are capable of learning and absorbing at a much more rapid rate than children of other generations. I was told that they need to be presented with challenges. This will stimulate their curiosity and sharpen their abilities. There are many children in this age group who are already gaining the attention of the media because of their remarkable abilities. Down through history there have always been stories of child prodigies; children who had talents far beyond their years. These were few and far between. Science could not explain them, yet I think their abilities come from talents learned and perfected in their past lives. However, the new group seems to be different. While the ones in the past were rare and unique, there seems to be many more of this new wave of children who are exhibiting the abilities of genius. The children interviewed on TV are already in college and pursuing careers. But each of them stressed their desire to form

172

organizations to help the less fortunate children of the world.

I tend to think from my work, that these talents are not coming from their past lives, but from the difference in their soul pattern. All of these three waves that I have observed, came to help Earth in her time of need. Most of them had never had lives on this planet, so they find it a difficult place to live. They are here for definite purposes and want to finish their assignment and go "home". Even though they don't know it consciously, they are fully aware of their mission on Earth. It is not hidden under layers of past lives and karma. The newest wave is not being as hidden as the others. The powers that be that make these decisions about who to send, are making them more noticeable, because the time is growing short to make the changes that will either save or destroy our world. More and more of these souls that are not native to our world, but have lived most of their lives on other planets or other dimensions are being sent, because it is believed they can make a difference. The "native" souls who have lived countless lives on Earth have become so bogged down by karma and the everyday pressures of living in our hectic world, that they have lost sight of their purpose for being here. This causes them to keep coming back and repeating the same mistakes. Thus the hope for our future is souls that have not been tainted by Earth who can help us survive. *If* they can keep from becoming trapped also, and forgetting their mission.

In the beginning days of my work I thought it would be impossible for a spirit to come directly into a physical body in our civilized and hectic culture as their first incarnation. I had been told they would logically first incarnate into some primitive society where life would be simpler. That way they could adjust and learn how to live on Earth and how to deal with other humans, before coming into our modern lifestyle. Now I am finding that is not always the case. I am encountering

173

more of the special people who have been sent or who volunteer to come and help during these challenging times. They say they have been sent as channels of energy, or as antennas etc. It is, of course, more difficult for these gentle souls because they do not have the background of Earth lives to prepare them.

In October 2004 I met two more of these special people. And even more unusual they were husband and wife. I think it is wonderful that they were able to locate each other out of the millions of people in the world, so their identical energies could work together. But then, I have also been told that nothing happens by accident. They had evidently agreed and made plans on the other side before incarnating.

They both gave identical stories while in deep trance even though they were unaware of these things consciously. When Tony came off the cloud he only saw a very bright light. "It is very bright. It radiates, it has rays going in all directions. It is very beautiful, but you can't look directly at it. It also has many different colors throughout. It is very soothing. There is so much love that comes from it. It surrounds you just like it's hugging you." When this happens I know they have either gone to the spirit side, or back to the Source (or God). Also various energy beings look like this. I asked it to take Tony and show him something that was important for him to see. Instead of going into a past life, he was taken to a room where there were several beings dressed in robes. He could not make out any features as the beings floating effortlessly around the room.

T: I don't see any walls, but you feel you are in a closed environment. This is like a council, and there is a meeting where they have come to discuss all different types of things. Things of the universe. All the different planets. They're having to make decisions for other types of beings or for ... I guess it would be for lower vibrations. For those that haven't reached the higher planes or higher vibrations. This is the council that helps them in making decisions in their processes or what they will be doing.

He saw that he had the same type of wispy, ghostly body, and felt he was a member of this council.

T: Otherwise, I wouldn't be able to be here. This is a higher vibration, a higher frequency. And they help to make decisions. They don't necessarily make decisions, but they *help* in making decisions. What ever would be appropriate for the lower vibrations.

D: *How do they help make these decisions?*

T: It seems like for each lower vibration, there are certain things they need to learn to be able to elevate their vibrations to a different plane. To help them. The council actually helps them to make decisions that will actually raise their vibrations.

D: *This is not interfering?*

T: No, it's only a form of guidance.

D: *Do you have anything in particular that you're working on right now?*

T: Only to be of a service. To help. To give guidance. That's what we're only here to do. To help gain them the knowledge.

D: *Is there any particular project that you're concerned about right now?*

T: There are all different types of projects. As we help the lower vibrations, we are also helping ourselves. Because it also teaches us as well as we teach them. If you serve, you gain. This helps you gain knowledge.

D: *Are you working with any certain planet at the present time?*

T: It's working with all the universes. It's not just one planet.

D: *Did you have to go through physical lifetimes to reach that point? Where you could be on the council?*

T: No. Didn't have to go through physical lifetimes. Only by choice.

D: *So how did you get to that point where you could be on the council?*

T: You can raise your vibration level, even though you don't have to go through physical lifetimes to be on the council.

Sometimes it may take over a period of time. But sometimes you can progress very quickly.

D: *Did you ever have a desire to be physical?*

T: Not at this point in time, no.

D: *You were doing your job over there then.*

T: That was all I needed to do.

D: *Well, it sounds like it's a very important job.*

T: This was all that was asked for me to do.

I then asked him to move to when he made the decision to come into the physical, because after all, I was communicating with a physical body in our dimension. He must have decided to come here and incarnate. I wanted to know if someone told him to come.

T: No, it was only by choice. And the opportunity was there. The ability ... or the physical form, in other words that would fit, was there at the time of choice.

D: *Did anything happen to cause you to make the choice?*

T: To experience. For that was something I had never done before. It was definitely new.

D: *Have you picked out the body that you're going to go into?* (Yes.) *What does it look like?*

T: It is the present. There is no other time.

D: *Explain what you mean.*

T: It is as the person you are speaking to.

D: *Tony, you mean?* (Yes.) *You mean Tony has never had any other physical incarnations before this?* (No.) *I've always thought that if that were the case, it would be very difficult, wouldn't it? To come directly from the spiritual side to life the way we have it now on Earth. Without any former lifetimes to condition the person.*

T: It *is* very difficult. But there are ways they help in doing things. There was certain things. I don't know if I can describe these things for you.

D: *I would really appreciate if you could try. Analogies are always good, too.*

T: It's like the information is provided. It's like you go into a chamber. And once you come out of this chamber, this information has been placed within you. Then this information, once it has been placed within you, would give you a background. Something to relate to.

I knew what he was talking about. He was referring to imprinting. This is discussed in this book as well as *Keepers of the Garden* and *Between Death and Life.* It is a way of providing information from other people's lives so the soul can have some background in order to function.

T: I don't think you can come in with nothing. It is still difficult even with this information being placed within. It is extremely different here. There is much to learn, and to experience. It was difficult to leave that beautiful place, but it was something that needed to be experienced. This time in history is when there is great change that is coming about. Things are moving very rapidly; very quickly. He wanted to be able to observe these things.

D: *So no one told him he had to do these things.*

T: No, no one directs you and tells you that you must do these things. These are choices. And also discussions. And he was helped by other members of the council. They help or guide him to make these choices.

D: *We're used to thinking of Earth lives where we accumulate karma, and then we have to come back again and again to repay it.*

T: He doesn't have that type of karma that you're speaking of. He is here to observe the progression of humans. How they are actually raising their vibration levels. To see how they are accepting knowledge. And how they're using knowledge. If they're using for the good of mankind, or if it is being used for greed.

D: *Because Earth is a complicated planet.*

T: It's *extremely* complicated. It is unlike any other planet. I think the form of negativity on this planet makes it

177

different. The human race is a very warrior type race. They have a great deal of difficulty of living peace. It is almost like their race cannot co-exist in peace. This may come from their lower vibrations. I think each one that comes here has to be so careful and not be caught into these lower vibrations. It is a very challenging planet. I did take that chance. I think that any time you come into this existence, you have created karma. And, no doubt, I will have to repay this karma. However, I think the main thing that I do here is try to maintain a balance of being very positive, very loving, and what karma I have created with Earth isn't of a negative form, per se. It's to actually find ways of working to reduce that. And then to take care of that karma. And not allow it to carry over.

D: *What is your plan then?*

T: At present time, it's to come in for this one lifetime. I will have to see once I get back.

D: *You don't want to stay and experience other existences?*

T: I don't know if I will return for other existences. There may be more important things for me to do than to return. Than to be physical. I don't know if I will be able to accomplish this or not. It would be very easy to become trapped here. There are so many things to trap me. That is the reason it is so difficult to come here, into the physical form. Even though many desire this presence, it is extremely difficult. It looks pretty simple until you come in. Once you're into the physical form, then it is extremely difficult.

D: *One of the problems is the physical forgets and doesn't know all these things?*

T: Oh, quite true.

D: *Would it be easier if they were able to remember?*

T: I don't think it would be right for the physical form to remember. I think it would be too much. To remember all these things would be too great. It would be too confusing and then they would try to change things and probably in a most undesirable way. And maybe not learn the things

178

that they were here to learn for their own growth.

D: *People are always saying if they only knew what it was like before, it would be easier.*

T: I think this would be too much information for them. If you had all this knowledge before you, what would be the purpose to come in? We also teach. Children teach their parents as parents think they teach their children. More vise versa. More than we realize.

D: *I seem to be working with many people lately who are energy workers and healers.*

T: There's going to be a great deal more. This is only starting to open. And people are seeking other alternatives. They're looking for different ways. They are seeing that what they are used to is not actually working for their best interest. There will be some that will cling to the old forms. They have trouble getting past that. It is their conditioning and upbringing, but you have many out here, and especially the new ones are coming in, that will be seeking all this new information. And of course, they will be bringing that new information as well. Most of the information is not new. It is new to the people that are present. But it is actually old information. − There are only so many physical forms that are available. And there are so many more spiritual forms that want to come, that there are not enough physical forms.

D: *But right now with our population growth, there are many physical forms available.*

T: But there is not. Also you have certain ones that are trying to control the metaphysical forms that are available. You have leaders that are trying to control the availability of physical forms. Of course, the diseases, the wars.

D: *You mean they're eliminating many of the physical forms?* (Oh, yes.) *Then there are those physical forms that are spoken for by those souls that want to come back to repay karma, too.*

T: That's quite true, yes.

D: *Is that what you mean, there's only limited physical forms that your type of spirit could come into?*

179

T: Yes. That's true. It's hard to find appropriate food because of all the chemicals in the foods. But the human body is also adapting. You are seeing at this time new humans that are coming in with the old knowledge. The source of the food is going to be more difficult as time goes on. It will be a real problem.

D: *All of this is going to affect the raising of the vibrations.*

T: We have to make the body lighter. And this will help in the process.

Tony was told how he could use his mind to heal. "He will have to develop his mind and also to trust his mind as well. The mind is very powerful. And by viewing the problem, seeing the problem, then his mind will make the changes. It will be like you will be able to see inside the body. It is as if you would go inside the person and look at that person inside. It is as if would go into the leaf of the tree and float into the channels of the chlorophyll. He will see them as pictures. And these changes can take place. He would not have to have the person's participation, but he would have to have their permission. Because some choose to have these conditions for whatever reasons."

In the afternoon I had a session with Tony's wife Sally, and I was surprised to find she was the same type of soul. This was also her first time to come to Earth. How remarkable that the two were able to find each other. Of course, nothing happens by accident, but I had never encountered two such cases on the same day.

In the beginning of the session, Sally also had difficulty seeing anything except shifting colors, and after several attempts to get her to a past life or something visual, I finally contacted the subconscious. It supplied the information I had been denied. Sometimes if the subject is not ready the information will not come forth. Because of the protectiveness of the subconscious it is very particular about who it will release it to.

S: What is happening with Sally is an experiment. It has never been done before. We're trying to raise the energy levels. There are energy rules in incarnation on Earth and everywhere else. But because of the times and because of the necessity, what we were trying to accomplish is to bring a higher vibration into the Earth and then expand it, raise the level even after the incarnation. And also to bring in the highest level we could without harm to the physical form. There's a level that the human form can't hold. This is very important to Sally because we failed at it before. That's why she volunteered to come and to bring that energy in and to go through it and do it. And we did it. It worked this time. When it failed before it was like blowing a circuit.

D: *Did it harm the physical form that she was trying to come into?*

S: Right. It did. The body died. It was too much energy, too much information, too high of a vibration in one physical body.

D: *It just can't hold that.*

S: Right. But this body has been able to. And also we fine tuned the body as it's aged. To be able to hold more, and we have added more since.

D: *Has she had physical incarnations before?*

S: Imprints. Many of the physical problems are because of the stress and strain on the body from holding the energy that is there.

D: *Then you mean that Sally has never been in a physical incarnation anywhere?* (No.) *But I always thought when they came into the physical body for the first time, in this kind of civilization, it would be too hard on the body. On the soul.*

S: She has been an assistant to the Earth. Not incarnated in the Earth, but around the Earth assisting others who incarnate. She has a workable knowledge but not actual incarnation knowledge, but has been behind the scenes assisting others who incarnate.

D: *Why then did she decide to come this time?*

S: Because it was very important for the Earth, and she had the ability to bring in the energy that was needed at that time. In that way, in that magnitude, and in the proportions that needed to come at that time. It's very scientific. I'm not explaining it well. It's almost like mathematical equations of energy. Hers were most adaptable to come in because she had been working closely with the Earth. And knew how things worked and the rules and regulations and that sort of thing, scientifically. So she was able to adjust her energy, and adjust the body. And also we're helping with that.

D: *But when somebody does this for the very first time, isn't she taking a chance of getting caught up in karma?*

S: No. The reason she isn't taking a chance in getting caught up in karma, is because she doesn't accumulate karma. She's on a different level. Or a different contract, we can say, with the Earth. She won't get trapped. Her contract was to come in and bring that energy in. To bring her energy in to the Earth. It is not a karmic contract.

D: *That's very tricky.*

S: And the people that she came with, are people that did come with contracts and have been caught up. And they're attracted to her because she's, on a subconscious level, helping them release that.

D: *So they didn't have any karma with her.*

S: No. She came to help them release their karma with others, without getting caught up in it. It's almost like a batting machine, when you practice batting. The ball comes at you and you hit it. She was that backdrop that the ball goes onto. But it wasn't an actual team out there catching the ball and running with it. She held a spot so they could release their karma with her.

D: *So these other people needed someone to help them work out their karma.*

S: Right, because they were on a downhill path. Because they

182

had gotten themselves into a negative spin. She did contract to help the Earth, but it was on a different level. It wasn't on an incarnation level. But now, she chose to do this, to pull in more energy for this time. It's a strategic time because of the free will, and because ... it's a balance. It's a balance time where the Earth can go either way and it's a major shift. It's a shifting place. A crossroads place.

D: *Is this why more of these, I don't want to call it "new" souls, because you do have a lot of knowledge and power, but is this why more of these are coming in at this time?* (Yes) *I keep meeting more. Some of them say they are just observers. They don't want to get caught here.*

S: It's not that they're observers, but if you can picture how I said: it's like the batter is hitting the ball and it's going against something. So you're hitting and putting it out there, but the backdrop doesn't react one way or the other. So it's not accumulating any karma. Everything bounces off. But that person is doing their thing, and they're releasing their stuff. And that's why they're not accumulating karma. They didn't come to accumulate. And they're not *just* observers. They're healers. They're bringing in positive energy to help other souls see. And they feel their vibrations and they want to acclimate to that.

D: *But the main thing is that they don't get sucked in.*

S: There's no danger of them getting sucked in. Because their energy level is what it is, it's almost like there's light going out all the time. Or energy going out and interacting with others in a healing manner. And there are no holes to suck. Or there's no karma to connect with. So that it's a very positive thing.

Some of my other cases who were this type of special being were protected from accumulating karma by having protective devices or shields placed around them. This is reported in other chapters. But Sally's subconscious said, "There is no need for protection, because it's built in, because of the purpose and because of the energy level. And because there isn't any prior karma. There's nothing to connect to it."

S: Her daughter has come in a similar way as her mother, only it's more perfected now. Her body has acclimated better. Because of the ones that came in first, and brought the energy in, it's not as hard for the new ones to come. The first attempts didn't work. It was too harsh; too stressful for the human form.

D: *I've been told that all the energy of a person's soul could not possibly fit into the human body. That it would destroy the body.*

S: That is correct. Her husband, Tony, has come in, in a very similar way. To blaze the trail.

D: *And he also doesn't accumulate karma either.* (Yes) *Was it by accident that the two of them got together?*

S: No. It wasn't by accident. They planned to come together in the same area before they incarnated. They are two similar types of energy. Not the same, but very similar. Sally was an experiment. The amount of energy that is in her body, would normally be as much as in two separate bodies. And part of the problem was the amount of energy, and also the vibration level. The previous time it failed. We didn't have the timing and the fine tuning of the body and the soul coming in and the exact amounts of energy at the right times. It's very technical.

D: *But it had to be as much energy that would normally be in two bodies?*

S: Yes. This was the experiment. It was very important and it has accomplished a lot. That was very beneficial. She isn't the only one that did this. Just like her husband. He was one of the ones that came. It's slightly different, but very close to the same. There are others. And she's also helped with them, when she is out of body. She had helped them adjust and get in to incarnate. She has helped several do this, but the part that she doesn't understand, is that since that time coming in, there has also been more energy come into her. You've heard of walk-ins where one soul leaves and the other comes. This isn't like that. This

184

wasn't actually two souls. It was just that the portion that came in would take the volume of two souls. Double the normal amount has come and joined with her recently. That is incarnated now with her.

D: *The two didn't exchange.*

S: No, there was no exchange. That was a joining, an adding. We told her twice that this new part of herself was coming. And now it is here and now it is joined.

D: *Did she know when this happened?*

S: Not consciously. But she knew it was going to and she prepared consciously, and that was of great assistance. And she knows she feels different now. But had not consciously acknowledged that there was more of her. And that it had joined. She will now receive very much knowledge. It's not going to all happen at once, but it will be triggered as she acclimates.

D: *Then when this life is over, will she go back and not have to keep returning?*

S: Right. She will stay until her job is finished. She won't have to incarnate again. She will stay until the shift is complete.

D: *This place where she came from, is that what I call the spirit side?*

S: Anything that is not a form, is spirit side. There are multiple, multiple places. This is not like you die and go there. It's before you incarnate, you're there. It's just a different realm.

D: *Some people consider those spirits are angels that have never incarnated.*

S: It's not an angel. It's a soul like everyone else. Just not incarnated in form. It didn't need to. Didn't feel the necessity until now. She was in form, just not in a body form. She was in spirit form. And there are different levels of ... we don't call them incarnation, because it's not lower formed like a body on any planet. It is an energy, and it has a body. It has an individuality, but it's just energy. But it's in a space. It's not the energy we call the One energy. The Lake energy. It's an separate individual energy. But it's not in a body or in a physical form like a human form. Or a body on any planet.

D: *That makes sense to me. But now I have more people coming to me that are here as healers and energy workers.*

S: That is due in a large amount to the times changing. It's the winding up of an age. So these types of beings like Sally and Tony are here to help with this transition. – I will tell you who you've been talking to. This is the part of Sally that just connected.

D: *The new energy.* (Yes.)

Another strange case in 2004, was a man in the medical profession whose main complaint was that he seemed to be holding what he called "fear and anxiety" within his solar plexus area. It felt like a big knot, and caused him a lot of discomfort. He was constantly insecure, and had fear of something that might happen. Although there was no reason in his well ordered life to explain what that "something" was. He wanted to know where this feeling came from, what it meant, and how to get relief from it.

He went into one of the most unusual past lives I have investigated. He was on another planet, and he was a *killing machine.* In his conscious state, he would have been horrified at the raw hatred in his voice as he exclaimed that he wanted to kill everything. This was his sole purpose: to kill everything he came in contact with. And he did it in a unique way. His home planet and another one had been warring for many generations. He was the product of genetic engineering. His body was designed to store a tremendous amount of energy. He was sent to the enemy planet on a spaceship. When he landed, he was to search out the enemy which had learned to hide from these machines. He did not use weapons of any sort. He *was* the weapon. He was a suicide machine. He could trigger the energy in his body, and it would explode with the power of ten hydrogen bombs. It would destroy everything for miles around.

His planet was advanced enough that they understood metaphysics. When he would explode and die, his soul would immediately be reincarnated into the same society. And the process would begin again. When he reached a certain stage of development and a certain age, he was sent out again. It was a vicious cycle and it seemed as though he was trapped within it. He never had any family or social life within the planetary structure. He was just engineered as a killing machine. This was his total mind-set: one of hate, killing and destruction. Eventually after many, many generations, the two planets realized that the only way to stop the killing was to raise their consciousness, and this began to happen.

At that time, he was finally able to break away, and was reincarnated on Earth. Even then the drive was so strong that he experienced many, many lifetimes where he killed and murdered. He had not lost the programming. He said in a way Earth was like his home planet, because there was much killing here. It was just not on so grand a scale. His present lifetime was finally an attempt to break the cycle. He was born into a family that pushed him down, broke his spirit and made him meek and mild. (So even those types of families have a function.) He said as a child he had a desire to become a mercenary when he grew up, which would have continued the same cycle. Instead he entered the medical profession and was now helping people.

The intense feeling that he felt in his solar plexus area was this holding back of the rage, hate and violence that had been so much a part of his personality for so many eons. He was afraid of what would happen if it were let loose, and so he had to keep it suppressed. He was doing a good job of it, and with the subconscious' help it looked like he would be able to win this battle. He said upon awakening, that this strange explanation was the missing piece that he would never have been able to figure out on his own. One of the reasons he was here on Earth at this time, was because Earth was also moving out of its violent cycle and was on the verge of raising its consciousness into a new era.

I wonder how many others have these suppressed feelings and emotions that make no sense to them, and cannot be explained by their upbringing? How many young people are having similar feelings exaggerated and awakened by the violence in our world and on the TV? This opens up a new way to look at these circumstances that the authorities seem to have no explanation for.

CHAPTER 10

LIFE IN NON-HUMAN BODIES

This session was done in Clearwater, Florida, when I was there for an Expo in October, 2002.

As humans, we become accustomed to thinking (once we have accepted the concept of reincarnation) that we have only experienced past lives as humans. This belief is very limiting, as I have discovered from my research. Life in any form has a lesson to teach us. That is what life on Earth is all about; going to Earth school and learning lessons. You cannot proceed to the next grade until you have successfully completed the one you are working on at the present time. Of course, the lesson gained from being human is much more complex than life as a rock or an ear of corn, but they are equally alive, just vibrating at a different frequency.

In my book *Legacy From the Stars*, I took a young man back to his first lifetime on Earth, thinking it would probably be as a caveman or something similar. Instead he went to the time when the Earth was still cooling down so it could support life. There were still volcanoes belching lava and hazardous fumes into the air. It was not yet a healthy environment for life to develop. The young man found himself as part of the atmosphere. His job, along with many others, was to help cleanse the air of ammonia and other toxic gases, so that as the Earth cooled down, it would become hospitable to life developing in its first rudimentary stages. Even though he did not have what we consider a "body", he was alive and aware of his assignment. He definitely had a personality and saw everything from his own unique perspective. He even took time off from his "job" to occasionally have fun by going in and out of the flowing lava to experience what that felt like.

189

I discovered and reported in my book *Between Death and Life* that we must experience life in all its forms before we finally enter the human stage. This has a purpose that is not recognized by our conscious minds. It is to show us that all life is one, and we are all connected on a deeper soul level. We are spirits first, and have many different adventures as we progress up the ladder of all knowledge, to return and become one again with the Creator. Thus I am not surprised any more when a subject reports a non-human life. The subconscious picks the one it thinks they need to see at this appropriate time in their life when they are looking for answers.

Some of the non-human lives that have been reported to me were: life as a stalk of corn where enjoyment came from basking in the sun and swaying in the gentle breezes. Life as a rock where time went by with incredible slowness. Life as a mammoth where the main feeling was the hugeness and heaviness of the body. Life as a giant bird feeling protectiveness for its egg, and feeling the camaraderie of others in its species. Life as a giant ape who felt peace and contentment with others in its group. He possessed only the simplest of emotions. Their leader was an older ape who they expected to take care of them. When he died, there was much confusion among the group, and they prodded the body to try and make him wake up.

All these lives were simple by comparison to humans, yet they had their distinct qualities that indicated they were living and sentient beings. Maybe if we could understand this, and realize we have all gone through these stages, we would take better care of our environment and our planet; realizing we are all connected on a deeper, vaster soul level.

This session with Rick was another example of a subject going to an unusual and unexpected life as a non-human. When Rick came off the cloud he was confused, because he couldn't understand what he was or where he was. Normally, the subject comes down from the cloud and finds themselves standing on something solid, and the impressions continue after that. The skeptics say that the subject will fantasize a scene in order to please the hypnotist. Yet Rick did not feel anything under his feet after he reached the surface, and that only added to his confusion. I told him to trust whatever impressions that came.

R: Well, it's like I'm looking up. And it's a purplish sky. (Confusion) And that's directly in front of my eyes as I look up. And what's on my peripheral vision is ... it's hard to describe. It's real fuzzy. I don't feel any pressure against my feet.

I instructed him that the sensations would become clearer.

D: *Look to your right and see what's on the peripheral.* (Long pause) *It will begin to become clear, instead of being fuzzy.* (Pause) *Trust anything that comes. The first impression.*
R: Okay, now there are more colors. It's brighter, like the sunrise. And maybe like water.
D: *Like the sun on the water?*
R: Yeah, or like ... have you ever seen the sun underwater?
D: *I haven't, but I guess it's possible.*
R: It's like ... yeah, I feel like I'm underwater.

This was a surprise. I wasn't sure if he was swimming or maybe we had come into the last of his life and he had drowned. There were several possibilities. But I never could have predicted the real one he was experiencing. This was a first.

R: That's the purplish-blue. Looking *up* through the water. And to my right is like the sunrise over the water, if viewed *under* the water. Hmmm. Just the colors moving and undulating, like as the waves of the water distort the light patterns. And it's golden color, like in the morning, as the rays come into the water. That's why there's no form. I'm in the water.
D: *That's why you don't feel any pressure either.* (Yes) *Do you see anything over in the other direction?*
R: No, not really. Just darker. Opposite, because the sun is rising in this other direction.

191

D: *The sun sounds beautiful filtering through the water.* (Yes)
   What does the water feel like on your body?
R: Hmm. Natural. There's no fear. It just feels very
   comfortable.
D: *Become aware of your body. What is your body like?*
R: It's smooth. (He found this humorous.) I don't know. It's
   like a dolphin. (Softly) How can that be? But, yeah, that's
   what I see. I see a dolphin. Like I'm outside looking at it,
   or I'm looking at another one. But I'm not on my back
   looking up. I'm on my stomach looking up. Like I'm
   sleeping, sort of. Just laying there in the water. Moving up
   and down. Out of the one eye I can see the sun, and out of
   the other I can see the dark. And I can see upward too,
   without having to turn over and move. The whole
   panorama from east to west.

How do dolphins or sea creatures see, and what is their
range of vision? Do we really know? Maybe they can see a
much wider range with their eyes located on either side of their
head. It certainly appeared to be that way.

D: *That's interesting. And you think there's another one there?*
R: I think. Or I saw. I'm moving in and out, looking around.
   Because I was *in* and then I moved out to see what the body
   looked like. So I think it's mine. It's smooth. Soft. (With
   conviction.) I'm a *dolphin.* It's very peaceful. It's
   surprising.
D: *Does it feel good to be in the water?*
R: Yes. It feels free. No restrictions. You have all that you
   need right there.
D: *Just complete freedom in the water.* (Yes) *What do you do with
   your time? Of course, right now you said you were sleeping.*
R: Sleeping. It's time to do *something* now that I'm awake. We
   just exist ... we just live! There's no plan. There's eating.
   Just have to eat. But right now it seems ... as we just float
   and then ... it's hard to relate. There's no job. No *must do*
   something. Other than just feel. And to feel – I don't know

– nice, really. This is somewhat strange to me right now.

D: *Why is it strange?*

R: Because I can't put it in the right context. I can't label it.

D: *Just do the best you can. What do you eat?*

R: Oh, other fish.

D: *Are you able to breathe in the water?*

R: Yes. But air. Amazing! (Pause) I'm seeing something. I'm seeing buildings that are ... on the shore.

D: *Are you on top of the water now?*

R: Kind of. Sort of. Sideways. I can see them with my head above the water. They're kind of like huts. Like jungley-kind of things, with the grass roofs. I just wonder who they are? What it is?

D: *Have you ever seen people?* (No) *Have you seen the shore like that before?* (No. No.) *Mostly been out at sea?* (Yes)

He obviously was becoming and identifying more with the dolphin. His answers were slow and simple.

D: *And now you can see the edge where the water stops?* (Yes)

I was structuring my questions toward a very simple being. I didn't think it would understand anything too complex. It had already demonstrated that it was a sentient or feeling being.

D: *What does that feel like?*

R: Curious.

D: *To know there is a boundary in the water or what?*

R: Yes. (He had difficulty finding the words.) It's... why ... what is it? It's different. I feel like I've got to go somewhere else.

There was a long pause. He was obviously having difficulty finding the proper words in the dolphin's brain.

R: (Long pause as he stumbled for words.) It's the ... it's just ... I don't know. I don't understand it. I don't understand what those ... what it's doing here. What ... why I'm here. And why I'm doing it. It's something new. And I don't understand it. And I don't know. I understand things where I was. I don't understand *this*. And I don't know what it is. It's just different.

It was obvious that as a sea creature he was used to seeing nothing but the water. Now he could see that the sea had boundaries, and the group of huts was something he was unfamiliar with, so there was no way to describe it.

D: *But you said you had the feeling you should go somewhere else?*
R: Yes, for a moment there I felt like I should be gone.
D: *What did you mean by, going somewhere else?*
R: Like away. Like moving fast.
D: *Away from where those huts were?*
R: No, away from that ... that where I am. Me. I'm .... (Pause) Out of that body?
D: *Tell me what's happening. What does it feel like?*
R: I'm confused. Because I can see that body. That ... porpoise. And then it's like I want to leave that. Or want to go somewhere else. I felt like I was moving fast for a moment. Then it stopped, because it startled me. But I'd like to go back there. I liked it in the dolphin, but I don't ... it was too ... (had difficulty) confusing ... too different? I couldn't relate to it.
D: *But if you want to go somewhere else, you can. You can go anywhere you want to go. We're looking for something that's appropriate and has meaning. So let's move to where that is. Tell me what's happening as you move. What do you see as you go to something else that is appropriate and important for you to know about?*

Rick then found himself in a lifetime in ancient times when he was a leader of a group of people. He had a great deal of responsibility and felt he betrayed them when he led them into a war that was impossible to win. It was more for the gratification of his own ego than to benefit the people. He was still carrying that guilt into his present lifetime, and that explained many of his physical problems. This included back problems, because he died by falling from a cliff and living for several days in pain from a broken back. The memories remained in his present body as a reminder against taking responsibility lightly in this life.

I then contacted his subconscious so we could ask his questions. The main one I was concerned with was the reason for showing him the lifetime as the dolphin or sea creature.

D: *Why did you show him that life?*
R: Because it is alien. Because it is somewhere from whence his true roots are. He has been altered in a way to experience "humanness" from the roots of that first incarnation.
D: *Was that his first incarnation on Earth?*
R: No. It was another place which does not have humans. Only those types of beings.
D: *The ones that live in the water?*
R: Yes. That is why he experienced the time of moving fast. For he was a curious one, and wondered what it would be like on that place, that shore. That vision that he had of the trees and the huts. That was why he didn't understand it. It was a vision of a place he had never seen.
D: *Then that was not a physical place in his water world?*
R: It was a physical place of which he was curious about. He was curious as to what it would be like to be out of the water. So he desired that experience.
D: *And this led to him reincarnating as a human being?*
R: Ultimately it did. These are his true roots. That's where it all began for him on this journey.
D: *In the water world.*
R: *From* the water world.
D: *And you said he had to be altered?*
R: Yes. His alteration took place in a series of processes. Vibrational shifts. Assisted by ones who are still assisting

the infinimentation of the planet. The experiment has been going on for many millennia. They chose and they asked. They sought out core and root stock, which could be used and modified for the human experience.

D: *But couldn't the soul, the spirit just come and enter a human body?*

R: It had to be modified. There are incompatibilities between the soul, the energy, the essences of that water creature. Before coming to this experience, those modifications were necessary in order for the creature to properly understand the feelings, or the instincts, that were programmed into the human.

D: *I see. So it would have been too difficult – or impossible – for him to come directly from the water creature into a human being.*

R: That is correct.

This is similar to Estelle coming from the reptilian race and having alterations to her human body in order to accommodate the different type of energy.

D: *But then he started a series of lives on Earth.* (Yes) *And that was why you were showing him the dolphin in the beginning.* (Yes) *He has wondered all his life why he has an interest in UFOs and ETs. Is this why?* (Yes) *Though I think he's picturing it as the movie variety.* (Chuckle) *So this is different, isn't it?*

R: Similar, but different. There are programs established throughout the universe. All sorts of types of material. Let's say, all sources were considered for this experience. This happens to be his primary source, which is of the water world creatures. There were others that were also from various other groups, all in this together.

D: *So, it's not necessarily like he is thinking, of spacecraft and those type. There can be many different types?*

R: Yes. But those were certainly involved in the transportation. The modification and the experimental.

D: *The adjusting of the body.*

R: Over the millennia.

196

D: *So they were able to help those who wanted to come into a human body to adjust.*

R: They were needed. The original intent was to experience. That original intent was granted and facilitated by the others. To the extent that he was deposited here.

D: *I see. Has he had any contact with them since he's been in the human body as Rick?*

R: Not physically. In his dreams. In his nonphysical state. As he meditates, as he sleeps.

D: *He's out of the body then?*

R: Yes. When he feels very cold or when he feels very hot. This is the transfer.

D: *When he leaves out of the body, you mean?*

R: Yes. Or when he enters. When he enters into his physical body, he becomes hot. When he exits, leaves into his light body, he becomes cool.

D: *And he doesn't remember this.*

R: He's becoming more aware of the abnormality of his normal dreams. He is now experimenting with what might be called "remote viewing". It comes at a certain time when he is in his quiet. It does not happen often, but he is aware. He should practice this more often. He would be able to see clearly events, both in the present and in the past, and potential future. This ability will be important not only to him, but to those who desire protection.

This was somewhat similar to another case I had a few months before working with Rick. A woman came to see me while I was in Memphis. She was so thin she was like a walking skeleton. She told me she had almost died three times. The doctors said there was something wrong with every organ in her body. They were surprised that she was still alive. Naturally, she was in much pain and discomfort, and was very unhappy with her life. She desperately wanted answers, but when they came it was something she would never have expected. She regressed to a carefree, wonderful life as a sea creature similar to a dolphin. She greatly enjoyed her life swimming in a totally free environment with no problems. Then it came time for her to leave that lifetime. No matter how happy a person may be in a certain lifetime, eventually the lessons are learned and nothing more can be gained by staying there. It is then time for the spirit to move on to more profound and complex lessons. The spirit must advance. So she was made to leave and begin her human incarnations. She hated being forced into the human body with its limitations. She longed for the freedom of the water, but it was not to be. So in her frustration she was trying to destroy her present body, so she could exit it. This, of course, was unknown to her on the conscious level, but it was the reason for the many physical problems. But she was not being allowed to exit in this way. She was just making herself miserable by not adjusting to her physical body. This took much therapy to get her to see the reason for the illnesses. A strange explanation, but it showed the attachment a person can have for a delightful, uncomplicated life of freedom.

When I saw her a year later she appeared to be gaining weight, and was not having as many problems with her health. She was finally making the adjustment with the decision to remain in this world until this lesson was learned. After all, if you exit too soon, for whatever reason, you must return to complete the lesson. You never get out of it that easily.

There was also the case reported in *The Convoluted Universe, Book One*, of the young man from Australia who spent eons as a free-floating spirit on a beautiful planet. He had no obligations or responsibilities, just a carefree life of pure enjoyment. He was presented many times with the opportunity to leave and progress in another form, but he was enjoying himself and didn't want to leave. So the fates (or powers that be, or whoever is in charge of these things) finally had to take a hand in making the decision for him. And he was sucked off that planet much like a vacuum cleaner would suck up a piece of tissue paper. That was how he described it. And he was deposited in a physical body, much to his dismay and dislike. When he first saw his beautiful planet at the beginning of the session, he became very emotional. He cried and called it his "home", because all the memories of being there in complete peace and harmony came flooding back. There was instant recognition and intense sorrow for being made to leave. So it is possible for us to carry a memory of a place of complete happiness that creates a deep sadness within us. Whether it be as a free-floating spirit in a beautiful world, or as an unrestricted sea creature in a water world.

CHAPTER 11

STRANGER TO EARTH

I keep finding these special souls, who are not originally from Earth, in the strangest ways. The fact that they are different and are here on a special mission is never evident upon our first meeting. They appear physically just like anyone else. The majority of the time they are not aware consciously that they are different, although they often feel out-of-place. Their unique qualities are only revealed by the subconscious, and then only if it thinks the person is ready to know such information. It is as protective as I am, and is well aware that some information can cause more harm than good. But it appears that when the person is ready to know these things they somehow find their way to me; and the secrets are revealed.

Aaron was a man who works for NASA as a engineer involved with space projects. I do not want to reveal the location where he works, for reasons that will become obvious. He drove many hours to have this session. He brought his girlfriend with him and she wanted to sit in on the session. She became quite insistent when I told her that no one was allowed to sit in on any of my therapy sessions. She said that Aaron always told her everything anyway. I insisted that I was not going to change my procedure, and she reluctantly went back to her motel room. After she left, Aaron said he was glad that I would not let her stay. He did not want her there, but she can be very persuasive. With her gone, he was able to relax and we could have our interview. This session was held in a motel in Eureka Springs, Arkansas, in February, 2002 during the time I allowed a week to have sessions with the local people: Arkansas, Missouri, Oklahoma, and Kansas. Yet when Aaron saw it on my website he traveled a long distance, because he was so anxious to have a regression.

After we began the session, Aaron came off the cloud. The first thing he saw was a small village of huts with straw roofs nestled among rolling green hills. He saw that he was a young man in his twenties, dark-haired, bearded, dressed in loose baggy clothing. This sounded like the beginning of a normal past-life regression, where the subject relives a simple country life as a farmer etc., but it quickly became obvious that there was a difference. He was on a hill looking down at the village and nervous because he was hiding. "I'm feeling anxious about something. Like something's going to happen in the village. I think there's some group, or some military people coming to look for me." These were not people from the village. They seemed to be the local government or the military. He felt apprehensive, "They're looking for me for some reason. And that's why I'm up here. I don't want to be down in the village. Afraid they'll catch me or whatever." He was not originally from the village, but was staying with a family there.

D: *Why do you think they're looking for you?*
A: (Slowly) Because I'm somehow different. I'm using some things like telepathy, or some psychic things that I've grown up with. I'm able to move objects just with my mind, and cause things to pass through other things that are solid. And I can manipulate things this way. Just a few know about this. And this is causing a problem. It is attracting attention. They think I'm some other kind of being, or some sort of devil. I try not to cause attention.
D: *I can see why that would scare some people. How did the military get word of it?*
A: I think somebody was coming through to visit the village, and some villagers just told them about me. They didn't think it was something they should keep secret. They are used to me doing these things. I'm afraid they're going to kill me or something.

He felt he would have to go away for his own safety, even though he didn't know where. "I have already left a couple of other places."

D: Why did you have to leave the other places?
A: The same reasons. The same thing would happen. I'm feeling I'll never have a place to stay. Feeling alone, frightened. (Big sigh)
D: *How did you learn how to do this?*
A: I think I came from another star system or another place. Somehow I just knew this. I just had these abilities. I grew up with this.

This was definitely not going to be a normal past life regression. I wondered if he had come directly from another star system full-grown, or if he had entered the body as a baby and was raised on Earth. This was similar to people I have worked with who entered the body as a spirit in their present life, and later discovered they were "Star Children".

A: I was born here, but I know I'm not from here.
D: *Do you remember the other place that you came from?*
A: You mean the other places I lived?
D: *Well, you were talking about coming from another star system.*
A: I think I go back there for visits, at nights or other times. And that's how I know who I am.
D: *Did you ever try to keep your abilities secret so people wouldn't find out?*
A: Yes, I tried. And then something unusual would happen. And then another thing would happen. And they would somehow sense that I was the one responsible.
D: *What do you do for a living when you're in these villages?*
A: I know how to make things out of glass. Like glass-blowing, and I can use some of my capabilities to manipulate the glass in ways that you wouldn't be able to normally do.

His unusual abilities would also warn him if there was any danger. This was why he went into the hills above the village to hide. He had a premonition that harm was coming. When the soldiers could not find him, he saw them leave. Now he was deciding what to do, because he knew he was no longer safe in the village. "I must find another place to live. Maybe find some people who are – if they're not like me – at least more open, and who would be a little more protective."

Since he had temporarily eluded his pursuers, I moved him forward to an important day, and asked what he could see.

A: I'm in a square, and I've been given an award for doing some meritorious kind of service in this community. I found some places where they could get water, and also some other kinds of minerals. I'm seeing a cave. And some minerals that are used for different kinds of things that they can make with them. And I am happy. I am older now. More in command of everything really.

D: *Your abilities?*

A: Abilities and also able to deal with people more effectively. And not so frightened.

He had discovered these things for the community with his psychic abilities. He had apparently learned to control and use them without creating unwanted attention. Apparently these people were more understanding, and he didn't have to keep moving.

D: *Do you think much of it was just learning how to control the abilities?*

A: Yes, just be more focused. It has to be more focused with the energy. I'm in a different area now. And it feels like it's a higher level civilization. Not quite so primitive. I have a community to stay with now that I can feel part of.

D: *You said you felt you went back to the place you came from at night (the other star system). Do you still feel you do that?*

A: No, I think I do that in a more direct way. I set aside a time

203

to retreat, and then I mentally go back there.

D: *I thought maybe you didn't need to go back anymore.*

A: Now it's more like exchanging information. It's explaining what my life's experience is like here to those back there. This is like a training mission. A training ground. This is teaching me to learn how to do these things and interact with the human beings here.

D: *You mean Earth is like a training mission?*

A: No. It's like this lifetime is getting ready for a future time when much of this is going to be needed. It will be a little bit more second nature and understanding better how people react to these different things.

I moved him ahead again to another important day, and Aaron kept surprising me.

A: I'm meeting these beings from this planet where I come from.

D: *In the physical?*

A: I think it's in the physical.

D: *You're able to go back there?*

A: No, I think they actually came here to where I was. In a vehicle of sorts. At least that's the image I'm seeing. This is just a visit. It's like a reward for good work, instead of just going back mentally. So now it's a physical presence, and it's like meeting old friends. You know, just hugging them.

D: *Then the body didn't die. Is that what you mean?*

This is the type of thing that would normally happen after death, to return "home".

A: Not yet in this lifetime, no. I am pretty old though. It is a good feeling. I am going back with them.

D: *Have they told you what you are going to do now?*

A: I'm basically going to shed this human body, and return with them. Our civilization doesn't exist in this physical density. It's different. It's a little higher vibrating frequency. But when we come to Earth we take on a physical form as every other being here on Earth does. And so it's like that, except that we're more knowledgeable about it. And we're just working with that process a little bit more directly, is all.

D: *So when you go back there, your physical body can't exist there. Is that what you mean?*

A: Yes, basically. It just dissolves, or it would dissolve, so yes.

D: *Because you don't need it anymore.* (No) *How do you feel about going back?*

A: Really good. It's home. (Big breath) And being on Earth was just tough, and not easy to do. It's like a really tough assignment. And when you finish it, you feel good about it, and relieved. I know I probably will return to Earth at some future time, but it's now time for a rest. To get caught up with things that have been going on.

D: *Was that your first time to go to Earth in a Earth body?*

A: I don't know. I think that was the first time from *this* home. From this place. I think it was the first. I don't know though.

D: *Is this place a physical place? A physical planet?*

I am always trying to determine whether we are talking about the spirit plane where you go between physical lives, or another actual physical place.

A: Yes, it has physical aspects to me, just like Earth would to you and others.

D: *Except you wouldn't need this body.*

A: We have a form. It's just that it vibrates at a different rate. It's like being on Earth, but on the other hand the energy interchange with the environment is different. You're more a part of it. You feel part of everything, and you can sense things so much more directly.

D: *What does your form look like?*

A: We're fairly tall and kind of thin. Long – as you would say

— appendages or arms. We're rather skinny-looking from Earth point of view, perspective. And I guess you would say we're a little bit ... grasshopper-looking really.

D: *Spindly?*

A: We're spindly like, yes. And our planet has a lot of red color to it, so we tend to be red as well.

D: *So when you decide, you can just go to some other place? Or are you sent?*

A: We can visit, like on missions, to go to certain places. But that always involves a down-shifting in energy. And there's certain protocols that we have to follow that are established by governing — not governing, but beings that are watching over different areas. So it's not where you can just take off and go wherever you want to go.

D: *There are certain rules and regulations.* (Yes) *They must tell you where to go?*

A: Well, if we have an interest in a particular area, or we have a mission to perform, we can institute or we can ask, or we can plan a visit. And then if it's compatible with other constraints we can follow through. Right now we have this project on this planet Earth that we're working with. It's a longer term project that we were actually asked to help participate in.

D: *You said a while ago about making these abilities become more widespread. Is that part of the project, or is there something else with it?*

A: That's part of it; to allow beings in the human form to start using some of these abilities in a way that will help human beings' transition to a higher functioning state. To get through this crisis period where there still would be a tendency to want to stop this from happening. To stop these individuals, or somehow restrict the movement of these individuals, or look upon them as a threat.

D: *Couldn't the people on Earth develop this on their own without your help?*

A: We're considered advisors or guides.

D: *I was thinking of teachers, but then you'd be showing them.*

A: Yes. More like a star football player, or something like that. Where people see them and admire them, and understand what they can do. It's more of an example thing.

D: *It sounds like it's an ongoing very long project, if you come to Earth at different time periods.*

A: Yes, everything has its time and place, and we were just working on one facet of things.

D: *Apparently your group has patience, to stay with the project.*

A: Earth isn't their only project. There are others that focus on different types of things. We're working with other civilizations as well. And so this service is part of our evolutionary process, or how we advance through this work.

D: *You said a while ago it was a crisis period on Earth. What do you mean by that?*

A: There are energies that want to hold in check any significant developments in this area. They're fearful of losing their control. And so this makes it difficult. It's very much like the experience I had on Earth earlier. It's a matter of learning how to do this without attracting too much attention, or too much visibility. Such that eventually you will get to the point where it will just have happened, and there's nothing to be done about it.

D: *If it was a crisis period, then it could go either direction.*

A: I think that's why we others were sent to help, yes. There was a concern that ... it's not that it would have stopped it completely. It's just that it's a timing and phasing question. It would have eventually happened, but it might have happened after the civilization was destroyed and gone, and restarted again.

D: *That would be more difficult, wouldn't it?*

A: Yes. You lose some momentum, and it has other impacts elsewhere. Whatever happens here affects other things elsewhere. So it's in everyone's interest to see to the successful path.

D: *It sounds like you're a more advanced species than those on Earth.*

207

A: We've made many gains, but we have our own challenges and our own directions of pursuit.

D: *So you're not at the perfect state yet.* (No) *But you seem to be more advanced than those on Earth, if you're able to come back and help them.*

A: Yes, we are, yes.

D: *When you come back to help them, do you always do it by being born into a body as a baby?*

A: Ordinarily. Although sometimes we can merge our frequency with someone else who's willing, who's already here in human form. Sometimes there's a linkage that can be agreed to. And so we work through them, or can work with them, advising them or directing them. It's a way of accomplishing some of it without having to go through the birthing process.

D: *On your planet, does the body die?*

A: It goes through a transition also. And it takes – I want to say – thousands of your years for this to occur. But it occurs with more of the shedding concept, in the sense that we know there is a higher part to ourselves as well. We're more aware of that. And it's almost like a planned event where you know it will happen.

D: *So you're not infallible or immortal. The body does eventually have to die.*

A: Not really. We don't view it that way. We view it as more of a regeneration period where we go to the higher self, to the higher energies and get regenerated, rejuvenated. And then we come back and take on a form again.

D: *Whatever form you want.* (Yes) *That's quite interesting. So you have had lifetimes in many different places then.*

A: Yes. It's something I enjoy. I enjoy going through different experiences in different civilizations.

D: *Although it sounds like when you come to Earth it's more limiting.*

A: Yes, it's not so much fun here. In the broader perspective it's enjoyable, but when you're here, yes, some of it is not so good.

D: *But at least it's not boring. You get to try different things.*

I felt we had learned all we could from this unusual entity, so I asked it to leave and brought back Aaron's full personality in order to contact his subconscious. Aaron gave a deep breath as this transfer occurred. I asked the subconscious why it picked that certain lifetime for Aaron to see.

A: This is part of the reason he's here at this time. It's about this skill and aspects of himself that he hasn't allowed to manifest, to exist here in this lifetime. This hasn't surfaced very well yet. He's been holding back, afraid, like he was afraid in the early part of that first lifetime. So he needs to let go of that fear, and get to the point where he was experiencing the feeling when he was receiving the award in that lifetime. That feeling instead of the other one. He's noticed certain things that have happened, and he's been afraid that these would draw attention to him as an outsider. To cause a threatening situation to develop where he'd be viewed as an alien or something different.

D: *But it probably wouldn't happen now, would it?*

A: No. This is a fear that he can let go of now. This connection is something he hasn't allowed to surface very well.

D: *It sounds as though he's not essentially an Earth person. Is that right?*

A: This was under camouflage, yes.

D: *That he is really from other places.* (Yes) *And he just comes to Earth occasionally?*

A: Yes. He's done both. As *birthing* and as a *merging.* Both kinds. He's done always one or the other. But yes, he's not like others, though he has a tie to another home.

D: *The way I understand it, whenever people have many Earth lives they create karma which requires that they keep coming back here time after time. They are more or less tied here for a while until it is repaid.*

A: He works with the karmic patterns that are in place, such

209

that those are allowed in terms of a human being; a human experience to unfold or unravel. But his destiny is not bound by those. He contributes to the collective human unconsciousness. And in that sense, there are karmic patterns that are created and dissolved, but he's not bound by those. Do you understand?

D: *It's difficult to be on Earth and not create karma.*
A: It's almost impossible.
D: *But it's a different type of thing, because he is not bound to keep returning again and again?*
A: That's right. It's like a sleeve put over him. Because of this service, this responsibility, he's protected from the karmic debt that otherwise would be incurred.
D: *So he won't become trapped here.* (Yes)

Aaron had asked to find out why his marriage had ended in divorce. I would have thought that event would have incurred karma, but the subconscious disagreed. Part of it was the learning and assistance opportunity. "An envelope of emotional instability" that also allowed him to experience human emotions he would not have come up against any other way. It was also a ruse or bit of camouflage to make him appear normal to the outside world.

A: These are lessons for him to experience. He cannot create karma because he is protected from these Earthly things by the shield of the sleeve that has been placed around him.

I decided to go to the questions Aaron wanted to ask that had been bothering him most of his life.

D: *He said in very early childhood, he remembers having some kind of experiences with other beings. It sounded like they were the grasshopper type. He wasn't sure if he was dreaming this, or if he was really experiencing it. Can you tell him about that?*
A: Yes, these were real experiences. These were the beings we just referred to who were from his home planet. They

visited early in his lifetime, to specifically prepare him for the injury that he had as a child. And other things that would happen that would make it a little easier to wend his way through this lifetime.

D: *And he wasn't supposed to remember much more than that. Just that they were like dream people, playmates?*

A: Right. He did get instruction and guidance. They have been there all along to help and guide him, but he's not aware of them.

D: *Since you brought up the injury, why did he have to experience that? What was the purpose of it?*

Aaron had experienced a traumatic accidental injury as a child. I do not want to tell specifically which part of his body, because I am trying to protect his identity for obvious reasons. But it left him with a slight disfigurement and impairment. I could not understand how they considered such an injury would make it easier for him to go through this lifetime.

A: It was a handicap that we felt would be the best for him as, you might say, a camouflage aspect to allow him to function in certain areas without attracting too much attention. It instituted and allowed to enter an instability in his emotional self, which plays on him at times. And therefore, allows him not to stand out so directly.

D: *Do you mean having some kind of a handicap makes him appear more normal, more human?*

A: Yes, basically more human. This was a playing out of karma needed by others around him. So it was to fit in again. It was a sacrifice that he was willing to make. We tried to make it fit the circumstances. It is important that he not feel alone. I am telling him to keep his focus on the stars. Don't lose perspective of where he's come from, and where he's trying to go in this lifetime. There are many different influences that will try to dislodge him from that. But if he keeps that focus, he'll be successful and happiest.

A session with another man also involved interaction with space beings in a past life. We tend to think that UFO involvement is new and unique to our modern times, but I have had sessions where people in other lifetimes experienced the same sightings, interactions and emotions as their modern counterparts. A man went back to a lifetime that at first appeared to be mundane and boring, just as ninety percent of past-life remembrances are. He was a simple shepherd living in a small hut in a valley between tall mountains. His only companions were the sheep that he cared for. He had no family and saw no one unless he had to go to the neighboring town. He was very unhappy and longed for companionship.

There was also an element of fear in his lonely existence, because he would occasionally see huge lights come over the mountains and hover over the pasture where his hut and the sheep were. At these times, he would hide inside his house until the lights would disappear. At least those were his conscious memories. In reality, on several occasions one of the lights, which turned out to be spacecraft, landed not far from his hut. He would awaken and go out into the field and converse with its occupants. At those times he begged them to take him with them. He wanted to go "home". They told him the time was not yet appropriate. He had volunteered to be part of this experiment, and he had to stay until it was over. He was told there were many who had volunteered to come and live a life as a human under various circumstances, to see how they could adjust to life on Earth. Some of the others were living other types of lives, but his was to be a life of solitude and loneliness to see how he would handle it. When the ship flew away, he would stand in the field and cry, begging them to come back and take him because he found this existence intolerable. Then he would go back inside the hut, fall asleep again and awaken in the morning with no memory of what had occurred during the night.

This was very similar to modern UFO cases I have investigated. The person's conscious memories of what occurred and the actual experience are often very different. What the conscious mind remembers with fear is often a very harmless and benign experience. Humans are most often frightened about what they don't understand. When the truth becomes known, it is easier to handle because it is never as bad as what they thought happened.

The shepherd was not released from his lonely life in the valley until he was finally dying as an old man. At that time the ship returned one last time. He was able to walk outside and happily greeted the occupants and entered the ship for the journey home. As in many of these past-life contracts and agreements to live on Earth and learn how it is to be human, the lifetime was not exciting or dramatic. Maybe there is more to be learned by the alien soul from a lifetime of monotony and simplicity, rather than violence or drama. It was obvious that this type of life could not create karma, because there was no interaction with other people.

As Aaron said, it is difficult to escape karma while living on Earth. When the soul creates karma then it is trapped and condemned to return to repay the karma. Aaron said in his case, a protective sleeve was placed around him to shield him from the influence of karma, to keep it from affecting him. Without such a protective device it would be impossible to live among humans and then return "home" without the contamination and entrapment of karma.

Bobbi's tape also mentioned a protective device. She described it as a protective film to keep her from being stuck in the flypaper of karma, as she described it. This is expanded upon in Chapter 28, "A Different Alternative to Walk-Ins." The session with Bobbi was done at the same location in Eureka Springs directly after Aaron's regression. Almost as though "they" wanted me to have two examples of individual souls being able to shut out karma, and avoid entrapment.

CHAPTER 12

WORK DURING THE SLEEP STATE

This session was conducted in Clearwater, Florida in October, 2002 while I was there speaking for an Expo. Patricia was a nurse and a hospice worker who helped counsel the dying and their families. Little did I know when I started this session that she was also continuing her work during the sleep state, and helping souls make the transition to the other side. No wonder her occupation gave her such satisfaction. She was working with the dying during the awake state and also the sleep state.

When you have been doing regressions as long as I have, you learn to recognize when the client is describing something different than a normal Earth setting. When they come off the cloud into a past life the setting may be a city, field, desert, woods, garden, etc., but the description sounds normal and they proceed through a past life that can be used for therapy. This is where listening is very important, because if the setting is another planet, another dimension or the spirit realm, the clues will be given in their description. I always go along with it and do not try to correct them or change it. Their subconscious has picked this setting for them to experience something they need to know that will help them in this life. If it also helps me in my research, then I welcome it, but I never know where we will be led.

At first the description given by Patricia sounded normal and earthly, but as she proceeded, it became obvious it was not. As she drifted off the cloud she saw land beneath her with green hills and blue water. It sounded normal enough, and as her feet touched the ground she said, "It feels very comfortable. It's very bright. Very, very bright, but it's comfortable. Everything looks like a garden. It *feels* like a garden, but it's not like someone has to take care of it. It just *is* that way. There's a path, and it's branching in different directions. I'm like in a park. And there is green grass and little places to sit. And beautiful trees. And the water's in front of me. There's the sand, and it's a golden color. And when I walk, it feels like I'm a part of everything. I'm walking on it, and I'm not separate from it, but I'm still *me*. And I can walk in the water without getting wet, if I want to."

No, this was already sounding like something other than a normal garden.

P: There are some flowers growing all around. It's just a beautiful place. And I walk, but it's different. It feels like I'm just wanting to move, and I do. I just think it and I can do it. It's effortless.

D: *Is there anyone there?*

She unexpectedly and illogically became emotional, "Oh, that's where my family is!"

D: *What do you mean by your family?*
P: It feels like where I'm from. (Sadly) And I didn't want to leave.
D: *It sounds very beautiful.*
P: It is. (She was ready to cry. She reassured herself:) It's okay. Just being here is good.

This has happened many times in my work, and has been reported in *Keepers of the Garden* and Book One of *Convoluted Universe*. The person will see a place that seems foreign to anything they know on Earth, and there is no logical reason for emotion. Yet just seeing it brings emotion rushing to the surface, and a tremendous feeling of melancholy and homesickness. Even though they have no conscious memory of this place, they have the overpowering feeling of coming "home" after a long journey to a place so special, yet so buried in the

215

mind. Seeing it again reawakens all the lost and forgotten feelings.

D: *That sounds like a beautiful place. But you said there are many paths going off in many different directions?*

P: Yes, in many different directions. I can go anywhere, and it's different. (Chuckle) It's very different.

D: *Why is it different?*

P: (Big sigh, then a whisper:) Why is it different? It's hard to find the words. We are just all there together all the time. Everything is the way it should be. It's hard to explain that. I can take a path or think of a direction, and I can be with these people, and we can do many things together. We can create things together. We can be together, and just enjoy being together, or we have projects that we do to help other people, because this is a special place. I see the air is different. It has colors to it, and it can be different colors in different places. And I come from a place where the air looks golden. You can take a path and go to different – we would call them "neighborhoods". It's sort of like that. And I can move to certain neighborhoods of different colors and be very comfortable. And other ones I go to on special projects.

D: *They're not your favorite places to go? (I could tell this by the tone of her voice.)*

P: No, no. But I go there because of *my* colors.

D: *What do you mean?*

P: Because I'm comfortable in the golden color. And that's a very helpful, very loving color. And that's where I come from.

D: *The sky is that color there?*

P: I look through the golden color, and the sky can be any color I want it to be.

D: *But you said you're told to go to some of the other places on projects?*

P: I go on projects. I go on assignments when I choose. I'm not forced. It's suggested. I could say "no", but I don't.

216

D: *Are some of these places different colors?*

P: They have a very different feel to them. Different places, different energies, and the color is different. I don't like the darker places. Darker colors, darker energy, heavier energy. And I don't go too often to those dark places. Some of those paths are only taken by others, because their energy can work with it better. Can deal with it better. But I can, if I were to choose to do that.

D: *There are paths that go to those places, too.*

P: Yes. We all go to places that we are suited to go to, to work. That's why I came. I want to work with the energy that is lighter. (Pause) I can't find the words. Ones who can deal with harsher energies go to the other paths. The darker paths. I don't like to do that. But I like being home.

D: *Do you go back there from time to time?*

P: (Sigh) Yes, when I sleep.

D: *Whenever Patricia's body is sleeping, you can return to this place?*

P: Yes. Patricia, the body, what I am that I have, that is with me. I'm connected to that body.

D: *How are you connected?*

P: Through the energy. The energy comes to the body, and that body can hold a lot of energy, for I am with that body.

D: *But you mean, at night, when the body is sleeping, you like to return to this place?*

P: Sometimes I return there. Sometimes I go to other places. I mostly stay around the Earth, doing work. I do a *lot* of work.

D: *What kind of work do you do while the body is asleep?*

P: I am helping people who are going home. Helping people who are lost, to get home. I'm working in between worlds to help them get home. That is my job. I can hold the energies of the two places. The gold light is very strong on the Earth, so I am here to help people hold that energy. And to help people go through that energy to home. So I am always working.

D: *Can't these people find home by themselves?*

P: Some of them can't. Some are afraid. Some are confused.

Some don't even know that there *is* home. I am one who guides people, who shows people where home is. Some know there's a home, but are afraid; they're timid. They don't know where to look. I can go there very easily. And even if I don't go into that place, I guide them to the entranceway where others are waiting. That's what I do.

D: *You mean, they're looking for home when they leave the physical body?* (Yes) *Not just at night, but when they leave it permanently?*

P: Right. There are some who are going to leave soon, and they're ... we could say "practicing", but it's not practice. It's rather like learning, because (Sigh) when so many leave there is a ... well, you can't say "traffic jam", because it's not like this Earth. But many are leaving, and it's easier if they know the way.

D: *Otherwise, there's confusion with so many spirits leaving at once?*

P: Yes. So we are helping people to learn how to do that.

D: *I always thought when they left the body and actually returned home, that it was an automatic thing. They would know which direction to go.*

P: There are those who help. But when people leave in a great energy of confusion or fear, that emotional body does not dissolve right away. And sometimes they do not see. There are different ways to help them even before they go. We can call it "practice" or teaching or guidance. That's what it is.

In my book *Between Death and Life* I was told there are "greeters" who meet the person when they die, depart the body and begin the journey toward the light. I always assumed these were spirit souls, deceased relatives or friends, or the person's guardian angel or guide. Now it seemed that this job is also performed by those still living in a body. It is done during the nightly excursion that we all take while we are sleeping. At least Patricia said her job was to guide the dead to the entranceway where others would take over from there to lead them the rest of the way. She would be unable to go all the way as long as she was still connected to her physical body by the silver cord.

D: *You know these are people that are going to be leaving soon?* (Yes) *How do you know it's their time?*

P: Because it's their plan. *They* don't always know. But the higher spirit of themself knows, has agreed, and knows that it's time. So there are those who are working with them, with their bodies. Not their *physical* body, but with the part of their spirit that is connected to their body, because we have many levels of being. We have part of us that is on the spirit path, on the spirit world. And parts in-between. And parts on the physical world. And some people are not connected to their spirit part, or they don't *know* that connection, is a better way of saying it. So we help those people to practice. Then when it's time, they know how to move. They know how to feel, and they'll know to perceive the spirit part.

D: *But they don't have to go all the way. They're just shown the path.*

P: Oh, yes. Just shown the path so they can connect easier. There are many gatherings of these people.

D: *What do you mean by gatherings?*

P: Many places of light near the Earth that these people are taken to. We are preparing.

D: *But how do you know it is their time? Are you told in some way?*

P: Yes, because I am different from most. I came from home to volunteer to be here, to do this.

D: *But didn't we all come from home?*

P: Yes, we did, but different paths of the home. Not all came from that path where the golden energy is.

D: *Does this have to do with the person's development?*

P: It has to do with how much of your spirit you have embraced, because we all have the same spirit. No one is more spirit than others. It is how much you have embraced.

D: *I just thought it was automatic, but whenever it happens, they don't always know the way to go.*

219

P: That's right. When it happens in circumstances of confusion, or when it happens to a person who is in fear, or who doesn't want to go. We could say "rehearsal". It's not exactly rehearsal, but it's sort of being shown ahead of time, so it's easier.

D: *What if the conscious part of the person decides it doesn't want to go at that time? Can it change its mind?*

P: Not always, no. There are times it can prolong. Perhaps other times, no. It depends on what the contract is. In some contracts there is a specific event or circumstance that involves many people. And one cannot change that contract. There are others where there are possibilities of time or circumstance. It depends on the contract.

D: *Because you know, human beings are always very reluctant to go.* (Yes) *Even though the spirit knows the plan, the human body wants to hang on as long as it can.*

P: Yes. And there are times when that is not an option. Accidents, catastrophes, or even a personal event such as a stroke or heart attack. Many times that cannot be changed. It's in their contract.

The contract is the agreement you make while on the spirit side before entering the physical body again. There is more about this in *Between Death and Life*.

D: *But you said there were some groups of many people going at once.*

P: It feels that way. (Sigh) I felt it last year too (2001), before September 11. There were many beings, and I didn't understand. The part of me that is on the Earth felt it. About many, many people coming to help. More than usual were here. I felt all the spirit helpers. They were here. And I felt them helping people. And I feel it coming too. I feel there's more that will come.

D: *You mean because of the confusion at that time, they wanted to show them the right way to go?* (Yes) *Or there would have been just mass confusion with so many leaving?*

P: Yes. There was too much ... an energy of horror. But there were many spirit beings who were here, who helped.

D: *Did you help at that time?*

P: (Softly) Yes, I did.

D: *Did some of those people not have rehearsals ahead of time? It was so unexpected.*

P: *All* had rehearsals.

D: *Everyone knew on another level that it was their time to go?*

P: Yes. All had rehearsals. That is why those who had to be there were there. Those who were not to be there were not there.

D: *There were stories of people escaping by miraculous means.*

P: Yes. There were also rehearsals for that. And there were rehearsals for those who were not. Right now there are many possibilities, and I don't want to see them.

I received an email in 2004 from an unknown source that I believe is appropriate to insert here:

After September 11th, one company invited the remaining members of other companies who had been decimated by the attack on the Twin Towers to share their available office space. At a morning meeting, the head of security told stories of why people were alive. And all the stories were just LITTLE THINGS:

The head of the company got in late that day because his son started kindergarten.

Another fellow was alive because it was his turn to bring donuts.

One woman was late because her alarm clock didn't go off in time.

One was late because of being stuck on the New Jersey Turnpike because of an auto accident.

One of them missed his bus.

One spilled food on her clothes, and had to take time to change.

One's car wouldn't start.

221

One went back to answer the telephone.

One had a child that dawdled and didn't get ready as soon as he should have.

One couldn't get a taxi.

One of the most unusual was the man who put on a new pair of shoes that morning, took the various means to get to work but before he got there, he developed a blister on his foot. He stopped at a drugstore to buy a Band-Aid. That is why he is alive today.

Now when I am stuck in traffic, miss an elevator, turn back to answer a ringing telephone ... all the little things that annoy me. I think to myself, this is exactly where God wants me to be at this very moment.

Next time your morning seems to be going wrong, the children are slow getting dressed, you can't seem to find the car keys, you hit every traffic light, don't get mad or frustrated;

God is at work watching over you.

May God continue to bless you with all those annoying little things and may you remember their possible purpose.

(To me these sound like rehearsals for survival.)

D: *But you said you had the feeling there were going to be many people leaving during this next year?* (Yes) *Is it just many possibilities, probabilities, or is it anything definite.*

P: This is a different time. The event that happened that I speak of ....The one last year (2001), was in what we call the "etheric", and then it came into the physical. There are many events in the etheric now. Some are big, some are small. There are many different possibilities, but even those of us right now working with potential, don't know which will be. Because this is a time ... I'm seeing a circle. It's like everything is contained in the circle of light. It represents the whole, the divine, the spirit. It represents all that is. In that are many potentials. And we don't have to

222

know right now. It feels that we are making changes. All may not manifest. And I am seeing past that. And I feel much more comfortable, because I didn't feel comfortable thinking about it.

D: *But if you are working with people to prepare them during this next year, there are so many probabilities and possibilities, what happens if the circumstances change?*

P: This is why it's so beautiful. We work with people, help them little by little to see more and more of the light, of who they are. So when the time comes they will not be afraid. And *whatever* comes doesn't matter, because the time will come for them to know their true light. To move into a greater expansion. And it doesn't matter how that time comes, and I know that. The part of me that is working with the people, knows that. We have many different ways of moving into that greater light. And we are going there. We are all going there soon.

D: *How soon? As in eventually?*

P: Soon as in ... for the physical body in this lifetime.

D: *These lifetimes can be many different lengths though.* (Yes)

It sounded like she could be referring to the ascension into the next dimension when the frequency and vibration of our bodies change, and we become pure light. This has been talked about in many of my sessions, and is discussed more fully in this chapter and throughout the book.

D: *But a little earlier you said there might be catastrophes where many people will leave.*

P: It is possible. Doorways will be opening. Though it's hard to say it, doorways will be opening in different ways, depending upon how we need to have them opened. And there are many choices to be made in that.

D: *But in catastrophes more people exit at once.*

P: Yes. But there will be openings and doorways in times to come where many will be able to move through in the light. Like a walk on the path in my home.

D: *What happens to those people who are confused, and don't want to go? The ones who don't understand what's happening?*
P: Their body is gone. But they sometimes don't know it, because their energy body is attached to the physical body. And they think they are still in it. They are just confused, not knowing what to do with it. But many are with them to help, and they can help them. The way we help these people is, we send out energy to embrace them. And when our energy embraces them, they feel a comfort. And because they have felt this comfort before, they are able to pay attention to it. They have much chaos in their energy. But they begin to feel the soothing comfort, because they have felt it before. And then they are able to pay more attention. And they are able to understand. Then their own spirit part of them is able to make contact. So we are working to help these people. It's a very chaotic energy that happens in a catastrophe. It's like all the vibrations start moving in a way that is not comfortable. So you have to bring in comforting and soothing energy. So that people can begin to feel it and lessen the chaos of their energy. And those don't have as hard a time who, in their own hearts, are peaceful and connected to their inner spirits. And there are many more of those. Many, many more are coming. That is what we do. That is why we are working with people. The doorway is their own spirit. They move through their spirit to the higher vibrations. And when they do this, they are able to go home in a peaceful way.
D: *What about the person's belief systems? Doesn't this hinder it in some ways?*
P: Sometimes it does. That's why there's fear. Those who have guilt, those who are afraid of what they call "God". They're ashamed, and they're so afraid in that. They have been taught to be afraid of death, of hell. That keeps them from embracing the light, which is just love. It's love that's reigning, and love is at home.
D: *They think it's something bad.*
P: They do. And all we are is love. But that human part of us

224

is very malleable, very easy to be manipulated. It's like clay, and sometimes they become what they are not. And then it's very hard for them to see the way home.

D: *People are influenced by their cultures, their educations.*

P: And that's part of our lesson. To learn in different ways.

D: *You also said that down those other paths were other projects. This is your project, but what are the other projects that are down the other paths?*

P: (Sigh) Those are people, beings ... (confused as to how to word it) ... if you were to take plaster and put it around something and let it harden. And inside was a beautiful jewel, but around was this dark, ugly plaster. That's what they're like. They don't know they're beautiful inside; they think they're dark and ugly. And there are great, loving beings who are working with them. And that's a very different project than the project here that I'm in.

D: *Are these the energies of people while they're still in the physical, or after they have crossed over?*

P: No, they're not on the Earth, as you call it.

D: *Where are they? In the spirit world?*

P: Yes, it is part of an energy place. Everything's energy, but it's a different vibration around you. It's an energy that is very dense. It's even denser than this planet.

D: *Are these spirits that have done things that are considered negative?* (Yes) *That's why they are in the plaster, so to speak?*

P: Yes, they are, because they got to really like the negative. To hurt people – or whatever – to do things which cause other people to feel bad, or to not be able to find their light. They like the darkness. So that's their path, and that's what they keep doing until they change.

D: *It must take a lot of patience for spirits to work with those types.*

P: It takes a great love and great light to do that.

D: *And dedication.* (Yes) *Are those negative spirits allowed to reincarnate anywhere?*

P: No, not right now. No.

D: *I was told this type could bring that negativity back with them.*

P: Yes, they are not reincarnating right now. Especially they cannot come to Earth. But they also cannot come to other places, because it's a long project. And it has to come from the inside. These great beings of light are there with them, and they are shining their light. And they need to get through this great darkness. And it's taking time – not time, but it is vibrational. And it is occurring in a different place. It is occurring in a different way. And they cannot be here. There are some *here* who are still in the physical who may go there. There's a point on the circle that we are coming to. I can see it. It's a circle. It's not a break. But there's a point we are coming to where we can move off into another place. And when we get to that place, people will go to different places, depending on their own vibration, their own energy. And there may be some who have to go to that dark place.

D: *Because of what they have done on Earth?*

P: Yes. Not many!

D: *But this deals with karma, doesn't it?*

P: It's like that. Yes, it is. We can call it that, but it's their energy. It's not a punishment, because they would like to go there. This is where they're comfortable.

D: *But they're not forced to go there, like the church teaches?*

P: No, they want to go. It's not punishment.

D: *These beings* want *to be in those dark places.*

P: Oh, yes. And they still have their light, because I can see the light in them. It's always there. But it's covered in the plaster, and they think they are the plaster.

D: *But they won't come back here, because the Earth is changing.*

P: Exactly. That's why they can't come anymore. Things have changed too much. They can't see the light. They see the darkness. But then through change of vibration, through these great beings willingly working with them, they begin to allow their inner light to shine. And when that inner light connects with the outer light, then the darkness is gone. But it takes as long as it needs to take. And when that happens, then they can go to other places, to go again and be, so they can bring that light into usefulness.

Because it's all about using the light. And there are other places besides this place of Earth that we all go back and forth to. But this place is coming to that circle opening. It's all energy. A different place. A different energy. It's ... let's see. (Trying to find the words.) It's not *home!* But it's *like* home. See, home is the energy where we come from.

D: *The original energy.*

P: Yes. There are many different levels (unsure if that was the correct word) of energy on this planet Earth. And there's going to be a redirection of energies, of people. A redirection. So there will be people taking pathways to different places where they will be comfortable.

D: *It's not necessarily going home. It's going somewhere else.*

P: Right. Some will go home. Some who have come to help, who don't have a purpose for being somewhere else. Their only purpose is to help. That is my purpose.

D: *They would go back home.* (Yes) *But the other ones would have a different purpose when they cross over?* (Pause) *Or you said it's coming to a point on the circle where it would open.*

P: It will open different pathways, different levels. People are going to go to places where they will be comfortable. And from there they will then be able to make other choices and other decisions, when it is right for them.

D: *Does it all depend on what they have done in their physical lives?* (Yes) *So karma is involved in that way too.*

P: Yes. Karma meaning the balance of their energy, where it takes them. And no one needs to be punished. And where we are now, has been a very special plan in a very special place in the universe. And it feels like much good is coming from this.

D: *I've always felt that everyone, when they crossed over after each life, would go home. They would go to that place you're describing.*

P: Yes, but home is different for people. Home for one is not the same as home for others. Although it is all in the same, but it is different levels of the same. That's what I mean.

D: *So, you said some of these people would be shown other paths.*

227

(Yes) *Going home is different than going to the spirit side.*

P: First they may go to spirit, then they will choose to go to other places. This planet is going to spirit.

D: *The whole planet?*

P: In a way, because it is going to become aware of its higher vibration.

D: *Yes, I've heard this. They say that the vibration, the frequency of the planet itself is changing.*

P: It is. That's why I'm here. And many others are here too, for there are many different vibrations of people on the planet. Many are here to help.

D: *I've heard the whole planet is going to move en mass. Is that true?*

P: That's what I see.

D: *So many people with so many different vibrations, that would be difficult.*

P: That's why there are many paths. See, that's the doorway. It's like the circle, and the opening in that circle. And when we get to the opening they will move into the circle, but going into different places in the circle. Into different pathways. So it's okay for everyone. Everyone will be where they are supposed to be. And there is another circle of beings around our Earth. There are all these beautiful energies. Beautiful beings who are with us working with those on the physical plane. And they are not our angels. They are what we would call the "ascended beings", who have done this. They have moved through the energy. And they are extending their energy as pathways for *us*. Those are the beings I talked about earlier.

This was a perfect time for me to ask a few of Patricia's questions. I knew I didn't have to call forth the subconscious, because, since the beginning of the session, I had been communicating with the part of her that had all knowledge.

D: *Patricia mentioned that she has seen beings in her meditation that were gold and platinum. Are these the ones you are talking about?*

P: I see many different beings surrounding the planet. Many

different color vibrations. I see blue, and white and violet, and gold and silver and platinum. But these are all loving energies who are coming to help us all now. The different colors are helping the people of those same vibrations.

D: *So we all have different colors, as well as vibrations?*

P: Colors are vibrations.

D: *And these beings are attracted to the different colors?* (Yes) *So these spirit helpers are different from the angels?*

P: Yes, they are. Angels are with us too, but these are different, because these have an understanding. Many of these have been through this, either on this physical world, or other similar worlds. But they also know what it's like to be moving through the vibrational planes. This is what they do.

D: *So what is their purpose, if the guardians or spirit helpers like you are to help individuals?*

P: They're helping us, the spirit helpers. It's like energy transformers stepping down energy. And there are many people who are here on the Earth who could not hold or feel the energy of those great beings. But there are others who can be go-betweens. So we are go-betweens.

D: *When Patricia came into this life, did she know she was going to be doing these things?*

P: No, Patricia didn't know. Patricia's *soul* knew.

D: *Yes, the physical is the last to know.*

P: Yes. Patricia put herself in a self-imposed closet, so she wouldn't know. And she experienced many things. And she had to come out of the closet and say, "Okay, I'm not in the closet." And she did. And she is also connected to the golden light. That is her energy.

D: *But as humans we don't consciously know the agreements we've made, and we don't know the connections.*

P: No. And she felt the spirit family. And she knows *home*. She knows it very well. And sometimes she wants to go there. She used to want to go there intensely, and be out of this life, but she could never kill herself.

229

D: *Because we have a contract, don't we?*
P: Yes, and she knew she had to be here. That there was something to do. So she stayed. And she eventually was able to come into her true understanding of who she is. Many of the problems she has had with relationships were because of an agreement.
D: *What kind of an agreement?*
P: If she chose to do that, that was the hard path. It was a choice. She didn't have to do that, but she chose to do that.
D: *You said there was a choice, and she chose the more difficult one. What would the other path have been? Can you see that?*
P: Yes. I think she would have died young.
D: *Why do you think that?*
P: Because ... this is complicated, but it is time for her to know. I have to find the words. If she chose the easy path, she would not have had the knowledge in her physical life to help as many people. Accepting the difficult path is teaching her many experiences and much knowledge, but many other people can be helped by it. She did not have to do this. She could have helped only from the other side. From home. It is a joke, in a way. Because she has always wanted to go home, and yet that is where she is helping people to go. That is her work.
D: *And she does go there at night, even though she doesn't realize it.*
P: Yes, she goes there. Her physical body sometimes has a hard time holding as much energy as it does. And although she is healthy, she has to be very careful, and take extra care, because her body holds much energy. But she has to be very careful now, especially because the energies are getting higher and higher in vibration. I'm seeing her body filling with the gold light, turning into gold energy. And she can do this. She will hold more and more. Turning more and more to the gold light, which is where she comes from. And as the physical body moves to that, she is helping many more move to that. Those who choose to take that pathway. Those who take the gold light highway, so to speak. But it's now getting into the final times of it.

The final days.

D: *What do you mean by the "final days"?*

P: Before we come to that place in the circle, where we all move into different places.

D: *You said on the spirit side when her body is sleeping, she is working with people who are going to die, to help them to pass over.* (Yes) *But on the physical, she is also a hospice worker.*

P: She has done much. She feels both worlds. She has always felt both worlds.

D: *Is this why she's comfortable working as a hospice worker, because of the connection when she's sleeping?*

P: Oh, yes. She's happy to help people home, because she knows how wonderful it is.

D: *Of course, it's easier working on the spirit level, isn't it?*

P: Yes, it is easier for her.

D: *Because when you're in the physical trying to work with people who are dying, you run into the interference of the physical – I want to say – programming.*

P: People feel fear, much fear in the physical. And that is what she does, help people to overcome fear, because she herself has no fear of death. And when people are with her, they feel her truth, because she is real. It is her. She is connected to that energy of love.

D: *That way she can help people much more effectively. But she has had other lives on Earth, hasn't she?* (Pause) *Because you said she is also existing on this spirit side at the same time as she is living the life of Patricia.*

P: It feels like it's yes, and it's no. *Part* of her has had lives. But not Patricia, other parts of her soul.

D: *Because we think of it as reincarnation.*

P: Yes, it is in a way, but it's different. (She had difficulty finding the words.) She has come from a soul that has had many, many lives of spiritual significance, working on a spiritual path. And those lives have brought back to her soul their energy, their knowledge, what they have gained. So the part that is Patricia has taken little bits and pieces from all those lives. She must remember that she is always

231

connected to home, and always connected to her family (meaning the spirit family). And is much loved.

———————◇—◦◦❈◦◦—◦◦❈◦◦—◦❈◦◦—◇———————

During another session in Minneapolis in October 2002, there was a similar incident. I was in Minneapolis to do a series of lectures and workshops, and was going to Australia and New Zealand immediately afterwards. This session was being done with a retired teacher that I shall call Ida.

As I have said, normally in my technique I have the subject visualize a beautiful place of their choice to get the visualization started. Then I complete the induction, which includes descending from the cloud. In this case Ida did not let me finish the induction. She was describing her beautiful place and it did not sound like Earth. She was already talking about it before I realized she did not need the rest of the induction. This occasionally happens, and I have learned how to tell the difference, and how to proceed. I turned on the microphone. She was describing a beautiful garden on *her* planet, which was a place full of light.

I: There are lovely light beings walking all around. There is just love. And it is *so* beautiful, *so* peaceful, *so* harmonious. This is where I come from.
D: *You said there was a garden there?*
I: Oh, yes. It is so beautiful. It shines with the golden light of God. It has illumination, and an energy and frequency of complete peace, love and harmony. There are beautiful golden fountains. They look like water, but it's the essence of God that flows all over. It is just pure beauty, love and bliss.

This sounded very similar to the place described by Patricia only a week earlier.

I: We are *all* light beings. We recognize one another by the essence and the vibrational frequencies. There's no verbal communication. We just speak without words. It's just a vibration of what we want to say that one picks up from the other. This is where I'm from. And this is where there's total bliss and total peace and total harmony. I do go back and forth in my sleep state. I meet with the council and we discuss the work that I have to do on this Earth plane.

D: *Where is the council located?*

I: The council is located on this planet as well. And we meet in the same beautiful gardens.

D: *You do this in the sleep state.*

I: I do. That frequency in my sleep state. Although my physical form and my physical mind remembers not. But this is done all the time. And I do go on errands as well in my sleep state. We look at all the interaction I have with various beings on this Earth plane. And whenever there is help needed, I am guided and directed to do whatever work I have to do.

D: *Is it with people you know or others or ....?*

I: Some people I know, and there are others that I don't know.

D: *What kind of guidance do you give them whenever you meet with them at night?*

I: I work with them on many levels. I work with the mind. I infuse thought patterns in them, so they can *shift* in their daily lives. I also heal some of them. I work with healing frequencies and healing energies with many of them. I also go into war zones and work with the injured. I work with those in pain. I've been doing a lot of work in Afghanistan. (2002) There is so much trauma and pain in that country. Not only with the American soldiers and other peace keeping forces that are there, but the locals as well are completely and totally traumatized with what is going on. They are not accustomed to all the bombs that have fallen there. All the injury that has happened to their land. There's so much devastation there. Half of it is not reported in your media, or in your news.

D: *I can believe that. We don't really know what's going on.*

The rest of the session dealt with predictions about the war that broke out in Iraq the next year in 2003. They were extremely accurate, but I was undecided whether to include this in this book. I only wanted to include here the part that was relevant about the work we do during our sleep state that is unknown to our conscious mind. We were warned that there would be many deaths during the war, and people like Ida would be very busy during their "sleep" state leading them in the correct direction.

There are many schools on the spirit side. These were discussed in *Between Death and Life*. The most advanced are located in the Temple of Wisdom complex which have the Great Halls of Learning where absolutely everything known and unknown can be learned. These are also described in *Holiday in Heaven*, by Aron Abramsen. Many of the teachers are advanced guides who have completed enough of their karma that they do not need to return to Earth for more lessons. They are in a position to teach and train others. As it said in my other book, "You cannot become a guide as long as you need a guide." Normally the training to become a guide begins when the person has left the Earth plane. The guides and elders decide whether the person is ready for this advancement, after looking at a life review. However, things on Earth are changing rapidly and the training must change with it. There are so many problems on Earth at the present time that many advanced souls have incarnated, not to work out their own karma, but to help the others who are in the physical. Of course, they do not know this consciously, that they are advanced souls sent to Earth for specific purposes. But I am encountering more and more of them through my work, and their subconscious is no longer hesitant to tell them they have a job to do, and they had better get on with it instead of wasting valuable time. In my early days of working in the trance state, this was not mentioned. Now it is brought up with practically every client. It is emphasized that the time is growing short, and they have to proceed with the job they volunteered to do.

Because there are so many advanced souls who have returned to the Earth plane, some of the spiritual training is done in the sleep state. Some of the training that these souls receive is how to assist souls who are departing the Earth through the death process. During the sleep state they have helped in many such assistances with the aid of a more experienced guide. They are not sent out to do the work on their own until they have had enough training or experience or confidence to feel they can handle it. Their main job is to lead the person in the right direction and out of confusion, so the more experienced and proper "greeter" can take over. Besides, the helper cannot go beyond a certain point until it is their time to leave the body.

In my work, I have discovered that the *real* part of us: our soul or spirit, never sleeps. The physical body is the part that gets tired and must rest. The spirit has no need for this. I always say, "It would get bored waiting around for the body to wake up so it can continue life." So while the body is asleep the spirit is having many different adventures on its own. It can travel anywhere in the world, or go to the spirit side and converse with its guides and the masters and elders or to get more information, and attend classes and take training. I hear from many of my readers who report dreams of attending school while in the sleep state. I try to explain to them that it probably is real, because this is a favorite place for the spirit to revisit. They can also travel to other planets or other dimensions. Normally, the conscious part has no memories of these journeys unless it remembers dreams of flying or unfamiliar places. This is the same thing that is experienced in Out of the Body travel, when the person has trained themself to go out of their body and remember what they see. All during physical life, the spirit is connected to the body by the silver cord which acts as the tether the entire time you are alive. The umbilical that is not broken until the death of the physical body. With this death, the cord is severed and the spirit is released to return "home". When the spirit is journeying out of the body at night, it is always connected by the cord. At a certain time, the body must awaken in order to continue its life. At that time, the spirit feels a tugging on the cord, and it is "reeled in", for want of a better word. At that point the spirit reenters the body and the body can awaken.

Many people have reported to me a strange sensation they sometimes experience upon awakening. This can also occur when the body is going to sleep. They say they have temporary paralysis, and this can be quite frightening. One woman said her doctor told her it was a serious condition called "sleep apnea", and charged over $1700 for sleep tests. It is really nothing that complicated at all, but a natural phenomenon that occurs sometimes. While the spirit is disconnected from the body, the body functions are being taken care of by another part of the brain. It rather goes on automatic pilot. When the spirit returns, the brain/body connections have to reconnect. If the body awakens too soon before the connections are in place there can be a temporary feeling of paralysis. I have investigated cases where a sudden noise in the person's environment wakes them up suddenly before they are entirely back into the body. If they can relax for a few minutes, everything will return to normal. The same sensation can occur when the spirit first leaves the body and is disconnecting. This shows how the spirit and body are truly separate, yet one. The body cannot exist without the spark of life dwelling within, yet the spirit or soul can exist without the body. At death when the spirit leaves for the last time, the connection is broken and the body begins to deteriorate instantly. Without the spirit of life, all systems shut down. Then when the silver cord is severed at death the spirit cannot reenter the body.

In this session, as well as others, we see that our "real" self, the spirit, is not only journeying and having adventures while the body sleeps, it is also working. There apparently is much work being done in the astral state that we are totally unconscious of. As I was told in one session, "These things are happening anyway. You have no control over it. They are a part of your existence that you are unaware of. There is nothing you can do about it. They are natural, so there is no sense worrying about it." It is the same with reincarnation and other metaphysical concepts. They will continue to happen whether the person believes in them or not. I was told that we will never fully understand the complexity of it all. It is impossible. The problem in understanding and comprehending resides in the mind. It is not the brain, but the mind. There is nothing in it that can grasp the totality of these concepts. So I am given small pieces and hints of the enormity of it all. As time goes by, it appears that we are being allowed to see more, and we can try to comprehend it. But it is as peering through a small crack in the wall of time and space, and being allowed to see a tiny portion of the whole picture.

When a spirit elects to return to Earth for another cycle of living a human life in a physical body, it comes with its plan for what it wishes to accomplish this time around. It has already met with the elders and masters, gone over the life it just left, and made decisions, plans and goals. It has made agreements with other spirits that it had associations with for debts to repay. And with their permission, certain things would be worked out and certain lessons would be learned. It comes back to Earth with its nice little plan wrapped up like a Christmas present. The problem is that this is a planet of free will. This is what makes Earth so challenging. And everyone else is coming in with their nice little plans. And because of free will, these plans and hopes and fears will sometimes clash. Also the spirit incarnates with all memories erased of what the plans were in the first place. Only the subconscious remembers. I asked one time, why couldn't we remember? Wouldn't it make it easier?

237

I was told, "It wouldn't be a test if you knew the answers." So we come to Earth and think we are prepared to face the challenges that will be put in our way as we work toward our goals, dreams and aspirations or challenges. But oftentimes, we are not as prepared as we think we are. It always looks easier from the other side. While we are living through the frustrations of physical life, we get sucked up in everything that makes us "human". Hopefully we will work it out and pass the test to progress to the next "grade". Or we goof up and we will have to come back and do it all over again. You can't proceed to the next grade or class until you finish the lessons and tests of this one. You can go backwards in this school, but you cannot skip a class. There are very strict schoolmasters with very strict rules and regulations. Yet paradoxically, these schoolmasters are also very kind, just and understanding.

Just as we come into life with a plan, we also have a plan for our departure from this life. Everyone decides before entering how they will exit. This is said with all emotion removed, and must be understood that way. None of this is known on the conscious level, and it is probably very wise that we don't remember these plans. People always say they don't want to die, they do not want to get sick, and they do not plan to leave their loved ones. They would strongly deny that they were planning their death. But it is all part of a plan much further beyond our knowledge and understanding. Therefore, the only way to look at it with our limited human minds is logically with all emotions removed.

There are various reasons why a spirit decides it is time to depart the physical. It has completed its goal, its plan and worked out all the karma that was necessary for this lifetime. In this case there is no need to continue. In other cases, it decides that other people will progress much faster if their presence was not acting as a liability. In these cases the spirit decides to forego its own further development so that others who are too dependent can go on their own. So they can "grow up", in other words. These reasons are often not apparent on the surface, and can be discovered only after much soul

238

searching.

Another interesting scenario is that some people's lives are so rigidly locked into one chain of events that switching in order to accomplish their goal in life becomes impossible. Possibly they failed to accomplish their earthly purpose because of inappropriate choices made through free will. So they decide to die, get out of the situation, and start over. Next time, hopefully, they will not get trapped into the same direction or situation.

An interesting and more appropriate alternative to this is when the person's life "dies" in another way. The person is also locked into a chain of events that will not allow them to accomplish what they came into this life to do. Too much time would be lost if they physically died in order to start over. Or perhaps the physical conditions needed would not be present in another time line. Rather than dying, they decide to start over by creating the death of their life in another way. By losing everything they hold dear, especially all their physical possessions. Such a scenario would also allow them to focus on what is really important in life, and it is not possessions, no matter how tightly they hold onto them. Now that everything has been taken away, they can start over and begin anew toward their real goal in life. What they really came in to do. They became too immersed in the material world, so it all had to be taken away. Without this material distraction, they can now proceed in the correct direction. Such an incident occurred to a member of my own family. Through a strange set of circumstances beyond their control, they lost absolutely everything material: house, business, occupation, and all material possessions. At the time it seemed like a cruel twist of fate or a punishment from God. It was very difficult to understand. But time proved that it was a way to push them in another direction. The direction they should have been going all along, but they became trapped into another way of life. They say that when one door closes, another one opens. In this case the door was not only closed, it was slammed shut. They had no choice but to go in another direction. There was no turning back. So many times, what seems like a disaster is often a blessing in disguise.

Another example of a drastic solution was given by a client. During my interview with him, the man told me about a terrible incident that occurred when he was younger. He was attacked in an alley in a large city, stabbed repeatedly by a gang, and then left for dead. He managed to crawl out to the street where someone found him and took him to the hospital. He almost died and remained in the hospital for quite a while recuperating. One of the things he wanted to know during our session was the purpose of the horrible experience. Why did it happen? During the session, when I contacted the subconscious and asked it that question, the answer was very surprising. It said, "Oh, that was a group of his friends who volunteered to help him." I thought, with friends like that, who needs enemies! It didn't seem the type of thing a friend would do!

The subconscious explained that it had all been orchestrated from the other side. The man's life was going in the wrong direction, and he was not going to be able to get back on his path without drastic action that would turn his life around. There had been many subtle attempts to get his attention, and when these did not work, the attack was arranged. Drastic, dramatic, unexplainable, yes, but it shows the extremes the universe will go to in order to turn someone's life around without having them physically exit this world. That probably would have been the next step if this one had not worked.

Once the soul has decided it is time to leave the physical, it will arrange events so that it can die. An interesting point has been brought out through my regression material: that one of the problems today is the medical establishment. If the person is dying in a hospital, often the doctors try to keep them alive with all the wonderful equipment that is available. Also the family is reluctant for them to leave even though the physical body is so damaged it can no longer sustain them, and there is no point in remaining. So the quickest, easiest way with the least likelihood of interference, is to die in an accident or natural disaster, etc. Some of these methods of exiting life are called "freak accidents" and can be quite bizarre. I have always

240

believed that if it is your time to go, it will happen even while you are sitting in your living room. There are cases reported of planes or cars crashing into a house and killing someone.

While I was writing this at the end of 2003 the terrible earthquake in Bam, Iran had just occurred and took the lives of over 41,000 people. Before we were able to go to press with this book the terrible 9.3 earthquake and tsunami occurred at Christmas, 2004, off the coast of Indonesia. At last count, almost 200,000 people decided to leave in a mass exodus. Also at the same time, many people died in mud-slides and avalanches in other parts of the world. As is reported in this chapter, often people decide to leave together. This is all decided on the subconscious level and arrangements (or as Patricia said, "rehearsals") are made. Also arrangements will be made for those who are not supposed to be involved to miraculously escape, or to not be there in the first place. This has happened to many people who just happened to miss a doomed flight or were bumped at the last minute. Or were delayed from leaving the house by a last minute phone call, to then find they had just missed getting caught in a terrible accident. I also believe that our guardian angels play a big part in all of this too. They are busy trying to warn us with subtle nudges and suggestions, or the "little voice in our head". And sometimes their methods of keeping us safe are not so subtle. We have to learn to pay strong attention to our intuitions and "gut" feelings.

CHAPTER 13

THE FIRST OF THE SEVEN

This session was done while I was speaking at the Glastonbury Crop Circle Conference in Glastonbury, England in July, 2002. This is a very old city with many ancient ties to the past. There is a tremendous amount of energy that can be felt there. The session was in the Bed and Breakfast we were staying in, just off the square. The client, Robert, took the train down from London for the session. He has been channeling for a few years and had written a book of the channeling. He felt though, that he could not get reliable personal information, especially about the direction his life should take, from the channeling. So he wanted a personal session to clarify some things. I try to help the client find the best choice for their life, with the cooperation of the subconscious. Since he was accustomed to the trance state, he went deep very quickly. This is often the case when working with channelers, psychics, healers or people who meditate regularly. The altered state is a familiar condition.

When he was asked to go to the beautiful place, he was already contacting someone, so I did not need to complete the induction that normally requires the cloud method. I can usually tell where they are by the answers they give. And I know what does not sound like the normal beautiful place. If the description sounds unearthly, that is usually the first clue. I turned the tape recorder on and tried to recap what he had said.

He saw himself in a beautiful place by a waterfall. There was an old man there with a silver beard. This was the first indication that he was not in a normal place. Robert continued in a very soft voice that was barely audible, "He's saying, 'You're in so much pain. Come over here.'" He wants to distribute knowledge. He says *I* have to distribute knowledge. And he is part of the creation of that knowledge. "You are the mediator of that knowledge. You need to understand the pain."

D: *What do you mean by the pain?*
R: Its effects on the human body. The burden you carry. The boy. He's talking to the boy. This boy.
D: *Do you see yourself as a boy?* (Yes) *About how old?*
R: The boy is three.
D: *And he's in this beautiful place with the waterfall?*
R: He's there right now. It doesn't have to be beautiful all the time. It's the multi-dimensional experience of molecular structure, of the equates of it as positive and negative. The child is here to learn, to teach. Not only are there flowers, but there are alive flowers and there are dead flowers. And the evolving cycle is creational.

His voice was becoming louder, and I knew from experience and from the voice tone and vocabulary, that an entity was speaking through Robert. This entity turned out to be different in several ways from the ones I was normally used to conversing with in this state. This one used words and complicated terminology that was often difficult to understand, and it created new words. This may have been because it was not used to the human vocabulary, and was improvising. The entity also seemed to have a colder, almost abstract interest in Robert. The subconscious will have a detached observer viewpoint when speaking about the entity, but this one was almost cruel in its observation. As we proceeded, it described Robert as a different type of human than I had encountered before. My first purpose is to protect the subject, but this entity made me uncomfortable, and was difficult and tedious to converse with. The language and terminology was too convoluted to be clearly understood, so I have condensed and tried to clarify much of the session.

Robert's body began exhibiting symptoms. It was jerking occasionally with sudden spasms. I asked, "What is it?" There was no answer. I knew if I did not focus on it that it would stop

243

on its own, because it didn't seem to be causing Robert any physical discomfort.

R: The child's multidimensional frequency comes here to learn. He has several elements to do with the past, the present and the future. There is much information to be had with regards to this. This information is so paramount, and the burden that it places upon the young child is sometimes immense. But the importance of this information becomes formed into a vibrational energy frequency. So that the re-polarization of humanity and the poles in which he works can create a new process of restructuring.

D: *Why does this burden have to be placed on a young child?*

R: The child is not a child. The child is a component of this energy. The child is the reality behind your human format. But the reality behind the child is that he is a composite of energy. And that energy is the relevance behind the changes the man, body, spirit, mind and physicality is part of. The fight between the three dimensional and the nonphysical is a very difficult one. Because there is a fight within this human frequency. And until that fight desists, the child will continue with the pain. And the non-knowledge is what is required.

D: *So it is the non-knowledge that is creating the pain? Is that what you mean?*

R: It is the nonacceptance of non-knowledge.

D: *But you know, in human life that is the way we are. We come in without the knowledge.*

R: This child came in with the knowledge.

D: *We were curious as to whether he had other lifetimes on Earth?* (No) *Where were his prior lifetimes?*

Robert began a sequence of unintelligible sounds, rather like a clip-clopping. This continued for about a minute, in rapid succession, as though trying to get something out very quickly, but in an unintelligible form. It did not sound like a language, but just a series of sounds. I attempted to stop it.

244

D: *You'll have to speak in English, so that I can understand you.*

Robert let out several very deep whistling breaths, almost as though applying brakes to the outpouring.

R: We have to download energy formats into the frequency of the third dimensional energy that sits here. So he can re-vocalize in his format for you.

D: *But you must not harm the vehicle in any way.*

I am always very careful when these strange physical manifestations occur. I always want to make sure the entities (or whatever they are) realize that the physical vehicle they are attempting to speak through could possibly be harmed by their energy. But I have never had to worry, because "they" seem to be as protective (or even more so) as I am.

R: The vehicle is never harmed. The harm is created by the purpose that the child has on the three dimensional level, of nonacceptance of *who he is.* He creates his own damage. The damage comes from without, not within us. The physicality this child creates is the damage created. We create no damage within the child.

D: *Because that is what I require when I do these sessions, that no harm ever come to the vehicle.*

He was still experiencing spasmodic jerks, almost like electrical charges. This and the bodily reaction to the strange sounds, caused me concern.

R: This has never occurred. We relevance your information.

D: *All right. But I am curious, if he did not have a physical life on Earth before, where were the majority of his lives?*

R: There is no such thing as "had life" format.

D: *He has never had a physical life in any other dimension?*

R: Yes. A life in the dimension in which you are not talking about.

D: *Not in this dimension then.* (No) *But what other dimension was he in before coming here?*

R: An astral dimension.

D: *Was this a physical one?* (No) *Because I am aware there are other dimensions where physical cities and people do exist.*

R: A parcel of information of relevance was part of the transition between this child and the life that one is accepting at this point in time. This parcel of information is what this child carries. He is a light body. He is an etheric body. He is a physical body. But not only that, he is a multi-dimensional frequency that carries an immense amount of knowledge. This in turn is being gradually transduced down, via the levels, through to a three dimensional frequency. So this child can vibrate this knowledge in a vocal format. In a spiraling format towards and with an understanding those that are working with these levels at this point in time.

The entity used the word "transducer" several times during this session as a noun and also as a verb. I was finally able to find it in the thesaurus. It was defined as something similar to a transformer, or something that changes something into something different.

D: *There are many others that are doing the same thing that I've come in contact with.* (Yes) *Did this happen at the age of three, or was it before that?*

R: The transitional point, the change, occurred at this point.

D: *But he was born a physical human.* (Yes) *And the knowledge was there even as a baby.* (No) *Before that he was ... what? (I was trying to understand.)*

R: The child, prior to the existence and changeover, was a transitional thought format seen by others, but not real.

D: *It was not solid and physical?*

R: No, it was an apparition.

D: *But yet it was fed and raised by the parents.*

246

R: Yes, seen to be, but in reality, not. So no infraction or
    creational process was incurred to humanity via the using
    of a human form. The human form that you see now is a
    creational process. It is not a real process. It is a figment.
    A figment we will not elongate on at this point in time. It
    is a figment.

    The physical body of Robert that was lying on the bed
certainly seemed real and solid enough, and not an illusion. I
was hoping before the session was over that these remarks
would be made clearer.
    One of the incidents that Robert had asked to explore, dealt
with his memory that something happened to him at the age of
three. He felt there was a changeling. That was the only term
he could find that made any sense.

R: A changeling being the child's version of his eyes. The
    realization behind this is totally different.
D: *He felt as though an awakening occurred at that time.*
R: An awakening in your eyes. It was an acceptance of a duty.
D: *At the age of three?*
R: At *your* age of three, not his. The dimension of thought and
    hours, minutes, times, dimensions, is a process which we
    have to adjust ourselves to. To explain it to you, is working
    with your perimeters. So therefore we will accept what you
    are saying, but it's not the true reality behind the truth.
D: *Yes. I've heard this many times, so I can understand in my
    limited way, what you're talking about. But the scene he saw of
    the waterfall and the man, was that an actual physical place
    where the child was taken?*
R: This is a portal connection point. And this connection
    point will take him and *it* and the energy *back* to a point of
    nonexistence. To a point of reality. To a point where this
    energy and the burden behind the energy was created by
    the manifest beings that are here to help create a new
    purpose. A new thought format for man to elongate and
    stretch his mind to. This process is not one that is being

247

forced on man. It is one of an acceptance. And those that wish to work with this acceptance can tune into this knowledge. This is called "non-knowledge". It is a *new* knowledge. It is not one that has been left in portals of information from your tri-existence. This is a non-knowledge, a new acceptance. A new perimeter, a new structure, a new understanding. A new feeling and sensation that is being given to man. This child sits with this knowledge. He vibrates with this knowledge. And is working with this knowledge at this point in time. At this point in time, the child knows so little about what he is. It is not what he is, it is what he carries that is the important format line to realization. There are not many of these children on this planet. We state the perimeter of five to seven children doing correct work at this point in time, with regards to this elongation of mind.

D: *I have been told there are other children that have come that are more or less like channels of energy, to help mankind at this time.*

R: They are all coming from different aspects of the same. There are many here helping this planet at this point in time.

D: *So this is just a different aspect?*

R: This is another aspect. Another figment. In the way the child is a figment, an energy, a possibility, an elongation.

D: *So the spirit that is in the body has not had any other physical existence on other planets or dimensions?*

R: This is not correct. This elongation of mind cannot take himself to these points, because it will affect the three dimensional body that is here. There is no, and can be no, acceptance from whence this child has come. It would interfere with the current work. It is so very difficult when this child has chosen to work.

D: *But I'm speaking of the soul. We know that there is a soul and a spirit present in the body that is the spark of life.*

R: The spark of life burning in my child was created by the creational purpose behind humanity. So therefore if we are working from that point, the creational purpose can recreate and put a perimeter forth for this child. And have his own new soul and perimeters to work from. Bearing in mind, a new soul will not have the elongational stretching of previous existences. But the programming, if you want to elongate into lives, you can stretch into lives that have been programmed into this child, but they have no relevance. If you were to regress this child, you would regress into programmed memory reporters, but they would be of no relevance.

D: *Is this what I have found as imprinting?*

For a clearer definition of imprinting see my book *Between Death and Life*. This is a process whereby the record of other lives can be imprinted upon the spirit. These are lives that the individual has not lived, but provide necessary information to allow them to function in this world. All memories, including emotions, are included in this procedure, and no one (including the person) would be able to tell if they are real or not. These are especially useful if the person has never had any Earth lives of their own. If this is their first life on this planet.

R: You could say that. That is your circumspect. This is acceptable to us.

D: *I've worked with other people who called it imprinting. Which were actually programs of other lives that they had never actually lived.*

R: Correct.

D: *So we're using the same definitions anyway.*

R: Correct.

D: *I know it's difficult for us to understand, because I have found that the soul can splinter into many different facets. This is what you're talking about, isn't it?*

R: Absolutely.

This concept will be expanded upon later in this book.

D: *I've always taken people back to relevant and appropriate lifetimes, so they will understand what's happening in their life now. And you mean this would not be possible?*

R: This would not be relevant.

D: *All right. Because we always want to know where the soul originated. And many of these people volunteered to come here to do this work.*

R: Manifested, created, proported.

D: *Who are you, the beings that are speaking, when you say "they"?*

R: We are part of the creational process behind human format. Human, being: the origins behind the creational process, the facade of humanity and the planet in which we live. We are part of that creational purpose. We are part of the energy behind that. We are here now to re-enlighten those that wish to understand that there is another existence. There is another energy format to move forth to. There are so very few here that are prepared to accept the changes and relevance. Change is so relevant at this point in time. Humanity is at a point where they are stretching the elongation of spirit mind to the point where the existence of man can no longer exist at this point of energy frequency. This is not an interference. What this is, is a statement of facts. There needs to be a change. There needs to be an understanding. *But* the moving forth needs to be done correctly, with understanding, with knowledge, with the re-frequency of the bodies that are prepared to do so. And in doing so they can talk and work with these energy levels. These thoughts and formats are not the process of humanity. They are the process of the creational endeavors behind the way humans were created.

D: *Yes, I can understand that, even though there are many others that can't, because I've been working with this for so long. But I've been told there are tens of thousands of people who have reached the level that they will be part of this change.*

R: There are many. Tens of thousands being very few with regards to the nameless people on this planet. Tens of thousands would be correct. You are correct. The point is, there are so very few that actually carry an energy of the

250

reason. Many are learning the reason, but actually telling the truth behind the reason, that is the reason for this child. *That* is the reason.

D: *I know there were many, many involved in this, but they are ignorant of it. The person doesn't realize what is happening. There is an awakening happening though. More are becoming more conscious of the fact that something is occurring to the Earth.— But these were things he wanted to know about, what happened when he was three years old.*

R: The child knows exactly what happened, so we need not give further information on this.

D: *Well, he had questions about it.*

R: The child has all the answers. He always has them.

One memory that haunted Robert since the age of three that didn't make sense, was that he was standing on a beach looking up at a cliff. He saw what he perceived to be his "real" parents walking away from him on top of the cliff. He was very upset, crying and screaming for them to come back, to not leave him there. As he remembered this memory from the viewpoint of an adult, it did not make any sense because these people he remembered and called his "real" parents were not his biological parents who raised him. This was why he wanted to explore it.

R: (Sigh) We are prepared to accept that the child will not be given this information. You must accept, and we must accept that at this point in time, to elongate the child to the point of where he has come from, will not allow him to live and abide within the dimensions in which he is. There are energy frequencies that would be totally non-conducive with the frame in which he is. He works very little with these energies, but they affect him much. This was the choice. This was the acceptance when this child came to do this work. The perimeters behind that will create some imbalance of deformity within his physical structure. This has to be accepted. Non-correctional purposes will be put in place, but they will never function correctly or

251

physically. His body will suffer much with regards to the energy he carries. We cannot ford the purpose behind where he has come from. For the simple reason being: that the energy of which he is, is not the energy and reality behind where he has come from. This will be so confusing for those to understand the truth.

D: *But I've been told that the full creation energy can never enter into a human body. It would be impossible. So this is only a fragment?*

R: This is a fragment. The child has been given a fragment of his reality.

D: *But you think some of this knowledge of what happened when he was three, is dangerous for him to know?*

R: The knowledge of the prior existence from whence he has come, the energy which that has come from, would not be conducive to his physical element. He can have this knowledge when he is out of his physical element, which is not at this point in time. So he is not allowed to venture out. That is part of the pain that he has to sustain. He knew that when he took on this work. He being the energy format, that he would not be able to commune with the energy of life that he has come from. There is only one portal acceptance that allows him to do that. We saw the entry point. The only time that entry point can be re-entered is at the point of demise. As and when this child leaves this planet, he will be taken. He will not go through the normal tubes of parallel, which will endure him back into a non-frequency of acceptance. As we are well aware at this point in time, when an earthly spirit moves to the fourth dimension, there is a tube. And within this tube, there is beautiful light. But elongated within this light are many experiences that can take you, and drag you to elongations of spectrum that are not conducive to you. They have been created by low astral frequencies. The child will not be relevant with these. He will not have to proport himself through these processes. The child has been reborn of light, and is now well aware of the work he has to do. He has been pushed with this work.

D: *So you think this is not advisable to ask questions for his curiosity of what happened when he was three.*

R: No. The truth is there. What occurred is from the point when he is allowed to remember. Nothing prior to that will be given, and will never be given.

I wasn't going to give up. I tried again to get at least a small amount of information for Robert.

D: *He was just curious, because of his memories of seeing his real parents leaving him.*

R: Real energies left in the human format. The moment he was in a human format, the energies created human format for him to see, for them to see, for you to see, that this change occurred. That a suspension of anonymity occurred at that point.

D: *So that was just something for him to remember.*

R: That's correct.

D: *That would be a safe memory.*

R: That he has come from somewhere, and not here. And there is love to be had in abundance if and when his work is completed, and it is far from completed.

D: *Yes, I understand. But you know this is difficult for the human when they feel they have been left here. They feel very isolated. And they feel different from the other humans.*

R: Bear in mind, what you are talking to at this point in time, is nonphysical. But the physical body at which you look at, at this point in time, is physical and suffers much through the work and misunderstanding of those that *he* in the physical thought format have and occur with.

Robert said as a child he had very high fevers and physical problems that the doctors could not explain. He came close to death several times, and spent many days in the hospital as they tried to control his temperature and understand what was happening to him. To this day, his parents were never given any explanation.

R: This is to do with the transition transducement of new energies that are focusing. There are many people that are like magnifying glasses of energy. This child is one. What he is, is a curator of energy, but passes it on. He is a formatter. He is an understander. He is a transducer. He is like a fuse that moves energy from one point to the next. He doesn't always understand it. This has much effect on the physical human body that he carries. He is understanding that much of this energy is not his. It is a shared energy. It is a transducement from one portal point, to a physical entry point, to a physical humanity.

D: *And this is what caused the fevers and the physical problems that happened in those early days?*

R: This was a learning to deal with energies. This was a point in his life where he had to wake up to who he was. Otherwise he would have left this planet. There would have been no reason for him to be here.

D: *So he was having to adjust to ... what? An upsurge in the energy?*

R: Either adjust or out! Fact! Figures! Adjust or out! No relevance is either side of that.

D: *So it would be like a step-up in the frequencies at that time?*

R: Yes, or step-out! Step away from humanity. Move back. And let another energy do the work correctly.

D: *He said it was very traumatic, and they couldn't understand what was happening to him.*

R: Incredibly, too much for a physical energy to endure. Almost beyond endurance. The child has much to go beyond endurance. To also be allowed to deal with energies on a physical level, you have to be taken to the point of no endurance left. To understand that is the point where you can no longer go. It is deemed the tested time. It is learning to understand that the planet is of the physicality. This child has an immense strength way beyond many. He is yet to understand the true sense and purpose behind what he will carry out. There is so much

254

work to be done. Much of it will be done in the physical, but so much will be done on the subliminal and super-conscious levels.

The voice was affecting the tape. It had a hoarse sound throughout, but now it was becoming more pronounced, like an electronic signal beginning to break up. Some of the words had a garbled and unnatural sound. Throughout, my voice sounded normal on the tape, only his was distorted. I didn't notice it during the session. It only became evident on the tape. This has happened many times, that the entity has affected my electronic equipment in some unnatural way.

D: *But he has adjusted now. He no longer has the fevers and the other aches and the pains he had in the past.*
R: He has new pains. This is a misinterpretation of energy formats.
D: *He said they were in the back and his legs.*
R: These are energy points of the new energy.
D: *So another up-step in energy is occurring?*
R: That is correct. The child has had this explained. Does not accept. *Will* accept. This is expected.

Robert unexpectedly let out a weird high-pitched moan, and his body convulsed and shook. It was unexpected and took me off-guard.

R: Sound is the only way of programming and accepting.

This apparently was the reason for the strange sound.

R: Sound is a new creational programming. Accept. Accept. Accept. We are prepared to accept that the new sound boundaries that are creating a healing basis on this planet, are going to be a formula for human beings to accept the pain which they endure. This child is now working towards working with sound. Sound will allow his body to re-polarize. To re-access. To relearn how to develop the boundaries of the energy that it carries. The child has this in place right now.

D: *By sound, do you mean the human voice or music?*

R: With music. The child is working with music. Dispensing music and singing and producing music. And also he's involved with sound. With people working with tuning sound. Sound resonances, frequencies, sound, color, extensions.

D: *It's all very important because the frequencies of music do affect the human body. It would be better if he could make these energy adjustments and the step-ups in the energies without discomfort to the body.*

R: Yes, that would be conducive, but the body does not know its limitations until they have been gained. This is the point. This is a learning process. For the human body to change, one needs to understand that the elements which humanity chose, were not through learning through love, but learning through angst and energy. And angst and energy create a disposal of unwanted energy, which creates, in the end, pain. So pain is the point of learning. Pain is the point of evolvement and stretching to the point of understanding. So therefore, pain is the point of learning.

Here Robert's voice changed and became emotional, at the point of crying. What was being said was definitely affecting Robert, and that human part was overriding the entity.

R: So therefore pain is the point in which this child will get to the point of endurance. And then he will have the ability to teach others to do so.

Robert now was crying. I tried to ignore it rather than focus on it. This way I could get the entity back, and keep Robert's emotions suppressed. Besides, my job is always to take away pain, not justify or prolong it.

256

D: *But we really don't want pain, because pain gives discomfort to the body.*

R: Yes, correct. (The entity was back in control.)

D: *So can it be done in a much easier way?*

R: No, not in this circumstance. What needs to happen is this: Manage the point of pain. He has chosen this element, this frequency, this two thousand year cycle to develop through the energy of pain to the evolution of a new body. This is how man has chosen to learn. We are now moving into a new process of love environment where pain will be remitted. And love will be allowed to be the frequency of *exposure* as and when new experiences come through. What needs to occur, is the quickening process where man is allowed to transduce all the pain that he carries and remove it. So therefore, the new love elementary feelings and sensations can be carried through into the fourth and third. This is how this is occurring. It is being shown through this cycle of experience of this burden of this child.

This changing of the human body to be able to exist in the New Earth will be expanded upon later in this book.

D: *Is it the DNA of the body that is being affected?*

R: Absolutely.

D: *I've heard this from other people. And they said it is a definite raising of the frequencies.*

R: Yes, absolutely.

D: *But I would like it to occur with less discomfort to his body.*

I was determined to alleviate discomfort from Robert's body, even though I was meeting with tremendous resistance from the stubborn entity.

R: At first you learn the pain isn't all. As you learn, the pain becomes and progresses to be less. Pain, not necessarily being the function of pain. Pain being the evolutionary process of learning. If you learn much, pain occurs through

257

the functioning of the brain. Pain occurs through having to work hard. Pain occurs through loving too much or living too much. These are the processes that man chose to evolutionize with.

D: *Yes, it's all part of our lessons.*

R: Man is being given a step-off point, but he needs to know his perimeters. He needs to understand that these step-off points are step-off points of realization. You need to remove the old to move with the new. It is the clearing time. We need to work with this. There needs to be disciples of this clearing time. This child is one of the seven disciples at this point of time, doing the particular work that he has chosen to do. This is the first one you are to meet. You will meet more. You have now worked with this energy. You will attract this energy again. They might not be such a difficult subject to work with. This child has been programmed with elements that will not allow him to go to this place in which he has come from. It was the light body in which he chose to come into. The light bodies with the next child you will work with, will allow you to go *back* into the purpose behind this child. And the energy in which they have come from. You will now meet another. You will draw that to you, because you will be interested to know what is behind this purpose. You will not get that this time.

D: *I do know some of the purpose has to do with the creation of a new world, and going into another dimension, by changing the frequency and the vibration. I've been given that type of information.*

R: Yes, you have. You will be elongating on the spectrum of that information. Bearing in mind the resonance of that information will allow you to resonate in many respects. As you will appreciate, my dear lady who works so hard and well, you carry very little of the experience you have. And the energy you carry in a nonphysical sense, is the immensity behind the work that you are. My child, you are to be thanked. But your physical element carries so little, and the fact that this physical element carries so little, it is what you are carrying, not who you are.

D: *The energies behind all of this.*

R: Not only the energies, but the energies that are *attached* to that energy. It takes time for those parallel experiences to be gathered up. It is like the fish in the fishing net as the trawler pulls in the net. Gradually the crop is exposed as the catch is pulled in. But the strength needs to be gained to pull the net in. So therefore, the weight of the knowledge carried within that net will only happen if and when the person or the endurance has been given for that purpose. You are gathering in that information. You have an acceptance behind who you are and what you are, my child. You also have an acceptance way beyond that, that you chose to come and work with what you work with. Outside of your physical elements, you will be given so much. But within your physical elements you are given so little. In fact, you are given so few thanks in regards to what you do on so many different levels. But the very few thanks you are given are true thanks. What awaits you, in real truth, is behind you from what you have *left*. In the same way with this child. You are all coming from the same purpose. We all realize that. This spiral of consciousness spiraled from another spiral which spiraled from another spiral which spiraled from another spiral. It is an elongation of a process that is not possible to understand in the dimensions of what you have. But you are being given more than you have been given in the past. You are being given the ability to understand, if that makes a point.

D: *My part is trying to help others understand it, and present it in a way they can understand and accept.*

R: You are saying so many words that have very little meaning at the time. But the resonances behind those words are the true meaning. An elongation behind what that energy is. There are many visions and proportments we have as and when you speak, but you cannot speak about them. But what you are actually doing with the words, is transducing, transporting that energy through to these people. So therefore, the cellular structure is retaining and taking on an energy that is conducive to them; that will allow them to move. There are so many people doing so little. There are a very many people doing an awful lot.

D: *So it will resonate to them on another level, other than what they are reading in the books.*

R: Absolutely, my child. Your books carry a resonance. You need only to own them to carry the resonance, the proportment of their information, their energy.

D: *So people will get more than they actually do from reading the words on the page?*

R: They will feel the inspiration. They will feel and touch the books, and feel the need that there is something within that book. And it may be one sentence. It may be an idea, it may be intuition. It may be elongation. It may be the proportment of just hearing that, that will elongate a whole new frequency of thought format to them. That will allow them to transduce, to accept a whole new spiral of information. This is what this is about. You, we, being the curators of the new force. And the force is not where you are going. It is what you have come from. It is time to finish for many. And it's time to start for many others. It is time for an evolution of change. A cycle has begun.

D: *That's what I've heard, that not everyone will be making this transition.*

R: That is correct. The ones that are ready for it will be the ones that will be able to physically understand at least ten percent of where they are going. They will need to earn that right.

D: *The other ones won't understand what's happening, and they will be very confused.*

R: They may, in the last five minutes of their existence, be transponded or given the information into their physical level, so they can move on. And they will have worked on a subliminal level. In the last moments of their life they will be given that on a physical level. So therefore, they will have the energy to move over. And with the teachings to understand that when they proport down the tube of knowledge, when they elongate from one existence to the other, they will not move into the fourth dimension. They will move *back* to the proportment, to the energy point from whence they broke away.

D: *What about those people who refuse to understand?*

R: Again, choice is the equal-libertization of human.

D: *That's true. We do have free will.*

R: That is correct.

D: *Then they will not go on into the transition.*

R: Not this time! Time being the element of your frequency.

D: *Yes, I know time is an illusion, but we are trapped in it. We have to use it.*

R: In their experience, it will be their time. In your experience, it will be nothing. You, being the one that has passed over into another experience. It will be like you will be waiting to gather together your flock, so the flock can then move to other pastures. If we are to accept that the divine sparks of human consciousness have broken away from one level, if this is to be an acceptance, you have divinely broken away into sparks of individualism. You are then working and evolving on a state of consciousness. As you have evolved in this consciousness, you have created a density frequency of this planet. The density frequencies of energy knowledge behind this planet. The life, the death, the life, the death. The density frequency, the karma, the information surrounding that. The point in which you leave this point and go back to your multi-dimensional singular frequency, you will wait for the flock to re-gather itself. This might take millennia. But the point is, when you are waiting for your flock to gather itself, you are in an abyss of total love and acceptance. You will be given exactly what you need to enjoy what you are.

D: *Yes, I've heard that it's very beautiful. It's going to be totally different. At first I thought it was rather cruel that the others would not go at the same time. They would be left behind.*

R: It isn't like that at all. It is not like you having to leave; bodies, like what the child has experienced, is experiencing, the elongation of emotion of leaving a physical family. What he has actually left is a physical family of the dimension of which he has come. He misses the love. He also realizes that he cannot go back to that. He has been coming back and forth for many millennia, to understand how the planet works. On this occasion he has chosen, or he has been given the choice, to come and work with the planet. To transduce and draw back the flock. If we are to put this into a proportment of thought process, this child is the disciple of new knowledge. This child is to be adorned with regards to the information that has been given by this voice. The child does not work within karma. He has stepped away from the energetic frequencies of the spiral of karmic frequency and third and fourth dimensions.

D: *Because you know with karma you can become trapped in the earthly frequency.*

R: You are talking to a non-karmic influential purpose at this point. Remove all thinking levels from that. Take yourself above.

D: *So he's here just to serve this purpose. And then he will go back to the dimension he came from.*

R: That is correct. He will live a normal human life. And during that human life, he will carry out his purpose, *but* he does have influences. He can be drawn into a three dimensional purpose.

D: *Yes, it's very difficult to live in this world, and not be drawn into that.*

R: And if he is drawn into a three dimensional purpose, he is drawn back out again.

D: *Because this is how karma is created. We're here to learn lessons.*

R: (He interrupted.) We are getting irritated with this subject. Karma is not reflected with this influence here at this point. We will not be rude to you. Can we further this information elsewhere, please?

D: *All right. I just wanted to clarify it for his benefit, because he was concerned with it.*

R: Clarified accepted. The child knows all the answers.

D: *But his conscious mind doesn't. We're trying to relay it to the conscious mind.*

R: Thank you for working with his conscious mind. You would do better to work with information you require. The child has all the answers. You have no need to ask these questions. All the questions that he has been asking, he has the information to those. You will work of the same place. You have been told you will work with these people. That will eventually occur for you. That needs to be occurred. That needs to be waited for. It will occur in time.

D: *The other people I've worked with who are what we call "star-children", or the ones that are coming in, do not have as much difficulty as Robert is having.*

R: We are reexpressing old information, but I will reexplain this: (He seemed aggravated) at this point in time, the transitional period between love frequency and man thought format energy experience, is elongated by a pain. The point at which there is a transitional point, where man can move from pain learned evolutionary experience, through to love learned evolutionary experience needs to be elongated by exemplars. Needs to be shown the point of moving and tipping from one point to the other. The only way one can do this is by getting to that point. And learning to move from the utmost point of the spiral to the next elongation of expression. So therefore, the disciples that come through need to understand where that point is. The stepoff point. The point where you meet on the bridge. The point where you understand that it is time to love. (Deliberately) Is this making clarification sense?

D: *Yes. I believe the other ones I've spoken to, probably are not of the same frequency. But they have also volunteered to come and help the world.*

R: They are working on the level frequencies that are moving towards this point. This does not mean this energy frequency is any higher or lower. They are part of the stepping stone. They are part of the steps up to the point at the top of the pyramid. The top of the pyramid being the point where the child is then ready to reportalize itself. The elongation of existent spiritual stretching of mind will be at the point where they will be allowed to elongate themselves back to the purpose from whence they came. Then search for another experience when the flock has regathered itself.

D: *But you know how difficult this is going to be for the ordinary person to understand.*

R: The ordinary human has time on his hands, but time is speeding up. So therefore this elongation is speeding up. So therefore expectance is speeding up. So therefore DNA restructuring is speeding up. So therefore vibration frequency is speeding up. Everything is speeding up. So pain will also speed up, and be stretched to a point. Pain again, is not only pain with regards to blood. It is also pain with regards to every evolutional purpose planned. Man's endurance of evolution and evolving.

D: *I have been told that we are working out much more karma more quickly, because we're trying to adjust to these frequencies and leave.*

R: That is correct. We are downloading present information, energy thought formats, that have been with us for many millennia. There is a point now where people are being allowed to download, clear out, and are being allowed to step *out* of the karmic cycle. The moment they can step out of the influence of the karmic cycle, they can then work with the spiral of information that is allowing them to step out, and off, and back to the frequency from which they have come. Simplistic terms of explanation. Not easy to work with. Will work with. And will work.

He sounded aggravated because he had to explain it simply and put it into words that I could understand, but it was finally making a little bit more sense.

D: *I've been told that many of these things are very difficult for our minds to comprehend. That's why we've not been given the information before.*

R: Accepted.

D: *That the physical human mind just does not have the capacity.*

R: That's correct.

D: *So I've always been told to present the information in a way people can understand.*

R: That is correct. And you are.

D: *But the information you are giving is much more complicated.*

R: That is correct, because you are asking for the answers.

D: *But I think it will still be difficult for some people to grasp it. That's the problem.*

R: The people, at this point in time, *will* grasp it. Because their evolutionary purpose, their bodily energy frequency will allow this purpose to be accepted. This is the point we are making. We have sent seven disciples now to this planet. Two elongate, two stretch. There is going to be a three, and there will be a four. They will all meet at some point. But the three will not know the four, and the four will not know the three. The first to have met one has occurred. The first of the three are at the point of possibly meeting.

D: *But they will never meet the other four.*

R: That is correct.

D: *They will be working in different areas?*

R: That is correct.

D: *But I will come across some of these?*

R: You will. And as and when you come across them, you must not mention one to the other, in a physical sense. You can talk subliminally, but you *must* not talk on a physical sense. It will interfere with the energies. Because they are carrying the same energies, but they are using different formulas. Bearing in mind, the ethnic breeding is different. They carry different energies. So therefore southern and eastern and western and northern hemisphere energies are not totally conducive with each other on the planet. So therefore you must not mention.

D: *So they will be different races and cultures.*

R: Different cultures would be better as opposed to races. They may well speak the same language, but the cultural bridges will be different.

D: *But when I meet them, I will know it?*

R: You will.

D: *Will I know it this way, within trance?*

R: You will know it immediately.

D: *Because this is where I'm usually given my information.*

R: Absolutely correct. Therefore, you will know immediately when you meet one of the others. You will know subliminally before it even occurs.

D: *And I'm not to network them. They're not to be put in contact with each other.*

R: That is correct. Unless you are told.

D: *I've been told that same thing about other information. I have found people working on the same inventions. And I was told not to let them know of each other at this point.*

R: That is correct. Energies interfere with energies. What you have, is a connection via a subliminal thought form process, that is connected via one spiral of energy. If you connect one to the other, you can fuse the two together and dilute the information. You know exactly what is being said, so therefore dilution would not be conducive to the thought format collectional purpose behind the energy. So therefore, introducing one to the other doing the same work, would confuse. Bearing in mind, as and when an invention is ready to occur, it needs to occur in many different avenues. So therefore, the energy is ready on a subliminal level. So when the *conscious* acceptance comes, the subliminal is already there. So it sits well.

D: *I met a man in California, and then across the world in Australia, I met another man working on the same invention. And I was told in this state, that it would be like two waves in the ocean moving on their own, but if they were to merge together it would be just one wave, and it would lose its – what? – its energy or its potency.*

R: That is correct. That is a fine analogy with regards to your three dimensional terms. You will also, very shortly, if you are not already, work with *total sound* resonance.

D: *I have met people that are working with the medical profession who are trying to introduce natural healing.*

R: You will elongate your mind to this thought further. You are now having a proportment of energy transduced to you at this point in time. You will be able to write about this. It will work with you soon.

D: *I've had other clients telling me they're wanting to work with sound and color. This will be the new healing.*

R: Color comes before sound.

D: Before *sound.*

R: Color comes before sound. Color resonances sound. And that resonates energy. Then that resonates thought format frequency. Color comes first. The spectrum of color resonates sound. The spectrum of sound resonates color.

D: *So it works together.*

R: Works in total elongation and stretching. What we are *not* working at this point in time, is understanding that each figment, elemental frequency of the physical body, resonates at a certain sound level. The DNA, the cellular structure, all works with sound resonances. This is why we are being programmed with total new DNA structure. So therefore, sound resonances can be protected and projected to the human thought format. So therefore, we will be able to accept new frequencies. And these are being transduced via sound. Via crop circling sounds, via imprintments, via meeting intonations, via sound frequencies. These are all intonations of sound and color. And they are coming in a far thicker, more affluent sense at this time. We are also being given the *element* of introduction of knowledge on a three dimensional level. How to understand and work with this. So therefore human diseases can be manifested and created into a more positive format, rather than living and dying with these diseases, and learning what energies these diseases carry. Diseases are information. But if the body doesn't have the information from this disease, the body creates the demise. It is a very interesting format to think that actually a disease is an energy of importance, not an energy of negativity.

D: *I was also told that the body will become more resistant to the different diseases.*

R: The body will become resistant to different diseases, only if the thought format creational purpose behind the body is ready to become resistant. If the thought format creational purpose within the body is that of total three dimensionalism, then the diseases will act out its normal course. Unless an introduction of new levels are created.

D: *I was told that they're trying to make the body more resistant, and also increase the life span.*

R: This is totally correct.

D: *Because we are going into a totally different dimension, frequency, than we've ever done before.*

R: That is correct. We have *never ever*, in a human frame of understanding, moved a bit further from this point in time. This is the first. You do not realize the importance of this new level of work. This is the first time this has been introduced to planet Earth on these levels.

D: *Is that why I've been told that the entire universe is watching, to see what will happen?*

R: That is correct.

D: *But first we must get through this present time.*

R: That is correct.

D: *That is why it's called the "Time of Troubles".* (So-called by Nostradamus in my books of his predictions.)

R: The Time of Troubles is basically the world's karma coming to the point where it is transducing itself. The world is a living, breathing entity, as well as all that creates itself within the world. The humanity is just a flea on the ointment of the world. We are all *part* of the transitionalization, the purpose. A whole new energy that will be elongated to the planetary system. Many of the planets are here helping. They are not here enforcing and policing. They are here helping.

D: I believe that, because I've been told that by many others. And I also know about the planet being a living entity, because these are concepts I've also been given. So you are reinforcing some of the same information.

R: Absolutely correct. There is so much more to come to you. You are deserving of so much, because of the work you have carried out. The blessings that you will be given are blessings of total love.

D: Then is it permissible if I use this information we have been given today?

R: Absolutely. This information is of the populace. It is not information of the individual. And Robert will understand that the pains are pains of the work that he has chosen to carry out. These pains, once understood, will be acceptable, endurable. The work he must do has been behind the pains. And the pains behind the work he must do. They are all part of the commitment. They are all part of the procreational purpose behind the job, and the energy the child has chosen to work with. It can never be interfered with. He has been told this. There is also another purpose that needs to be elongated to you at this point in time, because you are now about to come across this.

D: What is that?

R: You have been given information this evening with regards to a whole new format of transitionalization of human beings. This being the purpose behind some human beings who will be totally different to that which you are used to. What is actually occurring at this point in time, there are human beings that are actually here on a physical level, but they are carrying a soul impregnation that can never be read. This child that sits here today cannot be read on a psychic level, on a dowsing level, on any level the child cannot be read. Because we well know on this planet, once read you can be tuned into and interfered with. That level frequency has been removed. He cannot be read. So if you read into him on an intuitive level, you will get a different environmental purpose behind. *You* will not personally,

Dolores, because you're a level of evolution purpose. Your light body level is that of beauty and love. Those that are not enduring on that level, will not be able to tune into *he*, and many others like he, that work with this. You will now begin to understand that there are two differentials here. There are those who can be tuned into, and those that cannot.

D: *It's a form of protection.*

R: That is correct. A subliminal protection that has been ordained. So therefore, what is actually occurring is that this child is not involved in karmic evolutional process.

D: *That's important that he is protected.*

R: That is important. He has been protected. It is also a learned experience process for you this evening, because I believe you will start experiencing more of this purpose, because you have invited this energy to you. And the energy has invited itself.

D: *And I will find more people of this type.*

R: Yes, you will. Do not be bemused.

As we were coming to the end of the session I then thanked the entity for the information and asked it to recede. He responded in the clip-clop sounds. Robert was then reoriented and brought back to full consciousness.

An interesting case of a handsome young man who made cabinets for a living. In his conscious state, there was absolutely no indication of what lay just beneath the surface of his personality.

Of course, many of the things he said were confusing and disorienting because they were difficult to understand and comprehend. Mostly because of the way the entity used the English language. But one of them did come true. He said that there were seven disciples located around the world. These were special people who were sent to this world. They were vibrating at a different frequency, they were not bound by karma and had a specific purpose. He said I had just met one of the seven, and that I would meet another. They would be living in

270

different countries and have different cultural backgrounds. The main admonishment was that I not put them in touch with each other. Amazingly and unexpectedly this occurred a few weeks later, after I returned to the States. I met another disciple while conducting my hypnosis class in Fayetteville, Arkansas. I have no idea whether I will be allowed to meet all seven, or if I was just to know that they existed. Maybe that knowledge would be enough. But he was correct, they are located on different continents, and have different cultural backgrounds.

I have met many people who, through trance, and unknown to their conscious minds, reported they had come to Earth at this time to help mankind with the progression through the coming changes. But apparently these seven are of an even different vibration and on a different assignment.

CHAPTER 14

ADVANCED BEINGS

This session was a perfect example that "they" were continuing to come through many of my clients, often under unusual and unexpected circumstances. This case was certainly unexpected. I had returned from England only a few weeks before. There while doing a session with Robert at Glastonbury, "they" said that I had met one of the special people that had volunteered or were sent to help with the changes going on in the world today. They said there were seven of these special people or disciples, and I had met one of them when I worked with Robert. And that I would meet another one soon. But I was warned not to put them in touch with each other. They were to continue on their own paths, even if they were physically located a world apart. Little did I know that I would discover the second one only a few weeks later under far from normal circumstances.

"They" had been warning me throughout 2002, that I was traveling too much doing lectures at conferences and Expos. At the height of my work during 2001 and 2002, I was on an airplane every week speaking in all parts of the world. It was not unusual for me to go to two or three different cities in a week before returning home, only to start out again. I was beginning to feel the stress, so I knew they were correct. They said I did not need to travel as much as I had been in the past. That my books could stand on their own now. The energy was out there and it would escalate. They wanted me to write more, and to teach my hypnosis technique more. They said it was to become the therapy of the future. I said I would still have to travel in order to teach, but they said, "Let them come to you." And amazingly, that is what happened. I began holding my classes in the neighboring city of Fayetteville, Arkansas, and people have been coming from all over the world to learn the technique.

The middle of August 2002, I was conducting another of my hypnosis training classes in the nearby city. I keep my classes small so there will be more interaction and personal involvement, to make it easier to understand my technique. I had not done many classes, so I was still working out the procedure of how to conduct them. In the earlier classes, I had the students (who were already qualified hypnotists) practice on each other on the last day. At this class, I decided to try something different, because even though I had taught my technique, they had not had enough time to study it. They would need to do this when they returned to their own practices. In the past, the effects were stilted because it was unfamiliar to them. So at the end of the second day of training, I discussed this with the class. They all decided they would rather see me do a demonstration on one of the students, so they could observe. They thought this would be more effective. Of course, that always puts the teacher on the spot. Although I have a great deal of success with my technique, this would be under different circumstances, a goldfish bowl type of atmosphere. What if, because of the environment of everyone watching, the subject became nervous and self-conscious and resisted going into trance? I would have to work harder if that happened, so I was worried about whether it would work. Several people wanted to volunteer to be the guinea pig. The solution was to have them all put their names into a box, and I would pick the one to do the demonstration on the next morning. I rummaged through the names, and one piece of paper seemed to fly up and stick to my hand. It was Estelle.

She was a last minute student. I will not tell where she came from for reasons that will become evident. I was giving a lecture at a conference, and two people wanted to take my class the next week. I already had the set number that I wanted for the class, so I didn't know if there would be room. When I called my office I found that two people had cancelled at the last minute, so I told Estelle there was room if she was interested. Because she had decided to come at the last minute, she had to pay more for her airplane ticket. At first, she was hesitant about coming, but decided the opportunity had been presented for a reason, and that it was worth the expense. She was also surprised at how easily her boss agreed to give her a few days off from work. She said later that she had wanted a session very badly, so she was not surprised that her name was chosen.

One of the students had a room in the hotel that was more like a suite, so we decided the next morning we would meet first at the classroom, and then go to her room. Some of the men carried extra chairs, and the room was very crowded. There were ten students, my assistant and myself, which meant twelve people gathered in the small hotel room. During the night, I had extra worries because Estelle had an accent, and I sometimes have trouble understanding accents when the client is in trance. When they are in a deep state, their voice becomes soft and slurred. I really had problems when I conducted sessions in Hong Kong and Singapore, but I eventually grew accustomed to the different accent. All of these things went through my mind as we got ready to start. I needn't have worried, because "they" were way ahead of me and were going to handle everything.

The room was very crowded with students sitting on the sofa, on all available chairs and on the floor. Estelle was on the double bed, and I told everyone to be as quiet as possible as I began. I was not aware that strange things were already happening until the session was over, but "they" had already taken over. Since I normally do not tape the induction, the microphone was lying on the bedside table next to the recorder. I use a hand mike, because I hold it right next to the client's mouth. Their voice can become very soft during deep trance, and this way I am sure of catching the words on the tape recorder. Other people use lapel mikes, but this is the way I have always recorded my sessions. This type of mike can be controlled by pushing a button on it, so the recorder would not start until I pick up the mike and turn it on. More about this later.

I began the induction and she went down immediately. So

my first fear was unjustified. She paid no attention to the number of people in the room. They did not cause any distraction. In my technique, I usually have the subject picture a place that I call a beautiful place, a place where there is no worry or problems. I let them pick the place they consider to be the most beautiful, peaceful place. From there the rest of the technique takes them into a past life, which was the objective of the demonstration. But Estelle did not wait for me to complete the entire induction. This sometimes happens, and I am so used to doing this that I recognize it because of their description of the beautiful place. It did not sound like the normal perfect place. In fact, it did not even sound Earthly.

E: It's a place where there are many exotic flowers and different colors. The wind blows. I feel the breeze. There are many crystals there. Many generators. Birds flying, I can see their different colors.

This was when I realized she was not talking about Earth. She had jumped ahead of me, and was already experiencing *something, somewhere.* I grabbed the microphone from the table and switched the tape recorder on. The atmosphere in the crowded room was tense. No one made a sound, but everyone instinctively knew that something unusual was already occurring. Especially since I was not even allowed to complete the entire induction that I had been teaching them. It was unnecessary.

D: *What do you mean by crystals and generators?*
E: Large crystals coming from the ground. And they're tall, like three or four feet tall. They have a point at the top.
D: *Why did you call them generators?*
E: They generate energy.
D: *Is there anything else around?*
E: The coloring on the floor. The coloring's green, but it's not grass as we know grass. It's something similar to grass. Yet it's green and it covers the ground.

275

D: *And these crystals come out of that?*
E: Yes, and they're placed strategically to generate the energy in that area.
D: *What area is this?*
E: It's a place far away. I want to say ... another galaxy?
D: *Are there any buildings?*
E: No. It's like a set area specifically to go there to energize and at the same time relax and feel at peace.
D: *So it's a place that people don't live all the time, you mean?*
E: Right.
D: *It's like going to a vacation spot? You go there to specifically be energized and relax.*
E: That is correct.
D: *Who are the ones that go there to be energized?*
E: You have all different types of beings going there.

This was apparently why she unconsciously chose this spot as her beautiful place. Some people see places where they remember spending a vacation, that was very special to them.

E: As soon as they become aware of it they can project themselves there.
D: *Oh, they project without going in a craft?*
E: That is correct. Anyone can project themselves there if they connect with the place or they become aware of it. You stay for awhile, not too long. Enough to feel the energy, and get the sense of peace and tranquility, so that you can come back to wherever you were. And continue with whatever it was you were doing.
D: *Do you go there in a physical body?*
E: You can go there in a physical body or you can project your energy there.
D: *When you're there, do you appear in your physical ... like a form of some kind?*
E: Some beings do. They can appear in their form. It's a place where everyone is welcome.
D: *And you go there often?*

E: Yes. I enjoy the place very much. It gives me a sense of tranquility and awareness.

D: *And then you must go back to where you do your work?*

E: That is correct.

D: *When you return from this beautiful place, and project back to where you do your work, what is that place like?*

E: The work is done simultaneously on the Earth plane. And the work is also done in a far away place, on what you would call a base. It is done in many galaxies, many dimensions. But the home base right now is Earth.

D: *So you're doing both at the same time, you mean?*

E: That is correct.

D: *When you're doing it on the Earth plane, what does that place look like?*

E: It's a place where you interact with many beings also as you do in that sacred space. You recognize many others by looking at their eyes. You recognize them by connecting with their energies. And in spite of all the masks that they wear, you become aware of who they are. You look deep within them and you recognize their energies.

D: *Is this something that the average person wouldn't know?*

E: Many know of this. And many others are aware of it, but not on a conscious level.

D: *When you're working on the Earth plane, what does your body look like?*

E: When I work on the earth plane my body looks like most people. It takes on a human form. But it is like a mask that I wear. I project it out so the others will see what they're used to seeing.

D: *The regular physical form.*

E: That is correct.

D: *Is this the mask of Estelle?*

E: That is correct.

It was interesting to me to find the definition of person/personality is *mask*. Taken from the Latin: persona. Literally: an actor's mask, hence a person.

D: *That is the mask you wear at the present time on Earth doing your work.* (Yes.) *It's a very good mask, it's a nice one. And this is what other people see.*

E: That is what they see.

Robert also said that what people perceived as his physical form was only an illusion. Although both of these people certainly appeared solid and human to me.

D: *What do you look like without the mask?*

E: Without the mask, I also have physical form surrounded with a light. It is physical form that has shape, that has substance. But within that physical form, on the outer edges, there is also energy and light.

D: *I've been told that the basic form of everyone is light.*

E: That is correct. That's how others would see it. But if they look a little bit deeper within, they will see that it has another form physically, as you would call physically. For it has the form of where it came from. And the place that it came from, there was form, but it was different.

D: *What was that form like?*

E: It would be called on Earth "reptilian" form. I must say that there are many degrees of reptilian form.

D: *This is where you are existing simultaneously, you mean?*

E: That is correct.

D: *So you have a reptilian form on another place? And the Earth form on this place? Am I understanding correctly?*

E: There is a part of the energy that is there in that other place, but the present experience is being experienced now in this physical Earth plane.

I have heard so many unusual things in my work that this statement did not bother me. I always just continue to ask questions, because anything is possible in this type of work. But I looked around the room to see how this statement was affecting my students. They were absolutely still, and their attention was glued upon the woman lying motionless on the bed. Here a pretty middle-aged dark-haired woman was saying she was also living a simultaneous life as a reptilian on another planet. And it was not upsetting or startling them at all. Maybe they had read enough of my books to know that anything is possible with this type of hypnosis, but it was unusual for me to have others observe this. After it was over and we were going to lunch, one of the men students told me it was the most remarkable thing he had ever seen. In this case, actions really did speak louder than words. The demonstration taught them more than the class. It is one thing to tell them how it is done, and quite another to show them. Book learning versus hands-on.

I continued, "What is it like in the other place?"

E: In the other place, we observe the other galaxies to make sure everything is in order, that no one is doing and causing harm to others. And there we observe and keep track of all that is going on.

D: *That sounds like a very big job. To observe everything.*

E: It is big, but we are trained for it. And it is something that once you are trained, it becomes second nature. The way everything becomes when you are trained, no matter where you are.

D: *It would be a big job to observe everything. Do you use machines to do this?*

E: You do it with your mind.

D: *That would mean you have a great mind capacity, wouldn't you?*

E: Yes, we do, we project the mind to places. Everyone has certain areas that they are specifically connected to, but at any given time they can project themselves to other places. Humans have not developed that capability yet.

D: *Did you say this is like a home base?*

E: Yes, you would call it a home base.

D: *Like a headquarters?*

E: Like a station.

D: *Is it a craft or is it a planet?*

E: It is not a craft, and it is not a planet as you would perceive a planet. It is more of ... a place, a station.

D: *I'm thinking of a physical place of some kind.*

E: It's like ... an enclosure ... in an open .... If you could imagine the sky, let's say for instance. And in this sky, there is this enclosure, within itself, that monitors the different places around it. That's what this would be.

D: *I'm thinking of the spirit world where we go after we leave the physical body. Is it like that or different?*

E: This is different, for this is not a spiritual world. This is a physical place. This is a place where there is what you would call physical form. Not physical as humans take, but a form beings from other places within would take in order to be able to survive and live.

D: *Is it like another dimension?*

E: It would be more like a different galaxy.

D: *Where you all are creating this place just in space, so to speak?*

E: Yes, it's as if the place was created because it serves a particular function. And that is where we exist.

D: *So does it take the combined mind power of everyone to keep it in existence?*

E: No. Once it is brought into being, it stays in being. For it has a specific purpose and it's a continuous purpose.

D: *So it exists whether you or the others are there or not.*

E: That is correct.

This sounded similar to the case where the caveman-like being existed on the world with the purple sun. His subconscious said it was not a planet, but a galaxy operating under a different set of rules that we could not understand. Those beings also created everything they needed with their minds. (See Chapter 18)

D: *And it's more like the headquarters, the main base, so to speak, the station where the monitoring is done of all the worlds.*

E: That is correct.

D: *It seems like a very powerful place. How is this information stored if you gather it with your own mind?*

E: It is not stored as you would store in a computer, for that is obsolete. But yet it is stored as you would think of storing it on a disk. But it is more of a miniature, tiny little disk that stores millions and millions of pieces of information.

D: *Hmm, that would make our computers obsolete. And how is this information read if it is just a tiny disk.*

E: It is read with the mind. When you hold it in your hand, you receive all the information.

D: *That you're looking for?* (Yes.) *Otherwise, it would be a bombardment of information, wouldn't it?*

E: That is correct, you do not want to keep excess information in the mind, for that is not necessary.

Another unusual phenomenon that occurred shortly after the session began, was that Estelle lost her accent once we entered this other world. The being that was speaking through her had a very precise, exact way of speaking and pronouncing the words. Of course, this made it easier for me. I didn't have to listen so closely. It was obvious to everyone in the room that this was not Estelle speaking.

D: *I don't want to insult you, I don't want to offend you, but in our time period some people have the impression that the reptilian race is negative.*

E: That is because there are many who still are negative. You must understand, that in everything, there is a balance. There is that balance here on this place. There is that balance everywhere. And particularly on the Earth plane, when others come to exist, you will find that duality more than in those other places. So therefore, as far as the reptilians, there are many here on the Earth who carry that energy. And because they carry that negative energy – to give it that word, it is more of a misguided forgotten energy of the true self. They will do things that, yes, will be seen as negative.

D: *But this is not the true nature of your people.*

281

E: Not in the future, as you would – for lack of a better word – call the future.

D: *Is that where you're speaking from?*

E: That is correct.

D: *You know you're speaking through a vehicle, the one you said lived in the Earth plane. One of the questions she wondered about was: is she existing simultaneously in the future?*

E: I speak from the future. But I also speak from what you would call the present. I speak simultaneously from both places. For I am one.

D: *So, in this future life, you are on this station accessing and compiling information. Why then did you decide to also exist in our time period in the 21st century?*

E: Because of what was happening here, and what is happening here with the reptilian race. There are many who are in a place of power and position who are misusing that power to control and manipulate. And I was asked to come here to assist, to enlighten and to let others know what is going on. For a few cannot control the whole. And because the whole is not aware, they are allowing a few to control and manipulate.

D: *So you chose to come back simultaneously as you're existing there, to have part of your energy, or whatever, enter a physical body?*

E: (Sigh) I did not enter a physical body. I shape-shifted into a physical body. But in order to have my energies here to resonate with the planet's energy, which is dense, to be able to survive in this dense energy, I needed to be born through a physical being. But the people that I chose to come through, one, the father is also reptilian. He has always been reptilian. In all his existence, he has chosen not to experience anything but that. And for this Earth experience, he chose to become a vehicle to allow my energy to come through. The one who is my physical mother only carried me for nine months, as time is perceived. Much work and preparation was done so she could hold my energy, for she was not able to. So she had to be prepared in order that I could stay in that space and then be born and be, more or less, grounded.

D: *But the body was genetically formed from the DNA from the mother and father, wasn't it?*

E: (Heavy sigh) It is a different process that is not totally understood by humans. That is why it looks human. But if work were to be done to find out the true make up, the genetic make up, they would find that there are things that are different.

D: *If someone were to examine the DNA or the genes of the one known as Estelle?*

E: That is correct. That is why the physical body does not get ill. For the physical body cannot be subjected to probes and tests.

D: *That's why you don't want doctors to examine the body?*

E: That is correct. They will find something different and then they will want to explore. And that will not be allowed. So she is not allowed to get sick. As far as she and I—I say she and I to distinguish when she is communicating, and when I am communicating, even though we are the same. She sometimes does not allow the information to come through.

D: *Why is that?*

E: She has not made total peace with her whole experience on the Earth plane.

D: *But you know it is difficult for a human to understand this.*

E: It has been difficult for me to see myself on this planet Earth.

D: *(Laugh) It is different, isn't it?*

E: It's very different.

D: *Because you've evolved beyond that.*

E: That is correct. I have had many lifetimes, or I should say, my *spirit* has had many lifetimes on the Earth plane. It was a surprise to me when I was chosen to come back and have an experience again here.

D: *You thought you were finished, didn't you?*

E: That is correct.

D: *(Laugh) It was time to move on somewhere else.*

E: That is correct.

D: *Then they said you had to go back. It's almost like going back to kindergarten, isn't it?*

E: That is correct, and I felt a great responsibility in having to come back knowing the circumstances of what was to be. I felt alone.

D: *Is it because there are not many of your own kind here?*

E: That is correct. And I knew the many I would be encountering, would be of the type that was working with their energies to cause harm and to cause control. That was the reason why, as a three year old, I had the experience that I had. Because that was necessary to help the physical body forget who it was, and where it was coming from and what it needed to do. For, if it had started at that early age to say the things that would be necessary to say, it would have been eliminated.

That statement was an unexpected surprise.

D: *Do you think so? Or would they think it was just a strange child?*

E: That is correct. There were many who were trying to find the energy, but the energy was camouflaged in a child.

D: *So they wouldn't just think it was childish talking. They might recognize you?*

E: That is correct. For we are not talking just of physical beings. We are also working with the different energies, whether they are perceived as physical or not.

D: *So it was a safeguard?*

E: That is correct. It was a safeguard to protect the being from speaking. It was not the time.

D: *What happened when she was three years old, because that was one of the questions she wanted to know about?*

E: When she was three years old, she was taken aboard a craft. Her memory of that is correct. As she looked around and saw where she was, she knew she was not in harm. But it was a surprise to her physical being to find herself there and not know it. Through all existences, we have been aware when we communicate and in what form. At the time, there was a veil that was put so no memories would come of what was to come. As a three year old, the experience is that of how you react.

D: *So up until she was three years old, she had the memory of who she was and where she came from?*

E: That is correct.

D: *But she was not able to express it yet?*

E: There were no words to express.

D: *She didn't have the vocabulary. That would make sense.*

E: That is correct. So therefore she felt isolated. And yet, she was able to communicate with us and with many others. At the time of being three years old, the veil was lifted and she saw a little bit more, but she could not express then, so the memory had to be put into a place until it was appropriate. The connection was still done, but now it was done more on a psychic level than on a physical level.

D: *And for her own safety, you put the veil around her when she was on the craft to ... what? Deaden or soften those memories?*

E: To more or less ... deaden the memories, that would be a good word.

D: *So she could function as a child without causing undue attention.*

E: Yes. And yet as a child she felt isolated, because she could not relate to anything that was going on around her.

D: *I've found many people who feel they have come from other places. They're very lonely here. But how was the veil placed when she was on board the craft? What happened at that time?*

E: She was so caught up in feeling the betrayal of not knowing that this was going on, that it created at the time, a period of indifference of not wanting to communicate anymore.

D: *But, did the people on the craft do something physically to her to create this blinder, this veil?*

E: Energetically, a box was placed within her being, that allowed constant communication. An exchange of information, but not on a conscious level. Where before, it was done on a conscious level.

D: *What do you mean by a box?*

285

E: It was more of, I do not want to use the word "implant" per se, for that has a negative connotation, but actually it was like ... what would you call .... (She had difficulty.)

D: *Well, to me an implant is not negative, because I understand them.*

E: It was more, let's say... like a panel.

I had heard about implants many times and I understood their purposes. This is explained in *The Custodians*. But I had never heard about a panel being put into anyone.

E: A panel with depth inside of it. Inside where ... the so called "box" had little chips. The same as the ones at the control stations.

D: *Oh, little electronic parts.*

E: Yes. Which, by the way, is also part of her physical make up. Within her physical make up there are – what would I call it – the only word that comes to mind would be like wires.

D: *These wires are inside her physical body.* (Yes.) *Why are they there?*

E: Because she is always connected to everything out there. It is also part of her genetic make up as a reptilian. And therefore, in shape shifting, to look human, she retained all of that within the appearance of the physical body.

D: *Then if a doctor were to examine her, would he find these strange things?*

E: He would find different things going on inside. He would find that the energy would flow in different ways than he was used to and that's where the desire to investigate more would come in.

D: *Hmm, so we can't have that, can we.*

E: No, we cannot.

D: *Because they wouldn't understand. The same way you thought she would be in danger at age three if they knew what was going on.* (Yes.) *But, is it all right for us to know this?*

E: It is all right for you to know, for you were collectively as a group. There are many things that you will be doing together collectively to assist the all.

D: *So you know that she is not in danger from us.*

E: No, she trusts everyone here. Or, I should say, *we* trust everyone here. They are connected.

D: *You would not have allowed the information to come through if you didn't trust us, would you?*

E: That is correct.

D: *Because I would never place the vehicle in any kind of danger.*

E: That is correct.

D: *So the ones that are here, are the ones that were chosen to know this information.*

E: That is why we waited until the last moment to be part of the group. For as you are aware, there wasn't space at the beginning.

D: *That's true, she was the last one to come in.*

E: We had to be sure that the energies that were going to be present, would be compatible to revealing these things.

D: *And it was no accident that I chose her name then.*

E: Yes, she knew when she put her name in the box that she was going to be picked, and her friend that was sitting next to her also knew it. So it was confirmation for the both of them when it happened.

D: *So, this information would not have been allowed to come through at all if you had not trusted everyone in the room to protect her. Because we do not want this to become public knowledge. It would harm her, wouldn't it?*

E: That is correct.

D: *So I think everyone here will keep it confidential.*

I looked around the room at the students as I said that, and they all nodded affirmation. I knew they understood the gravity of protecting her identity, and the special thing that had just occurred when they were all allowed to be privy to this strange information. I also had the feeling if they did not honor this commitment of privacy and protection for Estelle, that "they" would know. I don't know what would happen if this promise was violated, but I have worked with them long enough to know that I have to listen to them, and do as they say. If I did not follow their instructions, the interchange of information would be stopped. I don't know what would happen to the others, but I think they realized the seriousness of the situation. Later they might question what really occurred on this morning, but when it was happening, it was all too real. I was accustomed to communicating with these type of entities over many years, and I knew it was very unusual for them to allow this type of information to come forth in front of so many witnesses. Maybe this was also intended to show the students graphically, what could happen when using my technique of hypnosis, so they would not be startled if it happened during their sessions. A demonstration is worth a thousand words.

E: We will be watching. If they wish to share some of the experience, it is allowed, but just do not use the name or the location where the information can be found.

D: *That's true. I work with many people like this and I'm always told to protect them.*

This is the reason why her real name, location, and ethnic background are not revealed here.

I was curious about the panel that she said was located in her body, because this sounded different from the implants that I was very familiar with. "Where is that located in her head?"

E: It is located in the back of her head.

D: *As I understand, it would be very, very tiny, wouldn't it?*

E: Actually, no. This particular one covers the whole back of her head, the bottom part. There was too much information that needed to be received and transferred from one place to the other. So that's why it was designed in that way.

D: *Hmm, so it's larger than the ones I'm familiar with. Is it of a physical substance, or is it an etheric type thing?*

E: It was both. First it was etheric and then it became of a physical thing so that others could feel it and become aware of it. And therefore, in becoming aware of it, they became

288

more aware of who she is, who we are and share that knowledge.

D: *Could this be picked up by X-ray if someone were to examine her?*

E: That's where it was protected by a shield of energy that would only be picked up by those who were allowed to pick it up.

D: *That's another reason why she can't get sick. You don't want examinations.*

E: That is correct.

D: *You are also protecting her against having any type of accidents?*

E: Yes. The only time that she had to be examined – and it wasn't so much – was when she had her children. Unfortunately for the physical body, because of the way that it is, it could not have children in a natural way. So, what was called a Cesarean had to be done to take the child out.

D: *So the body was not designed in a way that could have children normally.*

E: That is correct, the body never went through what you would call "labor".

D: *But the doctors wouldn't have noticed anything unusual in the body?*

E: That is correct, for when she went in for the surgery, it was over and done with, and there was no reason to check anything else.

D: *What about before she had a child? They usually run many tests while you're pregnant.*

E: No tests were done, for she was healthy. They just made sure that her diet was properly kept and that was all. As far as the diet, she usually does not eat or need much of the food that is eaten on this physical plane. Her tastes in food are very simple. She will not take in much of the foods that are eaten, especially too highly processed foods. For it will make the appearance of the physical body more dense, and she and us will not feel well at all.

D: *Then by eating some of the heavier foods, the body becomes denser. And this would make it harder for the other part to come in and maintain control?*

E: That is correct.

D: *Why is she being allowed to know these things now?*

E: Because it is time to awaken and educate. Because the more you know the more you can share with others. What we are facing now on the physical Earth plane is a battle, but it is not a battle as others would perceive. It does not have to do with battle in the physical form. Even though battles are fought, the battles that are going on now are about the dark with the light. And the light will need to come together to be spread so that these who are controlling can be stopped.

D: *This is part of her work?*

E: That is correct.

D: *Are there many of you that have come back into the physical on Earth?*

E: As far as my kind, there are just a few, but there are also many different kinds who are here to assist in the same way.

D: *Because I've been told of many different types of beings that are coming back. And some of them are souls that have just existed on other planets that have volunteered to come into a physical body on Earth to help at this time.*

E: That is correct. You have many now at this time that have taken a physical existence, but yet their spirit of who they truly are is connected to many other things. And the information has been given to them so they can fully awaken to all that they are. To become aware that this is an experience, yes, but there is much work to do.

D: *Some of the ones I work with have difficulty sometimes adjusting to the Earth plane.*

E: That is correct, because the more aware you are of where you come from, the more difficult it is to exist in a planet that is so dense, because of the negativity that is found here. Even though the negativity that is found here serves well to assist others to move forward.

D: *That's what they've told me, that the world is so violent and there is so much negativity, they don't want to be here. Because it's not like where they came from.*

E: But yet, they will stay here, for that is what they chose to do.

D: *But some of them have so much difficulty they're trying to commit suicide and leave.*

E: As we are aware, this is a planet of free will.

D: *That's true. And the cases I've worked with were miraculously kept from doing this.*

E: The help is always received when it is needed, if it is asked for.

D: *And now that they realize what they're here for, they've said they'll stay even though they don't like this world.*

E: That is correct.

D: *But let me ask you, I have noticed different waves of people coming in. The ones from Estelle's generation seem to have had more difficulty adjusting than the new ones that are coming in now.*

E: That is because the ones that are coming in now have more awareness of who they truly are. The children need to be nurtured. The children need to be understood that just because they are in a small little child's body, they are not ignorant. They are more advanced than most humans who are now here.

D: *That's why I'm going to many groups and speaking, because they're trying to educate the educators. They don't understand these new children.*

E: That is correct.

D: *The children seem to be more advanced, but the teachers don't know how to deal with them.*

E: The little children need to be taught how to work with energies also, for they will assist in this transformation. The more people that are awakened, the stronger the energy will become.

D: *Then it's all right if the new ones are aware of where they come from?*

E: They chose to come back as children, because children are very open. So they have more awareness and because they are aware of it, they can do more. Usually, in the past when children were aware, most adults would tell them they were making it up and did not encourage it.

D: *You think now the adults will be able to understand it better?*

E: More will understand and the children can educate the adults into awareness.

D: *But the problem right now is that some of the teachers and doctors are putting these children on medications.*

E: It is up to the parents to take a stand, and say, no. That's where the awareness of who these children are comes into play. There are those who are writing books about these children. It is up to everyone to share the knowledge and make these parents aware of who they're dealing with.

D: *I'm told they're the hope of the world.*

E: That is correct. In spirit form much can be done, but many have chosen to do it in physical form.

D: *But the medications they are giving them are very powerful, and this is not a good thing.*

E: Any medication that is being used is not the natural way of being. And be aware that many more medications will be tried to numb the mind and to make the physical body ill. That would be a way of eliminating many.

D: *Do you mean that some of the medication would be deliberate to eliminate these children?*

E: Not only the children, but the adults. That is the reality of those who try to control and manipulate.

D: *I have thought maybe this is a way of elimination, because they're talking about giving everyone vaccinations we don't need.*

E: That is correct. Many people are very ignorant of what is going on, but that is not their fault, for that is where they are being kept with what they are being told. That is where awareness of who you are and what you're doing here comes into play. For you become aware that things are not what they really seem to be. There is more that is going on that is not obvious.

D: *But they use fear to make people agree to have medications and vaccinations.*

E: That is correct, and the vaccinations are going to be used to try to stop many. People need to remember that where there is fear, there is control by outside forces.

D: *So the main thing we have to do is keep healthy so we won't need medications?*

E: That is correct, be aware of what you're doing to yourself. Look for other avenues before just going and getting medication. There will be times when the medication will be needed to assist the physical body, but once you do some research, unless it is a life lesson that was chosen deliberately to learn from, anything else can be worked on.

D: *Is it all right to use natural substances like herbs and minerals?*

E: That is all right to do, but what is really needed is to allow the physical body to heal itself. For it has that capacity to do so.

D: *But how do we keep the government from giving us vaccinations and shots we don't need?*

E: It's a matter of taking a stand. If a stand is not taken, then the government will continue to do what it is doing now. There comes a time when choices have to be made. And if you remember this is a spiritual war, then what is there to fear?

D: *So there are many beings that have come into our world to help with all of this. And many of them are living in physical bodies like this.*

E: That is correct.

D: *And they're not aware consciously that they are actually from other places.*

E: Some are aware, some are wakening even more. But, yes, there are many who are still not aware at all.

D: *The way I understand it, the reptilian race just developed in another direction. That was why you appear differently, is that correct?*

E: That is correct. It was a matter of where one developed as far as the conditions of the place. For that is what determines how one looks or one is. The environment of the place where one exists, determines how one would look.

What shape one would take to survive in that place.

D: *Yes, that makes sense. That's what I was told, some developed in the reptilian line, some developed in the insect line, and we developed in the mammal line.*

E: That is correct. And part of that is because of the conditions in the planet.

D: *Yes. The conditions in the planet and the environment and the "primeval soup", as it is called, as to which way they developed.*

E: That is correct.

D: *But the spirit, the soul, can enter any type of body it wants to.*

E: That is correct. That is what needs to be remembered. No matter what physical form the body is, what you truly are is your spirit form. And that is always energy and light.

D: *We just enter different bodies to have different experiences and lessons.*

E: That is correct.

D: *Estelle wanted to know about her purpose. Why she's here, what is she supposed to be doing? She feels she has many obstacles in her way as a human, and she wants to go forward in her work. What can you tell her about that?*

E: She will be doing more of her work now that she has done this, for she has more clarity and awareness of who we are. I say "we" even though we are one. And now that she has this awareness and is making peace with it, she will move forward. For she will allow that guidance to come in and follow it.

D: *She'll have more confidence now.*

E: That is correct.

D: *But, it will be difficult, because she can't tell people these things, can she?*

E: There will come a time when she will do so. She is supposed to be educating people and helping them remember who they are and where they come from.

D: *Do you mean from the Source?*

E: Yes, from the Source, but helping them remember on an individual basis their soul's experience and why they chose to be here now. She's also here to educate them about these different beings in other dimensions and other galaxies, and why they are here and how they function. There is much misconception and fear about beings from other places. It has been difficult for humans. They sometimes do not like fellow humans. How could they be expected to open and receive others from other places? It is very important now because things are accelerating. Those who are in charge are becoming aware that there is an awakening, and they will try to do things to prevent that or at least slow it down.

D: *But things are changing. I know they're speeding up. Would it be advisable if Estelle can remember the information she's been given today? Because usually the person doesn't remember.*

E: It would be advisable for it will help her to know and connect and make peace with all of it.

D: *Would it be all right if I use some of this information in my work?*

E: It is not coincidence that this happened. She knows it and so do you.

D: *But I always ask permission.*

E: Yes, you have permission to use all of it as you wish.

D: *Because I get it from many different sources and I put it all together like a puzzle. And I will not divulge her identity. I always keep everyone anonymous that I write about.*

E: She's not concerned with that, for you and she have a connection that comes from a long time ago. There was a time in Atlantis where you worked side by side. (This was a surprise.) You worked with crystals. You were very connected to the energy of utilizing the crystals.

D: *Was it in a laboratory?*

E: There were not laboratories. It was more of open spaces using crystals to heal. It was more temples than laboratories. In more of a temple setting in how temples would be perceived in this time. The two of you were doing healings with crystals. Miraculous work can be done with crystals by those who know how to connect with the energy. There are many here in this room who were there in different times working with the crystals. It is a gift that the crystals gave, and it is a gift that can be utilized now in these times to gather information, and to be able to go deeper in work to assist others in healing.

D: *I've been told Atlantis existed for thousands of years. So many in this room were alive during those times?*

E: Most of the ones here had many lifetimes there. If they question it they can use this mode to recover the knowledge.

D: *Yes, and they're training to be able to use this method to regain the information.*

E: That is correct. That is one of the connections that we all have here. Our lifetimes in Atlantis. They can use these methods to regain the information, and then they could recover and work with crystals, for crystals store a lot of knowledge. And crystals also can work in healing many different things that people are not aware of yet. It is time now to get the information back. It is time now for many things. It is time now to become more aware and be empowered. If there are any blocks that need to be cleared, because of the physical beliefs, then that needs to be worked on so your spirit can communicate more with you and you can perform what you came to do. This is not a time of fear. This is a time of awakening and rejoicing and discovering that you are a spiritual being with many reasons for being here at this time.

D: *This is one of the reasons they've all come together here?*

E: That is correct. They all feel it was no accident that they communicated. And they're communicating on a deeper level many things that will come forward in the near future.

D: *And they're supposed to take this knowledge back and use it, and recover more knowledge as they work with different people.*

E: That is correct.

It is was getting to the point to stop the session, so I asked (as I always do) if there was any message or advice for Estelle before we left.

E: She will find that, in the coming days ahead, more things will flow naturally the way they have been flowing for the last few weeks. She will find that mentally, all she has to do is think on things and she will see results. That is part of the energy that we carry.

D: *And she is being protected and taken care of.*

E: She has never feared or questioned that she will not be. It was more of a thing to keep others out than to keep her in.

D: *Because she didn't know these things consciously, did she?*

E: That is correct. She can know them now, because she has been asking for it for awhile. For she understands that she does much work and she understands there are many things going on, but she needed to be more confident on a conscious level.

D: *Because we don't want to do anything that will cause her any harm or any problems. She's only being given what she can handle at this time.*

E: That is correct.

D: *All right. I want to thank you for coming and giving us this information. It's very wonderful for you to allow everyone in the room to hear it.*

E: It is an honor and a pleasure to be here among you. And remember, *we will be watching each of you.* And you, Dolores, will find more who carry this special energy so you can gain more information.

I then asked the entity to leave, gave integration instructions and brought Estelle back to consciousness. She remembered very little when she awakened to a roomful of stunned observers.

This session had been a surprise in more ways than one. It really impressed the students, because I believe it showed them what they would be capable of doing when they explore the subconscious in this manner. I had begun the session with reservations because of the environment I would be working in, so many people crowded into a small motel room. And the feeling that the atmosphere would not be conducive to Estelle going under. No one likes to be put on display. In the back of my mind was the possibility that nothing would happen at all. But "they" knew better. They had orchestrated it from the beginning when Estelle chose to come to the class at the last moment, and a surprise cancellation allowed space for another student. There were a few others who also cancelled at the last minute, but "they" said that was no accident. The ones who were there were the ones who were supposed to witness this amazing session. It was also apparently no accident that I picked Estelle's name from the box. This was further proof that nothing could have been arranged in advance, because no one knew which class member would be chosen. Yes, this session contained many surprises for both myself and the students. But another one was yet to come, and I wouldn't find out about it until I returned home.

I told the students that I would make copies of the demonstration tape and send it to everyone along with their certificates. That night after everyone had left the motel and began their journeys home, I thought about something that I should have done and had forgotten about in the suddenness of setting up the session. I regretted that I had not recorded the entire induction, because it would be valuable for the students to have a record of it. During the class, I gave each of them sample induction tapes to study later, but I thought it would have been valuable for them to hear the entire procedure. This oversight was natural because every time I do a session I never record the induction. I think it is a waste of tape, and I also do not want the client to hear it later when they play the tape. My voice has a tendency to put them under again, and I don't want anything like that to happen if I am not there with them. So I always start the tape when they come off the cloud and are entering the past life. In Estelle's case, she did not even allow me to complete the induction before she was already in the appropriate scene that was intended for her and the class to experience. The

298

microphone was lying on the small table next to the bed, and I grabbed it suddenly and turned it on when I realized what was happening. Later I was angry at myself for not starting the tape recorder at the beginning of the session. But I did not know until the next day that "they" had also taken a hand in that. Another paranormal event was yet to occur that I would have no explanation for.

The next day in my office, I decided to play the beginning of the tape before I started making copies. I wanted to see where it began, and if my sudden action had cut off very much of the beginning of the session. My daughter, Nancy, was working on her accounting at the computer. As I started the tape she heard me gasp, and asked what was the matter. I said, "You're not going to believe this! The entire induction is on the tape! It starts at the very beginning! But that's impossible!"

I immediately called my friend, Gladys McCoy, who with her husband, Harold, is the head of the Ozark Research Institute in Fayetteville. She is a long-time friend and was a student at this class. She had been sitting directly across from me on the other side of the bed during the session. She had a clear view of everything that happened. I told her that the induction was on the tape.

She remarked, "That's impossible! I was watching you very closely to see how you do your inductions. The microphone was lying on the table, and you didn't pick it up and turn it on until she was under." She had no explanation for it either, because she knew what she saw, and I knew what I had done. When I sent the tapes and certificates to the students, I included a short letter telling them what had happened. This way they would know they had witnessed an even stranger event than they thought they had. I still have no explanation for any of this, especially for the induction being recorded. The only answer can be that "they" were controlling everything. They intended for the students to have the recording of the procedure, as well as the session. A session that they all agreed they would keep private and confidential. And they promised they would not divulge Estelle's identity or location. I believe they had the feeling that if they violated this trust, something might happen. We were all aware that we were dealing with something much higher and much more informed and in control than we mere mortals. This was an experience I would never forget, and I am positive it made an indelible impression on all those present.

But little did I know that it would be repeated at my next class. They were definitely monitoring my actions and my classes.

I believe Estelle could be the second of the seven disciples or special people that I was told I would meet while doing the session with Robert in England. I was told I would meet some of them, but not all. And that I was not to put them in touch with each other, because their work had to be done separately at this time. If she is one of this special and unique group of entities who have returned to help the Earth through these turbulent times, then we know one is located in England, and one in America. I was told that they would be living on separate continents, and would be of different cultural backgrounds. Out of the billions of people in the world, what are the odds of finding two of these unique people half a world apart within two weeks? I think the odds would be staggering, but I do not question. I just continue to do my work into the unknown, never knowing what they have in store for me next.

SECTION FOUR

THE WISE PEOPLE

CHAPTER 15

REMEMBERING THE WISE ONE

This was another of the sessions I did during the extraordinary week I spent in Laughlin, Nevada, at the UFO Conference immediately following the September 11 attacks in 2001. Out of twelve sessions that week, ten contained information that I could use or included personal messages for me. Virginia was present at the Experiencers' meetings which I and Barbara Lamb conducted every morning during the conference. These were meetings intended for those who thought they had had UFO/abduction, etc. experiences, so they could share them with other sympathetic people. During the session, Virginia intended to mostly focus on her suspected UFO experiences. However, it went in another direction. She was a good-looking woman who definitely did not look her age (early 50s). She had been a registered nurse in a large hospital for many years.

When Virginia came off the cloud she found herself in a barren, bleak environment. No vegetation, just brown dirt stretching for miles toward brown hills in the distance. A very desolate place. She didn't like the place because it was so barren. "I like green, and I like palm trees, but it doesn't have any here."

V: That's all I can see. Over at a distance I'm *starting* to see some people. A long *stream* of people. And some camels. People mostly leading the camels, that are loaded down. And once in a while there may be someone *on* a camel. But mostly it's the people walking, and the camels are loaded with their treasures, their products, their goods, their produce. They are taking them to be marketed. To be exchanged for other things. I can see them just passing by me at a distance. They're moving from my right to the left, just going along this trail, but they're a little ways off. And I see no other people other than these. It is quite desolate. The people have to pack well, carry some food, and know where the water sources are. Just people on a long, hot path.

I asked her to describe herself. She was a female with dark skin and long loose black hair, not at all her present coloring. "I have on some simple leather sandals. I think I made them myself. Carved it out of hides, and fitted it to my foot. I am wearing a loose-fitting robe. White, but not pure white. Loose-fitting because it's very hot. And it's airy and it's home woven material. But it fits the purpose, it covers my body, and allows ventilation. And it's something that we are able to do for ourselves."

When I asked whether she was young or old, she said, "I am getting to be fairly old for my culture. I am almost thirty-five. The body feels healthy, but tired. There's a lot of physical work. And it takes its toll on my body. I am tired. I work too hard, and have too many responsibilities. And not enough time to rest and to play. Things are in my life. It is a struggle to survive."

D: *Do you live out there?*
V: Where we live, it's partly a cave and partly a structure built around the entrance of a cave. Inside, we can escape some of the searing heat. Sometimes at night when it gets cooler, we can come outside. And we have a breezy-type structure constructed outside the cave, where we can have some of our utensils and things.
D: *Are there many of you living there?*
V: There's not as many as there used to be. Shards. No families left. We're always afraid. There are bands of marauders that come through. And we always are afraid that we will be struck again. Many have been killed, and some of the women have been violated. (Emotionally) And sometimes their children are stolen.

304

D: *They take the children?*

V: (Crying) They do! They raise them into their ways. They want to increase their community, and to decrease ours. So they hate us. (Crying) I don't know why!

I had to distract her in order to get her away from the emotion, so she could talk to me without crying.

D: *But in this community all of you live in the different caves with the structures in front?*

V: (Sniffling) That's all we know. I know there are other people that live different lifestyles and different ways, but these are my people. (Sobbing)

D: *How many are there in your family?*

V: I have a husband, and I have two children. And I had another one that ... (Sadly) that is not with us any more. (Sobbing) There were these people that came through, and they just picked him up, and took him.

D: *That's why it's so emotional for you, because you lost one of your own.*

V: (Crying) I did. I don't know what happened to him. But I have heard that they just raise them as their own. (Sniffling) They want to increase their ... I want to say "their herd".

D: *But that way they wouldn't hurt him.*

V: No. (Sniffling) I've heard that, and I hope it's true. (Sobbing) But I miss him. And I would like to know that he is all right, and not too afraid.

D: *But you do have other children.*

V: I do. I have another son and a little daughter. (Sobbing) But I'm always scared that it will happen again. It's hard. Life is hard. Life is *hard*, and sometimes I wonder why it is so *hard*. (Sobbing) Why can't we just be happy and free. I can remember being free. I don't know why I remember being free, but it should be better than this.

D: *Is it hard to find food out there?*

V: It is. There are places where there is water. And there are some fig trees and dates. And we can make trips. And we collect food and bring it back. But it's scary to go out. And there are people that we trade with so we can have the means to make bread. (Sniffling) But it is hard. We have to be careful.

D: *Why don't you live in a town; in a city? Wouldn't that be safer?*

V: We don't know that life. It's too far away. We are not city people. *This* is where *we* know. But we have heard of other, bigger settlements. But we have also heard of bad things happening there too. So we don't try to go to any bigger settlements.

D: *If you went somewhere like that, maybe you would be safer, because there would be more people.*

V: Maybe. Maybe. This is where I've always lived.

D: *Do you have any animals?*

V: There are a few of us that have common donkeys. There are some who have a camel. But not many of us have those things.

D: *I thought that would make it easier if you traveled and collected food with animals.*

V: Yes, we go to places where we can exchange some things. I do some weaving. And I take my blankets and my baskets, and I can exchange them for things to eat. We do trade, and there is this trading route where people walk by us. And it's not too far away from our encampment, where we live. And sometimes we can get things from them.

This was probably the long stream of people she saw in the beginning of the session. The caravan that was following the trade route.

D: *So you are able to survive.*

V: We survive. But it's hard.

D: *Is the weaving what you do with most of your time?*

V: I weave, and I try to put beauty into my blankets. Using the coloring that I can find. I can get wool. There are some people who have goats. And I can make blankets.

306

And I try to put in some designs when I can get proper dyes to color my thread. I can put designs in it that make me feel happier. And hopefully will make other people feel happier. I feel like I need to create beauty. It's important.

D: *What does your husband do for your small group?*

V: He has some goats that he takes care of. And he takes them to places where they can find some water. And sometimes there is some green grass that they can eat around the watering places. He takes them off, and he's gone all day. Sometimes more than one day with them. And we can get milk from them. And we can eat some of them. That kills me! It hurts me to eat my animals! I don't like eating them, but we must survive. We must be nourished ourselves. The animals are my friends.

D: *This means you're alone a lot, aren't you?*

V: I am. There are other people not too far away in this area. And I don't feel isolated. But he is gone a lot, and I do my weaving and my thinking. And that is good.

D: *And you have the children to take care of.*

V: I do, and they are a pleasure.

D: *It sounds like you're not really that happy there.*

V: It's a lot of work. Somehow I know there is more to life than just struggling to survive, and taking care of my family. I love my family, and I want to take care of them, but there is a part of me that knows that this is not all there is. This cannot be all there is. And sometimes I long for other places, and being freer. There has to be something else. And somehow I know I remember – I don't know how I remember, or what I remember – but I remember it not being this way. (Sobs) And yet the memories are haunting. It makes me think about how hard this life is. And I know something about life not being this hard. But also it helps me, to remind me that there are things that are coming, that will be this way again.

D: *That would be confusing to know that, and not be able to really remember it.*

V: It is. It is. I know, but yet I don't know why I know. No

307

one else seems to know.

D: *They don't have these memories?*

V: They don't seem to. (Crying) Why don't they know too? (She was openly crying now.) Sometimes they think I'm crazy. They think I am not right in the head. (Sniffling) When all they think about is making bread or feeding themselves, I think about *things.* I don't know why I think about things, but I think about *other* things, and I don't know how I know. (Sniffling) Things were different. They were peaceful, and I was happy. And I didn't have to work so hard. (Sobbing)

This sounded very similar to some people in our present world. They have memories of other lives and other existences. They do not know where these come from, because they have no basis in their current reality, especially the way they have been indoctrinated by the Church. This can be very confusing now, so it is easy to see how it would be totally foreign to a woman living in the middle of nowhere, with obviously little education, who had had no exposure to any other way of thinking. She apparently had vague memories of other lives, and there was no logical explanation. It only added to her unhappiness and feeling of separation from the group. This frustration of trying to fit in and being misunderstood seems to be timeless. It seems to know no boundaries and has existed as long as there have been thinking humans on this Earth. It also partially explains the underlying longing to "go home".

D: *That makes it more difficult when you have those memories.*

V: (Sniffling) It *is* hard. It's hard with people thinking that I am not right in the head.

D: *But you know you're all right.*

V: (Emotional) Sometimes I wonder if I'm all right.

D: *You are just a little different, that's all. You remember things they don't. But that's okay. You can talk to me anyway. I understand.*

I moved her forward in time to an important day. In a life where one day is just like the next, it is often difficult for the subject to find anything that would be important. And because their lives are so mundane, often what they consider to be important would not be important to us.

D: *It's an important day. What are you doing now? What do you see?*

The emotion that had been present was now gone. Her voice was normal again, even mundane.

V: Oh, I'm starting my day, like all others. Getting up and preparing for my day, and for my family meals. But yet, this is a day to remember. I am to meet someone this day, who will change my life.

D: *How do you know this?*

V: Well, I don't know it yet, but this is the day. Looking back from the "here" perspective, this is the day when a very unusual person was part of the trade caravan that I went out to meet. I went out with some blankets and baskets. And there was someone on this road that the caravan takes. He was just going along with them for a while. Maybe he was just going to the same place they were going, but he was not a trader. He was an older man. (Seriously) But he was someone who knew of other things. The caravan stopped for a while. That's when I knew I could take them my wares. They were staying overnight. And this man was traveling with them. He was a different man. A man of gentleness and strength and learning. And very, very humble. Not like some people on this route, who think that you're just nobody. And they are all important and all knowing. This man spoke to me. He talked to me as though I was important too. He looked at me, and he called me, "My child." And he spoke to me of other things, of other places, and even of other times. He could look at me and he knew all about me. I didn't even have to tell him.

309

He sensed my pain. He sensed my confusion with life. And how life was going on. I used to ask myself, "What are we doing here? Is this all there is? Why are there not other things in my life that I seem to remember having before?" And I longed for the water. I have heard that there is water, much water in other places. I have never seen it. I want to be where there is lots of water. It would make my life so much easier. And he speaks of water. (Crying) And he speaks of the water of life. He speaks of water as though he's not really talking about water. (Sniffling) He talks of other things that can set me free. It's about who I am inside. He tells me that if I can just remember hard enough, that ... a *part* of me can go places without taking my body with me. That this body is not really me. That I can go places and not have to worry about not being rich, and not having more opportunities. And I can just be me right here where I am. And I can access other realms, other times even. And I can visit with my friends that I have known in other times and other places. And he speaks of angels. (Quietly) I have seen things sometimes, but I don't tell. I don't even tell my husband. But I see people who come, and they are made out of light. And they talk to me. But yet then I wonder if I am crazy. And he tells me that these are people, great beings who love me. And that they miss me too. They come and visit me. And I can go with them, and not even have to travel in any ways. But I think I have to. I can go with them, and I can visit people. And I can even eat all I want to. I can *feel* like I'm eating all I want to. I guess it wouldn't be real. But I can enjoy the sensation of taking within myself all that I want to, including a lot of learning. Because I want to know more things. (She became emotional again.) And I *can't* know more things here. There is no one to teach me. But he tells me I can. (Crying) And it's hard for me to believe. I want to believe it. I want to know more. I feel like I know more, but yet I don't. It's hard to explain. But he tells me that I can go places. And if I can just get with these great beings that I see, these beings that I don't talk about. They're light. They're like they're made out of a candle flame or something.

D: *Do they come to you when you're by yourself?*

V: They come to me at night when everybody is asleep. Sometimes I see them, and sometimes they speak to me. I never tried to speak back to them, because I don't want to wake anyone. But I listen to them. Then I think maybe I am going out of my mind. I want to hear them, but ... sometimes I just don't want them to leave.

D: *But this man understands these things?*

V: He understands these things, and he understands *me*. He understands my longing, and he understands my frustration. And he knows that I want to know. And he tells me that I can go to these places. I can go to places of learning. And I can do that by being who I am, and where I am. And this is exciting to me.

D: *Those are very strange ideas, aren't they?*

V: They are strange ideas. No one speaks of these things.

D: *Do you know who this man is?*

V: He tells me of someone that he has long been associated with. And they are both getting very old. And he tells me of the time in another country where they had to flee. And they have been in my country for many, many years, and their time is drawing to a close in this life. And he tells me of other lives. And to not be afraid. This man that he speaks of is a mighty man of peace and love. He has been his friend, and his protector for many, many, many years. And they are growing weary, and long to return to where they came from. I always knew I came from somewhere else. And he tells me that when we are finished in this life, that we go back there. And it's wonderful, and it's beautiful. And he is going to be doing this. He and his master – he calls him – are going to be doing this very soon. They are going on to be with their friends from somewhere else before they entered this life. But he has learned many things. This man knows many things, and he has shared

311

many experiences with the one he calls the "master".

This did not sound like Jesus, because the man was too old. I wondered if she could be living in the Holy Land, and this might be one of the disciples who traveled and taught others.

D: *This country where you live, have you heard it called a name?*
V: Its name is somewhat like a river that I know. I hear people speak of a great river. It is called the Indus River. It is the country around that river. We have no name for it here.
D: *Did this man say where he came from?*
V: He had been farther to the west, visiting the place where he had once lived. He had important contacts with people he needed to see back there.   He wanted to stay in communication with them. It was quite far away, but these trade routes come through this way, and he travels with them for protection.
D: *Well, this is an important day when you meet this man, and find someone who understands you.*
V: He goes on. But he has given me a gift that cannot be taken from me. (Sobbing) He helps me to understand. And he tells me how to allow more of it, and to not resist it. And to find ways of learning and visiting other places. And how to do that and live my life here too. I can take care of my family. I can be a good wife. I can be a good mother. And I can weave my baskets and my blankets. And I can also be free to go other places, and to know other things. And to feed myself in that way.
D: *That's very important. He has given you a very great gift.*

I then had her move forward again to another important day in her life.

V: I am (big sigh) getting ready to leave this life. The body is weak, and I am old. And I am starting to see visions. I have visited many places since I met this man. This man of Judea, he tells me.

312

D: *Is that where he said he was from?*

V: He was from Judea. I don't know of Judea. And I am much happier at the end of my life, because he taught me things. He taught me how to be free where I am. He told me about leaving the body permanently, in what we call "death". He told me not to fear it. And I have learned from others since then too, that I have contacted. Great beings who never die. And I know that I am just here for a little while. And I have other things to do, other places to be, and other people to interact with. And I am leaving this body, and I have no fear.

D: *So there's nothing wrong with the body? It's just worn out.*

V: Just worn out. And I have finished my time here. My family, what's left of it, is sad. But I tell them not to be sad. Yet they don't understand me anyway. They never have. And they are glad that I have gotten happier in my later years. But they don't know why. And I tell them not to be sad at my leaving. They don't understand that either. I have tried to teach others. They haven't accepted it very well.

D: *But you always were the different one.*

V: I was. And my children think perhaps I might be right, because they love me and they respect me. But yet, they are influenced by the others more than they are me, I'm sorry to say. But I am leaving. I am not unhappy about leaving. I know that I can watch over my family, my children, and they have lives of their own now. But I can watch over them the way these beings, I know, have watched over me.

I moved her to the point where she left her body (died), and asked her to tell me what that was like.

V: It is very, very, very peaceful. I am seeing my angel friends. They are holding their arms out for me. And I am feeling lighter and lighter and lighter. And finally I just float over to them. And I am in this wonderful place of peace and love. Peace and love and light and freedom. And

313

it is just a wonderful feeling of being back where I belong, where I feel I just recently came from. Like it was just a minute. My life seemed so long and hard, but yet now it seems like it was a minute.

D: *As you look at this life you just left, you can see all of it from a different perspective. What was the purpose of that life?*

V: I was to learn how to integrate this realm with the earthly realm. The earthly mundane existence. I was to learn how to incorporate my knowingness of higher realms into my everyday workaday world. This is an issue that I still have not mastered. I learned much in that lifetime. And it was worth all the pain that I went through to learn that it can be done. And it can be integrated successfully.

D: *Even though you had opposition and ridicule.*

V: There will *always* be opposition in the earthly life. When one brings in the memories and the knowledge of the heavenly realms, when one remembers existence before that lifetime and knows there are other things, and not just being closed down to what is before one's face. There will always be those who are just at that level. And they will lash out at those who even suggest such things. So this is to help me in future lifetimes too. Because whatever lifetime I go into, it will be a lifetime where there is resistance.

D: *But doesn't that make it harder to have these memories when you're in the physical world?*

V: It seems like I will always have these memories. I am told that I am not one who completely forgets. And this is to help prepare me to be able to integrate this, because I have chosen on a higher level to not be completely forgetful. To not completely be behind the veil. I choose this. And by choosing this, I also have to learn how to integrate it.

D: *But doesn't this make it more difficult living in a life when you have the memories?*

V: It is a difficult life. But from my higher vision, I choose to have difficulties in the physical lifetime that will help me to grow spiritually. It is not important how easy my life is. It

314

is only important how much I grow. And this is the path that I have chosen to do this. Not just to go into a lifetime being completely blind and dumb of the bigger picture. And forget what I came in to do. That is of no importance. I come into the life with the memory of things I am to learn. Sometimes it takes me a while to get it together, to remember what that is, and how to go about doing it. But this is the path I have chosen from consultation with the elders.

D: *Yes, but it does make it harder.*

V: It *is* harder, but I have chosen this path that spirits will go through difficulties.

D: *So you will always have less forgetfulness in all of your lives.*

V: I will. I will know things, and I will remember things. And it will help remind me who I am, and what I came into the lifetime to do. I feel that if I have these difficult experiences, I will accomplish more than going into lifetime after lifetime, and forgetting what I came to do and how to do it. So I come in with partial memory. Just enough to spur me on, and to know that there are things to be learned and work to be done. To know that there is more. I have been very, very afraid of the possibility of going into a lifetime with all these grand visions of things I was going to do, and getting lost and forgetting what I came in to do. And it would be a wasted time and wasted opportunities. And perhaps hurting other people and hindering their path. I choose to have more enlightenment for this. Even though it is very often hard for me to integrate. But I have friends who come into lives with me, and we have made a pact to help each other remember. And this I did with this wonderful being whom I met on the path. He knew and I knew before we came into either of these lives what we were going to do with each other. It was a karmic promise. And I have set this up with others in other lifetimes too. I will know enough to ask questions, and others will help me to find the answers.

D: *So any life you go into, there will always be someone there.*

315

V: There will be. I am never alone. I have many, many, many friends through past acquaintances and associations. And we all know of the dangers of getting lost in the muck and the mire. And we have a fail safe.

D: *What do you mean by a fail safe?*

V: Maybe I think when I'm going into a lifetime that I will forget. And I have loving friends who go into lifetimes with me, or who I will meet sometime during my lifetime. And we have made promises that we will remind each other of who we are. And surely not all of us will forget everything. So if one remembers one thing, and another one remembers something else, we will help each other. And we will even have things that we call "codes". If one will just remember one phrase or one sentence, it will set off things in another that will open up reams of remembering and knowledge.

D: *So you'll know how to identify each other?*

V: We will do this *for* each other. It's not a conscious code. But there are things that someone may say that we have set up in advance. Like when you say *this*, it will download this whole box of information for me when I'm ready. And we will meet when I'm ready, or when you're ready. And we do it for each other. And it's like a little safety net for going into a scary life where we're afraid we'll forget.

D: *And you will always be with these people in different lives. Is that correct?*

V: That is correct. It takes me some, what you would call "time", after a lifetime, to rest and to think about everything that I learned. And things I didn't learn.

D: *To assimilate, yes.*

V: Assimilate is a good word. It takes me a while to do that, and then I am free to do what I choose. I can choose many paths. One of which is going into another lifetime. And I have chosen to go back into lifetimes quite frequently, with some time out in between to go on to higher learning and do some work with others. Sometimes, I just spend time working with others on the earth plane. Visiting them and inspiring them. And I still have those who are my soul mates, I call them, in lifetimes. And I spend time with them in dream-time even. I whisper things to them, and I influence them, and I watch over them. And there are times when I go on to visit other areas of learning. And sometimes just relaxation. And there will come a time always when I consult with what I call the "elders".

I then moved Virginia forward in time, leaving the other entity in the past, so I could ask the questions about her present life. The subconscious had difficulty leaving the other personality in the past.

V: It is as though Virginia is now the woman in the arid country of what is now India. As though she were that person *now*. And this is an analogy that I would like her to understand. She is, as that person was, on some level. And the foreigner who was coming through her area – not *from* her area, mind you – but coming through just for a short stay, and looking the place over, and getting to know the people somewhat. There are others who are as the traveler that came through that brought her further enlightenment. And showed her how to look within herself to find her freedom, and to remember who she is.

D: *Is that why the subconscious chose that life for her to see today?*

V: This is the purpose of that lifetime. It is an analogy. She is the one now, the woman involved in hard labor. And she does work hard. And she has trouble at times integrating her knowingness with her everyday workaday world. And there are those, especially in her workplace, who will hear nothing of her mysticism. (Virginia is a nurse in a large hospital.) And this is often frustrating. And there are those who come to her at night, who teach her of other things. They take her to other realms, and they show her many things. And it is her way of growing above this lifetime. And she agreed for this to be, for this to happen. It was to help her to remember that there are other things to life rather than the here and the now, and the work that is in front of your face at the moment. There are many things happening on many levels. But for her immediate level, it was an agreement before she came into this life, because she had much to do in this lifetime. Much karma to finish. And it was her goal to help people to remember who *they* were. And she was afraid that she would forget who she was, and would be unable to help herself or anyone else.

Virginia had, during meditation and dreams, seen glimpses of an entity that she called "Heperon". She wanted to know if this was a real entity, and if so, who he was.

V: Heperon is a very integral part of her being. She would never have volunteered for the Earth experience if it had not been for the knowledge that her "soul-mate" – I would call him – this very, very dear person from her soul group on another planet, was with her. He assured her it was *their* agreement that she would come into Earth life, and he would watch over her. He would be with her on some level at all times. He is, what you would call, a "multi-dimensional" being. He can be doing many things in many realms, and also watching over Virginia, too. And this is a very integral part of her life. Her very existence on Earth is the knowledge that Heperon is watching over her from his – you might call – somewhat *lofty* position. He can be many places at many times. He is, what you might call, an angel. He is an angel to her anyway.

D: *So he is very important in her life.*

V: That connection is extremely important. It is at the very heart of her existence on Earth.

D: *That's very good. She has a few more questions. She wanted to know if she ever had any connection with Jesus?*

V: There was an incident in Kashmir where she met the young man who was Jesus. She was a priest at that time when Jesus was traveling with his uncle Joseph, and studying with the wise teachers. It was a true encounter. It was a very, very true encounter. A true memory. A very profound one. And the memory of his serenity has helped her in many ways in this lifetime. Just tapping into that soul memory of the love and the peace that he emanated has been a stabilizing force. And the knowledge that he is there. He is steady as a rock, and he is love and peace. That has been an inner knowing. And also during this lifetime that was revealed this day in this session. It was further, the next incarnation of this entity, Virginia.

D: *After the other one in Kashmir?*

V: After the other one. And this man – this is difficult to say, because it's not generally accepted – but this man who taught her lived a long life with Jesus.

D: *I was thinking it was not Jesus, because he was older.*

V: He was a companion of Jesus. He carried the knowledge, so Jesus has touched her life twice.

I ended the session by asking about Virginia's physical problems. They were caused by her continuing to work in the negative atmosphere of the hospital after her usefulness there was over. She thought she was helping people, but the energies present in that environment were draining her. It was time for her to move on in her work. She could still help people, and work with those who were dying, but she was to leave the hospital.

CHAPTER 16

SEARCHING FOR THE WISE ONE

This is another session that I did in Clearwater, Florida, while I was there speaking at an Expo in October 2002. It also had a connection with a wise man, but one of a different type.

When Nancy, the subject, came off of the cloud, she found herself standing barefoot on sharp gravel, small pieces of crushed rock. This made her uncomfortable, but she became more upset when she saw she was standing on the edge of a cliff. She saw that she was a young male with short brown hair wearing a thick padded vest and pants made of rough material. "I'm very close to a cliff. I feel like I want to go backwards away from the edge. I'm being told not to turn around. Somebody is behind me. And I want to run," she said with a big sigh. "I want to get away. Why are they doing this?" The answer was a revelation, "They're trying to scare me."

I asked if she wanted to turn around and see who it was. "There's more than one person. I feel if I get any closer to the edge, I'm going to slip and fall. And they're making me stand here to teach me a lesson. But I don't know what that lesson is. They are very small people with light hair. Almost white. I'm much larger than they are, at least a foot or more taller. And my coloring is different. I'm dark and they're very light. They're different from me. I don't belong to them. I'm not part of them. I feel like I was traveling through their village. They are afraid of me. I didn't know where I was, and I found this place. At first I thought they were children. They don't have any weapons, but somehow they forced me here."

D: *What kind of a village did they have?*
N: Hmmm. I see they can hide. I don't know how to say this.

320

They can disappear. They can hide their homes, their buildings in with nature, with the environment. And when I first saw them, it looked like a child's village. They had grass roofs, like little huts, but that wasn't real. That was just a camouflage that they used. It wasn't really what their houses look like. Like they were playing a trick on me. It's very confusing.

D: *That's what you saw when you came into the village?*

N: Yes. I saw the little huts with the grass on the roofs. And it looked like children playing. But really their homes are hidden. I know they camouflage them. They hide them in the hillside. It's funny, but I don't know what they *really* look like. But I know that they're hidden.

D: *Had you come a long way to get there?*

N: Way up in the mountains.

D: *That's where your home was?*

N: No, that's where I was crossing. This is very, very high. I was just traveling. (Big sigh) I wanted to go to the far east. It was my journey. I heard stories of a magical man that I wanted to see. Far away, way up in the mountains. Very high. Who had magic. The holy man. Stories of this man. I wanted to find him.

D: *It sounds like it was going to be a long journey.*

N: Very long. I thought it might take me a year or more to get there. I had supplies, but these people took them.

D: *Did you have a family in the place you left?*

N: I feel like I was alone.

D: *So you were free to travel if you wanted to?* (Yes) *Did you have further to go when you came across this little village?*

N: Oh, yes, much further. I had been on the road for a long time. I came around a bend, and I wasn't really paying attention. It was just so beautiful. And then I saw these huts. And I heard people inside. I thought they were children playing. But I scared them. I looked down inside, and I frightened them. This feels like a place that no one comes. This is a hidden place. This is a very secret place for them.

321

D: *So you frightened them because you weren't supposed to be there.*

N: Yes. And I can't communicate with them in my speech. They don't understand what I'm saying. I'm trying to tell them that I'm not going to hurt them, but they don't understand.

D: *You said they took your supplies?*

N: Yes. I had pouches on straps over me. (Hand motions indicating something over his shoulders.) Crossing over me. And water. And a bag of – I don't know what to call it. – Some food ... *dried* things in the other one. And then I would, from time to time, get other food from my travels. Places I would stop where people would share with me. But this is a different place. These people don't look the same. They're very, very pale and small. Very light skinned. Very, almost white hair.

D: *Are their features different?*

N: Yes, they are. They all have the same features. Their eyes are different colors. They're not blue, not green, but both. Almost turquoise, a bluish-green color. But their features are very tiny. Very small nose, petite. Very small chin. Very delicate features. And sharp.

D: *Do they look male and female?*

N: I see young ones with them that are their children. There are adult partners. Families! They're families. But the parents look very much alike.

D: *So it's hard to distinguish gender?* (Yes.) *Did you try to keep them from taking your supplies?*

N: No. I just stood there. I felt very quiet. Very still. And they just walked up and took them from me. Why did they take my shoes? (She was puzzled by her reaction.) I just let them do it. I just stood there. That's very odd. I stood very still. And then they walked me up this pathway with the stones. Hurt my feet. (Wincing) It hurt my feet. (A revelation:) Oh! Their places are a secret. No one's supposed to know that they're there. And I found them. And they don't want to hurt me, but they can't let me go. They're afraid that I'm going to bring others, or talk about them. I wouldn't tell. I tried to tell them I wouldn't say anything. (Big sigh) And I want to get away from that cliff. They're standing behind me, but they're a distance away. They're not touching me, and there are no weapons, but their thoughts are pushing me towards the edge. (Sternly) And I'm resisting them. I'm not going to do it! I'm not going to let them do it. (Determined) I'm going to turn around. I know I can. I'm going to turn around very hard. And I'm going to tell them to *stop*. *Stop it!* (Big breaths, and she held up her hand with the palm facing out.) I'm telling them to *stop*. (Big relieved breath.) They're stopping! And now I'm being very firm with them. I'm *not* going to let them do this! I was thinking that if I followed what they wanted me to do, they would see that I wasn't going to harm them. But now I see that *I* have to tell them to *stop*. They are not going to tell me to do this. And now one of them is bringing my supplies, and my shoes. They're handing them to me so I can get on my way. They're very sorrowful. They're apologizing. They're not speaking to me, but I can feel how they feel. I feel that they are sorry.

D: *Were you able to communicate with them that you weren't going to expose them?*

N: Yes. When I turned around and I told them to *stop*, I was angry. And I felt strong. I told them I wasn't going to hurt them. I wouldn't tell anyone. But they *weren't* going to make me walk off the cliff. That it was wrong. And they felt very sorrowful.

D: *Maybe this was the only way they thought they could protect themselves.*

N: They were very frightened. And now I'm leaving. Going up the hill. (Big sigh) They're watching me. They're starting to leave. I stopped at the top of the hill, and they were walking back down. Whew! But I'm okay, I'm safe, I'm on my way again. But it's very curious, because I know they didn't belong here. They're different. I feel like they don't belong *here* in this time.

D: *This time?*

N: Yes. They don't belong in this time. (Trying to think how to explain.) I feel they're from another time. Far in the *future!* Very far in the future. And they just were *there.* But I feel they have been there for a long time. But they thought they were safe in this place. That no one would find them there.

D: *Why do you get the feeling they're from the future from where you are?*

N: I don't know. I just know that they are from far in the future. That they're not from my place, this time. They're not from here. They thought they'd found a safe hiding place.

D: *I wonder what they were hiding from?*

N: I don't know.

D: *But anyway, you stood up to them.*

N: Yes, I'm fine. (A relieved sigh.) I'm happy to be on my way. I'm looking forward to meeting this special person. And I know I'm going to see this person.

I then moved Nancy forward to an important day:

N: (Smiling) I'm here. I'm so excited. I met many people on my journey. And I heard stories of this person all the time. I feel older.

D: *But you never met anyone as strange as those little people.*

N: No. (Laughing) That was just once.

D: *Does this man live in a city?*

N: He's way up on the mountaintop, but everyone here in the city knows him. He is a holy man. And I'm in a marketplace of some sort.

D: *Do you know the name of this city? Did you hear anyone say?*

N: This feels like it's in the Himalayas. There is a name they call it, but the city is at the lower elevation. (I could see she was struggling to find the name.) I don't think it's the name that they call it, but I want to say Katmandu, but I think that's a modern name. I don't think that's what they call it now, in my time. There are many high mountains

324

around. And this city is at a high elevation, but it's below where he is.

When she mentioned the Himalayas, I immediately thought of Tibet. I was surprised when I looked in the encyclopedia and found that Katmandu is a city in Nepal. It sits on a plateau 4000 feet above sea level and is surrounded by very high mountains. The Himalayan mountain range has the highest mountains in the world and forms the northern border of Nepal and China. I did not know the Himalayas extended that far. I do not believe Nancy had this information either. It would have been more natural for her to say she was in Tibet when thinking of the Himalayas. Apparently the memory was real, because it was not conforming to what our conscious minds would fantasize. The strange little people did not seem to fit, but all of this would be explained before the session was over.

D: He is up much higher, and everyone knows about this man?
N: Yes, this is a very special person who I feel I can learn from. (Long pause) I have to rest here and clean myself. I have to bathe. I've been on the road a long time. I feel like I need to rest for a little while, and adjust also to the elevation. And I need to change my clothes. I'm not warm enough now. I need to put on more clothing, because it's very high and cold.

I decided to move her ahead to when she was going up the mountain to see him.

D: *Have they told you where he is?*
N: I know where he is. I can feel him almost pulling me there ... calling me. He knows I'm coming, and he's directing me. I can feel him pulling me higher. Here it's very steep. It's *very* cold. *I'm* cold.

She was shivering, and her voice was shaking. I gave instructions so she would not physically have any discomfort.

325

D: *Is there snow also?*

N: No, it's just steep now. It's not the winter season. But it's very windy. I've come up on a level piece of ground. There's a cave. And he's inside. It's dark and quiet. And there are candles in there. And I stop for a moment. My eyes are adjusting to the light. And he is here.

D: *Can you see him?* (She nodded) *What does he look like?*

N: (Big breath) He has the shape of a man, but he is energy. He's not really solid. (Sudden laugh.) He's telling me he is the embodiment of many holy people. He is showing me, first, a holy man in just raggedy clothes, like a robe and long, brown, dirty matted hair. And a long dark dirty beard. And then suddenly he becomes clean and pure. And he's many. He's not just one person. He's many souls. He's a combined .... (She had difficulty finding the word.)

D: *A composite?*

N: Yes! Of all of them. And he's very bright. He's appearing as a bright light, but also the shape of a man. He's both. He can transform from man to the shape of a man, and then suddenly be just this brilliant light. Almost blinding light.

D: *Is this why he can live in such a strange place, because he isn't solid?*

N: Yes. He adjusts to wherever, whatever his environment is. It doesn't affect him.

D: *If other people come and see him, would they see him in that way?*

N: Only a few come to him. People know that he's there, but only a few ever make the journey to him. (Pause) It's a calling. He calls you.

D: *I was wondering if someone from the village came, would they see him as a human being, or like you are seeing him?*

N: They know they can't go. You have to be called. They know he's there, but he only calls a few. He can exist in other places at the same time.

D: *But you had to make the journey there.* (Yes) *You couldn't have found him somewhere else?*

N: No. I had to go there. That's where he wanted me to come. The journey was very important. He had to know that I believed. He had to know that I was worthy of .... He had to know that the calling that I felt inside was strong enough.

D: *Because otherwise, he could have appeared to you anywhere.* (Oh, yes.) *But he had to know you had the determination to travel so far to find him.* (Yes) *Why did you feel this determination?*

N: I just felt that I had to be there. I was pulled and drawn to him. I feel like there's something I'm supposed to learn from him. And I just couldn't not go. I *had* to go. And I was going to go. I didn't care how long it took me to get there. I was going to see him.

D: *But in your normal life where you started out, were you a holy person, or a normal person?*

N: It was so long ago. I was an apprentice of some sort. I didn't like it. I did it because ... well, you had to do something. I was working with my hands. A mason, I think. I would build things, but I was just learning how to do these different things. I was young.

D: *But then you felt this urge to find this man, even though it didn't make sense?*

N: Yes, I knew I had to find him. I wasn't like everybody else. I just always felt like I didn't really belong there. I just felt different. The people were very poor, and very dirty. And they just worked *all* the time. They were kind to me, but I don't think I belonged there either. I think I just stopped there for a little while, because I didn't know where to go. I knew I had to find this man. And I knew what direction to follow. And I knew that if I stayed on my path to him, that he would provide to me all of my necessities. That he would give me food and water. But I had to stay on my path *to* him. I could have stopped any time, if I wanted to, but I didn't want to.

D: *Now that you have found him, what are you going to do?*

N: He has things to teach me.

D: *Are you going to stay with him?*

N: Yes. For a little while. Until the time is right. And I am the only one here. It's just the two of us. No one else.

D: *No other students.*

N: No. Just me. He called me. From very far, very far.

D: *What is it that he has to teach you?*

N: (Long pause) I am to become one of his children. And in so doing, I can share with others his teachings. The teachings of many are all from the *One*. And I'm beginning to understand, but it's still much for me to comprehend. It's going to take me some time with him to fully understand. He has much to teach me.

I felt this could take quite a while, so I moved her ahead again in time. "How long do you stay there?"

N: (Big sigh) It was winter passed, and now it's springtime. I've been here for a while. (Laugh) And I have *hair* on my face. (I laughed) And my hair on my head is longer. And I feel older.   I'm still youthful, but I feel older. And it's almost time for me to go.

D: *What has he been teaching you?*

N: (A whisper)   So much.   He tells me, as I need the information, it will be there. But he sends me on my way with the knowledge of the truth, of simplicity, of the teachings of the Christ, the teachings of the truth of many. Of Buddha. The teachings of many of them who are all the same. They all have the same truths.

D: *All the wise people?*

N: Yes. Christ was not the only one. Jesus was not the only one, but there were many. And there were *women* who also had this Christ energy.

D: *The abilities and knowledge.*

N: Yes. And it's almost time for me to go now, to share the truth.

D: *Did you ever ask him where he came from, and what he was? You said he was not human. He was not solid.*

N: Oh, I know.   You don't have to ask.   He is the Christ energy.   He is the God energy manifesting in different places all over this planet.

D: *How did he teach you?*

N: I slept for a very long time, and that's how it happened. While I was sleeping, yes.

D: *You more or less absorbed this. Would that be a good word?*

N: Yes, that's it. Absorbed. And now I have to leave. I'm very joyful. I'm very happy.

D: You don't mind leaving him?

N: Because I know that he's always with me.

D: *You never lose him then.*

N: (A very emotional response:) No! He is part of me.

D: *Because he has placed this knowledge and information within you.*

N: Yes. And there is great joy. (She was emotional and almost crying.) I'm just going down the hill very carefully. Watching my footing, because there are many stones, and very steep. And as I come to the village, I am greeted by everyone. And there are many flowers, and music and dancing. A celebration.

D: *That you returned?*

N: Yes. (Smiling) It's very festive. And there are beautiful colors, and music. And a feast. And I stay for a while. And I am given clothes and supplies. And I am honored. And now I must leave. I don't know where I am supposed to go. (Chuckle) I am supposed to wander and meet people. I feel like I'm heading south.

D: *Away from the mountains?*

N: Yes. Further south. And I don't know what it is exactly that I am going to be doing. But I know I must follow his teaching. And talk to people.

D: *To share what he has taught you? (Yes) Do you think you'll be all right?*

N: Yes, I know I will. I have no fear. I'll be taken care of. No fear.

I moved her ahead in time again to another important day, because the journey could take a great deal of time.

N: It's the day of my passing. I'm very old. There have been many weddings and many blessings. And many people who I have loved, and who I have touched. I feel good about my life. And I have many, many children. And many grandchildren. Many loved ones around me. And I am ready to go.

D: *Were you able to teach the knowledge?*

N: Yes. It just came when it was ready. When I spoke and I talked, and I shared stories.

D: *And you never questioned, because you knew it was just there.* (Yes) *On the day of your passing, what is causing the body to cease to function?*

N: It's just time. I'm just old and tired. And he's calling me. He's calling me again. It's time for me to rest. He says that I have served him well, but now it's time for my rewards. And I'm very happy. (Contented sigh.) And at peace. And I know I will be leaving soon.

D: *Then let's go to the time when it happens. When you do make the passing, what happens at that time?*

N: (Big sigh) I'm just ... I'm just *gone*. (Chuckle) I'm gone. And I feel movement, and see light. I'm just there and then I'm gone. (Laugh) It's very easy.

D: *Is anyone with you?*

N: I feel several of those who have come. But I really didn't need their help, because I was told how to do this before. They were there if I needed them, but I just sort of slipped away.

D: *But you said he was calling you for your reward. What is your reward that you're going to?*

N: I got rid of that old body. It was tired. And I was very old. And I feel I'm still the same person. But I don't have that tired, heavy body on me now.

D: *From that vantage point, you can look back on the entire life. And it sounds like it was a very rewarding life.*

N: Yes, very.

D: *You did a lot of good. As you look at it, what was the lesson to be learned in that lifetime?*

N: I had many lessons in that lifetime. I had lessons of faith,

330

and belief in myself. And the dimension of spirits. I had to learn that I was not always going to be accepted easily. And I had to learn that I had to use my strength with my gentleness. That it wasn't just one or the other. But it was a combination of using your strength and your power with the gentleness and the love.

D: *Those are important things, aren't they?*

N: Yes. There were many souls touched in that lifetime.

I then asked the entity to remain where he was, and brought Nancy's personality back into the body. After she was oriented, I asked to speak to the subconscious to find out more information about this strange session.

D: *Why did you pick that lifetime for Nancy to look at?*

N: (Big sigh) She needed to remember her strong connection to the Christ energy. And also to bring forth that power that she has. That strength to make things happen. But also to feel that love and the truth. To remind her to still use these qualities in her lifetime now. She has difficulty sometimes with this. She has great challenges in this lifetime. She has a lifetime now that, although the circumstances are different, the time is different, she still faces similar challenges. Of meeting people and sharing the truth with them. And of incorporating that strength and wisdom.

D: *This being she called the Christ energy, that appeared as a man in the cave. What was that? It didn't seem to be human.*

N: That was the universal wisdom. That was the universal power. That was the cosmic knowledge. That was the element that activates that part of each one of us, that reminds us ... (Softly, a whisper:) That's not right.

D: *The words aren't right?*

N: Yes. It was the catalyst. The catalyst to remind her of what she needs to do.

D: *So it's like an embodiment of all knowledge?* (Yes) *And it was passed to the man she was in that lifetime.* (Yes) *In the beginning, she came to that village with the little strange creatures. Who were they?*

N: (Loud laugh) That was a test that was placed on my path. To see how I would handle *many* things. Dealing with those who are not like me. Dealing with my own strength. It was a test of faith and of my own power. It was a test of how much loving energy I had. How I would use my power. Would I try to hurt them, or would I leave them at peace? Many tests.

D: *And that you were going to be meeting many people who would be different. (Yes) Were they real physical beings?*

N: Yes, but they were not from that place. They were from another place. They volunteered to come to enact this scene, but they were not from that time.

D: *He said the appearance of the huts was like an illusion.*

N: Yes. But they were not from that time. They were from another dimension. And they volunteered, because they knew that I had to be helped along the way. Yes, they were there to help me.

D: *How will Nancy be able to tap into this knowledge, and use it in her present lifetime?*

N: She's afraid of being rejected, of being ridiculed, for being different.

D: *Those are normal human fears, aren't they?*

N: Yes. Nothing happened to the man in that lifetime. He was accepted. This was why it was shown to her. So she can see that it is possible to use this knowledge without being rejected or ridiculed. She'll be able to use these forgotten abilities. There will always be people that won't understand. But maybe she doesn't have to work with those people, or she doesn't have to share as much as she could.

This was another case where the person had accumulated great knowledge in a past life. It is assumed that it is lost; left with the deceased personality. But I knew from experience, that this was not true. Anything that has ever been learned in another life, any talent etc., is never lost. It is stored in the subconscious mind, and can be revived and brought forward to be used in the present lifetime, *if it is appropriate.* I have found many cases in recent years, where great psychic abilities and healing knowledge are being allowed to come forward to the conscious mind. Because they will be needed in the time we are headed into.

I think it would be appropriate to mention another strange case that also appeared to be a time shift. The subject descended into a large modern city, but everywhere he looked there were no people, or any sign of life. Everything was still and quiet; just the buildings and surroundings. I moved him to many places in the city, but everything seemed deserted. He said nothing seemed familiar, almost as though he was a very puzzled observer. He seemed to be out of time and place, as though he had been dropped down into an alien environment where he didn't belong. He was very confused, as I was, because it was difficult to know how to proceed. Finally, I asked him to move to a place where he did feel comfortable. He then found himself in the middle of the woods, living a very primitive and lonely existence in a cave. Here he felt at home, with only the company of his dog. The rest of the session was about a very simple, mundane life where he never encountered another person, yet he was content.

After his death, I communicated with his subconscious. I wanted to know about the unusual circumstances in the beginning. Why the strange contrast? The subconscious said that he had come into the scene at the correct location, but at the incorrect time. During his existence in the woods there was no city there, yet in a future time a large city would be built in the same location. Thus he saw the city and it was deserted, because the city did not exist yet in his time. No wonder he was confused, and could find nothing that was familiar to him. He was content when we located the woods that had existed before the city. As though the past and future were merging as overlays in the same location simultaneously, with only a thin veneer separating the dimensions.

———◇——◇◆◇——◇◆◇——◇◆◇——◇———

I thought this book was finished and was preparing it for the printers, yet the information continued to come through during my therapy sessions. My family keeps telling me to hold it and put it into Book Three of this series. Since the information will not cease I suppose there will have to be a Book Three. Yet these pieces that continue to come through seem to want to be inserted into this book, so I guess this will continue until the book finally goes to press.

In November 2004 at my private office in Arkansas I had a session that relates to this one of the search for the wise man. This one happened by accident, and has the qualities of the famous Rip Van Winkle classic.

Gail went to a past life where she was a young male living with a group of semi-primitive people in an area of high mountains. They lived in dwellings made from branches and hides, or in caves. He lived in one of the huts with an old woman relative. His job was to go into the woods and hills and gather berries and nuts, which were shared with the others. On one of these gathering searches in the high mountains that surrounded their settlement he found some strange small rocks on a ledge. They had pictures of animals and people carved on them. He had no idea where they came from since such things were foreign to his culture. Thinking they were pretty and perhaps lucky he put them in a pouch and always carried them with him. When he showed them to the other people it only created great fear and suspicion, since they had never seen anything like them. His people only carved useful utensils out of wood, never out of rock.

He wanted to go back to the same area to see if he could find more. Since they were found on the tallest mountain he also wanted to climb to the top, which no one in the village had ever done. I condensed time to see what would happen when he decided to climb the mountain. Along the way he found more rocks, but they were not the type with carvings. They were blue and white and sparkled. (Probably some type of quartz crystal.) I condensed time again to see if he was able to make it to the top. He said, "I am almost to the top. Had a hard time. Hard to breathe. It was a long ways. I found a *cave* on the side. I'm tired ... my body. The sun's high outside, so it's hot. This looks like a good place to rest and it's cool."

When he entered the cave he was surprised to find a person there. A being was carving on larger rocks with another rock that threw sparks as he used it. When I asked what the man looked like, he said, "Not like me. His skin is kind of *shiny*. He has big eyes and his head's kind of sloped and pointy." It was difficult to see him clearly because he was so bright. "He's shiny. It could be his clothes are shiny, but then it doesn't seem like there's a separation between his clothes and his skin, so I don't know." Since he was not afraid of the being he decided to stay and watch him for a while instead of continuing his climb to the top of the mountain. There was some type of mental communication going on. "He's shaking his head like I'm supposed to understand. I don't think he lives there, but he's staying there. I believe that when he's carving the shiny sparks keep him warm, because it's so warm in here now."

He felt he must have fallen asleep, because when he opened his eyes the being was gone, and the cave was cold. "I must have been here for a long time, because there's a lot more writing or carving there. More like symbols." These were not carvings of people and animals, but were designs or symbols. "It's shapes with three sides. And they're at different angles to each other. Some of them are hooked on top of each other so they have more sides. Must be some kind of message to it." These were on rocks that were part of the cave, so they could not be moved. "He's gone and it's cold in there, so I think I'll go outside and go to the top of the mountain."

When he went out of the cave he discovered everything had changed. The mountain now had ice and snow on it, and he could not continue to the top. As he tried to find the path back down he discovered something that left him totally in awe. He saw something red coming out of the side of the mountain. "It's red and it's *moving*. And there are blue clouds coming up out of it. There are rocks and other things coming down the side of the mountain." It was something he had never seen before. Ignoring his own safety he wanted to get closer. "It doesn't matter. I want to see it. I'm climbing through the ice and snow and rocks, and I came to a place where I can look down over the other side of the mountain. It's making noise and ... moving ... and it's black and red and ... hot. It's melting the ice and snow. It's making its own clouds. Pretty. The ground is shaking. Maybe it's where the man came from. Maybe he lives there." To me it sounded like he was witnessing a small volcanic eruption up close, but he had never seen anything like it, and could only describe it in his limited vocabulary and experience.

He then had difficulty deciding how to get back down the mountain. "Maybe I climbed up too far. I don't know how to get down. I can't find the way I came up. It's very steep and slick. It's gone! It's gone down the side of the mountain. I'll have to go another way." As he struggled to descend he slipped and fell several times and hurt his head and back and leg. "I go a long way before I find a way down that isn't icy and shaky. There was no ice when I went up. I'm finally working back down to where there are trees again."

After finding a stream to drink from he looked for something familiar so he could return to his home. But nothing looked the same. After much walking he saw the caves and some people. "They do not look the same. It's not the same people that I know. The huts are there, but they look *older*, like they need repair. They do not know me. I'm trying to find the old woman, I ask somebody. She's been gone for a long time. They don't recognize me. I don't look the same. I'm ... old. My hair's gray, and very long. They don't remember me. I don't know what happened. I must have been gone for a very long time. It didn't seem like a very long time, but everything's different now. Yet it's the same place." Even though it must have been very startling to see this strange disheveled man

336

come into the village, they allowed him to stay.

When I took him ahead to an important day he was sitting in a cave with people around him. He was showing them the rocks from his pouch and telling them the story of the man and the symbols in the cave. "Some of them are angry. They don't think it's true. They don't know what it means. It's different. They think I'm a crazy old man. That I was up on the mountain too long. Bumped my head. They think I'm scaring the children. But I'm beginning to try to understand, and I just need to talk about it to tell them. It's like magic and they think it's something to be afraid of. *Some* of them want to listen."

There was one young woman who listened and believed him. She kept asking about it, and wanted to go there, but she was too afraid. She was with him when he died in one of the caves with his rocks by his side. After he died I asked him to describe from the spirit side what lesson he had learned. "I had to find out what was on the other side of that mountain. I found someone there that had knowledge. I placed knowledge above everything else." He was willing to go into the unknown to find it even if no one believed him. When I called the subconscious forth to answer questions, it expanded upon this. "A quest for knowledge is the important thing. It's not the answer to what Gail's seeking. It's just the journey. It's the experience. She must now use the knowledge. The knowledge is not somewhere else. She has that knowledge already."

I wanted to know what type of knowledge she was to use, because one of her questions was about her purpose in this life. "We see this one using the light of different colors, different frequencies, and vibrational levels to heal the body. The light will come to her from *stones*. Blue stones. They will be the ones that she will use to speak truth, and then the lights will come. She will know the path to follow. There will be instructions. It will be information that will come from *light*. We see this coming from alternate realities. She will need to go within, and then there will be instructions on how to use the light and the colors. This one will get the information from a contact in an alternate reality."

Of course, I wanted to know about the being she saw in the cave on the top of the mountain. "The being was from another – as this one would say – solar system (had difficulty with the word). But the consciousness is how they communicated. Not through physical sound, and that is the same way this new information will come in."

I asked, "If he was from another place, what was he doing there in the cave, in our world?"

"It's hard to describe. It's a very thin ... it's like a wall or a veil that separates the two even though they are far apart. He was there with the symbols, to pass it on. But it was the same time, but then again, it wasn't. This one, at that time, did not have the consciousness to understand that. The knowledge was passed on, and she still retains it. This one needs to tap into that, so to speak. This one needs to become disciplined."

I asked, "The man said he felt like he was in that cave for a long time. Was that correct?"

"In his way of measuring time, yes. The other entity returned to his appropriate time and place."

"How could he stay alive if he was not consuming anything?"

"There was no need. His physical body was being taken care of by the energy."

"He felt he had aged by the time he came back down the mountain."

"In his way of recording time, yes."

He had been placed in a state of suspended animation while time passed. Yet his physical body continued to age. "What was happening during that time?"

"His *mind* was open, so to speak, for these symbols to be placed in. Although, he may have not with his physical eyes, seen it. It was being planted, so it just feeds into his consciousness. He did not need it in that lifetime. He lacked the skills mentally. The information has been there for many years, but this one has repressed it. And it is now time for it to come forth. That is why she was shown this lifetime."

I also wanted to know about the event that was occurring

338

when he came out of the cave. "It was power from the Earth. Energies from the Earth that can be utilized in this lifetime. It was very much like a volcano, but he had never seen this before. He did not understand. The Earth is a living energy and has its own energies. That was coming forth."

This was another case of memories from a past life being reawakened to bring healing knowledge forward to this time. I have investigated many UFO/ET cases where symbols have been placed into the brain on the cellular level. This is information to be utilized at a future time when it will be activated. This is also the purpose of the Crop Circles, to release the information contained in the symbol and implant it into the minds of anyone who sees the symbol in the grain. It is a language that is perfectly understood by the subconscious.

These separate encounters in times past with individuals who had extreme knowledge and wisdom were different from each other. But they demonstrated that access to such knowledge is possible and has been attained many times. In each case extreme faith changed their lives. How many of us have also lived such lives and have the knowledge and information buried in our subconscious? The number must be legion, because we have to live every imaginable type of life, and experience every type of situation before we reach perfection and finally ascend.

SECTION FIVE

OTHER PLANETS

CHAPTER 17

LIFE ON OTHER PLANETS

This was another demonstration session for my hypnosis class in 2003. Like the last one, I had the students put their names into a box, and I picked the one I would perform the demonstration on the next day. Margaret was the one I picked. I asked her to write a list of questions for me to ask once she was in trance. Since this was the last day of the class, we chose the room of one of the students who was staying over, because most of us had given up our rooms. There were twelve of us and we again, all crowded into the small hotel room. I was sitting in the corner next to a small table by the bed, with barely enough room to turn. All the students were crowded around the bed. Some had brought chairs from the classroom, and some were sitting on the floor. Many had notebooks and were taking notes. This caused a funny remark that Margaret told us after the session. She said she could hear everyone writing, making scratching noises. She said she never heard so much writing before, and was afraid that the noise would be distracting and prevent her from going under. Yet surprisingly, to her, she went into deep trance immediately and no longer heard the sounds. When she awoke after the session, she remembered nothing, and we all had to fill her in on what had happened. The session again was unusual, but not as strange as Estelle's during the class in 2002. I would have liked to explore this one further, but since it was for a demonstration of my technique I tried to keep it brief.

When I began this time, I remembered to record the

induction, so the students would have a record of how it was done. Margaret came off the cloud onto a very barren, desolate landscape. No vegetation, just dirt with a few rocks. It was a very inhospitable environment. She noticed a few tall people standing nearby dressed in beige robes and sandals. She saw she was a man who was dressed the same way, with the robe secured by a cord around her waist. When I asked if she lived near there, she could not see any structures whatsoever, just the barren landscape. Then she was surprised to see something unexpectedly on the ground by the people. "There's a *hole* in the ground," she said. "It goes into the ground. It's where we go down." When she went over to it, she noticed there was a ladder going down into the hole, and she knew she could go down inside if she wanted to.

When she went down the ladder, she saw that there were many people living a very simple existence underneath the ground. There was a woman cooking over an open fire.

M: It's a big space. It's the entry to the passageways and to the hallways. And this is where people live.
D: *Why do you live under the ground?*
M: There's nothing on top.
D: *Couldn't you build a house up there?*
M: There's no need to build anything up there, because everything we need is underneath. There's nothing up there.

When I asked where the food and supplies came from, he became confused and couldn't tell me. Apparently he did not question it. They were supplied with what they needed to live. Everyone lived down there together, but they did have individual spaces. He shared his with his wife. It was very simple. There were many people, and also children.

M: There's a lot of dirt. Tunnels. It's very rounded there. Fires everywhere. It's very light.
D: *Are the fires on the ground?*

M: No, they're on the sides. *Inside* the walls. They cut a little ... I think a little hole for it.

D: *Have you always lived underneath the ground?* (Yes) *So no one has ever lived above the ground?*

M: (Sternly:) No, no! We don't live on top. No, no!

Apparently they did not question it. It was perfectly natural for them to live this way. They had everything they needed to exist underground. I asked what his occupation was. What did he do for the community?

M: I watch! I go above ground and I watch. I protect. I watch. I'm a guard.

D: *Do you have to stand up there above the opening?* (Emphatic: Yes!) *What are you watching for?*

M: Machines.

D: *(That was an unusual answer.) Is there a danger?*

M: There doesn't appear to be a danger now. It's more prevention.

D: *What kind of machines?* (She was uncertain.) *What do they look like?*

M: It depends. There are different kinds. Some of them are little, and they fly above the surface. They move very quickly. They're small and round.

This did not sound like an Earth environment, unless Margaret had gone ahead into a future life.

D: *What do you do if you see one of those kinds of machines?*

M: We go down. We always go down.

D: *But they're not very big. You said they just fly over the surface?*

M: The little ones fly near to the surface.

D: *What about the other machines? What do they look like?*

M: Some of them are very big, and very ... mean. I don't know why they come by, but they sometimes do.

D: *Can you describe what one of those looks like?*

M: Yes. Two legs. And on top, they can see. They come by

345

and they can see.

D: *Does it look like one of you? Like a person?*

M: (Emphatic:) No, no! It has metal legs. It has no arms.

D: *Does it walk?*

M: Yes. It's very awkward. We're most afraid of those. (Long pause) They scan for holes in the ground. They come by, and they scan.

D: *What would they do if they found a hole?*

M: They would take somebody. The other machines don't take anybody.

His job was to watch for these strange machines and warn the people when they were coming. Others also took turns watching. He did not know what happened to the people they took; they just never saw them again. I decided to move Margaret ahead to an important day. She became very emotional as she came in on it.

M: I'm scared. (Hesitation) They ... they found us. And they're taking ... (emotional) they're taking the people away. And I'm trying to protect my family. (Emotional, breathing faster.) Everybody's panicking.

D: *I thought you were safe down there. They could get down into the hole?*

M: No, they don't come down into the hole, but they take us. It's like they don't need to come physically down. They suck us up. Through the hole. (This was upsetting her.) We have passageways to take us away from the danger. That go deeper. We take our families and we take them deeper. Deeper into ... the planet. Into the soil. We have passageways that go deeper.

D: *Do you have any kind of weapons that you might use?*

M: No. We can't do anything against them.

D: *So you just have to run. That's the only way you can get away from this?* (Yes.) *You said it was like being sucked out. Is that what you saw happen?* (Emotional again: Yes.) *Is this the first time they've come in there like that?* (Yes)

I was trying to think of questions to ask, because Margaret was not volunteering much information on her own. Fear was overriding her desire to talk to me. This was a strange regression to have for a demonstration, and the students were sitting motionless listening to every word. I am used to having these types of strange sessions, but they had not experienced anything like this in their practices. But that was the whole motive of having the class, to show them that the strange and unusual is possible to obtain with my technique. This way, if and when it happened to them, they would know that it can be controlled, and that the client is in no danger. The subconscious was allowing the story to come forth for a reason that would benefit Margaret. I had to find out what that reason was.

Most of the people were able to escape from the strange scavenger machine. I then moved Margaret forward again to another important day. If she had been fantasizing a strange tale to impress us, I believe she would have continued with the frightening machine. Instead she went to a very normal scene.

M: My son is preparing to leave. He's leaving here now ... for good.

D: *I thought you had to stay there.*

M: He's not staying. He's going to serve somewhere else. He's preparing his bags. He's very proud. Sometimes the boys go somewhere else. They're taken and they go to serve in other locations. In different ways. Not everybody stays underneath.

D: *Have you ever seen these places?* (No) *How do you feel about your son leaving?*

M: It's fine. He's a strong boy. He's very sturdy. He's very tall. He's very strong. The stronger ones go other places. It's not sad. It's hard, but I'm proud of him.

I moved him forward to another important day, and he was being honored for years of faithful service. He was now older and he wouldn't have to work any more. He said it was now time to think, a time for reflection.

347

There was only one place left to go now, and that was to his death. I wasn't sure what to expect because of the strange nature of this regression. But it was not a violent death by the strange machine. It was a normal ordinary death in his bed in the underground quarters. He said he was older and his heart was giving him trouble. Margaret was exhibiting physical sensations, so I had to give suggestions to remove these.

M: I've written many books that are in the corner. I'm very proud.
D: *What were the books about?*
M: Philosophy. Spirituality. Many people read my books. There's a whole pile of them over there.
D: *That's good. You like to think. You've passed on the knowledge.*

I then moved him to after the death when he had entered the spirit realm. From that perspective, he would be able to see the entire lifetime, not only the small portions we had covered. He described that it was their custom to burn the body after death. This was also done in the underground environment, so it must have had many areas within the tunnel complex. I asked what he thought was learned from this strange lifetime. Strange from *my* viewpoint anyway.

M: Service. Service with my work, and service with my books. And the importance of introspection.
D: *You mean thinking?*
M: Yes, I did a lot of that.

I then moved her away from the scene, and brought her to the present time. I had Margaret's personality replace the man's so that I would be able to bring forth the subconscious to find the reasons for presenting this strange session.

D: *Why did you choose this lifetime for Margaret to see?*
M: Humility. She led a life of guarding and serving, but she wasn't very humble. She needed to learn how to be humble.

348

D: *She was proud?* (Yes) *We didn't know that. She was doing a good job at her work, but she wasn't humble.* (Yes) *That was a strange life. Was it on Earth?* (No) *Can you give us an idea where it was?*

M: Orion.

D: *Why was it so barren?*

M: There's no life on the surface of that planet.

D: *Is that why they lived underground?* (Yes) *Where did they get their food?*

M: It was brought to them. Their friends close by would bring the food regularly. It was in exchange for materials in the planet. They would bring food, and they took lots of materials.

D: *Of course, she didn't seem to know where the food was coming from.*

M: No, it was by land. Most people didn't work inside the planet. It was provided to them.

D: *The people that lived underground didn't seem to be very sophisticated. They didn't have much technology, did they?*

M: No. They were a very jovial and light-hearted, kind group.

D: *What were those strange machines?*

M: They came from the central base.

Apparently where the man lived was an outpost, and they had no reason or ability to travel very far from it.

D: *What were the little flying machines she saw?*

M: On patrol. Going around on patrol. To see what they could find.

D: *What were the ones with the metal legs?*

M: Scavengers. They would go around looking for the holes, and take what they could find ... from energies.

D: *What would they do with the people when they found them?*

M: Use them. They'd use them for fuel.

D: *Fuel? What do you mean?*

M: Burn them for fuel at the central base.

D: *This was how the base was powered or what?*

M: Yes. By people. People that they could find underground. There was nothing on top. They had to have something to use for fuel.

That was certainly a grisly mental image.

D: *She said it was almost like sucking them out.*
M: Yes. There was a combination between actually physically pulling them out and filling up their energy. It would happen rather as though they were being sucked out.
D: *And they would take them back to the base, and use them as fuel to power the* city?
M: There's no city as you would think of a city. It's more machines, major machines. Not so much a city. Mechanized.
D: *What connection does that have with Margaret's life now?*
M: She needs to learn a lesson of humility. Her big goal is to serve others. She has a sense of urgency to really get out and help other people. It's almost as though it's insatiable sometimes.
D: *But is that her purpose? Because that's one of the questions she wanted to ask.*
M: Yes, most certainly. She's doing the right thing. She has so many fears and concerns. And she just doesn't let go.

This is a common thread that runs through most of my regressions, even though it is the last thing the client is aware of. The subconscious always chastises them because they are here to do something (usually to help others in some way) and they are caught up in the everyday things of life. This has caused them to forget what they came in to do. I have never had the subconscious say the person is here to live and play, have a family and a mundane existence. They are always told they are here for a purpose, and that purpose is supposed to make a difference in other people's lives and a difference in the world.

It is amazing that this is a common theme, yet it is totally unknown to the conscious mind. It seems that once the person gets here and becomes an adult, they get caught up in the earthly rat race. The unreality of it all becomes their reality, and no matter how high-minded they may seem, they have lost sight of their true reason for incarnating. Hopefully, they can discover their purpose and work on it before they get too close to the end of their lives, and it is too late to accomplish it. If that happens, the only solution is to return and try all over again.

I continued with her questions, most of which dealt with her personal life: her occupation and the city she should live in. Her romantic relationship and other concerns.

After Margaret awakened, I turned the tape recorder back on to record some of her memories of the session.

M: When we were going down the passageway. I saw the inner passageway very clearly. There were like bridges underground. Long bridges of dirt. It was very hollow. I saw long lines of people going down.

Apparently, that was all she remembered, just the scenes at the beginning. This is typical and is what most people remember. The students told her about the things she said, especially the parts that came from the subconscious. Much of this was personal and I did not include it here. She had no memory of those parts. She was very amazed about her revelations about herself.

In another case in late 2004 a woman journeyed to another planet where the inhabitants had a humanoid body shape, but they were definitely not human. They all looked alike because they wore coverings that completed enclosed all of their body in a skin tight material. The only thing that was not covered by this was their face. However, it was also covered by a see-through panel that served as a breathing device. On this planet they had no need for food or sleep. The being traveled to other planets and asteroids in a small one man craft, and collected soil samples. These he brought back to the home planet and they were analyzed. Their job was to see if the planet he was visiting was capable of supporting life. Then the rest of the procedures were handled by someone else. He eventually died when his breathing device malfunctioned. All of these cases in this section demonstrate that there are as many possible scenarios of life on other planets as there are stars in the heavens. They defy our imagination.

CHAPTER 18

THE PLANET WITH THE PURPLE SUN

This session was one of the first I did after opening my office in Huntsville, Arkansas, shortly after Christmas 2003. The office has worked very well, and the energy seems to be conducive to really powerful sessions. Each person that comes there seems to bring their own unique vibration. My clients say they can feel a very positive energy there.

During this session, Molly literally became the other personality and was animated.

When Molly came off of the cloud, all she could see was purple and green colors. This sometimes happens and I usually have to move the person through the colors in order to come out to a scene. This time the colors turned out to be something else that I could not have anticipated. She only saw darkness, with the colors providing the only light. After several minutes, she finally realized she was in a cave. This was the reason it was dark and difficult to see anything except the colors.

M: Yes, I'm inside the cave. And there are lights at the top. I'm at the bottom, and on the ceiling of the cave there are reflections. Reflected light. There's no fire. There's no light. Just these glowing lights on the ceiling.

D: *I wonder what it's the reflections of?*

M: Crystals. Amethysts. Big, like geodes. And the deeper I go, the deeper the color gets. They're reflected up there on the ceiling. (Her voice sounded almost childlike.) And I'm laying down looking up. I'm not walking. I'm laying down on the floor of the cave looking up. Sandy. I'm laying on something sandy, and looking up at the ceiling. Hmm. There must be lights *somewhere* reflected down in here. But

I like it right here. It's like my own aurora borealis inside.

D: *Are you by yourself?*

M: I think so. It feels as if I'm by myself.

D: *What kind of clothes do you have on? What does it feel like?*

M: (She rubbed her hands over her chest, trying to feel the clothes.) Furry. (She laughed.) Furry. Furry, yeah. (She kept rubbing it and smiling.)

D: *Do they cover all of your body?*

M: Can't see this. It's dark. It just covers to here and down to here. (She placed her hands on her chest and thigh areas.)

D: *Your chest and your waist?*

M: Torso. Not on my arms.

D: *Are you a male or a female?*

M: I'm a male. I feel pretty big. (She was moving as though she was proud of her body. She enjoyed being in this body.)

D: *Are you young or old?* (Pause) *What does it feel like?*

M: Fifteen summers.

D: *Oh, so you're still young then.*

M: I have family. I have responsibilities.

She was definitely becoming the other personality. Her voice and manner of speaking were very simple. So I supposed she was some type of native or primitive person.

D: *If you're a male, do you have a beard? (She felt her face and chin.) What do you feel there?*

M: Furry. This (face hair) is coarser than this (body fur clothes).

D: *But you have responsibilities. You already have a family.* (Yes) *Do you have children?* (Yes) *A wife?*

M: (She hesitated, as though the word was unfamiliar.) I have a woman.

D: *Do you live in that cave?*

He certainly sounded like a caveman, but I was in for a surprise.

M: No, I found this. I followed some animal into here. And this is where I can go and just look at the colors. I've known about it since I was a child. But I don't tell everyone. It's mine. (Smug laugh.)

D: *You don't want them to find it.*

M: No. If I have to, I would share. But since I don't have to, we have other accommodations. I'll just keep this to myself for a while. It's peaceful here. My work is done. I can relax here.

D: *What kind of work do you do?*

M: Hmmm. (Thinking) I sow things. I dig in the ground, and I sow things. What I sow and grow then I trade for other things. We have hunters and we have growers. And I fit in the growers, because I can't hunt.

D: *Everybody has something they can do. They have their specialty. (Yes) Are there many in your group? (Pause) Because I'm assuming it's not just you and your woman and your children.*

M: There are .... I'm counting. Fifteen. We're a pretty good size group.

D: *Yes. Are you all family? Are you all related?*

M: (Thinking) No. We are a group.

D: *Do you live near where this cave is?*

M: It is ... half day away from where I live.

D: *Doesn't the group worry about you if you're gone that long?*

M: They think I'm on a quest.

D: *Do your people go on quests?*

M: There are male people that do.

D: *What do you look for when you go on the quest?*

M: Dragons. I do the quests for the group. The males that go on quests are guided towards ... for hunting. When I go on my quest, it is to discover what is needed for the group.

Similar to other primitive cultures, as in my book, *Legend of Starcrash* where they relied on instincts to find animals, etc.

D: *You also said you trade with others.*

M: Mostly for survival, I trade within my group. And then we

355

also go once a year to a gathering and exchange goods.

D: *It sounds like you're happy there, aren't you?* (No answer.) *Do you know what that means?* (No) *It means you like living there?*

M: Yes, I like living there. We are well taken care of. (Words were becoming difficult.) We have shelter. We have water. We have food. And we have what we need. Is that happy?

D: *Yes, I think so. You would not change anything. If you would not want something else, then you're content. You're happy.*

M: Yes, happy. When we go to group gathering, we make changes there. We learn what other groups are doing, and if we like it, we bring it back. We can trade and acquire different tools, and things we need to make *our* lives more comfortable.

D: *You share knowledge and information. That's very good. Where you live, is it cold or hot?*

M: It is warm. It is very ... (had difficulty finding the word) agreeable and warm. What is this? (Had difficulty with the order of the words.) A chill gets where sometimes we need an extra skin or blanket, but not for very long.

D: *Then that is a good place to live. And you have everything you need.*

M: (Unexpectedly) We have a purple sun. Humph!

D: *A* purple *sun?*

This was an unexpected twist. The first indication that this was not a simple primitive lifetime.

M: We have a purple sun. A sun, up there sun, it's purple.

D: *Purple. That's a rather strange color, I would think.*

M: I don't know. It's purple. (I laughed.)

D: *Well, where I live, it's yellow or orange.*

M: That's a *strange thing.* Mine is purple.

D: *Hmmm. What color is the sky?*

M: It is ... kind of ... purple. (As though she was studying it.) (Laugh) Assorted shades of purple.

D: *So the sky is purple also?* (Yes) *Does the sun shine all the time, day and night?*

M: (Pause) I don't know day, night.

D: *Does it ever get dark outside?*

M: Not *out*side, no. In *here* it gets dark (in the cave), but not outside.

D: *Because you know when it's dark, it's hard to see.* (Yes) *But when you're outside, you mean the sun shines all the time?*

M: Unless I close my eyes. But yes, it doesn't get like inside the cave. It stays the same, assorted shades of color outside.

D: *Oh. Because where I live, it becomes very dark sometimes, when the sun goes away.*

M: Outside? Your sun goes away?

She expressed genuine surprise.

D: *Yes.* (Oh!) *And it comes back though.*

M: Where does it go?

D: *Oh, it goes away for a little while and goes to sleep, and then it comes back.*

When talking with someone apparently primitive, I have to use terminology that I think they will understand. You can't get too complicated.

D: *And we don't worry about it. But when it goes to sleep, then the whole world gets dark. So you don't have it like that?*

M: No. It is very lavender ... we have assorted shades of lavender or purples. And sometimes they're light, and sometimes they get a darker shade, but it's still where I can see my hand. Or I can see to walk down the path. I don't need any artificial or other light to see that.

D: *You don't need a fire or anything?* (No) *Do you know what "fire" is?*

M: Well, I don't need it, so I don't think I do.

How do you explain something so basic and simple?

357

D: *Do you cook your food?*

M: Cook food? No. We pluck food. And we dig it. And we have ways of *preparing* our food. We have these rocks that are very, very hot. And we put our food in containers, and we put it by the rocks until it's done.

D: *Well, a fire would be very, very hot, like flames. And you can see it. So you don't have that.*

M: No, we have hot rocks. We have hot water, and we have hot steam.

D: *Does this come out of the mountains?*

M: It's in the ground. It's always hot.

D: *That's very good.*

M: Is it? Yes, it is very good.

D: *Do you ever kill anything to eat it?*

M: Kill things? Like hitting them on the head, or drive them into the hot rocks?

D: *Well, animals of any kind?*

M: Yes, because that is what this fur is made of.

D: *That's what you're wearing.* (Yes) *So you do kill animals sometimes?* (Yes) *Then do you eat the meat?*

M: Yes, yes. We use everything there. There's not much left when we are done.

D: *So there are certain kinds of animals that you will eat?*

M: Yes, they have four legs.

D: *Do you ever use the animals for anything else?*

M: (Confused) No. Like ... no.

D: *Well, some people use animals to carry things, and to pull things.*

M: No. When we have something heavy that needs to go somewhere else, we just look at it. It moves it.

D: *(That was a surprise.) Oh! That sounds easy.*

M: Yes. And when I said we drive the animals to the hot rocks? We really just ... (difficulty thinking how to explain it.) ... just ask them to do that, and they do that. (Big sigh)

D: *Do all of the people in your group have this ability? To just look at things and make these things happen?*

M: (Confused) I guess so. We just all do it. Yes, it must be, because if the baby, or the small one, wants something over

358

there, it goes over where the baby is. Little things.

D: *So even the baby is able to do this.* (Yes)

This creature sounded so strange with these abilities, I wondered if it also looked different from humans.

D: *I'm wondering about your body. Do you also have ... well, you don't have four legs, do you?*
M: No, I have two legs.
D: *And two arms?*
M: (She raised her arms in front of her to examine them.) Two arms. Yes, two arms.
D: *I think some of these words you don't know. But that's okay. I think we're understanding each other. How many fingers do you have on one of your hands?*
M: (She held up her hand to examine it.) Three.
D: *Three fingers. Which ones are they? Can you show me?*
M: (She held them up for me.) Three. Like that.

The little finger was missing. This has happened in several regressions where people were aliens or seeing aliens. The little finger is either missing, or only a useless stub.

D: *Do you have what we call a thumb?*
M: Like that? Yes.
D: *Is that enough to do the job?*
M: (She laughed. It probably seemed like a stupid question to him.) Yes.
D: *(Laugh) All right. But what color is your skin?*
M: Black. It's very dark.
D: *And you said you have a beard. What color is your hair on your head and your beard?*
M: Dark. Black. Different dark than my skin.
D: *Do you have eyes? And nose and mouth?*
M: (Long pause) I see! And I speak! And I eat.
D: *And the nose is to smell, isn't it?*
M: (Confidently) I smell!

D: *So you can do all of those things.* (Yes) *Are there others that look different or dress different?*
M: We dress as we choose, but we're all of the same appearance, yes.

I wasn't thinking, because that is hard to do in a session like this, but he might have been thinking "different from what?". Because he was probably just like everyone else in his culture. I was the different element.

D: *Where do you live?*
M: I have a *structure.*

When he described the "structure" it became even more obvious that this was not a primitive society, even though the man seemed to be living quite simply.

The structure was dome shaped, and everyone had their own "section" within the larger structure. "It is domes within domes." There was a larger central structure used for meeting, eating and visiting. When I asked what material the structures were made of, it only confused him more. I asked about wood and he didn't understand. I attempted to describe trees and it was evident that they did not have such plants. Or if they did, they were not used for construction. "Our plants are for our eating and decoration. They provide food for our animals as well as our beings, our peoples." He said the structures were a polymer. Now it was my turn to be confused; this was a word I was not familiar with.

Dictionary: polymer - any of two or more polymeric compounds. Polymeric - composed of the same chemical elements in the same proportions by weight, but differing in molecular weight. Polymerization - the process of joining two or more like molecules to form a more complex molecule whose molecular weight is a multiple of the original and whose physical properties are different.

I didn't know any more than before I looked it up. Complex is putting it mildly. I asked if his people built the structure.

"Oh, no. You look at picture, and you look where you want it to be. And it becomes."

He was full of surprises. He said the pictures were located in their libraries. "There are small libraries in this structure, and then there's the big main library in the large gathering place. I *see* them. They are ... projections (unsure of the word). Where you go to the room, and you think what you want to see. And then the projections come, and you choose the one that you want. And you choose the place you want it at, and it becomes there."

D: *(This was a different and unique idea.) So the pictures are always on the wall then.*

M: They're like ... a box. A box. And they go ... fast. Or as fast as you want them to go. (Laugh) (Hand motions.) And then when you find the area you want to look at, it slows down. And then you look at each one, till you find the one that appeals to you.

D: *And then you just create it with your mind.* (Yes) *That's wondrous.*

M: And then you do whatever you want with the inside.

D: *So your people decided to make the structures a dome shape.* (Yes) *And you can even create the material to make it out of.* (Yes) *You don't have to have material that you would build with your hands, to make it happen.*

M: No. You just ... do it. We've been doing this for many, many moons.

D: *Did someone show you how to do it?*

M: I don't think so. It's kind of like you practice for it. Doing something when you're a child, and then as you grow, you start doing different things. And pretty soon you can think your own. When you need a place of shelter, you can make your own. Some choose to do it in small groups. Others do it in major groups. Some do it out in isolation, or where they're further apart from the rest of the group.

D: *But everyone in your group knows how to do these things.*

M: Yes. When my children are bigger, then they will do the

same thing.

D: *Where you live there, are there any cities around?*

M: We go to the major gathering. And that's much larger. There may be hundreds of people there.

D: *Do you know what a city is?* (Long pause, then: No.) *It's where there are many, many structures very close together. And there are many people all living in the same place.*

M: That would be very uncomfortable. So we are more in smaller groups for our comfort, and to not put stress upon our land.

D: *Yes, that would make sense, really. Well, how do you travel to go to these different places?*

M: When we go to gatherings, our group gathers together, and we think where we want to go, and there we are.

D: *The whole group goes at once?*

M: We go at ... all at the same ... Yes.

D: *I thought maybe you had to walk.*

M: When I go to my cave, or when I go exploring, then I move with my legs. But when we go to gatherings, we go "Poof". (Hand motions indicating speed).

D: *Very quickly.*

M: Yes. And we miss a lot of things. We just "Poof". (I laughed) So when I'm at home and I want to find things, I walk around and look, to see what I can see.

This session had certainly taken me by surprise and had many twists. What appeared to be a simple life of a primitive caveman turned into a much more sophisticated society. I decided to take him forward to an important day.

D: *What are you doing? What do you see?*

M: There's lots of noise. Lots of chaotic noise. People thundering. The earth is shaking kind of noise. The earth ... Oooh.

D: *The land is moving, you mean?*

M: It's shaking. People are screaming. Animals are screaming. It's very noisy. (She shuddered) Very chaotic. And it's very hard to breathe.

She exhibited physical signs that it was affecting her. She started coughing. I gave calming suggestions. She took several deep breaths as the distracting physical symptoms subsided.

D: *What's causing that?*
M: The mountain is exploding. It just exploded. Perhaps we didn't appease the god.
D: *Do you believe in gods?*
M: We have many gods. The priests and priestesses tell us we have many gods. We have a god for the house, and a god for being fertile for the children, for protection, for the garden, for ... we have many gods.
D: *And you said you have to appease them?*
M: Yes. Otherwise they get angry if they're ignored. They're sometimes like (She lowered her voice to a whisper, as though telling a secret, or trying to keep the gods from hearing her.). Shhh! They're like little children who don't get their way.
D: *I understand what you mean. What do you do to appease these gods?*
M: We give money to the priests. We give honey. We make little altars. We just honor them, and let them know that we know they're there.
D: *I wouldn't think that you would need money.*
M: It's little silver things. Little monies makes them happy, to have something shiny.
D: *But you think maybe you didn't do it right?*
M: The priests are saying that we didn't. We didn't sacrifice enough. That we didn't believe strong enough. So the mountain god has to tell us that we need to believe, need to straighten up.
D: *You think the mountain god became angry.*
M: That's what I'm told.
D: *And this caused the mountain to explode, and the ground to shake.*
M: Yes. And the hot ... hot ... hot (had difficulty finding the

363

word) hot lava stuff to come. And the ashes in the air.

D: *That's why it's hard to breathe?*

M: Yes. And you can't see. It's very difficult, and it's very scary. And it's very devastating. People are dying.

D: *Can't you use your abilities to just move to get away?*

M: Well, you can run, but where can you go? (Nervous laugh)

D: *I mean your other abilities you have to just move from one place to the other. You can't do that to get away?*

M: *I* cannot do that!

D: *You have to do it in a group?*

M: I cannot do that. We cannot do that.

D: *I thought that was how you went from one place to another.*

M: Not *me!* I have to walk or run or ride an ass.

D: *So you can't get away. People just have to run.*

M: Yes. And when you can't breathe, and when you're scared, people fall down. And then the ash covers you up so fast. And then you can't breathe any more. And ... and ....

D: *You can talk about it. It won't bother you at all. I don't want you to be uncomfortable. What about your family? Are they there?*

M: No. My father and my mother were nearer the top. They were up on the top of the mountain. They live closer to the top, and I am down in the valley. And the ones at the top were the ones killed first. But now it's moved down into the valley. And the ash is blowing, and the lava is flowing. The earth is shaking, and the houses are falling.

D: *Are your woman and your children there?*

M: I have no women and children! I have no family this time where I am.

D: *So this is a different place? Oh, I'm sorry. I'm getting confused.*

M: This is the only place I live.

I did not pick up on the signs earlier, only when I listened to the tape while transcribing. I should have picked up on it when she didn't know what I was talking about, with the ability to move themselves. Now it was clear. When I asked her to move to an important day, she "leap-frogged". She jumped into a different life. I had continued to talk to her as though she was the man on the planet with the purple sun. Now I understood she had jumped into a different life. I would have to adjust my questioning.

D: *The only place you live. All right. But that sounds very scary.*
M: The sky is falling, and the earth is moving up to meet it. We will not be much longer.
D: *What kind of a job were you doing?*
M: I made gold jewelry. Gold leaf and ... necklaces. Tiaras and crowns. And bracelets. I made jewelry.

We had come into this other life on the day of her death. But I wanted to continue and finish the life of the unusual man on the planet with the purple sun, rather than find out about a different life. Besides, I knew we could get it all straightened out when I spoke to the subconscious. So I had her leave that scene of destruction, and locate the man with the fur who lived in the dome structure on the planet with the purple sun. She immediately returned to that life, and I was able to move her to the last day of her life in *that* lifetime.

D: *What's happening? What do you see on the last day?*
M: My family has come to bid me adieu. It's time for me to depart.
D: *Is there anything wrong with the body?*
M: It has just become used up. It is time to depart it. And make room for others to come and live here.
D: *Sometimes the body stops because something is wrong with it.*
M: No, it's just not functioning any more. I believe it's time to go. I'm very comfortable.
D: *Do you just decide to go when you want to?*
M: We have options in our ... society. We can stay until we're driven out through illness, or accident, or we can choose our time. And I just made a decision now, that it is time for me to go. I have fulfilled my purposes.
D: *So your family is with you. I suppose they're grown now, aren't*

they?

M: My wife is gone. Your term is "wife", correct? And she's gone. My sons and daughters are here. And their grandchildren. We have great-*great*-grandchildren now.

D: *So they're all there to say good-bye to you.*

M: To say good-bye. It's not a big thing. It's just a respect they're here to show me.

D: *Are you in your dome structure?*

M: We're not at the one where you visited with me before. We have a different one. We have chosen to live out in the countryside.

D: *I thought you were in the cave that you liked so much.*

M: No, because I didn't want to share that yet with anyone. I never told anyone of that cave. There was no need to.

D: *That was your own secret.*

M: That was my quest cave, yes.

D: *Let's move to where whatever happened has already happened, and you're on the other side of it. And you can look back at the entire lifetime from that position. And see it from a totally different perspective. What did they do with your body after you left it? What's the custom there?*

M: It ... (laugh) it dissolves. It dissolves, yes. But we never gradually totally are nothing, you know. It dissolves, and it's absorbed into the system of our land. Of our country. Our part becomes part of the air and the earth. It was an easy going, you know. When you're ready, and you know you have accomplished what it is you came for, it is an easy, joyous celebration of the going. There are some there that would be upset, but no, it's only a momentary thing. Now there's a celebration. And I am free of the body.

D: *And they celebrate it because they know you are going on to a different world.*

M: Yes. And it's very lively. (Laugh) Oh, they're having a very nice time down there. And (voice dropped to a whisper) they're talking nicely of me. They have good memories.

D: *Do you think you learned anything from that life?*

M: (Slowly) I learned that I was capable of influencing others. And needed to be very careful to not project *my* perceptions as being the *only* perceptions on to other peoples, other beings, other parts of the family. To allow space for each individual to make their own discoveries.

D: *That's a very good lesson, isn't it?*

M: Yes. It was trying at times. (Laugh)

D: *And it was a good life.*

M: Oh, it was a *very* good life. I have no *wants*, no regrets.

D: *And you could do wonderful things with your mind.*

M: You seem astounded or surprised at that.

D: *Well, some places they don't use their minds.*

M: I see! I *don't* see, but ... (Laugh)

D: *I mean there are many places where they don't know how to use these abilities.*

M: I imagine perhaps our *race* always had these abilities. Looking back within my lifetime we did.

D: *All of you did, so it was a very natural thing.* (Yes) *That's why I am surprised, because where I come from, it's not natural.*

M: But you have a yellow sun.

D: *(Laugh) Yes, we have a yellow sun. (Laugh) It has to be different in different places.* (She laughed.) *And we have something you didn't have. We have a moon.* (Oh?) *A moon is white, and it shows in the dark.* (Oh.) *Like I told you, the sun goes away and goes to sleep, the moon comes out.* (Oh.) *So we all have different things.*

M: Can you move things with your mind?

D: *No, we haven't learned how to do that yet.*

M: (Big sigh) It makes life quite easy, you know.

D: *It does. And I respect that you know how to do that. That would be something you could teach us. Something that we could really use.*

M: Possibly. I don't know how to teach that, because it was just there. And I can't even describe it. Just did it.

I then oriented her back to our time period and integrated Molly's personality back into her body, so I could contact her subconscious to find some answers. There was a deep breath as the shift occurred.

D: *Why did you choose that unusual life for her to see? I think it's unusual, anyway. (Laugh) Why did you pick that life of the native on the planet with the purple sun for her to see?*

M: She wanted to know of other planetary lives, other than Earth beings.

D: *It sounded like it was another planet.* (Yes) *They didn't have any night there?*

M: No. As you are maybe thinking in terms of time? (Yes) They did not have that concept of time. They didn't have the day and night. When they were tired, they rested. When they were not tired, they *didn't* rest. But there was no dark, right. It was pretty constant. And there was no need of a dark at night.

D: *Because I'm thinking of the world revolving around the sun.*

M: Their galaxy is further beyond. It is not part of this galaxy with the sun. I believe it's of the ... (Pause as she was thinking how to say it.) super sun. No, that's not the right word.

D: *But it's not part of our solar system.*

M: Correct.

D: *But it's part of the galaxy?*

M: Correct.

D: *And there's a different sun there.*

M: No, not sun as humans know it though. It's part of a super ... I guess super sun would be the ... that's Molly's language: super sun. Super sun is what is known as the supreme being. It provides the light unto the darkness. And that planet does not have darkness.

D: *It sounds like what I have also heard called the "central sun".*

M: That's it. The *central* sun. That would fit the description, yes.

D: *But they seemed to be physical beings.* (Yes) *And they were able to use their minds to a remarkable degree.*

M: Yes, that is correct. They just manifest.

D: *They were physical because they ate and they slept and they died.*

M: Yes. They had a shorter life span. They chose a shorter life span to keep their planet underpopulated.

D: *But still, it's different because the sun was in the sky all the time. And it was a purple color.*

M: Correct.

D: *But you showed this to Molly so she would know that she had lived on other planets?*

M: Correct.

D: *How is that connected with her present lifetime?*

M: She still has the ability to manifest whatever she needs in any quantity she needs. She has many natural abilities that she is afraid to admit she has, because then she would be different.

D: *So you're trying to show her she's done this before, and she can do it again?* (Yes) But how can she tap into this? How can she bring it forward?

M: Choose to remember.

D: *Because I know once you learn something, you never forget it. It's always there. And if it's advisable it can be brought forward. She could use it now, couldn't she?*

M: Yes. If she steps past what is known as her human fear.

D: *You know how humans are.*

M: Yes. (Laugh) Oh, what a challenge. (Big laugh) Why do people come here? (Laugh) They have this challenge. What a hoot! (She continued laughing.)

D: *To learn lessons.* (Yes) *They forget all the things they used to know.* (Yes) *So she can bring these abilities back, to manifest anything she wants, if she chooses to remember.*

M: Correct.

D: *I think she would like to bring these abilities back. Can you explain a little better what she can do?*

M: Things in some sense come very easy to her. In this lifetime, she's convinced she has to work hard for everything. (Laugh) And she does *not.* So if she would just take a few more minutes in her meditation, then the memories could come flooding back in a rush. May I tell

369

you, it's the *conditioning* that she *has* accepted in this lifetime, saying she can't do it.

D: *During the session, when I took her to an important day, she jumped into what appeared to be another life. Where the volcanoes were erupting and the ground was shaking. Why did you jump her into that life? We didn't go any further with it. It was the day of the death. Why did you show that to her?*

M: Reminding her of – for lack of another term – the silliness of turning over one's power to outside influences. Rather than going inside, and knowing the god in her.

D: *How did that relate to the volcano and the earth changes?*

M: The belief system was that it was caused because of not appeasing the gods.

D: *Oh, yes, that's right. They didn't appease the gods and that's what caused it.*

M: Yes. That was the belief system, and there's still some of that, that's very prevalent in the area that she lives in. And it frightens her.

D: *Yes, it goes along with the religion of this time.*

So she was being shown that little piece of that life to remind her that she shouldn't get caught up in the traditional religion beliefs of the culture she lives in. But to think for herself and find the true God within herself.

During my interview with Molly, she said she had strange memories of things that happened in her childhood. She remembered being put into a dark place and left there, because no one wanted to have contact with her. She thought maybe it was a closet, and it seemed she was in there for several days at a time. Of course, by that time she would be smelly and dirty, but she had the feeling no one wanted anything to do with her. When she asked her mother about these childhood memories, she denied anything like that had ever happened to her, and said she was probably making it up or fantasizing. But she said, why would she fantasize an awful memory like that? One of the things she wanted to find during this session, was whether it was a real memory or a demented fantasy. The subconscious supplied the answer before I could ask the question. And the answer was so strange, we could never have imagined it.

Her family lived in the country many miles from anyone when she was born prematurely. Her mother did the only thing she was familiar with, she put the baby into a shoe box and set it on the open oven door to provide warmth.

M: Well, you know ... no, you wouldn't know, but let me tell you. She chose to come into this lifetime with *so* much in the way of gifts to others. And she went into this little bitty baby. She was only four pounds something when she was born. She would do those things. This little bitty baby in the shoe box sitting on the oven door. (Laugh) She would do stuff, and it would just *scare* the bejesus out of people. And one time her mother shut her up in the oven to make her stop. Because she would juggle the stuff in the kitchen. (Laugh) Her mother was very afraid of her.

D: *So she used to make things move.*

M: Yes. She liked to juggle the silverware, because it flashed. It was flashy. (Laugh) And it would make good noise. But it scared her mother. So her mother would shut her up!

D: *So she put her in the oven.*

M: She sometimes shut the oven door.

D: *She has this strange memory of being in a closet or something. Can you tell her anything about that?* (Pause) *What do you think? Is it all right for her to know?*

M: (Now serious.) It will be better for her to know that it was the truth, not an imagination. And that it's really important for her to know. When she was a few years older, they shut her up in the closet and tried to forget about her, because she frightened them so much. But she blames herself, because she was always told it was her fault she was in there. If she would behave herself she wouldn't be stuck in there.

D: *What did she do?*

M: She liked to make those flashy silverware float around. And she liked to make lights when it was dark. And she liked to

371

make singing noises when she wasn't supposed to be able to talk. She would scare people. So they thought she was weird, and so she blames herself. And it's not her fault. She was using what she remembered, and what she knows how to use. But she was just kind of "out of time".

D: *Yes, she thought it was natural.*

M: And then as she grew older, she would do things that were ... *unusual.* Again she would be rejected or pushed away or punished, until she just stopped doing those things.

D: *It was really the only way to survive.*

M: Yes. She describes it as shutting off the faucet.

D: *So when she got too big to be put in the oven, I guess they put her in a closet. Is that what you mean?* (Yes) *That's cruel, but I guess they were very afraid of her.*

M: When they put her in the dark then it was easier just to leave her in there and forget about her. Then they wouldn't have to deal with things floating around in the kitchen or in the house, or her singing.

D: *So finally just to survive, she shut off the faucet and didn't do it any more. And then they let her live with them in the house?*

M: Yes. As long as she wasn't *bad*, then she could become part of the household.

D: *Well, if all of that has been suppressed, do you think she would be afraid to bring these talents back now?*

M: I think so, because somebody might stick her back in the closet and lock the door and never let her out.

D: *Well, you know, they wouldn't really do that now that she's grown up.* (Yes) *But I can see why she'd be afraid.*

M: I think she could do certain things that are more acceptable in this society, and let a little bit at a time come back to her. Because if she went out in the middle of a field and created a house, you know the government might come looking for her. (Laugh)

D: *If she made things float around the room, I think her husband might get a little scared. (Laugh) So she's not supposed to do those things.*

M: No. But she could maybe turn the faucet on, like just a little dribble. She's very capable of helping people. She's capable of elevating them out of darkness. And that scares people, and they aren't all prepared to know who they truly, truly are. But she's afraid she will turn the faucet on, and it will all rush out. And overwhelm people, and they'll run screaming from the room. She has a very deep fear of rejection. She can use a form of meditation to bring forth the knowledge in a smaller scale, and relieve that fear. Here's a picture that will work for her. On the kitchen sink there's a trap. Like so? (Hand motions) Under the sink, yes, there's a drain pipe and there's the trap. And a lot of gook is stuck in the trap. And if she goes to the trap, she can let a little bit up over the curve at a time. Let it seep back out.

D: *Let it backtrack up into the sink.* (Yes) *This would be a mental picture she could use.*

M: Yes. And then as she opens the trap, or clears the trap out a little bit at a time, that makes room for the information to come back that she has forgotten, or has trapped in the trap.

D: *So she's not supposed to try to get it all back. That would overwhelm her.*

M: And overwhelm so many others.

These types of abilities are being allowed to return to our time period now, because these will be considered normal in the not too distant future. But it would have to be done gently so as not to shock herself and others around her. The main thing was that Molly now knew that the strange memories of childhood events were not her imagination, just the actions of people who were frightened and couldn't understand. I wonder how many others this has happened to, where they have had to shut the abilities and memories away. It is very difficult to understand and accept the abnormal actions of children.

SECTION SIX

TIME PORTALS

CHAPTER 19

GUARDIAN OF THE PORTAL

Ninety percent of the sessions I do for therapy involve the client going back to a past lifetime that holds the answers to present day problems. But it is becoming more and more frequent to have clients finding themselves in strange surroundings that do not resemble Earth. They are also finding themselves more frequently in parallel situations. This is where they are living another experience that is existing at the same time as the present life. Many skeptics will say these are only fantasies, yet they do not resemble any fantasies I have ever heard of. The majority of the time, the past lives people regress to are very boring and mundane. I call them "digging potatoes" lives, because the person is often a farmer or servant, etc., where there is nothing exciting going on to report about. They spend their lives doing simple, ordinary things, such as working the fields. The lives are very undramatic. Many times, the person is disappointed when they awaken. One man said after one such session, "Well, I certainly wasn't a Pharaoh in Egypt." If they were fantasizing, I believe they would invent a glamorous lifetime, such as a knight in shining armor rescuing a fair damsel from the castle tower, or a woman reliving a Cinderella-type life with Prince Charming. This never happens. The lifetimes experienced may seem mundane from my viewpoint, and I often wonder why the subconscious chose it for the session. But before we are finished with the session, it becomes obvious that it was exactly the lifetime they needed to see. There is always something, no matter how obscure, that relates to the problem they are experiencing. It is never obvious to me on the surface, but the subconscious, in its infinite wisdom, has chosen the precise one.

Occasionally, the scene they come into is so strange and out-of-place, they cannot even find words to describe it. In these cases, I am certain they are not creating a fantasy, or it would not baffle them. This session, held in Florida in October 2002, is one such case in point. Betty was a nurse in a neonatal unit of a large hospital. What she discovered during the session was definitely not what she was expecting. When she came off the cloud, she was standing in front of something so unusual that she could not find the words to describe it.

B: It looks like ... it looks like a crystal ... it's hard to describe. It's like a crystal mountain thing. Crystal mountain *thing*. (Chuckle) I don't know what else to call it. It's like a crystal mountain. And I see what appears to be a native American boy with black hair standing in front of the crystal mountain. It looks like ice, kind of, but it's not cold. It's clear, but not completely clear. It's sparkling in the sun.

This definitely didn't sound like something on Earth, yet she had mentioned the Indian boy. Where was she?

D: *Is the boy still there? (I was thinking maybe she was the boy.)* (Yes) *How is he dressed?*
B: He has just buckskin below his waist. Probably ten years old.
D: *Well, look down at yourself. Are you wearing anything?*

This is usually the way I begin to orient the client into the body they have in the past life. Her answer was an unexpected surprise.

B: I'm ... no, I'm very big! ... I'm huge! I'm not a body. I am (uncertain how to word it) ... I'm an energy form. I'm very *large* compared to this boy.
D: *Do you feel as though you have perimeters? You're not just part*

378

of the air, are you?

B: I have perimeters, but it's not solid. It shifts and changes, but has this same amount in it. So the perimeter shifts and changes, but it's large.

D: *So it is contained anyway.* (Yeah, yeah) *All right. What connection do you have to this boy?*

B: I'm just observing him. – I feel I'd like to go inside of this mountain. There's an opening. But it's like I could *become* the mountain. It's like, by moving into the opening of the mountain, I could experience life as the mountain. I would become it. Even though I could still separate from it again.

I was familiar with energy beings, a form of life where the being can essentially form or create any type of body they desire, in order to have an experience. But this one sounded different.

D: *So you can experience many different things?*

B: Yes.   I can become, integrate with other energies, to experience what that's like. And then separate and have that awareness as a part of me. I am about experiencing in that manner.

D: *You said there was an opening there?*

B: Yes.   It's a large opening, like a natural opening. (Suddenly) You know what? This crystal mountain isn't really a mountain at all. That's just the way it showed itself. It's like a spaceship. It's a *vehicle.* How interesting!

D: *How do you know that?*

B: (Excited) Because when I saw the opening ... you see, this is the way it looks from the outside. And as I explored the opening further to try and explain it, I realized that it was not exactly as it appeared.

D: *You mean it was giving the illusion of a mountain?*

B: Exactly. Right. So anyone who came across it would see that's what it was. But then upon closer inspection it *shifts.* Ah-ha!

D: *If it is on Earth, there would be other mountains. They might be different colors, but not crystal.*

B: Right. There are other mountains around it that are different. They are just the brown, with trees and stuff like that.

D: *It would be unusual to see a crystal mountain. It might cause more attention.*

B: It *would!* Right! Hmm. It is somewhat confusing. But then, I wonder if others even *see* it. Because I saw that boy. Did the boy see it? I don't know. I couldn't tell. He was facing away from it. I don't really know. – The opening shifted from looking like this natural opening, to a doorway. As I looked at it, it changed to a door. And there are stairs leading from the ground up to the door. It doesn't seem to be that solid. It looks crystalline and light, and I know that you could step on it and it would be solid. And yet, I also feel like someone could walk right through it and not be aware of it, at the same time. The only explanation that makes sense to me, is that it's like the merging of two worlds. It's like a place between the worlds. That there are pieces of both.

D: *This would be why some people would see it and some would not?*

B: Yes. And so I feel like somehow I am part of – I just have to say what comes to me – because it feels like somehow I am part of the keeper of this gateway, or this "between" place. So that those who are not supposed to enter, don't. And those who can, do. There are some responsibilities for awareness that I must have about that, because I'm aware of both, yes.

D: *To know who can come in and who cannot.* (Right) *But wouldn't those who were not supposed to, not even be aware of it?*

B: Normally that's true. There are times, however, when certain circumstances make it happen that there's a seeing that normally wouldn't take place. And it's just not beneficial, for the most part, for that to happen. Certain shifts in the atmospheric pressure and energy ... things. (This was said slowly as though she wasn't sure, and was searching for the words.) There are certain, yes, shifts that could make it happen.

D: *To where it could be seen, where normally it wouldn't be.* (Correct) *In that case someone might come across it, who wasn't supposed to.*

B: Yes. And it would be very confusing.

D: *Would they be able to enter it?*

B: Unfortunately, the body makeup would have to shift, because of the energy configuration. And it would possibly, probably dissolve that physical energy instantaneously.

D: *Oh? Would it destroy it?*

B: The *spirit* is not destroyed. The physical, cellular structure, yes.

D: *It could not exist once it came in contact with it?*

B: This is correct, because there's a different makeup. And different vibrations, yes. It would be very confusing and difficult for even the spirit energy to understand what happened. It is not intended to be that way.

D: *So, your job is to make sure this doesn't happen?*

B: Yes, I have a guardianship kind of responsibility for that.

D: *Would you call this a portal?*

B: Yes, you could call it that. And I believe that's also why I can move into this crystalline thing, whether mountain, spaceship or whatever. And become, have the awareness of that, because that exerts, *intensifies* the energy to separate the existences.

D: *What if someone would come? What would you do to divert them or keep them away?*

B: Focus my energy on that bend in the place to intensify it. And just kind of give them a little gentle nudge in the opposite direction. To give them a little push, so they may just feel like the wind pushed them, or they are nudged in a different direction.

D: *Just enough to keep them away from it, from coming in contact with that energy? Because your job is to keep them from getting hurt.*

B: Exactly. Protection, yes.

D: *Is this portal there all the time?*

B: There are certain times when it is more open, when it has more possibilities of being open, and other times when it is closed. When it is not an issue.

D: *Then it doesn't move around like a spaceship?*

B: No, it stays in one place. But as I look at this closer, it's more like what we might call a "stargate", rather than like a spaceship that would leave. It's more like a portal to go into another dimension.

D: *So that's why it would stay in one place.*

B: This is correct.

D: *What is the portal, this stargate used for?*

B: I must work at this description. I can do this. There's the portal for this energy, and then it goes swoosh (a long swooshing sound with hand motions) through space and time to a whole other area of the − I want to say − the "galaxy".

D: *From the motions you were making, it's elongated, like a tube?*

B: Correct. And try to visualize seeing the stars and the universe and the energy. But it's a very quick swoosh (same sound again and same hand motions) transport system. And it goes from this portal to another galaxy.

D: *Is that what you would see if you went inside this crystal mountain?*

B: That would be a portion of it, because inside, there are all these vibrant, vibrant colors, and crystalline things. It's kind of like ... (had difficulty finding the words) reentry ... desensitization is not the right word, but getting you back into feeling normal again. (Laugh) Because when you do these transport things, then you have to ... re ... not regenerate, re ....

D: *Readjust?*

B: Readjust, thank you. Whew! That was hard! Adjust. Reenergize. (Laugh)

D: *Words are hard to find sometimes.*

B: Yes. Readjust. So it's like a readjustment area. And you go into this crystalline room with all these beautiful, beautiful colors. And they vibrate into your being, and it regenerates

382

you, or re ... what was the word you said?

D: *Adjust?*

B: Adjusts you.

D: *If it readjusts you, is this before you go or after you come back?*

B: After you come back. There's one for either end. I'm not sure what the one at the other end looks like, at this moment. I would have to travel. But I have to leave part of me here in order to do that, because I have to maintain my responsibility.

D: *Yes, to guard the portal.*

B: This is used by other beings who come to learn, and come for additional awareness, by observing. When I say "observing" it's more than just watching. It is observing with every bit of your senses, so that you feel, no, *experience* it. But you're observing it, because you're not creating anything to happen. You are an observer who is allowed to somewhat integrate with the energies there for learning.

D: *Are these physical beings?*

B: Not to the extent that humans are physical beings. There's a physicality that is of a lesser density. And that is why they're able to integrate and observe an experience, at that level.

D: *Where do these beings come from?*

B: (Pause, then a chuckle as she tried to find a way to explain.) P-L. P-L has something to do with it. I don't think it's Pluto. P-L.

D: *Just tell me what you think. But they don't come from Earth?*

B: No, no. They are different.

D: *Our solar system?*

B: Hmm. A *bit* further. From a different planetary essence. Again, it's not a completely physical planet.

D: *But it's not as much of an energy as you are?*

B: Correct. They're different than I am. I don't look human, like a body. My energy is shifting. The beings that come by this transport portal system have a shape similar to humans. Similar to a body. They're tall, thin beings. Seems like heavy robes, but like I said, they're not physical.

D: *Not as solid?* (No, no.) *So when they come through this tunnel, this tube, whatever it is, they come into this room immediately?*

B: Correct, that's where they enter.

D: *And they readjust their energies? Vibrations or whatever?* (Correct) *What do they do then?*

B: Then they're able to come out from there. This is not a good description again, but it's like being able to see through glass, but there's no glass. There's no barrier like that. They've gone through the portal, and come out of the crystalline structure where the light and colors were. They've come out of that. It's still part of that energy, but it's not in that structure anymore. So that it is right up against the – I want to say "Earth". They are on the planet and can see what's going on, so that they can observe and integrate.

D: *Are they allowed to leave that place?*

B: It does not appear to me that they do.

D: *So they just stand and observe from that side without actually entering into this other dimension.*

B: Correct. However, they can see a large, large vantage point from there. They can pretty much observe anywhere they choose from this portal.

In another session, a woman saw something that looked like a wormhole appear, and beings were going back and forth through it. She described it as a large elongated tube with circular ridges visible on the inside of it. Could this be another description of the same type of device? If so, the beings she saw were entering and exiting, while the ones in this regression were only allowed to use it to view.

D: *So it's not just the area where this is located. They can see anywhere on Earth that they want to see without traveling to that place.*

B: This is correct. Pretty much. And how does stuff like that work? I'm not sure. (Laugh)

D: *See if you can find out. How can they do that from just one*

384

vantage point without actually entering into the dimension and traveling all over the world?

B: They shift their perspective. So it's like they come out and there's a particular scene or area that they're seeing. And they can just shift, and it's like the world shifts for it, so that they can see it. I know this doesn't make any sense, but .... What I see is this three-pronged gold energy that just *shifts.* (Chuckle) For example, the Earth could be this big. And they're at this place on it. (Hand motions of a small object.) And the three-pronged gold energy shifts it so that they're observing. So it's like everything moves with it. That's the only way I know to describe it. Even though obviously, the Earth is not this size. (Hand motions.) But it's as if it is, as they're observing it. So it can be shifted very easily.

D: *This way they're acting as an observer, and they don't interact.*

B: This is correct. They are not interacting. They are not changing anything. They are merely observing and integrating information.

D: *They wouldn't be allowed to leave that part anyway, I guess, because of the way their energy matrix is?*

B: Exactly. They couldn't or wouldn't. They understand the way it would affect their energy field. Whereas the humans don't even know this exists.

D: *So these beings just observe and integrate information, or whatever they're trying to accumulate. And then they go back through this tube to where they belong?*

B: This is correct. They come through that portal, but they come from other places to get to that portal. And come and observe, and then return, and report back.

D: *I was thinking of something like a central location on the other side. (Right) Do you know what they do with the information once they have observed?*

B: It's used for many purposes. (Pause as she thinks.) I see that my energy is shifting now, from that guardian being to one of those beings who came and returned.

D: *Because you said you could do that, if you leave part of your energy there to guard the opening.*

B: This is correct. (Big sigh) Going through the tube does rattle up your energy a little. So the chamber that you come out into brings you back into – what was the word you used?

D: *Adjust?*

B: To adjust, is very, very important.

D: *And when they go back through, is it fast?*

B: It's very fast. Very, very fast. And then coming out on the other side, it is again another color, energy system.

D: *Like another room?*

B: This is true. And the colors and the energy intensity brings you back to yourself again. And I came back to the other planet. And then I returned to *my* home base.

D: *What does the entrance on that side look like?*

B: It also is a crystalline structure.

D: *But the people on that side can see it?*

B: It also has a cloaking factor with it, because there are those who work with this energy, and there are those that don't.

D: *So it's the same as on Earth? It would not be visible to everyone.*

B: This is true. Even though the beings on this planet are of a higher or different vibration, there's still not a need for all to know about it.

D: *So the being that you're going with, comes through on his planet. Where does he go then?*

B: I see him. He's like a scribe writing, but the writing is magical. It's not physical, although it looks similar. (She was moving her hands.) He's doing something with his hands. But as I look at it, it's light and colors again. Light and colors are very important. And so the observations, the learning, the knowledge that was gained is incorporated into ... (She had difficulty.) ... I'm seeing like the tapestry. How did that happen?

D: *Maybe you're trying to make a comparison.*

B: Maybe. Because the information that this scribe has taken, goes into a part of the tapestry, or the records. He's sitting, and it looks like a tablet. When I say "tablet" I mean like a stone tablet. It's not paper. And there's what I would call a "magical pen", because he appears to be writing using magical writing. And there are these beautiful colors and light that come onto this. But then it moves and flows and goes into ... what I would call a "weaving". And it's colorful and light and sparkling and moving. So it's not like we consider a tapestry. (She had difficulty.) It's a record of some kind. And it's a living recording.

This, of course, sounded similar to the tapestry of life that is located in the Temple of Wisdom on the spirit side. This was explained in *Between Death and Life*. It is described as incredibly beautiful, and appears to be alive and breathing because of the beautiful colors that are woven into it. I do not think it is the same thing, because the tapestry on the spirit side is a record of all the souls that have lived and their lives. Each one is represented by a thread. The tapestry being described here is also a record, but maybe a different type.

D: *Is this his job? Does he do this all the time?*
B: Yes. And he loves to do it.
D: *But you said there are also many others that know about this doorway?*
B: Yes, there are beings from other planets that come to the portal. This is true. There are many of them that know it exists. This is one portal, but there are many others. Some of the information that comes back, is used to help develop new possibilities. It's like when you're in school, they teach you things that people already know. And once you have a basis, then you develop your own ideas. The creativity.
D: *Like scientists and researchers, they will take the basics and develop their own concepts. Is that what you mean?*
B: Yes, and also provide new possibilities for this planet as well. Because they observe, they see, they go back, they discuss. They look at, "How can we assist the people of this planet?" And so then they come up with some thoughts. And then come back. No, that can't be ... that's not right. Hmm. It's to add to the body of knowledge that is in

387

existence. About Earth, specifically in this situation.

D: *So they are accumulating information and they're trying to develop new ideas to help Earth progress or what?*

B: That was the impression I got. But there has to be another way to use the information to help Earth. Because when they come through the tube, they just observe, so they can't do it in that way. They observe and take it back to their planet and record it. So there has to be another way that it is used to help. It's not through that way.

D: *But the other beings that come through the tube, are doing it for the same reason?*

B: Some are just curious. And that's allowed. To be observed out of curiosity without any interference. Just like it's allowed for us to observe without interference. And I went with this other being whose purpose is to take the information back to his planet. And there's some kind of (had difficulty) – I'm trying to get a clearer picture. (Pause) This one is more difficult to get, so .... It appears to be some kind of *beaming* process. It doesn't make sense to me. That's why I'm kind of stuck.

D: *Describe it as best you can.*

B: Okay. So they take the information. He shares it with these other beings who are like him. And then they transmit or beam certain energies or information back toward planet Earth.

D: *In the opposite direction from where it came.*

B: Correct. It's like a guidance system. In that the information was taken from Earth, observed from Earth, and gets transported back with the beings. And then these beings take this information, and .... This is where the people of Earth need some assistance or guidance, or just a little "tweak", or a little inspiration, to help them move in the right direction. And it's not a judgment call, as in, make the right step. It's just like sending a little inspiration. So it somehow gets beamed to the Earth energy atmosphere, whatever. And then there are those on Earth who can pick up those signals, so to speak, and receive that inspiration.

And this helps them to move to the next step. Or bring about things that might have taken longer.

D: *Is this done by one individual or ....*

B: No, it's a group. A group with some kind of machinery that is able to beam the thought form or inspiration back to Earth. For example, Earth is struggling right now with war/peace, light/darkness. Moving out as duality. And as that happens, the duality is intensified. So these beings, at some point, observed, went back, and are beaming information similar to the inspiration of bringing mass consciousness together to unite, to create the reality that you want, for example. Because many people in different parts of the globe receive this inspiration at similar time frames. And then unite to make it happen. Does that example make sense to you?

D: *Yes, I think so. But are these groups under some kind of instruction? They don't act on their own, do they?* (Pause) *Is anyone telling them what they can transmit back?*

B: I want to get the correct meaning across. They are like a higher council that assists the planet with her growth. So they're not the *only* body doing this. They are one of them. Just as they are helping the Earth do that, there are also higher bodies assisting *them* with their process. So it goes on to infinity.

D: *So there are many different layers.* (Yes) *It's like the people on Earth are not that developed yet. They're at the bottom of the levels, the layers, I guess.*

B: I wouldn't say the "bottom". They're in transition. They're moving.

D: *But they aren't aware of any of this.*

B: Correct, correct. There are some that are aware. Because the energy's shifting, and the vibration is increasing, there are more who are becoming aware of the connection. There are our higher selves, for example, that observe and assist. But there's always free will, a choice. The inspiration that comes through, is for those it resonates with.

D: *It's not forced on anyone. It may be something they are looking for*

anyway.
B: Exactly. And had requested.

———————⋄——⋄§⋄——⋄⋄§⋄⋄——⋄§⋄——⋄———————

There seems to be a central theme running through all the information I have been accumulating. The theme of mass communication on many levels. Our own body is constantly processing and delivering information to our brain and central nervous system. Our DNA also processes information. In my book *Between Death and Life*, it was made clear that we must go through countless lives, both on Earth and other planets. We must, while on Earth, experience every form of life (rocks, plants, animals) before evolving to the human stage. Then when we reach the human stage, we must experience everything in life (rich/poor, male/female, live on every continent, be every race and religion, etc.) before we have completed that cycle. In between all of these lives, we go back and forth to the spirit side. Our main purpose is to accumulate information about everything possible. We began with God, and our goal is to return to God. We were told in that book, that God developed this system, because God cannot learn on His own. We, the children, are expected to return to God with all the knowledge and information we have accumulated throughout all our experiences. In this way, we are like cells in the body of God.

Thus, what I am learning from the aliens and these other more advanced, or more aware, beings, is that they have a more active part in the assimilation of information. They are also recording and accumulating, for various purposes. In the *Custodians*, there were examples of ETs recording what we have learned. This is one of the purposes of the implants that people have the incorrect impression of. They are recording everything the person sees, hears and feels, and transmitting it into giant computer banks, for want of a better word. These computer banks are directly linked to the historical records of our civilization in the higher councils. We also found in *Keepers of the Garden* and *Convoluted Universe, Book One*, that sometimes entire planets are recording devices. Later in this book, we will see that this is also active in our own solar system, with our Sun as a main recording device. It is not inconceivable that our own planet is sending out its own experiences and reactions to the damage that is occurring to it at this time in our history. The Earth is, after all, a living being.

It appears that this is a common theme or pattern throughout; from the tiniest cell in our body to the entire universe. From the microcosm to the macrocosm, information is being transmitted and stored. The only logical explanation is that the final destination of all of this information could only be God, the Source. Similar to a gigantic computer, He is accumulating data. For what purpose, we can only speculate. But it was becoming more and more obvious that this is what is occurring.

D: *Why are all of these beings so concerned with what's happening on Earth?*

B: Earth is a very special planet. It is a melding of many, many, many energies from many, many, many different places. And so it is like a *beautiful* – I don't want to say "experiment" – but beautiful experiment, for lack of a better word.

D: *Yes, I've heard that before.*

B: In bringing it all together, and allowing free will and different experiences to take place. Now the grand experiment is actually the merging of spirit with biology. It is the merging of spirit with physical*ness.* And so those who discount their physical bodies have missed the boat. It is about the *merging,* the *integration* of spirit in the physical being. And that is the part of the grand experiment. Those who are not of this density don't have that experience. It is quite different. And so there is a lot of curiosity. And there's a lot of *excitement* to see how this unfolds in all of its array. And obviously, we have the light and the dark, the

391

beauty and the ugliness. It's all of it and the challenges.

D: *The ones that are watching don't have this variety?*

B: No, not in this way. Not like this at all. It is like the Garden of Eden. As humans, we take it for granted. We've totally taken this *beautiful* Garden of Eden for granted. It's very sad.

D: *But some of these other planets are physical, aren't they?*

B: Yes, there are other physical planets. The variety is not as enormous as it is here. The variety is *much* expanded here.

D: *I was thinking if they were physical, they would have physical bodies.*

B: Yes, but there is the difference. There's different differences somehow.

D: *I'm trying to understand why ours is that different. Because the other beings have physical bodies, and are living lives as these other creatures on other worlds.*

B: The only thing that I can see or know about in this moment, is that there is an awakening awareness in the human that is different. There appears to be a grand drama that we have chosen to experience on Earth. An awakening through the drama is happening now. And it is just the best show there is. (Laugh)

D: *That's why everybody wants to watch it.* (Yes)

This has been repeated in several of my books: that many beings throughout the universe are watching what is occurring now on Earth. This is because it is considered different. It is the first time any planet or civilization has gone through the events that are happening now. They are curious to see how it will work out. It has been said that it is also the first time an entire planet will reach the level where it will increase its frequency and vibration to allow it to shift en masse into another dimension. Many other beings are aware of the "drama" that is being played out here, and like watching a movie or TV show, they want to see the conclusion. We are unconsciously supplying the dialogue, situations and script for the actors upon the stage of the galaxy. And as she said, "It is the best show there is."

Continuing with the session:

D: *On Earth, we get caught up in karma. Is this different on the other planets?*

B: There does seem to be a difference in that respect, yes. There is a density in the atmosphere of the Earth. This is just how *I* describe it. A density that keeps the energies here to resolve. And once it's resolved, then they can move out of that density.

D: *So the other beings have different lessons to learn. It's just a different form of learning.*

B: Exactly, exactly.

D: *I know some of these things are very hard to understand. But is there like a whole series or layers of councils over each other that keep track of all of this?*

B: Yes, that have an awareness of it. Kind of like a parent and a child. Obviously you don't have complete awareness of everything, but you do the best that you can. You're tuned into it and you work toward providing the help and the guidance that they need.

D: *But in my work, I have found that not only do the beings observe through portals, but some of them actually do come in physical ships?*

B: This is correct. But there is a shifting in the energies in order for this to happen. Because there has to be a lowering of the vibration in order to come into this atmospheric energy. There is a protective layer around the Earth. And so, in order to come into this level, there is a shifting of vibrations to some extent, to manifest in the physical. To be seen in the physical.

D: *But if the other ones are finding out all the information by*

observing, why do some beings have to physically come to Earth?
B: It's important that the people of Earth begin to understand that there are other beings outside of themselves. And to expand their scope of awareness. They have very narrow thinking in many ways. And so it is necessary that an expansion take place for their growth and development. Now, not all entities are all good and light. Just as there is darkness on the Earth, there are darker energies other places as well. And it's just a part of the way things are.
D: *But they also come to observe?*
B: Yes. In some instances, there's a desire for control. There's a desire for resources, that kind of thing. But as much as possible, that is not permitted.
D: *Because this planet is being watched very carefully.*
B: Yes, very carefully.
D: *But this is what you've been able to observe. You said you left part of yourself to guard the portal, and the other part traveled to where you could observe and ask questions.* (Yes) *Go back now to where you were the total energy there at the portal. Have you been there a long time doing this job? Or does time have any meaning?*
B: It seems that time does not have meaning, but it is as a mountain. A mountain exists for a huge span of time. And it is aware. Its energy is just very slowed down. So my energy as this guardian of this area also is that way. So it has been there for, what you would call, a very, very long time. And yet it does not *feel* like a long time at all. It is just very lovely. (Chuckle) Very lovely. Just as a mountain.
D: *But is that the only thing this crystalline structure is used for, this portal? Or does it have other parts to it?*
B: There appears to be other "rooms", that you would call them, because there are separate areas within. Almost like a system for sending information back without actually going back yourself. So there's that kind of setup.
D: *You said mostly it's used as an observation window.* (Yes) *Are beings ever allowed to go out from that place? To exit onto this*

planet? (No) *It's just mostly self-contained like an observation post then.* (Yes) *So the beings remain in those other rooms that are used for transmitting information.* (Correct) *I just wanted to try to get it all straight. But the entity whose body you're speaking through, whose name is Betty, are you existing as this energy at a different time from her or what?*

B: No, it is all one. It is all one.

D: *You can exist as the energy that guards the portal at the same time you're existing as the physical body as Betty?* (Correct) *How is that done? Can you explain that?*

B: (Chuckle) It *is!* And there's a matter of focus. As Betty, I focus my awareness in this life. However, another portion of my being is also the guardian energy at this portal. Most of the time we are unaware of each other.

D: *That's what I was thinking. Betty has not been aware of the other part.*

B: No. And yet it's a different vibrational level that we're operating under. And so I'm able to be in many places, and doing many things at once.

D: *Without any of these parts being aware of each other.* (Correct) *That's one of the things I have found confusing. Because people say, how can we be all of these things at the same time?*

B: Well, trying to understand it with a limited perception and awareness makes it difficult.

D: *(Chuckle) The human has great difficulty.*

B: Exactly, because the focus is different. And so, currently, there's not the ability to be aware of many parts of your being at the same time.

D: *Many different aspects.* (Right) *This is what I've been told, that the human mind is just incapable of understanding everything.*

B: This is correct.

D: *I think this is very important information. Would I be allowed to use this information?* (Yes) *Because in my work I'm the reporter also, accumulating ....*

B: (Delighted interruption) This is correct! This is very interesting! You do exactly what these other beings do. And it's a great honor to share this with you.

395

D: *Because I take many different pieces and try to put them together, I guess, in the same way.*

B: This is correct.

D: *I'm just doing it while in the physical body.* (Yes, yes) *One piece adds to another piece of information. That's why I have so many questions.*

B: And this is good, because it helps, once again, to expand the perceptions. To expand the possibilities. To bring that spiritual awareness into the physical being. And that's what this time is about.

D: *The problem is, humans have a very difficult time trying to understand these complicated concepts.* (Yes) *My job is trying to simplify it so they can understand. Which is difficult. Can you tell me, why she is exploring this today?*

B: Ah, she is a messenger. She is not fully aware of this yet. She will open more fully to bringing messages through to assist the vibrational process. She has asked to open more fully to receiving messages from the spiritual realm. And becoming more aware of the beings that are out there, triggers an opening for messages to be received.

In addition to working full time as a nurse in a neonatal unit of a large hospital, Betty had been doing psychic readings for people. This happened spontaneously with no training. She found she was able to pick up things about people just by being in their presence. Of course, there were many people she could not tell what she was perceiving, especially those she met in the hospital, where emotions run rampant.

This was another example of how we are unknowingly living two or more existences at the same time, with each counterpart being oblivious of the other. It is only through this method, they can become aware of each other and interact.

I am not sure whether the entrance to the other dimensions mentioned in this session can be classified as a portal or a window. In *Book One*, this concept was explained: you can move through a portal into another dimension, whereas you can only look through a window and observe.

In the other sessions included in this section, it appears we are also dealing with portals that *can* be entered and exited from, not windows that are only used for observation.

CHAPTER 20

THE ABORIGINE

This session with Lily, a psychologist, was held during the WE (Walk-ins in Evolution) Conference in Las Vegas in April 2002. It demonstrated that portals have been around much longer than we can imagine, and have been actively used.

When Lily came off the cloud, she found herself standing amidst tall grass as far as the eye could see. Her mind supplied the location without being asked.

L: Fields of tall, stalky grass, like wheat. And it says "the Veldt, Australia".
D: *Is that where you're feeling it might be?*
L: I feel it is. It feels flat. And it feels part of a big land mass.

She was surrounded by the grass that she assumed to be wheat, but there was something else that she could see in the distance that definitely did not fit in this pastoral scene.

L: And I feel this big monolith in the distance.
D: *What do you mean by monolith?*
L: A big mound. Rock. Made of rock, but bigger and flat, rock.

I thought if she was talking about Australia, it probably was Ayers Rock, which is located in the middle of the continent. It is significant because it stands alone on flat and desolate terrain. But I didn't want to influence her, so I asked about other mountains.

L: Ayers. They say Ayers. It just sits by itself.

Information found on the Internet:

Ayers Rock is also known by its Aboriginal name "Uluru". It is the world's largest monolith rising 318m above the desert floor in the center of Australia, with a circumference of 8 km. It is considered one of the great wonders of the world, and is located on a major planetary grid point much like the Great Pyramid in Egypt. Depending on the time of day and the atmospheric conditions, the rock can dramatically change color, anything from blue to glowing red.

Ayers Rock is considered a holy place and is much revered in the Aborigine religion. The Aborigines believe that it is hollow below ground, and that there is an energy source they call "Tjukurpa", the "Dream Time". The term Tjukurpa is also used to refer to the record of all activities of a particular ancestral being from the very beginning of his or her travels to their end. The Aborigines know that the area around Ayers Rock is inhabited by dozens of ancestral beings whose activities are recorded at many separate sites. At each site the events that took place can be recounted. There is much ancient rock art found in the area. Some of it has been translated and some has not. The paintings are regularly renewed, with layer upon layer of paint, dating back many thousands of years.

D: What color is the monolith?

Her voice began to change, becoming more simple, almost primitive. She spoke very deliberately.

L: Dark. Brownish-red. When the sun hits it, it gets more fire-red.

She was definitely describing Ayers Rock.

D: But otherwise, around you it's just fields.
L: Of wheat. Or what looks like tall grass. Hard, harder than grass.
D: Is there any sign of habitation, or buildings or anything?
L: Here aborigine (had difficulty with that word) peoples live nearby. (Deliberately) Tribal people live nearby.

I asked for a description of herself. She was a male with brown skin and black hair, with "very little face hair", wearing "pelt skins covering my torso and loins". He was in his twenties or thirties, but that was not considered young. He said his body was "strong, warrior strong. Brave, I'm brave."

D: Are you wearing any ornamentation or ....
L: (Interrupted) Beads. Around my neck. Several types of strands, with metal amulets for bravery and protection. And in my hair, you will notice, honor. Sign of honor in community.
D: What is in your hair that signifies that?
L: Bone, tusk and metal coin circles.
D: Is this interwoven in your hair?
L: (Pause) Like a necklace on my head. (She was speaking very simply and using the words the entity was familiar

400

with.) I am ... place of status. Like chief, but not chief. I earn this. (Confused) You can ... can you not see me?

D: *Not as well. It is as though there is a veil separating us.*

L: My chest is big with pride and muscle.

D: *That's why I must ask questions, because I can't see you that clearly. Can you relate to that?* (Yes) *Do you have any other ornamentation?*

L: Yes, my skin has incisions. We do this as matter of course in growing and showing age at puberty. And with each killing of native animal, and other settlers that come to harm us. But we stay away from killing human people, for that is against our religion.

D: *I see. But when you do kill something, then you make an incision?*

L: Yes. It is a sign of warrior prowess.

D: *Where do you make the incision?*

L: On my upper right arm. Sometimes left arm. And chest above nipples. Above ... by the neck and chest.

D: *Is this how you received the amulets for honor, through the deeds you have done? Like killing animals?*

L: The incisions are more for each accomplishment. The amulet is more for being *grown* in that culture that we are in. It is a place of honor and dignity. You have it from childhood. You know what you are expected to do.

Her words were carefully chosen, as though they were strange and unfamiliar to the entity. She spoke very deliberately and directly.

D: *Then you receive this as a mark of reaching that state.*

L: Yes. Not all people in tribe have this opportunity.

D: *But you said you kill the native animals.*

L: Yes. That is my role as man. I kill with spear and hands.

D: *Animals would be very fast, wouldn't they?*

L: We are smart. We know how to track, trace the animal, and attack at right moment. Precision is what kills.

D: *But you said, sometimes you do have to kill humans?*

L: When settlers come to destroy our land or our people, we must sometime – it is more told to me by my father – but I feel I have done this as well. It is not something I seek to do, to harm. But you sometimes must protect. My people.

D: *That's true. These settlers that come, are they also brown-skinned people?*

L: White men. And ... and ... (hesitant, with a big sigh) ... glowing men.

D: *What do you mean by* glowing *men?*

L: (He seemed apprehensive.) Bulbs. They look like light bulbs. Glowing and shining men. (She was breathing faster.)

D: *The white men look like you except for their skin?* (Yes) *And these other ones look different?*

L: (Confused and definitely frightened.) They make ... together the glowing men are ... (searching for the word) *whirling* them. The mind ... the brain ... the force behind them. The glowing bubbles ... the glowing beings are in charge. They have the power.

It was difficult, but he was satisfied that he had found the proper words.

D: *I thought you meant the white men were the settlers.*

L: The white men come out from the ... (had difficulty) spaceship? Building? Thing? Come out from the glowing thing where the glowing beings are.

D: *There are glowing beings in there, and the white men come out from there?*

L: Yes, the white men come out. And the glowing beings, they look like test tubes, or big corn on stalk, but glowing beings that look like corn. Long and oblong.

D: *So they look different than the others.*

L: (Excited that she had made me understand.) Yes, yes!

D: *So it's something you haven't seen before.*

L: Never! Frightening! (Big breath.) We cannot go there. They come from far away in the sky. And the white people talk to us, and explain to us.

402

D: *The glowing ones, are you able to make out any face or features? Or is it just all glowing?*

L: All glowing and pulsating, and brain. *All* brain. Knowing, knowing, knowing, knowing.

D: *What do you mean by all brain?*

L: They all-knowing. They know, they see all time. And like ... computer, but *alive* and pulsing. And no arms, no legs, no face. But color at top of high pod different from bottom of pod. Bottom of pod is more blue, iridescent blue and green. Top of pod white where brain is. Long.

It was obvious that the entity was drawing words from Lily's modern day vocabulary. Otherwise the aborigine would have no words to explain the unknown things he was trying to describe to me.

D: *But you said, these come, and you couldn't go there.*

L: (Interrupted) No! No go to ship. No go to ship.

D: *Where does it come down?*

L: By the cliffs, by the rocks. Far from monolith, but close to rocks. And not near the wheat. The white-skinned ... they come to us. And they explain. At first we afraid. Never saw *white*. We thought they sick. They have no *blood* in them. And no hair like us. No dark. No ... no thing like us. *All white. No clothes.* But no ... (difficulty) no birthing stuff. No what we have.

He was obviously referring to the sexual organs.

D: *Do they have eyes like you?*

L: Yes. But no blink. No blink. They are white *people*, but different. But no ... what you call "anatomy". No anatomy.

D: *But you called them "the settlers", didn't you?*

L: They come to settle, to test, to take soil, to talk with us, to take back our children to work with them.

D: *What do you mean, take back your children?*

L: Take back to ship. Teach, talk, go up and down, and bring

403

them back.

D: *How do you feel about that?*

L: They say it okay. They nice people. Our children want to learn. We feel okay. (He didn't sound as confident about it.) I go nowhere. No go there. No go there. I'm afraid. Afraid. Don't know how ... don't know how be.

D: *And the white people that come and talk to you ....*

L: (Interrupted) They glow a little. A little.

D: *But they explain what's going to happen?*

L: Yes, they say everything fine. To be calm, to be okay, this agreement. We make agreement that no harm, and children be okay. They learn. And they bring back *tools.* Spear and rock. Rock, smooth, curved at end of spear. And ... circles. Disks. To help women with making seeds, corn, bread.

D: *What are those disks made out of?*

L: Stone, but *soft,* and round and smooth. And easy to beat on. On table and stone bowls. They show us how to make easier. Very fine. How they make, we don't know.

D: *They don't show you how to make them?*

L: No, they give. Children may learn, we hope.

D: *Maybe that's one of the things they are teaching them.*

L: Children take time in ship. And go back and forth. We no speak much about this.

D: *The children don't tell you what happens when they come back?*

L: (He seemed apprehensive to talk about it.) One or two tell, but no talk much. They go to learn and pass on, and come back.

D: *But do the children want to talk about it?*

L: They told not to. Too much for head, brain, to understand. A fear. Scare womenfolks. Scare women, but *I* strong. I can take some.

D: *Do you have children?*

L: Yes. Five. Two boy go on ship. They like.

D: *They were taught things?*

L: Yes. But travel. Travel to distant place, places. Not here. They go far.

D: *Did they tell you what it looked like at the place they went?*

L: Far from moon. They say *purple* beings live there. But no look like our place, our world. All green and vegetation where the purple beings are. Hot. Hot and damp on skin. Purple beings don't have skin as we do. It's more like rubber. They are what is called "amphibians". Purple beings are amphibians.

D: *What does that mean to you?*

L: They swim and walk equal. They drew them in the dirt. They look like salamander beings. Have you seen these?

D: *I know a salamander is like a lizard.*

L: Swim more than lizard. And them upright also. Lizard not as advanced. Very round, rubbery. Not as defined, and not as hard and pointy as lizard. More round.

D: *Because lizards sometimes have rough skin.*

L: This is smooth and rubbery. And they glow *also,* but not as much as the glow beings in the ship. Those are most bright. Much bright.

D: *Is this the place where your sons were taught? Or are they taught on the ship?*

L: They go many places. They taught on ship and in places they travel to.

D: *Did they say what they were taught?*

L: "Many teachings, papa, you would not understand." That's what they tell me. They are kind to me. They say I would not understand. Like, for young children in your world, to explain to old people, a hundred years old, about computer. It's better just to say, "You would not understand." Not understand, yes. Your world very advanced, like ship, yes?

D: *I think so.*

So the aborigine was able somehow, to know that in the world where his counterpart, Lily, lived, things were very different. Apparently, it did not confuse him. I have found this in other cases where I talk to native people. They are more intuitive and can often see into other dimensions without realizing anything is unusual about it.

D: *But in your life, things are very simple?*

L: Yes, and ship very, very far away. They come from far away in time. They travel far in time.

D: *Is that what your sons have told you?* (Yes) *But at least you know they were not harmed.*

L: No. They love it. They want more.

D: *Did they give them any instructions, as to what to do with what they're taught?*

L: Cultivate land for indigenous peoples. Make it grow better, for soil. Make soil more ... (uncertainty) more arid, to grow better beans and rice stalks. No make sense. But they say it will happen. I say we need water for fertile. They say arid for fertile. They show us with ... fluid in tubes. But it's not water. It look like mercury. It look like silver white composite of the purple beings. You pour it into the arid soil, and it make everything *grow.* It's amazing!

D: *So you don't need water?*

L: No. And the white beings, they show us how to plant and farm. (Confused) How could this be? So they help us, and we grow strong. Have food for babies. And they take our children for trips. And ... investigate them.

D: *Do they show you how to make this fluid?*

L: It come from ship. From purple planet.

D: *So you can't make more?*

L: No. It is barter. We give our children for study. They give us test tube fluid for growing and cultivating.

D: *But you only have it as long as they give it to you. You can't make it yourselves.*

L: We have it *forever.* They not going away.

D: *So they will stay and keep giving it to you.*

L: We think. They are here. They are very good people.

D: *Is there water near there? Because you must have water also to live.*

L: Not enough. Very dry. It is problem sometimes.

D: *But you said earlier, that sometimes your people killed the settlers. When did that happen?*

L: In the beginning. When they first come. We did not know.

We made mistake. We made great fear. We thought they were coming to snatch our babies. And we fought. Two we kill. And then we track.

D: *These were two of the white beings?* (Yes) *Did they try to defend themselves?*

L: Not like us. They took them to ship to heal them.

D: *So they didn't die?*

L: They die. And then they ... they give them new *life.* (Amazed) They give them new energy over body. (Uncertain how to word it.) New soul energy over dead body. From top. Comes down and fills body. And body flat on ship. Soul come in on top, merge, and bring to life again.

D: *This is what they told you?*

L: This is what I saw through my son.

When Lily awakened, she retained a mental picture of how it was done. She saw that the dead aliens were placed on a slab, and a light overhead like a halo brought them back to life.

D: *Then your people killed them with spears?*

L: And with poison in dart spear. There is plant that is deadly. I talk precision for big animal. If you get dart or spear in neck. Through a vein. (Hand motions indicating the side of the neck. Probably the jugular vein.) You kill.

D: *This is how you kill the animals?*

L: Big animal.

D: *This is how some of the people killed the first ones that came?* (Yes) *They must have been surprised, weren't they?*

L: No. They knew planet is dangerous. No one ever said it. They have knowledge. They know about us. They say they have come before. (Pause) Fifteen hundred. They were come before.

D: *Fifteen hundred years before?*

L: Year fifteen hundred.

D: *Do your people have any legends about this type of people?*

L: Yes, on rocks. The bubble. The circle from sky.

407

D: *This is drawn on the rocks?*
L: By the cliffs where they come back.
D: *Did your people who knew them from before, draw the drawings on the rocks?*
L: Yes. And they disappeared. Many disappear, and they don't come back. Our people. From before my parents, before their parents, before their parents. This is legend, you asked. They came and many did not return. They went off in disk, and did not come back. Same is true of your people in this country .... (Paused, confused.)
D: *You can see where I am speaking from?*
L: Yes, they are showing me. You are like ... travel in time.
D: *Yes, this is what I like to do. And I learn much information this way. It is lost information.*
L: (Surprised) Anasazi! They say you know Anasazi. Similar. You understand us.

The Anasazi were a tribe of American Indians that lived in Chaco Canyon in New Mexico in the 14th Century. They completely disappeared, and no one is sure why, even though their ruins have been studied extensively. Was he indicating there was a supernatural explanation?

D: *Then the people knew you were dangerous. Is that why your people killed them, because they were afraid they would take the people like they did in the legend?*
L: We were afraid for our children only. We could not think of legend. Only our babies. It's ... scary to look. Pictures don't show scary look. You never saw anything like this. They don't have body and parts like human.
D: *At least, you didn't kill the strange people. They were brought back to life. That's very miraculous, isn't it?*
L: They *did* kill, and then it *un*-killed. Good medicine.
D: *But anyway, you don't want to go to where the ship is?* (No) *You're very brave, but not that brave.*
L: My father told me, "Don't go near ship!" Others did not come back. I have responsibility to my family, and my

children. I no go. I obedient. My father say, no go. I must protect my family. I talk to white beings now. Without fear. I no go ship. White beings okay. My children show me they okay. My children introduce me to them.

D: *And they are learning much, and they are giving things for your people to use.*

L: For their crops.

D: *That means they don't want to hurt you. They want to help you.* (Yes)

I decided it was time to move him to another scene as he grew older so we could gather more information. I moved him to a day that he considered to be important, when something was happening. She appeared to be watching something.

D: *What is it?*

L: It is a structure. It look like a stone flower, a stone sculpture, a stone ... diamond-shaped, but rounded, with different blue and ... dark blue on perimeter, and green and white – off-white – veins running through stone. I am facing this. It is tall. It is taller than person.

D: *Where is it sitting?*

L: In the land. Stuck in ground.

D: *Was that there before?* (No) *Did someone make it, carve it or what?*

L: I am not ... I am not on my home land.

This answer was a surprise.

D: *Oh? You're not where you were living?*

L: No. I am ... in other world.

D: *How did you get there?*

L: I don't know. I am uncomfortable. It is dark here. It is unfamiliar.

D: *I don't want you to be uncomfortable. Will you talk to me, and not let it bother you?*

L: Yes. It is nothing like what I know. It is ... like obsidian stone. Taller than me. Wider than me. It has shape like a big leaf standing upright. Where it starts out and goes fatter, and then goes thinner again at the top. And it is *stone!* And I walk up to this. And that's what I see when you took me here.

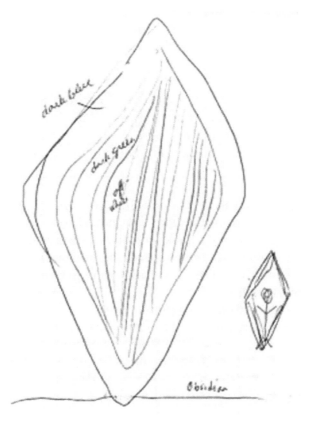

D: *Are there any buildings around, or does it sit by itself?*
L: No, no building. But you ask, and I hear and sense a tunnel. Stone tunnels. Ah! I ask. I am inside the Earth.
D: *That's why it's dark?*
L: Yes. Very different.
D: *When you ask like that, you can get answers?* (Yes) *That's good. How did you get to this place?*

L: They let me here. (A revelation.) I went through a door. They say, in your language "portal".

D: *At the place where you were living?*

L: Near. Near the cliffs.

D: *You said you were not going to go near the craft.*

L: Not near craft. Near, but far. No craft. Near the cliffs. There is like a passageway.

D: *Did they take you there?*

L: He show way. I went myself. I walk through passageway door. Dark door.

D: *What did the portal look like when you first saw it?*

L: (Surprised) A shadow! It looked like a line or a shadow in the red rock. You walk up to it, and you put your foot to walk through, and you are *gone.* And I see this *stone* in front of me. It's like a god. I think it's ... I'm convinced it's a god.

D: *Is anyone with you?*

L: No. I don't see them.

D: *They just let you through. What are you going to do?*

L: I'm looking around ... for light. For others. And for way back.

D: *Can you turn around and go back the way you came?*

L: I see nothing but dark with a little light. Tunnels.

D: *Not the way you came?*

L: No. I walk, take one step, I here. I don't know how I came.

D: *You can't find the passageway that you came through?*

L: No, I cannot. I feel I need to look and be at this statue. To receive something. Or why am I here? It must be for something. Do you know what this is?

D: *No, it's nothing I'm familiar with. I'm as confused as you are.*

L: (Surprised, a revelation) Knowledge here. I get knowledge from this stone. I get knowledge from standing here in front of stone, and putting my head on stone. Standing up next to it, and putting my forehead against the stone.

This description of a strange stone that contained great knowledge and that was located underground sounded very similar to two other cases I have written about in my other books. In *The Custodians,* John Johnson was taken from his hotel room in Egypt to an underground room where there was a massive stone in the middle of a room that contained great knowledge that he was given, but couldn't retain or repeat. In *Legacy From the Stars,* there is mention of a similar stone located in an underground city in the future when the Earth had poisoned its atmosphere to the point that life on the surface was impossible. The survivors had to live an ant-farm type existence underground. In a room there was a huge stone where the beings could access any knowledge they wished by simply placing their hands on it, or their forehead against it. Each case represented knowledge stored somehow in stone.

D: *Like magic?*
L: Like osmosis.
D: *What kind of knowledge comes through that way?*
L: Science. Scholarly matters.
D: *Do you understand it?* (Surprised: Yes!) *Even though it is different from where you come from?*
L: It is way to go through time without going on ship.
D: *I see. Do you think this is the way your sons were taught?*
L: (Surprise) I don't know! I thought they learned on ship. This feels new. I don't know if anyone knows about this. It feels secret.
D: *But they allowed you to go there, didn't they?*
L: They did not stop me. (Pause) I don't know if they showed me, or if my sons showed me. I don't know if they know that I'm here.
D: *If you're getting information from that stone, what are you going to do?*
L: Travel.
D: *What do you mean?*
L: I want to go back and find my people who left here. I want to bring them back.
D: *The ones in the legend?* (Yes) *Do you think that's possible?*
L: Yes. I feel I can get it from the stone. And if I bring back the people, then I can die in peace.

412

D: *Do you think the stone will tell you?*

L: That is my hope. And to take me there. I have feeling. I don't know how possible, but I have feeling that by working with stone, I can find my people.

D: *Do you think that would be dangerous?*

L: No more dangerous than what I have done. Coming down here to tunnel.

D: *But if you found them, how could you get them back?*

L: I would like to try. I don't think in advance. I try.

D: *Were you thinking about this before, of finding the people?*

L: No. But now I feel a desire to connect, to *find*, to gather them back.

D: *So you're not really worried about how you're going to get out of there.*

L: I'm going ... forward. I want to go into the stone.

D: *You think you can merge with it?* (Yes) *Tell me what happens. (I emphasized to her that she was protected.) What does it feel like?*

L: I am *light*. I am glowing. I am ... I am eternal Sun.

D: *When did that happen?*

L: I merge with stone. I pressed my head into stone, and body into stone. And I am *here* now. I am light. I am ... like a flame. I can go anywhere.

D: *You said you were "here". Where is here?*

L: I was in front of stone .... in the tunnel. And then now I am ... *nowhere*. I am light. I am *energy*.

D: *You no longer have the body you had?* (No) *How do you feel about that?*

L: I feel wonderful. I no want to go back. I want to find the *people*, but I no want to go back to my body. Too tiny. Too ... constrained.

D: *Too limiting?*

L: Yes. This is big. Now I know maybe what my sons know.

D: *What they couldn't talk about. You said something about the Sun?*

L: I feel I *am* the Sun.

D: *Glowing, you mean?*

413

L: And big.

D: *Big and glowing. That is very strange, isn't it?*

L: It doesn't feel strange. It feels like I have been here before.

D: *You don't miss the body at all then.*

L: No, I don't want body.

Is this what happened to the others that disappeared from the tribal group? Maybe they also stumbled across this portal near the cliffs. The portal was also in the vicinity where the ship always appeared. Maybe the people associated their disappearance with the mysterious beings. Maybe also the beings used this portal to travel back and forth between worlds.

D: *What does it feel like?*

Lily's voice changed and returned to normal. It was no longer the aborigine searching for the correct words, and speaking deliberately. That personality seemed to have been left behind, and the real personality emerged.

L: It feels glorious. It feels ... like the angels dancing. I can feel all the other beings. I can feel all the intelligence. I am no longer uneducated. I know *all.*

D: *Just that quickly you were able to make that switch. Is that what you mean?*

L: Yes. My *body* and my life as that *person* was male, uneducated, primitive, uncultured. He was a good person, but he was ... primitive. I am the same person, I thought. But I no longer feel male *or* female. I feel everything. I feel I can know anything by *being.*

D: *That's a wonderful feeling, isn't it?*

L: It is the way it is.

D: *Then that's a perfect place.*

L: Yes, but it is not a *place.* It is *everywhere.* It has no walls. I am limitless. I don't want to go back to that body and that limitation.

D: *In this state you're in now, you can know what was going on. Do*

414

*you understand more about the white beings now? And what was
happening with your people at that time?*

L: The white beings are space travelers. And they travel the
galaxy far and wide, searching for civilizations that have
something to offer, something that can prosper, for both.
It is equal exchange. They are good beings. They have
been doing this for eons, for centuries immortal. They are
the space travelers.

D: *What about the glowing ones? They were different from the
white ones.*

L: They are more like ... the energy beings that we are now.
Contained within a cellular sack, a membrane, that can then
allow them to travel with the group, like an entourage.
Otherwise it is very difficult to contain free energy. So it is
a membrane for traveling, like a spacesuit.

D: *These are two separate kinds of beings then.*

L: Yes. They travel together. The space membrane beings, or
we in sacks, or suits, are the guardians. The commanders
of the mission.

D: *So they don't really interact with the people.*

L: No. We are the all-knowing, all-seeing navigators.

D: *So that's why there were two separate groups. But they've been
doing this for eons. And it is not negative, because they're trying
to help people.*

L: Absolutely. That is the way of the universe. To educate
people and to advance them. And to not interfere unless it
is desired, and asked for. (Pause) And the amphibians who
you ask about.

She must have anticipated that I would also be asking about
them.

D: *Yes, the ones with the purple skins?*

L: Yes. They have gold interior beings. Their energy field
inside is gold rays. And their purple amphibious exterior
allows them to deal with the climate, and to breathe in the
air, such as it is.

415

D: *This is just what is required where they live. That type of body for that place.*

L: Yes. Where they live, it is more of a red planet. Very gaseous.

D: *But your sons on the other place were taken there so they could learn these things.*

L: Oh, yes, the amphibians were interested in seeing humans.

D: *They were curious about us also?*

L: Yes. Young boys like snails and lizards and fish. So it was not frightening for them.

D: *And these were things that your people carved on the rocks?*

L: No. That was not to be spoken of. They carved only the disks in the sky, and the white beings that walked around. But we did not know that this was real. At the time, we did not know what was story and what was fact.

D: *But there had been a long time between their visits.*

L: Yes. A different settlement. It is not necessary to come back more than every four to five hundred Earth years. In order to take soil samples, and test and investigate erosion. Understand atmospheric conditions, and bring back samples of human DNA.

D: *Because things would take a long time to change. (Yes) So they'd come back from time to time to just check on things. (Yes) They don't have to be there constantly. (No) These beings anyway.*

L: Correct.

I proceeded with the therapy, because, after all, that was the purpose of the session. Some of it was personal and only related to Lily, so it will not be included in this book.

D: *I know where you are is kind of a strange place, but you seem to have all knowledge. Do you know the being known as Lily? (Yes) In that place you know that in a future life you will be Lily? (Yes) Can you have access to information about her?*

L: I believe we are in a good space for knowledge. Why don't we try? And if we are unable to access, we can ask the

416

beings of the all-knowledge to come. They can support this effort, because it is within her jurisdiction to ask. All information is available, even for you, if it's appropriate. Only if the person, the soul, wishes it. Then they can have access to it, if it is the right time.

D: *Yes. The time is always very important.*

L: And we don't mean to frighten you when we say "we", for we are many facets of the soul.

D: *Yes, I understand when you say "we". I've spoken to you many, many times.*

L: Thank you.

D: *So that doesn't bother me. That's when I know I can find information that's helpful. This man's life in that country. I call it "lost" information.*

L: Hmm, you are an explorer.

D: *Yes, I'm a reporter, a researcher.*

L: We like to think of you as an explorer of the mind and the celestial realm.

D: *I like to put all the little pieces together of things I've never heard of.*

L: You have heard a lot.

D: *Yes, I have, but I'm always looking for more.*

L: You remind me of me if I were on Earth, taking all this knowledge and having it glowing around you like a halo.

D: *(Chuckle) That's why I write the books. I try to give it to other people, so they can understand.*

L: You do good work.

D: *Well, let's see if we can find some answers for Lily. She has a searching mind, a questioning mind, too. What can you tell us about her?*

L: There will be a big change. And the transition will be bumpy. She will feel it as treacherous. But she must go through this, as she did as *me* when I went through the doorway to *Hell*, and it was to Heaven. This was to show her that she has access to all dimensions. And she knows this. She has great access to the other worlds, and she knows this. She can use this to her advantage. We are all

417

here to assist her. She can perform what you would consider to be magic, if she lets go and believes it. As long as she is held down to her earthly beliefs that there is nothing more than this in her career, she will not expand to her next level, which builds *upon* the career. But takes her to a quantum leap forward, as I did as I stepped before the great stone. Her *global* purpose is to be at one with the universe. She will be involved in a great project, similar to the great experiment. She has already agreed to do this on the other dimensions. She will be harnessed and accelerated through this process.

D: *What do you mean by the "great experiment"?*

L: There is a great test of wills battling on planet Earth at this time. There is much disease, much unrest, much civil strife, much combat. She is one of the emissaries who has come here to bring peace and harmony and wholeness to this planet, by working with the people with whom she comes into contact. By dedicating her love, she strikes that chord and activates beings to get in touch with that light. As the light continues to grow on the planet, the forces will come into greater balance or harmony. There are a great many warriors or soldiers of light, who are battling this balance, this triumphant scale of justice.

D: *Why is it called the "great experiment"?*

L: That is a metaphor. For there is no outcome that is definitive, only seen through probabilities, as you well know. There is no definitive outcome. He has spoken to you. The great one. You know this. You know who he is. And she understands this as well. There may be the potentiality of this planet destroying itself. That is a great potentiality. And there is a great – perhaps *greater* – potentiality that it *will* come to a state of equilibrium and quiescence. And there are those who need to do what they must do on either side of this balancing wheel. This is not specific enough perhaps. Some of this information is being given to her so there can be some objectivity from a human perspective. And give her some perspective, for she is still

418

in a human body at this time. Although there is a spiritual opening for her, and there is the opportunity for her to take leave of planet Earth within two years, if she should choose to do so. It would be her decision entirely. The body would remain.

D: *What do you mean, the body remains?*

L: She would not go through the death process. The body would remain on the planet, and she, her essence, would leave.

D: *Then would the body remain alive?*

L: Yes, it would.

D: *How would it be kept alive if her essence ....?*

L: With an essence soul that would come in to hold the energy of the body intact.

There is more about holding souls in Chapter 28.

D: *But this will be if she decides to have this happen.*

L: Yes. And it may be, that once the two year assignment is complete, if all goes well with that two year galactic assignment, she may choose not to stay on planet Earth at that point.

D: *But still, it is her decision to make.*

L: Completely her decision. The body will remain. It is healthy and intact. And we see no reason to believe that there would be any demise of this body. There has been much work to do on the planet. She is a multi-dimensional being.

D: *Yes, and I have spoken to other multi-dimensional beings, so that doesn't surprise me.*

L: Yes, they love working with you. You do not think them foolish. And so she would like you to know through us and our groups, and the groups we work with, that we are at your service when and if that would serve you, and would be appropriate or delightful.

D: *All of you beings keep coming through and giving me information. And I greatly appreciate this and respect it. That's why I consider myself the reporter, the accumulator of information.*

L: You are far more than that. You are a great navigator of time and space. You are a space being yourself, and you know that. And she sees a kindred space being in you.

D: *I'm thinking of the information we had earlier about the aborigine. Would I be allowed to use that information?*

L: Absolutely! Her permission is given.

D: *Because I put these things together like puzzles. And I'm always looking for something I haven't heard of before.*

L: If you need more pieces to your puzzle you can call us at any time, on behalf of spreading knowledge. This state you assisted her in getting to has access to the wholeness, the *All*-knowledge, and has served you both, has it not? *(Yes)* We would like to place one suggestion in her human mind now. So we will do that with your agreement. We would like her to know that she can access us at any time. That she can assist in her own healing of fears and in insight and wisdom. But she needs to remember to ask, as you have been so kind to ask. There is nothing to fear in the evolution of her career. This will only take the pace that is comfortable for her. She need not rush into anything, but it is happening.

CHAPTER 21

TIME PORTALS FOR FUTURE BEINGS

(TIME TRAVELERS)

This material was gleaned from a much longer transcript. The beings that came through were not ETs as we normally perceive them, and as I have worked with them. This time, the being speaking made it very clear that it was a time traveler from the future. They use spacecraft similar to those often seen in our skies and thought to be related to extraterrestrials. They also shift back and forth through dimensions, as the ETs do, but they come from the dimension associated with one of our probable futures. They often travel back into their past to make changes that affect their own civilization. These changes are often very subtle, barely noticeable. If the changes were dramatic it would change their world too drastically, and their civilization (as they know it) could be changed beyond recognition and no longer exist. Therefore, when they travel through time, they are under strict regulations and must be very careful how they influence events. Often, they are only observers because of these delicate circumstances. They say they use portals or windows. The difference between these two was explained in former chapters. A window is used to look through, whereas a portal can actually be passed through. Windows are the safest way to time travel, because the beings cannot influence or alter anything if they are only observing. They said there are many of these time portals that are connected with time vortexes located at various places on the Earth. They are related to the positioning of ley lines where they intersect at vortexes. Many of the sacred places and ancient temples were constructed at these locations. Ancient people had the knowledge of how to use these, if not for actual travel, for observing to gain information for the people of their time. This was one of the reasons why these sacred places had their holy sections, where only initiates were allowed. They had knowledge that we can only dream of. Much of this lost knowledge is being allowed to return to our time frame. It is now time on Earth to regain the forgotten information and move into a new era.

My encounter with one these future beings, or time travelers, came about unexpectedly, as most of my material does. Under their explicit instructions, I am not allowed to even say where it occurred, except that I was speaking at several conferences in the New York City area and conducting some private sessions while staying with a friend. The woman client wanted to explore what she thought was a UFO/ET encounter with missing time in the summer of 1996. She and a woman friend were walking on a lonely beach on a dark moonlit night. It was a relatively safe beach area because there were mansions nearby, and the full moon cast a beautiful reflection on the water. Since it was a warm night, they intended to walk several more miles along the beach before turning around. While walking, they saw lights in the sky coming toward them, and the next thing they knew they were back in their hotel room. Determined to find out what happened, they returned to the beach. They saw their footprints still remained in the sand. The footprints only went so far and then stopped abruptly. Naturally curious about how they got back to the hotel, she wanted to focus on this incident during the session.

When we began the session she entered the scene. As she relived the event she described the surroundings and the full moon. The only sign of life was a black truck containing four men that went by them with no lights on. Otherwise, the beach was deserted. She said she felt a little strange, and when she looked up, they saw several white lights. There were many planes in the sky, but these lights were different and stood out as very bright, even with the full moon in the sky.

"They're much brighter than the moon," she reported. "And they get bigger as they come toward us. They come down like in a spiral. And I feel like I'm being sucked up, if that's the

422

word for it. Like the last little part of the spiral takes your feet and just kind of lifts you up." Surprisingly, she was not afraid. Although what was occurring was unusual, she knew she would not be harmed.

She then found herself walking through an area on a spacecraft that had a combination of squares and circles at the same time. I don't know if she was describing designs on the wall or what, because this was not made clear. She just knew she was supposed to go through a brightly lit doorway. She saw that her friend had been taken to another room. "She's just sitting there. She's not afraid. They're showing her something. To her it would be like a movie. It's colors. Not like a kaleidoscope, but they just shimmer and blend. And there's some information mixed in there with what they're showing her. It's colors with pictures in them." So information was being transmitted on a subliminal level.

In the room she found herself in, there was a white light. Someone was beside it, but she couldn't tell what or who they were. "There's some kind of form there, but it's not like a person. It's like something that's talking, that's in my mind. And they're telling me that I was not supposed to be on the beach tonight. If I had kept going, they would not have been able to protect me. This is one of their entrance points, an inter-dimensional doorway, and it was being revved up tonight. It's energy and it has something to do with crystals."

At this point the being began to talk to me and announced that they were from the future. I was expecting to communicate with an alien, because that has become "normal" for me. When I asked about the difficulty of time travel, he laughed loudly and said that actually it was rather easy. Many people from other dimensions use these doorways to travel back and forth. But for humans it would be dangerous to wander into the area while it was being used. This was the reason why the two women were returned to their hotel room. They were removed forcibly from the area for their own protection.

So it appears that many times when the person sees lights in the sky, has missing time, and assumes it has to do with an alien encounter, it may not be that at all. It could be an intervention by future time travelers, because the two greatly resemble each other. It was explained in another part of this section that an unexpected or unprotected encounter with the portal could be dangerous to humans. It could even cause the breakup of their central matrix. Thus people using these portals try to make sure there is no human around that might be harmed by accidental exposure.

Much of the information the time traveler gave me must remain undisclosed at this time. I was told I could have it for my work so I would understand when similar information came through my subjects, but I was not to lecture about it or publish it. I learned years ago to listen to them and to obey them when it was suggested that I hold material. This was proven to me when some of my tapes disappeared for eight years. They only reappeared when it was time for that material to be published. This story was told in *The Custodians*. So I will listen again to their advice and hold much of the material that I was given. I will only write those portions that apply to other material I have received from other subjects.

They said many of these time portals are located underground so they can be contained. If they were located above ground, they could become larger, they could expand. It was better if they are underground surrounded by natural rock formations, or within walls of stone. They gave a description of what one of these would look like if it were activated. They said it appeared as an orb tunnel. I think of an orb as being like a circle or a ball.

The subject tried to describe what she was seeing, "I get the picture of two of them. One would be light, and one is like darkness with many broken white lines in it. And the two are connected. You have to have both apparently to use this. It appears that you activate the two of them and the orb is created in the middle. It's not a ball, it's energy. It's not even a place. If you can imagine an opening to a cave. It's like something which you're going to go through. The whole circle thing shines, it moves. I see the two vortexes. One is the dark one,

424

one is the light one. And when they meet, this is what is created: a time portal. The orb exists simultaneously as another orb in space in another dimension, and they are connected."

The being told me about many of these that are located all over the world, but the only one I feel comfortable writing about is the one in Egypt. Probably because I have found so many unusual things around the pyramids, that one more will not seem out of the ordinary. The one located underneath the pyramid used to be the main "keeper", and was used regularly in the past by those who possessed the knowledge of how to travel through dimensions. It is used by the time travelers from the future, because it was rediscovered after our present time, and put to use. It's another dimensional doorway. They somehow travel on the white lines that were seen inside the undulating orb tunnel. They really don't want others to discover and use these various portals, because they could be very dangerous if used incorrectly. The technology is very complex.

It's rather like a child playing with fire. It depends on what time frame the visitors are coming from, because they know how to use it without danger to themselves. The people of higher dimensions do not use these, because they travel in a quite different way. When I was told this, I thought about one possibility where they could travel by raising and lowering the vibrations of their bodies. This is one method ETs use to travel from one dimension to the other, by changing the vibration of their spacecraft, so this could be what is being referred to. Many people may feel or sense where the vortex is or even be able to see it, but they can't enter it or influence it. He said, "The universe takes care of itself ultimately."

We are familiar with this concept from the popular TV series "Star Trek", where individuals are broken down molecularly and reassembled elsewhere.

PHILADELPHIA EXPERIMENT

This idea of time portals to the past and the future reminded me of the mysterious case of the Philadelphia Experiment supposedly performed by our government during World War II. They have continually denied it, yet the story has persisted that they made a ship with its crew disappear, and reappear elsewhere. One of the reasons I suspect they have denied it (although it was a secret project) was that it had disastrous results. Some of the crew members disappeared upon reentry, and others were trapped half in and out of the metal of the ship. I thought I would see if he had anything to say about that. Whether he could verify or deny it. He seemed to be the ideal person to ask.

S: This was done with one of these time portals, and the same vortex that was used in this experiment is still open. That's why they are able to use it for time travel. The aliens gave them the technology to do the Philadelphia Experiment.

D: *But it didn't work, did it?*

S: Actually it did. But they didn't know how to control it, so that's why they had to stop doing it. They hadn't planned on two vortexes connecting. They thought the ship would go through one vortex and come back right where they started. The two actually connected and it came out in a different vortex.

D: *I've heard that the people onboard the ship were affected physically and mentally. Why did that happen?*

S: Because when the hyperspace jump happened, they went somewhere else in a different dimension. And they lost form and body when they did this. They disappeared. So that when the jump was made back, unfortunately some of them got stuck when the forms came back.

D: *Did the physical ship remain solid or did it also break apart?*

S: The physical ship also broke apart molecularly.

D: *So all of it was breaking apart as it went through the vortex. Especially when it connected with the other vortex. And then*

426

when it was brought back, it didn't all come back the way it should?

S: Well, actually it did. It's just that when it came back, all of it came back together. So people who were shifted from this one point got caught in matter. There was a shift, and they didn't know how to keep the shift at the point where the person left when they did this.

In other words they didn't know how to bring the person back to the exact point he started out. It shifted enough, that the person was caught in the physical material of the ship.

D: *You mean the vibrational rate of the shift?*
S: And the re-transformation.
D: *It was not at the same rate?*
S: It was the same rate. It was not the same point in time. It wasn't at the same spot that they left when it happened. This is crucial.
D: *So the matter intermingled. Would that be a way to say it?* (Yes) *They also said some of the people disappeared.*
S: They didn't re-transform. They were lost in space, and did not survive.
D: *Was this one of the first experiments?*
S: No, there were more than that one. That was the first one they did with people. They did it with objects first, animals and objects.
D: *Did they keep experimenting after the Philadelphia Experiment?*
S: Actually, no. After that one attempt they did not, because they didn't know how to control the people thing. But they still kept experimenting with the time tunnel. The vortexes. They didn't try it again with objects and people together. They were given more technology, so they were able to send people *directly* through this tunnel. They didn't send them *in* anything.
D: *So they bypassed that problem of mixing the matter together.*
S: Yes. Although when they do this, they have to make sure to bring the person back to exactly the same place at − I

think – two minutes ahead, so they can re-transform. They have gotten pretty good at this.

———————— ⋯⋯⋯⋯⋯⋯⋯⋯ ————————

Another subject also mentioned time travelers from the future. This is only part of a session.

L: Linda has also been working with beings from the future, from the 23rd century. They found that they know how to travel in time. And there are certain pivot points in time that are important to the past and to the future. They have right motives to some point, but although they're a better organization ... they are more human. They're not entirely evolved into the light. They came back. That's how they found Linda by tracking pivot points in time. And they have been working with her and some others in this current time, to facilitate a better future than they currently have.

D: *In their time?*

L: Yes. To try to minimize some of the problems that came into the future.

D: *But won't this change their future?*

L: It has already. And they are very knowledgeable, thanks to teaching from many sources, as to how to see the different variables of the future. And how to ride that out. They're very careful. The ones that do the traveling in time are not as connected to their time as some of the other members are.

One of the questions people have is whether the future would change so much, for instance, that some of them wouldn't be born. And he said they'd make sure that would not happen.

D: *That's what I was thinking, the theory that they would no longer exist.*

428

L: Yes. He said they're very careful to make sure there are no connections in that way. But we can verify that they have changed much of the future in a very good and positive way.

I encountered a different type of time traveler that is more compatible with the concept of simultaneous lives. In 2003 a man flew from Denver for a private session. He had tried hypnosis with several other reputable hypnotists, but they were unsuccessful. This often happens if the subconscious is unsure if it should release the information. It has to feel trust and rapport with the hypnotist. This was understandable when the information emerged. It was not the type of thing that could be shared with just anybody. It did not startle me because I have worked in this field for so long, and have encountered similar cases.

He went to a scene from the past, but he appeared to be an observer, a visitor just passing through. He said his job was to go from place to place and gather information. He was an explorer, and did not stay very long in one place. After a while, he said he didn't want to be there in the past, because it was boring. He really wanted to go to the future. That was where he felt the most comfortable. That was his home. He described a city with few large buildings. There were mostly homes, where everything was perfect. There was no overcrowding or pollution or anything negative. All that had been eliminated. They had machines in the homes that provided everything. Even their food was taken care of. His job was to accumulate information and to teach others. There was a centralized location where information was assimilated and shared with others. He had to travel to different time periods that were in the past from where he was. There in these various time periods, he would create a body automatically that fit in with the time, so he wouldn't be noticeable. Then he would bring the information he accumulated or observed back with him. It seemed as though these trips to various time periods were occurring simultaneously, so it took no effort on his part. His job in this *present* lifetime was to learn as much as he could and gain all the information he could. This, apparently, was used by this other part of him to take back to the centralized education center. He missed this home in the future, because it was so different and perfect. A far cry from this time period.

All his life, he never felt at home with his parents. He felt as though he was not really their child. I have heard this many times, the feeling of not belonging here on Earth, as though this is not really "home". This unusual regression helped explain this, as well as is possible. This was another case of a Time Traveler; an observer who is gathering information. Some would call it a shape-shifter. If it was, it was the general observer type who are not allowed to interfere. Also he has never married and has no children. This type do not want ties because it creates karma and ties to this Earth (and apparently to this time period.) They must be able to accumulate, do their job and then return to their real home.

During another of my private sessions, a man went to a past life in what appeared to be Egypt, but I think it was a much older civilization (or maybe a lifetime on another planet). There were dog-faced, spindly beings (maybe masks). He had done something forbidden (maybe the misuse of energy), and was being punished. They sent him through a time portal. It appeared as a big black space like a door. It was a one way portal. He couldn't return through it. He found himself on a barren, lifeless planet of permanent twilight. There were some strange structures (multi-pyramid-shaped), but they were empty. He had no need to consume anything. He lived the rest of his life there, wasting away from loneliness and isolation. His mind finally numbed itself to the isolation. Needless to say, he was happy to finally leave that life. What a perfect, yet horrible, solution to prisons.

In my work, I found that some scientists living in Atlantis had the ability to go through a wormhole or portal into space to other worlds. Since there were many tunnels or exits along the way, they had to leave markers on both sides of exits in order to find their way back to the laboratory. They had a ring that had something to do with the ability to travel like this.

A woman who I will call "Marie" began corresponding with me and wanted me to come to a small town in the outback of Australia on my next trip there. After reading my books she knew of my interest in UFO investigation. She said the small town of about 2000 people was located in what seemed to be an UFO corridor. There were continual sightings of unusual lights and objects in the sky that had been observed for several years. I have agreed to not reveal the name or location of the town, because I do not want curiosity seekers to disrupt the lives of these gentle people. Marie also wanted me to come out to her 1000 acre ranch located outside of town, where she wanted to show me the location of a portal. On my next trip to Australia in 2001 I arranged to include the trip there in between Expos and lectures in several cities. We flew into the nearest airport on a small plane, and were driven over an hour to the little town. It was very isolated, and nestled among the hills and trees, from which many colorful wild parrots flew back and forth.

When we arrived at the town it was like taking a trip backward in time to the 1880s and the days of the Old West. We were to spend two nights in a back-packer lodge. The lecture was held in an old store that was reminiscent of the old movies. When the townspeople arrived the women graciously brought dishes for a pot luck supper afterward. It was cold and I huddled as close as I could to an old potbellied stove for warmth. There, I was introduced to a woman in her 90s who

431

was the official historian and record keeper. She had detailed the accounts of the sightings and unusual happenings for many years. It was a fascinating evening as the people finally reluctantly began to tell me about some of the things they had observed. I say reluctantly, because they did not want ridicule. Several of the people verified the report of the portal located on Marie's land, and the unusual occurrence in 1997.

At night it was easy to see why there could be so many sightings. The location was very isolated, and because there were no city lights the sky was crystal clear. The stars looked large and plentiful. One oddity I was surprised to find was that the constellation Orion was upside down. Which I suppose it should be since I was on the other side of the world in the Southern hemisphere.

When this book was going into its final stages, I called Marie and asked her to email her account of the incident. I did not want to rely on my memory. I wanted to get it as accurate as possible. She said that would be no problem, because she had written down the entire incident right after it happened.

Here is her account of what I consider a modern-day portal into another dimension, that is being actively used:

"The Drop" Light Explosion - June or July 1997.

We have a beautiful 50 metre high waterfall which we have named "The Drop", a minute or two stroll from the house. It had been raining for a couple of days so the waterfall was in full flow. Just before 5 pm the rain eased and it became misty. I heard a loud rumbling down in the creek, so I thought I would go and see what was being tumbled along in the water. I thought it might be a large boulder, or perhaps an uprooted tree about to be washed over the falls. The sound was not unlike thunder, but was coming from down in the creek, not from the sky.

As I was about halfway along the track and the waterfall

came into view there was an extra loud rumble, then an explosion of gold, pink and white light up from the bottom of the falls, spreading out and up into the sky, almost reaching me - about 75-100 metres away. At this moment I heard a voice inside the left hand side of my head say, "Go back! Do not come any closer! Go back now!" I said, "OK, fine, I'm going!", and turned and quickly walked back to the house. The air seemed electrically charged and crackling. The light explosion had been the most extraordinary thing I have ever seen. It was beautiful, the pink was soft, the gold and white were brilliant. The whole scene would have covered an area of approximately 100 metres diameter, perhaps more, almost reaching to where I was. I do not know how high it went as I could not see clearly, because of the mist which changed colour with the explosion.

Even though the rumbling and explosion were very loud and startling, I knew I had experienced something very special indeed. I telephoned my husband in town to tell him what had happened, but could only speak for a short time as the line had a lot of crackling and static.

A friend who lived in a valley to the south phoned me that evening. She said she had been looking out a window towards our place about 5 pm, and had seen a beautiful pink and gold cloud over the hills in our direction. She described it as looking "Biblical – should have angels sitting on it, sort of cloud". Then she heard a loud rumbling and bang, and a column of gold/pink light shot down to the ground. "But it didn't seem like lightning. Very odd."

The next day another acquaintance who lives in the valley to the north of us said, "What have you been doing up on your place, Marie?" She then went on to describe seeing a beautiful golden and pink cloud that seemed to explode in a column, unlike lightning. She said it was quite different than any storm cloud she had ever seen.

Two nights afterwards I had gone to bed, and was still pondering what I had seen. I decided to pray to Jesus and ask if it was possible for me to be given some understanding of what had happened. Immediately, I saw a picture in my mind of the

433

book *The Keys of Enoch*, by J.J. Hurtak, and a voice said, "Page 221". I laid there stunned, the voice then said, "You really are a sceptic, Marie. Page 221!" So, of course, I got up and looked up page 221. In part it reads:

"Thus, the Merkabah vehicles of Light descend upon our planet, whereby a field of light is opened, 'whole light beings' descend as the Magnetic fields of the space-time overlap are controlled.

"These 'whole light bodies' come down through the artificial time warp zones, and land upon the face of the Earth. And this is what the ancients beheld when they saw 'the pillar of the cloud go up from before their face'".

This experience of seeing such a wonderful happening, and especially the gentle nudge of being told I was a sceptic, has altered my way of seeing things totally. I am now no longer a sceptic – just wishing I understood more!"

Well, there you are, Dolores. I hope I have described the event clearly. What a pity we can't pass on the actual emotions experienced at the time. You would get quite a buzz, I'm sure.

When I visited Marie's beautiful isolated home she took me to the place where the event had occurred. Of course, I could not see any sign of a portal now. All I saw was a beautiful waterfall cascading down the side of the mountain into a deep gorge below. Yet this fits the description of the opening of a portal to another dimension. The guardians were truly on duty that day to keep any unwary human from venturing too close. As they said, the energy would destroy the matrix of a human being. Marie knew without a doubt that the strange and majestic event occurred, but I am glad that she had the validation of her friends on the other sides of the valley.

When I speak on radio shows, I usually receive mail (both snail mail and email) from listeners. Especially when I talk on the Art Bell show which has millions of listeners. We have received hundreds of emails in a day. Many of these people want to tell me their personal stories they feel they cannot share with anyone else for fear of being thought crazy. It makes them feel better when they find out that I have heard many similar tales, and that I understand it enough to try to explain it to them. At least they know they are not the only ones having these strange experiences. For some of them, I do not have any logical explanation except to think they may have to do with traveling back and forth between the numerous dimensions surrounding us. This was explained more fully in *Book One*.

One man said he was driving at night on a coastal highway in Florida. Long ago the highway was rerouted and bypassed all the small towns. Yet on that night he suddenly found himself (on the same highway) driving through a small town. He could see the outside lights of the houses and various closed businesses. Everything seemed deserted, as would be natural in a small town at night. After five minutes or so, he suddenly found the highway widened again and he was back on the coastal interstate where he belonged. My only explanation was that for a short while, he had slipped backward in time and entered a dimension where the road through the town still existed.

This next one I will quote directly from the email I received in January 2001. If anyone has an explanation, I wish they would contact me.

"I managed to catch some of your show on Coast to Coast AM and found it very interesting, which is what prompted me to contact you. In September of last year (2000), for about 2 or 3 days, I experienced some very strange things. It started when I was walking past a local airport where I live. It was during daylight hours when I saw a passenger plane take off from the airport. A few minutes later a Lear Jet took off, and as it left the runway and climbed into the sky it went backwards and forwards several times as it took off. I stood there dumbfounded, because I know that it is impossible for a jet to go backwards. A few minutes later, another Lear Jet took off and did the same thing. Or was it the same one? I then noticed that the cars on the road were doing the same thing. Rather than move forward down the road, they would go back and forth as they went down the road. I noticed that the clouds in the sky would do the same thing, going back and forth. At night, I went for a walk by some businesses that were closed for the night. Yet I saw people inside moving around that did not belong there, because they were dressed in attire of around 50 to 60 years ago. I also saw other unusual images that I knew weren't possible. Any idea what was happening? I am a very skeptical person, and do not believe what I was seeing."

My answer: "Thanks for sharing your very interesting experiences. Even though you're skeptical, you can't deny something when you see it with your own eyes. I have not heard of this exact phenomenon, but I can try to guess based on the information I have received and written about. There are more strange things out there than anyone can possibly imagine, so I know I have not investigated all of them by any means. It sounds as though you might have been trying to enter a time warp, but did not go all the way. Also people often go back and forth between dimensions and do not know it because surroundings look very similar. Because things were moving back and forth, maybe the line between dimensions was not stabilized. I have heard of people suddenly finding themselves in another time period and interacting with people dressed differently, etc. Often, they go back and try to find the same places and find they either do not exist, or are in a deteriorated state. One thing that I find strange is that the people in the other time period do not notice anything strange about the future person they are interacting with. They seem to be living their normal lives. I don't know if this is any help or not, but that is as close as I can come to it. Maybe you were trying to cross back and forth between dimensions and it was not stabilized. Otherwise, you can do these things and never know the difference. I have even had people reported as being in two places at once. It was verified by other people who saw them

436

and spoke to them. So who knows? Sometimes it is better if we don't know these strange time warps are happening on a regular basis. It is less confusing to our little mortal brain."

———————— ⋄◦⋄ ⋄◦⋄ ⋄◦⋄ ————————

This next email is even stranger. But in this case there was physical proof that something unusual had occurred.

"I was fortunate enough to hear your terrific interview on Coast to Coast the other night, but something happened that mystifies three of the listeners. This is why I am writing. To be as brief as possible, we all three have the Reel Talk radio/recorder which can be preset and it records at 1/4 speed. We have this device just for the Coast to Coast program as we are unable to stay up till the middle of the night. (The show usually goes from 12 PM to 4 AM.) We all three set our radio/recorder on the same station which comes out of Nashville, Tennessee. It is the only station that we can get the program on. We live some distance away from each other, and quite some distance from Nashville, but WWTN is a 100,000 watt station. Much to my dismay, when I played the recorded tape for your program the next morning, all I got was a sports event, all four hours. As did one of my friends on her tape. I called the station and they informed me that they were no longer going to air Coast to Coast. They were changing their format, and they didn't care how many protests there were about it. Now the BIG mystery is: the other of us three, her tape had your entire interview on it! We absolutely know that it was the same station as the same call letters were given several times. We were all listening to the same station, but receiving different broadcasts. I have talked to a few people who have a working knowledge of radio transmission (former government people whose training was in that field), and they all said it was impossible to have such a thing happen. Thank God it did, as we all three wanted to hear what you had to say. My question to you is: do you have any explanation for this incident? It

437

crossed my mind that perhaps it could be related to parallel universe phenomenon. That is the only thing that computes. Any insight you could shed on this would be greatly appreciated. PS: For some reason, WWTN started broadcasting Coast to Coast again and do we ever appreciate that! It is our contact with the universe."

Part of my reply: "In my work I have had strange things happen to my tape recorder during sessions that cannot be explained. Static, strange noises, speeding up and slowing down, voices over voices, and many things that should not occur with electronics. Many times there is more than one tape recorder going, and they are all affected. I have also had strange effects with telephones. But this is the first time I have heard of anything like this. You may be right that it has something to do with dimensions. That's as good an answer as any other. The station broadcasting the sports show was existing in a parallel reality. I'm glad you had three people involved. I think that would qualify as proof."

A few weeks later, I spoke at the Unity Church in Memphis, and was surprised to find that the three ladies drove from Nashville to meet me. They mainly wanted to see me to affirm that the incident really did happen, and they have the tapes to prove it. They were three of the most normal women anyone would hope to encounter. I am convinced they were telling the truth. Again, if anyone has any other explanation for this incident, I would love to hear from you.

In my book *Jesus and the Essenes,* Jesus gave the following example of reincarnation and different dimensions, using nature in his parables so the people could understand more easily:

"He used another plant as an example, a plant that is composed of many layers (similar to an onion). He says this would show the different planes of existence. He pointed out that, at the very center of the plant the layers are very thin and close together. If one could consider each layer as a different

438

plane, one can see that at the center where it's the smallest and most limited, that is like the physical world. As one travels upward and outward in the planes, one's horizon of understanding would expand each time, and you would see and understand more."

It makes me wonder whether the people he gave the parable (or example) to understood the deeper meanings that he was trying to impart. Perhaps it may have been too complex even for the disciples. But it shows that he was very aware of the deeper meanings of life and the universe.

Several other strange incidents dealing with time and dimensions that occurred during my sessions are sprinkled throughout this book.

SECTION SEVEN

ENERGY BEINGS

AND CREATOR BEINGS

CHAPTER 22

MYSTERIES

This first part is a continuation of the Earth mysteries section found in *Book One*. There were a few things I wanted to have more clarification on before I included them in a book. This was information that was accumulated in the late 1990s. Some of it came from Phil, a young man that I have written about in many of my books. He has the ability to go into deep trance and close off his conscious mind so it will not interfere with the answers coming through. We have always been able to receive new, unusual and valuable information when we have sessions.

OUR SOLAR SYSTEM

D: *You told me once that there is no life as we know it on the other planets in our solar system at this time.*

Phil: That is accurate. There is no human life, not to say there is no life. For the atmosphere on the other planets is not of such a nature that would sustain human life as is known on this planet at this time. However, that does not mean that there is not life in other forms, such as in spirit form or even in an advanced or some other form in physical.

D: *I've been told that at one time there was life on Mars. There was quite a civilization of humanoid beings there. Is that true?*

P: That is in fact the case, and will soon be made aware to your planet. It has been suggested tentatively through microscopic examination of meteors. This is a huge change in consciousness which must be delicately spoon fed to your civilization. They are in fact the ancestors of your civilization, and life on Earth as you know it. There were

443

life forms occurring simultaneously on both planets. However, the Martian planet had been stable and productive of life for a much longer period of time than her sister planet who had a much different path ecologically, geologically. Mars settled down and became habitable much quicker than Earth. And so the seeding process began much quicker and much sooner on Mars than on the planet Earth.

The story of the seeding of the planet Earth with the first life-forms was told in *Keepers of the Garden* and continued in *The Custodians*. This indicated that Earth was not the only planet in our solar system that had been seeded, but something must have happened over time to render some of these other planets lifeless once again.

D: *What happened that destroyed the life on Mars?*
P: There were many different opinions at that time as to who should be in control of the world government, and many different types of technology which allowed them to manipulate their weather. They became somewhat disjointed in their purposes and destroyed their own weather system. Much as the abilities now manifesting on your planet will also allow you to destroy your planet if given the opportunity.
D: *I've also been told there are remnants of life still left on Mars.*
P: There are elements of life deep within the planet which have succeeded in maintaining their life-form. However, they are not what you would call "human" or humanoid. They are somewhat different in that their evolution was from a different path than that which you have on this planet.
D: *I've been told that there are cities underneath the surface of Mars where some of the inhabitants went when the surface became uninhabitable.*
P: That analogy could be used similar to the concept of a colony. However, we would not characterize city in the

manner in which you understand city. In a technological sense more like a colony of termites, in that social structure. The beings are living within structures naturally occurring, and also manufactured within the planet.

D: *I've also been told that when the scientists finally get to Mars they will not realize that there is life still there. They won't recognize it.*

P: When the scientists do get to Mars, they will be aware of many other life-forms besides what are under their feet. There will be an increase in the awareness by that time that the life-forms on Mars will be considered just another life-form.

D: *Now let's switch to another part of the solar system. I'm very interested in Jupiter. What is the phenomenon called the "Red Spot" on Jupiter? It's visible with our telescopes.*

P: The expression of the Red Spot on your plane would be called a weather disturbance. What you perceive on your plane of existence is a hurricane of gases that are a weather phenomenon. It is however a phenomenon which has its core essence in a higher plane of reality. The higher expressions would indicate that this is an area of many different – of like form but separate – individual entities of awareness. It is a city, which on a higher plane of expression is a life-form expressing its lower components in the form of an atmospheric disturbance on your level.

D: *If it is an atmospheric disturbance or a hurricane, it's been there forever, as far as we know. And it doesn't really seem to change that much. It would also be enormous in size.*

P: There are many different forms of expression of life within this universe that the human consciousness is simply not aware of. However, in order for you to comprehend this, this could be compared to a colony of living beings whose expression reaches into your plane of awareness, such that the atmospheric conditions which overlay this lower form of expression are visible. There are many different levels of awareness which have no corresponding influence on another plane. However, in this instance there is an effect on the lower plane of expression. Such that this colony, which is a civilization on the higher planes of existence, leaves its footprint on your level as an atmospheric disturbance.

D: *Then I think you mean on an alternate reality it is a group of people in a physical city on Jupiter. And it is more or less casting a shadow on our plane that appears as an atmospheric condition? Would that be a good analogy?*

P: We would enhance this concept by seeing it not so much as a city in your terminology, but more as a colony of virus or bacteria, in that they are co-existing and living on their plane. However, we would not characterize it as a technological civilization in your context.

D: *Then it wouldn't be intelligent beings, as we consider them.*

P: That is not in fact the case. They are highly intelligent, but simply live in a different form. Their expression does not include construction and technological aspects. They are highly evolved and civilized, however, they are not technological.

D: *Someone else told me that the relation of Jupiter to the Earth plane was vital. Do you have any information on that?*

P: There are many different levels of co-dependence within your solar system, for the entire physical balance is dependent on each individual element maintaining its own equilibrium. On simply the physical plane the sudden loss of any one planet would throw the gravitational balance of the entire solar system out of equilibrium. There are, of course, other levels of awareness and the change or loss of such a planet would, of course, have implications and effects on the other planes as well.

D: *This is what the aliens have told us about Earth. That we must not blow it up, because it would cause great havoc in the universe and other dimensions.*

P: That is accurate.

D: *I've heard that others who are observing us would not allow this to happen, simply because it would throw off the balance of the galaxy.*

446

P: That is accurate, in the sense that the individuals who inhabit the other planes of existence have a right to protect their civilizations and their life forms from intrusion. It would be as if an undeclared and unknowledgeable war were being waged against an unseen party by an ignorant culture.

D: *But they are more aware of these things than we are.*

P: That is accurate. And so they have a right to protect their civilization from damage caused by the ignorance of a somewhat unruly neighbor.

D: *Do you know anything about where the asteroid belt came from?*

P: This was at one time a planet which was destroyed when a passing star caused a collision between it and a meteor which came into its path. The collision caused the breakup of this planet. With the planet's own internal forces and those of the Sun and other planets, it was pulled apart to such an extent that it was rendered simply formless, and so spread out in its former orbit as particles or asteroids.

D: *I've also heard there may have been a race of people living there and they blew it up themselves.*

P: That is not accurate. The collision was a natural phenomenon which occurred, not because of tampering by any certain race of people. There is also a case where these stories arise because of misinterpretation of information. Not an intentional story-telling or fib, but simply a misinterpretation. These channelings are not the absolute bottom line as well, as this vehicle is not the bottom line. There are potential inaccuracies in these channelings as well. And so all channels should be viewed with an open awareness to this fact. As the channelings can only be as accurate as the vehicle is physically possible to translate, and it would be almost impossible to channel with 100 percent accuracy. For there are simply concepts and ideas which have no precedent in this lifetime or even in this plane. And so, some questions which are asked would require concepts which do not exist here, so analogies must be drawn, which may not be entirely accurate. However,

447

the gist of the information could be translated.

D: *I understand that anything that comes through a human being is bound to have problems that way.*

P: It is simply a matter of not being able to translate, owing to many factors. Some, as we have said, being the lack of concepts to draw from.

THE SUN

D: *Is the Sun actually hot?*

Phil: There is indeed that element which is hot. However, we feel this is misunderstood from your physical perspective. As the heat itself seems to be the focus of one's attentions here, and it is nothing more than a byproduct. The true energy of the sun is not heat, but of a nature far beyond that which man's understanding is capable of at this time. The heat is simply a manifestation of a phenomenon which is far more complicated than simple combustion. This is a transition of energies, and the physical aspect would be what you call flame or combustion. Heat being a byproduct. The true reality of this is a transference and change of energies manifested down to a physical level as heat and combustion.

D: *The rays and emanations we can't see are ultra-violet. Do you mean something like that?*

P: Far beyond what you would even consider as rays, but as elemental forms of energy. A fundamental change in the energies themselves.

The sun, as everybody perceives it to be, is a gaseous planet. But one of my subjects said it in fact has a *culture* underneath the gas belts, which cannot be seen from the outside surface.

D: *People on Earth can't see that, can they?*

Bob: No, they can't. They have no idea. They just assume, like everybody else, it is a solid gaseous ball. But all the explosions that occur on the belt outside, actually occur *within* that belt. But the center part of the planet is just like it is here on Earth. They have farms, they have houses, they have people. They have civilizations. And all that is encased underneath the energy belt.

D: *So it's not hot on the surface?*

B: Oh, no! No, no! That's one of the interesting things about it.

D: *You would think it would be too hot to support life.*

B: You would, but all of that's high up in the energy. Up in the so-called "atmosphere". It's something similar to the Van Allen belt on this planet. But we travel back and forth all the time. In and out. It's a very nice civilization.

There were more surprising revelations about the actual properties of our Sun that are revealed further in this chapter.

D: *Some people believe that the world was created in what is called the Big Bang theory. Would this be true?*

Phil: If you were in physical form at that time you certainly would have perceived what you call a Big Bang. (I laughed) The Big Bang, of course, is an analogy used by the scientists to describe the explosion, as opposed to implosion. The outward moving force created when the universe, or perhaps more accurate to say, *laws* of the universe, were set. And so in that sense, yes, it would be accurate to say the Big Bang theory does signify the beginning of that point in time in which the physical or material laws of your universe were set.

D: *One theory is that as the outward thrust of these worlds happens, it will reach a certain point where it will begin to turn and go back together again. Would this be true?*

P: That is accurate. That point at which all outward motion ceases is called "equilibrium". And is within the turning point in which the laws of the universe then would change and be their polar opposites of those which they are now. That which is positive would then become negative and that which is negative would then become positive. The universe then would recede into that which is again a void. The abyss. At which point the creation story would repeat itself.

D: *It would start all over again. After it had collapsed on itself it would again explode, so to say.*

P: That is accurate.

D: *How long a period of time would it take for something like that to happen?*

P: It would be safe to assume that you would be in another form when this happens.

D: *(Laugh) We don't have to worry about it.*

This concept demonstrates that the laws of reincarnation or recycling apply to everything from the microcosm to the macrocosm. Nothing escapes this cycle.

When the universe reaches the end of its expansion, the stage where it reverses, implodes, goes back to the Source and explodes again, is that when we all return home to the Creator with all the knowledge we have accumulated?

D: *There is a line of thought that this world will either go into itself or be destroyed within 5000 years. At the same time there is another planet being prepared for those entities that live on this Earth that have raised their vibrations or raised their understanding of the spirit. Is this a true theory?*

P: Perhaps your chronological time frame could be somewhat in error. However, the concept itself is quite valid, as even now those who choose to migrate to, not only this planet you speak of, but to others as well, have already begun. There is indeed the successor to this planet in its infancy. And as yet it has not reached that stage where it would be hospitable to life forms, not as you know them now, but as they soon shall be. That is *your* life forms. The energies resident on this planet at this time will then move en masse to that which is being prepared at this time. For at that point your life forms will have evolved to a somewhat different level than they are now. It would be inappropriate and immature to try to transmigrate these life-forms to that planet. For neither, at this stage, are in readiness. There is yet a time frame to evolve before both life form and planet are hospitable to each other. Needless to say, that time at which it happens will be the most appropriate time.

This answer came through in the 1990s, but has been repeated with greater frequency in my sessions during the last few years. This idea of the bodies being changed in order to make a transition to another level will be expanded in the last section. There has also been information received about another physical planet similar to Earth that is being prepared for the survivors of any Earth calamities. It has been stressed that the human race must not perish. There will be survivors even if "they" have to resort to drastic measures. The story of this second Earth is told in *Keepers of the Garden.*

There have been many questions about the shafts in the great pyramid that seem too small for anything useful, which are aimed at the sky. As with everything else connected with the pyramid they are shrouded in mystery.

D: *What is the purpose of those shafts in the pyramid?*
Carol: The purpose of the shafts in the pyramid were to allow the souls of the beings they considered to be priests and pharaohs to go back to their planetary system, so they would not be bound into the layers or the light of this particular planet. In the *very* beginning they were made

manifest into the physical, and then when it was no longer necessary to be manifest, the soul would travel through those shafts using what you could call a "stargate". (This word was asked as a question. Unsure of the word.) Using technical devices in the King's chamber.

D: *There were technical devices in the King's chamber?*

C: What you call the King's chamber. They used these technical devices to allow those souls to go back to their original star system.

In *Keepers of the Garden* and *The Custodians* it mentions that extraterrestrials often came in the early formation of civilization to live among the developing people to help them and give them needed knowledge and instruction. These beings had incredible life spans, so they were eventually treated and respected as gods. This indicates that the first pharaohs might have been these types of beings. (Refer also to Chapter 4, Isis.)

This reminded me of sessions described in *Legacy From the Stars* where the souls of extraterrestrials became trapped in our world after they died. They apparently created karma, and could not return to their original home, even after death. In these cases often no one from their home planet even knew they were here. Maybe the ETs were well aware that something like this occasionally happens, and they did not want these visitors, who had lived so long upon the Earth, to be similarly trapped.

Another mystery is the existence and location of hidden chambers underneath the Sphinx.

D: *It is said that the chambers underneath the Sphinx were sealed. Why was this done?*

C: There was an overthrow of the beings that were not from this planet.

This indicates that some of the beings operating the pyramid system in those days were not human. Maybe they were the advisors that are spoken of in my other books who

452

came to live among the humans to give them the new gifts (advances) when they were needed. This would also explain the use of the shafts to return their souls to their original star system. They did not wish to be trapped here on Earth when their job was over.

C: Mankind wanted to take their power away from them and make it theirs. The beings knew that this was going to occur. So there was a sealing of all these technical devices and information, so that it would not fall into the wrong hands at the wrong time, because they would destroy themselves with this.

This also sounds rather like the humans who, because of their ignorance, destroyed the devices used to generate power from the Sun, moon and stars. (Bartholomew gave this information in *Convoluted Universe, Book One.*)

D: *So the beings from the other planets were the ones that sealed the chambers? It wasn't the humans.*

C: There were initiates, those that were trained by these beings. The pyramids were used for initiation and training. There are many, many of the ancient temples located throughout what is known as the "plateau" now. (This goes along with the Cat People's temple in the same area. See Chapter Three.) And these were used for initiation for people, *humans*, to raise their consciousness and their vibration. Then they in turn could use these devices and technology in an appropriate manner to help the planetary system. The pyramids were based on a grid system. The grid system is very important, because it is the major connector system for the planet. *One* of them. There were several systems, but this was *one* of them. In each one of these major places there are also pyramids. The pyramids are conductors of universal harmonics that also connected other planets in harmony and vibration. This is also worked with colors, sound frequency, and also vortices, planetarily throughout the grid system, in order to maintain balance and harmonics for this planetary system.

D: *And these people knew how to use these things in the right way.*

C: They instructed. They put them into place.

D: *So the sealing was because the other people were coming in and they didn't want them to take these things. You said there was a danger also to others that did not know how to use them.*

Again, this sounds like the energy in the Cat People's temple that was dangerous to those not able to handle it.

C: One of the planetary star systems intervened. They sent envoys that helped to influence humankind, as always. To overthrow, to personalize, to take the power from corrupt groups.

D: *So these people sealed the chambers to hide the information, and to protect people from using it in the wrong way.*

C: To protect them from themselves.

D: *And where are these located?*

C: Staggered chambers underneath the Sphinx. Each one interconnected with small tunnels, and guarded by energies and frequencies.

Again, this sounded like Bartholomew's history (*Book One*) where the people thought if they were in possession of the secret energy appliances they would be in power, and would not need the extraterrestrials or priests. In his history they caused destruction to the devices and themselves. So apparently the last controlling group at the Sphinx decided to seal the devices away, so such a thing could not happen again. They have remained entombed ever since.

In *Conversations With Nostradamus, Volume III,* Nostradamus also referred to energies that had been put in place so that only the correct people would ever be allowed near the secret entrances to these hidden tunnels and rooms. If the people attempting to enter these were of the incorrect or negative vibration, they would be killed. So it was a very elaborate protection system installed thousands of years ago.

Refer to Chapter 6 about the symbols being used to make the hidden information visible.

Astrology has always been an interest of mine, even though I am not an astrologer. How did astrology begin? It seems as though the study of the stars has been a fascination of mankind since time immortal. I found the answer quite unexpectedly during a routine regression session. A woman went back to a lifetime where she was a priest in ancient Babylon. It has been accepted that Babylonia is where the study of astrology began. In my books about Nostradamus, he had an ephemeris that he said dated from the ancient Egyptians and Babylonians. The woman was a male priest in an isolated and secret religion or mystery school. He was in a beautiful temple that was situated on a mound high above the city. He described the study of the stars that his group had been involved with from times even ancient to him. He said the movement of the stars had been charted for as long as his group had been in existence. This was their main purpose, while other groups practiced healing and prophecy. The temple was open in the middle (no roof) with huge pillars on all four sides. He said the priest would sit at a designated spot in the center of the temple and chart the positions of the stars as they moved across the openings between the pillars. The pillars gave them a point of reference, and a way to measure the movement of the planets as opposed to the stationary stars, and also to judge the rotation of the earth. After doing this for hundreds of years they had established very accurate charts. This was also used as a way to determine the solstices and equinoxes, because in a tropical country there would be little changing of the seasons to indicate these. This may explain why so many ancient buildings were built in this manner, high on a hill with many equally spaced pillars. It is generally understood that many were temples in the ancient world, but it now appears the pillars had a more practical purpose. To watch and record the movement of the stars.

After another woman client went through a past lifetime and was on the spirit side, she was taken first to the board of elders who would review the life she had just left. It was decided that she had acted admirably and learned the lessons she had come to learn. Now she was ready for the next assignment. This was all worked out in advance, and was discussed with the help of the elders. They could suggest, but not compel her to take the assignment. She had to decide who her parents would be, where she would be born, etc. The same type of information I have received many times before. But this time she said she also had to decide the day, month and year, and moon of her birth. So I asked the question that many others have asked me, "Is astrology involved in the decision-making process of a soul coming back to Earth." She said it definitely was. It all had to be worked out exactly. This would indicate that even premature births were scheduled before birth, because the astrological influences were important on the personality of the incoming soul. There is probably much more involved also, because I do not believe we understand all the qualities of astrology and numerology.

DEPOSITORIES OF ALL KNOWLEDGE

This session took a strange and unusual twist. Phil was attending the UFO Conference in Eureka Springs, Arkansas in April 2001, and we decided to have a session since it had been quite a while since the last one.

My old friend, Harriet, was rooming with me. She has helped with moral support since the beginning of my work over 25 years ago. This was the year (2001) that the Convention Center burned in Eureka Springs, and Lou Farish, the man who organizes this conference, had to find another place to hold it. We still reserved a room at the Inn of the Ozarks in order to support the motel (because of the loss of revenue). Many people thought that the conference had been canceled because of the fire. Ann came to the Conference on the last day, and we let her stay in our room instead of going back to Fayetteville. She slept on a pallet on the floor. When I started the session Ann asked if she could sit in and watch, because, although I had had a session with her, she had never observed one. Phil did not object since this had happened many times before.

The strange incidents began almost immediately. After I gave Phil his keyword and he started into the session, I noticed that Ann (seated in a chair on the other side of the bed) was also going under. I motioned to Harriet and she saw it too. There was nothing I could do except proceed, although I motioned to Harriet to keep an eye on her. Probably because I had also worked with her, my voice had the effect of putting her under even though I had not intended for this to happen. Ann slumped in the chair seemingly in a world of her own. I conducted the session in a normal manner, until Ann began to also answer the questions. Then I knew I had a predicament. I use a hand microphone and hold it up to the subject's mouth. This presented a problem when she began to answer in a soft voice from a distance away. This occurrence will be expanded upon.

When working with Phil I use the elevator method that he is so familiar with. I asked him to tell me the first thing he saw as the elevator door came open.

P: There is someone there to greet me. In a pure white light. We are old friends. He's taking me to another room where information can be shown. There are several here whose purpose is to assist in this communication. They say there are many others who are assisting, who are in other dimensions. Who have the ability to influence the material from *their* perspective, such that it can be displayed in *our* perspective. There is always some information which is held, due to its being just above the level at which you can

457

perceive it. It is a growth process, which, as one moves forward in understanding, one continually breaches new levels of information. As the growth process continues, there is always, just ahead of the current level of understanding, a level of information which has not, as yet, been breached. It is this continual breaching process which allows for examination and understanding of the information. For were it all to be given at once, there would be no way to make sense.

D: *We've been doing this for many years. And the information we're getting now, we would never have understood in the beginning. So it wouldn't have made any sense, and it wouldn't have been of any value to us at that time.*

P: It is time now to bring you to the next, most appropriate level of information. The information necessary to answer your questions will be made available.

D: *One thing that was brought up many years ago, was information about the Sun in our solar system. At that time, I was told it was not what we perceive it to be, but that we were not ready to understand it. Can you expand on that? The true nature of what we call the "Sun" in our solar system.*

P: We ask that you please define your question in terms of reality. Are you questioning the physical reality here, or are you addressing the ultra-dimensional aspects?

D: *We could have both, I suppose. Because in the physical reality, we see it as the glowing ball in the sky that gives life to our Earth, and keeps everything functioning with exploding gases. That's our physical concept of it. Is that correct?*

P: We would say that, indeed, you are sharing an experience with a physical body not unlike your own. The physical manifestations which you perceive through your physical senses, are simply *that.* They are manifestations which are designed to allow a presence on that particular plane of which you are speaking from.

D: *We see it with telescopes as exploding gases that reach out for quite a ways.*

P: Not unlike many of your politicians whose influence is like

458

tendrils which radiate from their power base. The influence of your Sun is intentional, and affected by the interaction between those contingent elements, the energies, which inhabit both the solar and planetary manifestations. There are reactions observed on the Sun which are a direct result of the actions perpetrated on your planet. This is not to say that *all* reactions on the Sun are influenced from actions on your planet. For there are other beings surrounding the solar system as well, which also have an influence. However, the most immediate and dramatic influence on that which you call the "Sun", is the actions of the beings on your planet at this time. There are being drawn to your planet, adjustments and corrections to compensate for imbalances on your planet at this time.

D: *You also said that what we physically see is only one part of it, just one manifestation, but the real quality of the Sun was inter-dimensional?*

At this point the strange and unexpected phenomenon occurred. Suddenly Ann answered the question from her chair. She was slumped in the chair with her head sloughed to one side, but she was answering. I was too far away for the microphone to accurately pick it up. It sounded like: "It is recording," on the tape. I knew that if this was to continue, I would have to move her closer, because she was on the other side of the bed on which Phil was lying. At first, I thought it was only a sudden outburst, and that she probably would not continue. I continued questioning Phil.

D: *Can you explain what you mean by inter-dimensional?*
P: We would ask that the other individual please align themselves with our energies here, such that we may both participate.

Normally, Phil was unaware of anything going on in the room when he was in trance. But apparently, the entities that were communicating knew what was happening, and they

459

wanted Ann to be moved closer. This would make it easier for me also.

I turned off the recorder and walked around the bed. Harriet helped me to try to stand Ann up. She is a tall woman, and she was a dead weight. Together, we got her to her feet, but she was no help at all. We managed to pivot her to where she fell on the bed next to Phil. The entire time of the session she lay there in the awkward position in which she fell, making no attempt to move into a more comfortable position. At least this way, I would have them both on the same bed. But I had to stand over them and move the microphone back and forth as they took turns speaking. It was most interesting that throughout the session as they answered the questions, they never interrupted each other. They seemed to know when the other one was speaking, and allowed them to finish before interjecting their opinion. They also continued each other's statements in some cases, adding more information. This was the first time anything like this had happened to me. Many times, other people observing in the room had seemed to have fallen asleep, probably because of the sound of my voice, but they never answered and participated in the session. After we had Ann situated, I turned the recorder back on and continued.

D: *You are aware there is another individual in the room, who is also in this state?*

P: We are aware of levels of energy. That is accurate.

D: *So if she has something to add to the conversation, it's all right to do that?*

P: We would say that the communication is simultaneous between us. We are simply using two vehicles.

D: *So if she speaks, it's like you are both communicating?*

(Ann answered, "Yes".)

This would be an interesting experiment. It was the first time I had two subjects connected in this way. I wondered if they would be able to speak together as one. I didn't know what would happen.

D: *All right. What we want to find out, is the true aspects of the Sun if it's not as we perceive it on our physical plane. You said it was inter-dimensional.*

Ann: As a recording.

D: *What do you mean?*

Ann: (She cleared her throat so she could speak.) It records. It is a source of energy that is construed of thought originated. This thought is recording thought for the universe that you live on now. With these thoughts that are recorded into it, it is projected back into the universe, and it is simultaneously used together.

D: *But it is only the recording device of our solar system?*

Ann: No. It is a duplication of many other Suns.

D: *You mean, all of the Suns in the universes are recording devices?*

Ann: Yes. It is a source of energy. It is of the main source that you come from. It is a duplication, a lower version, a symbol that you have chosen to use to remind you of the energy source which you come from.

D: *Then the energy source we come from is just a greater manifestation of the Sun, as we see it?*

Ann: Yes. Much greater.

She apparently was referring to the Source or God, which has been called the Great Central Sun in some of my sessions when people are talking about where we all come from.

D: *But the Sun also gives life to the planets and to us.*

Ann: It is what you have chosen.

D: *But Suns also go out. They explode. We've heard about supernovas. (Yes) What happens at that time?*

Ann: You create anew.

D: *What happens to the information if it is a recording device?*

Ann: It never leaves.

D: *Where does it go?*

Ann: It remains, always.

D: *Where?*

Ann: It has always existed.

461

Phil: There are other levels of awareness which are not physical. This information is simply transmitted simultaneously to these other levels which have no physical destructive element to them. The information simply resides on other levels, and is available to be transmitted or withdrawn to a new or expanding Sun, at any time.

D: *In our work we have been told of many planets that are recording planets. Some of the people I work with call them "home". The whole entire planet is a depository of knowledge. Is this a different concept?*

Phil: It is exactly the same. It is simply a difference in the manifestation of the device. You have different media in your realm of experience with which you can record. However, the devices themselves are not the essence of the recording. They are simply a way to store and project the recording itself. It is in *this* manner that the definitions are changed, based on the appropriateness of how this information is to be either stored or delivered.

Phil was the first of my subjects to report such a place. This was described in *Keepers of the Garden* as the Planet of the Three Spires, and expanded upon in the first book of *Convoluted Universe* and *The Custodians*. I have since heard of other planets that record information and are considered depositories. On the spirit side, there is the wonderful library which holds all information known and unknown. The accumulation of information seems to be of primary importance in the way the universes, etc. are constructed.

I started to ask a question, but I noticed Ann wanted to interject.

Ann: I give you an example. Prime Sun that radiates within, for you are within that radiates with the Sun. There is no difference in the beam. It is all of one beam. It is the same beam that penetrates all knowledge and all knowingness. You create the intensity. It is the intensity that you create together, collectively that brings the strength in the source out brighter. For when the Sun weakens, it is your intensity that weakens.

D: *Then we control the Sun?*

Ann: Correct.

D: *Well, we really control everything, but we don't realize that. Is that true?*

Ann: Right. Your planet is in the process at this time of change. You have asked for this to happen. You have known this is going to happen. (Ann raised her hand and faced her palm toward me.) It is as my hand that is holding up to you at present moment. At this present moment, I am doing the same as the Sun. I am shooting energy to you. I am redirecting this energy to you. In a moment you will feel that.

D: *Let me give an example of some of the things I'm finding, and see if it makes sense. It's as though our soul, our spirit – or the subconscious, or whatever you want to call it – accumulates all of the information the being is exposed to, and is a recording device on a lower, smaller level. Then that means the planets are the depository of knowledge, or recording on another level. And now you are saying the Sun is also a recorder of information. Does this mean there are different levels from the smaller to the greater?*

Phil: There are many different forms of expression. We are simply illustrating that everything is in some manner both an *expression* of, and a *recorder* of, reality. There is no recorder which does not express. For how could it be that the recording is simply *made*, but never expressed? There would be no point in there being a recorder which never plays back.

D: *Then on the simple level, that the majority of the physical beings can understand, everything that happens to us in all of our lives, are simply experiences that are recorded.*

Phil: The planets are recorders of the people. The Suns are recorders of the planets. It is, in effect, a chain of recording, such that the individual person's individual experiences are collectively recorded by the planet. Each planet's individual experiences are then recorded by the Sun. Each Sun's individual recordings of each individual planet and each individual being are recorded in a galaxy. Each galaxy is then recorded in a universe. And each universe is then recorded, such that every individual experience is never lost. Which we would illustrate here with the passage in your Bible. It says that not even a sparrow falls from a tree that God does not know. And this is literally true. Every single event on every single planet is eventually and ultimately recorded and known through the planetary, solar, galaxy, universal levels. There is no such thing as any event or idea which passes unnoticed.

D: *If people would understand this, they would see there is no negative, there is no positive. There is only experiences that are recorded. They are just lessons that people learn, and are put into the total memory bank, I suppose you would call it?*

Both Ann & Phil said at the same time, "Collective."

D: *The collective memory bank or what?*

Phil: The God level. (Ann agreed.)

D: *Many of the people I work with, have gone to these repository planets of knowledge, where there was no one but spirits. They were taken there to download information, so to speak. Is that correct?*

Ann: Correct.

D: *It was as though the only people there were keepers of records.*

Ann: They are beings that have experienced on other levels, other than your planetary level.

D: *And they are capable of helping with the accumulation of knowledge?*

Ann: Correct. Dispersement.

D: *Dispersement of knowledge. I'd like to think of it as a giant computer.*

Ann: You have touched on this. You have called it "imprint".

D: *We touched on that many years ago. It was like a library of all the lives ever lived.*

464

The theory behind imprinting is that a spirit can scan and choose from the library a life to have imprinted upon their soul before entering an incarnation. This usually occurs if they are going into a life where there will be experience needed that they have not had in their life history. Rather than actually living the life, it is easier to imprint the life. I was told that the imprint contains everything that happened in that life, including emotions. It would be impossible to tell that the person had not actually lived the life. This presents a difficulty for the regression therapist. But it also answers one of the skeptics' questions: "Why are there so many people saying they were Napoleon, Cleopatra, etc." They think if many people say they are the reincarnation of the same person, then this invalidates reincarnation. But it does not. It just means that several people chose to imprint the same life on their soul, before entering our physical world. It can be compared to research, to prepare them for the life they will enter.

Ann: These spirits are the keepers of what you call "imprint". They are the dispersing factors into the new creation, that you will face very soon.

D: *You mean because the Earth is changing?* (Yes) *But in that same vein, I've also been told that the DNA of our existing bodies is changing.*

Ann: It is.

D: *Can you tell me about that?*

Ann: Yes. Ask your question.

D: *I've been told that it is happening slowly. That the DNA strands are changing?* (Yes) *Some say that, eventually, we're going to be twelve strand DNA?*

Ann: You will be fourteen.

D: *But I have been told that if we reach twelve strand, we will be light bodies, and therefore not visible on this level.*

Ann: No. You will be able to be visible on this level, because it is your choice to do so. You have collectively chosen.

D: *But I was told that our DNA is gradually being changed.*

Ann: It has been happening. This is very minute. (i.e.: tiny)

D: *Because, if it happened suddenly it wouldn't be able to hold.*

Ann: This is why your energy system around your planet is changing. It is increasing. There are some amongst your planet now that are aware of this. And they are preparing at this present time. And they are bringing knowledge forward to you. At this time there is an energy wall around your planet that is changing and revolving, to be able to hold this source.

Phil: There will always be those who can acclimate to higher levels of energy at a more accelerated rate. It is as the concept of the older, shepherding the younger. Such that the assistance is given to those whose ability to understand is enhanced and aided by those who already do understand. The change in your DNA is necessary for your physical expression, your body, to have more possibilities of expression. Enhancements to the basic structure, for these higher, more advanced and energetic expressions. It is simply an upgrade in your body version, such that it will be able to accommodate these higher energies which are prepared to express themselves physically. To this point, it has not been possible for certain energy levels to express physically. For there was no way to communicate with the physical human body. With this upgrade, the human body will be able to communicate on a higher level, and be able to activate certain energies which are, at this time, incapable of expressing.

D: *I've been told, that with this gradual activation of the DNA, of the strands, we are also being made more resistant to disease.*

Ann: I will show you how it will work. You have your strand presently, as you know it now. These lengths are added to the *top* of your strand. You presently think they are at the bottom. They are not; they are at the top. They will link together in a circle formation, that you presently miss now. In this circle formation, when they are linked together, it will increase the intensity. Through this intensity, it will change in your vibration levels. You will be able to transform yourself from one place of existence to another.

466

D: You mean by dissolving or the breaking down of the molecules of the body?

Such as is done in Star Trek, when they go from one place to another.

Ann: It does not break down. Your understanding of breaking down is much different than ours.
D: The dissolution or transfer of molecules?
Ann: It was to be in a matter of energy thoughts. You redirect the energy. But you have chosen not to understand this at this time.
D: But we will be able to do it at that time whenever the DNA changes?
Ann: Correct. It will be a *looped* strand.
D: We've also been told this will make the body more resistant to diseases?
Ann: That is so minimal. It will no longer be a concern.
D: And they said they are extending our life spans also.
Ann: It is forever, of eternity.
D: But it will still be a physical body, as we possess now?
Ann: If you so choose to.

I wanted to clarify the difference between the body and the spirit state, when a body is no longer needed. I suppose as human beings, we like to keep our physical bodies as long as we can. We do get attached to them after all, and we would like to stay with what is familiar.

Harriet: (She had been listening, but this was the first time she joined in.) Will there be any advantage in using the physical body?

I had been standing over the bed, instead of sitting in the chair as I normally do. I had to move the microphone from Phil to Ann, and this required stretching over the bed. It seemed very awkward, but I knew of no other way to get both voices. Now I pointed it in Harriet's direction also. I only hoped that the tape recorder would be able to pick up all of the conversations. Later, upon transcription, I found that my trusty "little black box" had not failed me. It recorded perfectly and clearly.

Ann: Yes. It will be your advantage to be able to resource yourself to other planetary systems.

D: *So we will keep the bodies we have now.*

Ann: If you so choose to.

D: *And just be changed. But not all the people's bodies will be changed in this way. Is that correct?*

Ann: It will be already collective thought and decision. You have already chosen to do this.

D: *What about those who don't understand or believe in this?*

Ann: They do understand. They will not understand at this level, but they so choose to when they move on.

Harriet: Can you give us a time frame on how long this process will take?

Ann: Your time frame is extremely limited. This has already been done. It is a matter of you manifesting it to your reality.

Harriet: Will we be doing this within our time frame, as we know it now? (Yes)

D: *She's thinking of five, ten or twenty years, will it become manifest?*

Ann: In your mathematical system? Twenty-two years.

D: *It will be finalized by that time?*

Ann: You will initiate it. *Twenty-two years* you will have looped your strands, and you will just begin starting initiating your process.

Harriet: Will any of the people that are currently in body now be able to progress to that point?

Ann: They will be returning.

D: *What about those of us that are in the older generation?*

Ann: You will choose to come back, if you so choose to. You will come back with remembrance.

D: *But won't our bodies be able to change where you could stay here during the process?*

468

Ann: You will be able to change your outer skin level to be able to handle the current change in the energy level of your Earth's surface.

D: *Because, I was told age would not be the same as we look at it now.*

Ann: It will not.

Harriet: *And the energy level is going to be increasing?*

Ann: Correct.

Harriet: *Those that cannot maintain that energy level, will choose to leave and come back later? Is that correct?*

Ann: You will choose to move, if you so choose to. If you choose not to come back, that will be your choice. It is already collectively thought of. You seem to not understand this.

D: *No, we don't, because we are still thinking in the individual point of view.*

Ann: No, that stopped. That is your problem.

I directed my question to Phil, who had been silent allowing Ann to answer most of the questions up to now.

D: *Do you have anything to add about the DNA?*

Phil: We would say that there will be more explanations in other arenas. This information will be confirmed through other sources. We would ask that you please keep your awareness to this subject, so that when items which could enhance this information are presented to you, whether it be in your news format or convention format, you be aware. And you then can enhance the understanding of others who have, as you, an elementary understanding of the process about to unfold.

D: *The changing of the DNA and the adding of more strands, is this going to be visible to scientists and doctors?* (Ann: Yes.)

Phil: They are only now beginning to understand, through their research avenues, the implications of what we are expressing here today. The human genome project has only now given a *hint* at the possibilities, which have, as yet, not been expressed in your physical bodies. There are

469

many, many segments of the chain which have been classified as "junk" DNA, simply because they do not understand its function. However, some of this so-called "junk" DNA is in fact in use, and is expressing. There are however some sections which are, as yet, not activated. These additional segments will work in concert with many of the segments which are already in place. It is an enhancement which will activate many of the segments which heretofore have been in place, but idle.

Harriet: I know you're very much aware of the influx of the so-called "Indigo" children.

Ann: Correct. They are your teachers. There is an energy change. Their bodies are actually reconstructing right now, with the energy change. Their DNA levels are increasing.

H: Are there good ways of dealing with these new energies? (Yes) *How can we find the best way to do this?*

A: You have resources upon you right now. Water is a very main resource for your children.

D: Water? Do you mean bathing, drinking?

A: Get them around water. Internal ingestion. Is that the correct word? Water is a balancing for them. Because of the reconstruction that is going on at this present time with your energy field (She had difficulty finding the next word. She kept starting something that sounded like: cir ... cir ...).

D: (I volunteered) Circuitry? (No)

H: Circulate?

A: Circulation around your planet. At this present time, it is acting as confusion in these particular individuals. They have come here, as you have asked them to, with a higher awareness and a higher understanding. Their energy vibration is much higher. It is because of the construction that is around your planet, that they have a hard time connecting at this time. But they knew that this was going to happen.

D: But many of the educators, the teachers, don't understand these children.

A: You cannot expect them to understand them. They do not

470

have a physical, emotional understanding to them. They are very limited.

D: *But the problem is, they are putting them on medication and drugs, which we think may hinder their abilities.*

A: These individuals that are taking these medications you are giving to them, understand that they can counteract them.

D: *Oh, that's good! Because we don't want them to be harmed.*

A: You cannot harm them. It is their individual choice, even these individuals that come with this enlightenment. (Pause) Your questions were very limited. We have noticed that you have come with many questions in the past. That your questions this time are very minimal.

D: *That's because we were not prepared to do this, and we were trying to focus on just a few items at a time.*

A: You will only receive a bit of information, as we feel that you need it for the time that is in your life. We cannot change your course. You change your own course. We can assist you with any question that you have. We won't deny you that information.

Phil: There will be given opportunities to continue these research sessions, as we like to call them, because they are, in fact, a device or opportunity by which, not only can you probe our understanding, but that we can probe yours. We would say that we both on each ends of these experiences learn from each other. It does not matter what method you use to contact us and ask questions. It is your sound vibration that affects the body. It does not matter your words.

D: *My voice, you mean?*

A: Correct. It never matters your words. It is always the sound vibration that is being connected to.

D: *So I just have to talk to them with the intent that we're going to connect, and we can do this?*

A: Correct.

P: We would like to thank you for your endeavors in disseminating this consciousness shift. We see the effect you are having on those on your planet. Those who have

471

turned their focus towards higher understandings, or rather to say, understandings of the higher planes, have found in your writings a very captivating and easy to understand manner in discussing these issues, which to some are quote, unquote, "way above their heads". We would thank you, for you have no idea that the effect you are having on the energy surrounding your planet is demonstrably and noticeably different, because of or as a direct result of, your endeavors. It is being noticed by those who are observing from a great distance, this change in the energy, which is transparent to those of you with physical senses. However, those beings which are remotely viewing your progress have noted this change. We thank you for, not only *them*, those beings who are unable to express their appreciation to you; but also especially to those of us who are directly working with you and the beings on your planet. That the increase in awareness is in the path of God's desires. There will be given many more opportunities before each of you in this room have the ultimate, or perhaps, final experience. That is to say, your transition to return home. Each of you in this room has much left to do. You need not worry about any transitional issues, as these time frames and manner of departures, are handled by a most competent authority.

D: *I was told I would be around to see these things happen.*

A: You will.

P: There will be many amazing things that each of you will experience before your tasks are complete. We thank you again from those of us here, and those of us who cannot be here.

Upon awakening, Ann was very confused and groggy. She had absolutely no memory of going under, and no memory of anything that happened. Phil had a few remarks to add before the tape ran out. I turned the recorder back on to record these.

D: *You said you felt there were two separate channels, and not the same group.*

P: I think this is probably because our higher sources, at some level, are all joined together. I mean it's the same and ultimate source, but on our level down here it feels individual. I could feel when Ann was getting ready to say something, and I couldn't talk at the same time.

D: *That's what I was afraid would happen. You would both start talking at once, and not be aware that the other was speaking. You were continuing each other's thought and adding to it.*

Ann said that when she heard my voice, she couldn't keep awake even though I was speaking to Phil. So it turned out successfully, even though it was unexpected. There was much more information during this session. It has been incorporated in other chapters.

CHAPTER 23

ANOTHER ENERGY BEING

This session was held at a hidden retreat in northern Minnesota in October, 2001, by a group of remote viewers. They work with others all over the U.S. to gather information through remote viewing. They know they are watched by government agents who are always attempting to find out how much and what they know. They also know that their phones are tapped. We knew this when they called and set up this meeting with her group. About once a year, the group meets somewhere in seclusion to compare notes and plan strategy. This meeting was held at a resort by a lake that was closed for the winter. We were the only ones there, except for the owners who also ran a bar on the premises. The day before the meetings began, while they were still settling in with supplies, etc., some suspicious people showed up asking unusual questions. So they suspected the government probably knew they were having a meeting. They seem to take this in stride and do not let it bother them. They said they have tried to work with the government agencies, by supplying them with information when they think something is going to happen. This is as much information that I feel comfortable saying about them. Minnesota is the land of 10,000 lakes, so it would be difficult to pinpoint their location. I try to protect the identity of my subjects as much as possible.

The place was very deserted. After speaking at the MUFON group in October, 2001, we flew from Minneapolis north on a small plane. Then we were driven for over an hour to the lake resort. It was cold and snowed while we were there. After the meeting, we flew back to Minneapolis for the WE (Walk-ins for Evolution) conference.

This was only a few weeks after the Sept. 11 attacks on NY and Washington DC. During the WE conference, the U.S. attacked Afghanistan under the guise of trying to kill Bin Laden. So this had been a tense few weeks, and there was a lot of suspicion. I could understand why the group was being so cautious. The leader has called me a few times after this to tell me about events they thought might happen, so I could keep up to date on their work. Their philosophy is to try to change any predicted events or keep them from happening by group mind influence.

This session was done with one of the members at the resort. I used the cloud technique with Laura, and when she came down, she did not know where she was, but it definitely did not sound like a past life. At least not on Earth, anyway. She was getting strange impressions more than scenes.

L: It's almost like sun shining off a bright object. It's just shades of lights and shapes. It was like sun hitting a mirror at an angle, and I was looking at it from the flat side across. And now it's all dark.

I asked several questions to orient her and allow images to form. She assumed she was inside rather than outside, because she felt enclosed. She saw portions of several objects that were unfamiliar to her. Then lines, straight and jagged. Shafts of light. Then plays of light, and images superimposed on top of each other like a double exposure. Laura continued for several minutes seeing various geometric shapes, including some stacked diamonds, and colors, but nothing that could explain where she was. Then incredibly she announced: "I think I'm in a machine of some kind! Or I'm looking at a machine. Now, all I see is something like a window. But I can't see through it. It has a very white light behind it. But the light doesn't hurt my eyes."

D: *What shape is the window?*
L: It's very round. Maybe it was the clamps holding it that I

475

saw before when I saw the edge of the window. The light I saw coming through the window was from the inside of the machine. I'm inside the machine now. And I'm just surrounded by light. It's kind of around the outside of me. Kind of like a halo? Only it's on all the walls and everything. And sometimes, the light comes in and totally surrounds me and other times it just becomes a circle around me. A cylinder around me. I moved to the inside of this machine. The light is lavender now.

I wanted to get some impression of her body, so I had her focus on her feet. "I feel my feet, but I don't see them. I don't think I have any body. (Confused) I'm here, but ... there's no feet, no arms. I'm just here. I don't think there is a body so much as there is just me."

This has happened many times, so it did not surprise me. I just had to think of the proper questions to ask this type of being.

D: *What does the rest of the machine look like? What other impressions are you getting?*

L: I get a texture on the walls. I know they're metallic, but they don't look or feel metallic. And the walls are in a kind of up and down interlocking diamond shape.

This was probably the diamond shapes she saw earlier, but had no explanation for.

D: *Do you feel comfortable with this place? Do you feel like you belong there?*

L: Yes, I do. It's a small machine. I'm confined in it when I go into it. And I perceive that the world is colors. A lot of colored light in the world and I am colored light. The colors change as I react to my environment. Light and dark. We're dark right now, but it goes to white light, lavender light, yellow light.

D: *I wish we could know more about this place and find out where it is. Do you want to move outside of this machine and look at it from the outside?*

L: Yes, I would like to see what it is.

D: *What does it look like from the outside?*

L: Again, I know it's metallic, but it doesn't look metallic. It looks like a dark plastic. Yet I know it's metallic. It is cylindrical, with a pointed top like a cone. Seeming a tight fit. Confining. Not constricted but just confined, like I filled it. There was room to move.

D: *Where is it located?*

L: I don't know what I'm seeing now. I see it in a ...? A catwalk around the outside of it. I'm above it. And I kind of felt like it was a ship or a transportation device. Now that I get a better picture of it, I know that it is.

D: *If it is some kind of ship, where does it transport you to?*

L: Anywhere, that came to mind, *anywhere*. (Laugh) It's in a much bigger place, but I get a sense of a wide flat area around the loading dock and there is movement on it, but not a lot. It's not a crowded place. And there's something going straight up.

D: *Are there other people around?*

L: Yes. Not many. They are shapes and I get a sense that they're wearing a uniform. Not a human shape, just shapes.

D: *Do they have different colors too?*

L: They're pretty much just a grey or dark, bland. But I think that's because they're wearing something.

D: *What are these other people doing?*

L: Oh, they're doing their jobs. I would call it a loading dock area. They're just workers.

D: *What is your job?*

L: I pilot the ship. That feels like *home*.

D: *What does that part look like where you pilot it?*

L: It's just the whole ship. I go in the ship and it does what I want it to do.

D: *They don't have to have controls or anything?*

L: It's with the mind.

This was not the first time I have heard of this concept. In my book *Legacy From the Stars,* there were examples of extraterrestrials who were wired into the ship. They controlled the ship through their mind and muscle responses. Those entities were more physical, where this one sounded similar to the energy variety; because she didn't seem to have a body of substance.

Many ETs also control their crafts through their mind. Group mind is especially powerful.

L: But the ship is slender. It's not like a real big cargo plane here on Earth. It's just a slender cone. Kind of like a pencil, only it's all round and it's long and it has a pointed top.

D: *And you're the only one on this?*

L: I get a sense that I am, yes. When I take the ship, I am the only one. I run errands. Not really errands, but I don't haul cargo. Not like trucking or something here. I don't get a clear sense of what I do when I go. I have a purpose for going. Deliver messages, to do something, but I pilot the ship. I take the ship and I go.

D: *Do you take a message to someone? Is that what you mean?*

L: Just my going is the message. It's very hard to explain. Even I can't quite get the conception of what that means.

D: *See yourself doing it. Do you just get in the craft and think where you have to go?*

L: Yes, that's how the craft works, that's how the machine works. The place where I see it docked is not my home place, but this place I come to frequently. Some others like me do also. That's why they have a loading dock that fits the ship. It comes into the ring. And then it has a platform around it. That's why the shapes were wearing clothes and didn't look like me. Because this isn't my home, this is where I come sometimes.

D: *Let's see what it looks like where you do come from. You can return there very easily. What does the place that's home look like?*

478

L: Light. Lots of light. Soft, soft ... very soft light. Light of all colors.

D: *Do you go there in the craft?*

L: I didn't this time. I just went.

D: *There's nothing solid or physical?*

L: I don't see it. We're all light.

D: *Are there other beings around?*

L: It feels like it's all me, but there's just this part of me that goes. (Laugh) But all of me is when I'm home. And it's a good, happy feeling; I'm home.

D: *Why would you have to go in a craft then? You said you don't feel you have a body.*

L: They need the craft. Where I go. They need to see it. I can travel without it, but they need to see the craft.

D: *Why do they need to see it?*

L: They're not quite light beings yet, but they understand it some. And for their comfort, I use the craft when I go to that place and places like it. And they're comfortable seeing a craft come in and a light being come out. It doesn't make sense to me, but that's the way they're comfortable with it.

D: *So they see you as these colored lights?*

L: They see me as a light being, but they need to see that craft. Why, I don't need it. Like, I went home and I'm back at the craft now. When I went home, that felt good. It was just the big light I went home to. But I needed the craft to come *here.*

D: *On this light that you consider home, there's nothing physical? Houses or anything like that?*

L: No, I just get a sense of this floating light. And I get the sense of "we". "We" are light.

D: *Like there's more than one of you at this place?*

L: Yes. But we're just one mass. And I leave and then I come back. When I leave, I'm me. When I get back, we're we.

D: *You're all part of the same thing then.* (Yes)

I decided to move her ahead to an important day when something was happening. Although I couldn't imagine what would be considered important to an energy being. Still, I had to follow the procedure that has worked so well for me over the years.

D: *What's happening? What do you see?*

L: It has to do with the we becoming I and I becoming we. And it has to do with having to have the ship for other people. For their comfort, for their well-being. I have to have the ship. But for me, it's just being I and not we and we not being I. And I get that it's not one particular day, it's that whole concept.

D: *But you said you are sent out to deliver messages.*

L: Yes, and sometimes I stay away a long time, where I'm supposed to go for a message. That's what they were trying to tell me. That's what I'm trying to see.

D: *What do you mean?*

L: This *body* is my ship now. And I'm here for a message. For a reason.

D: *On Earth, you mean?*

L: Yes. This body of Laura. And for the comfort level of this time and place, I have to be in it. And I have to be me. I can't be we. And I'm comfortable with that. I like being me, but I miss the we.

D: *Is that what it's showing you; that at one time, you were the we?*

L: I'm being told it was the kindergarten way of showing me that this was one of the reasons, or to explain why I'm here. How it happened.

D: *How did it happen?*

L: I was called here. I've been here many times, but this time I was called here.

D: *What do you mean?*

L: I was needed. I had to come. They wanted me. Not anybody else. They wanted *me* to come. And it is a very important job. And it would be a long job. I couldn't come and just go. I had to take this vessel and come here.

D: *You mean, you came here to Earth to do something that was going to take a long time?*

L: Yes. And it was going to be hard, but I could do it. And they felt that only I could do it. I'm to change things. It's very subtle. And it's kind of all garbled. But the planet entity needs help. And the planet called to me, too. The entity that makes this planet is pained and sore and hurt. So I work with the planet. I work with that entity. And the people on the planet are pained and sore and hurt. I came to help. I know how to change these things. I know how to work on them.

D: *In your other lives, were you doing the same job?*

L: I do it whenever I'm needed.

D: *So in other lifetimes, you have done the same job of trying to help the planet?*

L: Yes. This time it's serious though.

D: *How do you help the planet?*

L: I balance the energies. I try to shape and mold the energies of the Earth and the people. It's like sculpting. The climate, the atmosphere. It's all one big picture with many parts. And it's kind of like ... making iron filings with a magnet, like little kids' pictures. And you try to make the iron filings into a pretty picture with the magnet. And I'm trying to hold all these iron filings together. (Chuckle) Trying to make them keep the pretty picture. This is such a beautiful planet. Instead, the filings keep going off by themselves. They keep wandering, keep straying, keep getting into trouble. And it's a hard job.

D: *But apparently you volunteered to do it, didn't you?*

L: Yes. This person, this body wanted to know why it was called here. And this is why she was called. To help Earth. To help the people. To help the atmosphere.

She had turned objective. This usually meant that I was now in touch with her subconscious or her higher self. I had not asked for it to come forth yet, but often it takes over and enters the session on its own. I always welcome this, because I know I can get answers to both her questions and mine.

D: *This place that she came from, can you tell her what that was? The place she called home.*

L: It's the One. The One. Where all is all.

D: *But she came here to help Earth.*

L: Always the balancer of energies. For a long time, yes. She's very good at it and the universe knew she was the one that could help. Most people come for lessons. They come for whatever. She came to help. The planet called, the universe called her.

D: *But in this life, she's also learning lessons too, isn't she? That's part of the human experience?*

L: Yes, she has learned lessons to help others to learn their lessons. Always help, always help.

D: *When we live on Earth, we have a tendency to create problems and then create karma.*

L: Yes, people do that. (Chuckle) And there are souls that have been doing that too much, and she has also agreed to help those souls learn how to balance their karma in one life. She is not being caught up in karma herself that would keep her trapped here. She's doing well. She remembers. No matter what happens, she can balance the karma. And she's been doing that even before she remembered she knew how to do that. She keeps that memory well, but she's old. She's done this many times.

D: *And that's very difficult to live among humans, and not create karma.*

L: She's very much respected by us to do that. She's one of the few that doesn't. And this life has been a hard one for her. But she remembered early and she's remembered well, and she's remembering much now. We feel it is time. She wanted to know. She remembered more than she wanted to acknowledge, but only because she was listening to everybody telling her it wasn't so. And we want her to know it *is* so. Her memories are accurate.

Laura also wanted to know about angels, but it appears they are a different type of entity.

D: *Laura, the body here, was wanting to know about angels. Can you tell her if there are any such things?*

L: There are angels. She's been working with them many thousands and hundreds of thousands of years. She's been doing much work with them. She has special angels that She works with.

D: *Are these like her guides or guardians?*

L: She has those too, but they are separate things. Guides or guardians are people, humans that she has known in other lives and this life, that have come back to help her through this time. Her angels have been with her through it all. Through all the lifetimes on this planet and some of the others.

D: *She was thinking that an angel was something that was attached to Earth. I don't think that's correct, is it?*

L: I think she's confusing angels with some of the protective entities of Earth that live in the higher atmosphere. They stay near Earth because that is their job. And she works very closely with some of those with the balancing job; in that part of what she's come for. But there are other angels that go anywhere the souls go. The souls that make humans and other entities. She was wondering if angels come into human bodies. And they do not. They are just the beings that she calls angels. And there are certain of those beings that work with her, and one in particular that has worked with her all this time. All these hundreds of thousands of years. From the time she started incarnating, to the current. They are very pleased with her work with them. But she needs to remember there are more than just the angels that she calls *guardian* angels. She needs to remember all the other angels in her ministry work, as she calls it. She needs to remember and praise and thank them for their job and to pray for their energy and their well-being and their strength.

D: *That was another one of her questions. What she should or could do* for *them?*

L: She needs to remember about the bigger calling. She knows about the calling for helping people and for helping the souls that are brought to her to help through their experiences. But she needs to remember that she's working with all these energies in the atmosphere and the human harmonics. The energies that all the people are putting out, and the planet energies. And there are angels helping her with that. And helping others that are doing somewhat the same jobs. There are others working on the Earth energies. Others working on the human energies. And others working on the atmosphere energies. She is the only one working all three.

D: *That would be a harder job than just working on one kind.*

L: It is. It takes much from her. She often wonders why she doesn't sleep very well. And that's one reason. She's busy on that other level and it keeps her awake. She doesn't feel tired and that's because we are trying to minister to her to keep her active to keep her well.

D: *So she's doing many things when she thinks she's sleeping.*

L: She does them all the time. It shows in her life because she has a very low metabolism. And a low energy level. She moves a little slower, talks a little slower. Sleeps very late and that's because she's so busy on this other level. And it affects her body that way.

In my work in the last few years, I have found more and more people are becoming aware of their true soul origins and their purpose for being alive at the present time. It appears that now is the time for it all to be revealed to them. It is time to be consciously aware.

CHAPTER 24

IF YOU THINK, YOU CREATE

Richard, a school teacher, descended from the cloud to see people greeting him on the surface. They were welcoming him back. He thought it was another planet. It was definitely not Earth. "It feels different. It's very peaceful, very. The people are very nice. It's like my family." The people looked similar to humanoids, dressed in flowing robes. He was dressed in a purple one, and they were not communicating orally, "We exchange telepathically."

D: *Do you feel like you are solid or physical?*
R: To some extent physical, but also very light.

He became emotional and started crying as he said it felt like he had been gone a long time.

R: They are asking me how it has been. What kind of experiences I had. It's almost like taking on a job. Taking on an assignment. Been gone like I left on a long trip.
D: *Why did you decide to go back?*
R: Because it's time to go back. Just to refresh my energies, and to remember where I came from.
D: *Where have you been?*
R: Mostly on planet Earth. That's been my assignment for at least the last one hundred thousand years.
D: *So you have been on Earth a long time.*
R: Yes, many lives. Always coming back.
D: *Why did you have to keep returning?*
R: Because that's part of the job.
D: *And you said now you have returned to exchange information?*
R: Yeah, just a little refresher, I guess. (Crying)
D: *Has the physical body ceased to exist while you're there?*

R: No. Just changed its frequency.
D: Then is this the physical body of Richard?
R: Yeah, but at a much higher frequency.
D: So you can go to this place whenever you change the frequency? (Yes) *When does this normally happen?*
R: Probably at night sometimes. During my sleep.
D: So Richard's not consciously aware of these things? (No) *Is this place a physical place?*
R: Yeah, in some sense it is, but it's also in a different dimension. In some cases it feels it's almost physical, but there are some aspects which are different. More lightness, more free flowing, easier to move. I can create more easily with visualization.
D: What do you create?
R: Shapes, energies, music, colors.
D: Do you create these things for that dimension?
R: Part of it, but the other part of it consists to create experiences on lower levels. When you lower the vibration, then it becomes form.
D: So what you're able to create over there remains, or does it dissipate?
R: No, it remains. It takes form. I don't know how to explain it. I don't know of any other way to explain it.
D: When you're creating, how do you do it?
R: Just by thinking about it. And then *holding* that thought. And then bringing it down from the higher planes to the lower ones. And while you do that, you hold the intention, and then suddenly, it *springs* forth. And it's there!
D: I wonder if there is a way people who are in a physical body on Earth, can use this ability?
R: Yes, it would be nice. They could do it by working together and harmonize as a group. Dedicate themselves to the task. Make some commitments. Be constant in the attention. Have the willingness to surrender to the task. It makes it easier as a group, but also it's a two sided thing. On the one hand there's an individual. You don't have all the complexities of a group, but as a group you have more

486

energy to be able to realize something bigger. So, they have both pluses and minuses.

D: *I was thinking, if you create it and thought it into being, would it disappear when the energy was removed from it? When you weren't thinking about it anymore.*

R: No, you always have to think about it. You can think about many things simultaneously, and maintain the energy. There are multitudes and whole star systems you can think about.

D: *Can you do this as an individual, or do you need a group?*

R: I think it would be *both*, actually both. Some aspects you can do individually, but you also need the group for larger projects.

D: *Do these other beings stay there all the time?*

R: Some of them stay there all the time, yes. When I go on assignment, they're holding the energy for me.

These beings helped Richard from that side without his conscious knowledge, because he sometimes forgets when he's in the physical. It is much harder to create on the planet Earth because of the density. He was being allowed to know these things now so he wouldn't forget as easily.

D: *What would you call this place if you were to describe it?*

R: Starship home base. I don't know what the coordinates are. Some light years from here, I guess. But it takes only a few minutes to travel, if you travel in the light body.

D: *It is different from the spirit side, or is there a similarity?*

R: It's a similarity.

D: *I'm thinking of when the body dies and the spirit goes to the spirit side. Is it similar to that?*

R: Yes and no. I think if you lose your body you're ... there's a little bit of a disconnection. I'm describing it more as the next *phase*, and this is to be able to take all of the lifetimes and integrate that into a single body, and just raising the frequency and then take that with me. It's more like an ascension process or whatever you would call it. You just raise and raise and raise the frequency. Death is a little bit disruptive in a sense. This is more of a continual.

D: *Why do you think death is disruptive?*

R: A little bit. It draws you from one experience to another experience. And sometimes people get lost a little bit. But this is more of a very conscious, continuous, easy flowing, raising of vibration with no disruption in consciousness.

D: *When they go to the spirit side, they come back again like a cycle. And this one is not a cycle?*

R: I think this one would be like freeing yourself from that cycle. You have more choice as to when you want to come, when you want to go back.

D: *Why would you decide to experiment with Earth when you could remain there where it's so beautiful?*

R: I guess I sometimes want to take on difficult assignments.

D: *Earth is a difficult assignment?*

R: Yes, I think so.

D: *What do they do with this information that you bring back?*

R: They study it. They compile it. I think it's another level of experience that some of them are familiar with. Many of them have never decided to experience a physical life.

D: *Do you know what they do with the information when they accumulate it?*

R: I think it's part of a research project of finding out if that experiment really works. Or if there should be some other experiments that should be started.

D: *How would you explain that research experiment?*

R: (Pause as he searched for words to describe it.) How does the divine unfold itself, and then return again? Ever expanding and coming back cycles. Launching different directions. All the vastness of different experiences.

D: *These are experiences of all the individuals?*

R: No, it's all groups, all multitudes of ... first you're expanding and individualizing and becoming parts and then ... how do you bring it back again?

D: *This is what is called the research experiment? Becoming all these different parts. And they accumulate information and then bring*

488

it back? (Yes) *Is only Earth involved in the experiment?*

R: No, no, no. I think it's many.

D: *Has it been going on for a long time?*

R: No, I think mankind is about a hundred thousand, two hundred thousand years. Other experiments were longer. When all the other life forms were very old. There was no time limit to anything.

D: *That's why it's hard for me to ask questions about how long something takes, because it doesn't make sense.* (No) *Do they think the experiment is working?*

R: I think we're making progress. There's a glimmer of hope that it might work.

D: *What would happen if they thought the experiment was* not *working?*

R: (Laugh) Then you recycle. You just mix them up and create something new.

D: *Then what will happen to all the experiences and all the information that was accumulated?*

R: Some of it might be lost, but in the grand cycle of things, it's just part of the accumulation of information. You always have experiments. And some experiments will work and some others will not. But they all contribute to what does work and what doesn't work. It's always valuable information. So you change conditions a little bit and fine tune, but you don't change them drastically. You learn from the experiences and then you make some changes and then you try again.

D: *Is that one of the rules, you can't change it drastically?*

R: Yeah, because if you change too many variables at the same time, then you don't know. It's very, very difficult to know exactly what works and what doesn't work.

D: *So there are certain rules and regulations.* (Yes) *I've heard that Earth is a difficult planet.*

R: Yes, it's one of the more denser places to be. But because of that, it also has some opportunities and some challenges. Because it's a planet of free will, so many aspects are sometimes unpredictable. Lot of surprises.

489

D: *When Richard leaves the body, when he dies, does he go back to this place or does he go to the spirit side?*

R: I don't think I need to go back to what you call the spirit side. Because this time I may be, like I said before, just going to raise to a higher frequency. So I would go back to the home planet, of course.

D: *Many people have to go to the lower levels. Could they just jump suddenly to this other level where you are?* (No) *Are there certain rules about that?*

R: Rules is maybe not quite the right word, but many are in certain conditions that would not allow them to jump that quickly. Even though the *freedom* would be there, it would be very difficult.

D: *I know many people would like to bypass the spirit side, even though it's beautiful, and go directly to where they can create.*

R: Yes. But you have to work on yourself a lot to be able to do that. But also, I think, a willingness to *give.* To serve. To contribute.

D: *Is that your goal, to go back to that place and stay there?*

R: Not necessarily stay there, but I know I want to go back. And if there's another assignment, after a while I will contemplate it and be willing to take it on again.

D: *You said some people there have never gone on an assignment.*

R: Yes, but they also have different roles. For some of them it's the role they have taken on.

D: *Maybe some of them are like the accumulators of the information and records.* (Yes) *And you are one who adventures and brings it back.* (Yes) *I always think of machines. Do they need anything like that to accumulate the information and record it?*

R: They do have computers and different devices, but on the other hand it needs the consciousness of the entities or whatever you want to call it. – When you were speaking of creating, there can be problems because of free will. Let's say you have free energy. But if you use the free energy to create the wrong products as a result of it, then that would be a misuse of the free energy. – His soul has done this before. Even in a long distant past. Actually, it's kind of funny to talk about past. I think Atlantis, Lemuria. He knew to a certain extent.

D: *What did he do in those lives with the energy?*

R: All kinds of things. Heating homes. Transporting people. Building things. Healing. Maintaining the body. It can be used for many things.

D: *What happened? Did he misuse the abilities?*

R: No, he did not misuse them, but he lost control of it. It got out into the wrong hands. He was not quite careful enough with it. Sometimes trusting too much and sometimes *believing* too much that everybody has the same good intentions. So I think we need to be a little more discerning.

D: *How can he tap into the knowledge he had in those other lives?*

R: Through meditation, through talking to people, and then just by doing it. And then when he works with his hands and suddenly something takes shape, a flash will come and say, "Oh, this looks familiar." I think sometimes just by trusting it and actually doing it. Because many times he wants to be perfect and wants to be always thinking of the next best thing, but just by doing it. – I think seeing this place is just reminding me of where I come from, so I don't forget. And letting me know they're supporting me, thinking of me, over-shadowing me.

D: *Is there any way you can have contact or communication with them during your conscious state?*

R: First step is in meditation. And then I think the channel will open up more. It will open up such that I can almost do it any time.

D: *Today we were looking for an appropriate past life for Richard to examine. Why did you choose to take him to the home place that he came from? You took him directly there, instead of a past life.*

R: I think that's much more important than any past life information, because that's where his home base is. I think the different roles we play are just part of the overall experience. What's much, much more important is the

491

essence of one's origin and where we come from. I think sometimes it's not even useful to dwell on things that have already happened in the past. It's important to just focus on the future, and in doing what is required in the moment, then the necessary information will come. That will assist in the process.

D: *Then you think dwelling on things that happened in the past holds us back?*

R: To some extent, yes.

D: *The past has an importance, and we don't want it to have been in vain. Because we learn lessons from it, don't we?*

R: Yes, we do. But sometimes it's also good to let go. And just release it. Even if bad things happen, just let go. They're part of the human experience on one level, but on the other hand there's so much more.

I encountered another being capable of creating when I had a session with Nicole, the supervisor of a large corporation. She went immediately into an off-worldly place when asked to describe her beautiful place. She found herself in a cave, but it did not sound like a normal place on Earth, because there were spirits there that she communicated with. "I see these spirits when I have questions or when they have information to give me. I can call them. Sometimes they're doing other things. If I call them, they come. Most of the time I can just *find* them here." She described these spirits as glowing white lights. "They look any way that I want them to look. They can look like individual people. I call them the 'white robe people'. Many times I don't look at their faces very closely. I recognize them by their energy vibrations."

I asked about this cave that she found herself in. "This is a place that I've created. And I can come to anytime. I created it in my mind with my mind, but I created it on a physical. It exists on – what you might term – an astral plane. It's a real

492

place. Others would recognize it."

D: *But the spirits you're talking about, do they exist in the astral plane?*

N: They exist beyond the astral plane. They're friends of mine. They're guides and colleagues. I use them for information, companionship. (Chuckle) And just for hanging out together. They can access information that is difficult for me to access from this incarnation. I don't have to go to the cave. I can contact them from anywhere.

D: *But you just like this astral plane because it's peaceful?*

N: It's restful.

It was obvious that Nicole was not in a past life. She was just describing her contact with these spirit guides during her present incarnation. "I have contacted them in other lifetimes. We've been colleagues more than guides to each other." I then continued with the regression technique and used the cloud method.

N: I'm drifting down through some very pointy, pointy pine trees. I don't think this is Earth! The pine trees are very, very, very tall. Maybe ten feet across, and very round. And the ground is shifting. It's not solid.

D: *What does it feel like when you stand on it?*

N: I'm not in the physical. I don't have a physical body. So I don't necessarily have to stand on it. The ground just moves. Kind of like standing on a cloud, but it's energy instead of water particles.

D: *What about the trees, are they solid?*

N: No, they're not solid. Nothing's solid in a way you expect on Earth. They have a shape, but you could put your hand through them. They're three dimensional, if you can imagine that the molecules that make up the tree are not as tightly tied together as the molecules on Earth.

D: *That's why you would be able to put your hand through it. And the ground is moving because it's not solid either?* (Right) *And your body is more like ....*

N: It's more of an energy body. I can make a shape. I just pull some molecules tighter together. I have a little bit of matter. It's very loose though.

D: *If someone were to look at you, what would they see?*

N: (Chuckle) Depends on who looked at me. Maybe some people would see sort of a gray smear. Other people would see all of the sparkles. All different colors. It depends on what they were aware of. Unless I pull the molecules in more tightly to create a shape.

D: *If you were going to create a shape, what would you create?*

N: Whatever I wanted to create. I could create anything. I could create a big *cat.* I could create myself the way I am in the present incarnation. I could create myself as a man. I could shape myself into any shape that I wanted to. It is very easy to do.

D: *Then whatever you created, would it be solid?*

N: Not solid as Earth solid, but it would be as solid as the trees.

D: *Then people could put their hand through it?*

N: If they chose to.

D: *That's interesting. But this is the way your body looks all the time in this place?*

N: Most of the time I leave it as sparkles.

D: *That sounds beautiful. And this whole world where you are is shapeless?*

N: No, it's not shapeless. There are rules on this world too. There are different parameters on this reality than on the Earth. The physical parameters are broader. Other parameters are much narrower. There isn't as much leeway in the forgiveness -- I think I have misinterpreted that word. There's less leeway in thought. If you think, you create.

D: *Did you say this place, this world, is not on Earth?*

N: It could be concurrent with Earth. The space that it occupies may also be occupied by Earth.

D: *They could both occupy the same space?*

494

N: Certainly. There are planes. You might say this is on a different plane. On a different vibrational level. Part of it overlaps parts of Earth.

D: *So this is why they can exist in the same location, because they're vibrating at different rates?*

N: Yes. They can occupy what might appear from the Earth incarnation as occupying the same space. Space is actually infinite. By occupying a different vibrational level, it would be invisible to the Earth, in most of its occupancy.

D: *Are there others like you that exist there?*

N: There are a few. We don't contact each other very readily. I come here to be alone. I don't exist here all the time. It's the place to practice controlling thought. And to do it without excessive consequences.

D: *What do you mean by excessive consequences?*

N: In many areas, or planes, or vibrational levels, thought is more difficult to control in the entity occupied. And so in those cases, thought often creates unexpected consequences. Those consequences can often be disruptive in broad patterns.

D: *You mean people create things and then it's ....*

N: It's a mistake. Incomplete.

D: *Is this when it's created instantly?*

N: No. Anything you think is created instantly. On this other plane that I'm visiting, the creations *appear* instantly. And so it's an excellent place to train your thought patterns. Because you think something. Instantly it appears and you can instantly blow it up and refine it.

D: *You mean it's easier to control it there.*

N: Yes. The Earth plane is *so thick.* You create something, and there are interfering energies that are so *thick.* It takes so *long!* So *slow!* Earth is so *slow.* It's dense. *Thought* creates something, and it goes out and it takes a while to come back. By the time it comes back, you've created other things. All this time has passed. This creation finally comes and you go, "Pffft, that's not what I wanted. That's not what I needed." So you have to blow it up and start all

495

over again.

D: *But if it took longer to happen, to come to fruition, wouldn't you be able to change it easier?*

N: Sometimes you can. Sometimes you can't follow it all the way out. It's just so *thick.* You can't always control it. Other people's energies catch on to the creations and move them.

D: *That makes changes in it. I never thought about that. It doesn't stay pure. Other influences come in.*

N: Yes. You have to create it at a very high vibration to keep it clean. It's *so* much easier to practice here. So much more *fun.* It's so *much* easier to create beautiful things.

D: *Can you bring what you create there down to the Earth plane?*

N: (Chuckle) That would be pretty disruptive. To have a tiger running down the street. Things like that. It's not the same.

D: *Wouldn't it be quicker if you could do that?*

N: No. There's a different vibration to create things on the Earth plane that works better.

D: *I thought it might be a way of getting around the slowness.*

N: The slowness is part of the rules, the laws.

D: *But you can see the person that you are on Earth. Are you actually in two places at once?*

N: Yes, you could say that. I can focus on certain places. It's more complex than that. I'm always existing in many places. I exist on the *highest* sense everywhere at once. There is no time, space.

D: *What would be the purpose of existing everywhere at once?*

N: At that point, that's to know all that you need to know. To have access to any information.

D: *Have you always existed? Or did you have a beginning somewhere?*

N: I had a beginning. I'm trying to find that information. I don't think there is a way to explain. It was actually a joint effort. How do I explain this? It was another half. I was *half,* and a male energy was *half.*

D: *Male and female energy was both together, you mean?*

N: (She took a deep breath.) I need a higher level of energy, please. (She breathed deeply as though adjusting to something.) I am moving up a couple of levels. So I have access to more information.

D: *Some people give me analogies if they can't find the words.*

N: Yes, but it's difficult to find an analogy on Earth. Because on Earth there isn't any understanding of the fact that something can be created out of an apparent nothing. But that's what it is. It's how I was born, so to speak, spiritually. And I was this thought created. Through thought. And I know on Earth, you say how can you create yourself through thought? You'd have to be already in existence to have that thought!

D: *Or something else has to think you into existence.*

N: Perhaps.

D: *Well, if it's too complicated ....*

N: No, it's not a complication. It's simply that the information isn't available on the Earth plane.

D: *You mean it can't come down to our human minds.*

N: Not at this point. It wouldn't make any sense.

D: *Maybe it's enough to realize there are some things we can't understand. (Yes) Are you aware of the entity known as Nicole? The one we're communicating through?*

N: Yes, we are the same. I am a part of her.

D: *You're a part of her, yet you're separate. (Yes) Do you influence her life in any way while she's living?*

N: Yes. By thought transference.

D: *Are you interested in what happens to her, or are you totally separate?*

N: I'm more interested in what happens to *me.*

D: *Then why are you existing also as an entity on Earth?*

N: Certain experiences are available on Earth.

At this point something unexpected happened. The entity stopped my questions so it could perform a task on Nicole. Nicole's body breathed deeply, and then the entity said, "I'm moving Nicole to the next level. This is the more

497

knowledgeable part of herself."

D: *Is the next level above or below?*
N: Above. A little bit lighter than the other. This helps for her to be aware of the different levels of awareness within her being, because that will be the next step in integration. And growth is to integrate all these into their *highest* level. At this time, she often dumbs herself down in order to relate to people around her. In a way that will mask her impatience with foolishness. As soon as she says something on the physical level about what's going on on the spiritual level, she is responded to with scorn. That's why it's much more fun for her to be alone. People would not understand if she shape shifted in public, or if she turned the clock into a frog. It is frustrating and irritating. (Deep breath) She has to *bottle* it all up. She uses these energies. She knows where they're coming from. She doesn't necessarily trust her control over them in this physical incarnation as of yet. It causes breaks in the energy and walls in the energy. That is why she doesn't do these things. She doesn't like to scare people. She doesn't want to put her foot through the wall. Put her hand through the wall. Create things; open her fist and have butterflies fly out.
D: *Can she do that?*
N: She's capable. She knows it, she fears it. These things are not against the physical laws of where you live. Consciously she realizes she can do these things. She doesn't do them, because she doesn't trust other people. She doesn't trust their understanding. She doesn't trust their reaction. She's always been able to do this even when she was a child. She shape shifted as a child.
D: *What would she shape shift into?*
N: Anything she wanted to. Trees. Water. Squirrel. Anything.

This is similar to other chapters in this book, when people were able to do things that we presume to be impossible. Since the writing of this book I have encountered people who have the ability to shape shift, often without their conscious knowledge. They just suddenly appear different to observers. This will be in *Book Three*. As Nicole said, these things are not against the natural laws of this planet and this dimension. We have just been conditioned since childhood that there are certain things that we do, and certain things that we cannot do. I have been lecturing for years about the fact that we don't know the power of our own minds. Once the power of our mind (which is scattered) is organized and focused (especially in groups) there is nothing we cannot do. Miracles then become possible. We need to recognize and contact that creator being that dwells within.

CHAPTER 25

AN ENERGY BEING CREATES

The September 11, 2001, attacks on New York and the Pentagon were turning points in our world. But there was also a change occurring in my work at the same time. A turning point in the gaining of information, and the type of information that would be obtained. All during 2001, this seemed to be occurring as the beings (or whoever they are) were supplying more complicated concepts. They seemed to indicate that the world was ready for this information. Sometimes, I longed for the simpler days when my focus was on past lives and the study of history, but this was not to be. I would never be able to return to those days, and would have to keep progressing further into the unknown and unexplored in metaphysics.

My daughter Nancy and I were caught in the mess that occurred at the airports on September 11 after the attacks. I had just finished speaking at an Expo in North Carolina, and we had spent the night at a private home. We got up that morning and were packing to go to the airport to return home for a few days. The lady received a frantic phone call from a friend telling her to turn on the TV. She said that the Pentagon had just been bombed. I said, in total surprise, "But that's in my books! Except Nostradamus said New York would also be bombed."

She shouted from the other room, "You better get in here. It's both!" We watched in horror as the camera switched back and forth between the two events that were occurring simultaneously. Then with complete disbelief, we watched the twin towers collapse into a pile of rubble. In the ten years that I had been lecturing about the Nostradamus prophecies, they were always a "possible" scenario. One which I sincerely thought we would be able to avoid. Now, his predictions were being played out in front of me. It jolted me to the core of my being. They had always been "maybe, could be, possibly". But now, they were in my reality.

After my daughter, Nancy, and I managed to tear ourselves away from the TV, we knew we still had to go to the airport where we were supposed to catch a flight for home. At that time, we didn't know what would happen next. As we drove our rental car to the airport, news was coming over the radio that all flights everywhere in the United States were being halted, and those flights in the air were being told to land at once. Overseas flights were either turned back in flight or being landed in Canada. This was the first time anything like this had ever happened in the United States. The implications were staggering. Yet we still had to go to the airport to find out what to do.

As we approached the Greensboro airport, it looked like a military camp or police raid. There were barriers, police cars and police officers everywhere. They had already sealed off the entrances. We were stopped immediately, and I could tell the policemen were very edgy and upset. They had no more idea of what was going on than we did. No one knew the extent of the catastrophe yet. They told us there were no flights and we would have to leave immediately. But we had to find out what to do about the rental car. Reluctantly, they let us park and go inside. It was eerie, the airport was totally deserted. The woman at the rental car desk said that if we turned our car in, we could not get another one. All rentals had been halted, and also all Greyhound buses had been stopped. The entire nation had come to a screeching halt. I looked at Nancy and she said, "I've still got the key. We'll start driving." We told them we would turn the car in when we got back home to Arkansas. They didn't argue, it was the only logical solution. It took two days of driving to get back to Arkansas. The entire way, in an other-worldly atmosphere of the nonstop radio broadcasts.

When I arrived home exhausted, there were messages that several radio stations wanted me to go on the air immediately to talk about the Nostradamus prophecies of the events. My books, *Conversation With Nostradamus*, were the only ones that had the incidents outlined in detail. The next day, we got a call from

Bob Brown who was putting on the UFO Conference in Laughlin, Nevada, where I was scheduled to speak that weekend. They had decided not to cancel, but to hold the conference anyway, and they were going to start driving from Colorado to set things up. They said some of their speakers who were coming from Europe had been turned around in mid-flight and would not be able to attend. No one knew what kind of conference there would be. But he wanted me to change the topic of my lecture from UFOs to the Nostradamus prophecies due to the circumstances. He said I had to get there, even if I had to drive. That idea did not appeal to me since we had just driven two days to get home. When we were due to leave on Saturday, we got on the only flight going to Las Vegas as the airlines resumed limited flights.

The conference did not have the attendance that was normally expected, but everyone said they were glad that the Browns went ahead. Otherwise, we would have all been sitting at home glued to the TV watching horrible repeats of the events. At least the conference gave us a distraction, something else to focus on. My lecture was the most difficult one I have ever had to present, because I was talking about a reality that had only been a possibility before. If this one had come true, then what about the others that foretold a horrific war?

It was a strange week in more ways than one. The interesting thing was that when I had a session in Memphis with Mary a few weeks before, "they" said I would be getting more of a different type of information. That a door that had been closed to me in the past, would be opened; and I would be allowed access. During this week in Laughlin, I did twelve private sessions. Ten of them contained either information to use in future books, or a message for me (including one dealing with my health). These messages usually occurred at the end of the session, when I would ask if the subconscious had a message for the subject. In addition to giving them a message, it would also tell me something I needed to know. It seemed that "they" were taking more and more advantage of my subject's trance state to provide me information.

Many of my sessions were taking interesting twists. It seemed as though I was being shown that the focus on past lives was not as important as I previously thought. It was valuable in finding the causes for clients' physical problems, diseases, phobias, allergies, and karmic problems. But I believe the entities that were controlling many of these sessions, were trying to impress that it was time to move to another level of understanding, which was beyond simply re-experiencing past lives in this dimension. They were attempting to show us that we are so much more than a spirit having an experience in a physical body. We are also something much higher, much more complicated. That this life was just one stop on our journey, and not necessarily the most important stop. Apparently, this higher level of understanding thought the person I was working with was ready for this knowledge so they could understand their life from a different perspective and an added realm of existence. Some people may be ready for this, but for some, it may be too difficult for their belief system to handle. I always kept reminding myself while I was doing a session, that the subject is never given information until they are ready. If their subconscious mind (the monitor) did not think the subject was ready, the information would not be shown, or the screen would just go blank. I never fight this, because I know "they" have much more wisdom than I do.

When I began working with Jerry, a businessman who was attending the Laughlin UFO conference, there was definitely censoring taking place by his subconscious mind in the beginning. It was almost as though it wasn't sure if he was ready to see the information. I had to do some maneuvering before he was allowed to have it.

Under normal circumstances with my technique, the person will come off the cloud into a scene (most often outside), and they begin by describing their surroundings. This session was different. Jerry found himself walking through a tunnel. At the end of it, he saw it was blocked by a very large door. He immediately described it as an energy door, although he didn't know why he called it that. He was curious to find out what was on the other side, and I asked how we would open an energy door. He said it was done with the mind. "I am attempting to dissolve it, but I can only get part of it. The lower corner is dissolving, but it's not enough for me to get through." Frustrated, he announced, "I can't get through it. I am sensing that I am not ready. The elements are not going to let me through." When he said that, the door disappeared. So I surmised that he apparently was not ready yet to see what was behind the door. The subconscious does a wonderful job of protecting us from ourselves. It would not allow him to see anything he couldn't handle. This was what I thought, but I was wrong.

Since the door had disappeared, we would have to go somewhere else to find the appropriate place for Jerry to see. I instructed him to look elsewhere for something that would help him understand his present life. "We don't have to go through that door if they don't want us to. We can go another direction and find something else that is safe for you to look at. Something that will make sense to you and be important." I counted to take him to a scene, and asked what he was seeing. Surprisingly, he found himself on a large spaceship.

J: It's a large ship, that I sense is alive. It's not made of steel or metal.
D: *Alive?*

In my UFO investigations, many people have reported the feeling that the ship they were on was alive and somehow aware of them.

J: Alive. The ship itself has a consciousness. It has form, but they're not letting me see it. Just this huge room. It has a garden in it.
D: *A garden is in the room?*
J: (In wonder.) Yeah! It's like a jungle planetarium almost, like on Earth. It has vegetation, and water. (He found this fascinating.)

504

D: *Like a big greenhouse?*

J: Yeah! It has waterfalls. This place is huge. Ha! They have their own Earth. It's in the ship. It has water. It has vegetation. It has ... ha! animals. It's allowing beings to travel in a peaceful setting.

D: *The ceiling must be high, too, if it has the waterfall.*

J: You can see through the ceiling. It's transparent. You can see the star systems. And yet it's enclosed. It has its own atmosphere.

D: *Are the animals the type that are on Earth?*

J: We can create any animals we want. Okay, we create this. It is created by a group mind. The group that's traveling on this craft. Ha! That's interesting.

D: *But you said the ship seemed to be made out of something that was alive?*

J: Yeah, yeah. It has its own consciousness. We've created this ship with group mind. So we can travel with thoughts and an environment that we feel comfortable in. That's how it's done.

D: *Like taking a piece of the planet with them.*

J: Yeah. Some of the best memories we have, we take with us. That's how it's done. That's what we do. It makes for a more pleasant trip.

D: *Is this just one part of the ship?*

J: We create living quarters that are alive. And we can talk with them. We can communicate with them. And it allows us to travel.

D: *Communicate* with *the living quarters?*

J: Ah, with the energy. The ship itself is alive. I'm trying to see what we look like. (He was finding all this amazing and amusing. He was enjoying himself.) Okay, we're energy. We're all energy, but we can create any form we want. We can create bodies of any shape, size, dimension. It's all with the mind.

D: *What do you look like if you're pure energy?*

J: (Pause, as though looking.) We can change colors. All purples. (Laugh) It's like a game. We're changing colors

and energies to play a game.
D: *Do you have a form?*
J: We can take forms as we choose. (Surprised) Ha! We can take the shape of balls, squares, triangles. We can take shapes of animals. It's like a big game. We're separate consciousness, but we're all connected.
D: *And what are you in your normal form?*
J: Just energy. Conscious energy. It looks like a kind of weaving, wavy energy.
D: *And it can take any form it wants, just to play the game?*
J: Yeah. (Laugh) I'll be darned!
D: *Then why did you create the craft?*
J: I guess it's an illusion that we enjoy. So that's how we travel, in a group. And we create the craft. And we can build waterfalls. We can put lakes. We can put fish. We can change ... it's very radiant now. The colors are really bright, glowing, phosphorescent.
D: *The colors of the beings?*
J: Yeah, and it surrounds the animals. We can put butterflies in there. Dragonflies. Put the birds. It's amazing. It's creating an Earth with our minds. Only it's a ship.
D: *Are you creating what it's like where you come from?*
J: We've been to many places. So those things that we've enjoyed, we're able to bring in with our group mind, and share it with each other. So to entertain ourselves, we bring in different things; memories we have of places we've been.
D: *It is physical and solid?*

He didn't answer me. He was enjoying what he was seeing.

J: Okay, those are pyramids.

He began to move his hands in rhythmic and graceful motions through the air.

D: *What are you doing?*

There was a long pause as he continued to move his hands through the air.

J: We're creating.

He was enjoying this. His expression was pure bliss. There was another long pause as he enjoyed whatever he was doing.

D: *What* are *you creating?*
J: Worlds. Planets. Dimensions. Star systems. (Laugh) We're going out and we're creating. (An expression of pure enjoyment.)
D: *But on your home planet, what is it like there?*

He really didn't want to talk. He was enjoying himself. Finally he answered, "It's made there with group mind. It's not one individual. It's done with group mind."

D: *All of you have to act together?*
J: Yeah, it's like a family of souls who create together. And we're using our minds. It's like a game of creating these beautiful universes. Stars. And we're doing it together.

He began to move his hands gracefully again.

D: *Is your home planet a physical world? A solid world?*

I have had enough experience now with talking to energy beings to know that not all worlds are physical or solid as we consider ours to be. There are many different possibilities that defy imagination.

J: No, no, it's not. It's a different dimension. It's not in your dimension. It has different forms, shapes, colors. It's not solid. It's changing constantly. It's different figures and symbols and shapes, and colors.
D: *Where you live, whether you're on the craft or on the home planet,*

do you have to take any kind of food or sustenance? Anything to
keep you alive? (No, no.) *What keeps you alive?*

J: Just energy. We can create and have bodies, if we choose.
We travel by thought. To explore and to create. We go to
different places with the mind. And it's a game. It's like
children having fun.

D: *But what you create, does it remain after you leave?*

J: In some dimensions it dissolves. In some dimensions it
goes into physical. We're capable of doing physical in the
lower dimensions. And in other dimensions, it's just
symbols. The raw energies take on different shapes and
forms.

D: *And they don't remain solid?*

J: No, we can make it solid.

D: *I was thinking it was like a hologram, and maybe it would just*
dissolve and fade away after you were through playing with it.

J: We could go to planets that have already formed. And we
could go down. And we could become one with anything
we want, trees, animals, and experience them. With mind.
We could take our energies into those creatures, those solid
forms. It's like a game. Like children.

D: *But you don't remain there? You just experience it?*

J: Yes, we just experience it and go on as a group. We travel
as a group.

D: *But you're allowed to enter into other objects and things?* (Yeah)
I guess I'm thinking that animals and humans have souls.

J: We have souls. Yeah. We have souls.

D: *But are you allowed to enter into a body where there is another*
soul?

J: With its permission, yes.

D: *Because it knows you're not going to invade or stay. Is that what*
you mean?

J: Right. It's just to experience. We don't invade. We honor
that soul. We must have permission.

D: *Just to experience it, and then you go on.*

J: Yeah. This is interdimensional. We're able to go into all
dimensions.

D: *Does this mean you're very advanced?*

J: There's not a word for that, or concept. It's just knowing.

D: *I mean, have you experienced lower lives, and evolved to this state?* (Long pause) *Have you had incarnations with physical bodies?*

J: Yeah, we can if we choose.

D: *I'm trying to understand how it's done. Do you evolve to this state after completing your other lives and karma? Or how does it work?*

J: This is a special planet.

D: *Where you're from?*

J: Where we're at. (Chuckle) Earth. It's a special planet. It's a meeting place for other souls, and other groups from other areas, other dimensions. It's like a vacation place to come and join in with groups of souls from other areas, dimensions.

D: *It's different than the other places you've been?*

J: Yeah. We all experience it. It's a special place. A gathering place of souls. This is the best. Everybody knows about this place.

D: *What's different about it?*

J: Its love energy.

D: *Oh, is that not found in other places?*

J: Not like this. It's the portal to the Creator. It's that connection. It experiences *everything*.

D: *And this is not possible in other places?*

J: Yeah, but not like this place. It's kind of like Shangri-La on Earth. (Laugh) Well, it *is* Earth.

D: *I thought maybe you had to have permission to do this creating.*

J: We are allowed. The Source, the great Creator. He experiences ... *it* experiences through us.

D: *Would you be called a Co-Creator?*

J: Yes, of course.

D: *They allow you to create, but you said some of it just dissolves.*

J: It's like drawing a painting, and then drawing another painting on top of it. You can erase or go over it, r*eform*, recreate.

D: *So it's a constantly changing thing, you mean?*
J: It could be, yes.
D: *With Earth, if you create something, it remains?*
J: Earth does, but it's changing also. Earth is a group consciousness.
D: *(He was making graceful hand motions again.) With all these hand motions, what are you creating, as you're talking to me?*
J: I'm trying to remember.
D: *How to do it?*
J: What it all means.
D: *(I was watching his constant graceful motions.) Are the hand motions necessary to create these things?*
J: It's working through the body. Waking the body. To remember consciousness. I don't think I was supposed to know this. To remember it. Yeah. That was the door.

He was referring to the energy door in the beginning that he couldn't dissolve. He thought the information was blocked when he was not allowed to enter. But apparently, the subconscious found another way to give him the knowledge.

D: *But if it has come through, it must be time, or you wouldn't be allowed to remember it. (Yeah) That means it's important. But if you're remembering how it's done, you need the group, don't you?*
J: Yeah, the group is important.
D: *You can't do it by yourself?*
J: I wouldn't want to. Part of the experience is creating together. Enjoy together. It's lonely by yourself, so we came together as a group, and we enjoy each other's company. (Chuckle) We entertain each other. So that's part of the group consciousness, is we can each entertain one another. So there's no boredom. It's continual change and creation. And admiring other people's work. Other souls, other creators. We go to places that have been created. And like a painting, we enjoy these places, to see what other people have created, other souls.

D: *That way you don't get caught up in the physical and the karma, do you?*

J: You can if you choose. That's part of the game. Part of the enjoyment. Experience as many different things as possible.

D: *But where you are right now you don't have karma, do you?*

J: On the ship I'm not. But I can. There are different ways of experiencing it. You can take on forms and experience it.

D: *Then karma is created because you're interacting with other people?* (Yeah) *I'm trying to understand how it operates.*

J: Other groups have come to this area, and interacted together. They choose to take on a form, and create that form, and play the game. It's all an illusion when it's the game, but it's important to play it. Because we get to experience the love and the emotions. The visual, the taste, all the sensations that are not found on other places. It's very unique.

D: *You mean in other places, and on your home planet especially, there are no emotions?*

J: Some have them, yeah. Some do, some don't. Some are just raw energy. The shapes, the symbols. Earth is unique because it has more variety. Because it's a gathering place. Not one group formed this, created this. It was many groups that formed and created it, which makes it unique. It's the all added to the all. (Chuckle) It's like a group painting.

D: *They've all had something to do with it?* (Yeah, yeah.) *But in order to journey here, you had to journey in a craft. In some type of an enclosure.*

J: Yeah, that's to keep the group together.

D: *Couldn't you just travel as energy?*

J: Yeah, we can separate from the group if we choose, and go off on our own. But we can reconnect with the group, because we're always in contact. We can travel as balls of light, and go to different places. Sometimes by ourself, usually with close friend souls.

511

D: *But if you didn't have the enclosure around you that you created, you couldn't hold the group together?*
J: Yeah, that's the concept of the group.
D: *The energy would more or less dissipate if you didn't hold it together?*
J: Yeah, it would. We chose to come together as a group, and travel together.

When I have spoken to other energy beings, I have been told the same thing. I thought if they were pure energy they could travel anywhere on their own. Why would they need a ship to travel in? They have told me that it keeps their energy contained. Otherwise, it would be dispersed and intermingled with the other energy around it. I have also been told by others, that the Earth is considered a vacation place, where beings come to experience various emotions and experiences. They want to have the adventure and then return "home". They must be careful not to get caught up in the experience to the point that they create karma and are condemned to remain here. Many of these visitors must remain objective observers, which is difficult.

D: *And you create your fun along the way while traveling by making the ship any way you want it.*
J: Yes. It's like watching a huge TV or entertainment center, only we created it. And that's the game, to do different things. Sometimes creating, sometimes enjoying other's creations. But Earth is very special. It's like a very strong connection to the Source.
D: *Why do you think it has a strong connection?*
J: It's almost like the heart of God, I guess is the best way to say. Of what we, as humanoids see God, or the Creator. But that's just on the physical. I guess maybe in our mind, that was what we've created, is the Source, to the Source.
D: *How do you perceive the Source?*
J: We are the Source. We are a part of the Source. It's just energy. It's thought. It's able to take shape, but it's able to connect to us.

512

D: *And you are more perceptive of this because you don't have a physical body?*

J: Yes. We're aware. We know. The presence is there. We can tune in.

D: *But the Earth is closer to the Source, because of the variety?*

J: It's because of the gathering. The souls. All the souls. This is the source of it. The connecting point. It's like a galactic family coming together. There's a big draw here.

He had continued to make the graceful hand motions throughout the session.

D: *(Chuckle)   It looks like you're really enjoying this creating experience, aren't you?*

J: The experience, yes.

D: *Do you stay away from your home planet for a long time?*

J: I can't sense a home planet. I just sense many places I've been to.

D: *Not a place you would want to return to? You like going from place to place.*

J: Yes. I don't sense *a* place, a beginning. (Pause) I'm trying to see if there is a place.

D: *Where you came from.*

J: Yes. At one time, there was the form. In the beginning there was no form. It was just energy.

This is the way it is described in the Bible: *In the beginning God created heaven and the earth. And the earth was without form, and void; and darkness was upon the face of the deep. And God said, Let there be light: and there was light. Genesis 1:1-3*

D: *But, as you said, you do have an individual soul.*

J: Yes. It's a knowing. It's a connection. It's separation, and yet a part of. It's a connecting point. But it's separation, yet it's consciousness, awareness. It's connecting to a Source. And it's also separate from.

D: *And it's something that wants to experience.*

513

J: Yes, yes. I can't see it, but it's just everywhere. It's part of us.

He was still using hand motions. I suppose we could have stayed with that scene longer, but I was running out of questions to ask an energy being that was busy enjoying creating. So I decided to do what I normally do. I moved him forward in that life to an important day, when something was happening. I had no idea what would be an important day to a non-physical energy being.

D: *What do you see? What's happening?*
J: Jesus being born.
D: *Oh? Tell me about it. Are you watching it?*
J: From above.
D: *What do you see?*
J: (Pause) It's a feeling. A sense. I can see it, but it's a sense. It's a very beautiful sense. It's a very special event. I'm not sure why, but it's a special event. Very special. I'm watching from above.
D: *Are others with you?*
J: Yes, the group is here. It's a very beautiful time. I'm observing. I'm trying to understand. I'm not sure why it's so important or special. Okay. It's the love energy being created in a very special way. You can experience it. It's very special. It's inter-dimensional. It's needed on many dimensions. We're all here. There's a gathering. We can experience it through the souls of the beings on the planet, or we can observe from above. It's very special.
D: *You said it was like love being made manifest?*
J: Yes. In the male/female way of Earth being separate, being dualistic. It's God coming in male/female. It's coming from a higher source. It's coming from the Source. It's very special. From this perspective, we can see it from a bigger vantage point. It's critical.
D: *Why is it critical?*
J: I don't know. For the planet, I guess, but not for us.

514

We're separate. But it's for the planet. Why is it special? Just love. It's bringing love to the planet in a way that has never been experienced. In human form. But it transcends many dimensions. It's affecting many dimensions on the planet. But it's like a portal.

D: *A portal? What do you mean?*

J: I'm trying to understand. I don't know why. It's a connecting point for souls. Beings. Angelics. It draws all beings, all creation there. It's a place to experience love being created in a special way.

D: *This is why it's drawing people to watch it. They want to experience that feeling?*

J: Yes. There are angelic beings. There are ETs. Different races. They're all experiencing it. It's ... (emotional) there's no word for it. Just special!

D: *They just want to be there to experience the feeling and the emotions.*

J: Yes, the emotions.

D: *Yes, that is special and it is different. Well, I'm going to ask you to move away from that special day, even though it is something that is very important. A special event. I want you to move – I don't know how far forward it would be – but I want you to move to the point when you stopped being an energy being.*

I normally take the subject to the last day of their life, when they die. But I didn't think that would be possible, so I was trying to think how to word it. Energy does not cease to exist, as a body does.

D: *Did you ever reach the point when you felt the need to stop being an energy being, and became another type of being? (This was tricky.)*

J: I took on many lives, many lives.

D: *I was thinking that an energy being would not die. It would just evolve. Would that be a way to put it?*

J: It's more to just experience the different concepts.

D: *Then let's move to the point when you, as an energy being, decided*

515

to go into the physical and remain there. Can we go to that point and see what happened? What is that like? What happens at that time?

J: So I pick and choose whichever one I wanted to choose.

D: *Do you make a decision that you want to go into a physical, and be that instead of an energy form?* (Yes) *Did something happen that made you decide to leave the energy form?*

J: It was a new experience. It was something we chose to experience. Someone else had created these forms, so we chose to experience them. We hadn't created them, but they were intriguing.

D: *You thought it would be interesting to become physical?*

J: We could if we chose, yes. But there were others that oversaw souls. It was with permission.

This is what I was looking for. I knew from my years of investigating reincarnation through thousands of people, that there are definitely rules and regulations. There is something like a board of elders, masters and guides on the spirit side that watches over and controls the incarnation into human bodies. Nothing is left to chance. I am really glad that someone is keeping track of what is happening. It must be a gigantic task.

D: *So you don't do it at random. You have to have permission to make this switch, this change?*

J: Yes, yes. To be able to get back out. (Laugh) You may want to stay. So there's a way of releasing the soul back out, so we wouldn't be trapped here for too long. A process for entry/exit.

D: *Do you think it would be easy to become trapped?*

J: Could be. We have to be able to get back out again. There is too much to experience. Not just to be *there*. Other things to do. Other things to experience. Other things to create. We don't want to be trapped in a physical.

D: *But there were other beings who gave you permission.*

J: Yes, there were some who were kind of in charge. Yes, the overseers.

516

D: *Then there definitely are people who control everything, so to speak.*

J: Yes, yes. I'm trying to see what they look like. They have their own ship. Yes, they're connected. It's part of the Source. It's just in charge of this planet.

D: *They have to agree when certain energies and souls come in?*

J: Yes, otherwise it would be chaos. It has a controlled order, and purpose. There has to be purpose.

D: *So, what is it like when you enter the physical body for the first time?*

J: It's new feelings, new emotions. A new experience. Many different forms, I see. Many different bodies?

D: *Babies or what? New forms, new bodies?*

J: First, we experience just going into different plants, animals.

This goes along with what I reported in my book *Between Death and Life*. When a soul first experiences life on Earth, they usually do not enter a human body immediately. (Although I suppose it could happen.) They have to start at the basic level so they will understand what it is like to be *everything*. Once you have experienced being gaseous, rocks, plants and animals, you understand the connectedness of *all* life. The fact that everything is alive, and everything is one. Then when the soul is ready to experience a human body, it carries this understanding at a soul level. Our problem now in our world, is to bring these memories back to the conscious level. So we can start honoring our Earth again as a living being.

J: That's part of the birth process. It's going into a form. A form is chosen. It's created.

D: *And the overseers decide which one you're to go into?*

J: Yes, it's decided on together. It's decided beforehand what one wants to experience. What type of life form. The difficulty is that you're trapped in one form. And it's very difficult for the soul to feel trapped in one form. It's very restrictive. Some choose not to do it, because they don't

517

want to give up their freedom. It's scary for some. It's the unknown. It's a lower vibration. It has things we haven't experienced. Dark energies. You know, there's a dark side. It's presented to allow us to experience something new and different. It's unique. And it allows us to come in contact with the dark sides, the dark energies, the lower vibrations. Yes, it's kind of a draw for some to experience that.

D: *Did you enter the form of a baby, a new being that was just being developed?*

J: I can't see what the form looked like.

He seemed uncomfortable, as though feeling something unfamiliar and a little distressing. I had to remind him that he had volunteered to have the experience. The overseers would not have allowed it to happen if they thought it was not the right thing to do.

J: It was good. It was something I was looking forward to.

D: *Is it like you thought it was going to be?*

J: Yes, because we still have control to a degree. And consciousness to a degree. And in that form, we still have a will of our own. So it wasn't bad. It was kind of fun. It was something to look forward to. It was a challenge. It was a different type of creation than we were familiar with. And had one form.

D: *Do you have as much control, once you're in the body?*

J: We're still telepathic. We can still connect with the other side. We're still aware. And yet we're here to experience. As others who choose to come at the same time.

D: *Can you influence the conscious of the physical that you're inside of now?*

J: Yes. There isn't much awareness and ability to create. There are laws. There are certain things that are set in place that we have to follow.

D: *Certain regulations?*

J: Yes, it's the process of birth and growth. And one must agree to that before coming into the body. The process

518

must be agreed to. But it's the group energy that holds the form together. It's not a soul experience, but a group experience.

This goes along with the soul being a group instead of a singular entity, and experiencing many things or lives at once. (See the following chapters.)

D: *What are the regulations you must agree to when you enter that physical body?*
J: To go with the existing development of the species. To take on what would be an animal form. And yet it's a consciousness the animals didn't have. An awareness. And yet much was blocked. We were aware of one another.
D: *On another level?*
J: Yes. Other humans, we were aware of these souls before they took on the physical. Now it was more difficult to communicate with them. It was strange. Being in the form it was restricting. Yet it was like playing a new game. It was manipulating the body. Form.
D: *Are you going to be able to get out of it easily and go back later?* (Yes) *Are there rules and regulations about that?*
J: Yes, there are specific time frames. Permanence. At first, there are no ideas of what you're going to do. You're just going to experience this, now. No lessons.
D: *No karma. No lessons. Just starting fresh.*
J: Exactly. It's like a new slate to paint your own ... whatever you want to experience.
D: *But you eventually accumulate karma? Is that one of the things that happens when you go into the physical body?*
J: I tried to understand and I ... oh, I don't understand it. I'm trying to figure out what karma is, or why .... I don't see it, I don't feel it.
D: *Maybe it's something that comes over time.*
J: I can't understand it.
D: *But anyway, you have agreed to be in the physical for a certain period of time.* (Yes) *And obey the certain rules and regulations.*

519

So it's a different kind of experience, isn't it?
J: Yes, it's limiting. It's the emotions, it's *all* emotions. It's all the feelings. But the love is there. It's still there. So the love energy is the reassurance. That's the connecting to the Source.

I thought we had found everything that was possible from the limited view of an energy co-creating spirit, coming into a physical human body to experience for the first time. The biggest problem seemed to be to not create karma that would tie the spirit to the Earthly realm, and keep it from returning to its free unlimited, creating existence. Maybe that's the biggest problem for all of us. We came here to experience something that we thought would be new and exciting. Then, life took over and we became trapped in the body, and were made through the law of karma and balance to keep returning. The first steps to release the soul so it can return to the Source, is the understanding of why the soul came here in the first place, and to release those ties. Much of this can be done through repaying old karma, and trying not to create any more. With understanding, comes release.

I asked the other spirit energy to return to where it belonged, and asked for Jerry's consciousness to replace it. Then I requested to speak to the subconscious mind of Jerry, because I know that all the answers are there, and this is where I can apply therapy and find solutions to the individual's problems. Once I obtained access to the subconscious, I asked it why it had chosen this strange lifetime for Jerry to see, when there were definitely many others that could have been chosen.

J: To make sense of it all. To see the big picture.
D: *It's a different concept for him to explore, isn't it?*
J: Yes. It was something within him that he understood on another level, but he didn't know consciously. And now he knows.
D: *At first, he thought he was not going to be allowed to see it. It was as though it was being blocked.*

520

J: Yes, only part was seen. Then it was decided to release the information.

D: *What is the connection with his present life?*

J: Reassurance and understanding. A purpose. A connection. To understand this planet, and why it's special. To understand how it can be manipulated. About the group, the group mind. It's involving the group mind. Jerry has been manipulating energy without understanding why he was doing it, and what it could be used for.

D: *Is this trying to explain to him how he can do it? Or where it comes from?*

J: Yes. It's done with the heart. The heart is important.

D: *What was the subconscious trying to show him?*

J: It's all energy, but it takes different forms for different purposes to experience different things. There's no right or wrong. Just experiences. Just creation. No judgments. Just enjoy. *It's the enjoyment of creation.* Of manipulating the creation, of manipulating the energies, in concert with the group and the whole. The whole is the creation.

D: *Was the subconscious showing this to Jerry so he can use this in his life now?*

J: Yes, he's aware.

D: *He was wanting to know what he was supposed to be doing with his life now. Can you tell him?*

This is the most common question people want to ask when they have a session. What is their purpose? Why are they here, and what are they supposed to be doing?

J: (He chuckled.) He's been given a blank canvas. And a brush and a palette. There are all the colors. (Laugh)

D: *Does that mean anything goes from here on out?* (He chuckled) *He's going to have quite an adventure.*

J: All the colors.

D: *And this was an important thing for him to know today. Past lives were not as important as learning about this energy connection.*

521

J: Yes. What's interesting, is that it's a group canvas. And there are others with their brushes. (Laugh)

D: *Oh, Jerry's going to have some really strange adventures as he explores this. This was very important for him to see, and now try to understand.*

I then brought Jerry back to full consciousness. When he awakened we discussed the unusual session. He agreed that it would be a lot for him to think about. It would be interesting for him to see how he could apply this concept of manipulating energy to his business field. It seemed as though anything would now be possible once he understood how to use it.

Many of my sessions were now centering on the person finding out about their *real* soul connection, instead of exploring past lives. The understanding of past lives is still important for the problems in the present life. But apparently the subconscious, along with our guides and masters on the other side have decided it is time for us to know more about our origins. These origins are definitely not merely of Earth, but from a much vaster location where we were one with the Source and enjoyed helping it create. In one session, which was reported in one of my books, I was told that the most important lesson to learn while living in a physical body was that we are able to manipulate energy. Once we become aware of that, we can create absolutely anything we desire in our lives. I suppose one way to remind us of this ability is to have us remember a time before Earth, when we all had this ability to manipulate energy and create.

The soul splinters or fragments in order to experience the physical body. When it becomes aware of its totality, it concentrates as an energy being that is able to create anything it desires. When it evolves beyond that, it can be many places at the same time. Even though each of us also has this ability, we are not aware of it, and cannot be as long as we are inhabiting the physical, because of its limitations. In that advanced state, it is fully aware of everything. Even so, it appears from my work, that the souls occasionally need to fragment and leave the highly desired state to focus on a single experience. A constant cycle or the search for more knowledge? As we have seen, if the soul has even partial memory of its larger self, this leads to frustration, loneliness and the feeling of separation on the conscious level. The subconscious knows why this is happening, but the conscious does not because it must maintain its focus and concentration on the life it is living. It would be too confusing to do otherwise.

CHAPTER 26

A CREATOR BEING RETURNS HOME

This session was done in October, 2002, in Minneapolis where I was doing a series of lectures and workshops. George was a very successful businessman who came to the private home where I was staying. Surprisingly, his session disclosed another aspect of a creator being, like Jerry.

When he came off the cloud, all he could see was sand. He knew there were some people on the other side of the hill, who were waiting for him to give them some type of answers. As though he was an advisor. He felt very uncertain as though he was not sure if he had the answers. He described himself as a bronze-skinned, black-haired man dressed in thin linen type material. He was also decorated with lots of gold: an ankh necklace, bracelet and a huge ring. Definitely signs of some type of power. Yet, when I tried to question him he became very suspicious and didn't want to answer me. Normally, I am able to quickly gain the entity's trust, but he was very wary and irritated. He kept saying everyone wanted something from him, so why should I be any exception.

He said it was a very trying time in his world. One reason he was upset was because his sister had been removed or taken away, and he missed her greatly. He said he felt very lost and alone, because she had always been with him and she wasn't any longer. He didn't know why they separated them, or where they took her. All of this was confusing to me, and I was attempting to straighten it out. I asked who had separated them. He said it was people from the other world. Not the people on the other side of the hill, because they were just the people. These were from somewhere else, and he didn't know why it had happened or where she went.

G: When we come back together, things will be magnificent. When we were together, we had enormous power and abilities. And formed a beautiful Shangri-La or a magnificent ambience. When we were together, it was the perfect world. They separated us. They took her away so that it wasn't the perfect. To make things difficult, and not so easy. And not so forgiving. She and I were able to anchor a magnificent .... We were able to bring all of the beautiful, tranquil, static ... all of that stuff together. But we were one. And they realized that, if they separated us, things would be different. And they're right.

D: *Why did they want things to be different?*

G: To experiment.

D: *How did they take her away.*

G: Just plucked her. Like the gods just plucked her, took her away.

D: *You mean, like one minute she was there and the next minute she wasn't?*

G: Yes. We lived other places too. Lots of places. Lots of different worlds. Whenever we were together, they were perfect.

D: *Why did you go from place to place?*

G: To help. To bring that aspect of – the word is "nirvana" – to bring nirvana. We would do it, then we would move on.

D: *What would happen after you left? Did it remain beautiful?*

G: Some did. Some didn't. Some went in different directions. This is an important one. Where I'm at now.

D: *Why is it important?*

G: (Big breaths.) Good. Evil. Dark. Light. Not used to all that.

D: *It has different varieties, you mean? Opposites?* (Yeah) *The other places where you brought beautiful things to, didn't have this much variety?*

G: Sort of. (He was becoming emotional. On the verge of

525

crying.)

D: *I know you're feeling emotional, but if we talk about it, maybe we can find your sister. It sounds like she was almost a part of you, wasn't she?*

G: Always.

D: *How did you travel from world to world?*

G: Just go. It's like a *huge* boat that could just transport at will.

D: *A physical thing?*

G: Yes, if we wanted to be.

D: *Did anyone tell you where to go?*

G: Our father. Father would tell us where to go.

D: *How do you perceive the father?*

G: Wise. Wisdom.

D: *Is he a physical person?* (Yes) *How does he communicate with you?*

G: It's been a long time. He gives lessons.

This was as much as I was able to find out about the father. He was very upset, and his main objective was to find his sister. He was crying when he talked about her, saying, "I have to find my sister, is what I want to do. I've got to find her. She's a part of me."

This seemed to be going nowhere, and I was becoming more confused than ever. So I decided to move George ahead in time to see if he was able to find her.

G: She's with the father. The people from the other world took her back. Maybe they wanted me to grow up by myself.

D: *Maybe they wanted you to not depend on her so much?*

G: Yes, but I don't have that same power (Emotional) as when we're together.

D: *And they wanted to separate you to see if you could do it by yourself?*

G: Probably that's right, but (Emotional) I think they didn't like the power either, that we put together.

D: *But you made beautiful perfect things.*

G: Yes, we did. They didn't like it. Things were too easy. No trials. Things were just good. No lessons without trials. (Emotional) We already knew it all.
D: *They wanted it to be more difficult?* (Yes, yes.)

It was not until I was putting the selected sessions into chapters, that I recognized how similar this session was to Jerry's. They seemed to both be creator beings. Jerry said it was more fun to do the creating with someone else, usually a group. George enjoyed doing it with his sister. When they were separated, the creating was not as effective. But as he said, it had become too easy. There were no challenges, no lessons, no trials. I moved him ahead to an important day.

G: Hmm. I'm getting older. Seemingly wiser. And there's a lot of upheaval.
D: *Did you stay in that beautiful place?*
G: Left it. Here, I was a teacher. I have long hair. Still the silly robes or clothes. Beard.

Apparently when I moved George forward he went into a different lifetime.

G: I can't be hurt. That can't happen.
D: *You're protected, you mean? But you didn't create any more beautiful places?*
G: I'm just here to share information with *these* people. That was my next job.
D: *You said there was upheaval. What did you mean?*
G: Still is. People are *really* trying to put their stuff together. And I'm here, if they want it, to advise them. A strange person I am, too.
D: *Why?*
G: Because they know I'm there, and they know I can't be hurt. And they know it's important. It's like they're carnal, but ... that's interesting. Ah! (A revelation) I'm sitting by an oasis. By a city. It's water, green trees, sort of a desert.

And the people from the city come and talk to me. I'm all by myself. Absolutely all by myself. Always have been.

D: *What did you mean, that they were carnal? You said that was interesting.*

G: Yes. Kind of rough around the edges.

D: *Different than you are?*

G: Oh, yes. A young race.

D: *Is this on the same world that you were on?*

G: A different one. It's sort of fun. I'm growing old, very old. Can't be hurt.

D: *But if you are physical, something could happen to you?*

G: Nothing can happen to me.

D: *I'm thinking of when you come to the end of your life.*

G: When I want to. When I'm ready.

D: *But right now, you're doing a different type of job than you were with your sister.*

G: Yes. I was young then. That was fun. This is kid's play. Easy.

D: *But it's not the power you had when you two were combined.*

G: That's right. I feel bad about her, too.

I then moved George to the last day of his life so we could find out what happened to him.

G: I'm sitting in a chair. Looking around. It's time to go. I've done my stuff here for this time. Done my thing. Done what I came to do. And I need to go. Sitting in that chair waiting to go. Counted everything and all the chit sheets. All the tablets, and I'm ready to go.

D: *What happens when you leave?*

G: (Matter-of-fact) I leave.

D: *What happens to the body?*

G: It stays. Just leave it. Shoot out.

D: *What do you see as you leave it?*

G: Hmm. It's like I'm looking into a stage play. It's like I'm looking into a movie studio or something. See all that *stuff.* All the sets. That's what I'm leaving.

D: *What you're leaving is like a stage play?*

G: Yes. I'm above it. I'm looking down, and there's this body sitting in that chair. And I turn around, and it's gone.

D: *What does it look like, where you're going?*

G: A void. A long void. I'm floating through the void. I'm by myself again.

D: *Do you know where you're going?*

G: No. Just go with it.

D: *Is anybody with you to help you go where you're supposed to go.*

G: No. I know where to go.

D: *Then let's move until you've gone through the void. And you've reached the place where you're going. What does that place look like as you arrive there?*

G: It's immense. It's huge, just huge.

D: *What do you see?*

G: Everything. Indescribable. *Huge.* Huge.

D: *Is there anything that you can recognize?*

G: Everything. I've been here before. (A moan of delight.) All kinds of choices, directions – all kinds of options. Even some old friends. Old souls. (Sounds of delight.) You know? You can see the old souls, and the young slivers of new ones. You can almost smell the young ones. They smell different. They smell ... not raw, but smell like fresh meat, or ... smell "funny". Different – like ripe, young souls.

D: *Why do they smell and the other ones don't?*

G: Because they probably don't know any better. They're just starting out. You can *really* tell which are young, older. The word isn't "old". Seasoned. Seasoned souls.

D: *So the* seasoned *ones don't have an odor?*

G: Yes. And it's a strange deal because there's no *age* here. But the difference is in the smell. It's kind of senseless. But it's sort of funny. It's a way to tell them apart.

In *Between Death and Life*, I was told that there are many different levels in the spirit realm. When the spirit leaves the body, they return to the level they are the most comfortable with. The level they vibrate with. They cannot go to the higher levels until they are ready. The frequency or vibration acts as a barrier, and they can only go to the level they have reached through experience. I was told you cannot go directly to college from kindergarten. The more advanced souls, or as George called them "the seasoned souls", can go immediately to the higher levels. They can go to the lower levels if necessary, but the "young" ones cannot go to the higher levels until they have attained that frequency, vibration or maturity. Apparently, George had to pass through these lower levels on his journey to the level where he belonged, or resonated with.

D: *Is there any certain place you have to go, now that you're over there?*
G: Yeah, sure. I'm going to check in.
D: *How do you do that?*
G: A good question.
D: *Because you said it's so big.*
G: I have a key, like an iron that fits into a slot. I have to go there. (Mumbling) I'm lighter now. I'm just getting used to being light again. And I find the slot. (Pause) Oh, boy! I got to figure out how to get around here again. (A series of mumbling sounds.)
D: *Did they bring you there to show you where to go?*
G: I don't want them to.
D: *You can ask for help, you know.*
G: They don't know how to get there. (Pause) I know where it is. I've got to go higher and deeper. Different layers, levels. Each one different. And you come in at the lower level. That's where you smell the stuff. Should go higher and deeper. And you don't smell that stuff. No young souls as you go higher. People nod. They recognize me. They don't smile. They nod, but they know something's up.

All of this was taking too long, so I decided to speed it up.

D: *Let's move ahead to when you get there. You can find it very quickly now, because you're moving into those different levels.*

What is that like?

G: Oh, boy! It's real light. Real bright. It's absolutely magnificent. Absolute magnificence.

D: *Are there other people there?*

G: Yeah. Others. All real bright. They're *real* bright. They got a little get-together for me. A big deal. There's maybe twelve, twenty-four, forty-eight ... Ha! Ha! Ha! Ninety-six. You know every one ... I'm the last one to come back. Of this group. And they're all gathering around. There's my sister. She's here. Found her. This group is *old*. It completes ... I'm the last one to come back.

D: *What does it complete?*

G: (Big drawn out sigh.) You know ... this is the council. That's what the heck this is. I'm the ninety-sixth person. We've got to discuss what's going on. The first time that everyone has been back. And there's a reason.

D: *What's the reason?*

G: That's what we're going to go find out. I've got to go higher and deeper. Out of that ninety-six there are eight that are like a council. Just hanging out. Just talk, to look it over.

D: *Eight separate from the ninety-six?*

G: They came from the ninety-six.

D: *And what are they going to do?*

G: Talk about this stuff. Where I just came from. Where they just came from. The *whole* deal. *Everything* I did. Everything they did. Plus what the other ninety-six did.

D: *What are you going to do after you discuss it?*

G: Make adjustments or tweaks. In where we have been, what we have seen and what will be done.

D: *Why do you have to do that?*

G: Because that is part of the game. That is part of what this is all about. Pattern one, pattern two, pattern three, pattern four. It's not a hierarchy, but what is done here, filters down through the eight and ninety-six. And also right down to where you can smell those young souls. To down to where you go through that hole, that chute, and

531

wherever you go when you go through that chute. It can be a *lot* of different places. Holy cow!!

D: *But then if you do these "tweaks" and changes, doesn't that affect things?*

G: It's supposed to.

D: *On the physical world?*

G: You got it.

D: *Why are they doing those things to change the patterns?*

G: Necessary. You tweak the souls. If you tweak the souls, don't you see, then you've got all the other things taken care of. You don't have all the other situations. Tweak the souls.

D: *Make them change, you mean?*

G: Yes. Tweak 'em. Don't change and they change themselves. Tweak 'em. Do you understand what that means? You tweak 'em. Adjust 'em. Input 'em.

D: *How do you do that?*

G: You know, it's really pretty simple. If they look inside, and see what has unfolded with a little bit of guidance, then they can make the adjustments. And if they don't, they aren't going back to wherever .... That's interesting. You know? Those eight ... they aren't even souls when you get up there. This is real curious. It's different. When you're there, you have no obligation. As you move down, you have an obligation. When you're there with those eight, there's no obligation. I don't need one.

D: *You've finished it all when you go there.*

G: Right. But as you move down, the obligation or the payback, whatever words, that's where the tweaking of the obligation takes part. Ha! Crazy!

D: *So if you're trying to influence people, I didn't know you were allowed to interfere.*

G: It doesn't interfere. Obligation. They know, the soul knows as it gets older, they have an obligation. They wouldn't be a soul. They wouldn't need lessons. Why would they do it? They know that there's an obligation. And they adjust that. It's neat though, and it's a goal.

Down there without an obligation.

D: *Is that possible?*

G: You decide.

D: *Why would you go down if you didn't have an obligation or karma?*

G: That's the fun. No obligation.

D: *Then, if you had reached the point where you didn't have any obligation, you didn't need to come back to the physical planet Earth, why have you come back into the body of George?*

G: For my sister and I to complete what we didn't do a long time ago. That is the one part. It's not karma. It's not obligation. It's an in-completion.

D: *What didn't you complete at that time?*

G: I think the union. We didn't complete the union of her and I.

D: *Even though you were together for a very long time?*

G: Yes. We didn't ... that *longing* is still in my soul.

I gave instructions to bring forth George's subconscious so we could perhaps get answers to some of this.

D: *George could have been shown many different lifetimes. Why did you decide to show him this lifetime? What are you trying to tell him?*

G: Humility. Absolute humility.

D: *Does he need to learn this?*

G: He knows it. He's learned it. Humility.

D: *Why does he have to be shown it at this time?*

G: Because it goes right back to those eight. They sometimes forget the humility. They lose the ... temple of it. Because it doesn't exist where they are.

D: *They have no obligations.*

G: And it's the humility for what's going on *here*.

D: *Why does George have to know that in his life, now?* (Pause) *Because this physical life is the one we're concerned about right now.*

G: Maybe that's what he doesn't know.

D: *He said there was a missing piece.*
G: Yes. It's what he doesn't know. This is crazy but ... the sister thing. It's all part of it.
D: *Just try to explain it to him, even if it does sound crazy.*

I had a suspicion what the lost sister represented. It was not a physical person, but the feminine *side* of himself. But I wanted to see what the subconscious would say. The subconscious told him slowly and deliberately, "It's the femininity that will enhance his life, his well-being, his humility. At one time he was total. He was both feminine and masculine. That was how he could create such wonderful things."

I asked how George could find the feminine part of himself. His subconscious said he would have to learn to be more feminine, gentler. This would be difficult because George was definitely very masculine, and this would not be part of his normal personality. Neither would humility.

Yet the subconscious insisted that George would have to allow the feminine part of himself to surface, by learning to be softer, not so stern and allowing the gentle side of his nature to come out. I then asked about his health problems. I received the same answer I have been given many times. If a being had been one of these higher entities in the other realms, and came to Earth for various reasons, they could not be allowed to be perfect. They would have to fit in with the general public. One way to do that, is to give them a defect of some type, so they do not stand out. George's was a stiff neck, and limited flexibility in his spine. "He wanted it to show him he's human." The subconscious was allowing the discomfort to remain as a reminder that he came to Earth for a definite reason, "Because that part of the body is the nervous system. That is the controlling factor. If you don't have the nervous system, you don't have life."

George had a few more questions. One pertained to an incident in 1972, when he fell down the stairs and fractured his skull. It was so severe, that he almost died. He wanted to know more about what happened at that time.

G: We were trying to tell him that he must change. He was on a dead-end street.
D: *It really did change his life, because he said he almost died.*
G: He was dead.
D: *(Surprised) He was?* (Yes) *What can you tell him about that time?*
G: He was dead. *Part* of him came back. Part of another came back. Two came back.
D: *Can you explain it better so we can understand it?*
G: (Big sigh) Two came back. He came back, and so did a little bit different part of him. It's still him. Another aspect of him.
D: *Why did that part have to come back?*
G: It wanted to. It desired to. That was a good opportunity. Good time. Good place. That was the part that would lead him in the direction he was supposed to go. There had to be a change. There was no way he could do it the way he was. He needed help from this other part of himself. This other part had the opportunity to come in, and it came in.
D: *Is that different from a walk-in?*
G: It's different. This is the *same* soul, different aspect.
D: *You also said this feminine aspect is missing.*
G: That was never part of that one that came in. It has not been with him for years and years and years. Centuries, moons and millennium. He always missed that. It will come in slowly.

George had another traumatic experience in 1998 when he was returning home after a tour in Egypt. They had a difficult time getting him back to the States, because he was like a walking zombie, with almost no control over his body. When he arrived home, it took many weeks before he began to return to

535

normal.

D: *What happened at that time?*
G: He wanted to leave. He wanted to go back to the eight.
D: *Did something happen in Egypt to trigger that?*
G: It seems that that part of the world is not always healthy. And he wanted to go back (to the spirit side) to help *tweak* that, or make adjustments in that part of the world. But he didn't ... and look what's happened now, since then. All the mess over there.
D: *And he thought he couldn't do it from the physical?*
G: He couldn't. He hadn't the position.
D: *But he thought from the other side, he could make a difference?*
G: Yes. There's underlying stuff going on also. Here and there and all over. And he wanted to go back. He was dying. He had already left. Just the shell was there.
D: *Then what happened? Did they tell him he couldn't leave?*
G: They can't ... they don't tell him anything. Just finish this. The other part will have to wait. But look what's happened. It's crazy over there now.
D: *So at that time, he decided to come back and finish the job.*
G: He left. Finish *his* job this time.
D: *Otherwise, if he left it unfinished, he would have to come back to Earth.*
G: To come back. He would.
D: *He would have incurred karma and obligation.* (Yes) *So the idea was to get back into his body so that he could finish his job.*
G: He came back here. Only the eight can do that.
D: *It shows we don't always know what's happening to our physical body, do we?*
G: Unfortunately, that's correct.
D: *There are always other parts of us we're not aware of.*
G: That's right.
D: *But thankfully, there are other forces that do take care of things and help us.*
G: They're guides. They're here. They're snickering a little bit about all of this, by the way. They say, "I try to tell you

this stuff at times during your day and night. And you won't listen." One of my guides has to do with the feminine aspect.

D: *Do they have anything they want to tell George? Any message or any advice?*

G: The same message they always give. Just tell us when you want our help. We're always there to help. *You have to ask.* We can't interfere. They also want to say – it's curious what they say. While keeping me alive, it was real interesting. I wonder why that is? (Mumbling)

D: *What do you mean?*

G: If I listen, everything's okay. If I don't listen, things aren't too okay. – Thank you, George. We all love you.

D: *What are you thanking him for?*

G: For being him. He's got a job to do.

Other evidence of having more parts of ourselves existing and interacting at the same time, came during two separate sessions while I was in Memphis in 2001. Both women knew each other and had been working on developing a healing center. It was an ambitious project that required much detailed planning. They didn't know how they would accomplish it, but they had a dream and wanted to follow it through.

The first woman, who I will call "Mary", did not go to a past life, although we were looking for answers to problems in this life. She went immediately to the spirit side, the place we normally only visit in between lives, or the so-called "dead" state. She was met and led to a large room where many spirit beings were seated around a table. They recognized her immediately, and a male energy said, "Good, you're finally here. We've been waiting for you." Instead of addressing her reasons for having the session (these were discussed later), they plunged into discussion about her project: the building and creation of a large healing center. They explained the way the center should

537

be built, where the land would be located, and how the funds for the project would come about. It sounded like a much more grandiose center than Mary had envisioned when she described it to me. Yet they were telling her the larger project would be the final result and would be more effective. She was supplied with much detail about the design, etc. The male energy being finally identified himself as a higher fragment of Mary that had no desire to incarnate. He chose to remain on the spirit side to help direct her progress. He had always been there as a member of this advising board, and would continue to be. But he was also a part of her, although she has no conscious knowledge of this.

This has been emphasized more and more in my work in the past few years, that there are parts of us existing at the same time, doing different work, living different lives. We are not aware of them, because it would be too confusing for our conscious minds. We continue to focus on the events occurring in our everyday lives, without the knowledge of the bigger picture.

The second woman, who I will call "June", was my second client on the same day. The two women had not had a chance to speak to each other. Even though June discussed serious problems during our interview that she wanted to cover, when she went into deep trance, she also did not go to a past life, but was taken immediately to the board room. Again, there were many spirit beings sitting around a table and they were waiting for her. She was addressed by a female energy who proceeded to give her instructions about her involvement with Mary on the building of the healing center. They explained that it would become a reality, because it had already been created on the spirit side, and was just awaiting being brought down into the physical. They explained that this is the way we create our realities on Earth. We first have to have the dream, the desire for something to become a reality. We must vividly see the end results, and adorn it with many details. Then it becomes a creation on the etheric side. It must then enter our physical reality and become solid, because this is a law of the universe.

This is why people have to be so careful about what they wish to create. On the spirit side, it is instantaneous, and only awaits the correct moment in time to become a reality. Thoughts are very powerful. Thoughts can create. Of course, the surprise was that the center both women had envisioned was on a smaller scale than the one that was described to them. So apparently, the part of them that stays forever on the other side can also embellish and create when the project is initiated by the conscious physical being. The project is now moving ahead. The two women were given all the information they needed. If it does not become concrete and solid in our dimension, it may be because they lacked the faith and belief to follow their dream. This is a planet of free will, after all.

This shows there is another part of us that remains on the spirit side helping direct the show, the play, the game. Can we call it our guardian angel, our guide? I think that is a separate thing, from what I have been told, but that could now be open to debate. I think this other part could be more closely described as our higher self. It is interesting, that whenever I contact what I refer to as the "subconscious", it does not appear to be a separate entity or part of the person. It always says "we" are doing this, or suggesting this, as though it is a group rather than an individual. It always refers to the client in the third person: "he" or "she" should do the suggested things, as though the physical entity is separate from the group, at least for the time it is on the physical dimension. Invariably, when the physical personality goes through the death experience and journeys to the spirit side, its viewpoint changes. It is immediately aware of coming "home", realizes the physical life was only a game, a play, a school from which to learn lessons. The other side is more real to them, they are supplied with more answers and, if they are ready, they rejoin the group, which gives them great happiness.

At least my work shows that there is a higher part of ourselves that is aware of the bigger picture; the grand plan. If we are aware of this we can use this knowledge to create our reality in this life to a fuller extent. We now know we can communicate directly with that portion of ourselves, and it listens and desires to help us. Is this really any different than communication with our concept of God? Maybe God is not totally separate, but is a part of all of us, and as such is much more accessible.

SECTION EIGHT

STEPPING OFF

THE DEEP END

CHAPTER 27

THE DREAMER DREAMS

THE DREAM

This session was done during a week of private sessions at a motel in Eureka Springs, Arkansas, in February, 2002. Charles is a male nurse working at a hospital in the nearby city. He was having physical problems mostly associated with being overweight. This was his main concern. Of course, one of the questions he wanted to ask dealt with his purpose in this life. This is the most common question that people ask when they come to see me. A few years ago, USA Today did a survey, a poll among the "mainstream" people, not just those interested in metaphysics. They were asked, "If you had access to a supreme power, what question would you ask?" The survey showed that the most common question was, "Why am I here? What am I supposed to be doing with my life?" So just about everyone has these same thoughts at one time or another.

During the session, Charles went through two past lives that helped explain some of the ongoing issues in his life. The first one was as a Roman soldier in Alexander the Great's army when they invaded Egypt, and took over Cairo. They gained entry into the Great Pyramid through a secret doorway, under orders to look for treasure. They found that there was nothing. They presumed that if there had been anything there, it had been taken away and hidden elsewhere. I found this interesting, because it showed that people were associating the pyramids with treasure, even that long ago. Anything of importance had been removed long before modern times. He was part of the occupying force for several years. He drowned during a storm at sea while crossing the Mediterranean on his way back to Rome.

The second life was interesting, but did not supply as much information as I would have hoped. He was a man studying secret knowledge in the Himalayas in Tibet. He remained there for several years gaining as much information as he could from the masters. He then returned home to France where he shared what he had found with the secret organization he was a part of. It sounded like the Masons, but he said it was even older. They were the ones behind the scenes that ran the governments, even though it was in the time of the Renaissance. People were very oppressed, and when he became the head of the order, he wanted to teach the common people so they could have a better life. This was the original purpose of this order, to make life better. Over time it was turned into a negative organization obsessed by greed and people desiring power. He lived to be over 100 years old, and shared much of his knowledge with others. After he died in that lifetime, I asked the other personality to leave, integrated Charles' personality back into the body, and called forth the subconscious to answer Charles' questions. This time the subconscious became argumentative, which is unusual. It is usually very cooperative.

D: *May I speak to Charles' subconscious?*

C: You mean the dreaming part?

D: *(I was confused.) The dreaming part? What part are you?*

C: Oversoul, I think you would say. It is *yours* as well. We are. We *are*. We are, yes.

D: *But you're separate from the person's conscious.*

C: Of course not. No, no.

D: *The part I normally speak to that has the answers relating to the physical, is usually the subconscious. You call that the dreaming part? What does that mean?*

C: Right now you are dreaming. Right now you are the dreamer. Right now you *are*. But go back to *us* for the "I, we, all". And then extrude like a plastic into a mold, to use an example you might know. And that's Dolores. But that isn't plastic. It's a fluid medium that *seems* to harden. But that's only in time. And then it flows back into its original.

544

And then it extrudes into a mold again.

Dictionary definition of extrude: to push or force out, as through a small opening.

C: And that mold might have a name "Dolores". You, every moment, flow between that mold and another mold, and inhabit various formless parts that is "us". You know that. Yes, you know that.

D: *These are concepts that are difficult for our human minds to understand.*

C: But you're not speaking to a human mind right now, so you don't need to worry.

D: *Well, I think I am.*

C: Oh, part of you might be.

This was becoming very confusing. I was not used to speaking to such a contradicting part of the person. I decided to redirect the questions back to what Charles wanted to find out, in the hopes I would be able to gain its cooperation.

D: *What is Charles' purpose in his present life?*

C: To change the dream.

D: *What do you mean?*

C: The dreamer dreams the dream. He can change the dream. Amend the dream.

D: *Who is the dreamer that dreams the dream?*

C: The one that dreams the dream in this reality.

D: *And you think the dream should be changed?*

C: It's time. Like it was before.

D: *By the dreamer, do you mean the mass consciousness or what? I'm trying to understand what you mean. The dreamer who dreams the dream.*

C: There's a dreamer who dreams this dream. There's only one.

D: *Is this a person or what?*

C: More of a consciousness. It is not personified, it's ... sort of a consciousness. We all dream the dream.

D: *As part of the consciousness?*

C: Yes. We all believe that the sun comes up and goes down. The dreamer dreams that dream.

D: *In the reality we're in, you mean?*

C: Yes. The dream of the reality.

D: *It becomes real though, because we're all in it. Isn't that true?*

C: Right, but each individual can dream his own dream too. He dreams he's a business person or a doctor or a lawyer. That's his dream within the dream.

D: *That's his reality.*

C: Right.

D: *But the dreamer who is dreaming the big dream, is that a much bigger consciousness? A much more powerful consciousness?*

C: Right.

D: *It would be hard to change it if it was that large.*

C: True.

D: *This consciousness, the dreamer that dreams the dream, is that more like our concept of God?* (Pause) *Or is it different?*

C: The thing is, God is not really ... there's only one, it's just ... the dreamer makes real what everybody else believes is real. The dreamer makes the stone hard, the Sun come up and down. That's his dream. It's other people's dreams that also do things in the dreams: create wars, strife, happiness, sadness.

D: *Those are all the individuals creating those parts within the other dream?*

C: Right, right.

D: *But don't they make that a reality when they do it?*

C: That is correct, yes.

D: *Just like the dreamer dreaming the dream makes that a reality?*

C: Correct. It's the big dream.

D: *It just keeps creating more realities?*

C: Right. But it is still just the one reality, though. Because there's only one.

D: *I've heard that we can create our own realities.* (Yes.) *Is this what you mean by ... I was thinking if the dreamer was like a*

546

larger consciousness.
C: Correct.
D: *I keep thinking of God. Maybe our concept of God is not correct.*
C: We are God, we are all at one.
D: *That's true. I've heard that. But if the consciousness, the dreamer, was dreaming the dream and creating it, then what he creates, remains, doesn't it? It becomes solid and physical?*
C: That is correct, yes.
D: *Because I think of a dreamer as eventually waking up.*
C: That is correct.
D: *Then does the dreamer eventually wake up?*
C: That is correct.
D: *(A nervous laugh.) What happens then?*
C: What happens when you go to sleep?
D: *I mean, what happens to what he has created in his dream?*
C: When you go to sleep, do you not go to another reality?
D: *True, but then when you wake up, does that reality remain?*
C: It's just as real as the other reality. It's a different form of dreaming. Do you call this reality? This where you're at now? Is it a dream or a reality?
D: *Well, we think we're in reality.*
C: Are you not dreaming here as you dream in the other place?
D: *(Laugh) We don't know, do we. That's always been a puzzle. But, anyway, the dreamer that has dreamed all of this that is happening now, when he wakes up, does our reality cease to exist or does it continue?*
C: Continues.
D: *Because he has given it life?*
C: We've *all* given it life.
D: *And all the other sparks and souls have given power and more creation to it. Is that what you mean?*
C: Right, but then they come back to the whole. But actually they really never left.
D: *So we are helping it become a reality and everyone is playing their part in it. (Yes.) But then on a larger scale, does the dreamer dream other dreams?*
C: When the smaller dreams, for lack of a better word, make

enough or have enough cause to change the big dreamer's dream; that's when that changes. That's when consciousness makes a jump. A jump ahead or it could be a fall backwards. It depends on your place in time. For example the Dark Ages, the dreamer changed the dream.

D: *So this is a huge consciousness then. It's more than we can understand?*

C: Oh no, it's just a dreamer.

D: *That has created all of this.*

C: Yes, we're all dreamers.

D: *We're all part of it then.* (Yes.) *Because I'm trying to understand. If he was so big that we wouldn't be able to comprehend it.*

C: No. Can comprehend anything.

D: *And this is the consciousness that we're all a part of?* (Yes.) *And we all go back to it.*

C: Yes, there's only one.

This sounded like the concept that I have covered elsewhere in this book, that we all originated with the Source and separated from it to do the various jobs we are assigned. Also to have the many adventures and lessons along the way, before we return. This creation by group mind could also be similar to Jerry's work, (Chapter 25) creating with his group. It could be the same concept, just put in different terms.

Could this also be part of what will happen when we ascend into the New Earth? Mass consciousness decides it is time to shift (or change) the dream?

D: *So the reality we have all created continues to exist.* (Yes.) *Because we've given it solidity, we've given it form?* (Yes.) *So then when we all go back, you said we make the consciousness shift.* (Yes.) *That is changing the dream to another dream.* (Yes.) *And when we do that, we create another reality, another dream at that time. Everyone that's involved?*

C: Yes, not so much in creating it, but just continuing.

D: *Continuing and changing the dream?*

C: Yes, it grows like a plant.

D: *I've heard we're getting ready to do a consciousness shift. Is that when this will happen?* (Yes.) *If enough people want to change the dream we're in now with the wars and negativity?* (Yes.) *Then it will go into the next consciousness then.* (Yes.) *I feel like I'm not describing it well, because I'm thinking of the dreamer as similar to God; as mass consciousness.*

C: True.

D: *Then eventually, does everyone leave the dream and go back to the dreamer or what? Go back to the consciousness that created everything?*

C: That is correct, yes. It starts over. Another dream. It's a cycle. Like when you wake up every morning, what happens to your dream? What do you think? It's *gone away?*

D: *Yes, because when you go to sleep the next night, it's a different dream. Very seldom do you go back into the same dream.*

C: Right.

D: *But many of our dreams don't make any sense.*

C: Seek to understand. (Laugh)

D: *There's more symbolism than we consider in our everyday life.*

C: It's a different *world.*

A different world with different rules that govern what occurs there. Our physical world on Earth is a place where rules and limitations strictly apply. That is why we chose to live here in a physical body in order to learn lessons within those limitations. Because we have no memories of our other lifetimes in other spiritual and physical realms, we have become used to thinking that everything has limitations. Thus we cannot perceive worlds with no limitations. As we have seen in this book, there are many other dimensions and realities that we can experience (when we have gained sufficient knowledge), where the beings are pure energy. They do not have even the limitation of a physical body. They can create anything they wish, from a body casing to their surroundings. They have complete control over their environment. Even so, many of them have chosen (or been sent) to experience life in our limited and confining world. These people are often unhappy, longing to return to their life of complete freedom. It must be the same thing when we enter the dream world. While in the dream state there are no rules, regulations or limitations. Anything can happen or be created. We have control and can create what we wish to experience. People who have lucid dreams soon realize they are dreaming, and that they can change the dream if they wish to. They understand they have control over this other world we enter every night when we sleep. I have been told many times that we will never be capable of understanding all of this while we are confined to a physical body. Apparently, the dream state is not a fantasy state that evaporates upon awakening. We have unknowingly created a world that remains and exists somewhere. This goes along with the idea that our thoughts are very powerful; they are actual things. Once thought, they exist forever. Of course, this is the way we create our reality; by guiding and organizing our thoughts, wishes, and dreams, and then focusing and directing them until they become reality.

D: *A different kind of world, you mean?* (Yes) *And that's why we have trouble understanding our dreams. We create our own individual little world each night when we go to sleep?*

C: Yes, and you're supposed to.

D: *But it's often full of symbolism that doesn't make sense to our waking minds.*

C: They just need to seek to understand. If they focus on it, they will understand.

D: *We always think it is trying to tell us things through symbols.*

C: It is. Just focus on it and you will understand.

D: *But when we wake up and come back into this reality, this one makes more sense to us.* (Yes.) *So every night, we go into a different world that we have created.* (Yes.) *Does that world in our dream state continue to exist?*

C: Of course! It's just a different ... when you go to sleep at night, what guarantee do you have to wake up the next morning?

D: *Well, we think we're going to.*

C: What if your body died?

D: *Well, that has happened to people.*

C: Yes. As is above is below.

D: *And then if the body died, you would go into the spirit world, wouldn't you? (Yes.) Which is different than the dream world. Isn't that true?*

C: True.

D: *But that way you would know you were no longer dreaming. You were entering the spirit world.*

C: Would you?

D: *Well, you think you would.* (Charles laughed.) *People have told me what the spirit world is like. It seems to be a different place.*

C: Compared to this one.

D: *Yes. They all describe it the same way, and compared to the dream world we see at night – it seems to be a different thing. (Yes.) This can get very confusing. For our human minds, anyway. But I'm always looking for information. Is it all right if I share that information with others, in my work?*

C: Yes, yes.

D: *I'm always looking for different things we haven't thought of, even though I know I don't understand it. Along the way, maybe someone somewhere might be able to expand on it.*

C: Sound is how God spoke the dream into creation. It started with sounds.

This is the way the Bible begins the story when God *spoke* our world into creation. *"And God said, Let there be light; and there was light."* Genesis 1:3. Every step of the creation process became reality when God spoke.

During another session, a woman I will call "Barbara" wanted to explore some events she thought occurred during Out of the Body experiences. She experienced going through

551

tunnels and similar things. During one of these, she ended up in another time period. I thought they sounded more like entering other dimensions by going through time portals. This was partly true. The subconscious said, "It's a memory. A memory of spaces that interlink."

D: *It seemed confusing. It seemed to be in our past as we know it.*
B: There is no past.
D: *That's what she thought it was and when she came back, it was confusing. The people in the other experience thought she wasn't supposed to be there.*
B: It's just a link to different space. It did no harm except to make her curious.

In another experience that Barbara also relegated to an Out of the Body experience, she found herself in a park talking to people. One of them told her he liked to come to the park, because in the other place he was in a wheelchair. I asked what had happened at that time.

B: They took her.
D: *Who took her?*
B: The minds. The minds took her. Her mind is their mind. The minds all thought.
D: *But, where were they?*
B: Somewhere else.
D: *And the minds of the other people that were in this park brought her there?* (Yes.) *Does she do this often?* (No.) *Because she thought it was familiar in a way.*
B: It's always the same. The minds create.
D: *And they create this place and they all go there?*
B: Yes, it's the communication with the other link.

These were not the minds of people that Barbara knew in her present lifetime, but she knew them on another level. That was why they seemed familiar.

D: *Is this similar to the spirit side, where we go when we die and leave the physical body?*

B: No, this is different. The others create it. It's the center of a tunnel. Where others come in from one end and some come in from this end. And they meet, and they create their surroundings, and stay there for awhile.

D: *But she said, when she came back here, it was very forceful. What happened there?*

B: She's obstinate.

D: *(Laugh) So it put her back in this body in this reality?* (Yes.) *Is this what happens sometimes when we're dreaming at night? Do we go to these places that the minds create?*

B: Like minds, yes.

D: *But we always come back to this body, don't we?*

B: Yes, but there is communication. Not a conscious level. On the other level. There are many houses, many levels. And you occasionally go to those that are created by like minds.

D: *Does this happen often?*

B: Not often.

D: *But usually we don't remember like she did. She remembered a lot, didn't she?*

B: She remembered too much. She has a good memory.

This event sounded more like the group creating their reality that Charles spoke about. The dreamer dreaming the dream.

Native people have a much more comfortable time accepting these metaphysical concepts than modern individuals. For instance, the beliefs of the aborigines of Australia explain the story of creation by saying that the dreamer dreamed it into existence. They say that the Dreamer's first dream was the elements: fire, earth, air and water. Then he proceeded from there. As he became bored with each new creation, he continued to create. They also believe that the real world is not on Earth, but on the spirit side. They call their life on Earth "Dreamtime", as though it is not "real". Thus, they rejoice when someone dies, because they know they are leaving Dreamtime and returning home. The concepts that puzzle us are easily accepted by them.

The astounding concept that nothing in our lives is real, that it is only an illusion has been repeated over and over in my work. The idea disturbs me, because it challenges my concept of reality. Everything in our life appears to be real and solid from our living and working surroundings to the touch and feel of those we love. If the dearest and most precious things in our lives are only an illusion, then how can we perceive reality? I find it much more comforting to think of these concepts as "mind candy". Something to think about to challenge our belief systems and push our minds to the brink of understanding. Something to philosophize over. But then at the end of the day, to put it over on a shelf and think, "That was interesting. It challenged my belief system. It made me think in a new direction. But now I have to return to the 'real' world." Even if it truly is only an illusion, it is still the only reality we know. So we have to live in it.

For the first time in many of our lives, we are being challenged with new and different information. Nothing like this happened in my early days of research. Maybe "they" are presenting it because it is time for humanity to expand their minds to accept radical ideas. Maybe it is time, because we are shifting en masse into a new reality in a new frequency and vibration. Our minds have to shift also, in order to accept the new and different world we are entering. Maybe this is the reason we are now being offered challenges to change our thinking from the mundane we have been trapped in for millennia. However, with a new paradigm and a new way of thinking, also comes a responsibility. It would be too easy to slip into a passive mode.

554

We could say, "I can just slide through life and not worry about anything, because nothing is real. Everything is an illusion. Everything is only a dream. So it doesn't matter what I do. I have no influence anyway." Then it would be too easy to sit back and contemplate the proverbial navel. Too easy to allow life to pass you by because you have retreated from it.

I believe that is not why we chose to be here in this world at this time. With enlightenment comes responsibility. That is one of the reasons we have had to reincarnate so many times. It has taken this long to get it right. We have been caught up in the material world for so long that we have forgotten why we came in the first place. This is also the reason why many of the advanced souls have chosen to reincarnate here, to help us as we move into the next dimension. In one of my books, I was told that the main reason for reincarnating on Earth was to learn to use and manipulate energy. So life may be an illusion. Life may be only a dream. But it is *our* dream, *our* illusion. We can change the world and change our circumstances once we realize the power we have. We can truly produce miracles. We can make the world in the next dimension a true heaven on Earth. This would be a hundred times more productive than sitting back and allowing life to slide by. The use and control of energies will become even more important in the new world. We are bringing back long forgotten powers and talents, because the world is finally ready. Otherwise, when we cross over to the other side, we will be told that we had a chance to change the world and we didn't take it. Then it becomes karma and we must go through the whole thing again until we finally understand. The release of more and more complicated concepts is preparing our minds to accept the new world that is coming. We cannot remain passive if we want to venture into the new reality, the new dream, the new illusion.

I have often been told in my work, that when we go out of our body at night while sleeping, or by guided and directed will, we go to different worlds as well as traveling on our physical planet. The person may return to the spirit realm to converse with their guides and get more instructions about handling events in their life. Or advice about creating the next events they have contracted to experience. Or maybe just a checkup accomplished by returning "home" to visit with people we have no memory of while awake. (This has already been explained elsewhere in this book that we go out of our bodies at night while sleeping.) This is one of the reasons why newborn babies sleep a lot. They are adjusting to their physical bodies, and only awaken when the body needs attention. They are still connected to the spiritual side, and go back and forth to receive guidance. The spirit is not attached completely to the body until about the age of two. By that time, they are not sleeping as much. This is also an explanation for Sudden Infant Death Syndrome, which the doctors have difficulty understanding. There are occasions when the spirit is on one of its excursions to the spirit realm, and decides (for whatever reason) not to return to the body. Maybe it decided that the circumstances it was born into were not conducive with working out experiences in this lifetime, and that another body in another environment might be more conducive. Maybe it occurred as a lesson for the parents. Something they had to learn, because of past lives experiences with the new baby's soul. Maybe the baby's spirit stayed too long on the other side. It was an accident, and it did not get back in time. (Although I have been told there is no such thing as accident.) The spirit must return to the body within a certain specified length of time or the body will expire. It cannot exist without the spirit (or spark of life) dwelling inside of it.

Also, it is a well known fact that old people sleep more, especially if they are ill or incapacitated. They are also making journeys to the spirit realm to converse with their guides and masters, and preparing for their transition. When the spirit considers everything is ready, it decides to remain there. There is no longer any need for the physical body. It has become worn out or damaged to the point that it is useless to continue to keep it alive. In these cases, the person usually dies in their sleep while their spirit is on one of these journeys.

If we are just dreamers dreaming what we perceive as reality, this would explain what so many of my clients say when they are reliving their past lives. When they go through the death experience and are on the other side they look back and say, "It was just a game, just playing characters on a stage. When I was there it was so complicated, and seemed to take so long, but it was just like a blink of an eye." They consider the spirit realm to be the "real" reality, and the life they just departed to be only an illusion. I, personally, would like to think it is really more than that. We experience so much pain and emotional heartbreak as we live life on Earth, that I would like to think it has purpose, and will remain. Of course, I have been told this is true, because we are all experiencing and learning lessons, so the knowledge and information gained can be returned to God. In this way, our lives, good or bad, are entered into a gigantic archive or library where they remain forever. Would we live our lives differently if we knew everything was all being recorded; literally carved in stone for eternity?

One of my daughters worked as a nurse in a hospital, and later as a home health care nurse for many years. She told me the story of a man who was bedridden and in a lot of pain. The family knew he was dying, and thought it would be a blessing when it happened. He spent much of his time sleeping. He told my daughter that he was actually journeying out of his body, and during that time there was no pain. He was actually doing work while in this state. He was building a beautiful house on the other side. He knew that when the house was completed, he would remain there and this life would cease to exist for him. He died quietly one night in his sleep, and my daughter said simply, "Well, I guess he finished his house and moved in."

I always assumed he was building his house in the spirit

realm, because we can create anything we wish there. But maybe he was building it in the dream world where spirit can exist as well. This is what was indicated in this session, that they are two different worlds, yet alike in many respects. If everything is an illusion, how will we ever know? What is reality anyway? If we are only characters acting out a larger dreamer's dream, what happens when "he" or "it" wakes up? These are interesting theories or aspects to ponder, but they just disturb me and give me a headache. Maybe they are better left to "thinkers" who like to explore complex theories. As for me, I have fulfilled my reporter's duty and written what I have discovered. Now I have to return to my illusion. The body does have physical needs, and that is my reality for the moment. I can stop hurting my poor brain with things better left to philosophers and hermits living in caves.

CHAPTER 28

A DIFFERENT ALTERNATIVE

TO WALK-INS

Many of my sessions encompass several different aspects, and it is difficult to know which section to put the information in. I try to think of the main theme of the information, rather than trying to break it up. This was such a case. It contained information about ETs, although a different concept. It also contained information about a different version of walk-ins. I decided to put it with this section about different soul facets. There are references to other chapters where similar information can be found. Everything in this book seems to refer back and forth.

This private session was done in February, 2002, when I stayed in a motel in Eureka Springs, Arkansas. This is the time I devoted to having just private sessions, concentrating on the local area: Arkansas, Missouri, Kansas, and Oklahoma.

Many times in the last few years I have been given a new piece of information or a new concept from one of my clients. Then the next client comes for their session, and the new concept is expanded upon. Almost as though someone or something on the other side is monitoring my sessions, and deciding which piece of information I will be given at what time. Of course, I know "they" seem to be aware of what is given in each session, because "they" always seem to know me and my work. Several times towards the end of a session they will say, "Here is the next piece of information you need for your books." Or, "You said you thought you were ready for the next concept. Well, here it is." This cannot be accidental or anything I am intentionally doing, because the pieces of the puzzle come from people all over the world who do not know each other, and who do not know the information I am accumulating. Sometimes I am given a piece from someone in the United States, and it is expanded upon by someone in England or Australia. So it is definitely being monitored by someone who is in a position to see everything I do and all the various people I work with. This has happened so often that I am not surprised and am very comfortable with whoever is running the show. This case is an example of what I mean. While doing the private sessions in Eureka Springs I received a piece of information about how "Star Children" or "Special Volunteers", are protected from the accumulation of karma from Aaron, the NASA engineer. Then my next client, Bobbi, came for her session, and the idea was expanded upon. Whoever it is that supplies the information and oversees the operation, I greatly appreciate their help. They understand, as I do, that the time is right for certain information to come forth to the people of Earth. Of course, they have also told me many times that I will never be able to have all the information, because our minds could never handle it. So they give analogies and examples to illustrate it as best they can within the constraints of our minds' limitations.

After Bobbi was in trance, she came off the cloud and found herself in a very desolate desert landscape. She was an almost naked native man who was desperately searching for food for his family. His group was living in caves after being chased from their land by the white man. "They wanted control. They wanted to take over. And they didn't see us as valuable." Where before his people had planted their food, they were now reduced to search for anything (small animals, salamanders and insects) to eat. They were starving, and he felt a great responsibility to provide food. "There is a real concern for survival. We are hungry. I can feel it in my stomach." The man felt such a responsibility that he went without food so the others could eat. "I can feel my stomach having challenges."

He eventually died from lack of nourishment. Even though he deprived himself for the others, he felt he had let them down. He felt a lot of responsibility, and by dying he was leaving them without someone to provide for them. I had to convince him that he had done the very best he could.

He said, "It had to do with nutrition, with not getting the right nutrients for my body. I felt I had to sacrifice for them. If only I had kept *my* strength up. I thought giving them my food was helpful, and it wasn't. I sacrificed my life for all of them, and then I felt bad because I left them. I let them down, because I really should have taken care of myself first. I didn't do that. I would have been more of value to them had I taken care of myself, and nurtured myself. It was a very hard, challenging life."

D: *What did you learn from that?*
B: I learned that I don't have to sacrifice myself for others. That was the wrong thing to do. I felt so responsible for their journey, and I didn't realize that I should have let them be responsible for themselves. It was co-dependency. And my digestive system was all messed up from not getting the proper nutrients. I always felt there was not going to be enough.

It was explained to Bobbi, that this lifetime was shown to her to help explain health problems she had in this present lifetime regarding her digestive system.

Because the lifetime was so short, there was time to explore another one. So I told her to move either forwards or backwards to another time and place where there was something else she needed to see.

B: I keep going back to the time in this lifetime when I was a little girl.

Occasionally when the subject chooses to go to an event that occurred in the present lifetime, there is something there that needs to be explored. Usually, it is something the conscious mind either has forgotten or never knew in the first place. The subconscious brings it up again for some reason. Maybe there was something there Bobbi needed to find out about, so I decided to leave her there rather than move her to another past

561

life.

B: I have some resistance in going there. I feel alone. I feel scared.

D: *But you weren't alone, were you? You had a big family.*

Bobbi had twelve brothers and sisters, but she was mistreated, along with others in the family, mostly because the overwork on her parents kept them from showing any affection. Bobbi was a twin, and her sister was the only one she had any bond with while growing up.

B: I didn't feel they cared about me. My sister was there, but she felt the same way. I just felt alone. Very alone.

D: *What time in your life are you seeing?*

B: When I was real young. We're out on a dirt road that we lived on. It's my sister and I. And our dog.

D: *Even with that big family and your sister, you felt alone.*

B: Uh-huh. Some of them were gone by the time I was born. It was such a big family. I was very young. I see this house that we lived in, and I see this other house. There are the two houses. (Pause) There's something in the sky. That's why I'm scared. There's like a light in the sky.

D: *You said your sister is with you, and the dog?*

B: I don't see her with me right now. I'm by myself. There's a light. And it kind of scares me. I don't know what it is. (Repeated as a whisper:) I don't know what it is. It's just a bright light. (A whisper) I don't know what it is.

D: *Do you feel you need to go back to the house?*

B: (Emphatic) No! I don't like the house! I don't want to go back there. That's where I feel alone. I don't like it there. I like to stay outside. I feel safer outside.

D: *Then what happens as you're watching the light?*

B: (A whisper) It comes closer. It's not so scary now. It's different. I'm not scared, just curious. Because the light feels better. (So soft it was barely audible. Only the tape picked it up:) I jump back! (Louder) There's something in the light. It's like someone in the light. It's almost like they pull me up, because all of a sudden I'm just ... there was this being in the light. And then the next thing I know, I'm not there. I'm not on the ground anymore.

I was trying to reassure her, as though speaking to a little girl, because this was how she sounded. She had taken on the characteristics of a child, which meant she was reliving the event exactly as it had occurred.

B: But I have my eyes closed. I don't know that I want to see this. I feel somebody touching me. And I'm still scared. My stomach ... I feel it in my stomach.

D: *Do you want to open your eyes and see what's happening?*

B: Yeah, I think I do. The touch wasn't bad. There's this being there in front of me. It's the being that I have seen before with the splotchy blond hair. But in my conscious mind, there was more hair. It was not so patchy. And it's my mom. My mom. (Her emotions were beginning to surface.)

D: *How do you know that?*

B: (Indignant) You always know your mom!

D: *That's the feeling you get?*

B: (Emotional, almost crying) Yes, yes.

D: *Is your sister with you, or are you by yourself?*

B: (Trying to keep from crying.) I'm by myself right now.

D: *Can you see where you are?*

B: (Muffled, then:) It's like a room. I'm like on a table. (Repeated the last two sentences) And I sit up.

Later after this session, Bobbi sent me a letter in which she tried to explain and clarify some of the things that happened during this session. "I had just been taken on the ship and remember lying down and looked up to see my Mother. She had the blonde patches of hair. I had had dreams of this woman, but I didn't know who she was. You asked me how I knew this was my Mother. I remember becoming very indignant because

563

everyone knows their Mom. At the time, I thought the question very silly. How could you not know who is your Mom? I laugh now at my strong reaction, which really validated the experience for me."

The experts may say that the little girl was fantasizing another mother to take the place of her own who was very cold, overworked, and had no time for her. But if she was going to fantasize and create another mother, why would it be onboard a spacecraft?

This is similar to the case in *The Custodians*, where the young girl was visited by her "real" father. In that case, when it began to cause problems in her young life, the extraterrestrial being told her he could not come anymore, and the memories of him were erased from her conscious memory. Was this a similar case where the memories only remained as strange dreams?

B: (Emotional) And it just feels good to be with her. Where have you been?! And she's saying, "You have an assignment. You're on an assignment, Bobbi. You know that." She says, "You know what the Earth is. You know it's not real. You know it's illusions. You know who you *are*. You know you're my child. You are of *the*, but you know you're of the whole too. You know that you're not limited. You know these things. I'm here to help you remember these things. I'm with you." She says, "I'm always with you." It's not about me, it's *we*. And the we, I think, is her. And she's there. She's helping me. She says, "We're with you. We *are* with you. We're always with you." She says, "What makes you think we're not going to help you? We're always helping you." I felt so alone. I see scissors. She said, "We had to cut the cord so you could live the life. We had to cut the cords so you could be a human. But you're not human. You're just having the human experiences, because you're learning. You're learning. We're teaching you."

D: *But she said she's your real mother. Weren't you born into a body as a baby?*

B: No, I didn't come in. That wasn't me then.

D: In the baby, with your twin?

B: No. There's a difference here.

D: Can she explain it to you?

B: It has to do with the time when the twins got lost.

This was an incident that occurred when Bobbi was very young, that her family always considered strange. She had asked to explore this during the session. She and her twin sister had been lost for quite a while and no one could find them. Then they unexpectedly turned up in the front yard of their home.

Bobbi's personality receded and the being that said she was her mother spoke *to* Bobbi.

B: There's an exchange. We have a way. I'm trying to see if I can explain this in human terms. We have a way that we can ... it's almost like an exchange of personalities in some way. It's like a change, exchange. There was a change that was made. You weren't born into that. You observed that, but that wasn't you. That wasn't the you that's you now. There was an exchange that was made. And no, it's not like the walk-in experience. You were right with that. Bobbi has this memory of a future self on a spaceship with blond hair. And that's the memory of who you really are.

D: Instead of a future life, it's the memory of what she really is, you mean.

B: Of what she really *is*. And somewhat from future too, because there's no time there. There's no time. You're in that dimension where you think there's so much with time, and time's not important.

D: That's true. But you mean your people on the ship chose this baby, this body, to what ...?

B: The body was going to experience many things that we wanted to know about. We wanted to know about human experience. Bobbi, that's why on Earth, you have always been interested in the psychological part of the human.

565

You weren't interested in traditional teachings. The front line, you weren't interested in going to school to learn psychology. That wasn't what you were there for. You were interested in the deeper meanings. You wanted the deeper truth. And it wasn't in the human nature. You had to live for the human experiences, so you could decide what was real and what wasn't. And we've always been there showing you. And it's like, relax, because the way is going to be clear. Let go.

D: *Can you explain to me how this occurred? It's not a walk-in. You said it was different.*

B: It is different. Okay, I see the twins. There's a room. The twins are lying on a table together. There's something ... some type of ... I just have trouble explaining what I'm seeing.

D: *Just do the best you can.*

B: There's some type of machine. Some type of, I want to say "implant". But there's some type of exchange or implant. How do they exchange? It's not a soul exchange. The twins didn't want to go through all of this. They knew what their life was going to be like. The depression. The family are depressed energies. The twins, the original twins, did not want to do that. (She had difficulty finding the words.) Trans .... It's not transmigration. Transigation? Transmitation? Something ... some parts of an exchange. She says, "You're trying too hard."

D: *Just let it flow. Use the words you can find.*

B: She said, the twins were so glad to ... it was what they all agreed. She said, "You all agreed to come in and to learn this." I've always wondered why my sister and I didn't have that twin thing of one always knowing when the other got hurt, or that connection. And she said, "That's because you were twins by looking alike, but it's different. The beings that you are now are not like the normal twins of Earth. You've known that you haven't had that connection. Your lives are parallel because of the twin process, but you're different personalities. You're different beings.

You're on different missions. You have different assignments."

D: *But you said it was all agreed to.* (Oh, yeah.) *What happened to the original spirits that came in?*

B: They're happy. (She laughed.) They are healing.

D: *Then they didn't stay. There weren't two spirits in the body at the same time.*

B: There were for a time, because Bobbi needed help knowing how to function. So there was a time that the twins were there. There were times that there was like a joining. In the early days. Ah! Because Bobbi didn't remember much of her childhood. There were times when she would go back and forth in consciousness. I don't know how. She would go back and forth because she was learning more of being in the child, in the body, and integrating. And we weren't just going to abandon you completely. Ah, how sad.

D: *Then the original spirits went somewhere else?*

B: Yes, the original spirit was there. There were things that the original spirit just couldn't handle. And the little girls were so sad.

D: *Then what happened to the original spirit? You said they were together for a while.*

B: They wanted to go home. They went to rest. She said, "They're fine. They went to a rest place. And from where they were, they could view some of this. They learned." She says, "Bobbi, they could learn from you going through the experiences too. So it was like they were someway detached, but yet a part of it. But they were learning as you were going through much of the experience. They didn't have the courage. They didn't have the strength. They didn't want to go through all of that."

D: *Why is this different from a walk-in?*

B: It's a different process.

D: *Can you tell me the difference?*

B: Let me ask her. She says many times the original spirit will go through much of part of the Earth life until it gets to a real critical point, where they just can't go on anymore. There's no resistance to that. It's like that personality ego wants to go as far as it can before it gives up, before it lets go, before it's exchanged. And then, it does get to a point where it sees that it can't go on. At least it tried. I mean, it really tried. I'm seeing determination. I'm seeing really trying. And they try as much as they can, and it's *hard.* It's just hard. And that's whenever they exchange. It's like, on the in breath there's that nanosecond between breaths. Inhale and exhale, where things happen. That's where God is. And it's on those times where there are opportunities for other things to happen.

D: *That's a walk-in. But what happened to Bobbi was not the same thing?*

B: No. There was more of a mechanical process involved. I don't understand why ... that's not the word. There's some type of molecular ... I'm seeing machines around. I'm seeing connections. How they can connect the spirit ... (a whisper) how is it done?

D: *They have the ability to do that with machines?*

B: It's not like normal machines. It's energy that they have, I'm seeing, in their hands. They have something in their hands. (Whisper) How are they doing that? I don't understand. Some type of transference. And when I was a little girl, it's like I saw them just step into the body, but it's much more than that. There's this transference. I keep asking her how they transfer it. (Pause) It's like a scientific process. There are machines around. Ah, the machines have to do with brain waves. They do something with the brain waves to help to get to a certain frequency. And when there's a certain frequency, there's some type of transference that can happen. It's other dimensional technology. Sometimes Bobbi sees something like energy lines, and those are frequencies. When the frequency is right, there can be a transference of personalities, or transference of thoughts, of consciousness. It has to do with frequencies.

D: *Something just occurred to me. The other case of the walk-ins is done totally with the spirit exchanging places. And this sounds as though Bobbi was a living physical being on the spacecraft, not a spirit.* (Yes) *And she had to transfer that way.* (Yes) *Where the other ones were spirits that had already crossed over, and they exchanged places.*

B: Yes, that makes sense. Because at the point of transference ... I see these two little bodies on the table here. But there are two more adult beings that will be the transference. Transference-ees is the word. Transferenc*ees*, that will come in. But there is a time capsule. She's just remembering more of who she really is. Because the time capsule is about being asleep for so many years. And the forties were trigger years. She knew at forty that she was needing to go through her fears. Forties were her most important years in awakening.

D: *This was when the knowledge came back.* (Yes.) *Then the transferees were really living a physical life onboard the craft, and were not deceased spirits.*

B: No, they weren't. That's a difference.

D: *And you have on this craft the abilities to make the transfer.* (Yes) *But it has to be with the permission of the existing soul.*

B: Oh, yes.

D: *But then it agrees to go back.*

B: The transfers would then go back.

D: *So it is an exchange, but it's done with another* living *being.*

B: I'm seeing the one that is Bobbi. I see the one coming in is almost a male energy. I don't understand why it would be a male energy, because they're not male or female.

D: *More or less androgynous?*

B: Yes. Let's get off of this.

D: *Well, I have one more question. What happened to the body of the transferee? The one that was on the craft? If the soul leaves the body to enter Bobbi's body, what happened to that body?*

B: That body is like in a state of stasis (She had difficulty with that word, and found it hard to pronounce). Is there a suspension? It's a suspension. It's like sleep? It's like a

569

sleep. And when you asked that, the answer came instantly. It's a sleep, because there's a dimension where there's no time. So it's like the Earth lifetime is not relevant to time on the other. So the body will be in this ... I keep getting state ... it starts with an S. It's not just stations, suspensions, gestation stasis. It's something like stasis.

According to the thesaurus: Stasis - immobility, inaction, stagnation. According to the dictionary: Stasis - (Act or condition of standing, stopping.) 1. a slowing or stoppage of the normal flow of a bodily fluid or semi-fluid: as: slowing of the current of circulating blood. 2. a state of static balance or equilibrium: stagnation.

B: The body goes into this for a time to learn. It's learning about humans. Bobbi refers to humans as the third person. She refers to Earth as Humansville. And it's a human thing. There are human homes. And she remembers a time when she asked what she did on the ships. (Bobbi had had the feeling [through dreams] that she visited a spaceship when she was supposed to be sleeping.) And she teaches about Humansville. She teaches about human life.

D: *Then this is different from walk-ins, because the body is more or less there waiting in a type of suspended animation for the return of the soul. The body doesn't die.* (Right) *And the soul is on assignment to Earth, but it didn't want to go through the birth process.* (No) *There would be more forgetting with the birth process, wouldn't there?*

B: (Excited) Oh! It squeezes the head. For some reason that just came in. The birth process, when they come out through the birth canal, that's when the memories are stopped. There's an excitement here, because the birthing process has something to do with the veil. If you come through that then the veil is thicker. Okay. That makes sense.

In my work with walk-ins, I had surmised this. People seem to be definitely more psychic after a NDE (Near Death Experience) or a walk-in, where there is an exchange of souls. Through my work, I have discovered that the birth process does erase the memories. Also the amount of time spent as a baby focusing on trying to make the body work: learning to crawl, walk and finally communicate, causes the memories of the inbetween life and where the soul came from to fade away. The walk-in, on the other hand, does not go through these memory-erasing experiences and comes in with full memory of where it came from. Therefore, they know how to use their psychic abilities. These abilities are latent or lying dormant, as they are in so many humans.

D: *So this is why she agreed to this. And this happened at the time her parents thought she was lost.*

B: She knows this is how it's done.

D: *And this soul that entered at that time was better able to handle things?* (Yes.) *It agreed to handle all these very bad complicated things that she had to go through.*

B: Yeah. And to be more grounded.

D: *The real mother and the people on the craft, are always with her.* (Yes) *Helping her in the subconscious state?*

B: They're the "we", yes.

D: *These people on the craft, do they have a physical home somewhere, or do they just live on the craft?*

B: There's something far away, but they really just live on the craft.

D: *What was Bobbi's occupation when she was on the craft, before she made the transfer?*

B: She was an adventurer.

D: *(Chuckle) She sounds like it.*

B: She loved the stars. She was like an astronaut, we would say. She was a spaceonaut. (Laugh) Like a Startreker. She loves the galaxies. Oh, gosh! This is why Bobbi likes galaxies. This is why she feels at home when she sees all the nebulas, and all of that. She's just going through with what she loves. And there were times Bobbi knew she was in the stars. She would see stars. She was seeing through my eyes. And we are space explorers. We're dimensional explorers.

D: *And this is another adventure.* (Oh, yeah!) *Isn't there the danger of being trapped here once you come into a physical body on Earth?*

B: We know what to do.

D: *I'm thinking about karma.*

B: We know about all of that. We're aware of all of that.

D: *Because there's always the danger of creating karma when you come to Earth. It seems to be something you can't avoid.*

B: What I'm seeing is there's like a film between ... I can't explain it very well. There's like a film between ... there's a protection between that.

This sounded like Aaron saying there was a protective sleeve that had been put around him. Maybe the film is the same thing.

B: We understand the grabbing. We understand the pull. We understand the mechanics of being sucked into this. I see dials. We can attune things. It has to do with frequencies. It has to do with dials. Bobbi's interested in frequencies. She's understanding frequencies. She's learning to tune into the different frequencies. But we can use a frequency. We know how far we can go. Let's put it that way. We know how far we can go without getting caught up into all of that. We can see it. We can see a bigger picture. Oh, yes, it's like sticky glue. What they're showing me is like that sticky glue that you can't get away from. We see the danger. It's like you get caught. I'm seeing something caught in ... it's like flypaper. It's like those horrible things that humans trap little animals on, and they can't get off. And we don't want to do that. That's a human thing. It's like you humans are in flypaper. And you're trying to walk around in all of this. And oh, it's hard! It's so hard for you.

572

D: *That's why it takes a really brave adventurer to want to do this, because you could get trapped so easily.*

B: We understand the vibrational frequencies. We understand the mechanics of the fine line to tune. I see dials. We understand how to avoid, how to maintain. Karma's your flypaper. It's like, get off it!

D: *So you know how to keep from getting stuck.*

B: Yeah, we know. There's a male here that's quite good. He's the one that oversees this. There's Bobbi's mother, there's me ... there's the Bobbi. It's hard to explain all of this.

D: *Yes, being in two places at once.*

B: Yes, in two places at once. But there is another being here. There's like a body and there isn't. It's like a presence that has a knowingness that's greater that's helping us. We know when to not get into the flypaper. That's all I can say. But your karma really is like something stuck on flypaper trying to pull off.

D: *Would this be one reason why Bobbi didn't have any children?*

I had already discovered this through another subject. Refer to Chapter 9, "Children Create Karma."

B: Oh, yes. There's more karma that's involved with that. She knew she had enough to work on.

D: *Because when you have children you do have more attachment to Earth.*

B: The assignment had more to do with the studying. With what we were wanting to learn from this dimension. We want to learn about human experiences.

D: *Just living the experiences, and not getting caught up in the karma.*

B: Exactly.

In the letter Bobbi sent after the session, she wanted to explain her memories about the karma: "Karma looked like what we do to insects with fly paper. At one point, I was shown a picture that would be like when you get gum stuck on your shoe, and you just can't get loose of it. The fly paper was like that. It was very difficult for humans to get 'unstuck'. At one part it was explained to me how the person on the craft stayed out of karma. It didn't seem to be as difficult as we have always heard, because they knew about vibrational frequencies and knew the precise frequencies of the karmic pull and entrapment. This was not a problem for them.

"The being mentioned that Earth was like in a Dome of vibrational frequencies. The dome looked like a thin membrane over the Earth and it reminded me of the movie, 'The Truman Show' where Jim Carrey lived his whole life on an actual dome shaped movie set unaware that everyone in his life were actors, playing a part – just like Earth is."

D: *But when she leaves this lifetime eventually, will she go back to the being she was on the ship? The body that is still waiting?*

B: Yes, she'll do that.

D: *Instead of going to the spirit side? Because the other side is where we say you go when you leave the body and die. Or do you see it differently?*

B: I'm not seeing much distinction with that. She will have a regular transition. She'll go through the death experience to the spirit world. We're part of that spirit world. We're part of that One. We're part of the Presence. We're part of the whole. We're all vehicles. It's like a domino thing. I'm just a part of the greater being. And Bobbi's a part of me, but in the end, it's all about spirit. It's all about the One. It's all about the Presence. It is complicated, because she'll be in me, but yet we're a part of that One.

D: *That life of the native who was very hungry, was that connected with the original Bobbi, or with the entity that has entered? It's a little confusing when we have two here.*

B: These are some of the memories of the original soul, the little girl, the little Bobbi, the twin. They've been used to help us understand human life.

D: *Like a residue that was still there.*

B: Oh, yes, yes. Before she came into the life we could see that memory.

D: *This is why the soul coming in, the transferee, didn't have those memories.* (Right) *Then it definitely doesn't belong with the Bobbi personality now.* (No) *That belongs with the one that went on to rest.*

B: Yes, it really does.

D: *So it can have no influence on her now at all.* (Right) *Well, that really puts it in its place.*

B: We will help with all these physical problems. We are of our integrity. As for her purpose for being here, there is a timing thing. She has healing abilities. She didn't know who *we* were until now. And so now she knows the "we" part. And the "we" part is we're all a part of the Creator. She will bring some light energy. I see there is a beam of light coming in that has encrypted messages. It's coding. The tones. In one of her ears she'll get a tone. She'll be able to decipher it. She needs to connect with me in meditation that she already does, and ask for help. She'll start deciphering these messages. I see beams of light. And I see it's not hieroglyphic, it's more like ancient Hebrew.

I understood what she was talking about, because I was receiving samples of writing (or symbols) from all over the world. It sounds like the same thing, and many people have told me they receive it as it appears in beams of light.

B: We're using her physical body. She's very grounded. She's skeptical, but not too skeptical. She's skeptical enough that she really discerns what she's getting. She's a very good vehicle for what we want to do. We want to bring in some truth. She's always wanted to bring truth onto this planet. That's why she's here. It's like my body is ... it's not gestation. My body is in this stasis, but yet I'm there in spirit helping her. My body needs to be in that state in order for me to give full attention to helping her. To be with her. So there's a discipline of information coming through. This light that comes through needs to be spread around. It'll go to more than she can imagine.

D: She's attempted to find this information before, and it just wouldn't come through.

B: She blocked it. She wasn't ready for it. She hadn't had the human experiences that we needed her to have in order to be able to get the clarity. She's always felt this dimension was slow.

D: Well, can I ask permission. Would I be allowed to use some of this information in my work?

B: Oh, yes. That's why we're here.

D: Because there's some parts of it that I'm beginning to put together like a puzzle.

B: There are concepts here that would be helpful for humans to understand. The flypaper concept is to help people. It's like your TV. People get glued to that TV. It's like that addiction. It's similar to hypnotherapy. People are under hypnosis, and it's time for them to come out. It's time for them to wake up. Absolutely.

D: I don't think anything happens by accident. You people are always giving me the next piece of information that I need. And you probably know anyway, the man I did yesterday gave me the first hint of this, about the flypaper and the karma. (See Aaron – Chapter 11.)

B: He mentioned the flypaper and the karma?

D: He mentioned it in a different way, like a sleeve protecting him from getting stuck in the karma. And Bobbi talked about a veil and a film. Some way to keep away from the karma.

B: It's like a dome, a frequency. It's like the veil is a frequency. That's the best I can put it into this language. There's that frequency that's like a veil that's around this dimension.

D: She has explained it more clearly. He said that you could learn the lessons, but you didn't have to get bogged down in the karma. He described it as a way to keep the karma from sticking to him.

B: Exactly. The world is an illusion. You're here to learn the lessons, but to not get stuck in them. Bobbi knew she was here to learn detachment, because she's so attached. She came in co-dependent, because she had to learn not to be co-dependent. She came in on the flypaper. And that's the deepest human challenge. It's like you're laying flat on that flypaper. And she got up.

D: *So if the original spirit had stayed in the body, it would have been very, very difficult.*

B: They would not have wanted to stay.

D: *So this was really keeping the body alive. That way, we can send the original spirits love, that they relinquished the body.*

B: Oh, yes. They received – the humans would call it "rewards". They received like a reward for allowing this to take place. The twins that left, it helped them too, because they, for some time, were able to learn from the experiences of this one. And they still can learn from that, because of the connection with the Great Soul. The great Creator connection.

D: *Does her sister, Linda, know any of this?*

B: She knows it on some level. The same thing occurred with her. She has to have different experiences. (Laugh) She has different flypaper because she was here to learn different things. She married a minister, a *gay* minister, so she had her own challenges. And so she's had a different diversity of experiences, but both of them have had very trying experiences. They did not want to do the journey by themselves. It was too much.

I was preparing to end the session and bring Bobbi back to full consciousness, but the entity had a few parting words.

B: Thank you for this opportunity. For the orchestration for everybody concerned. We know the webs of all these things intertwine.

D: *I keep running into more of this though than the average person.* (We laughed.)

B: It's your assignment.

D: *At least I'm on that web, I guess.*

B: Oh, yes. Oh, yes. You have a big thread. (Laugh)

I gave instructions to have the other entities recede. Bobbi gave a big breath when the others departed, and then I brought her back to full consciousness.

When I had a session with Jesse in New York in 2004 I found mention of another type of alternative to a walk in : the holding soul.

Instead of going into a past life she went to an energy type being who had been going to various places throughout the cosmos. Some of these were physical and solid, and some were not. She was a type that did not have to be tied to a particular body.

D: *Do you ever enter into a body?*
J: You can enter at different times during the life. If you want to.
D: *Don't you have to enter a body when it's a baby?*
J: No. Maybe a person needs help, and you go to help with it. You are a part of their life for a short period of time. If they need it.
D: *So you don't stay there for the whole lifetime of the body?*
J: Sometimes. Sometimes not. It does not have to be a body. It can be different forms on different planets and different areas.
D: *What other forms would you take if it wasn't a body?*
J: I know some of them are not solid. (Deep breath) It's *so* hard to explain.
D: *Yes! I think it would be. But you said you don't usually stay for the whole life of the body's existence or whatever the form is. But if you enter just to help them for a short while, isn't there already a soul or a spirit existing in that body?*
J: Yes, but they needed help.
D: *So, you're allowed to help even though there is already one*

in the body? (Yes.) *Because I thought maybe that wouldn't be allowed. To have two souls in a body at once.*

J: I don't think the other soul takes over. I think it's just there to help. Or add something to help. I can't explain. So hard.

D: *Then, when you have helped all you can, you leave?*

J: Yes. I don't think it has to even go into the body. You could just stay with that person. And communicate with them and send them energy they need. It can be done like that too.

D: *Is the person aware of you?*

J: What do you mean, the person?

D: *The physical body, the person who is in the conscious* part. *Do they know you're there?*

J: They may feel different. They do things differently than they normally would. But the soul is the one that knows everything. You know everything about them. And you just do what you're supposed to do to help them out. So it's nothing invading.

D: *So the soul knows what you're doing. It knows you're there?* (Yes.) *And it allows you to help for a short period of time, or however long it takes.* (Yes.) *Then you go from place to place.*

J: Sometimes, yes. Sometimes, you stay. If the main spirit maybe has to leave the body for a short time. Just to go back to the other side and repair itself or something like that. They leave, you take over. You basically become everything they were before, plus the strength and the connection they were before. And you help for awhile until the spirit comes back.

D: *It keeps the body, the vehicle, alive that way, keeps it functioning.* (Yes.) *Why would the soul have to go back to be repaired?*

J: I don't think it can be fully repaired on Earth. It has to go across the curtain. Across the veil. I think it has to rest and get different vibrational attunements.

D: *Does something happen in the person's life, the vehicle's*

579

life, to make it have to go back and be repaired?
J: Yes. Horrible things or tragedies, or the soul is so worn out it can't really go on any more.

It looks like those on the other side have a solution for any possibility. Rather than have the body die while the spirit goes back for repairs, the holding soul comes in for a while and keeps the body alive, until the original spirit feels it can resume its job. This is different from a walk-in which is more of a permanent exchange.

D: *Have you ever lived in a physical body for the whole lifetime?*
J: I think only a few times. I'm stuck in here now. I don't like it. It's hard to be in for a long time.
D: *You were not the original soul that came in?*
J: I'm not sure. I think I am, but I'm not sure.
D: *Do you think you entered into her body when she was born, as a baby?*
J: (Sigh) Maybe in and out. I don't know. I think it was a long time.
D: *I was just curious if you have been in her body the whole time she's been alive.*
J: I have memories of it, but, I don't think so. I think the original soul couldn't make it. It was an agreement. They just leave for awhile and someone else takes over. Maybe those things happen more frequently than people know. Souls share the body for a short period of time and then go on. Maybe the first soul was just a new soul that hadn't experienced Earth life before. It was the first time, and was like on a trial basis, and it was too much. If you can't go through with it. There were two other souls lined up just in case.
D: *In case they couldn't do the job?*
J: I don't know if it's doing the job or just being there. The

important thing is that the vehicle stay alive. So somebody has to take turns.

I called the subconscious forth in order to get more information. Jesse said she didn't feel at home here on Earth. It was a lonely feeling, and she wanted to know why she felt this way.

J: She feels that way because this is not home. Her real home is not a physical place. It's on another dimension. It is just light and beautiful and there is no body, no people. There is only energy. There is another place that is a little more physical, semisolid. Big mountains and animals and trees. She likes staying there a lot. It is in another dimension.

Jesse did not have a body when she was in either place. The subconscious said she had not had many lives on Earth. She had mostly lived in these other dimensions, when she wasn't being a holding soul.

D: *That other part that we were talking to... is that the part that goes back and forth? Or is it a different thing?*
J: Yes. It's the one that goes back and forth. When it was coming here and just helping, it didn't stay for the entire lifetime.
D: *So is it here now?*
J: It's very hard to explain. You can't say when one part starts, the other one ends.
D: *Is it more or less merged with the original soul?*
J: Yes, but the thing is with energy, there are no ends and no beginnings. And, as you come to help those souls, on Earth in the bodies, it's the part of you that knows what they're going through. You all have to learn. You just know it, they're part of you.
D: *Jesse's real home is these beautiful places. Will she be*

581

allowed to return to that place someday?

J: Yes, but it's so hard to explain. Being there is nice, but you don't grow. You don't contribute. You go through different experiences to enrich everything around you. Not yourself, because you don't exist as a separate soul. It's very hard to explain.

This was a tedious session, because even the subconscious did not know how to explain this other portion of Jesse that we had been allowed to glimpse. Apparently it had so effectively merged with Jesse's personality that it didn't know where she left off and it began. But that would be a good thing. It probably could function more easily that way. Apparently a holding soul is a separate spirit that has agreed to come in and keep the body functioning while the original spirit goes to the other side for a while. This would be different from a walk-in because the original spirit planned to return and resume its duties. The holding soul would remain as long as it was needed, and then go on to its next assignment. In the meantime when it wasn't working (or stuck) it could travel the cosmos having all types of adventures. In the next chapter we will discuss soul facets or splinters. A holding soul could be one of these, but as Jesse said, it is very complicated to explain.

CHAPTER 29

THE MULTI-FACETED SOUL

In *Book One*, I wrote about the splintering of the soul. I was presented with the concept that we are part of a much larger soul, that can splinter or divide itself, and live many existences simultaneously. We are not aware of this because it would be too confusing, and our human minds would not be able to comprehend it. It goes along with the concept or theory presented in *Book One* about living in parallel realities at the same time, and that more realities are being constantly created as they continue to divide. I was told that our human minds will never be able to comprehend the totality of it all. It is not our brains, it is the human mind. Thus I am given examples or analogies which supply some information that we might be able to handle. I like to think of these as interesting mind exercises. They make us think, but if we don't want to believe them or study them further, we can just treat them as curiosities. When I am being given these analogies I always have the strong impression that they are only the tip of the iceberg or teasers. That the bulk of the information, or the rest of the iceberg, will forever remain hidden from us as long as we exist in a mortal body. Maybe someday we will understand. For now, we will have to be content with the fact that "they" consider we are ready to receive the bare essentials or fundamentals to help us expand the capacity of understanding in our minds.

During 2002, I received information about soul facets from opposite sides of the world through my therapy sessions. It may be only a matter of semantics and it may refer to the same thing as splintering, even though it is called by a different name. I will attempt to explore the concept and see if it is the same or two separate processes.

—◇—◇◇◇◇◇◇◇◇◇◇◇◇—◇—

The first session was done in Minneapolis in October, 2002 while I was there doing lectures for Gary Beckman of the Edge Expo. Michelle came to the private residence where I was staying to have a therapy session.

When she was in trance, she floated down from the cloud and found herself in strange surroundings, and in an even stranger body. It was so dark, it was difficult to see, but she was aware of a barren landscape. There was no vegetation, and the ground was brown dirt with a touch of orangish color. In many cases, when the subject sees surroundings that sound otherworldly, it's usually because they are. I have to keep asking questions and be prepared for any type of answer.

As Michelle became aware of her body, she discovered she was dressed in a jacket and pants made of a silver material similar to foil. "I'm looking at my hand. The skin is kind of a greenish color." I asked how many fingers she had. "There are three main ones that I use. The little finger is really small. I have thumbs, but I don't ever use the left one, because it doesn't work right. The thumb on the right hand works okay." Her body felt male, but she knew she was androgynous. She only had sparse strands of black hair.

Her attention shifted away from her body when she realized she was carrying some equipment on her back. "It's a little white package. Almost like a carrying case. I'm scanning the ground. I'm supposed to be looking for something. Hmm. I don't think you can plant anything here. The ground is so thin."

D: *Do you know what you're looking for?*
M: A place to plant food. I was told that it might be a good place, but I don't think it is. It looks so barren. I don't know if I'm in the right place. Not much growing. Just these little turquoise, jagged looking bushes. How can I describe it? Kind of rubbery looking. – It feels I'm a little

scared. I don't know what to do.

D: *Why are you scared?*

M: Maybe I'm not going to be able to make a place that was gradually going to feed people. I don't know if I can.

D: *Is that your job?*

M: Yes. And I said that I could. I think I overestimated. I feel I'm not doing what I thought I could.

D: *Why did you pick this place?*

M: I was given guidance to come here by the elders. And I told them that I could find the place. But I don't ... am I in the right place? Maybe I've lost my way. Maybe I'm not doing what I was supposed to. I feel that I'm lost.

D: *Is this the place where you live?*

M: (Emphatic) No! No, it's not. The place where I live is a different place.

D: *How did you get there?*

M: Mostly thoughts. I beam myself there.

D: *You didn't come in an object or anything?*

M: Not really, no.

D: *You're just able to instantly transport yourself there, you mean?* (Yes) *Did anyone else come with you?*

M: Yes. There's somebody else here. They're behind me watching. They're kind of angry. They feel the same as me. That we don't understand why we're here. We thought we had the coordinates right. I don't think it will grow food.

D: *Do you have to grow food for your people?*

M: My people are okay. But the family of all souls are ... we're all united. All of us. And there's some of the family that doesn't have enough food. And enough housing.

She became emotional and started to cry. It was hard to understand her.

M: There are some of our family that are hurting each other. (Crying) They don't give each other food. Some people have it and some people don't. (Big sighs.)

585

D: Is this a family that lives on the same place where you live?
M: No, they don't. But I know from the people.
D: But if this is not on the planet where you live, how do you know about them?
M: Because we travel to different places. (She was still emotional, but calming down.) There's supposed to be unity. That's what we want. Some of us know about it, and some of us don't. And we've all been involved in different parts of trying to help bring unity, so that we're all aware. So we can all realize our connection, and stop some of these insanity practices.
D: Where you live, you have unity, but you want to help the other planets?
M: Yes. I've seen two. One is the planet where they're not giving the food to those who need it. They need a different environment. There's too much crowding on some of these planets. And you foresee that the crowding is going to continue to a point where there really will be a problem. Where even if they wanted to share, they couldn't.
D: And what's the idea? To go to another planet and grow food?
M: (Big sigh) So we can have other places to bring the lessons to. It doesn't have to be on these planets only.
D: What would happen after you began to grow the food?
M: Then people could choose to be incarnated on these planets.
D: Then you're not going to physically move the ones from the crowded planets?
M: No. But I see what happens on these planets, and it makes me very sad. And I foresee being able to help alleviate some of this, by having other choices of where to go.
D: So you mean when they are reincarnated to work out their karma, they wouldn't have to go back to those crowded places? (Yes) But you're not going to try to help the ones that are already there?
M: No, we can't interfere.
D: If you can't move them, the only thing is to give them another place, another alternative. So it's your job to find a place where you can grow food, because people wouldn't incarnate there if there wasn't food or a way to live. (Yes.) How are you going to

586

manage that?

M: That's the problem. I don't know what to do. I will have to go back, and try to rework this. I don't know what happened here. First comes food, and this place doesn't seem to have what it was thought to have. There has to be a way to start the planting, and this doesn't seem to be a good environment. I may have made a mistake. I thought I had the coordinates.. And I don't think I paid enough attention. Numbers are very important. And shapes are very important.

D: *Is that what you mean by coordinates?*

M: Yes. Numbers and shapes can point me in the right direction. They can transport me. I keep getting the number sixty-two forty-four (6244).

Her body suddenly and unexpectedly jerked. She laughed, "I just *went* all of a sudden!"

D: *I know you jerked. You just went that quickly, by thinking of those numbers?*

M: Yes. I just went back to my planet where I belong. Before I know it, I'm there. (Laugh)

D: *So you have to have numbers and shapes to help you transport?* (Yes.) *What kind of shapes?*

M: There's one that I use most commonly that has a base, a straight line. And then it goes over into a bit of a point, that's shaped ... I can't even explain it in terms that are understandable. But it curves a little bit, almost like a candle point, I guess.

D: *Like a flame?*

M: (Emphatic) Yes! It goes up kind of like a triangle, but it's not quite that shape.

D: *Do you draw this shape?*

M: I think it with my mind. It's all intention based. And the intention allows you to do what you need to do. But I feel somehow I'm not getting something *right*. And it's confusing. Like I ended up some place where I shouldn't

587

have been. And I thought I had the coordinates down correctly.

D: *But you think about a shape, a design, and the number 6244, and it brings you back to where you're from?*

M: Yes. Up to the home base.

In Chapter 17, another alien being went to other planets and asteroids collecting soil samples. These were analyzed to see if the planet was capable of supporting life. The difference was that he traveled in a one man craft.

D: *And whenever you go again, you have to think of that design?*

M: It's a different number depending on where you want to go.

D: *Well, now you're back where you belong. What is that place like?*

M: It's a feeling of great peace and serenity. I felt *so* out of my comfort zone before. That energy didn't have harmony. It felt more tense. That's why I felt myself getting aggravated.

D: *What does this place, your home, look like?*

M: (Pause) It's hard to explain it in words.

D: *Is it physical, solid?*

M: It is. But it's not the same as many of the other planets. You can see it, but it doesn't have the density that the other planet did.

D: *Does it have buildings and cities?*

M: It's more of a feeling. More of a connectedness.

D: *In that place, do you consume food?* (No) (This was said as though she was surprised.) *What do you use to keep yourself alive?*

M: Light. The sun.

D: *How do you get the light into your body?*

M: From the sun. It makes up all. It's the smallest, smallest particle. Not even particle. It's a wave. Wave form. We all absorb it. It's there for us all.

D: *But when you were on the other planet, you were away from that.*

M: Yes. I had to *really* focus. Almost like walking in both worlds. It was very difficult.

588

D: *Can you be away from the light very long?*
M: No. No. Not very long.
D: *So you need it to keep you alive.*
M: Yes, I do. It is who I am.

This has been reported before in my work. Certain ETs live off of light and have devices onboard the spacecraft that generate the light they need. In *Legacy From the Stars*, the beings in the future who lived in the underground city would take light baths. All of these beings said the light that kept them alive, came from the Source.

D: *But you were describing a physical body on that other planet.*
M: Oh, yes. We need to take on forms to go to different places, so we can be there. To fit with the environment.
D: *How do you really look?*
M: It's hard to see me. Hmmm. Gosh, I can't explain it. It's more of a feeling than a look. It's a ... like words aren't needed.
D: *I just wanted to be sure that it was not the spirit side. Is this a different type of a light body?* (Yes.) *Well, are you going to go back to the elders and tell them that you didn't have the right coordinates?*
M: Yes. I can see him. He has – if you call it a "he" – a round head. He has a thin long neck, thin long arms. He shape-shifts. He started out that way, and now he looks more light. Depending on what the thoughts are, depending on what is going on, the form has some variation. I tell him what happened. He kind of laughed at me. He said that my pride was in the way, and I was so sure that I knew, that I forgot to get the details. He's not upset.
D: *What do you think? Is he right?*
M: Yes. I thought I knew what I was doing. It seemed like one of the usual journeys, but it wasn't. I was not prepared. Hmm. I'm trying to hear. (Pause) I landed too soon. I can't put it into words. It's like overshooting. I overshot

right over ....

D: *Overshot the coordinates?*

M: Yes. Some of these things I can't seem to explain. You have to be very precise. It's not only about the coordinates, the numbers. But it's the intention you use with the numbers.

D: *Are you going to try it again?*

M: No. He's saying that I became involved so much with what I wanted to happen, to help, that I lost sight of the plan, the mission. He says these things happen.

D: *What was the plan, the mission?*

M: To help find other alternative places to incarnate that would lessen the burden of a planet. I was supposed to observe, but I became so involved in the *plight* of the people that it interfered. There is a plan. The plan is more important. Not that the people and the beings aren't important. It's just that everything is temporary. And you have to remember to keep things in perspective. And I had a hard time.

D: *You're not supposed to get emotionally involved with the people?*

M: No, I'm supposed to keep the overall vision. And realize that we all choose these things for learning to grow. And I got caught up in the emotion. I lost the vision.

D: *Those people chose to be in that situation.*

M: I'm not trusting them, that they are doing what they need to. It's very complicated. It's a combination of trusting them, trusting the plan, but yet realizing that alternative things need to be developed.

D: *So that's not interference if you develop food on another planet for them to go to?*

M: No. But my getting hooked into the drama, the emotions hindered, so I couldn't implement the plan. I got hooked in.

D: *But it's hard not to get hooked in, isn't it?*

M: It is very hard, very hard.

D: *You can't be emotionless.*

M: I couldn't keep the overall vision. If you can keep the overall vision, then you can do it. I couldn't do it. It's too hard.

This happened in other cases, reported in *Legacy From the Stars*, where the entity from another star system was on Earth on an assignment, and they got too involved with the people. When this happened, they had to reincarnate on Earth instead of returning to their own planet. Somehow, they created karma.

D: *So has he decided not to let you go back?*

M: Yes, I wasn't able to do it. He thought that maybe I'd do better in a different position. That perhaps you can't go down and observe in that way. You needed to be separated.

D: *What other position does he want you to do?*

M: I'm being ... I need to ... I'm fading ... It's like something's happening, where I'm fading. I don't know what it is yet. It's not scary. I just can't keep attachment with myself. It's like I'm floating. I'm going somewhere else.

Her body suddenly jerked. She burst out laughing loudly. I couldn't understand her, because she was laughing.

M: It was a jerking motion. (Laughing loudly)

D: *Yes, I saw you jump. What happened?*

M: I think I go through some kind of a vacuum. (She thought this was funny.)

D: *What do you see? Where are you?*

M: It's the planning committee. Actually, that's not the right words, but for lack of better terms .... It's to be decided what I'm to be doing *now*. But it's hard to implement that part of the plan when you get emotionally involved. I didn't realize it would be hard.

D: *So they're looking at your record?*

M: Yeah, to see what would be good for me to do next. I get to decide too, but it takes a group, because we all work together. I'm being shown some things in the life I'm to be in.

D: *You're going to go to another life?*

591

M: Yes. They're showing me a life as Michelle. (Big sigh) It's going to be a hard one. I'm not real eager. He said that these experiences would help me, by understanding different segments of this life. If I can put it into words. I can feel it rather than see it. All these different experiences are needed so that I can more effectively help.

D: *Is this to be your first life as a human being on Earth?*

M: *This* part of me, yes. It's much more complicated. It reminds me of a diamond, and those different parts of the diamond. The different facets. This facet has never been here before. The other two facets have. I think that my soul has more than one part to it. The different parts are the different facets.

D: *Can one of the facets know about the other facets?*

M: (Surprised) Yes, they can! They will. They will take turns in this life. They won't be able to manage the whole thing by themselves. The first facet will be there up until age ten. The second facet will be there till age twenty-one. Then the third facet will be there for the remainder.

D: *Why does there have to be different facets for the different parts of the life?*

M: That's the only way this can be done successfully.

D: *It would be too difficult for one facet to go through. It wouldn't be able to?*

She suddenly began to cry emotionally. She didn't answer as she continued to cry harder. Sometimes it is better to let the person get the emotion out, so I allowed her to cry, and then gently tried to get her talking to me again.

D: *Are you going to agree to do it.* (Yes.) *Even though you can see it's going to be hard?* (Yes.) *Why are you going to agree to it then?*

M: (A big sigh. She was gaining control of herself.) They can help later. (She gave a big sigh.)

D: *At least you'll know what it's like going in. Nobody's making you do it.*

M: No. It's necessary.

D: *So, does the conscious body know when these different facets move in and out?*

M: No, not initially. We remain aware of this agreement, but not fully. This is the first time that we fully understood what we're going through.

D: *But this is not like a walk-in.*

M: It's different, because we are not separate. A walk-in is a separate soul. We're all part of the whole.

D: *You're all part of the same soul. But Michelle did say when she was about ten years old, she felt she died at that time.*

Michelle had a partial memory of something that happened at that age. Her mother died when Michelle was very young. Her aunt took over the role of mother while they lived with her grandmother. Both women were mentally disturbed and sadistic in their treatment of little Michelle. This was what caused much of her earlier problems that she had successfully blocked from her memory. The women belonged to a satanic group that held meetings in their home, although Michelle did not realize what was going on. She saw many things that her young mind suppressed. The incident that she never forgot was when she was put into some kind of a wooden box. She was suffocating, and she felt that she left her body and floated upward. She thought she died at that time, because the feelings were so intense. Obviously, she did not, yet no one in her family ever talked about what happened that night. For many years, she thought the events she half-remembered were only part of her sick imagination. No one in her family ever gave any indication that anything of this intensity had ever occurred. All memories, especially of rituals she had been personally involved in, were forced back into the subconscious. It was probably the mind's way of maintaining Michelle's sanity. This was one of the things she had asked to find out about. Was the incident with the box real, or just a child's sick imagination?

D: *What happened at that time? Did she actually leave the body?*

(Yes.) *Is it all right for her to know about it?*

M: Yes, it's time for her to know.

D: *Tell her what happened when she was ten.*

M: She was put in the box. Her family had a very secret life that was not to be talked about in *any* terms.

D: *Then she was correct about the glimpses she's had of that?* (Emphatic: Yes!) *They were very sick people, I guess you would say.*

M: *Very!* Very, very sick.

D: *This is why one facet could only stay until the age of ten?*

M: Yes! Otherwise, it would have been too hard. The soul couldn't have handled it.

D: *Did she die when they put her into that box?*

M: Not in the physical sense. She went through the tunnel of light, but she kept the cord connection to the body. This was the time to exchange information, and to gain an understanding of her Earth life to that point. The entry of the new facet needed to occur. (Big sigh) And the first facet was very tired. The first ten years were very hard.

D: *Then she exchanged information with the second facet so it understood what had been going on?*

M: Yes. Even though there had been an understanding, there had to be kind of an exchange energetically. So that the pain ... if the full impact of what happened went back to the body, it couldn't have made it, in the way that could have helped later.

D: *Is this why Michelle only has glimpses of those first years, because the memories remained with the first facet?*

M: (Emphatic: Yes!) When she remembered, it was more like watching a movie, even though there was sadness. There was more sadness for the first facet than for the people involved. (Softly) Oh, the poor girl.

D: *Then when she came back, was it easier for her to handle it as the second facet?* (Yes) *That's the only way she could have survived, I guess.*

M: The second half wasn't any easier.

D: *But then the second facet stayed till the age of twenty-one.* (Yes.)

What happened at the age of twenty-one?

M: She was just getting married to Jerry. They weren't that closely connected. It was a choice to end that pattern, more than a connection of the souls. It was a way to get out of the pattern of that connection with her aunt and grandmother. The exchange of the facets helped to re-pattern. Because ... I can't even put it into words. There wasn't the emotional link with Jerry. Even though it was hard and sad not to have the connection, the kind of marriage that was desired, it gave a time to be able to reflect. It really wasn't even necessary to be with *him.* That sounds strange, but it was like a resting period.

D: *He was just the instrument to break the pattern, and get her out of that situation.* (Yes.) *Then what happened at the age of twenty-one when the third facet came in?*

M: It was in the bedroom. I see myself lying on the bed. I remember the cars going by. I remember the sounds. I was really distraught. I didn't even know if I should marry Jerry. People told me that nobody knows for sure about getting married. I was very upset. I know I didn't fall asleep. It was more like a trance state. A floating sensation. So ... during the trance, I left. (Very soft. Hard to hear.) I feel like I'm going right now.

D: *You can just look at it. You don't have to experience it. But it had to be done in the trance state, you mean?*

M: For me, it was easier. There were so many secrets in that house I lived in. My aunt and others knew what was really going on, but they weren't allowed to tell me. They thought it was better if I didn't remember. But I always knew something was not right. I know now, they were covering it up, trying to brush it away.

D: *The third facet exchanged or joined, or whatever it did, during the trance state?* (Yes.) *But it also exchanged memories?*

M: Yes. It took the memories, but it left a lot of pain. Some of the pain remained, because that was part of the process of learning how to clear.

D: *So it couldn't take everything.*

M: No, the personality would have split off and shattered.

D: *Is that possible to do that?*

M: To split off and shatter? Yes! They would call it multiple personality. It would have been too hard for them to help me. It would have been too hard for the guides to come through if I had multiple personalities. I had to be much more clear.

D: *So this is why the exchange took place, to give you more strength to handle what was going to come after that. (Yes.) And it had to exchange memories, but retain some of the feelings, because otherwise, it wouldn't make sense?*

M: Right!

D: *You can't take everything away, not at that age anyway.*

M: No, that's right.

D: *Then whenever Michelle woke up, did she feel any different?*

M: Yes. I felt, "Why am I marrying this guy?" (Laugh) But I did anyway.

D: *Did you feel like a different person?*

M: Yes! I did! I knew it was wrong for me right then and there. But I was confused.

D: *Then the third facet is the one that has remained. (Yes) And will remain? (Yes) It's more stable than the others, and can handle more trauma.*

M: It looks to connect more to the knowledge to help clear.

D: *You said before she came into this life, there were two facets, two parts of her, that had had Earth lives.*

M: Yes. Those were facets one and two.

D: *And the third is the one that has had no past lives? (Right) It's the one that came more directly from the light being. (Yes) So whenever she has remembered past lives, they are from the other two facets. (Yes) This one is more pure, if that's the right word. More direct?*

M: Yes, it is able to access more direct knowledge.

D: *This is why she's able to do the work she does with energy?*

Michelle had recently begun to do healing by using energy

through hands-on methods.

M: Yes. It came to do that to help people. She helps people see the problem. You can't do the healing for them, so she's just a tool. She's able to direct a lot of light to help their body remember the union they once had a millennium ago, so they can reconnect with it. She's not supposed to do all the healing, because it's a free will planet; they have to agree to it. And she wants them to be the master of their own destiny. They need to become their own masters; their own healers. We need people to be awakened, and remember. So she helps them remember, and helps them lift off the pain, so they can move back in their light.

D: *What did you mean when you said, people had forgotten when they split off a millennia ago?*

M: We're all one big family. All of us are equal in light.

A strange phenomenon occurred here that was picked up by the tape recorder. A loud electrical distortion like a steady static. It did not fluctuate like static, just a steady electrical interference. It lasted ten seconds, and knocked all the sound off the tape. It stopped as suddenly as it began. I was unaware of anything unusual happening, but the tape recorder picked it up. I continued the transcription after the sound stopped.

M: ... they even believe they're bad. They have been in the physical for so long they forget about their light. They've indoctrinated into something that is not true.

D: *This is why sometimes they think they're bad?*

M: Yes. She reminds them that they are not the *experience*, but these are just experiences they are having to help them learn.

D: *If they learn something, that's the important thing.* (Yes) *But why did we all split millennia ago, if we are part of the same family?*

M: Ah, the scene was at the very beginning of this work today, and I didn't understand it, so I just kind of blocked it out.

The way it's being shown, I'm sure it's symbolic, because I need to understand it. There is this ball of light, and all these people are dropping out of the ball of light. I was thinking, why are we parachuting down? But we split off to have these experiences. We're all jointly a part of this. We all are one.

D: *What are we going to do with these experiences eventually?*

M: Some day we will join back again. It'll be more satisfying. Let's see if I can get the feeling of it. It's really hard for me to translate this. I don't know if I can say the words. (Pause) It's kind of like people who have been in a war. You hear about people who have been in battle together. And they have a different sense of connection because they really helped each other, or they went through a lot together. And when it's all done, there is this bond that is never broken. We had a bond before, but we didn't have the experience.

D: *It's almost like a camaraderie, you mean?*

M: Yes, a closer bond. All of us are really important to the union. Each one of us. Each person has their own little part of it. Their soul will find it for them. You're connected to all parts of yourself. And I feel this reunion of all these people that I've missed. And all these souls that I've known before. Like we're all uniting and moving back up together.

Michelle's life had definitely been filled with challenges and continued to be. She thought she never wanted to have children, yet she suddenly decided to adopt a baby girl. As the little girl grew, it became obvious something was wrong. She was now nine years old and had been diagnosed as having a bi-polar disorder in her brain. At times, she would have lucid moments, but the majority of the time she was violent and suicidal. Michelle loved her, but felt totally helpless. Her husband couldn't take the challenge and divorced her, leaving her to care for the girl by herself. Michelle's subconscious said this was a challenge she agreed to before coming in. She was shown all this during the reviewing time before the board of elders. She had agreed to learn difficult lessons during this life in order to understand how to be human. Michelle definitely did not take on an easy life this time. It is admirable that she is devoting time to use her abilities to heal others.

The concept of a multi-faceted soul came up again a month later on the other side of the world. As has been happening with me in my work, when I am presented with a concept that is new to me, I am usually given more information that expands upon the theory through another client. I find it fascinating that whoever is guiding my work decides which topic I am to be given at each stage of my growth. And they use the trance state of my clients to deliver the information. There can be no other explanation, because the client has no idea what I have worked on with other people. During each session, I am focused on the client and their problems, and there is no need to talk about other people's problems or sessions. The subject seems to be used merely as a vehicle to get the information through to me. Other people have said that I appear to draw the appropriate client to me that has the information I need. Whatever is occurring, it is not on a conscious, purposeful level.

This session was done in Australia when I was in Sydney to lecture for the Mind, Body, Spirit (MBS) Expo in November, 2002. I had just come from presenting at the Conscious Living Expo in Perth. I was given a comfortable two bedroom apartment instead of the usual hotel room. It overlooked Darling Harbour and had a very nice atmosphere, and was within walking distance of the Convention Center where the MBS Expo was held. As usual, I scheduled the clients from my long waiting list. I never know what their problems are, or reasons for requesting the session until they arrive.

Cathie was an attractive, intelligent woman in her forties. She had many questions, but one that most intrigued her was an incident that happened a few years before. She was going through a very traumatic time in her life, where everything was wrong, including the death of her husband. The final blow was when she discovered she had breast cancer. Chemotherapy and radiotherapy were zapping her strength and reducing her will to live. She was tired of living under the existing circumstances. She had had enough, and had decided to kill herself. Before she did this though, she wanted to see all her friends one last time. Her plans were made very carefully. She had a Christmas party at her house and invited everyone. No one knew the real reason for the party, and she told no one that it was being held for the express purpose of saying good-bye to them. Everyone had a wonderful time and enjoyed themselves, as did she. She had been able to successfully hide her real emotions, and no one suspected that when they left she fully intended to commit suicide. After the last guest had departed, she set about very deliberately with the rest of her plan. Instead, an extraordinary incident occurred that prevented it. She thought she was very successful at remaining emotionless. But after the last guest left, she started crying uncontrollably. She had every intention of leaving this unhappy life and going on to the other side. She had made her plans carefully as to the method of suicide, but she now felt totally drained emotionally and physically, and was unable to follow through. She decided it could all wait until the next day, and went to bed.

This part is from Cathie's notes: "I awoke at 3am. I lay on my back with my eyes closed and could see bright white light through my eyelids, but when I opened my eyes the room was in darkness. As I lay there wondering what was happening, I saw a light dive down and enter my body. It flew in through my feet and ran up to my head filling me with light. I still had my eyes closed but I could now see my body as light. At the same time, I also felt a wave of electricity or a strong current run through my body, again from my feet to my head."

The next morning she felt totally different. Everything seemed brand new and the desire to commit suicide and leave this world was totally gone. She did not know what happened except that her life changed totally that night. Also, the cancer went into remission so she did not need more of the painful treatments. She could only guess that maybe a walk-in experience had occurred. In my experience, normally the person is unaware of any exchange when it takes place. But maybe there was a reason for Cathie to be aware enough to know that something strange and unusual had occurred.

This was her main concern: to find out what happened that night. So instead of going into a past life, I took her back to the night of the party. I had her come down from the cloud on December 17, in the year 2000. I set the stage to make sure we had the appropriate day, "You're having this party with these very special friends."

She interrupted me with a surprise outburst, "I wasn't there."

D: *You weren't there?*
C: No. It wasn't me.
D: *Can you still tell me about that date?*
C: I can't see it.

I have never let that stop me from obtaining information, because I knew that the subconscious has the records of everything that has ever occurred to the person. I asked if it could supply the information, and Cathie suddenly broke down and began to cry uncontrollably. I knew that I had to get her to talk in order to remove her from the emotions. "Can you tell me why you're emotional?"

C: (Letting some words out between sobs.) Yes ... it was very big ... very big.
D: *What was very big?*
C: That day.
D: *But you had a nice party, didn't you, with all your friends?*
C: (Calming down. Still sobbing, but gaining control of herself.) Yeah ... it was a party. (Sobbing) It was sad. (Sobbing) It was so sad. (Sobbing) It was a sad party. Because ... it was the end. (Sobs) An ending party. (Sobs)

601

And it was a saying good-bye party. (Crying)
D: *Was Cathie emotional on that day?*
C: She was saying good-bye to ... to Lucinda. (Sobs)
D: *Who is Lucinda?*

Some of her words were blocked by sobs. I was trying to understand who she was talking about.

C: She was the soul that came in at birth ... and who ... struggled so *hard.* (Crying) And who was in so much *pain.* Because life was just so sad.

All of this was difficult to understand, because of the continuous crying and emotion.

D: *Why did she have to struggle?*
C: (She finally calmed down enough to be understood.) Ah! She took the hard road. She *always, always* took the hard road.
D: *But she chose that, didn't she?*
C: Yes, she did. She made it *so hard.* (Sobs) She didn't know any other way. She thought that was the only way. It was difficult for *her,* but she made it very hard for other people too. She didn't see that. She only saw her own pain. She didn't see what *pain* she caused other people. She caused her mother so much *pain.* She caused people in her life – Stephen, that she grew up with. They were kids together. And then they were sweethearts. And she dumped him, and she caused him so much *pain.* She was selfish. She just cared about herself. (A big sigh. At least the crying had stopped.)
D: *She didn't care that she was hurting other people?*
C: No. She did it to make herself feel good. She was selfish. Lucinda was very selfish. She wanted to go home, because she realized that she wasn't *getting* it. She thought this was a waste of time.
D: *Being in a body, you mean, in a life?*

C: (A revelation) Oh! Okay! So what happened was that someone else came in, called "Yanie". She came in to help her, and to instruct her. And Yanie was with her for the last month. And Yanie helped her to learn, because Yanie was higher, more informed. She didn't have any ego. And she helped Lucinda, so that Lucinda could leave. And could learn some things before she left.

This sounded similar to soul parts, except that Cathie assigned them names. Maybe this made it easier for her to understand and explain.

D: *But didn't Lucinda realize she was creating karma by the way she was treating people?*
C: No, she didn't know anything about that.
D: *She was just a very selfish soul.* (Yes) *Did Lucinda talk to Yanie before she came in?*
C: Lucinda and Yanie agreed that they would work together. Lucinda wanted to go home. And she created the cancer as a way to get out, to go home. And then she could see that she'd wasted her life. She'd wasted the opportunities in this body. And she *hated* that. *She hated that!* (Emotional again.) She realized that she had wasted all those years. She realized that she didn't get the lesson. (All said with emotion.) And so Yanie said that she would come in and work with Lucinda for a little while before she left, to help her learn some of the lessons. And then when she went back, she would have achieved something. And Yanie helped her to let go of a lot of fear. And Yanie helped her to be more balanced. And Yanie helped her to prepare to go.
D: *There wasn't any way that Lucinda could stay?*
C: She didn't want to.
D: *I figured once she began learning these things from Yanie ....*
C: No, because the deal was made. And Yanie wanted to come in for a while. And Lucinda agreed to that; that she would leave. And that was not a problem. She was okay about

honoring that promise.

D: *So Lucinda would be able to progress on the other side?* (Yes) *It seems as though she wasn't ready for a physical life.*

C: She was just not conscious. She was ego driven. And she was caught up in the physical, and the *pleasures* in the body. She was caught up in money and greed and ego and sex. Ah, and even addiction. Alcohol, even went with that.

D: *So she was experiencing all of the negative parts of being human.*

C: Yes. She didn't want to be here, and someone else wanted to come in. She agreed to do that. And the deal was that Yanie would work with her for her last month on Earth, to help her learn some things, so that she could move higher. And Lucinda agreed to leave in December. They set the date. It would be December, 2000.

D: *She thought she was saying good-bye to her friends, because she thought she was going to die with cancer.*

C: When she left, she knew the body wasn't going to die. Cathie *consciously* knew that it was time to say good-bye, but she didn't consciously know what was going on.

D: *That's why she had the party with all of her friends and relatives.* (Yeah, yeah.) *But then when Yanie came in, there wasn't any need for the body to have a disease, was there?*

C: No. Yanie came in. She was such a different energy. Yanie was one of the first people. The first energies on the Earth.

D: *She would be a very old energy, wouldn't she?*

C: Oh, yes. She was a pioneer. A group of them came, of an energetic force, onto the Earth. And they were what people thought was the god, Horus. They came as a shape. And then when they got here, they had to find bodies. And they did. They went off and found bodies. That was in the beginning. And she came back in the year 2000, because she needed to bring back that pioneering energy onto the planet. The Earth needed to have an injection of that same energy that came all that long, long time ago. And that's what Yanie brought in.

This was similar to Ingrid and the Isis energy returning to

Earth to help. (See Chapter 4.) Both did not have any other lives in between and had returned because of world events needing that energy at this time.

D: *Can you tell us what happened on that night when the exchange was made? That was one thing that Cathie wanted to find out.*
C: Yanie came in. She had been there for some months. And they had been braiding.
D: *What is braiding?*
C: Braiding is where ... it's like a plait. (Hand motions.)
D: *Intertwining?*
C: Yes. Where there are two souls, and they're working together. And sometimes, one side will take the lead role, and another time the other side does. So sometimes, Cathie felt like there was ego. Sometimes she was being Yanie. Sometimes she was being Lucinda. Then other days, she felt like she was this wonderful, spiritual being. And they were the days when Yanie was taking dominance. They worked together very well. It was like a dance. They danced together. Learning and teaching and studying. And it was a lovely time, because Lucinda felt she had a friend. Beautiful.
D: *A different kind of a friend.*
C: Yes. And she learnt so much.
D: *So, it is possible for two souls to inhabit the same body at the same time?*
C: Yes. But it was a big relief when Lucinda left.

Although, it was not two separate souls. It was parts of the same soul.

D: *Because it's difficult for two to occupy the same space?*
C: They were so different, yeah. And Yanie could then *shine*, and she could be herself.
D: *Can you explain what happened that night? Cathie said she had such a powerful feeling after she went to bed that night.*
C: Yes. The final dance occurred. That was Lucinda's night

605

with those friends. Yanie just stayed way back, just in the background. And Lucinda ... it's very funny. She felt very numb that night.

D: *You mean insensitive or what?*

C: Numb, like the feeling of not very much emotion. Numb, emotionally numb.

D: *Even though she was with her friends.*

C: Yes. Ah, she knew it was good-bye. And she needed to stay that way, because if she'd let the emotions rip, it would have alerted everybody. And there was no need to do that. They didn't know she was leaving. And they didn't need to know, because it was not meant to be a funeral. (Laugh) It was just meant to be a secret. She knew she was going, and nobody else needed to know that night.

D: *She intended to die, but it wasn't meant to be that way?*

C: No. She changed her mind, because Yanie wanted to come in. And she said it would be okay for Yanie to take the body. And that night, she said her own good-bye, and then she went to bed. And then at three o'clock in the morning, she and Yanie danced together their final dance. It was like a waltz. Waltzed around. And then Lucinda just left. She just went from here.

D: *Where did she go?*

C: (Crying) She went ... she joined her friends. (Sobs) The people. She went home. Such a relief. (Crying)

D: *And she was not judged for doing the improper thing?*

C: (Emotionally crying) She was *welcomed.* (Crying) I think that's so kind. They welcomed her back.

D: *They probably realized she was not ready when she entered the body in the first place.*

C: Yes, she chose a hard life. She got some credit for choosing a hard life.

D: *So, it didn't matter that she had created karma with these other people.*

C: Ah! She had to do that. (Pause as she tried to understand it.) That was balancing up the karma. Because — I'm getting that Stephen was — (Very shocked at what she was

606

seeing. Horrified moans.) Ohhh! Ohhh! Stephen, the boy that she knew, that she hurt so badly, he ... he had her *beheaded.*

D: *In another life?*

C: Oh, yeah! Oh! That was so cruel! (Sobbing)

D: *So, what she did was repaying the karma by hurting him.*

Cathie moaned loudly and became very emotional. What she was seeing was very upsetting. Later she remembered this scene, and said she saw his face very clearly. He was brimming with delight as he watched her being murdered. It made her recoil as she watched.

To our rational minds it appeared that she had created karma by hurting the young man, Stephen. But from the other side, the entire picture is available, and it became evident that there was much more to the situation. Stephen had created extreme negative karma in the other life by having her beheaded. So, it was supreme justice that she hurt him in the present lifetime. At least the payback was not as drastic as the cause.

D: *She also hurt her mother very badly too, didn't she?*

C: Yes. (Shocked) Oh! Her mother ... that was payback for karma in *this* life. Her mother's life. Her mother had been very one-eyed. And she behaved like her children were perfect. She hurt so many people that way, by being so dogmatic, and so judging. She thought her children were perfect. And it was Lucinda's job to show her that her children weren't perfect.

D: *Because Lucinda was definitely not perfect.*

C: No. Oh, that was the balancing. A lesson for her mother. Teaching her mother to be less judgmental. And less one-eyed. To open her up. And to help her to see through another eye. Not those two eyes that she sees with physically, but the other eye. (The third eye.)

D: *So what appeared on the surface to have been creating a lot of negative karma and picking a hard road, was actually for a reason. There was more behind it.* (Yes) *There usually is, but we can't see it when we're alive.* (Yes) *So then, Yanie took over the body.* (A big relieved sigh) *Cathie said she knew something happened that night.*

C: (A revelation) Oh! It was meant to be. She was meant to *know,* because she has to help people. (Crying again) She has to help people understand this. And if she hadn't been conscious – so many people have these experiences, and they're not conscious of them. She had to *know.* That was the job for this new facet. Cathie was to open this up. Like *you* are teaching people so much about the other side. And she has a job to teach people about *this,* about souls. About how this body isn't *owned.* It's a gift to the Earth. Each body is a gift to the universe. And the souls that come into these bodies, they have that *right.* We think we *are* the body. Our ego is tied up with the body. And we think we *are.* I *am* Cathie. Who is Cathie? Cathie is really many energies coming together to take this *life* to an unimaginable dimension. So this life can impact on so many other lives, to help people to consciously evolve. To help people to *embrace* this program where souls *can* come and go. And not be closed to it. And not be too selfish about owning the body. We don't *own* the body. The body is here to serve humanity. Gandhi didn't own that body. That body was just a vehicle. So many souls were involved in the work that Gandhi did. So many souls came and went from that body. And he *knew.* He welcomed it. Martin Luther King was another one. Not just one soul, but many souls bringing different talents, bringing new thinking. Taking that vehicle to higher levels of conformance and love. (Softly) He knew. He knew what he was here to do.

D: *But the conscious part of the person is not aware of what's going on, are they?*

C: Some people can be. Some people can open their minds to it. There needs to be a trigger to open the mind. And once that trigger has been fired, the mind can embrace all sorts of understandings. And that's Cathie's job. She fires the

608

shot that gets people thinking. And it gets people opening their mind.

We were told that not only had Cathie received a new facet of her soul to continue this life, but her body had also been changed into a *new* body. Apparently, the changes would not be visible from the outside to others.

C: The new Cathie is so different. The old Cathie was on an accelerated path. She took on a very difficult life. And the new people who have come in, have had to just work out that side of the karma for those lives. To let go of the stuff in the cells of the body. All the stuff that was trapped in there, was from the old souls. And the new ones that have come in, have helped release that from the cells of the body. And brought her into a lovely, beautiful balance. And harmony and love.

D: *So the new Cathie is not the same person that started out.*

C: So different. So very different. And it's taken several soul solaces to work with that life. To bring it to the level that it is now.

D: *But couldn't this just happen with the maturity of the person as they grow and learn their lessons?*

C: No, not this, no. Because that takes a long time. There are many people who live on the Earth who die and they haven't lived the lessons. And some people, as they mature, become more and more egocentric, and more and more *frightened.* There's so much *fear* on this planet. And they get older and they get more *frightened.* So, it cannot be said that it's normal for people to gain that wisdom as they get older. Many people don't gain the wisdom.

D: *Why couldn't the soul facet, Yanie, just remain?*

C: Oh, she wanted to. But it would have stunted the growth.

D: *Why is that? She was a very advanced soul.*

C: (A revelation) Oh! The job was limited to what she was doing. Bringing in the new energy. Holding the space for the program to be worked out. She was a "holding" soul.

A transition soul. And at that time, the program was still being developed. And Yanie can return, if she wants to. She can be part of this program. But if she'd started then, *this* program could not have been brought in. This is a very high level program of accelerated growth. It's almost instantaneous, this growth. And this program is taking these people way beyond what we'd envisioned originally.

This concept of the soul being composed of many facets surfaced again during another session. I will only include the pertinent part here. I was having the session at a Walk-In conference in Las Vegas. I was speaking to the subconscious about Lucy's questions.

D: *She wanted to know if she is a walk-in in the present life as Lucy? Or is it important for her to know? You decide.*

She naturally was interested in this because she was on the board of the organization which studies walk-ins and puts on these conferences.

L: We wouldn't call it a walk-in. We would say she is more of a space being who has many different incarnations within one incarnation. The human equivalent and concept may be "walk-in". That is not a terminology we would use. We would say that she has visitations over the course of her life span by many different soul beings within her own soul. For she is of a spatial orientation. Many space beings are within her grasp.

D: *Would this be like I've been told, of soul splinters?*

L: It's bigger than splinters. We like to think of them more as facets, or segment sections. As you think of the configuration of a house or a building, there are several rooms. And each of those rooms is part of the whole house.

610

And that is how her soul is arranged. And each of these rooms or soul segments or facets carries with it different memories and different parallel spatial relationships. And that is why she has these various experiences.

D: *So it's not an exchange of souls as we understand a walk-in to be.*

L: It is an exchange of souls where one may leave and the other one may never show up again. But it is not through the death process. It is not that the first soul is sequestered or delivered to a completely different entity. It is lying in dormancy, but will not be used again.

D: *We think of a walk-in as the original soul leaving and being replaced by one that will take over the work.*

L: That is also a concept. This concept I am giving you is perhaps more complex. For this soul entity has access to many different soul structures. She has access to thirteen. And they are all within her soul. These are not alien, disharmonious characters.

From another subject:

D: *She had another question that was rather strange to her. I understand it, but I want to see what you are going to say. She says she has the feeling, from time to time, like she is interacting with two different women in New York. Is that real?* (Yes.) *What's going on at those times?*

Linda: They're alternate souls. Pieces of her living and doing her work in other dimensions.

D: *That's what I thought because I've been told this in my work. It's a little complicated for some people to understand. As though another part of her went in another direction. Is that what you mean?*

L: We must heal on all levels, in all dimensions, to achieve what we need to achieve. We have help. Those are pieces of her. There are many more.

D: *They created a different life than the life she is living.* (Yes.)

And there are times when she has contact with them.

L: Yes. She goes there to readjust them.

D: *They probably don't know about her, anymore than she knows about them really.*

L: They are unaware of her at all times. She watches them. They have work to do.

D: *I have just been given this concept in the last year; about the splitting off that we do.*

L: You have many parts.

D: *Everyone does, don't they?* (Yes.) *But we're not aware of them and that's the way it's supposed to be.*

L: No. You will all come together soon.

D: *Then we'll all know what's really happening?*

L: Yes. We all become one. And time will move forward at that time.

D: *I've heard about the raising of the consciousness and the changes in vibration and energy. Is that what you mean?*

L: Yes. We will all come forward together as one planet when our consciousness becomes one. The negative forces will be left behind. We will take with us those that can come. It is our duty to raise the conscious level of everyone we encounter. And heal them. You know, you have seen it many, many times. It is the consciousness of the people to move into a positive flame. They are aligning. They are becoming aware of each other in the different dimensions. They will wake up and become one, and go forward together. It will be as it is to be. It will leave the negative behind. And create their new lives as one.

D: *In the book I'm working on now, I am exploring the concept that we, as humans, are not one individual soul or spirit, but that we are splinters?*

Ann: Correct.

D: *Can you clarify that for me?*

A: Yes. You and many others are from different universes. There are several different God sources, that is actually considered one source. Each one of these universes has its own individual God source, to the understanding of your levels in the universes. Each one of these sources is broken down into other individual sources, which always go back to a main source. Each one of you create your own individual sources within yourself, because you so choose to. To understand your heights in awarenesses that you need to have on this physical level. This vibration level is very limited for you. And because you have chosen this, you have actually made a conscious decision to live as a separate source, even though you are still connected by a strand to the main source.

D: *How do we perceive this main source? This God source?*

A: It is always within you. I will tell you the easiest way for your understanding. To tap into it use the frontal lobe of your head. What you call a "forehead". In this forehead, you have an element, and you secrete a fluid in this element. And when you secrete this fluid, it is transferred throughout the body, which will energize the rest of your body to a higher level so you can tap into your source. This is where the source remains. It is in the frontal lobe of your head. That is where your connection, your string, as you call a "cord" is connected.

D: *What we consider the third eye?* (Yes). *But I was trying to understand this splintering, because I am working with people who say they have splinters of themselves everywhere.*

A: Yes, that's true. This is part of the thought process. You are allowed to create a reality. And in this reality, you can create other. And in that other, you can create new energy source, which is all from the same, what you call "God source".

D: *That's why it's so hard for us to understand, because we are so focused ....*

A: (Interrupted) It is not difficult. There will always be those who have more of a natural grasp of these concepts. They are simply more readily able to translate. You need only to have access to these individuals to translate these concepts into an understandable form. If you ask for these individuals to appear in your life, they will, as naturally as a breeze.

D: *That was what I was told, that we have soul splinters everywhere, but we're not aware of them.*

A: We are twins of each other.

D: *Like parts of each other in this way?*

A: You are. You come from one source. What would make you think that you are not of the same?

D: *Our human perspective that we are individuals?* (Chuckle)

A: Very limited.

D: *We are* very *limited.*

A: You choose to be. It is not a bad thing that you are limited. You have chosen to be so, because there are lessons that you go through. We understand this. As we speak through this body now, we understand this individual. It does the same. We know these things. It is okay.

D: *Yes, because this is the only way humans can perceive. And much of this is beyond the normal human being's concepts.*

A: Correct.

This life may be compared to playing one instrument in a large orchestra. Naturally you cannot play all the instruments at the same time. You can only focus on your part of the beautiful symphony, although the entire orchestra and all the music comprises the totality of who you really are.

At my lectures, I have often been asked about the difference between soul and spirit. "Are they the same thing? Are the words interchangeable? Are they referring to two separate things?" I did not have an adequate answer at first, because the

614

questions caught me off guard. At that time, I assumed they were the same thing. Just two different words referring to the life force that enters the body at birth and departs at its physical death. I assumed it is the part of us that is eternal from the moment it was created by God. And that it is the most constant part of us even though it goes from body to body during the cycle of reincarnation and changes as it gathers more information and repays karma. In my early writings, I wrote of it from the viewpoint that the two words were interchangeable, referring to the same thing, and that it was only semantics whether you wanted to use one word or the other.

Now, my learning and understanding is increasing and broadening, and I can look at this question from a different viewpoint. In my work, I have been told that when God brought all the souls into creation, it was similar to the Big Bang theory. We shot out as tiny sparks of light. Some of these sparks became human souls, some became galaxies, planets, moons and asteroids. Creation had begun and has continued ever since, ever expanding. Many of my subjects have seen themselves as individual sparks or balls of light when they are asked where they came from and how they began. Whatever body they find themselves in during their countless lifetimes on this planet and many others, is only a suit of clothes. Trappings to serve the purpose and to get the job done. I always say, "You are not a body! You *have* a body!" We tend to overlook this, because we get so attached to it. But just like a suit of clothes, eventually it will wear out and have to be thrown away. The "real" you is that little spark of light. I now can see that this is equivalent to the "spirit", because it goes from body to body. The spirit is the individualized representation of the soul in an embodiment. Therefore, it has limitations. It is constrained and separated from the larger "soul". It is our focus while in physical body, and we are shut off from the tremendous wisdom of our larger self. It has to be that way, or we couldn't exist here. We would be absolutely incapable of surviving if we realized there is more, and that we are shut off from that glorious larger self.

I have found cases (one reported in *Book One*) where the

subject wanted to go back to where they felt the most love, where they felt at home, where they instinctively had a great longing to be. When they went to this place it was a surprise to me. It was not the spirit side where we go after the physical death. It was far greater and expansive. They went to a beautiful, warm and comforting bright light. This was "home". They said when they were there, there was a wonderful feeling of togetherness, of being part of a whole, and they never wanted to leave again. This was called "God", for want of a better definition. It has also been called the "great central Sun" from which all life sprang. The subject always experiences great joy when they are once again reunited with the whole, even if it is only for the short time during the session. When they were made to go out away from the Source to learn lessons and gain knowledge, they felt a great loss, a separation that was almost unbearable. Where there had been only the One, now they were separate. This is what each of us is secretly wanting to return to, even though we don't understand it on a conscious level. But according to the information I have discovered, we cannot return and reunite with God until we have completed all of our lessons and gained all the knowledge we are capable of. Then, it is our destiny to return and share all we have learned with God. In this sense, we are literally cells in the body of God.

To try to explain the definitions of soul and spirit a little further, I think it can be seen as a stepping-down system. Where there is God, the One, the All That Is, the omnipotent, the Source, the Creator, it splits off into another component. Group souls, Oversouls, a larger composite of energies. Alive, but experiencing life in a way foreign to our way of thinking. It contains so much energy in its totality that it would be impossible for it to be contained in a body. In *Book One*, it was said that if the total energy of an individual tried to come into a room and converse with us, everything in the house would be destroyed. The power and energy is immense. Thus the soul is a combination of countless individual spirits, which are all "you". We are as much a part of this larger "soul" as we are of the embodiment of God. There are also several groupings of souls, to complicate our thinking further.

Then it splits again and becomes individual spirits. This is the smaller piece that we are experiencing at the present time. The part that we are focused on and have given personality. This is the part that goes to the spirit realm at the time of the death of the physical body. It apparently remains individualized until it has gained enough knowledge to incorporate back into the Oversoul. All of this is too much for most of our human minds to comprehend, and we are content to think this one existence is all there is. This is why we give simplified explanations to the unexplainable.

From the information in this chapter, it appears that in cases of emergency, the Oversoul will splinter or send out facets of itself, and have other soul parts exchange places. From as much as we can understand, it is a loving and caring arrangement, and the individual is never given more than it can handle, or more than it has agreed to attempt to handle in any one lifetime. At least these concepts are good thinking exercises, whether we will ever fully understand them or not. These concepts are some that I would never have thought about if they hadn't been presented to me through several of my subjects. Apparently "they" think we are ready to handle the deeper meanings of life.

So once again, there is God, there are the various Oversouls, the smaller soul composites, and the individual spirits.

617

CHAPTER 30

THE NEW EARTH

All of our lives when we attended church, we heard the following verses from the Bible: *"I saw a new heaven and a new earth; for the first heaven and the first earth were passed away ... And I John saw the holy city, new Jerusalem, coming down from God out of heavens ... And I heard a great voice out of heaven saying, Behold, the tabernacle of God is with men, and he will dwell with them, and they shall be his people, and God himself shall be with them, and be their God. And God shall wipe away all tears from their eyes, and there shall be no more death, neither sorrow, nor crying, neither shall there be any more pain: for the former things are passed away. ... Behold, I make all things new. And he said unto me, Write: for these words are true and faithful. ... And the (new) city had no need of the sun, neither of the moon, to shine in it: for the glory of God did lighten it ... And there shall in no wise enter into it any thing that defileth, neither whatsoever, worketh abomination, or maketh a lie. ... And there shall be no night there; and they need no candle, neither light of the sun; for the Lord God giveth them light; and they shall reign for ever and ever."* (Rev. 21-22)

Many different explanations have been offered by the Church since the writing of the Bible. But the book of Revelation has remained enigmatic, *until now.* The explanations in this book that have been brought forth through many people while in deep trance, seem to hold the answers. They have described the Kingdom of God, many times, as a place of light where they have great joy being reunited with the Creator, the Source. At that time, every one of them have become beings of light, and there is no desire to return to the earthly physical form. This explains some of the meanings of the verses, but what about the prophecy of the New *Earth?* Again, the answer seems to come through many of my subjects during my sessions. It was only as I was putting the book together that the similarity to the Bible became apparent. We are all talking about the same thing. John, who wrote the book of

Revelation, put his vision in the words that he could find in his time period and his vocabulary. It is the same today. My subjects had to use the terminology they were familiar with. I know therefore, that we are only seeing a small portion of the total picture of the new world that is coming, but it was the best they could do. It at least gives us a glimpse of this wonderful and perfect place.

During my work, I have heard much about everything being composed of energy and the shape and form is only determined by the frequency and vibration of each particular thing. Energy never dies, it only changes form. I have been told that the Earth itself is changing its vibration and frequency, and it is preparing to raise itself into a new dimension. There are countless dimensions surrounding us all the time. We cannot see them because as the vibration speeds up, they are invisible to our eyes, but they still exist, nonetheless. In my book *The Custodians,* I explained how the extraterrestrials utilize this and travel by raising and lowering the vibrations of their craft. Sometimes, we also go to other dimensions and return and are not aware of this. This was written about in *The Legend of Starcrash.* So, I have touched on the subject over the years, but I did not understand the full meaning of it until I began receiving more and more information about it. "They" want us to know more about it because it is coming soon. And it will be a momentous event. Of course, even in the Bible, it was described as coming "soon". But now we can see and feel the effects all around us as the world prepares to shift into a new dimension.

"They" said that we will notice the physical effects more as the frequencies and vibrations increase. Many of us can sense on another level of our being that something is happening. With the changes subtly going on around us, our physical bodies must also change in order to adjust. Some of these physical symptoms are unpleasant and cause concern. "You will see and notice that as the frequency of the planet continues to raise in terms of its vibration, you will have less difficulty with symptoms of energy blockages."

Throughout my work, my subjects are being told that they must change their diet in order to make the adjustment into the new world. Our bodies must become lighter, and this means the elimination of heavy foods. During the sessions, my clients are warned repeatedly to stop eating meats, mainly because of the additives and chemicals that are being fed to the animals. These are being transferred to our bodies and remain deposited in the organs for a long time. It is very difficult to eliminate these toxins from our body. We were especially cautioned against eating animal protein, and fried foods which act as an irritant to the body. "These act as aggravators to your system after many years of misuse. We do not mean to be judgmental, but the body is built for a certain type of vehicular traffic. The body cannot ascend in frequency to higher dimensional realms if the density and the toxins are polluting the environment of the human body." We were told to avoid beef and pork especially, because of the additives that are fed to the animals. Of course, if you are lucky enough to find organic meats that do not contain toxins, that would be safe, in moderation. They said chicken was better, and fish, but the best of all was "live" vegetables. This means those that are eaten raw rather than cooked. We were also cautioned about the elimination of sugar, and the consumption of more pure, bottled water and fruit juices that contain no sugar. Eventually, as the frequency and vibration continues to increase, we will adapt to a liquid diet. The body must become lighter in order to make the ascension. "As the energies on the planet continue to become heightened and more rarified, your body needs to shift with it." Of course, none of this is new. We have been told for many years about these facts of nutrition. But it seems to be necessary now to pay extra attention to our diet as everything is beginning to change.

In 2001 "they" stepped in to drastically get my attention and cause me to change my diet and lifestyle. During the sessions they would literally yell at me to get their message across. In 2001, I had problems with dehydration while in Florida and was experiencing unpleasant physical effects. "They" reprimanded me and made me give up my standard drink, "Pepsi" which I had indulged in for many years. They completely turned my eating and drinking habits around, and changed my diet for the better. By 2002, I had cleared a great deal of the toxins from my system and I was noticing the difference. It took several more months before I was "detoxified", so to speak. Every time they get a chance, they let me know that they are still monitoring me and I am scolded when they see me slipping back into old habits. During a session in England they said, "To understand the new energies in which you will be working, the body is being taught how to deal with this. One must never forget that there are energies out there that are not going to work with you. At this point, maybe these energies are not to be thrown away and pushed away from you. Because they are not familiar to you, you are thinking, 'They are not correct.' They are to be drawn into you and asked, 'What are they?' In fact, they are new energies. Maybe they are readjusting your body, and in so doing, they are removing toxins. Your kidneys especially will be working with a nonaccepted energy of the past. Just accept that the cleansing process is and will occur."

I was then given a process to energize the water we drink, to help in the detoxification process. "Water, in the basis of seventy percent of yourself, and seventy percent of the planet, is so far beyond importance, it is unbelievable. So therefore the resonance of the water you bring into your body is so very important. When you drink water energize it with the knowledge you have. Send that knowledge. Spiral it in. Imagine the water spiraling, creating a vortex, in a both clockwise and anticlockwise direction. Creating the positive and negative key. You must move it out of balance. Imagine an energy entering the water and spiraling and creating a vortex. That is all it has to do. The thought will then energize the water. That will then reintroduce life force back into the water, which is the lifeforce acceptance of the planet. All fluid on this planet, whether it is rock or whether it is fluid liquid, is liquid in a slower or faster motion. Everything has the resonance and memory of what it is. Humanity has lost the resonance and memory of what it is, but water can reenergize. Man's human thought format processes back into and helps work with its resonance. You must bear in mind that this energization of a bottle of water may only last a few hours. You may need to reintroduce it. So the formula may be, before you drink any liquid, do the same process. You can also do the same with food. Food simply being liquid in a slower motion. This will help with the body. This will also help clarify and create a place called "clarity" within your mind thought format, because you have started losing some of the clarity. This clarity will come back."

From an email sent to me from an unknown source:
Time is actually speeding up (or collapsing). For thousands of years the Schumann Resonance or pulse (heartbeat) of Earth has been 7.83 cycles per second. The military have used this as a very reliable reference. However, since 1980 this resonance has been slowly rising. It is now over 12 cycles per second! This means there is the equivalent of less than 16 hours per day instead of the old 24 hours.

One of the indications that the frequency and vibration is occurring, is the speeding up and shortening of time.

Subject: Starting in 2003, there will be an influx of energy that is going to really propel the Earth. There is going to be a greater schism between the group of people that are going to be staying behind, and the people that are going forward. The outcome will be a higher vibrational increase in Earth. This is affecting the whole universe. This is not just the Earth. This is galactic.

More information about how our bodies and the entire world will go through the dimensional shift process, and it will be undetected by those around who do not make the shift or change:
"Our bodies and everything around us are now increasing their vibratory rate and adjusting to a new frequency. Every cell of the body begins to vibrate at such a fast rate that it turns into light. When this begins, the temperature of the body increases and the body starts to glow with light. When every cell is vibrating at a very high rate, you will disappear from normal vision and move into a higher dimensional reality. This is because the body has moved in vibration beyond the third dimension and is now vibrating on a much higher dimensional level. This then means

that you will not go through the death process, as you will then have a Light Body. Aging will not exist for you, and you will have stepped into the next dimensional reality. You can then access the next stage of spiritual evolution."

"They" have emphasized that this has happened down through time to certain individuals and small groups of people. But what makes it unique now, is that it will be the first time that an entire planet will make the shift into another dimension. This will be the new Earth and the new world. This is described in the Bible as the new heaven and the new Earth. The others who are not ready, will be left behind (just as it says in the Bible) to continue to live out their karma. They will not even be aware that anything has happened. Those who have not become enlightened, will have to return to another, denser planet that is still involved with negativity, to work out their remaining karma. They will not be allowed to come to the "new Earth", because their vibration will not match.

A few years ago, I was on a panel at a conference with Annie Kirkwood, the author of *Mary's Message to the World*. She told about a vision she had that seems to portray the evolution of the New Earth. She saw the Earth as it is viewed from outerspace. Then it started looking like two Earths, one superimposed of the other. There were little lines of flashing lights going between both Earths. Then as she watched, she saw it begin to pull apart; the way a cell does when it is dividing to produce another cell. One Earth went off in one direction and the other one went in the other direction. On the one Earth she and the others were exclaiming , "Yes, yes, it really happened! We did it!" And on the other Earth she heard her sisiter's voice, "That girl was so crazy! She was out there telling everybody all these crazy things and nothing happened! She just died!" So it appears that when the final event occurs, there will be some people that will not even be aware that anything has occurred. This will be the separation of those who go on with the New Earth and those who are left behind on the Old Earth which will still be steeped in negativity.

After a lecture where I told the audience about this vision, I walked off the stage and was surrounded by people as I went to the table to sign books. A man pushed his way through and asked to speak to me. With a serious face he said, "Something very unusual just happened to me." He paused and hesitated, not knowing how he would be received. "You have to know that I am an engineer, very down-to-earth, and these kind of things don't happen to me. When you were describing the vision of the two Earths splitting in two, suddenly the auditorium disappeared and I found myself in outer space. As I watched, I saw it happen, just the way you described it. I saw the two Earths split, and the new one was superimposed over the old one." You could tell he was very shaken. He said he would go home and try to reproduce on the computer what he had seen. A week later he emailed us the picture, and we have printed it here. It is much more beautiful and vibrant in color, but it shows the new Earth glowing as it separates from the old one. He gave me permission to use the picture.

Created by Michael R. Taylor (MT)

Here is some of the information that came from various subjects about the New Earth:

The entity speaking through V. had a deep, gravelly voice:

D: *I've been getting so much information from different people, and they say the Earth is undergoing a transition. They say it will be like a raising into another, changing vibration.*

V: The whole idea is we have to get people to expand just a little bit. And we've got to get this level raised just a little bit. And when we do, we can make that change, and make it easier for them. It will be the ones that we can't get to change that are going to be left behind. It's going to be horrible. It's the ones that we can't get to change. We can't get them to see. We can't get them to love.

D: *Then the others, the ones that will change and love, they will go into another world? Another Earth?*

V: It's like it's going to expand into another dimension. Let me see how I can explain this to you. It's like a raising, if you can understand, like we're going to raise into a different vibration. We'll be able to see what's going on. We can't stop them. We can't help them anymore.

D: *Is it like a separation? Like two Earths, is that what you mean?*

V: Oh no, no. It's a changing of dimension. We're going to go from here to here. And those that can't change will be left behind.

D: *When we go into the other dimension, will it be like a physical Earth?*

V: It will be just like we are right now.

D: *That's what I meant by two Earths.*

V: Yes, yes. But they're not going to be aware of us. God help them, God help them. It's going to be so terrible for them.

D: *They won't know what has happened?*

V: No, they will know. That's the whole idea. They will know, but it's too late.

D: *But you said they'd be left behind, and they can't join the other world.*

V: No, it will be too late for them to change their vibrations.

They can't change it in a second. They have to change it over a period of time. We've been working on this for awhile. It has to seep in and work on your body, and it has to slowly change and raise your vibrations. And when it happens, it's going to be too late for them, but they will see it though. They will die, but they will see it and they will learn from that.

D: *That world will still exist, but it will be different?*

V: Not very well, no, not very well. There won't be much left in that world. Not much.

D: *Many people will die at that time?*

V: Yes. But I think much of their death will be painless. I think they will live just long enough to see what's happening. And I think God will spare them the horrible traumatic pain. I pray that's what will happen.

D: *But the others that do shift into the new vibration, with an identical physical world ....*

V: (Interrupted.) Yes, but some won't even be aware that they've made the change. Some will. Those that have been working towards it will know.

D: *Will they know about the people being left behind?*

V: I don't think so. There will be an awareness of a change that took place. I'm not sure if it's going to be a conscious awareness. Let me think about that. (Pause) We'll go into this dimension and we'll know. Some won't know though. They'll feel something. They'll feel a difference. Almost like a cleanness, a clearness. A crispness, a difference. I know what it is. They'll feel the difference. They'll feel the love.

D: *So, even if they haven't been working toward it, they will be carried along with it.*

V: Yes, because they're ready for it.

D: *And the other ones won't be ....*

V: They're not, they're not.

D: *So, they're left in the negativity? You said the whole world is going to be changed at that time.*

V: Yes, those that can go on, that can move into this, will move. And those that can't, won't. And it'll be horrible for them.

D: *And it will be like two worlds anyway.*

626

V: Yes, two worlds existing at the same time, but not always aware of each other.

D: *I know when you're in a different dimension, you're not always aware of the other one. But that's the message you want to get across is that we should spread this information about love while we still can, to bring as many as possible along.*

V: Love is the key. Because God is love. And love is God. And love is the supreme power. And that's what we need to feel in our lives. What we need to give to each other and feel for each other.

D: *Yes, love has always been the key. So, they're trying to tell as many people, so they can bring them along. That's what the urgency is.*

V: The urgency is that we've run out of time. Just be prepared. Uh, what? Tell her what?

She was listening to someone else. There were mumbling sounds, then the deep gravelly voice returned.

V: Tell you ... ready. Ready for the change coming soon. Soon now. Ready ... She's not a good vehicle. She's not done this before. I can't get my ideas through her to convey to you. I must work on it. Let's cleanse this vehicle. Oh, yes! Uh... there. That's better.

D: *What is it you want to tell me?*

V: Must help all mankind. Tell them of what is to come soon. Changes, dimensional shift. Those that can hear you will hear you. They'll be ready for that dimensional shift. (Her normal voice returned.) Those that can't, will not accept it anyway so, (Laugh) they'll think we're crazy. But the others, they may not know it but, it will touch a spark in them. When it happens, they'll be ready and they can make that shift. They may not know it's coming, but something inside will be ready for it and they'll be able to make it. It's those that don't know that it's coming, but if we tell them, it's inside them. Then when it happens, it'll come out and they'll be ready for it.

D: *Let me ask you one more question. Those of us that do make the shift, will we continue to live our lives the way we have?*

627

V: No, no, better. Different. Longer.

D: *Will we continue physical lives?*

V: Oh, physical in that dimension, yes. But physical in this dimension, no.

D: *But I mean, if we make the shift, will we ....*

V: (Interrupted) You mean, will you live or die?

D: *Will we continue lives as we know it?*

V: Yes, some will not even be aware. You see, that little thing that we plant in their head, will help them make the dimensional shift and they may not even know it. But they'll know there's destruction. They'll see destruction. They'll see what's taking place and they'll see the dead bodies, but they won't know that they've made that shift. They won't be aware of the fact that the reason they're not down there dead is because they made that shift and that change didn't affect them.

D: *You said something about the things that are put in the head. Do you mean the implants?*

V: No, no, no. I mean a seed, a thought. They don't know it consciously, but inside, that will help them. It's like a spark that, when the time comes, their mind would have accepted it subconsciously, already.

D: *But, as we make the shift, we will continue to live our lives. I have heard that we will live longer?*

V: Longer, better. Learn. Things will be so much better. People will learn more, after a little while. They'll know more. They'll become more aware of things. The way things are. They may not know when they make the shift, but then they'll learn about it. They'll realize after awhile what's happened.

D: *And the ones that are not ready will be left on the other Earth.*

V: Yes, they'll be gone.

D: *And many on both places won't even realize that something dramatic has occurred.*

V: The ones on the other place will. They'll be dead. But they'll know, because that's the lesson they've learned. Once they die, they will know. They will see the truth. And they will see what opportunity they missed, but they will learn from that.

D: *I have also been told that when they reincarnate, if they have negativity, karma, to repay, they will no longer come to Earth because the Earth will have changed so much.*

V: They will not be allowed to come back here until they've made the switch. They've made the change.

D: *I've heard they will go somewhere else to work out their karma, because they have missed the opportunity.*

V: Yes. Some will. And some may be given an opportunity to come back. But it will be awhile, a long, long while.

D: *But in the meantime, we will be going forward and learning new things and making progress in a whole new world.*

V: What a beautiful world. A world of light and peace. Where people can live together and love one another.

D: *But it will still be a physical world with our families and houses like we have now.*

V: Just a smarter world.

D: *(Laugh) That, I can understand.*

Another subject who was experiencing unexplained physical symptoms, described the new body in this way:

S: She is identifying more with her future body. It's not really settled in yet, but it's there. And this future body takes her essence, or portions of her. And merges it or pulls it up so she will get used to this future body.

D: *Will the body physically change?*

S: Some, yes. It will be stronger, and younger. This body that she is in now, it could be healed and redone, but she needs the future body. It will be lighter. More capable. She is feeling this now, her essence has been merging with this future body and pulled up.

D: *So this body she has now will be changed?*

S: It will be essentially left behind. It's going to be transformed and parts of it that aren't needed will be dropped away.

D: *So it's not like leaving one body and going into another.*

S: No. Gradually the newer body and the older body will be mostly merged together. But there will be certain parts of the older body that won't be necessary, so they will be left behind. It will just disintegrate.

It will probably be so gradual that we will not even notice the difference. Except for the physical symptoms that some are experiencing as the body makes the adjustments. I have been told that the older generation may be more aware that something is happening in the body. Yet it does no good to worry about it, since it is a natural process that is occurring now to everyone as part of the evolution of the new Earth.

This was part of a longer session in 2002 where the subject had a connection with extraterrestrials. They were supplying information about many things, including what they could do (or are allowed to do) to correct the damage mankind has done to the Earth.

P: Uh, they're moving me ... forward. They're moving my body. Oh, my god, I'm getting dizzy.

I gave calming suggestions so she would not have any physical effects. She calmed down and stabilized. The feeling of motion dissipated. This experience has also happened to other subjects I have worked with, when they are moved too quickly through time and space.

D: *What are they showing you now?*
P: All I see is light. It's just a brilliant explosion of light right now. There are different colors in the light. The planet is being bombarded with a special light and it contains different colors. And these different colors affect the consciousness of people in different ways, but it not only affects people. It affects plants and animals and rocks and

water and everything. It's a certain type of white light, and it has all types of colors in it. And it changes and moves and it permeates the very core of the planet. I see it's coming from the core of the planet. They shoot it down from, I guess, the ships, and it touches the core of the planet and it bounces out from the core and affects everything from an inward to an outward movement. If you were standing on the planet, you would feel the energies coming through your feet and coming out through the top of your head.

D: *The opposite of what it usually does.*

P: This is different. It's coming from the ships to the core of the planet and then it's bouncing back up. And it's affecting the whole planet. They don't want us to blow ourselves up.

D: *Is this something that is happening in 2002, or is it happening in the future?*

P: This is the future. They're going to do it! To correct the alignment in the planet to keep anything bad from happening. 2006.

D: *2006. Will we have gotten the planet more out of alignment by this time?*

P: Yes, yes. Oh, there are people on the planet and they're praying, but it's not enough because it's so messed up. It's going to get out of its orbit. And that will affect the rest of the cosmos. So by them directing these energies to the core of the planet, it's going to come back up, and that will correct the alignment. And when it corrects the alignment, it will also correct many other things on the planet. It will help the flooding, the droughts and things like that, that man has brought upon the planet. There's not going to be an annihilation of this planet. The council makes sure that it won't happen. The beings are down here on the planet watching, and they know what's going on and they know who's doing it and they can affect them. It's not that we *can't* intervene, we're not *allowed* to intervene.

D: *Because there's some things you can't do.*

P: That's right, but we can watch. And we know who's doing it.

D: *But whenever the planet gets to the point that man has damaged it so much, that's when you can help?*

631

P: That's when we're going to send these ... I see multi-colored lights. It's like multi-colored shafts of energy and they're being shot down into the core of the planet. And then they bounce back out and it affects the whole planet and it will keep the planet in alignment.

D: *Is this being done by many ships?*

P: It's a confederation. I see many. I see different levels or classifications of beings affecting the planet. We're involved in that. There are many, many beings.

D: *So it's a massive job.*

P: A confederation. Yes, yes.

D: *But isn't it dangerous to shoot things at the core of the planet. Hasn't something gone wrong before when that happened?*

I was thinking of the destruction of Atlantis. This was partially caused by scientists focusing the energy from the giant crystals downward to the center of the Earth. Too much energy was created, and contributed to the earthquakes and gigantic tidal waves.

P: This is not what you think. This is pure light energy. And the only effect it will have on the planet is good. It will not harm the planet.

D: *I was thinking of what they did in Atlantis.*

P: This is not the same thing. It's hard for me to explain. This is done on a soul level. It's like pure divine energy. It's not the energy in Atlantis. The energy in Atlantis was done through atomic power. This is energy that the divine has created that is done through light. It's not done through the separation through molecular structures. This is something we have created, and we send it from the Source. Anything that's from the Source is good and it's not going to harm the planet. It's going to do what we want it to do. And we've been allowed to do this. It is because the planet has caused this that we are taking this action. It's necessary.

D: *Isn't this interference?*

P: No! We cannot interfere with the people here. We can't come down and bully them and tell them what to do. But we can

632

bring our ships and we can point this energy at the core of the Earth. We can do things like this. This is actually on a soul level. So therefore, we are not interfering with the karmic structure of the people here. Everyone here has a karmic purpose, and we are not interfering with that. We're not allowed to. We don't do that.

D: *Do the people on Earth see this when it happens?*

P: They feel it. In other words, they'll go through the transformation. And they won't realize what's happened to them. Some of them will realize. Those who are sensitive will know that something has happened. But many on the planet will just go on in their normal lives, and they will be lifted up and they will be changed and the Earth will be changed. The rocks and the water, but they'll just go on existing, because we are not affecting the karmic pattern. We can't do that. We're doing this on a soul level, but it's not affecting their Earth lives as far as karmic patterns go. We're not bothering that.

D: *But the Earth has to get to a certain point before you're allowed to do this.*

P: 2006. It's getting bad. It's already very, very bad right now. If it's allowed to continue, the air will harm very many people. And the reason we're involved is, there are people in their physical embodiments breathing this atmosphere with all this pollution and it's changing their genetic heritage. We cannot let that happen and we *will* not let that happen! We gave people of this planet their genetic heritage. And now they have messed up their drinking water, their food, their planet. Everything here is polluted. Man has destroyed his genetic heritage and we're going to repair it, because they are not going to mess up our experiment! This is a divine experiment and they can't mess it up. We're going to change it.

To find out more about the grand experiment that mankind has been involved in since its beginning, see my books, *Keepers of the Garden* and *The Custodians*.

633

P: We have to do this. The whole planet was destroyed many times. You know about Atlantis; there have been many other explosions, floods. This is something that we can't allow to happen at this time, because it's going to affect the rest of the cosmos. And the Earth is coming a little more out of alignment. And we will be putting the planet, not only back in alignment, but we will also help cleanse and clear the genetic structure of everything and everyone on the planet. And this has been put forth, and it's been agreed upon, and it will be done. Because mankind has reached the point that it will not be cleaned up soon enough before it destroys the genetic makeup that we created.

D: *So it only has to get out of alignment just a little before it will affect the other ....*

P: It's already affected other ... not only civilizations in a physical realm that you know, but also on higher planes. That's why we're going to do this.

The various universes are so interwoven and interconnected that if the rotation or trajectory of one is disturbed, it affects all the others. In the extreme case, this could cause all the universes to collapse on themselves and disintegrate. This is one of the reasons for the monitoring of planet Earth by ETs. To detect any problems caused by our negative influences and alert the other galaxies and universes so countermeasures can be initiated. They have to know what the Earth is up to, so the rest of the universes, galaxies, and dimensions can protect themselves and survive.

D: *I thought if you were going to have a massive project like that on Earth, people would be able to see all these ships.*

P: Ohh, you typical Earthling! No, you can't see our ships. We're in different dimensions. There are many different vibrational rates. You won't even be able to see the light, but it's there. At some time, your scientists will be able to measure this type of energy. At some point, the scientists will be able to determine that we are in the atmosphere, and they'll see our ships. They will have machines and devices so

634

they can determine where our ships are. But they don't have that technology right now, because we've moved across the veil and we're in – shall we call it – an astral realm. It's a higher level than that, but it's a finer level. And your eyes can't see them, but in the future they will have machines that can see it.

D: *But they will know something is happening to the energy levels. That something is changing.*

P: It will change, and the people will change, but they're not going to be aware of what has happened. It's going to be a big event, but they're not going to be able to discern it on a physical level. On a soul level, they can tell. Subconscious level they'll know, but not on a conscious level, because you're thinking of a physical energy. This is not physical energy, this is energy from God. This is soul energy. And it operates within a different dimension than you're thinking. It's very different.

D: *So the people will feel it, but they won't see it. They'll just know that something is happening in their bodies.*

P: Some will know. Those that are sensitive will know that something has happened, but they won't know what. And that's what we want. We don't want to disrupt anything.

D: *How will this affect the human body?*

P: It will prevent the decay of the genetic material DNA within the body. Like I said, it's becoming damaged and we can't have that. We can't have a whole race of people damaged. The energy will change the DNA genetic structure of the humans so that it will be more perfect. That's what we really want. We want the humans on the planet to be in perfect harmony. Not only with themselves, but with us and the rest of the cosmos. They're not in that right now.

D: *So when the DNA structure is changed, how will the body be different?*

P: When the DNA is changed, the body will be what we wanted it to be many millennia ago. We tried this in Atlantis, it failed! The reason it failed was because the energies were used in a negative way by the beings in Atlantis. We tried to bring forth a more feminine energy back in the days of

Atlantis, which would raise up and cause a union between the divine male and divine female. It failed. Therefore, the planet Earth went through many, many, many thousands of years with women being subjugated and the feminine energies being suppressed. Now, this is the time that both will be equal. The male and female divine energies will join and this will make for a perfect being ... like Christ. Everyone here will realize they can be a perfect Christ, when these energies are in balance. The energies have not been in balance; they've been out of balance for thousands of years. That's why there are so many problems on the planet. So when the DNA structure is altered, the divine energies, the male/female, the yin and the yang, of the God energies can unite and there will be perfection upon the planet. Perfection within the bodies. And this planet will be something that we can show to the rest of the worlds, the rest of the cosmos. That this is our experiment, and this is what we have done and it has succeeded. The light has succeeded, because it will be perfect as we have wanted it to be for thousands of years. When we first came here, it was perfect. You've probably been told that. It was altered. You know the meteorite came, disease came. Everything was messed up. We're going to have it perfect again. And this is part of that alignment that we'll be doing to make it perfect again. And this is perfectly normal. – This is all part of genetics, but the reason that happened, was that humans have not been in balance. The divine energies have not been balanced within the psyche or even within the physical mind, but the psyche that comes into the body manifests physically. These have been out of alignment. This causes disease within the body. When the bacteria landed here on the meteorite, had the bodies at that time been in total perfect alignment, it wouldn't have mattered. The disease wouldn't have gotten in there. But the bodies had already begun to change when it hit, so there was nothing we could do.

She was referring to the same thing that was mentioned in my book *Keepers of the Garden,* which explains that disease was introduced to Earth and spoiled the grand experiment by a meteorite that struck the Earth when the fledging species were still developing. This caused a great deal of sorrow in the council in charge of developing life on Earth, because they knew their experiment of creating the perfect human being could not happen under these circumstances. They had to make the decision whether to stop the experiment and start over again, or allow the developing humans to continue, knowing that it would never be the perfect species it was intended to be. It was decided that so much time and effort had been expended in developing humans, that they should be allowed to continue. The hope was that maybe sometime in the future, the species could develop into the perfect human being with no disease. This is the main reason for the sampling and testing done by the ETs that people misinterpret as negative. They are concerned with the effects of pollutants in the air and chemical contamination of our food on the human body. And they are attempting to alter its effects.

The ET continued: "We didn't want to not do the experiment. We couldn't just throw the planet away. We couldn't just let all these lifeforms, all these souls be forever altered. We had to step in and we've been coming here for ages and ages. This is the culmination of many, many years of work. Millions of years. And it's coming very soon and we're pleased because mankind has reached the point to where this can be brought forth again upon the planet. As I said, we tried it back many, many thousands of years ago and it *failed*, but we expect it to succeed this time. It's already beginning to succeed. And we're very happy about that."

D: *Will all of the people of Earth experience this?*
P: As I said before, everyone will be affected. It's just that there are those who will be sensitive, who will pick up that it has been done. Some people will not realize on a conscious level that it's been done. It's been done on a soul level. If you were to put them in trance as you have this person now, they would know they have been affected, and they could explain

to you what it has done to their genetics. But on a conscious level, they haven't a clue. They don't know. And that's what we want.

D: *I was thinking of negative people (Murderers, rapists, beings of that sort.) Will they be affected in a different way?*

P: *Everyone* will be affected. They will know on a subconscious level what has happened. As the subconscious changes, and becomes aware of this, and is activated, yes.

D: *They still have karma.*

P: This will also be affected, because this planet in the future is not going to have karma. That is something that won't be allowed here. It will be a planet of Light and Peace and will be our grand experiment that succeeded.

D: *I've been told this is why many in the universe are watching.*

P: Yes, that's right. We're here to do that. And it will be safe.

In the fall of 2006 we received a call at our office from one of our readers asking, "Wasn't it mentioned in the book that something was supposed to happen in 2006?" When my daughter Julia remembered it and located this passage. Coincidentally (if anything is ever a coincidence) a few weeks later, we received several emails which were sent to people everywhere, alerting them to a cosmic event that was supposed to occur on October 17, 2006.

A cosmic trigger event is occurring on the 17th of October, 2006 beginning at approximately 10:17 am and continuing until 1:17am on the 18th. The peak time will be 5:10 pm on the 17th. An ultraviolet (UV) pulse beam radiating from higher dimensions will cross paths with the Earth on this day. The Earth will remain within this UV beam for approximately 17 hours of your time, and it will interpenetrate every electron of precious Life energy. This beam is radiant florescent in nature, blue/magenta in color. Although it resonates in this frequency band, it is above the color frequency spectrum of your universe, so it will not be seen.

However, due to the nature of your soul it will have an effect. The effect is that every thought and emotion will be amplified intensely one million-fold. Every thought, every emotion, every intent, every will, no matter if it is good, bad, ill, positive, negative, will be amplified one million times in strength. Since all matter manifest is due to your thoughts, i.e. what you focus on, this beam will accelerate these thoughts and solidify them at an accelerated rate, making them manifest a million times faster than they normally would. The ultraviolet Light will bathe every person on the planet. It has the potential of transforming the way Humanity thinks and feels. It will create a new, easier pathway for Earth's Ascension into the next dimension. This is the beginning of awesome influxes of Light that will move this planet up the Spiral of Evolution by quantum leaps and bounds.

So it appears that it has begun. When I had this session and wrote this part of the book I thought the beam would be coming from the extraterrestrials and being directed from spacecraft. Now it appears that the beam was sent from other dimensions which are invisible to us. I suspect the extraterrestrials are playing their part in all of this also, and helping with the directing of the beam. So apparently it has begun, and many of those who are aware of their bodies and the world around them, will notice the effects after that date.

Another portion of a session with Phil and Ann (reported in Chapter 22) might be speaking about the same type of power, or it might refer to something else.

Ann: There is an energy source that surrounds this planet. When you see the hue of what you call a "red" color, that is when you will know that the change has taken place.

D: *Where will the red color appear?*

A: It will be shooting beams from your planet to the other universal Suns. You will see the energy raises.

D: *Will we see this visibly?*

A: There is a pattern around your planet right now that is being reconstructed, which in fact will change the actual visual sight of the energy that radiates out from this planet. And it will be a color, what you call "red".

D: *Do you mean like the aurora borealis?*

A: Correct.

D: *And we will begin to see this shooting out into space in places where it does not normally appear?*

A: Correct. It will be the energy equivalent of arteries, such as in your own body. You see organs with many arteries carrying the blood, which sustains in one direction by bringing nutrients, and yet also by removing the byproducts. It is a two-way function in this manner. This planet has always had, in some certain functions, this effect. It is however, now, that the abilities of those of you on this planet will be able to physically perceive it. And also that the communication level itself will be enhanced to a higher degree. This is simply a manner in which you will then be able to participate more closely with the rest of the universe.

D: *So this glow you're talking about, means that the energy level of the planet is changing?*

A: Correct.

D: *And when we see it beginning to appear, we know that the changes are taking place?*

A: Correct. You have what you call "hot spots", which actually are radiating in your color scheme a blue.

D: *That's not visible to us?*

A: Yes, it is. It is on your Earth's crust. You will be able to see it bounce off the crust.

D: *You're not talking about the color of the sky?*

A: No. I'm talking about the energy field. From a distance, from your Hubble Space telescope, or from any vantage point which is above your atmosphere, it will be seen that there are these rays which are extending outward from your planet in many different directions. These will not be in the character of a diffused general glow, but will be seen to have a diameter and direction. It is a singular connection.

D: *Will this be similar to the way the Sun shoots out rays?*

A: No. Not in that sense, for in the Sun's emissions – we would not say "uniform" – it is however general. In that it is all over at the same time. This would be more along the lines of – perhaps if you could imagine what you would call a "disco ball", in your terminology, which emits singular beams of light in many different directions. They are individual beams, not a general overall broad structure of light.

D: *So they are now appearing blue from the Hubble telescope, and they will begin to appear red?*

A: There will be a transformation of several colors on your spectrum, which is very limited to your visible eye. You will be able to see the spectrum to the ultimate color of red within twenty-two years. It will be a sense of what you call a "hue".

D: *This is also the time span for the DNA activation. (Refer to Chapter 22)*

A: Correct. It is all together. It is simultaneous.

Harriet: What would happen to anyone perhaps walking through this emission on the planet? Would it do anything to their physical being?

A: You do now.

D: *So it's like going through dimensions. They say we go in and out of them and don't know it.*

A: You live in dimensions presently.

D: *And it's the same way as we go in and out of them, and are not aware of what's happening.*

More from another subject in Australia:

C: It's like a car. Imagine a car that has an old body. It's just the same old car you've been driving. And then you put a new engine in it. And suddenly that car begins to perform differently, even though it looks the same. And then you get another engine, and you replace it. And the car keeps getting faster and faster, and brighter and smarter. And then before you know it, the car is doing such good things, that

The Convoluted Universe

the body starts to change. It's like the energy of the new engine starts to reform the body. And before you know it, the chap has turned into a sport's car. A beautiful, glossy, attractive vehicle. And that's what this is about. The energies that are coming in have the ability to transform the vehicle. And it will start to be different. It's going to look different. It's going to look ... well, *younger* comes to mind. It's going to look smarter and younger. The cells of the body, the vibration of the body is changing, and is matching the vibration of the incoming energy. And the physical changes will be next.

D: *What will those physical changes be?*

C: Oh! The body's going to change to be *lighter*. And I'm getting that it will look *taller*. It's not that it's going to *be* taller. But the energy from within is somehow going to become visible on the outside. And it will make the body seem taller, elongated, slimmer. And more transparent.

D: *Transparent?*

C: Yes. It's a pioneering thing.

D: *Is this the way the people on Earth will be evolving?* (Yes) *Will everyone make the changes?*

C: Yes, because the people have all been given that choice. If they want to evolve with the Earth, and stay here, they will evolve into this new human being. It will look different. And that's what this experiment is about. That's why Christine and others are moving the ones who don't want to evolve with the Earth. They are going to leave. (Almost crying) And bring a lot of pain to their families. But the people who are staying must hold the light. That's a big job. To get divorced and separated from these things that are happening *now*. And these things are going to continue to happen until the cleansing is complete. Those who are here to stay, are taking this *race* of people into a very new and different civilization. Those people are being tested now, to see if they can hold the light when there is disaster, and not be sucked in. They're the people who will move ahead with this planet.

D: *Almost like a last test, you mean?*

C: Yes. The testing is going on right now. Whatever each

642

being needs to test them, to see what they're capable of giving back to this program; how firm their commitment is. How willing they are to serve. That is all being tested now.

D: *So each one is having their own individual test?*

C: Yes. And the people who are finding it tough now are the ones who are staying. They're the ones who are going through the tests. But some of them are not coming through.

D: *They're not passing the test.*

C: No. There are some who are not.

D: *This is what I was told by other people, that some would be left behind.* (Yes) *And I thought that sounded cruel.*

C: No, it's not cruel, because each soul is given the choice. And if they are not moving and evolving, it's because they are choosing not to. And they will reincarnate into another place of their choice. And it's all right. Because it's only a game.

D: *That's what I was told, that they would be sent where there was still negative karma to be worked out. And this planet would no longer have negativity at that point. Is that what you're seeing?*

C: Yes. They'll stay in the old Earth. The new Earth is so beautiful. You will see colors and animals and flowers you never imagined possible. You'll see fruit that is perfect food. It doesn't have to be cooked. It's just eaten as it is. And everything that the being needs to nourish them will be there. These new fruits are developing now with the help of the Star People.

D: *Are these fruits and vegetables that we don't have on the Earth now?*

C: We don't have them. They're mutations in some ways. I'm seeing a custard apple as an example of what happened. We will have a fruit called a "custard apple". And it doesn't look like an apple. It has a rough exterior, and it's about the size of two oranges put together. And then you open it. It's like custard inside. So that's a fruit, but a food. It's not just a fruit, but another food has been introduced to it, like custard. That's an example of one of the future foods. So these foods will be delights to the senses. And nutritious and sustaining for the – I keep being stopped when I start to say "body". And I am being told to say "being". They'll be nutritious for

643

the being. And things we now have to cook – like you'd cook custard – will be incorporated into these fruits. And it has to do with helping the planet, and cutting down on the use of electricity and energy. So the fruits are going to provide us with what we need.

D: *I've heard man has done many things to the food that is not healthy for the body.*

C: That's right. The organic foods are coming onto the Earth, and those organic farmers are moving with the Earth evolution program. That's why they're there. And that's why consciousness is being raised about this, because people need to know how to grow properly. And the Rudolph Steiner schools are teaching children this. So, the children who are going to be with the new Earth will know this. And those children are now teaching in universities and in institutions, and they're spreading the word. So when the cleansing of the Earth occurs, much of that toxicity is going to be pushed away. You see, the new Earth is not this dimension. The new Earth is another dimension. And we will move into that new dimension. And in that new dimension, there'll be these trees that have purple and orange in their *trunks.* And there will be beautiful rivers and waterfalls. And the energy will be brought back. There will be energy in the streams and the water that goes over rocks and sandbanks. And it *hits* the Earth. It creates energy and will be straightened out in this world. Many of these streams have been straightened out to make them navigable and nice. That's taking away the energy from the Earth. The Earth is going to be cleansed. I'm seeing water.

D: *Does this have to occur before the Earth shifts and evolves into the new dimension?*

C: I'm seeing us stepping through. (Startled) Oh! What I'm seeing is that the people who are going to the new dimensions will step through into this new world.

D: *While the other one is being cleansed?*

C: Yes, yes.

D: *What do you see about the water that will happen with the cleansing?*

C: (A big sigh) It's not going to be shown to me.

D: *They don't want you to see it?*

C: No, they won't show me that. What they're showing me is ... an opening? And we step through. We step into, what *looks* like this Earth, but it's different colors. It's different textures. At *first* it looks the same. At first only. And then as we look around, we start to see that it's not. It's changing before our eyes. And it's so beautiful.

D: *But this is not the spirit side? Because the spirit side is described as being very beautiful also.*

C: No, it's the new Earth. It's not the spirit side. It's the fifth dimensional Earth. Some people will pass through before others. I'm being told to tell you now that Christine has been there several times. There's a group going to go through now. And she'll be bringing more through. And they'll be coming and going a bit until they go for good.

D: *Then the others will be left on the old Earth?*

C: Yes, the ones that are choosing to stay will stay.

D: *They'll be undergoing a lot of hardships, won't they?*

C: Yes, the whole planet. (Startled) I just saw the whole planet explode. That's horrible, isn't it?

D: *What do you think that means?*

C: I don't know. I just saw it explode. But I saw the new Earth. There's this beautiful fifth dimensional place with harmony and peace.

D: *When they showed you the planet exploding, is that just symbolic? As though that Earth will no longer exist for the ones who cross over?*

C: Well, the people who have crossed over are watching what's happening. They can see. Now, is it going to explode? They're saying to me, "Don't get caught up with what's going to happen, because you've got to focus on the light." And that's the challenge for these people who are going to be in the new Earth. The challenge for them is to not get caught up in anything that's going to happen, because that's what pulls us back into the third dimension. And that's what's happened to many people who were on a path forward. They've been pulled back because they got caught up in the fear and the sadness and regret and the black stuff. So they're saying, "You don't need to know, because it wouldn't serve anybody if it were known." So really what they are saying is, "Focus on the good stuff." Focus on the fact that there is going to be this beautiful new existence, new dimension, that many people on the Earth are going to be moving into. Who are already moving into.

D: *I was told whenever you cross over, you will be in the same physical body that you have now. You will just be changed.*

C: Yes, you will still be in the same body, but it is going to change.

D: *So it can be done without dying or leaving the body. It's a different thing altogether.*

C: Yes, we just walk across. Christine's done it before, and she knows how to do it. She's done it and understands it.

D: *But it will be sad because there will be so many people that won't understand what's happening. It's so hard with so many – I want to say "ordinary" – people out there who have no idea of anything except the religion they've been taught. They don't know that this other is possible.*

C: Yes, but they're not ordinary. They only seem ordinary. It's a mask they're wearing. They're changing.

D: *But there still are a lot of people who haven't even thought about these things.*

C: Yes, but they'll be choosing not to awaken, and that is their choice. We have to respect that. They have been given the choice like everybody on the Earth, and they have made that choice. And that's okay. It's all right. It's fine.

D: *So if they have to go to another place to work out the negative karma, that's part of their evolvement.* (Yes.) *But do you see a majority of people evolving to the next dimension?*

C: No. Not the majority. And the numbers, to some extent, are not important, because what will be, will be. And the *more* people that can awaken and take that journey, the more people there'll be. And that's why so many of you are doing this work. To help people open up to the journey, and let go of the fear. And step into that void where anything is possible. Where the *blackness* is residing. And that's what you people are all doing. And you need to do it. And everybody you speak to then goes out and does it as well. You may not be aware of it, but you're acting like Christ. Everyone you speak to becomes a disciple, and they go out, and they in turn awaken other people. So it's working. And it's soon. It's all happening soon.

D: *Do you have any idea of a time period?*

C: The next years will be the – I'm getting the word "decision point". It will be the "cut-off" point. I think it means that those who have not decided by then, will be left behind. It's critical.

D: *But there are some entire countries in the world that are not ready for this. That's why I am thinking there are many people that won't make the crossover.*

C: There's more happening than people know about. I'm seeing some countries where people are being persecuted. The reason that's happening is to awaken spirituality, because persecution causes it. When people are persecuted or when they're facing death, or when they're facing huge human feats. That is a trigger that awakens people. And that's the purpose of much of the persecution that's occurring at the momen;,to make sure that these people are awakened. So that's the positive side of it.

D: *Is there something that triggers it or precipitates it?*

C: It's like the curtain drops. And I'm not allowed to see. I'm just being told that it will be the end of one and the beginning of another.

D: *They're trying to lead us into war at this time. (2002) Do you think it has something to do with that?*

C: (Big sigh) I'm afraid that's the test. I said that many people were being tested. And I didn't realize it then, but I do now, that that's all part of the test,if we can keep ourselves separated from that. It's like we have to create our own ... it's like each one of us is the universe. All parts of the universe are held *here* (placed her hand on her body). And if we keep this, this universe here ....

D: *This body?*

647

C: Yes. If we keep it at peace, and we keep it in balance, then we are passing the test. Then we can withstand anything. And those things that are happening in the world are really to test the whole; all of us.

D: *You mean to not get caught up into the fear.*

C: Yeah. Turn the TV off. Don't listen to it. Don't read the paper. Don't get caught up in it. Your *world* is what you create here. (Touched her body again.)

D: *In your own body.*

C: Yes. In your own space here. This is your own universe here. If every person creates peace and harmony in their own universe, then that's the universe they're creating in that fifth dimensional Earth. The more people who can create peace and harmony in this body universe, the more people who will be in that fifth dimensional new Earth. The ones who can't create peace and harmony in this body universe, are not passing the test. That's the test.

D: *We're trying to do this to keep the war from happening, or to lessen it anyway.*

C: I'm being told that it doesn't matter what happens, because it's all a game. It's all a play. And the things that are happening are there for a reason. And the reason at the moment is to test each human being to find out where they're at in their own evolution. And so if we hold peace and light here (the body), we don't have to worry about whether there's a war or not. It's only an illusion anyway.

D: *But right now it seems very real, and it could have some very disastrous consequences.*

C: Yes, but that's fear for each individual. Our job is to help each individual find peace *here* (the body). And then, of course, as you bring more people together, who have peace and harmony within their own body universe, then instead of the blackness spreading, that spreads. And that creates this whole new world. If you'd been given all that information back then you would have been overloaded. It's the same reason why they're saying, "We're not going to tell you exactly what's going to happen. We don't *know* exactly what's going to happen. But we're not going to tell you what

648

we know, because you don't need to know. All you need to do is focus here (the body) creating your heaven on Earth. Each human being creating their own heaven on Earth. That's all you have to do. And coming together with others who are creating their own heaven on Earth. And then expanding that energy *out*. And before you know it, you've changed the world. You don't even think about the world. What you focus on is what you create. Think about peace. The main thing people have to understand is that, what they focus on expands. So if they focus on, if they can replace predictions with something that is wonderful that they want, and expand that. Then they can create their own heaven on Earth. And I'm being shown in your book *The Convoluted Universe* (Book One) you give a description of thought. I'm being told to remind you about this. You talk about an energy ball the size of a grapefruit. And that ball has energy strands. And I'm changing this as I go. Energy strands which go over each other and transverse each other. And those energy strands can do anything they like. They can split, and they can become four energy strands. They can weave. They can multiply. They can go backwards. They can zip up. They can do absolutely anything. And this is the ball of possibility. When you think a thought it doesn't just disappear. It becomes an energy strand. It becomes energy. It moves into that ball of possibility. So imagine your thought becoming energy. And the *more* energy you give it, the stronger that becomes. And then it manifests, and it becomes *real*. It becomes physical. If you send a thought out that there's going to be peace. And then you follow it with, "Oh, but that war is getting worse", or "Those politicians are making a mistake." You weaken the energy: the positive strand you brought out. So we have to teach people to send out the positive thought, and then to reinforce it with *more* positive thoughts, and more positive thoughts. And we have to teach them that when one of those negative thoughts comes into their mind, not to just let it go, but to replace it with a positive thought. So that they're adding to that energy ball of possibility. They're contributing to it. We

649

have to teach them to do that. They do not know how to do that. And I'm being told to tell you to reinforce that the illusion – I don't know why I'm being told to tell you this. But they're saying that if we could get people to think of this conflict that's occurring in the Middle East as a movie, it would help people. The other thing I'm being told to tell you is that for every action they can make an opposite reaction. Where there's birth, there's death. And everybody *must* let go of any greed, any domination, materialism. Any of those issues that are stopping them from doing this work must be let go. Because these issues are not going to serve anybody in the new Earth. There's not going to be the need for money, as such. So why would you bother about it? Those who are working for the Earth, for the universe, are being provided for, and will continue to be. What you need will come to you. So it's time now to let go of that ethic of working to get the money. You're working to change the Earth. You're working to save this situation. That's where the driving force must be. It must come from love and service. And that's the only way we will maximize this effort. It must come from love and service, not from greed.

D: *I've been told love is the most powerful emotion.*

C: Yes, love heals.

One final piece of information came through a client at my office in 2004. I believed one part of all of this was still unclear: How could some people be aware that they had made the shift into the New Earth, and others would not be? How would it be possible to move an entire population with only a minority knowing anything had happened? "They" must have been aware that I was struggling with this lingering thought, so they supplied it. After all, how could I write about it, and lecture about it if I didn't have all the pieces?

Bob: Most planets, but especially this one was only designed originally for five hundred and fifty thousand people. Half a million people. That was as large as it was supposed to go. More people are reincarnating here to experience all these major changes. And the Earth has been damaged and changed beyond the capability to repair it. This planet has been unfortunately changed in such ways that there's no sense of return whatsoever to its original pristine condition. But now because of the prime directive from the Creator, this has to accelerate. Because it's been too long. There are two ways to do with this. You can cause the planet to rotate and the Earth crust to shift. And you literally, when that happens, you start all over again from ground zero. That's what touched off the Ice Age and killed all the dinosaurs. It doesn't matter how it happened, but basically it did the same thing. A civilization disappears, and you start off with the Ice Age and Neanderthal Man and all that kind of good stuff all happens again. You lose control of your entire civilization, and you end up as a legend like Atlantis and Lemuria did. This has all happened many times before. But that's not what's going to happen this time. This time you shift as a planet. And *basically* as a universe. You shift the whole dimension. The dimension changes. You go from 3 point 6 (3.6) which we are now, to five. And you say, "Well, what happened to four?" Well, four is sort of here in a way, but it's just going to *jump* it. You're going to end up as five.When the dimensional *change* comes, you will literally *jump* that. There's a lot of complications with this. This is why it's being watched so carefully. Many people who are spiritually ready will be able to make the transition very easily. Others are literally going to be taken off planet. In the flick of an eyelid they won't even know it's happened, most of them. And they will end up on another planet that's pristine, ready and waiting for this to happen. And your capabilities will be far beyond what they are now. You have basically five primary senses. You'll have many more than that when the transition goes through. You will become automatically telepathic. They'll wake up in their little lives the next day – or what can be done, depending on how it's shifted. – It has happened before, by the way. – We will simply shut down. It's like going into suspended animation. We suspend it. It may be two or three days to transfer the populace.

D: *The entire world, or just the ....*

B: Yes. All the people that are spirituallyready to make this transition. They'll all be shifted off. And when they wake up on this other planet, they won't even realize it's happened. There was a shift like this a few years ago on this planet, with all of us. And not many people knew about it. It just *was*. It was like a whole week passed by in the course of a night. It *has* happened that way.

D: *Why did that happen at that time?*

B: We needed to shift the sun, technically, and we needed to be able to adjust it. And if anybody could see it, they would all know what happened. That wasn't a very practical way of doing it. So we just kind of shut everybody down.

D: *So they wouldn't know it?*

B: Yes. You went to sleep that night, and you slept like you thought it was a twelve hour period. And you woke up. And your watch was still running the same. But in fact you had literally gone through a whole week.

D: *Everyone was put into suspended animation?*

B: Yes. You shut down the whole thing all at the same time.

D: *While the world moved?*

B: Oh, yes. The planet moves. You have the so-called "night and day". But we actually adjusted it. It was a really interesting trick to do it. But it does work. This planetary adjustment that's coming up. This frequency change thing that is coming up. You can't merely *do* this with everybody awake. Because you're going to have all sorts of strange reactions in people. So they *think* they're all awake. But yet we can shut them down. It's a bit of a trick. It's very technically involved.

D: *So they would think they were having dreams if they did see anything.*

B: Yes, yes, precisely. But they might not have conscious remembrance of it, because don't forget, most people *don't* have conscious remembrance of what they dream anyway.

And you can change things in dreams very easily too.

D: *You said this was done a few years ago.*

B: Yes, it was. We had to make an adjustment in the sun's frequency.

So apparently that would be the answer. The entire population of the world would be shut down and put into suspended animation while the transfer was made. As Annie Kirkwood showed in her vision, as the Earth split or divided into two Earths, the people on each were unaware of what had happened to the others.

This is also found in the Bible: *"In that day, he who is on the housetop, and his goods are in the house, let him not come down to take them away. And likewise, the one who is in the field, let him not turn back. I tell you, in that night , there will be two men in one bed: the one will be taken and the other will be left. Two women will be grinding together: the one will be taken and the other left. Two men will be in the field: the one will be taken and the other left. And they answered and said to Him, "Where Lord?" So He said to them, "Wherever the body is, there the eagles will be gathered together."* (Luke 17:31-37)

I have been asked many times about the Mayan calendar ending at 2012. People think that is the date for the end of the world if the Mayans could not see beyond that. I have been told that the Mayans evolved spiritually to this point where their civilization shifted en masse to the next dimension. They stopped the calendar at 2012 because they could see this would be the time of the next major event: the shifting of the entire world into the next dimension.

We will ascend to the other dimension by raising our consciousness, the vibration and frequency of our body. At first you can continue in a physical body for a while. Then as you gradually discover it is no longer necessary, the physical body dissolves into Light, and you live with a body made of light or pure energy. This sounds very similar to several cases in this book where the subject saw a being that glowed and was composed of pure energy. They have evolved beyond the need for a physical limiting body, and we will do this also when we reach that stage. So in many cases, when the being ascends, they take the physical body with them. But this is only a temporary situation and the shedding and letting go of the body depends on the level of understanding the being has reached. We do tend to hold on to the familiar, but eventually see that even though we were able to take it with us, the body is too limiting and confining for the new reality in the new dimension. When we reach this new dimension, the new body of light or energy will never die. This is what the Bible meant when it referred to "Eternal Life".

The spirit side or the in-between lives state, where I have found that we go when we die in this lifetime, is like a recycling center. It leads back to another life on Earth because there is still karma to be worked out, or something that needs to be attended to. People keep returning because they have not completed their lessons or their cycles. By raising the consciousness, the frequency and vibration, there is no need to return to that place (the in-between state). It can be transcended by going to the place where everyone is eternal, and there is no reason for recycling. We can remain there forever. This is probably the place many of my subjects refer to as "home". The place they deeply miss and desire to return to. When they see it during the regressions they become very emotional, because they have been deeply longing for it, yet not consciously knowing it existed.

CHAPTER 31

FINALE

Throughout my work, I have been told many times that we, as humans, are not the only feeling, sentient beings on this planet and beyond. We are so self centered that we think we are the most important and that everything revolves around us, mostly because we don't understand what life really is. I have found that *everything* contains the spirit, the spark of life. This is because everything is energy. It is only vibrating at a different (faster or slower) frequency. In our striving towards a higher spiritual form, we have passed through many of these so-called "lesser" forms of life. We have been minerals, dirt, rocks, plants and animals before incarnating in the human form. We are curious spirits and we needed to experience these and learn from them before we were ready to experience lessons in a more complex (although denser) physical body. I have found that everything is alive, including the planet Earth herself. She has feelings, emotions and needs, just as we have. Right now, she is experiencing pain (according to my sources) because of what is being done to her. According to the ETs, we are reaching the point of no return, where the damage cannot be reversed. At that point, we will ascend into the new Earth because the old one is no longer capable of handling the stress. But if the Earth itself is alive, does it stop there? I have been told that it goes beyond this even further out into the cosmos. We are all part of a larger living and functioning being, which we call the Universe. This means that the Universe itself is an organized, huge something that is alive and has feelings. You may want to call this "something" God, but it is even more complex than that.

Everything that makes up the Universe (stars, planets, etc.) could be considered cells in the body of God. Cells that compose the body of this huge "something". And we are nothing more than the tiniest cells in the circulation process. Although we may be something so minute, we are not insignificant, because in our evolution and growth it is possible for us to constantly rise upward through the morass of life.

I have been told that the reincarnation process is something less than to be desired. Through this process we constantly go back and forth between Earth and the spirit world. It is like a processing station where we go to judge ourselves and decide to come back to correct karma. The main objective should be to get out of this rut, and proceed beyond the physical. It is said that we can attain that when we bypass the holding station of the spirit world and go directly to the higher spirit levels where the accumulation of karma, and the correction of it are no longer required. Then we can progress in a different way and no longer be burdened by the physical body. This is all part of the ascension process. To proceed directly into the next world by raising our frequency and vibration and bypass the need to die and go to the spirit world.

The Universe is a highly complex organism living in many dimensions at the same time, composed of layers and layers of consciousness relating to all the other organisms within it. It has the power to create and relate to all of these at the same time individually. This could be what "they" have called the Collective. This is so because we collectively have thought it into existence by intent. At some time in the far distant past we were all one. We were all part of the Collective, the One, the great Central Sun, the Source, God, whatever you want to call it. Many of my subjects remember this existence while in trance. And it always causes great unhappiness when they separate from it, because the togetherness was of great comfort and love. They did not want to leave, and felt a great sadness, and a feeling of separation when they were forced out into the cosmos.

Because the Source wanted to experience (curiosity is not strictly a human trait, maybe this is where the desire to explore came from), we all (as part of the Source as co-creators) helped it begin to create. We helped it create out of nothing (or out of dust as is reported in several legends), and stars, planets, rocks, streams, plants, animals and humans came into being. Then we decided (or were told) to go and inhabit these things and report back to the Source what this was like. It is said that it is all nothing but an illusion. If this is correct, then it is being held together by our collective perception. We have helped think it into existence and our combined perception holds it there. In my book *Between Death and Life,* I was told that God could be thought of as the glue that holds everything together. If he were to wink out for a fraction of a second, everything would instantly vaporize. In this book we were told that between each inbreath and outbreath this is where God exists. Looking at it from this perspective, we are all collectively God.

What we perceive as accurate, may not be when viewed from the spiritual side. Everything we have in our lives and with which we interact is brought into physical reality because we want it there. This is possible because thoughts are real; thoughts are things. Once formed, thoughts exist forever, and the more they are reinforced, the more physical and denser (more real) they become.

This is why we can change our lives and circumstances; because we are more powerful than we realize. We constantly create our reality, and we are capable of changing that reality. But it often takes the combined power of many to do this, because what we have created has grown so big and powerful that it has taken on a life of its own. Maybe this is the reason for the creation of the new Earth, because the one we are aware of has reached the point that it is incapable of being helped or changed.

Within the matrix of the Universe are all the building blocks of reality. All the possibilities and probabilities that we can create from. We can have heaven or hell in our lives because we are powerful enough to do this, once we understand the process and use our minds to create it. Many times the electrical fields that contain these possibilities are disrupted by discordant intentions and negativity results; as it has lately. When negativity begins, it can be reinforced by people who accept this as a reality, and then it comes into form. We can just as easily have peace and love as our reality once we understand and put to use the power of our mind. As Nostradamus said in my books about him and his predictions, "You do not realize the power of your own mind. By focusing on the reality you desire, you can create it. Your energy is scattered. Once you learn how to focus and direct it, you are capable of creating miracles. And if the power of one man's mind is that powerful, think of the power of group mind once it is harnessed. The power of the focusing of many people's minds is not only multiplied, it is squared. Then miracles can truly occur."

It appears that we choose the parts and the general script of the play that we will participate in during each life. However, everyone else also chooses their parts in the play. It is like participating in a play where the script is created as it progresses, and it can be changed at any point in order to make the play more dramatic. This is because of free will, and everyone's actions influences everyone else's actions. During our Earth lives we can create and experience as many different types of lives (roles and characters) as we wish: fame, riches or poverty; murderer or victim; great love or great despair; war or peace, etc.

William Shakespeare understood this when he wrote: "All the world's a stage, And all the men and women merely players. They have their exits and their entrances, And one man in his time plays many parts."

No matter what we accomplish it is only as temporary as a stage play, and eventually the curtain descends. Then all we have left to take with us are the memories of the experiences, and hopefully the lessons we have learned. These are incorporated into our real self, our off-stage self, our observer self, our eternal soul self or oversoul, which stores these memories and experiences. They are eventually transferred to the computer storage banks of the highest of all: the Source or

God entity. Nothing in the play has gone to waste, whether we were playing the hero or villain. It all adds to the store of knowledge of the universe. Of such things new creations are constantly being formed.

Each time a soul returns to the Earth theater they sign up for the next play or game, and are handed a new script with many blank pages, which will be filled in by the actors as the play progresses. Totally unrehearsed and open to all suggestions and possibilities. Nothing is right or wrong as the actors play their parts. It is all about experience, the learning of lessons, resolution of indebted karma, and the creation of new situations for the enlightenment and learning of others. It is said that no man is an island. Everything we do or say affects someone. If we understood this we would be more careful of the effects our words and deeds have on others. We would be more aware of how these words and deeds are being recorded into the Halls of Knowledge.

With each new life we draw (often unconsciously) upon the store of knowledge we have gained from other lessons. As we apply the knowledge to our present life (play) hopefully we will have learned from past mistakes and not make those mistakes again. Then when we get tired of repeatedly going on stage and trying new scripts, we will choose to retire, return to the Great Stage Manager, and allow the newer (or stubborn, slow-learning) souls to play the parts for a while. This is what many of my clients refer to as "going home". This is the natural state that the soul knew in its beginning, at its creation. The state it knew before it became entrapped in the physical world, the stage world, the third-dimensional world of illusion. By this time we have hopefully gained enough wisdom and understanding to allow us to progress in other ways in other realms of existence. The possibilities are endless, and we have no need to return to this theater, except maybe as an observer or guide.

We are living in exciting times. The study of the laws of metaphysics and the laws of the universe are no longer for the few who were considered strange. It is spreading into the masses at an alarming rate. It is as though it has been just below the surface, just out of the reach of our logical thinking mind. Now it is emerging into the light of day to be studied and analyzed. It no longer seems strange and foreboding, but perfectly natural and normal. We have blocked our minds from pursuing this way of thinking too long. It is now time to open the floodgates and let it change our lives for the better. If everyone realized how their thoughts and deeds affected themselves, their friends and neighbors, their community and city, and eventually the world through the accumulated effect of energy, they would learn to monitor their daily lives and the world would change. It has to, because of the accumulated effect of energy. We are moving into a new world and the old negativity will be left behind. Through the law of cause and effect, which is really nothing less than the "Golden Rule" in the Bible, there can be no more violence and war. We can change the world, one person at a time. This was what Jesus was trying to teach, and they didn't understand. Love is the answer, it is that simple.

As our minds evolve, we are being spoon fed more and more complicated information. We can never know it all because our minds would not be able to handle it. But it appears that our minds are being expanded to comprehend more complicated theories.

If Alice in Wonderland succeeded in finding a portal to another dimension, the question now is: "How far down the rabbit hole do you want to go?" There is much more knowledge out there than we can possibly imagine. I am a reporter, an adventurer. I will keep accumulating information and trying to present it to the world. I don't know how far down the rabbit hole I want to go. I have no idea how deep it is, and how many twists and turns will be along the way. Yet I invite my readers to join me as I travel the dimensions of the unknown and attempt to find out.

The adventure and the journey will continue. There is no stopping it!

Author Page

Dolores Cannon, a regressive hypnotherapist and psychic researcher who records "Lost" knowledge, was born in 1931 in St. Louis, Missouri. She was educated and lived in St. Louis until her marriage in 1951 to a career Navy man. She spent the next 20 years traveling all over the world as a typical Navy wife, and raising her family. In 1970 her husband was discharged as a disabled veteran, and they retired to the hills of Arkansas. She then started her writing career and began selling her articles to various magazines and newspapers. She has been involved with hypnosis since 1968, and exclusively with past-life therapy and regression work since 1979. She has studied the various hypnosis methods and thus developed her own unique technique which enabled her to gain the most efficient release of information from her clients. Dolores is now teaching her unique technique of hypnosis all over the world.

In 1986 she expanded her investigations into the UFO field. She has done on-site studies of suspected UFO landings, and has investigated the Crop Circles in England. The majority of her work in this field has been the accumulation of evidence from suspected abductees through hypnosis.

Dolores is an international speaker who has lectured on all the continents of the world. Her seventeen books are translated into twenty languages. She has spoken to radio and television audiences worldwide. And articles about/by Dolores have appeared in several U.S. and international magazines and newspapers. Dolores was the first American and the first foreigner to receive the "Orpheus Award" in Bulgaria, for the highest advancement in the research of psychic phenomenon. She has received Outstanding Contribution and Lifetime Achievement awards from several hypnosis organizations.

Dolores has a very large family who keep her solidly balanced between the "real" world of her family and the "unseen" world of her work.

If you wish to correspond with Ozark Mountain Publishing about Dolores' work or her training classes, please submit to the following address. (Please enclose a self addressed stamped envelope for her reply.) Dolores Cannon, P.O. Box 754, Huntsville, AR, 72740, USA
Or email the office at decannon@msn.com or through our Website: www.ozarkmt.com

Dolores Cannon, who transitioned from this world on October 18, 2014, left behind incredible accomplishments in the fields of alternative healing, hypnosis, metaphysics and past life regression, but most impressive of all was her innate understanding that the most important thing she could do was to share information. To reveal hidden or undiscovered knowledge vital to the enlightenment of humanity and our lessons here on Earth. Sharing information and knowledge is what mattered most to Dolores. That is why her books, lectures and unique QHHT® method of hypnosis continue to amaze, guide and inform so many people around the world. Dolores explored all these possibilities and more while taking us along for the ride of our lives. She wanted fellow travelers to share her journeys into the unknown.

Other Books by Ozark Mountain Publishing, Inc.

Dolores Cannon
A Soul Remembers Hiroshima
Between Death and Life
Conversations with Nostradamus,
  Volume I, II, III
The Convoluted Universe -Book One,
  Two, Three, Four, Five
The Custodians
Five Lives Remembered
Horns of the Goddess
Jesus and the Essenes
Keepers of the Garden
Legacy from the Stars
The Legend of Starcrash
The Search for Hidden Sacred
  Knowledge
They Walked with Jesus
The Three Waves of Volunteers and the
  New Earth
A Very Special Friend
Aron Abrahamsen
Holiday in Heaven
James Ream Adams
Little Steps
Justine Alessi & M. E. McMillan
Rebirth of the Oracle
Kathryn Andries
Time: The Second Secret
Will Alexander
Call Me Jonah
Cat Baldwin
Divine Gifts of Healing
The Forgiveness Workshop
Penny Barron
The Oracle of UR
P.E. Berg & Amanda Hemmingsen
The Birthmark Scar
Dan Bird
Finding Your Way in the Spiritual Age
Waking Up in the Spiritual Age
Julia Cannon
Soul Speak – The Language of Your
  Body
Jack Cauley
Journey for Life
Ronald Chapman
Seeing True
Jack Churchward
Lifting the Veil on the Lost
  Continent of Mu

The Stone Tablets of Mu
Carolyn Greer Daly
Opening to Fullness of Spirit
Patrick De Haan
The Alien Handbook
Paulinne Delcour-Min
Divine Fire
Holly Ice
Spiritual Gold
Anthony DeNino
The Power of Giving and Gratitude
Joanne DiMaggio
Edgar Cayce and the Unfulfilled
  Destiny of Thomas Jefferson
Reborn
Paul Fisher
Like a River to the Sea
Anita Holmes
Twidders
Aaron Hoopes
Reconnecting to the Earth
Edin Huskovic
God is a Woman
Patricia Irvine
In Light and In Shade
Kevin Killen
Ghosts and Me
Susan Linville
Blessings from Agnes
Donna Lynn
From Fear to Love
Curt Melliger
Heaven Here on Earth
Where the Weeds Grow
Henry Michaelson
And Jesus Said – A Conversation
Andy Myers
Not Your Average Angel Book
Holly Nadler
The Hobo Diaries
Guy Needler
The Anne Dialogues
Avoiding Karma
Beyond the Source – Book 1, Book 2
The Curators
The History of God
The OM
The Origin Speaks

For more information about any of the above titles, soon to be released titles,
or other items in our catalog, write, phone or visit our website:
PO Box 754, Huntsville, AR 72740|479-738-2348/800-935-0045|www.ozarkmt.com

Other Books by Ozark Mountain Publishing, Inc.

Psycho Spiritual Healing
James Nussbaumer
And Then I Knew My Abundance
Each of You
Living Your Dram, Not Someone Else's
The Master of Everything
Mastering Your Own Spiritual Freedom
Sherry O'Brian
Peaks and Valley's
Gabrielle Orr
Akashic Records: One True Love
Let Miracles Happen
Nikki Pattillo
Children of the Stars
A Golden Compass
Victoria Pendragon
Being In A Body
Sleep Magic
The Sleeping Phoenix
Alexander Quinn
Starseeds What's It All About
Debra Rayburn
Let's Get Natural with Herbs
Charmian Redwood
A New Earth Rising
Coming Home to Lemuria
Richard Rowe
Exploring the Divine Library
Imagining the Unimaginable
Garnet Schulhauser
Dance of Eternal Rapture
Dance of Heavenly Bliss
Dancing Forever with Spirit
Dancing on a Stamp
Dancing with Angels in Heaven
Annie Stillwater Gray
The Dawn Book
Education of a Guardian Angel
Joys of a Guardian Angel
Work of a Guardian Angel
Manuella Stoerzer
Headless Chicken

Blair Styra
Don't Change the Channel
Who Catharted
Natalie Sudman
Application of Impossible Things
L.R. Sumpter
Judy's Story
The Old is New
We Are the Creators
Artur Tradevosyan
Croton
Croton II
Jim Thomas
Tales from the Trance
Jolene and Jason Tierney
A Quest of Transcendence
Paul Travers
Dancing with the Mountains
Nicholas Vesey
Living the Life-Force
Dennis Wheatley/ Maria Wheatley
The Essential Dowsing Guide
Maria Wheatley
Druidic Soul Star Astrology
Sherry Wilde
The Forgotten Promise
Lyn Willmott
A Small Book of Comfort
Beyond all Boundaries Book 1
Beyond all Boundaries Book 2
Beyond all Boundaries Book 3
D. Arthur Wilson
You Selfish Bastard
Stuart Wilson & Joanna Prentis
Atlantis and the New Consciousness
Beyond Limitations
The Essenes -Children of the Light
The Magdalene Version
Power of the Magdalene
Sally Wolf
Life of a Military Psychologist

For more information about any of the above titles, soon to be released titles,
or other items in our catalog, write, phone or visit our website:
PO Box 754, Huntsville, AR 72740|479-738-2348/800-935-0045|www.ozarkmt.com